South Pacific

Here's what the critics say about Frommer's:

"Excellent island-by-island information by Bill Goodwin, a writer who has been there and done his homework."
—*Chicago Tribune*

♦

"Amazingly easy to use. Very portable, very complete."
—*Booklist*

♦

"The only mainstream guide to list specific prices. The Walter Cronkite of guidebooks—with all that implies."
—*Travel & Leisure*

♦

"Complete, concise, and filled with useful information."
—*New York Daily News*

♦

"Hotel information is close to encyclopedic."
—*Des Moines Sunday Register*

♦

"I use a lot of travel guides when preparing my trips, but I have learned to especially trust Frommer's when it comes to picking lodgings."
—*The Orange County Register*

Other Great Guides for Your Trip:

Frommer's Australia

Frommer's Australia from $50 a Day

Frommer's New Zealand

Frommer's Southeast Asia

Frommer's®

South Pacific

by Bill Goodwin

IDG Books Worldwide, Inc.
An International Data Group Company
Foster City, CA • Chicago, IL • Indianapolis, IN • New York, NY

ABOUT THE AUTHOR

Bill Goodwin was an award-winning newspaper reporter before becoming a legal counsel and speechwriter for two U.S. senators, Sam Nunn of Georgia and the late Sam Ervin of North Carolina. In 1977 he sailed a 41-foot yacht from Annapolis, Md., to Tahiti; he then spent a year exploring French Polynesia and the rest of the South Pacific. Now based in northern Virginia, he returns to paradise as often as possible. He also is the author of *Frommer's Virginia* and co-author of *Frommer's Florida* and *Frommer's Florida from $70 a Day*.

IDG BOOKS WORLDWIDE, INC.

An International Data Group Company
919 E. Hillsdale Blvd.
Suite 400
Foster City, CA 94404

Find us online at **www.frommers.com**

ISBN 0-02-863475-6
ISSN 1044-2367

Editor: Matthew Garcia
Production Editor: Donna Wright
Photo Editors: Richard Fox, Michael Ross
Staff Cartographers: John Decamillis, Roberta Stockwell
Design by Michele Laseau
Page Creation by: Sean Monkhouse, Melissa Auciello-Brogan, Julie Trippetti
Front cover photo: Snorkeling at Tetiaroa, a small island just north of Papeeta, Tahiti

SPECIAL SALES

For general information on IDG Books Worldwide's books in the U.S., please call our Consumer Customer Service department at 1-800-762-2974. For reseller information, including discounts, bulk sales, customized editions, and premium sales, please call our Reseller Customer Service department at 1-800-434-3422.

Manufactured in the United States of America

5   4   3   2   1

Contents

9   Nadi & Viti Levu   235

10   Suva & Levuka   279

11   Northern Fiji   304

12   Samoa   321

13   American Samoa   361

14   The Kingdom of Tonga   375

Appendix: The South Pacific in Depth   419

Index   437

Maps

To my father,
with love, and thanks for the loans.

ACKNOWLEDGMENTS

I wish to thank the many individuals and organizations without whose help this book would have been impossible to write. You will become acquainted with many of them in these pages, and you will meet them in the islands.

I am particularly grateful to the friendly staffs of the South Pacific tourist information offices: Brigitte Vanizette, Taina Meyssonnier, Tehiva Galenon, Al Keahi, and Cathy Van Meter of Tourisme Tahiti; Sitiveni Yaqona, Keti Wagavonovono, and Eroni Puamau of the Fiji Visitors Bureau; Chris Wong, Karla Egglelton and Papatua Papatua of the Cook Islands Tourism Corporation; Sonya Hunter and Fasitau Ula of the Samoa Visitors Bureau; Virginia F. Samuelu of the American Samoa Office of Tourism; and Semisi Taumoepeau, Sandradee Fonua, Viliami Halapua, Senasi Tupou, Luisa Funaki, and the inexhaustable Bruno Toke of the Tonga Visitors Bureau.

My deep personal thanks go to Suzanne McIntosh, Nancy Monseaux, Max Parrish, Mark Miller, Curtis and Judy Moore, and Bill and Donna Wilder, whose generosity over the years have made this book possible; to my sister, Jean Goodwin Santa-Maria, who has consistently given much-needed moral support; to my dear friends Hina Kaptain and Cubie White on Moorea; and to Dick Beaulieu in Fiji, always a font of information, advice, and cold Stubbies.

I am truly blessed to have friends like these.

AN INVITATION TO THE READER

In researching this book, I discovered many wonderful places—hotels, restaurants, shops, and more. I'm sure you'll find others. Please tell us about them, so we can share the information with your fellow travelers in upcoming editions. If you were disappointed with a recommendation, we'd love to know that, too. Please write to:

Bill Goodwin
Frommer's South Pacific, 7th Edition
IDG Travel
1633 Broadway
New York, NY 10019

AN ADDITIONAL NOTE

Please be advised that travel information is subject to change at any time—and this is especially true of prices. We therefore suggest that you write or call ahead for confirmation when making your travel plans. The authors, editors, and publisher cannot be held responsible for the experiences of readers while traveling. Your safety is important to us, however, so we encourage you to stay alert and be aware of your surroundings. Keep a close eye on cameras, purses, and wallets, all favorite targets of thieves and pickpockets.

WHAT THE SYMBOLS MEAN

✪ Frommer's Favorites

Our favorite places and experiences—outstanding for quality, value, or both.

The following abbreviations are used for credit cards:

AE   American Express   MC   MasterCard
DC   Diners Club   V   Visa
DISC   Discover

FIND FROMMER'S ONLINE

Arthur Frommer's Budget Travel Online (www.frommers.com) offers more than 6,000 pages of up-to-the-minute travel information—including the latest bargains and candid, personal articles updated daily by Arthur Frommer himself. No other Web site offers such comprehensive and timely coverage of the world of travel.

The Best of the South Pacific

1

The magical names of Tahiti, Rarotonga, Fiji, Samoa, and Tonga have conjured up romantic images of an earthly paradise since European explorers brought home tales of their tropical splendor and uninhibited people more than 2 centuries ago. And with good reason, for these are some of the most beautiful islands in the world—if not *the* most beautiful. Here you can relax at remote resorts perched on some of the most gorgeous beaches the planet has to offer. Offshore awaits some of the globe's most fabulous diving and spectacular snorkeling.

Picking the "best" of the South Pacific is no easy task. I can't, for example, choose *the* most friendly island, for the people of Tahiti and French Polynesia, the Cook Islands, Fiji, Samoa, American Samoa, and the Kingdom of Tonga are among the friendliest folks on earth. Their fabled history has provided fodder for famous books and films, their storied culture inspires hedonistic dreams, and their big smiles and genuine warmth are prime attractions everywhere in the South Pacific. Personally, I like all the islands and all the islanders, which further complicates my chore to no end.

In this chapter, I'll point out the best of the best—not necessarily to pass qualitative judgment, but to help you choose among many options. I list them here in the order in which they appear in the book.

Your own choice obviously will depend on why you are going to the islands. You can scuba dive to exhaustion, or just sit on the beach with a trashy novel. You can share a 300-room hotel with package tourists, or get away from it all at a tiny resort on a remote island. Even out there, you can be left alone with your lover, or join your fellow guests at lively dinner parties. You can totally ignore the Pacific Islanders around you, or enrich your own life by learning about theirs. You can listen to the day's events on CNN, or see what the South Seas were like a century ago. Those decisions are all yours.

For a preview of each South Pacific country, see "The Islands in Brief" in chapter 2.

1 The Most Beautiful Islands

"In the South Seas," Rupert Brooke wrote in 1914, "the Creator seems to have laid himself out to show what He can do." How right the poet was, for all across the South Pacific lie some of the world's most dramatically beautiful islands. In my opinion, the best of the lot have jagged mountain peaks plunging into aquamarine lagoons. Here are some you see on the travel posters and in the brochures:

- **Moorea** (French Polynesia): Personally, I think Moorea is the most beautiful island in the world. To my mind, nothing compares with its saw-toothed ridges and the great dark-green hulk of Mount Rotui separating glorious Cook's and Opunohu Bays. The view from Tahiti of Moorea's dinosaurlike skyline is unforgettable. See chapter 5.
- **Bora Bora** (French Polynesia): James Michener thinks that Bora Bora is the most beautiful island in the world. Although tourism has turned this gem into sort of an expensive South Seas Disneyland since Michener's day, development hasn't altered the incredible beauty of Bora Bora's basaltic tombstone towering over a lagoon ranging in color from yellow to deep blue. See chapter 6.
- **Rarotonga** (Cook Islands): Only 32 kilometers (19 miles) around, the capital of the Cook Islands boasts the beauty of Tahiti—with hints of Moorea—but without the development and the high prices of French Polynesia. See chapter 7.
- **Aitutaki** (Cook Islands): A junior version of Bora Bora, a small island sits at the apex of Aitutaki's shallow, colorful lagoon, which from the air looks like a turquoise carpet laid on the deep blue sea. See chapter 7.
- **The Yasawa Islands** (Fiji): Unspoiled is the best description for this chain of long, narrow islands off the northwest coast of Viti Levu, Fiji's main island. Blue Lagoon Cruises goes out there, and the hilly islands have a few small resorts, but mostly the Yasawas are populated by Fijians who live in traditional villages beside some of the region's great beaches. See "Resorts Offshore from Nadi" and "Blue Lagoon Cruises" in chapter 9.
- **Ovalau** (Fiji): The sheer cliffs of Ovalau kept the town of Levuka from becoming Fiji's modern capital, but they create a dramatic backdrop to an old South Seas town little changed in the past century. Ovalau has no good beaches, which means it has no resorts to alter its landscape. See chapter 10.
- **Qamea, Matagi, and Laucala Islands** (Fiji): These little jewels off the northern coast of Taveuni are lushly beautiful, with their shorelines either dropping precipitously into the calm surrounding waters or forming little bays with idyllic beaches. See "Resorts Offshore from Taveuni" in chapter 11.
- **Upolu** (Samoa): Robert Louis Stevenson was so enraptured with Samoa that he spent the last 5 years of his life in the hills of Upolu. The well-weathered eastern part of the island is ruggedly beautiful, especially in Aliepata where a cliff virtually drops down to one of the region's most spectacular beaches. See chapter 12.
- **Savai'i** (Samoa): One of the largest Polynesian islands, this great volcanic shield slopes gently on its eastern side to a chain of gorgeous beaches. There are no towns on Savai'i, only traditional Samoan villages interspersed with rain forests, which add to its unspoiled beauty. See chapter 12.
- **Tutuila** (American Samoa): The only reason to go to American Samoa these days is to see the physical beauty of Tutuila and its magnificent harbor at Pago Pago. If you can ignore the tuna canneries and huge stacks of shipping containers, this island is right up there with Moorea. See chapter 13.
- **Vava'u** (Tonga): One of the South Pacific's best yachting destinations, hilly Vava'u is shaped like a jellyfish, with small islands instead of tentacles trailing off into a quiet lagoon. Waterways cut into the center of the main island, creating the picturesque and perfectly protected Port of Refuge. See chapter 14.

2 The Best Beaches

Since all but a few South Pacific islands are surrounded by coral reefs, there are few surf beaches in the region. Tahiti has a few, but they all have heat-absorbing black volcanic sand. Otherwise, most islands (and all but a few resorts) have bathtub-like lagoons lapping on coral sands draped by coconut palms. Fortunately for the environmentalists among us, some of the most spectacular beaches are on remote islands and are protected from development by the islanders' devotion to their cultures and villages' land rights. Here are a few that stand out from the crowd.

- **Temae** (Moorea, French Polynesia): The northeastern coast of Moorea, around the Hotel Sofitel Ia Ora, is fringed by a nearly uninterrupted stretch of white sand beach which commands a glorious view across a speckled lagoon to Tahiti sitting on the horizon across the Sea of the Moon. See chapter 5.
- **Matira Beach** (Bora Bora, French Polynesia): Beginning at the Hotel Bora Bora, this fine ribbon of sand stretches around skinny Matira Point, which forms the island's southern extremity, all the way to the Club Med. The eastern side has views of the sister islands of Raiatea and Tahaa. See chapter 6.
- **Huahine** (French Polynesia): My favorite resort beach is at Relais Mahana, a small hotel near Huahine's south end. Trees grow along the white beach, which slopes into a lagoon deep enough for swimming at any tide. The resort's pier goes out to a giant coral head, a perfect and safe place to snorkel, and the lagoon here is protected from the trade winds, making it ideal for sail- and paddle boats. See "Huahine" in chapter 6.
- **Muri Beach** (Rarotonga, Cook Islands): Wrapping for 14 kilometers (8.5 miles) around Rarotonga's southeastern corner, Muri Beach faces little islets out on the reef and the island's best lagoon for boating. The sand rather than the road serves as the main avenue among the Muri Beach resorts and restaurants. See chapter 7.
- **One Foot Island** (Aitutaki, Cook Islands): The sands on most beaches covered in this book are a tannish coral color, but on the islets surrounding Aitutaki, they are pure white, like talcum. Tiny One Foot Island has the best beach here, with part of it along a channel whose coral bottom is scoured clean by strong tidal currents, another running out to a sandbar known as Nude Island—a reference not to clothes but to a lack of vegetation. See chapter 7.
- **Yasawa Island** (Fiji): One of the most spectacular beaches I've ever seen is on the northern tip of Yasawa Island, northernmost of the gorgeous chain of the same name. This long expanse of deep sand is broken by a teapot-like rock outcrop, which also separates two Fijian villages, whose residents own this land. Blue Lagoon Cruises and oceangoing cruise ships stop here; otherwise, the Fijians keep it all to themselves. There are other good beaches on Yasawa, however, all within reach of the Yasawa Island Resort. See "Resorts Offshore from Nadi" and "Blue Lagoon Cruises" in chapter 9.
- **Natadola Beach** (The Coral Coast, Fiji): Although Fiji's main island of Viti Levu doesn't have the high-quality beaches found on the country's small islands, Natadola is an exception. Until recently this long stretch was spared development, but hotels and restaurants are coming. So far the locals haven't permitted buildings right on the beach. See "The Coral Coast" in chapter 9.
- **Vatulele Island** (Fiji): Nearly a kilometer (0.6 mile) of deep white sand fronts the deluxe Vatulele Island Resort, off the south shore of Viti Levu, Fiji's main island. Guests can have dinner out on the beach, or get a bird's-eye view from a private gazebo overlooking the sands. See "Resorts Offshore from Nadi" in chapter 9.
- **Horseshoe Bay** (Matagi Island, Northern Fiji): Home of one of the region's best small resorts, Matagi is an extinct volcano whose crater fell away on one side and formed picturesque Horseshoe Bay. The half-moon beach at its head is one of the finest in the islands, but you will have to be on a yacht or a guest at Matagi Island Resort to enjoy it. See "Resorts Offshore from Taveuni" in chapter 11.

- **Aleipata Beach** (Upolu, Samoa): On the eastern end of Upolu, a clifflike mountain forms a dramatic backdrop to the deep sands of Aleipata Beach, which faces a group of small islets offshore. On a clear day you can see American Samoa from here. See chapter 12.
- **Return to Paradise Beach** (Upolu, Samoa): This idyllic stretch of white sand and black rocks overhung by coconut palms gets its name from *Return to Paradise,* the 1953 Gary Cooper movie which was filmed here. Surf actually pounds on the rocks. See chapter 12.
- **'Atata Island** (Tonga): A gorgeous, wide beach wraps around the "tail" of tadpole-shaped 'Atata, off Tonga's capital of Nuku'alofa and home of Royal Sunset Island Resort. The narrow peninsula protects a colorful, coral-speckled lagoon on its western side. See chapter 14.
- **Ha'apai** (Tonga): The atoll-like Ha'apai Islands have several great beaches on their lagoons, but none is finer than the one in front of the aptly named Sandy Beach Resort. You can swim at any tide here, sunsets are magnificent, and on a clear day you see smoke rising from the active volcano on Tafuna island. See "Ha'apai" in chapter 14.

3 The Best Honeymoon Destinations

Whether you're on your honeymoon or not, the South Pacific is a marvelous place for a romantic escape. After all, romance and the islands have gone hand-in-hand since the bare-breasted young women of Tahiti gave rousing welcomes to the European explorers in the late 18th century.

Personally, I've never stayed anywhere as romantic as a thatch-roof bungalow built on stilts over a lagoon, with a glass panel in its floor for viewing fish swimming below you and steps leading from your front deck into the warm waters below. You'll find lots of these in French Polynesia, and a handful more in Samoa (more environmentally conscious, the other South Pacific countries won't allow anything like that to be built on their reefs).

One caveat is in order: Most over-water bungalows are relatively close together, meaning that your honeymooning next-door neighbors will be within earshot if not eyeshot. ("It can be like watching an X-rated video," a hotel manager once confessed, "but without the video.") If you're seeking a high degree of privacy and seclusion, therefore, they won't be your best choice.

On the other hand, the South Pacific's small, relatively remote "off-shore" resorts offer as much privacy as you are likely to desire. These little establishments would also fall into another category: The Best Places to Get Away from It All. They are so romantic that a friend of mine says her ideal wedding would be to rent an entire small resort in Fiji, take her wedding party with her, get married in Fijian costume beside the beach, and make the rest of her honeymoon a diving vacation. Most resorts covered in this book are well aware of such desires, and they offer wedding packages complete with traditional ceremony and costumes. Choose your resort, then contact the management for details about their wedding packages.

Meantime, here's what the two best honeymoon destinations have to offer:

- **French Polynesia:** The resorts here have the region's best selection of over-water bungalows. Invariably, these are the most expensive style of accommodation in French Polynesia.

  On Tahiti, which most visitors now consider a way station to the other islands, the **Tahiti Beachcomber Parkroyal** has over-water bungalows facing the dramatic outline of Moorea across the Sea of the Moon. Some of those at **Le Meridien Tahiti** also have this view. See chapter 4.

On Moorea, the now dated but nevertheless charming **Hotel Bali Hai** was the first resort to have them, and it's the least expensive choice today. Some overwater units at the **Hotel Sofitel Ia Ora** actually face Tahiti across the Sea of the Moon, and they're built over Moorea's most colorful lagoon. The more modern **Moorea Beachcomber Parkroyal** has bungalows partially built over the lagoon. See chapter 5.

On Bora Bora, the over-water bungalow dominates. A few of those at the **Hotel Bora Bora** look directly out to tombstone-like Mount Otemanu rising across the famous lagoon; along with Cook's Bay on Moorea, this is one of the most photographed scenes in the entire South Pacific. Others sit right on the edge of the clifflike reef, making for superb snorkeling right off your front deck. Ashore, the Hotel Bora Bora also has large, luxurious bungalows which boast their own courtyards with swimming pools; they are French Polynesia's most private quarters. The **Hotel Sofitel Marara** itself is not as charming or luxurious as others on Bora Bora, but about five of its over-water units are the most private in French Polynesia, and they have large, partially covered decks. Those at the **Moana Beach Parkroyal** are French Polynesia's most luxurious; they sit so far out on a pier that room service is canoe-borne. Sitting on a *motu* (little island), the **Bora Bora Lagoon Resort** has 50 rather closely packed bungalows over its reef, some with great views of Bora Bora's "other" peak, the more rounded Mount Pahia. Likewise at the spacious, nicely decorated units at the friendly **Pearl Beach Resort Bora Bora,** which also sits on its own island. More private, some beachside units at the Pearl Beach have fence-surrounded patios with Jacuzzi pools. On another islet off Bora Bora's east coast, **Le Meridien Bora Bora** sports 80 overwater units which are a tad small for the amount of furniture they contain. You'd also better like sand and sunshine, for Le Meridien is almost devoid of shade trees. See chapter 6.

On Huahine, units at the **Tiare Beach Resort** have the largest decks of any over-water bungalows (one side is completely shaded by a thatch roof). The **Hotel Sofitel Heiva** has six bungalows with views of the mountainous main part of that island. See "Huahine" in chapter 6.

On Rangiroa, the **Kia Ora Village** has them over the world's second-largest lagoon. See "Rangiroa" in chapter 6.

And on Manihi, units at the **Manihi Pearl Beach Resort** are cooled by the almost constantly blowing trade winds. Isolated on its own *motu,* the Pearl Beach here more closely resembles Fiji's offshore resorts than any other in French Polynesia. See "Manihi" in chapter 6.

- **Fiji:** For the remote island experience, Fiji has one of the world's finest collections of small offshore resorts. These little establishments have two advantages over their French Polynesian competitors. First, they have only 3 to 15 bungalows each, instead of the 40 or more found at the French Polynesian resorts, which means they are usually more widely spaced than their Tahitian cousins. Second, they are on islands all by themselves. Together, these two advantages multiply the privacy factor severalfold.

  Off Nadi, the atmosphere at the 16-unit **Turtle Island Lodge** and the 18-bungalow **Vatulele Island Resort,** both of which are in the luxurious, superexpensive category, is active, with guests given the choice of dining alone in their bungalows or at lively dinner parties hosted by the engaging owners. **Yasawa**

Island Resort sits on one of the prettiest beaches and has a very low-key, friendly ambiance. It has 16 very large bungalows, the absolute choice being the secluded honeymoon unit sitting by its own beach. If you can't get that, be sure to reserve one of the newer units, since a communal pathway runs just outside the bedroom windows of the older bungalows. See "Resorts Offshore from Nadi" in chapter 9.

In central Fiji off Suva, **The Wakaya Club** has eight of the largest bungalows in Fiji, and a staff that leaves the guests to their own devices, while the much less expensive **Toberua Island Resort** occupies its own tiny islet surrounded by a shallow reef upon which guests can play "reef golf" at low tide. See "Resorts Offshore from Suva" in chapter 10.

Out in Northern Fiji, motivational speaker Anthony Robbins and his wife, Becky, have equipped **Namale Resort** with some of Fiji's most romantic honeymoon bungalows, with double-sized chaise lounges strewn with pillows, mosquito nets hanging over heavy bamboo-poster beds, and huge bathrooms with Jacuzzi tubs and ceiling fans. See "Savusavu" in chapter 11.

On a dragon-shaped island all by itself in the Koro Sea off Savusavu, **Moody's Namena** is the most remote of all South Pacific resorts. All but one of its hexagonal bungalows are perched tree house–like on a ridge, providing both privacy and stunning sea views. "Occupied/Unoccupied" signs warn guests that someone else is already cavorting on four of the island's five private beaches. See "A Resort off Savusavu" in chapter 11.

Off Taveuni, also in Northern Fiji, movie stars and others with the bucks head to **Fiji Forbes Laucala Island,** the retreat of the late publisher Malcolm S. Forbes, Sr., off Taveuni. Staying there is like being a houseguest at a millionaire's private retreat (the staff will bring your meals anywhere on the island, including your own private beach). Nearby **Matagi Island Resort** is one of the region's best values and best family vacation spots. Of its 11 widely spaced bungalows, two are built 20 feet up in Pacific almond trees (they are reserved for honeymooners). Among my favorites are the 11 bungalows and stunning central building at **Qamea Beach Club.** Kerosene lanterns romantically light the 52-foot-high thatch roof of Qamea's main building, and each bungalow has its own hammock strung across the front porch. See "Resorts Offshore from Taveuni" in chapter 11.

4 The Best Family Vacations

There are no Disney Worlds or other such attractions in the islands. That's not to say that children won't have a fine time here, but they will enjoy themselves more if they like playing in the water.

Any family can vacation in style and comfort at large resorts like the two Sheraton resorts in Fiji, or Shangri-la's Fijian Resort, but here are some of the best smaller establishments that welcome families with children.

- **Moorea Beachcomber Parkroyal** (Moorea, French Polynesia; ☎ **55.19.19**): The most modern resort on Moorea, the Beachcomber has an attractive swimming pool, a calm lagoon, and the widest selection of water sports in French Polynesia. See chapter 5.
- **Bora Bora Lagoon Resort** (Bora Bora, French Polynesia; ☎ **800/223-6800**): In addition to a fine attended beach, this super-deluxe hotel has one of the largest and most attractive swimming pool areas in French Polynesia. It also has satellite TVs in every unit, great for parking the kids on rainy days. See chapter 6.
- **Muri Beachcomber** (Rarotonga, Cook Islands; ☎ **21-022**): There is no restaurant at the Muri Beachcomber premises—several dining options are a short walk

away along lovely Muri Beach—but what you do get here are one-bedroom apartments facing a swimming pool, so the folks can keep a sharp eye on the kids taking a dip. Or you can opt for one of three houses equipped with all the modern amenities of a little resort. The lagoon here is peaceful, shallow, and safe. See chapter 7.

- **Castaway Island Resort** (Mamanuca Islands, Fiji; ☎ 800/888-0120): One of Fiji's oldest but thoroughly refurbished resorts, Castaway has plenty to keep both adults and children occupied, from a wide array of water sports to a kid's playroom and a nursery. There's even a nurse on duty. See "Resorts Offshore from Nadi" in chapter 9.
- **Jean-Michel Cousteau Fiji Islands Resort** (Savusavu, Fiji; ☎ 800/246-3454): Parents are required to enroll their kids in this environmentally sensitive resort's educational program, the South Pacific's finest. It will keep the youngsters both taught and entertained from sun-up to bedtime. See "Savusavu" in chapter 11.
- **Matagi Island Resort** (Northern Fiji; ☎ 888/MATANGI): Born as a hard-core dive base, this low-key, family-run resort has adjusted to divers who want to bring the youngsters along. Parents do their two dives—or go snorkeling—in the morning, while those who stay behind help the staff keep the kids busy building sand castles. The children have their own mealtimes, but everyone is welcome to make visits to Fijian villages, go on picnics to fabulous Horseshoe Bay, or hike up to Bouma Falls on Taveuni. See "Resorts Offshore from Taveuni" in chapter 11.
- **Aggie Grey's Hotel** (Apia, Samoa; ☎ 800/448-8355): The grande dame of South Pacific hotels, family-owned Aggie's is not on a beach, but the complex surrounds a courtyard whose swimming pool has a coconut palm sitting on its own little island. Although the clientele is primarily adult, the friendly Samoan staff is adept at taking care of children. See chapter 12.

5 The Best Cultural Experiences

The South Pacific Islanders are justly proud of their ancient Polynesian and Fijian cultures, and they eagerly inform anyone who asks about both their ancient and modern ways. Here are some of the best ways to learn about the islanders and their lifestyles.

- **Tiki Theatre Village** (Moorea, French Polynesia): Built to resemble a pre-European Tahitian village, this cultural center on Moorea has handcraft demonstrations and puts on a nightly dance show and feast. It's a bit commercial, and the staff isn't always fluent in English, but this is the only place in French Polynesia where you can sample the old ways. See chapter 5.
- **Rarotonga** (Cook Islands): In addition to offering some of the region's most laidback beach vacations, the people of Rarotonga go out of their way to let visitors know about their unique Cook Islands way of life. A morning spent at the Cook Islands Cultural Village and on a cultural tour of the island is an excellent educational experience. For a look at flora and fauna of the island, and their traditional uses, Pa's Nature Walks cannot be topped. See chapter 7.
- **Fijian Village Visits** (Fiji): Many tours from Nadi and from most offshore resorts include visits to traditional Fijian villages, whose residents stage welcoming ceremonies (featuring the slightly narcotic drink kava) and then show visitors around and explain how the old and the new combine in today's villages. See "Sightseeing Tours" in chapter 9.
- **Devokula Village** (Ovalau Island, Fiji): About 13 kilometers (8 miles) north of Levuka, Devokula was constructed in the mid-1990s to look exactly as Fijian villages did before European traders introduced tin roofing to the islands. The

villagers perform traditional welcoming ceremonies, feasts, and dances for visitors. See "Levuka & Ovalau" in chapter 10.

- **Samoa:** The entire country of Samoa is a cultural storehouse of *fa'a Samoa,* the old Samoan way of doing things. Most Samoans still live in villages featuring oval *fales,* some of which have stood for centuries (although tin roofs have replaced thatch). The island of Savai'i is especially well preserved. See chapter 12.

- **Touring Savai'i** (Samoa): A highlight of any visit to Savai'i should be a tour with Warren Jopling, a retired Australian geologist who has lived on Samoa's largest island for many years. Not only does he know the forbidding lava fields like the back of his hand, everyone on Savai'i knows him, which helps make his cultural commentaries extremely informative. See "Savai'i" in chapter 12.

- **Tongan National Centre** (Nuku'alofa, Tonga): Artisans turn out classic Tongan handcrafts, and a museum exhibits Tongan history, including the robe worn by Queen Salote at the coronation of Queen Elizabeth II in 1953, and the carcass of Tui Malila, a Galápagos turtle that Capt. James Cook reputedly gave to the King of Tonga in 1777, and which lived until 1968. The center also has island-night dance shows and feasts of traditional Tongan food. See chapter 14.

6 The Best of the Old South Seas

Many South Pacific islands are developing rapidly, with modern, fast-paced cities replacing what were sleepy backwater ports at Papeete in French Polynesia and Suva in Fiji. There still are many remnants of the Old South Sea days of coconut planters, beach bums, and missionaries.

- **Fare** (Huahine, French Polynesia): Of the French Polynesian islands frequented by visitors, Huahine has been the least affected by tourism. As on Aitutaki, agriculture is still king on Huahine, which makes it the "Island of Fruits." There are ancient marae temples to visit, and the only town, tiny Fare, is little more than a collection of Chinese shops fronting the island's wharf, which comes to life when ships pull in. See "Huahine" in chapter 6.

- **Aitutaki** (Cook Islands): Noted for its crystal-clear lagoon, the little island of Aitutaki is very much Old Polynesia, with most of its residents still farming and fishing for a living. See "A Side Trip to Aitutaki" in chapter 7.

- **Levuka** (Ovalau Island, Fiji): No town has remained as much the same after a century as has Levuka, Fiji's first European-style town and its original colonial capital in the 1870s. The dramatic cliffs of Ovalau Island hemmed in the town and prevented growth, so the government moved to Suva in 1882. Levuka looks very much as it did then, with a row of clapboard general stores along picturesque Beach Street. See "Levuka & Ovalau" in chapter 10.

- **Taveuni Island** (Northern Fiji): Like Savai'i, Fiji's third-largest and most lush island has changed little since Europeans started coconut plantations there in the 1860s. With the largest remaining population of indigenous plants and animals of any South Pacific island, Taveuni is a nature lover's delight. See "Taveuni" in chapter 11.

- **Apia** (Samoa): Despite a sea wall along what used to be a beach, and two large high-rise buildings sitting on reclaimed land, a number of clapboard buildings and 19th-century churches make Apia look much as it did when German, American, and British warships washed ashore during a hurricane here in 1889. See chapter 12.

- **Savai'i** (Samoa): One of the largest of all Polynesian islands, this great volcanic shield is also one of the least populated, with the oval-shaped houses of traditional villages sitting beside freshwater bathing pools fed by underground springs. See "Savai'i" in chapter 12.

- **Neiafu** (Vava'u, Tonga): Although Nuku'alofa, the capital of Tonga on the main island of Tongatapu, still has a dusty, 19th-century ambiance, the little village of Neiafu on the sailor's paradise of Vava'u has remained untouched by development. Built by convicted adulteresses, the Road of the Doves still winds above the dramatic Port of Refuge, just as it did in 1875. See "Vava'u" in chapter 14.

7 The Best Food

You won't be stuck eating island-style food cooked in an earth oven (see "The Islanders" in the appendix), nor will you be limited to the rather bland tastes of New Zealanders and Australians, which predominate at most restaurants. Wherever the French go, fine food and wine are sure to follow, and French Polynesia is no exception. The East Indians brought curries to Fiji, and chefs trained there have spread those spicy offerings to the other islands. Many chefs in Tonga are from Germany and Italy and specialize in their native foods. Chinese cuisine of varying quality can be found everywhere. And a Kenyan-born Englishwoman has brought exotic tastes to the Cook Islands.

Wine connoisseurs will have ample opportunity to sample the vintages from nearby Australia, where abundant sunshine produces renowned full-bodied, fruit-driven varieties, such as Chardonnay, Semillon, Riesling, Shiraz, hermitage, cabernet sauvignon, and Merlot. New Zealand wines also are widely available, including distinctive whites, such as Chenin Blanc, sauvignon blanc, and soft, plummy Merlot. Freight and import duties drive up the cost of wine, so expect higher prices than at home.

- **Auberge du Pacifique** (Papeete, Tahiti): Award-winning chef Jean Galopin has been blending French and Polynesian cuisines at his lagoonside restaurant—with a removable roof to let in starlight—since 1974. He's even written a cookbook about Tahitian cooking. See chapter 4.
- **Le Lotus** (Papeete, Tahiti): The most romantic setting of any South Pacific restaurant is this over-water dining room at the Tahiti Beachcomber Parkroyal. Even without gourmet French cuisine and highly efficient but unobtrusive service, the view of Moorea on a moonlit night makes an evening here special. See chapter 4.
- **Alfredo's** (Moorea, French Polynesia): Folks who don't speak French or understand French cuisine can be intimidated at restaurants in French Polynesia, but not at Christian Boucheron's friendly establishment, where everyone speaks English and the selections are familiar and very good Italian fare. See chapter 5.
- **Te Honu Iti (Chez Roger)** (Moorea, French Polynesia): Assuming he has rebuilt it after a fire, you can dine right beside awesomely beautiful Cook's Bay at chef Roger Iqual's snack bar-cum-restaurant, where he gives some delightful twists to seafood prepared in the classic French fashion. See chapter 5.
- **L'Aventure Restaurant** (Moorea, French Polynesia): Here's another place for great French-style seafood, this time from the kitchen of chef Bernard Procuer. See chapter 5.
- **Bloody Mary's Restaurant & Bar** (Bora Bora, French Polynesia): The chargrilled seafood and steaks aren't reason enough alone to come to Bloody's, but stagehands built this remarkable thatch-roofed building after they had finished a movie here, resulting in the most unique and charming dining venue in the islands. See chapter 6.
- **The Flame Tree** (Rarotonga, Cook Islands): Born and bred in Kenya, owner Sue Carruthers brings the spicy cuisine of her native land to one of the South Pacific's

top restaurants. Sue has written a popular cookbook about The Flame Tree's offerings. See chapter 7.

- **Vilisite's Seafood Restaurant** (The Coral Coast, Fiji): This seaside restaurant, owned and operated by a friendly Fijian woman named Vilisite, doesn't look like much from the outside, but she offers a handful of excellent seafood meals to augment a terrific view along Fiji's Coral Coast from the veranda. See chapter 9.
- **Chefs, The Restaurant** (Nadi, Fiji): Perhaps the best restaurant in the islands, chef Eugeme Gomes' urbane establishment has gourmet cuisine, excellent service, and lots of little touches to make for a fine dining experience. See chapter 10.
- **Old Mill Cottage** (Suva, Fiji): Diplomats and government workers pack this old colonial cottage at breakfast and lunch for some of the region's best and least expensive local fare. Offerings range from English-style roast chicken with mashed potatoes and peas to sweet Fijian-style *palusami* (fresh fish wrapped in taro leaves and steamed in coconut milk). See chapter 10.
- **Sails Restaurant and Bar** (Apia, Samoa): Ian and Lyvia Black have turned Robert Louis Stevenson's first Samoan home into one of the South Pacific's best casual restaurants, complete with tables on an upstairs veranda overlooking historic Beach Road and Apia Harbor. You'll never forget Ian's Commodore Sashimi. See chapter 12.
- **Seaview Restaurant** (Nuku'alofa, Tonga): In a country where restaurants come and go, this German-owned establishment in an old waterfront home has for years provided Nuku'alofa's best cuisine. Tonga is the last island nation with an abundance of spiny tropical lobsters, so go for one here. See chapter 14.
- **Ocean Breeze Restaurant** (Vava'u, Tonga:): A native of Tonga, Amelia Dale learned to cook curries while living in London, and hers are the best in the islands (and that includes Fiji, where the population is almost half East Indian). In fact, I've never had better, even in India or Pakistan. See chapter 14.

8 The Best Island Nights

Don't come to the South Pacific islands expecting opera and ballet, or Las Vegas-style floor shows, either. Other than pub crawling to bars and nightclubs with music for dancing, evening entertainment here consists primarily of island nights, which invariably feature feasts of island foods followed by traditional dancing.

In the cases of French Polynesia and the Cook Islands, of course, their hip-swinging traditional dances are world famous. They are not as lewd and lascivious as they were in the days before the missionaries arrived, but they still have plenty of suggestive movements to the beat of primordial drums. By contrast, dancing in Fiji, Tonga, and the Samoas is much more reserved, with graceful movements, terrific harmony, and occasional action in a war or fire dance.

- **French Polynesia:** Hotels are the places in which to see Tahitian dancing here, with the best troupe usually at the Hyatt Regency Tahiti. Elsewhere, the resorts rely on village groups to perform a few times a week. The very best shows are during the annual *Heiva Tahiti* festival in July; the winners then tour the other islands in August for minifestivals at the resorts. See "Island Nights" in chapters 4, 5, and 6.
- **The Cook Islands:** Although the Tahitians are more famous for their dancing, many of their original movements were quashed by the missionaries in the early 19th century. When the French took over and allowed dancing again, the Tahitians had forgotten much of the old movements. They turned to the Cook

Islands, where dancing was—and still is—the thing to do when the sun goes down. The costumes tend to be more natural and less colorful than in the Tahitian floor shows, but the movements tend to be more active, suggestive, and genuine. There's an island night show every evening except Sunday on Rarotonga. The best troupes usually perform at the Edgewater Resort and the Rarotongan Resort, but ask around. The best public performances are during the annual Dancer of the Year contest in April and the Constitution Week celebrations in August. See "Island Nights" in chapter 7.

- **Samoa:** Among the great shows in the South Pacific are *fiafia* nights in the magnificent main building at Aggie Grey's Hotel in Apia. This tradition was started in the 1940s by the late Aggie Grey, who at the show's culmination personally danced the graceful *siva.* Daughter-in-law Marina Grey now plays that role, and the show has been expanded to include a rousing fire dance around the adjacent swimming pool. See "Island Nights" in chapter 12.
- **Tonga:** The weekly shows at the Tongan National Centre are unique, for this museum provides expert commentary before each dance, explaining its movements and their meanings. That's a big help, since all songs throughout the South Pacific are in the native languages. See "Island Nights" in chapter 14.

9 The Best Buys

Take some extra money along, for you'll spend it on handcrafts, black pearls, and tropical clothing.

For the locations of the best shops, see "Shopping" in chapters 5 through 15.

- **Black Pearls:** Few women will escape French Polynesia or the Cook Islands without buying at least one black pearl. That's because the shallow, clear-water lagoons of French Polynesia's Tuamotu Archipelago and the Cook Islands' Manihiki and Penrhyn atolls are the world's largest producers of the beautiful dark orbs. The seemingly inexhaustible supply has resulted in fierce competition by vendors ranging from market stalls to high-end jewelry shops. See chapters 4, 5, 6, and 7.
- **Handcrafts:** Although many of the items you will see in island souvenir shops actually are made in Asia, locally produced handcrafts are the South Pacific's best buys. The most widespread are hats, mats, and baskets woven of pandanus or other fibers, usually by women who have maintained this ancient art to a high degree. Tonga has the widest selection of woven items, although Samoa and Fiji have made comebacks in recent years. The finely woven mats made in Tonga and the Samoas are still highly valued as ceremonial possessions and are seldom for sale to tourists.

  Before the coming of European traders and printed cotton, the South Pacific islanders wore garments made from the beaten bark of the paper mulberry tree. The making of this bark cloth, widely known as *tapa,* is another preserved art in Tonga, Samoa, and Fiji (where it is known as *masi*). The cloth is painted with dyes made from natural substances, usually in geometric designs dating back thousands of years. Tapa is an excellent souvenir, since it can be folded and brought back in a suitcase.

  Wood carvings are also popular. Spears, war clubs, knives made from sharks' teeth, canoe prows, and cannibal forks are some examples. Many carvings, however, tend to be produced for the tourist trade and often lack the imagery of bygone days, and some may be machine-produced today. Carved tikis are found in most South Pacific countries, but many of them resemble the figures of the New Zealand Maoris rather than figures indigenous to those countries. The carvings from the Marquesas Islands of French Polynesia are the best of the lot today.

Note: Some governments restrict the export of antique carvings and other artifacts of historic value. If the piece looks old, check before you buy.

Jewelry made of shells and of pink or black coral is available in many countries, as is scrimshaw, but be careful when you shop, for items made of black coral and whale bone cannot legally be brought back to the United States and most other Western countries.

- **Tropical Clothing:** Colorful hand-screened, hand-blocked, and hand-dyed fabrics are very popular in the islands for making dresses or the wraparound skirt known as *pareu* in Tahiti and Rarotonga, *lavalava* in the Samoas and Tonga, and *sulu* in Fiji. Heat-sensitive dyes are applied by hand to gauzelike cotton, which is then laid in the sun for several hours. Flowers, leaves, and other designs are placed on the fabric, and as the heat of the sun darkens and sets the dyes, the shadows from these objects leave their images behind on the finished product.

10 The Best Diving & Snorkeling

All the islands have excellent scuba diving and snorkeling, and all but a few of the resorts either have their own dive operations or can easily make arrangements with a local company. For useful information on the Web, check out the Professional Association of Diving Instructors site ot **www.padi.com**. Rodale's *Scuba Diving Magazine* also has a helpful Web site at **www.scubadiving.com**.

- **Rangiroa and Manihi** (French Polynesia): Like those surrounding most populated islands, many lagoons in French Polynesia have been relatively fished out over the years. That's not to say that diving in such places as Moorea and Bora Bora can't be world class, but the best now is at Rangiroa and Manihi in the Tuamotu Archipelago, both famous more for their abundant sea life, including sharks, than colorful soft corals. Go to Rangiroa to see sharks; to Manihi to see more fish than you imagined ever existed. See "Rangiroa" and "Manihi" in chapter 6.
- **Northern Fiji:** With nutrient-rich waters welling up from the Tonga Trench offshore and being carried by strong currents funneling through narrow passages, Fiji is famous for some of the world's most colorful soft corals. This is especially true of the Somosomo Strait between Vanua Levu and Taveuni in Northern Fiji, home of the Rainbow Reef and the Great White Wall. The Beqa Lagoon and Astrolabe Reef also are famous for plentiful soft corals. See chapter 11.
- **Tonga:** The north shore of the main island of Tongatapu fronts a huge lagoon, where the government has made national parks of the Hakaumama'o and Malinoa reefs. The best diving in Tonga, however, is around unspoiled Ha'apai and Vava'u. See chapter 14.

11 The Best Golf & Tennis

While many resorts have tennis courts, both tennis and golf are secondary to water sports in the South Pacific islands. Except for Fiji, the countries in this book just don't have enough land for golf courses. In the Cook Islands, for example, the very flat courses on both Rarotonga and Aitutaki run under the guy wires of the local radio stations, making for some interesting obstacles but not particularly challenging golf. In

Tonga, the only course is a flat nine holes where the highlight may be playing behind the crown prince.

The best links in the South Pacific are those designed by Robert Trent Jones at **Centra Resort Pacific Harbour,** on Fiji's main island of Viti Levu. Unfortunately, they are in Viti Levu's rain belt, which caused the early demise of the original Pacific Harbor real estate development. See "Pacific Harbour" in chapter 9.

Across the road from the Sheraton Fiji and The Regent of Fiji resorts, **Denarau Golf & Racquet Club** has Fiji's most popular course. It's also the region's only tennis facility, managed by Peter Bourwash International. See chapter 9.

French Polynesia has only one course, and it's on the south shore of Tahiti, an hour's drive from Papeete. If you stay on Moorea, Bora Bora, or another island, leave your clubs at home. See chapter 4.

12 The Best Sailing

You would think that the South Pacific is a yachting paradise, and it certainly gets more than its share of cruising boats on holiday from Australia and New Zealand or heading around the world (the region is on the safest circumnavigation route). The reefs in most places, however, make sailing a precarious undertaking, so yachting is not that widespread. It has only recently gained a toehold in Fiji. There are only two places where you can charter a yacht and sail it yourself:

- **Raiatea** (French Polynesia): The Moorings and two French firms have charter fleets based in Raiatea in the Leeward Islands of French Polynesia. Raiatea shares a lagoon with Tahaa, a hilly island indented with long bays that shelter numerous picturesque anchorages. Boats can be sailed completely around Tahaa without leaving the lagoon, but both Bora Bora and Huahine are just 20 miles away over blue water. See "Raiatea & Tahaa" in chapter 6.
- **Vava'u** (Tonga): The second-most-popular yachting spot, Vava'u is virtually serrated by well-protected bays like the nearby Port of Refuge. Chains of small islands trail off the south side of Vava'u like the tentacles of a jellyfish, creating large and very quiet cruising grounds. Many anchorages are off deserted islands with their own beaches. See "Vava'u" in chapter 14.

2

Planning a Trip to the South Pacific

While they are similar in many respects, Tahiti and French Polynesia, the Cook Islands, Fiji, Samoa, American Samoa, and the Kingdom of Tonga have their own sources of information, entry requirements, currency, government, customs, laws, internal transportation, styles of accommodation, and food. Since the South Pacific can hold some surprises, wise planning is essential to get the most out of your time and money spent in this vast and varied modern paradise. This chapter gives a brief description of the islands and tells you how to plan your trip in general. It augments, but is not a substitute for, the information contained in the individual chapters that follow.

1 The Islands in Brief

The islands covered in this book are variations on an overall cultural theme, for most are part of the great Polynesian Triangle extending across the Pacific from Hawaii to Easter Island to New Zealand. Each has carved its own identity, yet each is fundamentally Polynesian. Only Fiji is significantly different. Living on the border between Polynesia and the Melanesian islands to the west, the indigenous Fijians look more like African-Americans than like their Polynesian neighbors. Their distinctly Fijian culture blends elements from both Polynesia and Melanesia. The Fijians also share their islands with East Indians, who add a starkly contrasting culture to the mix.

In the old days, islanders throughout the South Pacific lived in an environment that required little in the way of clothes, shelter, or effort to gather food, which grew abundantly on trees or could be found in the lagoons surrounding their islands. Although a growing number of young islanders are unemployed today, a perpetually warm climate, rich volcanic soils on most islands, and the islanders' strong communal family system mean that hunger and homelessness are virtually nonexistent. The islanders' extended family system is a testament to their strong sense of tradition, for they are consciously blending their old lifestyles with Western culture and amenities. While television and automobiles are a fact of life on all the main islands, so are many of the ancient customs, which adds a cultural richness to any visit to this area.

Let's make a quick tour to see what each island country or territory contributes to this fascinating smorgasbord.

TAHITI & FRENCH POLYNESIA

If there is a "major league" of dramatically beautiful islands, then Tahiti and its French Polynesian companions dominate it.

High and well-watered, **Tahiti** is the largest of the French Polynesian islands and was the first to be discovered by European explorers in the late 18th century. A great majority of the territory's population lives on Tahiti, especially in and around **Papeete,** the famous capital. Today this busy little city is so overrun by cars, trucks, and motor scooters that it can take up to 2 hours to commute to work from the outlying regions. A building boom has drastically changed Papeete's face in the past 25 years, and the town has lost its old charm. So I will say from the outset: If you're going to travel this far, don't just stop on Tahiti.

To find Polynesia, put your sights on Tahiti's companion islands. This is especially true of **Moorea** and **Bora Bora,** which surely must provide Hollywood with many of its choice stock shots of glorious tropical settings. Moorea's jagged, shark's-teeth ridges serrate the horizon like the back of some primordial dinosaur resting on the sea just 20 kilometers (12 miles) west of Tahiti. Tourism is not the main forte on the much larger Moorea, which although growing as a bedroom community for Papeete workers (housing tracts are beginning to climb its gorgeous mountains), is still primarily rural and laid-back. Bora Bora, whose famous tombstone-like central peak leaps out of one of the world's most spectacular lagoons, relies almost exclusively on tourists and their dollars—and lots of their dollars, too, for this is the South Pacific's most expensive destination.

Even more of old Polynesia exists on the territory's third most beautiful island, **Huahine,** which locals have taken to calling "wild" because of its undeveloped status. It's not all wild, however, for you can stay at a fine resort while exploring some of the region's most important archaeological remains. Nearby, the adjacent islands of **Raiatea** and **Tahaa** are even more natural. Raiatea has no beaches, and Tahaa has no resorts, but together they are French Polynesia's prime sailing grounds.

Off to the northeast, the great line of atolls known as the **Tuamotu Archipelago** boasts two top scuba diving destinations. **Rangiroa,** which encloses the world's second largest lagoon, is known for remarkably clear waters which are home to thousands of sharks. Much smaller and shallower, the fish-filled lagoon at **Manihi** makes it the world's largest producer of black pearls.

As the name states, this most eastern part of Polynesia is an overseas territory of France, and the Gallic *joie de vivre* is a mere overlay on the Tahitians' laid-back lifestyle, one of the most storied—and studied—in all Polynesia. The Tahitians' easygoing attitude about most things captivated Europeans of the 1770s, who saw in them the perfect example of Jean-Jacques Rousseau's noble savage, who lived in harmony with nature without artificial restraints. More than any South Pacific peoples, the French Polynesians—and their cousins in the nearby Cook Islands—have maintained this easygoing, relatively unrestrained lifestyle.

THE COOK ISLANDS

About 500 miles west of Tahiti, the tiny Cook Islands have much in common with French Polynesia. Barely 32 kilometers (20 miles) around, **Rarotonga** is a miniature Tahiti in terms of its mountains, beaches, and reefs—and in terms of development, it's like Tahiti was some 50 years ago. No other South Pacific destination has so many hotels, restaurants, daytime activities, and nightclubs packed into so small a space as does Rarotonga. Unlike Papeete, however, the Cook Islands' capital of **Avarua** remains a quiet little backwater, a picturesque village without a stoplight. Among the outer

The South Pacific

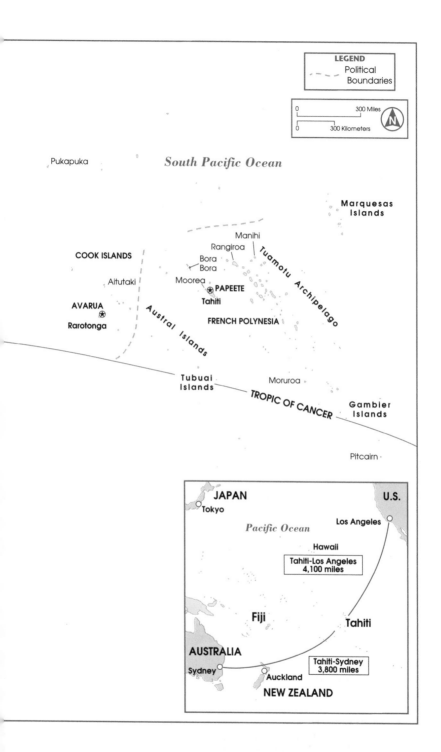

I wish I could tell you about the South Pacific. The way it actually was. The endless ocean. The infinite specks of coral we call islands. Coconut palms nodding gracefully toward the ocean. Reefs upon which waves broke into spray, the inner lagoons, lovely beyond description.

—James A. Michener, 1947

islands, **Aitutaki** bears the same relationship to Rarotonga as Bora Bora does to Tahiti, with a small central island surrounded by a shallow but spectacular aquamarine lagoon. It's worth a side trip to Aitutaki just to take a lagoon excursion out to the little islands fringing the reef. The beaches out there have the region's only pure white, talcum-like sand.

The Cook Islanders share with the Tahitians a fun-loving lifestyle, many of the old Polynesian legends and gods, and about 60% of their native language. Since the Cooks were a New Zealand territory from 1901 until 1965 and are still associated with New Zealand, Cook Islanders speak English fluently. This makes it easy for English-speaking travelers to take advantage of the South Pacific's most informative cultural tours and exhibits.

FIJI

Because its international airport at Nadi is the region's major transportation hub, Fiji is a prime place with which to begin or end a trip to the South Pacific. In fact, twice as many people of every income bracket visit Fiji each year as come to any other South Pacific island destination.

This lush country of 300-plus islands has something for everyone to do—from lying on some of the region's best beaches to scuba diving on some of the world's most colorful reefs, from cruising intriguing outer islands to hiking into the mountainous interior.

Although it's primarily a stop to and from more beautiful parts of Fiji, the **Nadi** area has two of the country's largest resorts and is awash with activities. From Nadi you can ride or trek into the tropical highlands or cruise out to the **Mamanuca** and **Yasawa** islands, all little specks of land which are home to fine beaches, a host of water sports, and a wide range of unpretentious off-shore resorts. Or you can take the Queen's Road south to the **Coral Coast,** Fiji's first resort area, and on to **Pacific Harbour,** known for its challenging golf course, great deep sea fishing, and diving on the nearby Beqa Lagoon.

The Queen's Road leads on to Fiji's cosmopolitan capital city, **Suva.** Although known for its rainy climate, Suva gives a glimpse of the bygone era when Great Britain ruled here. A 10-minute flight from Suva will whisk you to the island of **Ovalau,** where the country's first European-style town, **Levuka,** still looks like it did in the late 1800s before the government pulled up stakes and moved to Suva.

Up in Northern Fiji, the large islands of **Vanua Levu** and **Taveuni** will transport you back in time to the Fiji of colonial coconut plantations. Between the two islands lies the **Somosomo Strait,** home to the Great White Wall, the Rainbow Reef, and other world-class dive sites.

Fiji has the South Pacific's most fascinating mix of extraordinarily friendly peoples. About half are easygoing Fijians, most of whom still live in traditional villages surrounded by vegetable gardens. Slightly less than half are industrious—and sometimes abrasive—East Indians whose ancestors came to work the sugarcane plantations, which make Fiji one of the richest South Pacific countries, and stayed to found a class of intellectuals and merchants. Although the contrasting Fijian-Indian cultures have resulted in political friction, they also make this an interesting place to get into a conversation.

Fiji also has a great variety of accommodations, from romantic getaway resorts ranging from backpackers' hostels fetching just $5 for a bed to some charging more than $1,000 a couple a night—all-inclusive, I might add. In between wait a variety of fine establishments, affordable for all. Fiji also has many inexpensive restaurants, offering excellent value.

THE SAMOAS

Known until 1997 as Western Samoa, independent **Samoa** is like a cultural museum, especially when compared with its much smaller cousin, **American Samoa.** The peoples of both are related by family and tradition, if not politics. While Samoan culture still exists in the American islands, it is preserved to a remarkable degree in Samoa, relatively unchanged by modern materialism. Traditional Samoan villages, with their turtle-shaped houses, rest peacefully along the coasts of the two main western Samoan islands, **Upolu** and **Savai'i.** Time seems to have forgotten even the weather-beaten, clapboard buildings of **Apia,** the country's picturesque capital. Although tourism is not a major industry, the country has two luxury beach resorts and modern hotels from which to fan out and meet the friendly Samoans. Experiencing their unique culture and visiting their truly remarkable and undeveloped beaches (one of which was the setting for the Gary Cooper movie *Return to Paradise)* are highlights of any visit.

Tutuila, the main island in American Samoa, rivals the dramatic beauty of Moorea and Bora Bora in French Polynesia. The mountains drop straight down into fabled **Pago Pago,** the finest harbor in the South Pacific and the main reason that the United States has had a presence there since 1890. This American presence has resulted in a blend of cultures: the Samoan emphasis on extended families and communal ownership of property, especially land; and the Western emphasis on business and progress. The result of the latter is that Pago Pago harbor is dominated—and polluted—by two large tuna canneries. The road around it is often clogged with vehicles as American Samoans rush past their traditional villages on their way to the region's only warehouse-style shopping center.

Despite its economic development and Pago Pago's growing role as a regional transportation and shipping center, tourism plays a very minor role in American Samoa. Although there are small, simple places to stay, the territory's only modern hotel is in serious need of repair, and there are few quality restaurants. On the other hand, American Samoa is easily seen on a day trip from Apia.

TONGA

From his Victorian palace in **Nuku'alofa,** King Taufa'ahau Tupou IV of Tonga—all 300-plus pounds of him—rules over a nobility that carries European titles but is in reality a pure Polynesian system of high chiefs. Despite considerable grumbling among his commoner subjects in recent years, the king and the nobles control the government and all the land, of which they are obligated to give 8½ acres to every Tongan adult male.

Impressions

All the time our visits to the islands have been more like dreams than realities: the people, the life, the beachcombers, the old stories and songs I have picked up, so interesting; the climate, the scenery, and (in some places) the women, so beautiful.
—Robert Louis Stevenson, 1889

While the relatively flat main island of **Tongatapu** offers little in the way of dramatic scenic beauty, and accommodations here are below international standard, the
adjacent lagoon provides excellent boating, snorkeling, fishing, and diving. On the
other hand, hilly **Vava'u** in the north presents long and narrow fjords and a plethora
of deserted islands, which make it one of the South Pacific's leading yachting centers.
Neiafu, the only town on Vava'u, is a reminder of the old days of traders and beach
bums.

In between Tongatapu and Vava'u, the **Ha'apai** group of atoll-like islands also is a
throwback to an earlier time. The little village of **Pangai** looks as it must have when
the first Christian missionaries arrived in the early 1800s and proceeded to convert the
entire country.

Indeed, Tonga is the heart of the South Pacific "Bible Belt." While things are slow
on Sunday in most island countries, they stop completely in Tonga—for picnics at the
beautiful beaches and escapes to resorts on tiny islets offshore.

2 Visitor Information & Entry Requirements

VISITOR INFORMATION

The best sources for data about the specific island countries are their tourist information offices (see "Visitor Information & Entry Requirements" in the following
chapters).

A good source for general information is the **Tourism Council of the South
Pacific (TCSP),** P.O. Box 13119, Suva, Fiji Islands (☎ **679/304177;** fax 679/
301-995; www.tcsp.com; e-mail spice@is.com.fj), an international organization which
promotes tourism throughout the region. TCSP has marketing representatives at 475
Lake Blvd. (P.O. Box 7440), Tahoe City, CA 96145 (☎ **916/583-0152;** fax 916/
583-0154), and in the United Kingdom (☎ **181/3921-838;** fax 181/3921-318),
France (☎ **76/700-617;** fax 76/700-918), and Germany (☎ **30/2381-7628;** fax
30/2381-7641).

Another general source is the **Pacific Asia Travel Association (PATA),** whose
North American office is at 1 Montgomery Street, Telesis Tower, Suite 1000, San Francisco, CA 94104 (☎ **415/986-4646;** fax 415/986-3458; www.pata.org; e-mail
americas@pata.org). PATA's South Pacific Regional Office, P.O. Box 645, Kings Cross,
NSW 1340, Australia (☎ **02/332-3599;** fax 02/331-6592; e-mail pata@world.net),
directly handles the island countries. The association's Web site is linked to the home
pages of each island country's visitors' bureau.

The U.S. Department of State maintains a 24-hour **Travel Advisory** (☎ **202/
647-5225;** http://travel.state.gov/travel_warnings.html) to keep you abreast of political or other problems throughout the world.

ENTRY REQUIREMENTS

All South Pacific countries require new arrivals to have a **passport** that will be valid
for the duration of the visit, and an onward or return airline ticket. Your passport
should be valid for 6 months beyond the date you expect to return home.

U.S. citizens and nationals can obtain passport applications (form DSP-11) from
the **U.S. Passport Agency** (☎ **202/647-0518**), which has offices in Boston, Chicago,
Honolulu, Houston, Los Angeles, Miami, New Orleans, New York, Philadelphia, San
Francisco, Seattle, Stamford, Conn., and Washington, D.C. You can also get them
from U.S. post offices or download them from the U.S. State Department's Web site
at http://travel.state.gov. Applications are accepted by the Passport Agency and by
some 3,500 post offices and federal courthouses around the U.S.

VISAS   The South Pacific island nations do not require citizens of the United States, Canada, Australia, New Zealand, Japan, and the European Community countries to have visas for stays of 30 days or less (see "Visitor Information & Entry Requirements" in each country chapter). At press time, those visitors could stay in Fiji for 4 months. As a practical matter, Samoa and Tonga will let them stay until the dates of their departing airline flights. See "Visitor Information & Entry Requirements" in chapters 3, 7, 8, 12, 13, and 14 for details.

VACCINATIONS   The only shot required to enter the South Pacific countries is for yellow fever, and then only if you're coming from an infected area of South America or Africa. It's a good idea, however, to have your tetanus, typhoid fever, polio, diphtheria, hepatitis-A, and hepatitis-B vaccinations up to date.

DRIVER'S LICENSES   Valid home country driver's licenses are recognized throughout the South Pacific, although you will need to get a local license in the Cook Islands, Samoa, and Tonga. No new test will be administered; it's just a way for these two countries to raise a little revenue. I have never found an international driver's license to be useful.

3 Money

CURRENCIES
The Cook Islands use New Zealand dollars, and American Samoa spends U.S. greenbacks. Otherwise, each South Pacific country has its own currency (see "Money" in the following chapters for details). U.S., Australian, and New Zealand dollars are accepted widely in the islands, however, and the local banks will change most other major currencies. Accordingly, don't bother changing currency before leaving home.

Your hometown bank may not be familiar with the exchange rates for the local currencies. On the Web, the Fiji Visitors Bureau's home page (**www.bulafiji.com**) has a link to a site giving current exchange rates for the local currencies against the U.S. dollar. You also can find them by navigating through the *Washington Post* newspaper's Web site at **www.washingtonpost.com**.

HOW TO GET LOCAL CURRENCY
Banks in all the main towns will cash, and most major hotels, resorts, restaurants, and car-rental firms will accept, **traveler's checks** issued by American Express, Thomas Cook, VISA, Bank of America, Citicorp, and MasterCard. You won't necessarily be able to cash traveler's checks on many outer islands with limited, if any, banking facilities. Also note that banks in French Polynesia and some other countries charge fees of up to $5 per transaction.

Holders of VISA and MasterCard credit cards can get cash advances at Westpac Bank, ANZ Bank, and Bank of Hawaii. Between them, Westpac and ANZ have offices or major stakes in local banks in every South Pacific country except French Polynesia. Bank of Hawaii has branches in Fiji.

Banks in Tahiti and Fiji have **ATMs,** at which you can use your Visa or MasterCard to withdraw local currency against your credit card or check (ATM) card account. Check your card member agreement for charges, since Visa and MasterCard tack on a 1% currency conversion fee, and some banks add up to 5% to the transaction. You can avoid some of these fees by using your check or ATM card (as opposed to a credit card), in which the funds are withdrawn directly from your checking account. During my last trip, I used my Visa check card and got a rate of exchange up to 5% better than if I had changed traveler's checks, and I avoided the bank's per-transaction fee for changing traveler's checks.

Readers Recommend

Getting Rid of Local Currency. *"When you are leaving an island and want to get rid of your local currency, use it to pay part of your hotel bill. Every place we stayed, they allowed us to pay part of the bill like that and then we would put the rest on our credit card. It definitely beat getting the crummy exchange rate at the airport."*

—Laurie P. Floyd, Freehold, New Jersey

Don't forget you'll need a 4-digit personal identification number (PIN) from your bank in order to use the ATMs.

The American Express agents in Tahiti and Fiji will cash card members' personal checks.

CREDIT CARDS

Most hotels, car-rental companies, and many restaurants and large shops accept VISA and MasterCard, less so American Express. Diners Club is present but not as widespread. Always ask first, and when you're away from the main towns, don't count on putting anything on plastic.

American Express has full-service representatives in Tahiti and Fiji. If you lose your American Express credit card or traveler's checks in the Cook Islands, American Samoa, or Tonga, have the international operator place a collect call to American Express's number in your home country. United States cardholders should phone collect, ☎ **336/393-1111.**

WHAT WILL IT COST?

Granted, it costs a fair sum to fly across the thousands of miles of ocean to the South Pacific islands, but from a cost standpoint, many destinations—including Hawaii—have caught up with the South Pacific in recent years. Although some resorts in French Polynesia and Fiji can set you back more than $1,000 a day, some hotels nick you $20 or more for their breakfast buffets, and a beer in some Tahitian nightclubs can run more than $10, you can have a fine time here without paying more for food and lodging than you would on a comparable vacation elsewhere. Indeed, cost-conscious travelers can get excellent value throughout the islands.

The South Pacific has a wide range of hotels, in both quality and price. Even in French Polynesia, dining out should be no more expensive than in most American cities, provided you eat somewhere other than in the big resort hotels, whose restaurants and dining rooms charge a premium for food and drink.

All of the islands impose duty on imported goods, including foodstuffs, so you will find many items in grocery and other stores to be more expensive than you may be used to at home. This is especially true in French Polynesia.

The following chapters contain tables giving precise price information for each country and territory. As you will see, prices vary from island to island. If cost is a major factor, compare this information before deciding which islands to visit.

TIPPING & TAXES

One other cost-saving factor: In the South Pacific, tipping is considered contrary to both the Polynesian and Melanesian traditions of hospitality and generosity. That's not to say that some small gratuity isn't in order for truly outstanding service, or that you won't get that "Where's-my-tip?" look from a porter as he sheepishly delays leaving your room, but American-style tipping officially is discouraged throughout the islands. Nor will you be socked with a service charge on your hotel and restaurant bills. So forget that hidden 15% or more your vacation could cost in the U.S.

Island Time

There's an old story about a 19th-century planter who promised a South Pacific islander a weekly wage and a pension if he would come to work on his copra plantation. Copra is dried coconut meat, from which oil is pressed for use in soaps, cosmetics, and other products. Hours of back-breaking labor are required to chop open the coconuts and extract the meat by hand.

When the planter approached the islander, the latter was sitting in the shade, eating the fruit he had gathered while hauling in one fish after another from the lagoon.

"Do I understand correctly?" asked the islander. "You want me to break my back working for you for 30 years, and then you'll pay me a pension so I can spend the rest of my life sitting here in the shade, eating my fruit, and fishing in the lagoon? I may not be sophisticated, but I am not stupid."

The islander's response reflects an attitude still prevalent in the South Pacific, for here life moves at a much slower pace than what you may be accustomed to at home. The locals call it "island time."

The service rendered in most hotels and restaurants is not slothful inattention; it's just the way things are done here. Your drink will come in due course. If you must have it immediately, order it at the bar. Otherwise, relax with your friendly hosts and enjoy their charming company.

Hotel rooms are subject to an additional levy everywhere, and most countries impose a hidden "value added tax," but direct sales taxes aren't added to your restaurant, bar, shopping, and other bills as they are in the U.S.

4 When to Go

THE CLIMATE

The South Pacific islands covered in this book lie within the tropics. Compared to the pronounced winters and summers of the temperate zones, there is little variation from one island group to the next: They are warm and humid all year. Although local weather patterns have changed in the past 20 years, making conditions less predictable, local residents recognize two distinct seasons, which may bear on when you choose to visit.

A cooler and more comfortable **dry season** occurs during the austral winter from May to October. The winter trade wind blows fairly steadily during these months, bringing generally fine tropical weather throughout the area. Daytime high temperatures reach the delightful upper 70s (24°C to 27°C) to low 80s (28°C to 30°C) in French Polynesia, Samoa, and Fiji, with early morning lows in the high 60s (18°C to 20°C). Rarotonga in the Cook Islands and Tongatapu in Tonga are farther from the equator and see cooler temperatures, with the highs in the 60s or low 70s (15°C to 23°C). Breezy wintertime nights can feel downright chilly in those islands.

The austral summer from November through April is the warmer and more humid **wet season.** Daytime highs climb into the upper 80s (30°C to 33°C) throughout the islands, with nighttime lows about 70°F (21°C). Low-pressure troughs and tropical depressions can bring several days of rain at a time, but usually it falls during heavy showers followed by periods of very intense sunshine. This is also the season for cyclones (hurricanes), which can be devastating and should never be taken lightly.

Fortunately, they usually move fast enough that their major effect on visitors is a day or two of heavy rain and wind. If you're caught in one, the hotels are experts on knowing what to do to ensure your safety.

Another localized factor to consider is the location of where you'll visit. Because the moist trade winds usually blow from the east, the eastern sides of the high, mountainous islands tend to be wetter all year than the western sides.

Also bear in mind that the higher the altitude, the lower the temperature. If you're going up in the mountains, be prepared for much cooler weather.

THE BUSY SEASON

The dry and pleasant austral winter months of July and August are the busiest tourist season in the South Pacific. That's when Australians and New Zealanders visit the islands to escape the cold back home. It's also when residents of Tahiti head to their own outer islands in keeping with the traditional July–August holiday break in France. Many Europeans also visit the islands during this time.

There also are busy mini-seasons at school holiday time in Australia and New Zealand. These periods vary, but in general they are from the end of March through the middle of April, 2 weeks in late May, 2 more weeks at the beginning of July, 2 more in the middle of September, and from mid-December until mid-January.

With a few exceptions, South Pacific hoteliers do not raise their rates during the busy periods.

From Christmas through the middle of January is a good time to get a hotel reservation in the South Pacific, but airline seats can be hard to come by, since thousands of islanders fly home from overseas jobs and schools.

HOLIDAYS & SPECIAL EVENTS

The chapters of this book list each country's festivals and special events, which can change the entire nature of a visit to the South Pacific. The annual *Heiva I Tahiti* (or *Tiruai*) in French Polynesia, the King's Birthday in Tonga, and the week of Constitution Day in Rarotonga are just three examples, and every country has at least one such major celebration. These are the best times to see traditional dancing, arts, and sporting events. Be sure to make your reservations well in advance, for hotel rooms and airline seats can be in short supply.

5 Health & Insurance

STAYING HEALTHY

FACILITIES   Hospitals and clinics are widespread in the South Pacific, but the quality varies a great deal from place to place. You can get a broken bone set and a coral scrape tended, but treating more serious ailments likely will be beyond the capability of the local hospital everywhere except in Tahiti. For this reason, it's a good idea to buy a travel insurance policy that includes medical evacuation (see "Insurance," below).

Pharmacies are numerous, but their prescription and over-the-counter medications likely will be from France, New Zealand, or Australia and thus unfamiliar to most Americans and Canadians. Only the Lyndon B. Johnson Medical Center in American Samoa dispenses American-made medications. Carry an adequate supply of any prescription medications you may need in your hand luggage. Ask your pharmacist for the generic names—not the brand names—of your medications, and keep these with your passport. Eyeglasses are not easily replaced in Samoa and Tonga, so carry spares.

POTENTIAL PROBLEMS   The South Pacific islands covered in this book pose no major health problem for most travelers. If you have a chronic condition, however, you should check with your doctor before visiting the islands. Among minor illnesses, the islands have the common cold and occasional outbreaks of influenza and conjunctivitis ("pink eye").

Also present from time to time is dengue fever, a viral disease borne by the *Aëdes aegypti* mosquito, which lives indoors and bites only during daylight hours. Dengue usually starts with a sudden high fever, excruciating frontal headache, and muscle and joint pain so severe that it's also is known as "breakbone fever." Many victims also get a measles-like rash that can spread from torso to arms, legs, and face. The symptoms usually go away within 7 to 10 days, but complete recovery can take several weeks or even months. There is no vaccine, and treatment is strictly for the symptoms, with heavy emphasis on drinking lots of fluids and replenishing vitamins. Aspirin is not recommended. Dengue seldom is fatal in adults, but take extra precautions to keep children from being bitten by mosquitoes if the disease is present.

Malaria is not present in the islands covered in this book. If you're going on to Vanuatu or the Solomon Islands, check with your doctor well in advance of departure so that you can start anti-malarial medication a week before you arrive.

Cuts, scratches, and all open sores should be treated promptly in the tropics. I always carry a tube of antibacterial ointment and a package of adhesive bandages such as Band-Aids.

Special precautions should be taken if you are traveling with children. See "Tips for Special Travelers," below.

SUN EXPOSURE   The midday sun at these latitudes is intense, much more so than even during the hottest summer days in the temperate zones. Limit your exposure to the sun, especially during the first few days of your trip and, thereafter, from 11am to 2pm. Sunscreens with high protection factors are readily available in the islands; apply them liberally. Remember that children need more protection than adults do.

INSECTS & OTHER CRITTERS   Every South Pacific island has more than its share of mosquitoes, roaches, ants, house flies, and other insects. Don't be frightened by those little gecko lizards crawling around the rafters of your bungalow at night; they're harmless to us humans but lethal to flying insects. Ants are omnipresent here and will quickly invade if you leave crumbs lying around your room. Many beaches and swampy areas also have invisible sand flies—the dreaded "no-seeums" or "no-nos"—which bite the ankles around daybreak and dusk.

Insect repellent is widely available in island shops. Good local brands are Dolmix Pic in French Polynesia and Rid, an excellent Australian brand sold elsewhere. American brands such as Off also are widely available. The most effective skin repellents contain a high percentage of "deet" (N,N-diethyl-m-toluamide).

I light a "mosquito coil" in my non-air-conditioned rooms at dusk in order to keep the pests from flying in, and I start another one at bedtime. Grocery stores throughout the islands carry these inexpensive green coils. Although more difficult to find than others, I have found the Fish brand to work best; they're made somewhere in Asia by the Blood Protection Company.

Also, don't be surprised to see a multitude of dogs, chickens, pigs, and squawking mynah birds, even in the finest restaurants.

CHRONIC CONDITIONS   If you suffer from a chronic illness, consult your doctor before your departure. For conditions like epilepsy, diabetes, or heart problems, wear a **Medic Alert Identification Tag** (☎ **800/825-3785;** www.commedicalert.org), which will immediately alert doctors to your condition and give them access to your records through Medic Alert's 24-hour hot line. Membership is $35, plus a $15 annual fee.

AIDS   As I point out in the appendix, sexual relations before marriage—heterosexual, homosexual, and bisexual—are more or less accepted behavior in the islands (abstinence campaigns fall on deaf ears here). Both male and female prostitution is common in the larger towns, such as Papeete and Suva. The Acquired Immune Deficiency Syndrome (AIDS) virus is present in the islands, so if you intend to engage in sex with strangers, you should exercise *at least* the same caution in choosing them, and in practicing safe sex, as you do at home.

SMOKING   Although anti-smoking campaigns and hefty tobacco taxes have reduced the practice, cigarette smoking is still widespread in the islands. The airlines are smoke-free, but nonsmoking sections are scarce in restaurants, and only a few hotels have no-smoking rooms. Inquire when you make a reservation whether nonsmoking rooms are available.

TAP WATER   Tap water is safe to drink in the city of Papeete on Tahiti, on the island of Bora Bora, on Rarotonga in the Cook Islands, and in Fiji. Elsewhere you can buy bottled spring water in most grocery stores. See "Fast Facts" in the following chapters for particulars.

MORE INFORMATION   The U.S. Centers for Disease Control in Atlanta, Georgia, provides up-to-date overseas health information on its **International Traveler's Hotline** (☎ 404/332-4559 or 404/647-3000 for automatic fax service; **www.cdc.gov/travel/blusheet.htm**). You can also call the U.S. State Department's 24-hour **Travel Advisory** (☎ 202/647-5225; Web site **http://travel.state.gov/travel_warnings.html**) for advisories pertaining to health as well as crime and politics in foreign countries.

American Express has a "Global Assist" service, which provides emergency medical referrals and legal advice to its members who are traveling. Card members can call collect ☎ 301/214-8228 from overseas.

INSURANCE

You can buy insurance policies providing health and accident, trip cancellation and interruption, and lost-luggage protection, but the coverage you need will depend on the extent of protection contained in your existing policies. Your credit card companies may insure you against travel accidents if you purchase your tickets with their cards. Read your policies and credit card agreements carefully before purchasing additional insurance.

Many health insurance companies and health maintenance organizations provide coverage for illness or accidents overseas, but you may have to pay the foreign provider up front and file for a reimbursement when you get home. You will need adequate receipts, so collect them at the time of treatment. Some traveler's health insurance policies will pay the local provider directly, saving you this hassle.

Since many medical facilities in the South Pacific are not up to Western standards (see "Facilities," above), and evacuation by air ambulance in case of medical necessity is very expensive, I buy a policy that provides this service regardless of how much it costs.

Trip cancellation insurance covers your loss if you have made nonrefundable deposits, bought airline tickets that provide no or partial refunds, or paid for a charter flight and for some good reason can't travel. Trip interruption insurance, on the other hand, provides refunds in case an airline or tour operator goes bankrupt or out of business.

Lost-luggage insurance covers your loss over and above the limited amounts for which the airlines are responsible, and some policies provide instant payment so that you can replace your missing items on the spot.

Your travel agent should know of a company that offers traveler's insurance. Here are some American companies:

Access America, 6600 W. Broad St., Richmond, VA 23230 (☎ **800/284-8300**);

Travel Insured International, Inc., P.O. Box 280568, East Hartford, CT 06128 (☎ **800/243-3174**);

Travel Guard International, 1145 Clark St., Stevens Point, WI 54481 (☎ **800/ 826-1300**);

Travelex Insurance Services, P.O. Box 9408, Garden City, NY 11530-9408 (☎ **800/228-9792**);

The Divers Alert Network (DAN, ☎ **800/446-2671** or 919/684-2948) insures scuba divers.

Worldwide Assistance, 1133 15th St. NW, Washington, DC (☎ **800/821-2828** or 202/347-2025), is the American agent for Europe Assistance Worldwide Services, Inc., whose policies provide evacuation in case of medical necessity.

6 Tips for Special Travelers

FOR TRAVELERS WITH DISABILITIES

Unfortunately, the same sensibility that has led to ramps, handles, accessible toilets, automatic opening doors, telephones at convenient heights, and other helpful aids in Western countries has not made serious inroads in the islands.

There may be a cultural reason why the South Pacific lags behind in this respect: Usually shy anyway, the islanders traditionally have felt ashamed when something was "wrong" with them and were dreadfully afraid of being made fun of because of it. Even today, many islanders will stay home from work rather than have anyone know they have anything as simple as pink eye. This may explain the lack of political support in most island countries to provide programs and facilities for the disabled.

That's not to say that some hoteliers haven't taken it upon themselves to provide rooms specially equipped for the disabled. Such improvements are ongoing; I have pointed out some of them in this book, but inquire when making a reservation whether such rooms are available.

The airlines make special arrangements for disabled persons. Be sure to tell them of your needs when you make your reservation.

In general, there are more resources out there than ever before. *A World of Options,* a 658-page book of resources for disabled travelers, covers everything from biking trips to scuba outfitters. It costs $35 ($30 for members) and is available from **Mobility International USA,** P.O. Box 10767, Eugene, OR 97440 (☎ **541/343-1284,** voice and TDD; www.miusa.org). Annual membership for Mobility International is $35, which includes their quarterly newsletter, *Over the Rainbow.*

The Moss Rehab Hospital (☎ **215/456-9600**) has been providing friendly and helpful phone advice and referrals to disabled travelers for years through its **Travel Information Service** (☎ **215/456-9603;** www.mossresourcenet.org).

You can join **The Society for the Advancement of Travel for the Handicapped** (SATH), 347 Fifth Ave., Suite 610, New York, NY 10016 (☎ **212/447-7284;** fax 212-725-8253; www.sath.org) for $45 annually, $30 for seniors and students, to gain access to their vast network of connections in the travel industry. They provide information sheets on travel destinations and referrals to tour operators that specialize in traveling with disabilities. Their quarterly magazine, *Open World for Disability and Mature Travel,* is full of good information and resources. A year's subscription is $13 ($21 outside the U.S.).

Say "I Do"

Getting hitched in the islands is easy only in Fiji and the Cook Islands, where many resorts have wedding packages that include a traditional Fijian or Polynesian ceremony. They will tell you the documents you need to bring and what local formalities you will need to execute before your wedding. It's possible elsewhere, but the formalities are so complicated that you're better off having your wedding at home and simply honeymooning in the islands.

Travelers with disabilities may also want to consider joining a tour that caters specifically to them. One of the best operators is **Flying Wheels Travel,** 143 West Bridge (P.O. Box 382), Owatonna, MN 55060 (☎ **800/535-6790**). They offer various escorted tours and cruises, with an emphasis on sports, as well as private tours in minivans with lifts. Other reputable specialized tour operators include **Access Adventures** (☎ **716/889-9096**), which offers sports-related vacations; **Accessible Journeys** (☎ **800/TINGLES** or 610/521-0339), for slow walkers and wheelchair travelers; **The Guided Tour, Inc.** (☎ **215/782-1370**); **Wilderness Inquiry** (☎ **800/728-0719** or 612/379-3858); and **Directions Unlimited** (☎ **800/533-5343**).

FOR GAY & LESBIAN TRAVELERS

Although homosexuality officially is frowned upon by local laws, and by some religious leaders, an old Polynesian custom makes the South Pacific a friendly destination for gay men.

Here in the islands, many families with a shortage of female offspring rear young boys as girls, or at least relegate them to female chores around the home and village. These males-raised-as-girls are known as *mahus* in Tahiti, *magus* in Samoa, and *fakaleitis* in Tonga. Some of them grow up to be heterosexual; others become homosexual or bisexual and, often appearing publicly in women's attire, actively seek out the company of tourists. Some dance the female parts in traditional island night shows. You'll see them throughout the islands, especially since many hold jobs in hotels and restaurants.

On the other hand, women were not considered equal in this respect in ancient times, and lesbianism was discouraged.

More generally, **The International Gay & Lesbian Travel Association** (IGLTA; ☎ **800/448-8550** or 954/776-2626; fax 954/776-3303; www.iglta.org), links travelers with the appropriate gay-friendly service organization or tour specialist. Members are kept informed of gay and gay-friendly hoteliers, tour operators, and airline and cruise-line representatives. Contact the IGLTA for a list of its member agencies, who will be tied into IGLTA's information resources.

General gay and lesbian travel agencies include **Family Abroad** (☎ **800/999-5500** or 212/459-1800; gay and lesbian); **Above and Beyond Tours** (☎ **800/397-2681;** mainly gay men); and **Yellowbrick Road** (☎ **800/642-2488;** gay and lesbian).

FOR SENIORS

Just as children are cared for communally in the South Pacific's extended family systems, so are senior citizens. In fact, most islanders live with their families from birth to death. Consequently, the local governments don't provide programs and other benefits for persons of retirement age. You won't find many senior citizen discounts. Children get them; you don't.

In the United States, **Golden Companions,** P.O. Box 5249, Reno, NV 89513 (☎ **702/324-2227**), helps travelers 45-plus find compatible companions through a personal voice-mail service. Contact them for more information.

The Mature Traveler, a monthly 12-page newsletter on senior citizen travel, is a valuable resource. It is available by subscription ($30 a year) from GEM Publishing Group, Box 50400, Reno, NV 89513-0400. Another helpful publication is ***101 Tips for the Mature Traveler,*** available from Grand Circle Travel, 347 Congress St., Suite 3A, Boston, MA 02210 (☎ **800/221-2610** or 617/350-7500; fax 617/346-6700).

SAGA International Holidays, 222 Berkeley St., Boston, MA 02116 (☎ **800/ 343-0273**), offers inclusive tours and cruises for those 50 and older. SAGA also sponsors the more substantial "Road Scholar Tours" (☎ **800/621-2151**), which are fun-loving but with an educational bent.

Elderhostel, 75 Federal St., Boston, MA 02110-1941 (☎ **877/426-8056;** www. elderhostel.org), has escorted tours, some to the South Pacific, led by academic experts for those ages 55 and over. Most courses last about 3 weeks and many include airfare, accommodations in student dormitories or modest inns, meals, and tuition. Write or call for a free catalog, which lists upcoming courses and destinations. **Interhostel** takes travelers 50 and over (with companions over 40), and offers 2- and 3-week trips, mostly international. The courses in both these programs are ungraded, involve no homework, and often focus on the liberal arts. They're not luxury vacations, but they're fun and fulfilling.

FOR SINGLES

Having traveled alone through the South Pacific for more years than I care to admit, I can tell you it's a great place to be unattached. After all, this is the land of smiles and genuine warmth to strangers. The attitude soon infects visitors: All I've ever had to do to meet my fellow travelers is wander into a hotel bar, order a beer, and ask the persons next to me where they are from and what they have done in Fiji, Tahiti, and so on.

The South Pacific islands are relatively safe for women traveling alone; however, women should exercise the same precautions they would if they were in the U.S. or anywhere else in the world, and especially so in the main towns. Don't let the charm of warm nights and smiling faces lull you into any less caution than you would exercise at home. Do not—repeat, *do not*—wander alone on deserted beaches. In the old days, this was an invitation for sex. If that's what you want today, then that's what you're likely to get. Otherwise, it could result in your being raped. And don't hitch-hike alone, either.

The islands have three playgrounds especially suited to singles. Two are the **Club Méditerranées** on Moorea and Bora Bora in French Polynesia. The other is rocking **Beachcomber Island Resort** in Fiji.

Travel Companion (☎ **516/454-0880**) is one of America's oldest roommate finders for single travelers. Register with them and find a trustworthy travel mate who will split the cost of the room with you and be around as little, or as often, as you like during the day.

Several tour organizers cater to solo travelers as well. **Experience Plus** (☎ **800/ 685-4565;** fax 907/484-8489) offers an interesting selection of single-only trips.

Travel Buddies (☎ **800/998-9099** or 604/533-2483) runs single-friendly tours with no singles supplement.

You may also want to research the ***Outdoor Singles Network,*** P.O. Box 781, Haines, AK 99827. An established quarterly newsletter (since 1989) for outdoor-loving singles, ages 19 to 90, the network will help you find a travel companion, pen-pal, or soulmate within its pages. A 1-year subscription costs $45, and your own personal ad is printed free in the next issue. Current issues are $15. Write for free information or check out the group's Web site at www.kcd.com/bearstar/osn.html.

FOR FAMILIES

Infants and young children are adored by the islanders, but childhood does not last as long in the South Pacific as it does in our Western societies. As soon as they are capable, children are put to work, first caring for their younger siblings and cousins and helping out with household chores, later tending the village gardens. It's only as teenagers, and then only if they leave their villages for town, that they know unemployment in the Western sense. Accordingly, few towns and villages have children's facilities, such as playgrounds, outside school property.

On the other hand, the islanders invariably love children and are very good at babysitting. Just make sure you get one who speaks English. The hotels can take care of this for you.

Some hotels, such as **Jean-Michel Cousteau Fiji Islands Resort** and **Matagi Island Resort** in Fiji (see chapter 11), welcome children and have special programs to keep them safely occupied while their parents go diving. Most French Polynesian resorts welcome children, although most are oriented for couples. Others do not accept children at all; I point those out in the establishments listings, but you may want to ask to make sure.

Also inquire whether the hotel can provide cribs, bottle warmers, and other needs. Since tourism in French Polynesia traditionally has focused on couples, most restaurants there don't have children's menus, and you may have to ask for one in the hotel dining rooms.

Disposable diapers, cotton swabs (known as Buds, not Q-Tips), and baby food are sold in many main-town stores, but you should take along a supply of such items as children's aspirin, a thermometer, adhesive bandages, any special medications, and such. Make sure their vaccinations are up to date before leaving home. If your children are very small, perhaps you should discuss your travel plans with your family doctor.

Remember to protect youngsters with ample sunscreen.

Some other tips: Some tropical plants and animals may resemble rocks or vegetation, so teach your youngsters to avoid touching or brushing up against rocks, seaweed, and other objects. If your children are prone to swimmer's ear, use vinegar or preventive drops before they go swimming in freshwater streams or lakes. Have them shower soon after swimming or suffering cuts or abrasions.

Rascals in Paradise, 650 Fifth St., San Francisco, CA 94107 (☎ **800/872-7225** or 415/978-9800; fax 415/442-0289; www.rascalsinparadise.com; e-mail kids@ rascalsinparadise.com), specializes in organizing South Pacific tours for families with kids, including visits with local families and school children.

7 Getting There

BY PLANE

A few cruise ships visit the islands, but today more than 98% of all visitors arrive by plane. Since populations are small and the distances are great (7½ hours of flying time from Los Angeles to Tahiti, 10 hours or more to Fiji), flights are not nearly as frequent to and among the islands as we Westerners are accustomed to at home. There may be only one flight a week between some countries, and flights that are scheduled today may be wiped off the timetables tomorrow.

Once you arrive in the islands, most of the outer-island airports are unlighted, so there are few connecting flights after dark. Accordingly, it's always wise to consult a travel agent or contact the airlines to see what's happening at present.

Also, you may be limited to 10 kilograms (22 lb.) on the small inter-island planes, as opposed to 20 kilograms (44 lb.) on international flights (see "Baggage Allowances," below).

Always **reconfirm your return flight** as soon as you arrive on an outer island, primarily so that the local airline will know where to reach you in case of a schedule change. I avoid booking a return flight from an outer island on the same day my international flight is due to leave for home; I give myself plenty of leeway in case the weather or mechanical or scheduling problems prevent the plane from leaving the outer island on time.

THE AIRPORTS

Most flights to the islands from North America depart from Los Angeles International Airport ("LAX" in airline parlance). Australians and New Zealanders can get there from Auckland, Wellington, Christchurch, Sydney, Melbourne, or Brisbane, depending on the carrier.

If you don't live in a city where flights to the South Pacific originate, then you will have to pay to get there in order to make a connection. Some carriers offer "feeder" or "add-on" fares to cover the connecting flights. Be sure to ask about them.

The island countries each have just one main international airport: **Papeete** on Tahiti in French Polynesia; **Rarotonga** in the Cook Islands; **Nadi** (and in a few cases **Suva**) in Fiji; **Apia** in Samoa; **Pago Pago** in American Samoa; and **Tongatapu,** the main island in Tonga. Only Nadi (pronounced and sometimes spelled "Nandi") has enough international traffic to be considered a regional hub.

THE AIRLINES

✪ **Air New Zealand** (☎ 800/262-1234 or 310/615-1111; www.airnz.com) has the most extensive network to and from the islands. Consistently rated one of the world's top airlines, it has several flights a week between Los Angeles and its home base in Auckland which stop in Tahiti, Fiji, the Cook Islands, Samoa, and Tonga. From Los Angeles, its flights to and from Tahiti and Fiji are nonstop (you'll put down at least once on the way to the Cook Islands, Samoa, and Tonga). Within the islands, it has two flights a week directly linking Tahiti, the Cook Islands, and Fiji over its famous "Coral Route." From Vancouver, Canada, it has joint service to Fiji with Air Canada (see below), and it flies to several Australian cities, so Aussies can reach most of the South Pacific islands through Auckland. From Europe, Air New Zealand has nonstop flights from Frankfurt and London's Heathrow Airport to Los Angeles, where connections can be made to the islands. From Asia, it flies between Japan and Fiji, and it links Hong Kong, Singapore, Seoul, and Taipei to Auckland, with connections from there to the islands. From South America, Air New Zealand shares service with Lan-Chile Airlines (see below) between Santiago and Tahiti, with service on to Auckland.

✪ **Air Pacific** (☎ 800/227-4446; www.airpacific.com), Fiji's fine international airline, has five weekly Boeing 747 nonstop flights between Los Angeles and Fiji. The Wednesday flight leaves about 3:30pm Los Angeles time and arrives in Nadi 10 hours later (about 9pm Fiji time the next day, since it crosses the International Dateline). Air Pacific also flies between Honolulu and Nadi once a week. It also links Nadi to Sydney, Brisbane, and Melbourne in Australia. From New Zealand, it has nonstop service to Fiji from Auckland, Wellington, and Christchurch (some flights go directly to Suva). It provides nonstop service between Fiji and Tokyo in Japan. Within the region, it offers several flights per week linking Nadi to Samoa and Tonga, and it goes west to Vanuatu and Solomon Islands. It also flies between Nadi and Tahiti once a week. Given its frequent and convenient flights and special deals for visitors from North

America and Europe (see "Airfares," below), traveling on Air Pacific is one of the most convenient and economical ways to get around the South Pacific. All Qantas Airways passengers bound for Fiji actually travel on Air Pacific (see below).

Air Canada (☎ 800/776-3000; w3.aircanada.ca) shares service with Air New Zealand from Canada to Fiji. You get on Air Canada in Vancouver or Toronto and change to an Air New Zealand plan in Honolulu.

Air France (☎ 800/321-4538; www.airfrance.com) flies to Tahiti from Paris, Los Angeles, and Tokyo.

Air Tahiti Nui (☎ 877/824-4846 or 310/640-1860 in Los Angeles; www.airtahiti-nui.com), which is owned and operated by French Polynesians, flies a wide-bodied Airbus between Tahiti and Los Angeles four times a week, with departures scheduled for 1pm California time. That means you arrive in Papeete in time to connect to Moorea that same evening. The return trips are overnight. Air Tahiti Nui also links Tokyo to Tahiti at least once a week.

Ansett Airlines (☎ 131414 in Australia; www.ansett.com.au) flies from Sydney and other Australian cities to Fiji. Air New Zealand (see above) represents Ansett in the United States.

AOM French Airlines (☎ 800/892-9136; www.flyaom.com) flies several times a week between Paris, Los Angeles, and Papeete. The company often offers cut-rate fares to Tahiti, especially in connection with air-hotel packages. Its flights depart Los Angeles at night, but they usually make the return trip mostly in daylight by leaving Papeete at a civilized 9:20am.

Canadian Airlines International (☎ 800/426-7000; www.cdnair.ca) had been sharing service with Air New Zealand from Vancouver to Fiji, but at press time it was in the process of merging with Air Canada (☎ 800/776-3000; www.aircanada.ca).Call to find out if South Pacific services are available when you want to travel.

Canada 3000 (☎ 800/993-4378 or 416/674-0257 in Canada; www.canada3000.com), based in Toronto, Canada, has charter flights from Vancouver to the Cook Islands and Fiji from November to April. Reservations and ticketing must be done through a travel agent.

Corsair Airlines (☎ 800/677-0720; www.corsair-int.com), a French carrier, flies to Tahiti from Paris via Los Angeles and San Francisco. Although primarily a charter airline, individuals can buy seats, though not necessarily at the charter price.

Hawaiian Airlines (☎ 800/367-5320 in the continental U.S., Alaska, and Canada or 808/838-1555 in Honolulu; www.hawaiianair.com) flies from Los Angeles, San Francisco, Portland, and Seattle to Tahiti and Pago Pago, connecting in Honolulu.

LanChile Airlines (☎ 800/735-5526; www.lanchile.com) flies weekly between Santiago, Chile, and Tahiti by way of Easter Island.

Polynesian Airlines (☎ 800/644-POLY; www.polynesianairlines.co.nz) connects its homebase at Apia, Samoa, to New Zealand, Australia, Tonga, and Fiji, and it buys seats on Air New Zealand between Los Angeles and Apia. Its Polypass fare is a bargain (see "Airfares," below).

Qantas Airways (☎ 800/227-4500; www.qantas.com) no longer flies between Los Angeles and Tahiti, although it still has service between Sydney and Papeete. All its passengers fly to Fiji on Air Pacific planes, whether from Los Angeles or Australia.

Royal Tongan Airlines (☎ 800/486-6426 or 808/941-1701 in Honolulu; www.tongatapu.net.to/tonga/islands/royalt) connects its home country to Nadi, Auckland, Wellington, and Sydney, and it code-shares on Air New Zealand planes between Los Angeles and Tonga. Royal Tongan also flies a 44-seat turbo-prop plane once a week between Nadi and Vava'u in Tonga.

Cyber Deals for Net Surfers

It's possible to get some great deals on airfare, hotels, and car rentals via the Internet. Grab your mouse and surf before you take off—you could save a bundle on your trip. The Web sites highlighted below are worth checking out, especially since all services are free (you'll pay for the tickets, of course). Always call the airlines or a travel agent and ask the lowest published fare before you shop for flights online.

Arthur Frommer's Budget Travel (www.frommers.com)   Home of the Encyclopedia of Travel and *Arthur Frommer's Budget Travel* magazine and daily newsletter, this site offers detailed information on 200 cities and islands around the world, and up-to-the-minute ways to save dramatically on flights, hotels, car reservations, and cruises. Book an entire vacation online and research your destination before you leave. Consult the message board to set up "hospitality exchanges" in other countries, to talk with other travelers who have visited a hotel you're considering, or to direct travel questions to Arthur Frommer himself. The newsletter is updated daily to keep you abreast of the latest breaking ways to save, to publicize new hot spots and best buys, and to present veteran readers with fresh, ever-changing approaches to travel.

Microsoft Expedia (www.expedia.com)   The best part of this multi-purpose travel site is the "Fare Tracker:" You fill out a form on the screen indicating that you're interested in cheap flights from your hometown, and, once a week, they'll e-mail you the best airfare deals on up to three destinations. The site's "Travel Agent" will steer you to bargains on hotels and car rentals, and with the help of hotel and airline seat pinpointers, you can book everything right on line. This site is even useful once you're booked. Before you depart, log on to Expedia for maps and up-to-date travel information, including weather reports and foreign exchange rates.

Travelocity (www.travelocity.com)   This is one of the best travel sites out there, especially for finding cheap airfare. In addition to its "Personal Fare Watcher," which notifies you via e-mail of the lowest airfares for up to five different destinations, Travelocity will track the three lowest fares for any routes on any dates in minutes. You can book a flight right then and there, and if you need a rental car or hotel, Travelocity will find you the best deal via the SABRE computer reservations system (another huge travel agent database). Click on "Last Minute Deals" for the latest travel bargains, including a link to "H.O.T. Coupons" (www.hotcoupons.com), where you can print out electronic coupons for travel in the U.S. and Canada.

The Trip (www.thetrip.com)   This site is really geared toward the business traveler, but vacationers-to-be can also use The Trip's exceptionally powerful fare-finding engine, which will e-mail you every week with the best city-to-city airfare deals for as many as 10 routes. The Trip uses the Internet Travel Network, another reputable travel agent database, to book hotels and restaurants.

Samoa Air (☎ **684/699-9106** in American Samoa) flies its small planes between Pago Pago and Vava'u in Tonga.

AIRFARES

The Pacific Ocean hasn't shrunk since it took 10 days and more than 83 hours in the air for Charles Kingsford Smith to become the first person to fly across it in 1928.

Even though you can now board a jetliner in Los Angeles in the evening and be strolling under the palm trees of Tahiti or Fiji by the crack of dawn, the distances still run into the thousands of miles. Consequently, transportation costs may be the largest single expense of your trip to the South Pacific.

Be sure to shop all the airlines mentioned above to see who has the best deals. Keep calling if no attractive fare is available at first, since wholesalers and groups often reserve blocks of low-cost seats in advance but release some of them near the date of departure. Occasionally a carrier will hold a last-minute sale to get rid of unused seats, so always ask for the *lowest* fare.

SEASONAL & PROMOTIONAL FARES   Depending on the carrier, the South Pacific has four airfare seasons: High or "peak" season is from December through February. One "shoulder" season includes March and April; a second runs from September through November. The least expensive or "basic" season runs from May through August (when the weather is at its finest in the islands). Fares can change as much as 25%, depending on the season. When I checked recently, for example, Air New Zealand's regular mid-week round-trip coach fare from Los Angeles to Fiji was about $1,300 in peak season. It dropped to about $900 in the low season. Air Pacific was charging the same round-trip coach fare on its nonstop Los Angeles–Fiji flights.

SPECIAL FARES & PASSES   The airlines set aside a certain number of seats for discounted promotional sale, which usually are the least expensive available and must be purchased from 2 weeks to 1 month in advance. Always inquire what special deals the airlines are offering when you want to fly. Ask for their *lowest* fare, not just the best deal.

Several special fares offer savings if you're going to more than one South Pacific country, and if you can live with the restrictions that apply to each (always ask about restrictions).

On a regular basis, Air New Zealand has a **Coral Route fare,** which includes stops at Tahiti, the Cook Islands, and Fiji (one of my recommended itineraries) as well as Honolulu. When I asked recently, this ticket cost about $1,750 in peak season and $1,300 during low season, but special discounts may be available when you plan your trip.

Air Pacific offers a **Pacific Air Pass** to North American and European travelers, which permits trips from Nadi to Apia, Tonga, and Vanuatu for $462 coach class and $771 business class. The Pacific Air Pass must be bought in North America. Air Pacific primarily flies spoke routes among the islands; like the spokes of a wheel, most of its planes fly from Nadi or Suva to another country, then turn around and come back. A similar pass includes Fiji, Vanuatu, and Solomon Islands for $617 coach.

Air Pacific also participates in a **Pacific Triangle Fare** in conjunction with Royal Tongan Airlines. It's good for direct travel between Fiji, Tonga, and Samoa, eliminating the need to backtrack to Fiji. It costs $462 and must be purchased in North America.

Polynesian Airlines' **Polypass** permits unlimited travel for 45 days among Samoa, American Samoa, Fiji, Tonga, and Rarotonga, plus one round-trip to the islands from Los Angeles, Honolulu, Sydney, Melbourne, Auckland, or Wellington. A Polypass costs about $1,399 from Los Angeles, and $999 from Australia or New Zealand.

Polynesian Airlines and Royal Tongan Airlines participate in a **Visit South Pacific Pass,** which is sold in North America on a "sector" basis—a sector being one flight. One-way flights between Fiji, Samoa, and Tonga cost $175 each, which means you can fly Nadi-Tonga-Apia-Nadi (three sectors) for $525. Flights to and from New Zealand, Australia, and other Pacific islands are also available at higher costs. Among the restrictions, you must buy at least two sectors prior to departure from North America.

DISCOUNTERS & CONSOLIDATORS   Known as "discounters," many travel agents buy airline seats and hotel rooms at wholesale prices and then pass on some of their commissions to you. There are scores of them in the U.S. and abroad. Many of them run small ads in the Sunday travel sections of newspapers. *Consumer Reports Travel Letter* published a list of them in its July 1997 issue (volume 13, number 8). You can find an up-to-date list of them—plus information about current discount fares worldwide—on the Web at **www.etn.nl/discount.htm#disco**.

Here at home, ♦ **Discover Wholesale Travel, Inc.,** 2192 Dupont Dr., Suite 116, Irvine, CA 92612 (☎ **800/576-7770** or 949/833-1136; fax 949/833-1176; www. discovertravel.net; e-mail info@discovertravel.net), is one of the few discounters specializing in the islands. Owned by Mary Anne Cook, widow of legendary South Pacific tourism pioneer Ted Cook, it recently was offering round-trip Los Angeles–Tahiti tickets on Corsair Airlines for $480, a savings of more than $100 off the lowest regular fare at the time. It also discounts hotel rooms (see "Saving on Hotels," below). By all means give this firm a ring.

Many discounters—as well as some full service travel agents—sell tickets provided by "consolidators," who are sometimes called "bucket shops." Consolidators buy and resell seats on the major international carriers which otherwise would go unfilled, especially during the slow seasons. Consolidator deals can be riskier than direct buys from a carrier, but they can result in substantial savings on tickets that have fewer restrictions than you would get with an advance purchase ticket bought directly from an airline. Generally it's best to ask a travel agent to comparison shop for you. Always compare the deals he or she comes up with to those offered directly by the airlines, inquire as to any and all restrictions there may be, and pay by credit card.

Council Travel (☎ **800/226-8624;** www.counciltravel.com) and **STA Travel** (☎ **800/781-4040;** www.sta.travel.com) cater especially to young travelers, but their bargain basement prices are available to people of all ages. **Travel Bargains** (☎ **800/ AIR-FARE;** www.1800airfare.com) was formerly owned by TWA but now offers the deepest discounts on many other airlines, with a 4-day advance purchase. Other reliable consolidators include **1-800-FLY-CHEAP** (www.1800flycheap.com); **TFI Tours International** (☎ **800-745-8000** or 212/736-1140), which serves as a clearinghouse for unused seats; or "rebators" such as **Travel Avenue** (☎ **800/333-3335** or 312/ 876-1116) and the **Smart Traveller** (☎ **800/448-3338** in the U.S. or 305/ 448-3338), which rebate part of their commissions to you.

BAGGAGE ALLOWANCES

A "weight system" applies on international flights except to or from the United States and its territories (such as American Samoa). First-class and business-class passengers are limited to 30 kilograms (66 lb.) of checked baggage and economy-class passengers to 20 kilograms (44 lb.).

A "piece system" applies to all flights to or from the United States and its territories. All passengers are limited to two checked bags without regard to weight but with size limitations: When added together, the three dimensions (length, height, depth) of any one first- or business-class bag must not exceed 158 centimeters (62 in.) in length. Economy-class passengers may check two bags whose total measurements do not exceed 270 centimeters (106 in.), with the larger of the two not more than 158 centimeters (62 in.).

For example, if you fly Los Angeles–Papeete–Fiji–Honolulu–Los Angeles, the piece system applies only on the Los Angeles–Papeete, Fiji–Honolulu, and Honolulu– Los Angeles segments. The weight system applies to Papeete–Rarotonga and Rarotonga–Fiji. In other words, pack according to the weight restrictions.

Jet Lag

Except for Air Pacific's afternoon departures from Los Angeles bound for Fiji, flights from North America to the islands leave after dark, which means you will fly overnight—and which invariably translates into jet lag. There are probably as many theories about what to do for jet lag as there are travelers. Some people advise trying to adjust to destination time before leaving home by getting up early or sleeping late. Others say you shouldn't eat or drink alcoholic beverages on the plane. Still others advise not sleeping during the flight. Air New Zealand says you should drink lots of nonalcoholic fluids to counter dehydration that takes place at high altitudes, eat lightly, and exercise occasionally by walking up and down the aisle (all those fluids may send you to the rear of the plane whether you're in the mood to exercise or not).

Since I live in Virginia, I try to break my transpacific trips by stopping in either Los Angeles or Honolulu for at least one good night's sleep. I also make every effort to schedule flights during the daylight hours whenever possible. When I fly overnight, I eat lightly, and try to sleep as much as possible, comforted by visions of lazing the next morning away on a South Pacific beach.

Be sure to carry an **inflatable neck cushion,** which will make an enormous comfort difference on overnight flights.

In addition to a small handbag or purse, all international passengers are permitted one carry-on bag with total measurements not exceeding 115 centimeters (45 in.).

Many domestic air carriers in the islands limit their baggage allowance to 10 kilograms (22 lb.). Check with the individual airlines to avoid showing up at the check-in counter with too much luggage. Most hotels in the main towns have storage facilities where you can safely leave your extra bags during your side trips.

PACKAGE TOURS

Quite often a package tour (which is not the same thing as an escorted tour—most of the companies listed below offer independent packages) will result in savings, not just on airfares but on hotels and other activities as well. You pay one price for a package that varies from one tour operator to the next. Airfare, transfers, and accommodations are always covered, and sometimes meals and specific activities are thrown in. The costs are kept down because wholesale tour operators (known as "wholesalers" in the travel industry) can make volume bookings on the airlines and at the hotels. The packages usually are then sold through retail travel agents, although some wholesalers will deal directly with the public. It's worth a phone call to find out.

There are some drawbacks: The least expensive tours may put you up at a bottom-end hotel. And since the lower costs depend on volume, some more expensive tours could send you to a large, impersonal property. You may find that once you're in the islands, you want to shift to that cozy bungalow down the road; if you do, you may lose the accommodation portion of the money you've already paid. (Use the reviews in this guide to be a smart consumer.) Some hoteliers will endorse your vouchers to another property if you're unhappy with theirs; others will not. And since the tour prices are based on double occupancy, the single traveler is almost invariably penalized.

Most tour companies require payment to be made well in advance of travel. If possible pay by credit card, which will give you some protection in case the company doesn't come through with the tour. Also consider buying both trip cancellation and trip interruption insurance (see "Health & Insurance," above).

If you decide to go, read the fine print carefully. You may not want all the extras that are included, such as all meals (why pay in advance for all meals in places like

French Polynesia, where dining out can be a major extracurricular activity?). And don't think the free manager's welcoming party is any big deal; you may be invited anyway, whether you're on the tour or not.

Here are some companies specializing in the islands:

Air New Zealand Destinations (☎ 800/262-1234 or 310/615-1111; www.airnz. com) offers a variety of packages to Australia and New Zealand as well as to the South Pacific islands. Some of them recently started at $700 per person including airfare and hotel.

Brendan Tours (☎ 800/421-8446 or 818/785-9696; www.brendantours.com) provides packages to Fiji for Air Pacific Holidays. Some of its recent off-season packages have started as low as $800 for a week, including air and hotel.

Islands in the Sun (☎ 800/828-6877 or 310/536-0051; www.islandsinthesun. com), the largest and oldest South Pacific specialist, offers packages to all the islands. It was started in the 1960s by the late Ted Cook, who later sold the firm.

Jetset Vacations (☎ 800/453-8738; www.jetsettours.com), an Australian-based firm with offices in the U.S., recently offered luxury trips to Tahiti, including round-trip airfare and accommodation in over-the-water bungalows, for about $2,000 per person.

Manuia Tours and Travel (☎ 415/495-4500; e-mail manuiatours@earthlink.net) is based in San Francisco and specializes in Tahiti packages using Corsair Airlines' non-stops from the Bay Area.

Pacific Destination Center (☎ 800/227-5317; www.pacific-destinations.com; e-mail pdc@deltanet.com) is owned and operated by Australian-born Janette Ryan, who can offer some good deals in Tahiti, the Cook Islands, Fiji, Samoa, and Tonga.

PADI Travel Network (☎ 800/729-7234; www.padi.com; e-mail ptn1@padi. com) puts together packages for divers of all experience levels.

Pleasant Tahitian Holidays (☎ 800/377-1080; www.pleasanttahiti.com), a huge company better known for its Pleasant Hawaiian and Pleasant Mexico operations, offers packages to French Polynesia.

Tahiti Legends (☎ 800/200-1213; tahiti-legends.com) is run by former officials of Islands in the Sun. They specialize in French Polynesia.

Solace (☎ 800/548-5331; www.innovision1.com; e-mail solace@innovision1. com) specializes in Tahiti and French Polynesia, offering fares and rates below those published by the airlines and hotels.

South Pacific Holidays (☎ 800/940-1712; www.spac.com), based in Vancouver, Washington, offers packages to high-end resorts and less expensive diving destinations in Fiji.

Sunmakers Travel Group (☎ 800/841-4321 or 206/216-2900; www.lowest-fare.com), based in Seattle, Washington, is a consortium of small firms, many with island expertise (ask for its South Pacific department).

Sunspots International (☎ 800/334-5623 or 503/666-3893; www.sunspotsintl. com), based in Portland, Oregon, is an expert on the Cook Islands and Samoa and will arrange an itinerary for you anywhere else in the islands.

Tahiti Vacations (☎ 800/553-3477 or 310/337-1040; www.tahitivacation.com) offers packages to French Polynesia, the Cook Islands, and Fiji. The company is a subsidiary of Air Tahiti, French Polynesia's domestic airline, and it's the North American agent for AOM French Airlines, on which it often provides its least expensive packages to Tahiti. Some of its 1-week tours to Tahiti can cost as little as $800, including air and hotel.

Travel Arrangements Ltd. (☎ 800/392-8213; www.travelarrange.co.nz; e-mail talsonoma@saber.net) is owned and operated by Fiji-born Ron Hunt, a veteran South

Pacific travel agent who sells packages to Tahiti, the Cook Islands, Fiji, Samoa, and Tonga but specializes in tailoring itineraries (and weddings) to suit your whims and pocketbook.

Tropical Inspirations (☎ 800/976-5732; www.tropicalinspirations.com; e-mail tropicalinspirations@juno.com) is owned by Nigel and Carol Douglas, of the Matagi Island Resort Douglases in Fiji (see chapter 11). They specialize in Fiji's diving and small resorts.

Voyage Tahiti (☎ 800/473-9093 or 808/951-9107 in Hawaii; www.voyage-tahiti.com) is based in Honolulu but also has offices in California.

BY SHIP

Although the days of the great ocean liners are long gone, occasionally it may be possible to cross the Pacific on a cruise ship making an around-the-world voyage or being repositioned, say, from Alaska to Australia. Most of them, however, steam through the islands for a week or two at a time from a home port such as Papeete or Sydney. They are usually underway at night, with visits to the islands during the day.

Passengers fly to the home port, enjoy the cruise, and fly home, which means that cruises are no longer only for the idle rich with time on their hands. The cruise companies usually offer some form of reduced air fares on these fly-and-cruise vacations, so you'll save over the cost of booking the air and cruise separately. Many operators also offer land packages that enable their passengers to stay over for a few days or a week at a hotel at or near the home port, usually for a reduced rate.

The cruise price ordinarily includes all meals and double-occupancy stateroom or cabin, although their fares vary with the size and position of the quarters. You can save money by booking one of the smaller interior cabins on the lower decks. You won't have a porthole, but I can tell you from having served in the U.S. Navy that the lower amidship cabins tend to ride more smoothly than those on the outside of the upper decks.

Local cruise ships include the *Paul Gauguin* and the *Haumana* in French Polynesia (see chapter 3); and **Blue Lagoon Cruises,** which visit the beautiful and unspoiled Yasawa Islands in Fiji (see chapter 9).

Most other cruise ships visiting the region sail from ports in Australia and New Zealand to islands in the western South Pacific such as Vanuatu, Fiji, and Tonga. Their itineraries tend to change from season to season, and there's not space here to describe every possibility and price. Usually you have to buy your tickets from a travel agent, so contact yours to see which ships are going where.

You can get information from the major companies likely to have ships in the South Pacific. Most sell tickets through travel agents, although some now offer them directly to the public on their Web sites. Operators include **Crystal Cruises** (☎ 800/820-6663); **Cunard Line** (☎ 800/528-6273; www.cunardline.com), whose ships include the *Queen Elizabeth II;* **Orient Lines** (☎ 800/333-7300; www.orientlines.com); and **Princess Cruises** (☎ 800/774-6237 or 904/527-6660; www.princesscruises.com). In addition, **Abercrombie and Kent** (☎ 800/323-7308; www.abercrombiekent.com), a very upscale travel packager, offers nature- and culture-oriented cruises, some to the islands.

8 Suggested Itineraries

People often ask where I would go on a vacation in the South Pacific. It's a difficult question for me to answer. I am fond of the dramatic, breathtaking scenery of French Polynesia, the liveliness of the Cook Islanders, the ancient cultures of Samoa and

Tonga, the great variety of things to do in Fiji, and the enormously friendly people everywhere.

If you want to see it all, give yourself several busy months of island hopping. If you have only 1 week, then your time will best be spent in just one island country. Several companies offer attractively priced packages to individual countries, so you will save that way (see "Package Tours," above). If you have 2 or 3 weeks, here are some suggestions to consider.

FIJI–RAROTONGA–TAHITI

One of the easier and less expensive ways to sample the South Pacific is to fly with Air New Zealand over its "Coral Route," from Tahiti to Rarotonga to Fiji, or vice versa. Air New Zealand pioneered this route in the days of flying boats, and its jets now fly it twice a week. I highly recommend this itinerary because it gives a good sampling of Melanesia and the transplanted Indian culture in Fiji, of English-speaking Polynesia in the Cook Islands, and of Polynesia with a French overlay in Tahiti and its islands.

For a 3-week trip, spend one each in Fiji, the Cook Islands, and French Polynesia. Depending on flight connections, you can shorten your stays. As a variation, you can cut out Tahiti altogether and reduce your time in the Cook Islands by flying directly to Rarotonga from Los Angeles, Honolulu, or Auckland. See "Airfares," above, for information about Air New Zealand's excellent excursion fare over this route.

THE SAMOAS & TONGA

A tour through the "Bible Belt" of Polynesia includes Samoa, nearby American Samoa, and the Kingdom of Tonga. All three are very conservative, but by being so, they have maintained their traditional Polynesian cultures.

You can tour American Samoa in a day, so make your base in Samoa with its relatively unchanged Polynesian way of life. Tonga is worth a visit just to see all 300-plus pounds of King Tupou IV.

Air New Zealand flies directly to Samoa and Tonga from Los Angeles via Honolulu, or you can go on Air Pacific's Pacific Pass, Polynesian Airline's Polypass, or the Visit South Pacific Pass offered by Polynesian and Royal Tongan airlines.

FIJI–TONGA–THE SAMOAS

These three countries offer diversity, friendly people, fine beaches, reefs, and tropical scenery. Fiji is by far the larger, so give yourself more time there.

Air Pacific's Pacific Pass, and the Triangle Fare using Air Pacific to Tonga or Apia and Royal Tongan Airlines between the two, make visits combining Fiji, Tonga, and Samoa attractive, as do each country's reasonably priced accommodations and restaurants. The most expeditious routing is Fiji–Tonga on Air Pacific, Tonga–Apia on Royal Tongan Airlines or Polynesian Airlines, and Apia–Fiji on Air Pacific or Polynesian Airlines.

THE BACKPACKING TRAIL

Backpackers will have lots of company while traveling the islands on a shoestring, just as I did back in the 1970s: Young Australians and New Zealanders frolicking on school breaks, Canadians going or coming from work Down Under, Europeans out to see the world. Except in Fiji, which is well equipped for low-budgeteers, the number of low-end properties is limited. The result: a narrow trail of backpackers traveling through the islands. Once on the trail, you very quickly will meet fellow travelers coming from the opposite direction who will clue you in on which places are clean and friendly, who's offering the best scuba diving prices, and so on.

The most popular low-budget journey is via Tahiti, Rarotonga, and Fiji—essentially the itinerary I describe above. Because Tahiti is the most expensive South Pacific destination, most travelers spend less time there before moving on for a week or two in the Cooks, then on to Fiji, where prices for accommodation, food, and transportation are the South Pacific's least expensive.

Another popular route includes stops in the Samoas and Tonga between the United States and New Zealand or Australia.

9 Saving on Hotels

The South Pacific has a wide range of accommodations, from deluxe resort hotels on their own islands to mom-and-pop guesthouses and dormitories with bunk beds.

TYPES OF ROOMS

My favorite type of hotel accommodates its guests in individual bungalows set in a coconut grove beside a sandy beach and quiet lagoon. Some of these in French Polynesia and Samoa are super-romantic bungalows actually standing on stilts out over the reef (although I should point out again that these over-water units tend to be close together and thus less private than bungalows ashore elsewhere). Others are as basic as a tent. In between they vary in size, furnishings, and comfort. In all, you enjoy your own place, one usually built or accented with thatch and other native materials but containing most of the modern conveniences. Few of these accommodations are air conditioned, but they do have ceiling fans. Hotels of this style are widespread in the South Pacific.

With the exception of French Polynesia, the major tourist markets for the island countries are Australia and New Zealand. Accordingly, the vast majority of hotels are tailored to Aussie and Kiwi tastes, expectations, and uses of the English language.

Unlike the usual American hotel room, which likely has two humongous beds, the standard "Down Under" room has a double- or queen-size bed and a single bed that also serves as a settee. The room may or may not have a bathtub but always has a shower. There may be no washcloths (bring your own), but there will be tea and instant coffee and an electric "jug" to heat water for same. Televisions are becoming more numerous but are not yet common, but most hotels have radios whose selections are limited to the one, two, or three stations on the island.

Rooms are known to South Pacific reservation desks as "singles" if one person books them regardless of the number and size of beds they have. Singles are slightly less expensive than other rooms. Units are "doubles" if they have a double bed and are reserved for two persons who intend to sleep together in that bed. On the other hand, "twins" have two twin beds; they are known as "shared twins" if two unmarried people book them and don't intend to sleep together. Third and fourth occupants of any room usually are charged an additional few dollars on top of the double or shared twin rates.

Some hotel rooms, especially in Rarotonga and the Cook Islands, have kitchenettes equipped with a small refrigerator (the "fridge"), hot plates (the "cooker"), pots, pans, crockery, silverware, and cooking utensils. Establishments with cooking facilities but no restaurants often call themselves "motels" rather than hotels, especially in the Cook Islands. Having the kitchenette can result in quite a saving on breakfasts and light meals.

MONEY-SAVING TIPS

The rates quoted in this book are known in the hotel industry as **rack rates,** or published rates; that is, the maximum a property charges for a room. Hotels pay travel agents and wholesalers 30% or more of their rack rates for sending clients their way, and they may even sell blocks of rooms at even more of a discount during slow periods. Some hotels may give you the benefit of at least part of this commission if you book directly instead of going through an airline or travel agent. Most also have "local" rates for islanders, which they may extend to visitors if business is slack. It never hurts to ask politely for a discounted or local rate.

You can also save on hotel rooms by booking them through the airlines or a discounter. One example is **Air New Zealand's "As You Please"** program, which offers reduced rates at a number of establishments everywhere that airline flies. For example, it recently offered garden view rooms at the Tahiti Beachcomber Parkroyal for about $192 double, more than $100 less than the hotel's published rates, while the least expensive bungalow at the Moorea Village went for about $67 double, compared to a regular rate of $90. You book and pay for the rooms ahead through Air New Zealand's offices and agents (see "The Airlines," above). Ask the airline for an Air New Zealand Destinations brochure listing the hotels and rates.

Some discount travel agents also deal in hotel rooms. **Discover Wholesale Travel, Inc.** (☎ **800/576-7770** or 714/83-1136), for example, recently was selling rooms in Tahiti for $100 less than the published rate. This firm also discounts airfares (see "Airfares," above).

Some less expensive hotels that take credit cards may reduce their rates if you offer to pay cash. If you're going to spend a week or more at one hotel, ask about long-term rates or discounts.

Also ask how much the hotel charges for local and long-distance calls, because surcharges can more than double the cost. If so, make your calls at a post office or pay phone.

Most South Pacific countries charge a **room tax** which is added to your bill. Inquire whether these taxes are included in the quoted rate. The "Fast Facts" sections in the country chapters give the amount of tax charged.

3 Introducing French Polynesia

The largest and most heavily populated island in French Polynesia, Tahiti has evoked the magical image of an idyllic tropical paradise since canoes of young Tahitian *vahines* gave uninhibited, bare-breasted receptions to the European explorers of the late 1700s. Today its name often is used synonymously with this overseas territory of France.

Don't be surprised to find noise and traffic jams on Tahiti, especially in the territory's bustling capital of Papeete. A freeway runs across the mountains to a wealthy suburb along Tahiti's west coast, and tract houses scale the flanks of the island's serrated ridges. Papeete's sleazy bars that once made the town a den of iniquity are long gone. Chic bistros and high-rise shopping centers have replaced its stage-set wooden Chinese stores, and the glass and steel of luxury resorts on the edge of town have supplanted its cheap waterfront hotels.

But beyond Papeete, the awesome beauty of these islands is unsurpassed anywhere in the world. On Moorea, Bora Bora, Huahine, and Tahiti's other companion islands you will witness the other-worldly mountain peaks, multihued lagoons, and palm-draped beaches that have come to symbolize the South Pacific.

1 French Polynesia Today

French Polynesia sprawls over an area of two million square miles in the eastern South Pacific. That's about the size of Europe, excluding the former Soviet Union, or about two-thirds the size of the continental United States. The 130 main islands, however, consist of only 1,500 square miles, an area smaller than Rhode Island, with a population of 220,000 or so.

THE ISLANDS   The territory's five major island groups differ in terrain, climate, and to a certain extent, people. With the exception of the Tuamotu Archipelago, an enormous chain of low coral atolls northeast of Tahiti, all but a few are high islands, the mountainous tops of ancient volcanoes that have been eroded into jagged peaks, deep bays, and fertile valleys. All have fringing or barrier coral reefs and blue lagoons worthy of postcards.

The most strikingly beautiful and most frequently visited are the **Society Islands,** so named by Capt. James Cook because they lay relatively close together. These include **Tahiti** and its nearby companion **Moorea,** which also are known as the Windward Islands because they

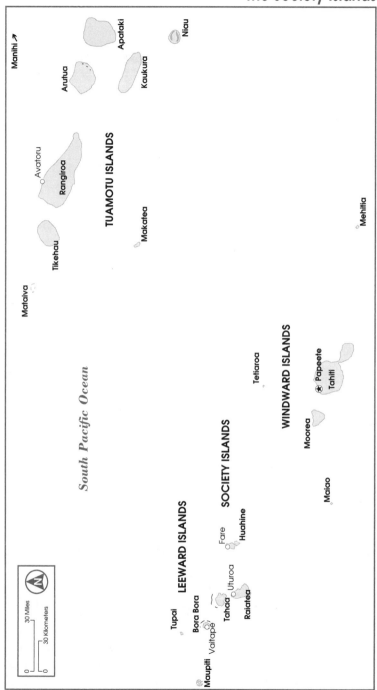

South Pacific Ocean

TUAMOTU ISLANDS

Manihi

Apataki

Arutua

Niau

Kaukura

Avatoru

Rangiroa

Makatea

Tikehau

Mataiva

Mehitia

WINDWARD ISLANDS

Tetiaroa

Papeete
Tahiti

Moorea

Maiao

SOCIETY ISLANDS

LEEWARD ISLANDS

Huahine

Fare

Tupai

Bora Bora

Uturoa

Tahaa

Raiatea

Vaitape

Maupiti

30 Miles

30 Kilometers

It is no exaggeration to say, that to a European of any sensibility, who, for the first time, wanders back into these valleys—away from the haunts of the natives—the ineffable repose and beauty of the landscape is such that every object strikes him like something seen in a dream; and for a time he almost refuses to believe that scenes like these should have a commonplace existence.

—Herman Melville, 1847

sit to the east, the direction of the prevailing trade wind. To the northwest lie **Bora Bora, Huahine, Raiatea, Tahaa, Maupiti,** and several smaller islands. Because they are downwind of Tahiti, they are also called the Leeward Islands.

To James A. Michener's eye, Bora Bora is the most beautiful island in the world. Others give that title to Moorea in a close race. It's all a matter of degree, for these are definitely the world's most dramatically beautiful islands.

The 69 low-lying atolls of the **Tuamotu Archipelago** run for 720 miles on a line from northwest to southeast, across the approaches to Tahiti from the east. The early European sailors called them the "Dangerous Archipelago" because of their tricky currents and because they virtually cannot be seen until a ship is almost on top of them. Even today they are a wrecking ground for yachts and inter-island trading boats. Two of them, Moruroa and Fangataufa, are used by France to test its nuclear weapons. Others provide the bulk of Tahiti's well-known black pearls. **Rangiroa,** the world's second-largest atoll and the territory's best scuba diving destination, is the most frequently visited. With a smaller and shallower lagoon, **Manihi** is the territory's major producer of black pearls.

The **Marquesas,** a group of 10 high islands, sit beyond the Tuamotus some 750 miles northeast of Tahiti. They are younger than the Society Islands, and protecting coral reefs have not enclosed them. As a result, the surf pounds on their shores, there are no encircling coastal plains, and the people live in a series of deep valleys that radiate out from central mountain peaks. The Marquesas have lost their once-large populations to 19th-century disease and the 20th-century economic lure of Papeete; today their sparsely populated, cloud-enshrouded valleys have an almost haunted air about them.

The seldom-visited **Austral Islands** south of Tahiti are part of a chain of high islands that continues westward into the Cook Islands. The people of the more temperate Australs, which include Rurutu, Raivavae, and Tubuai, once produced some of the best art objects in the South Pacific, but these skills have passed into time.

Far on the southern end of the Tuamotu Archipelago, the **Gambier Islands** are part of a semisubmerged, middle-aged high island similar to Bora Bora. The hilly remnants of the old volcano are scattered in a huge lagoon, which is partially enclosed by a barrier reef marking the original outline of the island before it began to sink. The largest of these remnant islands is Mangareva.

GOVERNMENT French Polynesia officially is an "overseas territory" of France; or as the French like to say, it's "an integral part" of France. Local voters cast ballots in French presidential elections and choose two elected deputies and a senator to the French parliament in Paris.

Although some changes were in the works at press time, the metropolitan French government decides matters of defense, justice, and foreign affairs, and it plays a significant role in law enforcement. The city of Papeete and a few other *communes* have their own local police forces, but French *gendarmes* are in control of many parts of the territory. The man wearing the round de Gaulle hat who stops you for riding a motorbike without a helmet is more likely to be from Martinique than from Moorea.

French Polynesians elect 30 members of a Territorial Assembly, which in turn selects its own president, the territory's highest-ranking local official (who often is referred to as the president of French Polynesia). Except for defense, justice, national police, and foreign affairs, the Assembly and its Council of Ministers decide most issues affecting the territory.

This may have changed by the time you arrive, for French Polynesians have been pressing for more autonomy from Paris in recent years. This is especially so since France stopped testing its nuclear weapons in the territory and told the locals they would have to go it alone economically by 2006 (see "The Economy," below).

A small but vocal movement would like to see the territory completely free of France. The village of Faaa surrounding the airport on Tahiti is a hotbed of such pro-independence sentiment. You'll see more English used in Faaa than anywhere else, as evidenced by stores with American-sounding names such as "Cash and Carry," "Magic City," and "Kiddy Shop."

THE ECONOMY   The territory would be bankrupt were it not for billions of francs poured in by the French government. Although many islanders gripe about the French, most Tahitians have readily accepted the largesse Paris has sent their way to pay for modern schools, roads, hospitals, airports, and other public projects. The result is a grossly inflated economy. In reality, French Polynesia has only two industries: tourism and black pearls (upwards of two million pearls are exported annually). Otherwise, little is produced or grown locally, including most foodstuffs. Yet professionals and government employees earn Parisian-level salaries. For ordinary workers, the minimum wage is about US$7 an hour—compared to US$1 or less on the other South Pacific islands.

No one pays income tax here, but everyone needs all that money just to exist, for heavy Customs duties and a value-added tax translate into relatively high prices for everything except bread, rice, sugar, and a few other basics. Most foodstuffs grown or produced in French Polynesia are more expensive than their imported counterparts; for example, you'll pay less for frozen vegetables from California than for locally grown produce. Tender beef and lamb from New Zealand are less costly than the fish caught offshore and sold in the markets. Frozen imported chicken is much less expensive than local pork, the traditional "Sunday meal" throughout Polynesia. Butter is cheaper than margarine. Just remember that you are not alone; local residents pay the same duty-inflated prices in their grocery stores as you will.

The good times may be rolling to an end, however, for when it began dismantling its Tahiti-based nuclear testing program in 1996 (see "History 101," below), France advised the territory to start earning its own living within a decade. Since tourism is the only industry capable of quickly creating badly needed private sector jobs (more than half of the population is under 20 years old), the territory has experienced a boom in hotel construction, much of it spurred by highly favorable tax treatment of hotel investments by French citizens. To bring in tourists to fill the new rooms, the territory launched its own international carrier, Air Tahiti Nui.

For us visitors, there's one saving grace: Since there's neither tipping nor a sales tax here, which can add 25% to your bill elsewhere, you should find that a meal at most non-hotel restaurants costs about the same as at comparable restaurants in American cities.

2 History 101

Dateline

- **6th century A.D.** Polynesians arrive (estimated time).
- **1595** Alvaro de Mendaña discovers the Marquesas Islands.
- **1606** Pedro Fernández de Quirós sails through the Tuamotus.
- **1765** Searching for *terra australis incognita,* Capt. John Byron on H.M.S. *Dolphin* finds some Tuamotu islands but misses Tahiti.
- **1767** Also on H.M.S. *Dolphin,* Capt. Samuel Wallis discovers Tahiti, claims it for King George III.
- **1768** French Capt. Antoine de Bougainville discovers Tahiti.
- **1769** Capt. James Cook arrives to observe the transit of Venus on the first of his three voyages of discovery.
- **1788** H.M.S. *Bounty* under Capt. William Bligh arrives to take breadfruit to the Caribbean.
- **1789** Lt. Fletcher Christian leads the mutiny on the *Bounty.*
- **1797** London Missionary Society emissaries arrive looking for converts.
- **1827** Queen Pomare IV succeeds to the throne.
- **1837** Protestants deny French Catholic priests permission to land. Irate France demands full reparations.
- **1838** Queen reluctantly signs ultimatum of French Adm. du Petit-Thouars.
- **1841** French traders trick Tahitian chiefs into asking for French protection. They later disavow it.
- **1842** Tahiti becomes a French protectorate.

continues

Surely Capt. Samuel Wallis of H.M.S. *Dolphin* could hardly believe his eyes that day in 1767 when an army of large brown-skinned men paddled more than 500 canoes across the lagoon at Matavai Bay, many of them loaded with pigs, chickens, coconuts, fruit, and topless young women "who played a great many droll and wanton tricks" on his scurvy-ridden crew. Secretly sent by King George III to find *terra australis incognita*—the mysterious southern continent that theorists said was necessary to keep the earth in balance—Wallis had instead discovered Tahiti.

The French explorer Louis Antoine de Bougainville was similarly greeted when he arrived at Hitiaa a year later. Bougainville noted that one young woman "carelessly dropped the cloth which covered her and appeared to the eyes of all beholders much as Venus showed herself to the Phrygian shepherd—having indeed the form of that goddess." With visions of Aphrodite, the Greek goddess of love, Bougainville promptly named his discovery New Cythère in honor of her hometown. It has ever since been known as The Island of Love.

Bougainville stayed at Hitiaa only 10 days, but he took back to France a young Tahitian named Ahutoru, who became a sensation in Paris as living proof of Jean-Jacques Rousseau's theory that man was at his best a "noble savage." Indeed, Bougainville and Ahutoru gave Tahiti a hedonistic image that has survived to this day.

The real Venus played a role in Tahiti's history when Capt. James Cook arrived in 1769 on the first of his three great voyages of discovery to the South Pacific. Cook's job was to measure the transit of the planet across the face of the sun, which if successful would enable navigators for the first time to accurately measure longitude on the earth's surface. Cook set up an observation point on a sandy spit on Tahiti's north shore, a locale he appropriately named Point Venus. His measurements were of little use, but Cook remained in Tahiti for 6 months. His studies of the island contributed greatly to the world's understanding of Polynesian cultures.

Cook used Tahiti as a base during his two subsequent voyages, during which he disproved the southern continent theory, discovered numerous islands, and charted much of the South Pacific.

CAPTAIN BLIGH & MR. CHRISTIAN   Capt. William Bligh, one of Cook's navigators, returned to Matavai Bay in 1788 in command of H.M.S. *Bounty* on a mission to procure breadfruit as cheap food for plantation slaves in Jamaica. One of Bligh's handpicked officers was a former shipmate, Fletcher Christian.

Delayed by storms off Cape Horn, Bligh missed the breadfruit season and had to wait on Tahiti for 6 months until his cargo could be transplanted. Christian and some of the crew apparently didn't want to leave, so much had they enjoyed the island's women and easy-going lifestyle. For whatever reason, the *Bounty's* 1,015 breadfruit plantings made it only to Tonga before Christian staged a mutiny on April 28, 1789. He set Bligh and 18 of his loyal officers and crewmen adrift in a longboat with a compass, a cask of water, and a few provisions.

Christian sailed the *Bounty* back to Tahiti, where he put ashore 25 other crew members who were loyal to Bligh. After searching unsuccessfully for a hiding place, the mutineers returned to Tahiti for the last time. Christian, eight mutineers, their Tahitian wives, and six Tahitian men then disappeared.

In one of the epic open-boat voyages of all time, Bligh and his crew miraculously made it back to England via the Dutch East Indies, thence to England, whereupon the Royal Navy sent H.M.S. *Pandora* to Tahiti to search for the *Bounty*. It found only the crewmen still there. Four eventually were acquitted. Three were convicted but pardoned, including Peter Heywood, who wrote the first English-Tahitian dictionary while awaiting court martial. Three others were hanged.

The captain of an American whaling ship that happened upon remote Pitcairn Island in 1808 was astonished when some mixed race teenagers rowed out and greeted him not in Tahitian but in perfect English. They were the children of the mutineers, only one of whom was still alive.

Bligh collected more breadfruit on Tahiti a few years later, but his whole venture went for naught when the slaves on Jamaica insisted on rice.

THE FATAL IMPACT   The discoverers brought many changes to Tahiti, starting with iron, which the Tahitians had never seen, and barter, which they had never practiced. The Tahitians figured out right away that iron was much harder than stone and shells, and that they could swap pigs, breadfruit, bananas, and the affections of their young women for it. Iron cleats, spikes, and nails soon took on a value of their own, and so many of them disappeared from the *Dolphin* that Wallis finally restricted his men to the ship out of fear it would fall apart in Matavai Bay. A rudimentary form of monetary economy was introduced to Polynesia

Herman Melville jumps ship, spends time in the *Calaboosa Beretane* (British jail). He later writes *Omoo* about his adventures.

- **1844–48** Tahitians wage guerilla war against the French.
- **1847** Queen Pomare acquiesces to full French protection.
- **1862** Irish adventurer William Stewart starts a cotton plantation at Atimaono.
- **1865** The first 329 Chinese arrive from Hong Kong to work Stewart's plantation. It fails, but most of them stay.
- **1872** Pierre Loti (Julian Viaud) spends several months on Tahiti. His *The Marriage of Loti* is published 8 years later.
- **1877** Queen Pomare IV dies at age 64.
- **1880** King Pomare V abdicates in return for pensions for him, his family, and his mistress. Tahiti becomes a French colony.
- **1888** Robert Louis Stevenson spends 2 months at Tautira on Tahiti Iti.
- **1891** "Fleeing from civilization," the painter Paul Gauguin arrives.
- **1903** Paul Gauguin dies at Hiva Oa in the Marquesas, apparently of syphilis. All of eastern Polynesia becomes one French colony.
- **1914** Two German warships shell Papeete, sink the French navy's *Zélée*.
- **1917** W. Somerset Maugham spends several months on Tahiti.
- **1933** Charles Nordhoff and James Norman Hall publish *Mutiny on the Bounty*, an instant best-seller.
- **1935** Clark Gable and Charles Laughton star in the movie *Mutiny on the Bounty*.

continues

- **1942** U.S. Marines build the territory's first airstrip on Bora Bora.
- **1960** Faaa International Airport opens, turning Tahiti into a jet-set destination. Marlon Brando arrives to film a second movie version of *Mutiny on the Bounty.*
- **1963** France chooses Mururoa as its nuclear testing site.
- **1966** France explodes the first nuclear bomb above ground at Mururoa.
- **1973** Infamous Quinn's Bar closes, is replaced by a shopping center.
- **1977** France grants limited self-rule to French Polynesia.
- **1984** Local autonomy statute enacted by French parliament.
- **1992** France halts nuclear testing, hurting local economy.
- **1995** Conservative French President Jacques Chirac permits six more underground nuclear explosions; anti-nuclear riots in Papeete; Japanese boycott Tahiti tourism.
- **1996** France halts nuclear testing, signs Treaty of Rarotonga (declaring South Pacific to be nuclear-free), tells French Polynesia to start earning its own way.
- **1997** Tourism rebounds, construction begins on several new hotels.
- **1999** Local officials propose increased autonomy from France.

for the first time. The English word "money" soon entered the Tahitian language as *moni.*

Wars were fought hand-to-hand with sticks and clubs until the *Bounty* mutineers hiding on Tahiti loaned themselves and their guns to rival chiefs, who for the first time were able to extend their control beyond their home valleys. With the mutineers' help, chief Pomare II came to control half of Tahiti and all of Moorea.

A much more devastating European import was diseases such as measles, influenza, pneumonia, and syphilis, to which the islanders had no resistance. Captain Cook estimated Tahiti's population at some 200,000 in 1769. By 1810 it had dropped to less than 8,000.

CONVERTS & CLOTHES   The "opening" of the South Pacific coincided with a fundamentalist religious revival in England, and it wasn't long before the London Missionary Society (LMS) was on the scene in Tahiti to save the souls of the "heathens" discovered by Wallace and Cook. The first LMS missionaries, who arrived in the ship *Duff* in 1797, were the first Protestant missionaries to leave England for a foreign country. They chose Tahiti because there "the difficulties were least."

They toiled for 15 years before making their first convert, and even that was only accomplished with the help of Chief Pomare II. The missionaries thought he was king of Tahiti, but in reality Pomare II was locked in battle to extend his rule and to become just that. He converted to Christianity primarily to win the missionaries' support, and with it, he quickly gained control of the entire island. The people then made the easy intellectual transition from their primary god Taaroa to the missionaries' supreme being. They put on clothes and began going to church.

The Protestant missionaries had a free hand on Tahiti for almost 30 years. There were few ordained ministers among them, for most were tradesmen sent to Tahiti to teach the natives useful Western skills, which the London Missionary Society considered essential for the Tahitians' successful transition to devout, industrious Christians in the mold of working-class Englishmen and women. Some of the missionaries stayed and went into business on their own (some island cynics say they "came to do good and stayed to do well").

THE TRICKED QUEEN   The Protestant monopoly ended when the first Roman Catholic priests arrived on the scene from France in the 1830s. The Protestants immediately saw a threat, and in 1836 they engineered the interlopers' expulsion by Queen Pomare IV, the illegitimate daughter of Pomare II, who by then had succeeded to the throne created by her father.

Sexy Skin

America isn't the only home of trendy tattoos. With their increasing interest in the ancient Polynesian ways, many young Tahitian men and women are getting theirs—but not with the modern electric needles used elsewhere.

Tattooing was unknown in Europe when the 18th-century explorers arrived in Tahiti. They were shocked, therefore, to find many Polynesians on Tahiti and throughout the South Pacific to be covered from face to ankle with a plethora of geometric and floral designs. In his journal, Capt. James Cook described in detail the excruciatingly painful tattoo procedure, in which natural dyes are hammered into the skin by hand. The repetitive tapping of the mallet gave rise to the Tahitian word *tatau*, which became tattoo in English.

Any Tahitian with plain old skin was rejected by members of the opposite sex—which may explain why members of Cook's crew were so willing to endure the torture to get theirs. At any rate, they began the tradition of the tattooed sailor.

Appalled at the sexual aspects of tattoos, the missionaries stamped out the practice on Tahiti in the early 1800s. Although the art continued in the remote Marquesas and in Samoa, by 1890 there were no tattooed natives left in the Society Islands.

When a British anthropologist undertook a study of tattooing in 1900, the only specimen he could find was in the Royal College of Surgeons. It had been worn by a Tahitian sailor, who died in England in 1816. Before he was buried, an art-loving physician removed his skin and donated it to the college.

When word of this outrage reached Paris, France sent a warship to Tahiti to demand a guarantee that Frenchmen would thereafter be treated as the "most favored foreigners" in Tahiti. Queen Pomare politely agreed, but as soon as the warship left Papeete, she sent a letter to Queen Victoria asking for British protection. Britain declined to interfere, which opened the door for a Frenchman to trick several Tahitian chiefs into signing a document requesting that Tahiti be made a protectorate of France. The French were in fact interested in a South Pacific port, and when word of the document reached Paris, a ship was dispatched to Papeete. Tahiti became a French protectorate in 1842.

Unaware of the document signed by the chiefs, Queen Pomare continued to resist. Her subjects launched an armed rebellion against the French troops, who surrounded her Papeete palace and forced her to retreat to Raiatea. The fighting continued until 1846, when the last Tahitian stronghold was captured and the remnants of their guerrilla bands retreated to Tahiti Iti, the island's eastern peninsula. A monument to the fallen Tahitians now stands beside the round-island road near the airport at Faaa, the village still noted for its strong pro-independence sentiment.

Giving up the struggle in 1847, the queen returned to Papeete and ruled as a figurehead until her death 30 years later. Her son, Pomare V, who liked the bottle more than the throne, ruled 3 more years until abdicating in return for a sizable French pension for him, his family, and his mistress. Tahiti then became a full-fledged French colony. In 1903 all of eastern Polynesia was consolidated into a single colony known as French Oceania, which it remained until 1957, when its status was changed to the overseas territory of French Polynesia.

A BLISSFUL BACKWATER   Except for periodic invasions by artists and writers, French Polynesia remained an idyllic backwater from the time France took complete possession until the early 1960s.

French painter Paul Gauguin gave up his family and his career as a Parisian stock-broker and arrived in 1891; he spent his days reproducing Tahiti's colors and people on canvas until he died in 1903 on Hiva Oa in the Marquesas Islands. Stories and novels by writers such as W. Somerset Maugham, Jack London, Robert Louis Stevenson, and Rupert Brooke added to Tahiti's romantic reputation during the early years of this century. In 1932 two young Americans—Charles Nordhoff and James Norman Hall—published *Mutiny on the Bounty*, which quickly became an enormous bestseller. Three years later MGM released an even more successful movie version with Clark Gable and Charles Laughton in the roles of Christian and Bligh, respectively.

The book and movie brought fame to Tahiti, but any plans for increased tourism were put on hold during World War II. Local partisans sided with the Free French, who gave permission for the United States to use the islands in the war against Japan. In 1942 some 6,000 U.S. sailors and marines quickly built the territory's first airstrip on Bora Bora and remained there throughout the war. A number of mixed-race Tahitians are descended from those American troops.

MOVIES & BOMBS   Even after the war, the islands were too far away and too difficult to reach to attract more than the most adventurous or wealthy travelers who arrived by ocean liner or by seaplane. Then two early 1960s events brought rapid changes to most of French Polynesia.

First, Tahiti's new international airport opened at Faaa in late 1960. Shortly thereafter, Marlon Brando and a movie crew arrived to film a remake of *Mutiny on the Bounty*. This new burst of fame, coupled with the ability to reach Tahiti overnight on the new long-range jets, transformed the island into a jet-set destination, and hotel construction began in earnest.

Second, France established the *Centre d'Experimentation du Pacifique,* its nuclear testing facility in the Tuamotus, about 700 miles southeast of Tahiti. A huge support base was constructed on the eastern outskirts of Papeete.

Together, tourism and the nuclear testing facility brought a major boom to Tahiti almost overnight. Thousands of Polynesians flocked to Papeete to take the new construction and hotel jobs, which enabled them to earn good money and experience life in Papeete's fast lane.

In addition, some 15,000 French military personnel and civilian technicians swarmed into the territory to man the new nuclear testing facility, all of them with money and many with an inclination to spend it on the local girls. The Tahitian men struck back, brawls erupted, and for a brief period in the 1960s the island experienced one of its rare moments of open hostility between the Tahitian majority and the French.

That's not to say there weren't hard feelings all along. An independence movement had existed since the guerrilla skirmishes of the 1840s, and by the 1970s it forced France to choose between serious unrest or granting the territory a much larger degree of control over its internal affairs. In 1977 the French parliament created an elected Territorial Assembly with powers over the local budget. The vice president of the Assembly was the highest elected local official. A High Commissioner sent from Paris, however, retained authority over defense, foreign affairs, immigration, the police, civil service, communications, and secondary education. This system lasted until 1984, when the French Parliament set up the present system.

3 The Islanders

About 70% of French Polynesia's population of 220,000 or so are pure Polynesian. About 4% are of Asian descent (primarily Chinese), and some 14% are of mixed races.

Impressions ————————————————————————————————————

I was pleased with nothing so much as with the inhabitants. There is a mildness in the expression of their countenances which at once banishes the idea of a savage, and an intelligence which shows that they are advancing in civilization.

—Charles Darwin, 1839

The rest are mostly French and a few other Europeans, Americans, Australians, and New Zealanders.

Members of the Polynesian majority are known as Tahitians, although persons born on the other islands do not necessarily consider themselves to be "Tahitians" and sometimes gripe about this overgeneralization. They all are called Tahitians, however, because more than 70% of the territory's population live on Tahiti, and because the Polynesian language originally spoken only on Tahiti and Moorea has become the territory's second official language (French is the other).

Of the approximately 160,000 persons who live on Tahiti, some 100,000 reside in or near Papeete. No other village in the islands has a population in excess of 4,000.

THE TAHITIANS

Many Tahitians now refer to themselves as *Maohi* (the Tahitian counterpart of *Maori),* a result of an increasing awareness of their unique ancient culture. Their ancestors came to Tahiti as part of a great Polynesian migration that fanned out from Southeast Asia to much of the South Pacific (see "The Islanders" in the appendix). These early settlers brought along food plants, domestic animals, tools, and weapons. By the time Capt. Samuel Wallis arrived in 1767, Tahiti and the other islands were lush with breadfruit, bananas, taro, yams, sweet potatoes, and other crops. Most of the people lived on the fertile coastal plains and in the valleys behind them, each valley or district ruled by a chief. Wallis counted 17 chiefdoms on Tahiti alone.

TAHITIAN SOCIETY   Tahitians were highly stratified into three classes: chiefs and priests, landowners, and commoners. Among the commoners was a subclass of slaves, mostly war prisoners. One's position in society was hereditary, with primogeniture the general rule. In general, women were equal to men, although they could not act as priests.

A peculiar separate class of wandering dancers and singers, known as the *arioi*, traveled about the Society Islands performing ritual dances and shows—some of them sexually explicit—and living in a state of total sexual freedom. The children born to this class were killed at birth.

The Polynesians had no written language, but their life was governed by an elaborate set of rules that would challenge modern legislators' abilities to reduce them to writing. Most of these rules were prohibitions known as *tabu,* a word now used in English as "taboo." The rules differed from one class to another.

A HIERARCHY OF GODS   The ancient Tahitians worshipped a hierarchy of gods. At its head stood Taaroa, a supreme deity known as Tangaroa in the Cook Islands and Tangaloa in Samoa. Below him was Tane, the god of all good and the friend of armies, and Tu, who was more or less the god of the status quo. *Mana,* or power, came down from the gods to each human, depending on his or her position in society. The highest chiefs had so much mana that they were considered godlike, if not actually descended from the gods. They lived according to special rules and spoke their own vocabularies. No one could touch them other than high-ranking priests, who cut their hair and fed them. If a high chief set foot on a plot of land, that land automatically belonged to him or her; consequently, servants carried them everywhere they went. If they uttered a word, that word became sacred and was never used again in the everyday language. When the first king of Tahiti decided to call himself Pomare, which means "night cough," the word for night—*po*—became tabu for a time. It isn't anymore.

The Tahitians worshipped their gods on *marae* built of stones and rocks. Every family had a small marae, which served the same functions as a chapel would today, and villages and entire districts—even islands—built large marae that served not only as places of worship but also as meeting sites. Elaborate religious ceremonies were held on the large central marae. Priests prayed that the gods would come down and reside in carved tikis and other objects during the ceremonies (the objects lost all religious meaning afterward). Sacrifices were offered to the gods, sometimes including humans, most of whom were war prisoners or troublemakers. Despite the practice of human sacrifice, cannibalism apparently was never practiced on Tahiti, although it was fairly widespread in the Marquesas Islands.

The souls of the deceased were believed to be taken by the gods to Hawaiki, the homeland from which their Polynesian ancestors had come. In all Polynesian islands, Hawaiki always lay in the direction of the setting sun, and the souls departed for it from the northwest corner of each island.

SEX   The sexual freedom that intrigued the early European explorers permeated Tahitian society, although it was not without its limits. Except for the nobility, sex was restricted to one's own class. Teenagers generally were encouraged to have as many partners as they wanted from puberty to marriage so that they would learn the erotic skills necessary to make a good spouse. Even within marriage there was a certain latitude. Married men and women, for example, could have extramarital affairs with their sisters-in-law and brothers-in-law, respectively. Since first cousins were considered brothers and sisters, the opportunities for licensed adultery were numerous.

The old rules have disappeared, and sexual relations in Tahiti today are governed by a mishmash of morals. Like elsewhere in the South Pacific islands, the coming of Christianity and its ethics has left Tahitians with as much guilt over adultery as anyone else. On the other hand, the European moral code was not accepted as readily as was the belief in God, and premarital sex has continued to be practiced widely in French Polynesia. Prostitution, which was unknown before the coming of the Europeans and their system of sex-for-nails, is widespread in Papeete's cash economy.

As in other Polynesian societies, homosexuality was accepted among a class of transvestites known as *mahu*, a fact that startled the early explorers and shocked the missionaries who followed. Mahus still abound in Papeete, especially at the nightclubs that cater to all sexual preferences and at the resort hotels, where the mahus perform as women in some dance reviews. Women were not considered equal in this respect in ancient times, however, and lesbianism was discouraged.

Note that the Acquired Immune Deficiency Syndrome (AIDS) virus is present in French Polynesia. Accordingly, visitors should exercise at least the same degree of caution and safe sex practices as they would at home.

Impressions

He had once landed there [the Marquesas], and found the remains of a man and a woman partly eaten. On his starting and sickening at the sight, one of Moipu's young men picked up a human foot, and provocatively staring at the stranger, grinned and nibbled at the heel.

—Robert Louis Stevenson, 1890

Tahiti has unique sex freedom. A bitter critic of the island has sneered that its charm is explainable solely in terms of the "erotic mist" that hangs over the island. . . . I remember as a boy poring over the accounts of early navigators and coming repeatedly upon that cryptic phrase "so we put into Tahiti to refresh the men."

—James A. Michener, 1951

THE CHINESE

The outbreak of the American Civil War in 1861 resulted in a worldwide shortage of cotton. In September 1862 an Irish adventurer named William Stewart founded a cotton plantation at Atimaono, Tahiti's only large tract of flat land. The Tahitians weren't the least bit interested in working for Stewart, so he imported a contingent of Chinese laborers. The first 329 of them arrived from Hong Kong in February 1865.

Stewart ran into difficulties, both with finances and with his workers. At one point, a rumor swept Tahiti that he had built a guillotine, practiced with it on a pig, and then executed a recalcitrant Chinese laborer. That was never proved, although a Chinese immigrant, Chim Soo, was the first person to be executed by guillotine in Tahiti. Stewart's financial difficulties, which were compounded by the drop in cotton prices after the American South resumed production after 1868, led to the collapse of his empire.

Nothing remains of his plantation at Atimaono (a golf course now occupies most of the land), but many of his Chinese laborers decided to stay. They grew vegetables for the Papeete market, saved their money, and invested in other businesses. Their descendants and subsequent immigrants from China now influence the economy far in excess of their numbers. They run nearly all of French Polynesia's grocery and general merchandise stores, which in French are called *magasins chinois,* or Chinese stores.

4 Language

The official languages in the territory are French and Tahitian. With the exception of some older Polynesians, everyone speaks French. English is also taught as a third language in many schools (especially those operated by the Chinese community), and many young Tahitians are eager to learn it, if for no other reason than to understand the lyrics of American songs, which dominate the radio airwaves here. Accordingly, English is widely spoken in shops, hotels, restaurants, and other businesses frequented by travelers (you're as likely to hear Europeans speaking to local residents in English as in French). Once you get off the beaten path, however, some knowledge of French or Tahitian is very helpful.

TAHITIAN PRONUNCIATION

Tahitian is the language spoken in most homes in the Society Islands, although the old local dialects are used on a daily basis in the far outer islands. Only after the Tahitians gained control over their own internal affairs in 1984 was their native tongue taught in the schools. This is one reason many pro-independence Tahitians view French as a symbol of colonial control over their islands.

No Polynesian language was written until Peter Heywood jotted down a Tahitian vocabulary while awaiting trial for his part in the mutiny on the *Bounty.* The early missionaries who later translated the Bible into Tahitian decided which letters of the Roman alphabet to use to approximate the sounds of the Polynesian languages. These tended to vary from place to place. For example, they used the consonants *t* and *v* in

Tahitian. In Hawaiian, which is similar, they used *k* and *w*. The actual Polynesian sounds are somewhere in between.

The consonants used in Tahitian are *f, h, m, n, p, r, t,* and *v.* There are some special rules regarding their sounds, but you'll be understood if you say them as you would in English.

The Polynesian languages, including Tahitian, consist primarily of vowel sounds, which are pronounced in the Roman fashion—that is, *ah, ay, ee, oh,* and *ou,* not *ay, ee, eye, oh,* and *you,* as in English. Almost all vowels are sounded separately. For example, Tahiti's airport is at Faaa, which is pronounced Fah-*ah*-ah, not Fah. Papeete is Pah-pay-*ay*-tay, not Pa-pee-tee. Paea is Pah-*ay*-ah.

Westerners have had their impact, however, and today some vowels are run together. Moorea, for example, technically is Moh-oh-*ray*-ah, but nearly everyone says Mo-*ray*-ah. The Punaauia hotel district on Tahiti's west coast is pronounced Poo-*nav*-i-a.

Look for *Say It in Tahitian* (Pacific Publications, 1977), by D. T. Tryon, in the local bookshops and hotel boutiques. This slim volume will teach you more Tahitian than you can use in one vacation.

USEFUL WORDS

To help you impress the local residents with what a really friendly tourist you are, here are a few Tahitian words you can use on them:

English	Tahitian	Pronunciation
hello	ia orana	ee-ah oh-rah-na (sounds like "your honor")
welcome	maeva	mah-ay-vah
goodbye	parahi	pah-rah-hee
good	maitai	my-tie
very good	maitai roa	my-tie-row-ah
thank you	maruru	mah-roo-roo
thank you very much	maruru roa	mah-roo-roo row-ah
good health!	manuia	mah-new-yah
woman	vahine	vah-hee-nay
man	tane	tah-nay
sarong	pareu	pah-ray-oo
small islet	motu	moh-too
take it easy	hare maru	ha-ray mah-roo
fed up	fiu	few

5 Visitor Information & Entry Requirements

VISITOR INFORMATION

Your best source of up-to-date information is **Tahiti Tourisme,** B.P. 65, Papeete, French Polynesia (☎ **50.57.00;** fax 43.66.19; www.tahiti-tourisme.com; e-mail tahiti-tourisme@mail.pf). The main Papeete information office is in Fare Manihini, the Polynesian-style building on the waterfront at the foot of rue Paul Gauguin on boulevard Pomare (it's also the welcoming center for cruise ship passengers). The staff members all speak English and are very helpful to visitors, especially in providing such information as when trading boats will leave for the distant island groups. Hours are 7:30am to 5pm Monday to Friday, 8am to noon on Saturday.

Other Tahiti Tourisme offices to contact are:

United States: 300 N. Continental Blvd., Suite 160, El Segundo, CA 90245 (☎ **310/414-8484;** fax 310/414-8490; e-mail tahitilax@earthlink.net).

Australia: The Limerick Castle, 12 Ann St., Surry Hills, NSW 2010 (☎ **02/ 9281-6020;** fax 02/9211-6589; e-mail paramor@ozmail.com.au).

New Zealand: Villa Tahiti, 36 Douglas St., Ponsonby, Auckland (☎ **09/360-8880;** fax 09/360-8891; e-mail renae@tahiti-tourisme.co.nz).

France: 28, bd. Saint Germain, 75005 Paris (☎ and fax **1/55426120;** e-mail tahitipar@calva.net).

Germany: Bockenheimer Landstr. 45, D-60 325 Frankfurt/Main (☎ **69/971-484;** fax 69/729-275).

Italy: Piazza Castello 3, 20 124 Milano (☎ **02/66-980317;** fax 02/66-92648; e-mail staff@aigo.com).

Chile: Av. 11 de Septiembre 2214, OF-116, Box 16057 STGO 9, Santiago (☎ **2/ 2512826;** fax 2/2512725; e-mail tahiti@cmet.net).

Japan: Sankyo Bldg. (no. 20) 8F-802, 3-11-5 Ildabashi, Chiyoda Ku, Tokyo 102 (☎ **3/3265-0468;** fax 3/3265-0581; e-mail tahityo@mail.fa2.so-net.ne.jp).

You can also get information from the **Tourism Council of the South Pacific** (see "Visitor Information & Entry Requirements" in chapter 2).

Travelers on a really limited budget can request lists of all the territory's less expensive "unclassified" hotels, pensions, and campgrounds. These are compiled by island, so ask for the lists applicable to your specific destinations. Most owners of these establishments don't speak English, so some French on your part will be very helpful if you stay with them.

Local tourism committees have information booths on Moorea and Bora Bora.

Once you're here, pick up the *Tahiti Beach Press,* a free weekly English-language newspaper which lists special events and current activities. Copies are available in most hotel lobbies.

ENTRY REQUIREMENTS

Most visitors are required to have a valid **passport** and a return or ongoing ticket. The immigration official may ask to see both. No **vaccinations** are required unless you are coming from a yellow fever, plague, or cholera area.

Visas valid for 1 month are issued upon arrival to citizens of the United States, Canada, Australia, New Zealand, Mexico, Uruguay, Japan, South Korea, Brunei, Malaysia, Singapore, and most European countries not mentioned below. Three-month visas are granted upon arrival to citizens of Germany, Austria, Belgium, Denmark, Finland, Greece, Ireland, Italy, Luxembourg, The Netherlands, Portugal, Spain, Sweden, and the United Kingdom.

Citizens from all other countries (including foreign nationals residing in the United States) must get a visa before leaving home. French embassies and consulates overseas can issue visas valid for stays of between 1 and 3 months, and they will forward applications for longer visits to the local immigration department in Papeete. *Note:* such visas do not entitle you to visit Tahiti without being stamped "*valable pour la Polynésie Française*"—"valid for French Polynesia."

In the United States, the **Embassy of France** is at 4102 Reservoir Rd. NW, Washington, DC 20007 (☎ **202/944-6000**), and there are French consulates in Boston, Chicago, Detroit, Houston, Los Angeles, New York, San Francisco, New Orleans, and Honolulu.

As a practical matter, your initial visa can be extended to 6 months if you still have your return air ticket, have sufficient funds, aren't employed in French Polynesia, and

The CFP & the U.S. Dollar

As a rule of thumb, $1 = approximately 100CFP, the rate of exchange used to calculate the U.S. dollar prices given in this chapter. This rate has fluctuated widely and may not be the same when you visit. Accordingly, use the following table only as a guide.

CFP	US$	CFP	US$
100	1	1,500	15
150	1.50	2,000	20
200	2	3,000	30
300	3	4,000	40
400	4	5,000	50
500	5	6,000	60
600	6	7,000	70
700	7	8,000	80
800	8	9,000	90
900	9	10,000	100
1,000	10		

have kept your nose clean. Applications for extensions must be made at the immigration office in the Faaa International Airport terminal building. Work and residency permits are difficult to obtain unless you are a French citizen.

Customs allowances are 200 cigarettes or 50 cigars, 2 liters of spirits or 2 liters of wine, 50 grams of perfume, two still cameras and 10 rolls of unexposed film, one video camera, one cassette player, and sports and camping equipment. Narcotics, dangerous drugs, weapons, ammunition, and copyright infringements (that is, pirated video and audio tapes) are prohibited. Pets and plants are subject to stringent regulations.

6 Money

French Polynesia uses the **French Pacific franc (CFP),** which is pegged directly to the French franc (5.5CFP per franc) and comes in coins up to 100CFP and in colorful notes ranging from 500CFP into the millions. No decimals are used, so prices at first can seem even more staggering than they really are.

The dollar has fluctuated on either side of 100CFP in recent years (it jumped from 109CFP to 116CFP per dollar during my last trip). I have used the rate of **$1 = 100CFP** to compute the equivalent U.S. dollar prices given in parentheses after the CFP prices in this book.

Helpful Hint: Think of 100CFP as $1, 1,000CFP as $10, and so on (that is, drop the last two zeros, and you have the approximate amount of U.S. dollars), then add or subtract the percentage difference between the actual rate and 100CFP.

To find out the current exchange rate, look in the financial section of your hometown newspaper, locate the number of French francs per dollar, and multiply that amount by 18.18. (Example: $1 = 5.5 francs x 18.18 = 100CFP.) You also can find the present CFP exchange rate in the business pages of the *Washington Post* newspaper's World Wide Web site (www.washingtonpost.com).

Don't bargain, for to haggle over a retail price is to offend the integrity of the seller, especially if he or she is a Polynesian.

HOW TO GET LOCAL CURRENCY   Banque de Polynésie, Banque Socredo, and Banque de Tahiti (the latter is a Bank of Hawaii subsidiary) have offices on the main islands. For specific locations and banking hours, see "Fast Facts" in the following chapters. All banks charge at least 450CFP ($4.50) per transaction to cash traveler's checks, regardless of the amount, so change large amounts each time to minimize this bite.

You can obtain cash advances using your Visa and MasterCard credit and check cards at ATMs at Faaa International Airport and at Banque Socredo and Banque de Tahiti offices on Tahiti, Moorea, Bora Bora, Huahine, and Raiatea. The simple operating instructions are given in both French and English. As I noted in chapter 2, I got more than the exchange rate for traveler's checks, and I avoided the bank's service charge, by using my Visa check card. You will need your personal identification number (PIN). See "Money" in chapter 2 for more information.

You probably will get a better rate if you change your money in French Polynesia rather than before leaving home.

CREDIT CARDS   MasterCard and Visa are widely accepted on the most visited islands, and American Express cards are taken by most hotels and car rental firms and by many restaurants. Don't count on using your Diners Club card except at the major hotels.

7 When to Go

There is no bad time to go to French Polynesia, but some periods are better than others. The weather is at its best—comfortable and dry—in July and August, but this is the prime vacation and festival season, so book your air tickets and hotel rooms as far in advance as possible. For the best combination of weather and availability of hotel rooms, the months of May, June, September, and October are best.

CLIMATE
Tahiti and the Society Islands have a balmy tropical climate. November through April is the summer **wet season,** when the average maximum daily temperature is 86°F (30°C) and rainy periods can be expected. Nighttime lows are about 72°F (22°C). May through October is the austral winter **dry season,** when midday maximum temperatures average a delightful 82°F (28°C), with early-morning lows of 68°F (20°C) often making a blanket necessary. Some winter days, especially on the south side of the islands, can seem quite chilly when a strong wind blows from Antarctica. Tropical showers can pass overhead at any time of the year. Humidity averages between 77% and 80% throughout the year.

The central and northern Tuamotus have somewhat warmer temperatures and less rainfall. Since there are no mountains to create cooling night breezes, they can experience desertlike hot periods between November and April. The Marquesas are closer to the equator, and temperatures and humidity tend to be slightly higher than in Tahiti. The climate in the Austral and Gambier Islands is more temperate.

French Polynesia is on the far eastern edge of the South Pacific cyclone (hurricane) belt, and storms can occur between November and March.

HOLIDAYS
Public holidays are New Year's Day, Good Friday and Easter Monday, Ascension Day, Whitmonday, Assumption Day, Missionary Day (March 5), Labor Day (May 1), Bastille Day (July 14), Internal Autonomy Day (September 8), All Saints Day (November 1), Armistice Day (November 11), and Christmas Day.

From a visitor's standpoint, July is the busiest month because of the *Heiva i Tahiti* festival (see "French Polynesia Calendar of Events," below). Hotels on the outer islands are at their fullest during August, the traditional French vacation month, when many Papeete residents head for the outer islands to get away from it all.

Tahiti Tourisme publishes an annual list of the territory's leading special events (see "Visitor Information & Entry Requirements," above).

French Polynesia Calendar of Events

January

- **Chinese New Year.** Parade, musical performances, demonstrations of martial arts, Chinese dances, and handcrafts. Between mid-January and mid-February.
- **Polynesian Cultural Traditions Exhibition.** Demonstrations of traditional tattooing, medicine, massages, basket weaving, and flower-crown making. At Place Vaiete, Papeete. Mid-January to early February.

February

- **Moorea Blue Marathon.** Prizes worth up to $15,000 entice some of the world's best runners to trot 42 kilometers around Moorea. Third Saturday.
- **Bora Bora Beach Run.** After Moorea, marathoners "relax" with a 7-kilometer jog around Bora Bora. 3 days after Moorea Blue Marathon.

March

- **Arrival of First Missionaries.** Gatherings on Tahiti commemorate anniversary of arrival of the London Missionary Society. March 5.
- **International Women's Day.** French Polynesia's own version of Mother's Day. Second Sunday in March.

April

- **Moorea International Triathlon.** A smaller version of the famous Hawaii Iron Man Classic includes swimming, cycling, running competition. Venue changes from year to year. Mid-April.
- **Maohi Sports Festival.** A chance to see traditional Polynesian sports, including outrigger canoe races (French Polynesia's national sport), fruit carriers' races, stone lifting, and javelin-throwing. Late April.

May

- **Taputapuatea Inaugural Ceremony.** Traditional outrigger canoes gather at Taputapuatea Marae on Raiatea. Early May.
- **Tahiti Pro WQS.** World class surfers compete on the big waves off Teuhupo'o on Tahiti Iti. Late May.
- **Week of the Outer Islands.** Papeete's Municipal Market becomes a big village featuring arts, crafts, and food from the outer islands. Music and dance, too. Last week in May.

June

- **World Environment Day.** Program at Point Venus emphasizes campaign to clean up the islands. Guided hikes to Fautaa and Papenoo valleys, Lake Vaihiria, summit of Mount Aroai. First Saturday in June.
- **Marquesas Arts & Crafts Exhibit and Sale.** Big crowds gather in Tahiti to see and buy exquisite crafts from the Marquesas Islands. Early June.

- **Miss Tahiti, Miss *Heiva,* Miss Moorea, and Miss Bora Bora Contests.** Candidates from around the islands vie to win the titles. Among biggest annual events on outer islands. Early- to mid-June.
- *Heiva Upa Rau* **(Polynesian Music Awards).** Artists from all over the islands compete to see who had the best song of the year. Mid-June.
- *Tane Tahiti* **and *Heiva Tane* Male Beauty Contests.** Day-long athletic contests lead to crowning the territory's most handsome hunk. Late June.
- *Heiva Vaevae.* Parade along Bd. Pomare in Papeete celebrates 1984 French law granting local autonomy. June 29.
- **International Pro/Am Golf Open.** Local and international golfers vie at Olivier Bréaud Golf Course at Atimaono, Tahiti. End of June to early July.

July

- ✪ *Heiva i Tahiti.* The festival to end all festivals in French Polynesia. It originally was a celebration of Bastille Day on July 14, but the islanders have extended the shindig into a month-long blast (it is commonly called *Tiurai,* the Tahitian word for July). They pull out all the stops, with parades, outrigger canoe races, javelin-throwing contests, fire walking, games, carnivals, festivals, and reenactments of ancient Polynesian ceremonies at restored marae. Highlight for visitors: An extraordinarily colorful contest to determine the best Tahitian dancing troupe for the year—never do the hips gyrate more vigorously. Airline and hotel reservations are difficult to come by during July, so book early and take your written confirmation with you. Contact Tahiti Tourisme for details (see "Visitor Information & Entry Requirements," above).
- *Te Aito.* Paddles fly at the Marathon Outrigger Canoe races, starting at Point Venus. Late July, early August.

August

- **Mini Fêtes.** Winning dancers and singers from the Heiva i Tahiti perform at hotels on the outer islands. All month.

September

- **Super *Aito* Individual Canoe Race.** Paddlers compete to see who's the "iron" man and woman. Second Saturday in September.
- **Floralies Day.** In the biggest flower show of the year, the Territorial Assembly Hall is bedecked in flowers and tropical plants in honor of Harrison W. Smith, the American who created the botanical gardens next to the Gauguin Museum in Papeari. Mid-September.
- **World Tourism Days.** Islanders pay homage to overseas visitors, who get discounts. Late September.

October

- **Iron Man Moorea Triathlon.** Top-shape athletes swim, bike, and run on Moorea. Second Saturday in October.
- **Camera Show at Faarumai Waterfalls.** Models in traditional costumes have their pictures taken before Tahiti's famous cascade. Mid-October.
- **Tahiti Carnival.** Playful parade celebrates Polynesian rhythms. End of October.

Impressions

The dance competitions—and other events of the Heiva festival—are unexpectedly tourist-free, a genuine people's celebration on which it is a privilege to eavesdrop.
—Ron Hall, 1991

November

- **All Saints Day.** Flowers are sold everywhere to families who put them on graves after whitewashing the tombstones. November 1.
- *Hawaiki Nui Va'a.* Local and international outrigger canoe teams race from Tahiti to the Leeward Islands. Early November.
- **Tipanie Flower Day.** After bedecking Papeete with frangipani flowers, Tahitians pick women with best flower crown and "Mama Ru'au" dress. Mid-November.

December

- **Tiare Tahiti Flower Festival.** Everyone on the streets of Papeete and in the hotels receives a *tiare Tahiti,* the fragrant gardenia that is indigenous to Tahiti. Dinner and dancing later. First week in December.
- **New Year's Eve.** Big festival in downtown Papeete leads territory-wide celebrations. December 31.

8 Getting There & Getting Around

GETTING TO FRENCH POLYNESIA

Air New Zealand, AOM French Airlines, Air France, Air Tahiti Nui, Corsair Airlines, and Hawaiian Airlines link Tahiti to North America. You can get there on Air Pacific via Fiji. Qantas Airways flies between Sydney and Tahiti, and LanChile comes here from Santiago via Easter Island. See "Getting There" in chapter 2 for details.

All arrive at **Tahiti-Faaa International Airport** on Tahiti's northwest corner, about 11 kilometers (7 miles) from downtown Papeete. See "Arriving & Getting Around" in chapter 4 for information about the airport and local transportation on Tahiti.

GETTING AROUND
BY PLANE

TO MOOREA   Shuttle service is provided between Faaa Airport and Moorea by **Air Moorea** (☎ **86.41.41;** fax 86.42.99), whose small planes leave Faaa on the hour and half hour daily from 6 to 9am and from 4 to 6pm, on the hour daily from 10am to 3pm. They turn around on Moorea and fly back at 15 minutes before and after the hour. There are no flights after dark or before dawn. Air Moorea does not take reservations. Its little terminal is on the east end of Faaa airport (that's to the left as you come out of Customs).

Air Tahiti (☎ **800/553-3477** in the U.S. or 86.42.42 in Papeete; fax 86.40.69) has daily morning flights between Papeete and Moorea and evening flights which link up with Air Tahiti Nui arrivals from Los Angeles. The daytime flights go on to Huahine and Bora Bora. Air Tahiti's terminal is on the west end of Faaa airport—that's to the right as you exit Customs.

The one-way **fare** is 3,200CFP ($27.50) on both airlines.

Pack carefully, for the **baggage limit** on both airlines is 20 kilograms (44 lb.) per person if you're connecting with an international flight within 7 days, 10 kilograms (22 lb.) per person if you're not. You will face a substantial extra charge for excess weight. You can leave your extra belongings in the storage room at your hotel or at Faaa.

TO THE OTHER ISLANDS   With a monopoly on scheduled service, **Air Tahiti** (☎ **800/553-3477** in the U.S. or 86.42.42 in Papeete; fax 86.40.69) provides service to more than 40 islands beyond Moorea. It has daily flights between Papeete and all the main islands, at least two daily to and from Bora Bora. Nevertheless, it's wise to reserve your seats as early as possible.

Air Tahiti's central downtown walk-in reservations office in Pomare (☎ **43.39.39**) is on the second level (the French call it the first floor, or *premier étage)* of Fare Tony,

The Best Seats & Something to Eat

For the best views of the islands, try to sit on the left side of the Air Tahiti aircraft when you're flying from Papeete to the outer islands. Sit on the right side when returning to Tahiti. And make sure you have your camera and a lot of film at the ready.

Most hotel dining rooms open for breakfast at 7am and close by 9:30am, so if you're catching an early-morning flight to another island, stock up on some munchies and something to drink the night before, and bring them along on the plane. Otherwise, you could figuratively starve or die of thirst before the dining rooms and restaurants reopen for lunch.

the building just west of the Vaima Centre on boulevard. Its airport office is in the west end of Faaa airport.

Air Tahiti is represented in Los Angeles by its subsidiary, **Tahiti Vacations** (☎ **800/ 553-3477** or 310/337-1040).

Following are one-way adult fares on the usual visitor's circuit (double the fare for round-trips between any two islands, half them for children) are the following:

Papeete to Huahine	9,240CFP ($92.40)
Huahine to Raiatea	4,620CFP ($46.20)
Raiatea to Bora Bora	5,355CFP ($53.55)
Bora Bora to Papeete	13,020CFP ($130.20)
Bora Bora to Rangiroa	21,735CFP ($217.35)
Rangiroa to Papeete	14,200CFP ($142.00)

Visitors can save by buying **"Passes"** over the popular routes. For example, one version permits travel over the popular Papeete–Moorea–Huahine–Raiatea–Bora Bora–Papeete route for 30,500CFP ($305), or 5,150CFP ($51.50) less than the full adult fares. Rangiroa can be added for a total of 45,500CFP ($455). Other passes permit travel to the Marquesas and Austral Islands. Restrictions apply.

Air Tahiti also has **day tours** to Huahine, Raiatea, Bora Bora, and Rangiroa, which range from about 23,500CFP ($235) to about 28,000CFP ($280), including lunch and land or lagoon excursions. They must be purchased within 7 days of departure.

An alternative to taking Air Tahiti's scheduled flights is to charter a plane and pilot from **Air Moorea, Air Tahiti, Wan Air** (☎ 85.55.54; fax 85.55.56), or **Air Archipels** (☎ 81.30.30; fax 816.42.99). **Heli-Pacific** (☎ 85.668.00; fax 85.68.08) and **Heli- Inter Polynesia** (☎ 81.99.00; fax 81.99.99) both charter helicopters and pilots. When the total cost is split among a large enough group, the price per person could be less than the regular airfare.

BY FERRY TO MOOREA

Two companies run several ferries daily from the Moorea Ferry Docks on the Papeete waterfront (opposite the Hotel Royal Papeete) to Vaiare, a small bay on Moorea's east coast. At least three of them are fast catamarans which take 30 minutes or less to cover the 19 kilometers (12 miles) between the islands. Competition on this route is fierce, and the two companies have been upgrading their vessels of late, so it's best to pick up printed schedules at the ferries' booths at the dock. Their ticketing personnel speak English.

In general, one or another of the boats depart Papeete about 6:25am, 7am, 9am, noon, 1:30pm, 3pm, and 5pm, with extra voyages on Friday and Monday (Moorea is a popular weekend retreat for Papeete residents).

One company operates the all-passenger *Aremiti II* and the much larger passenger-vehicle *Aremiti Ferry* (☎ **42.88.88** on Tahiti, 56.31.10 on Moorea), while the other has the *Tamarii Moorea VIII-Corsaire 6000* and *Tamahine Moorea IIB* (☎ **43.76.50** on Tahiti, 56.13.92 on Moorea). All are sleek, air-conditioned catamarans with bars selling snacks and libations. The older, much slower passenger–vehicle ferry *Tamarii Moorea VIII-H* (☎ **43.76.50** on Tahiti, 56.13.92 on Moorea) takes 1 hour to reach Vaiare. One-way fare on all ferries is 800CFP ($8) adults, 400CFP ($4) for children. Cars cost 2,000CFP ($20) one-way, plus 800CFP ($8) for your own passage (the actual fares will increase slightly as the local value added tax is raised). Reservations are accepted only for automobiles.

Buses meet all ferries except the 1:30pm departures from Papeete at Vaiare to take you to your hotel or other destination on Moorea for 200CFP ($2) per person. They take about 1 hour to reach the Club Med area on the opposite side of Moorea.

BY FERRY TO THE LEEWARD ISLANDS

The fast, jet-powered passenger ferry *Ono Ono* makes three voyages a week between Papeete, Huahine, Raiatea, Tahaa, and Bora Bora. The voyage between Raiatea and Bora Bora is absolutely beautiful, since the ship passes through the lovely Tahaa lagoon and then provides a gorgeous view as it approaches Bora Bora. It usually leaves Papeete at 9am on Monday and Wednesday and at 4:30pm on Friday. Return voyages are the following days. It takes just under 4 hours for the Papeete–Huahine run and about an hour between each of the Leewards. One-way adult fares are about 4,900CFP ($44) from Papeete to Huahine and 6,600CFP ($66) to Bora Bora. Each leg between the Leewards costs about 1,800CFP ($18). The Papeete ticket office is in a booth at the Moorea Ferry Docks on boulevard Pomare. For information or reservations, call 45.35.35 in Papeete, 86.85.85 in Huahine, 66.24.25 in Raiatea, or 67.78.00 in Bora Bora.

BY SHIP TO THE OUTER ISLANDS

Several cargo ships journey to the Leeward, Tuamotu, Marquesas, Gambier, and Austral groups, including the excellent cargo/cruise vessel *Aranui* (see "Seeing the Islands by Cruise Ship & Yacht," below). They keep schedules in terms of weeks or even months, not days. Their primary mission is trade—retail goods for fresh produce and copra (dried coconut meat)—with passenger traffic a secondary source of income. Accordingly, they leave an island when the cargo is loaded, not necessarily when their schedules dictate. They also are at the mercy of the weather and mechanical breakdowns.

There is a charm to riding these small ships. The sea will be an incredible shade of royal blue, and the sun setting through the clouds will split the horizon into colors spanning the spectrum. Your fellow passengers will be the salt of the Polynesian earth, with straw sleeping mats and cardboard suitcases. On the other hand, many passengers (perhaps even you) will spend the entire voyage with seasick heads slung over the rail. You will often experience choking diesel fumes, and you will seldom escape the acrid stench coming from sacks of copra. Your shipmates may include cockroaches seemingly large enough to steal the watch off your wrist, and some of the cabins—if you can get one—could pass for outhouses. In other words, you'll need lots of flexible time, tolerance born of adversity, and the patience of Job.

If you're still interested, ask Tahiti Tourisme for a list of inter-island schooners, their fares, and approximate schedules. Tickets should be purchased at least a day in advance of scheduled departure. Make sure you have obtained a 3-month visa to stay in French Polynesia. I once met a young Australian who took a boat to Rapa in the Austral Islands, expecting to return with it in a few weeks to Papeete. The ship broke down and went into the repair yard on Tahiti, stranding him for 3 months on Rapa, where he survived on coconuts and the generosity of the local residents.

✪ Frommer's Favorite French Polynesia Experiences

Watching the Sun Set over Moorea. No matter how many times I visit French Polynesia, I never tire of its incredible natural beauty. I always spend sunset of my first day on Tahiti's west coast, burning up film as the sun paints another glorious red and orange sky over Moorea's purple ridges.

Enjoying the View from the Belvédère. If the view from Le Belvédère Restaurant on Tahiti doesn't thrill me enough, the scene from the Moorea lookout of the same name certainly does. I never tire of standing there at the base of that cliff and watching dramatic Mount Rotui separate the deep blue fingers of Cook's and Opunohu Bays.

Gazing Across the Sea of the Moon. My neck strains every time I cross the hill behind Moorea's Hotel Sofitel Ia Ora, for there across the Sea of the Moon sits Tahiti in all its green glory. Whenever possible I stop and reflect on what amazement the early explorers must have felt when those mountains appeared over the horizon.

Toasting Happy Hour at Club Bali Hai. The other-worldly mountains and deep blue waters of Cook's Bay on Moorea are at their haunting best as the setting sun changes their colors from green against the blue sky to a mystical black against gray. The waterside bar has a Tahitian string band and half-price drinks from 6 to 7pm Tuesday, a balm for the pocketbook.

Snorkeling in Bora Bora's Lagoon. Shining with every hue on the blue end of the color spectrum, this watery playground is one of my favorite snorkeling spots. The Hotel Bora Bora has bungalows sitting right on the edge of a reef that drops precipitously to dark depths. I experience the exhilaration of flying when I glide out over that underwater cliff.

BY RENTAL CAR

Avis and Hertz have rental-car agencies (*locations de voiture* in French) on Tahiti, Moorea, and Bora Bora, and Europcar—known as National or Interent in the U.S. and Canada—is present on all the main islands. See "Getting Around" in following chapters for details. Not all rental firms permit their cars to be taken on the interisland ferries; check with them before driving on board.

Valid **driver's licenses** from your home country will be honored in French Polynesia.

Gasoline (*essence* in French) costs about 120CFP ($1.20) per liter (that's about $4.60 per U.S. gallon). Total and Mobil are the major brands. Service stations are fairly common on Tahiti, but only in the main villages on the other islands.

DRIVING RULES   *Driving is on the right-hand side of the road,* as in North America and continental Europe.

All persons in a vehicle **must wear seat belts.**

Helmets (*casques,* pronounced "casks") are mandatory if you drive or ride on a scooter or motorbike.

Speed limits are 40kmph (24 m.p.h.) in the towns and villages and 80kmph (48 m.p.h.) on the open road. The limit is 60kmph (36 m.p.h.) for 8 kilometers on either side of Papeete. The general rule on the Route 5 freeway between Papeete and Punaauia, on Tahiti's west coast, is 90kmph (54 m.p.h.), although there is one short stretch going down a hill where it's officially 110kmph (66 m.p.h.).

Drivers on the main rural roads have the right of way. In Papeete, priority is given to vehicles entering from the right side, unless an intersection is marked with a traffic light or a stop or yield sign. This rule differs from those of most other countries, so be especially careful at all intersections, especially those marked with a *priorité à droite* (priority to the right) sign, and give way accordingly.

Drivers are required to **stop for pedestrians** on marked crosswalks, but on busy streets, don't assume that drivers will politely stop for you when you try to cross.

Traffic lights in Papeete may be difficult to see, since some of them are on the far left-hand side of the street instead of on the driver's side of the intersection.

9 Seeing the Islands by Cruise Ship & Yacht

The Society Islands are ideal grounds for cruise ships, since it's barely an hour's steam from Tahiti to Moorea, half a day's voyage on to Huahine, and less than 2 hours each among Huahine, Raiatea, Tahaa, and Bora Bora. That means the ships spend most days and nights at anchor in lovely lagoons, allowing passengers plenty of time to explore the islands and play in the water.

Likewise, these are wonderful places to charter a yacht and set sail on your own. Two major yacht companies are based in Raiatea, which shares a lagoon with Tahaa, the only French Polynesian island which can be circumnavigated entirely within a protective reef. From Raiatea or Tahaa, short blue-water cruises will take you to Huahine in one direction, to Bora Bora in the other.

TAKING A CRUISE

As part of its effort to increase tourism, the territorial government has been encouraging cruise ships to operate in French Polynesia. By the time you arrive, there should be two if not three large ships plying the Tahiti-to-Bora Bora route, carrying more than 1,000 passengers among them. While the ships offer a high level of luxe, the downside is that all those people could be ashore on the same small island at the same time. You may also find that many of your fellow passengers work for the same company, since the ships are popular with corporate incentive groups.

THE *ARANUI*

The working cargo ship ✪ *Aranui* is the most interesting way to visit the out-of-the-way Marquesas Islands. Comfortably outfitted for 90 passengers, this 343-foot freighter makes regular 15- to 16-day round trips from Papeete to six of the 10 Marquesas Islands, with stops on the way at Rangiroa and Takapoto in the Tuamotus. While the crew loads and unloads the ship's cargo, passengers spend their days ashore experiencing the islands and islanders. Among the activities: picnicking on beaches, snorkeling, visiting villages, and exploring archaeological sites. English-speaking experts on Polynesian history and culture accompany some voyages, but the staffers mostly speak French.

Accommodation is in five air-conditioned deluxe cabins with their own showers and toilets, 40 air-conditioned first-class cabins (some of which share shower and toilets), and an air-conditioned dormitory-style cabin with 22 bunk beds (they also share showers and toilets). The ship has a restaurant and bar, boutique, library, video lounge, and swimming pool.

Fares for the complete voyage range from about 198,000CFP ($1,980) for a dormitory bunk to 399,5000CFP ($3,950) for deluxe cabins. All meals are included, but you'll have to pay your own bar bill and your airfare to and from French Polynesia.

For more information or reservations, contact **Compagnie Polynésienne du Transport Maritime,** B.P. 220, Papeete, Tahiti (☎ **42.62.40**; fax 43.48.89; www. aranui.com; e-mail aranui@mail.pf). The company has an office in San Francisco (☎ **800/972-7268** or 650/574-2575; fax 650/574-6881; e-mail aranui@mail.com).

THE *PAUL GAUGUIN*

Its interior trimmed with glistening chrome and polished teak, the sleek luxury liner
✪ *Paul Gauguin* spends most of its year making 7-day cruises through the Society
Islands. Twice a year it goes on 2-week voyages to the Tuamotu and Marquesas islands,
and it may even steam up to Hawaii and back over the Christmas season.

Built in 1997, this 156.5-meter (513-ft.), 318-passenger vessel has a crew of 206,
including French officers and an international hospitality staff. Adding local flavor,
eight young Tahitian women known as *Les Gauguins* serve as guides and stage cultural
shows in the ship's semi-circular Grand Salon entertainment venue.

The *Paul Gauguin* spends its time at anchor: 1 day at Huahine or Tahaa, one at
Raiatea, and 2 each at Bora Bora and Moorea, in that order. Its two swift tenders will
whisk you ashore for the same excursions I describe elsewhere in this book, but there's
plenty to keep you occupied without leaving the ship. From a stern platform, you can
swim, snorkel, dive, water ski, or kayak in the lagoons. There's even an on-board PADI
dive certification program. Up on the top deck, you can order lunch or a drink from
the al fresco Le Grill, grab the rays on the sundeck, take a dip in the swimming pool,
or shoot a round of mini-golf. Inside, there's a fully equipped spa, a library of books
and videos, a board games room, a casino with roulette and blackjack, and boutiques
offering black pearls and perfumes among other high-end merchandise.

Before dinner, you can take in the view over a glass of fine wine and a Cuban stogie
from the comfy, air-conditioned Connoisseurs Club. Superb French and Italian
cuisines are provided in the formal L'étoile and relaxed La Veranda dining rooms, both
with big windows wrapping around the ship's fantail. After dinner, you can dance the
night away at La Palette nightclub.

All of the ship's seven suites and about half of its 152 staterooms have private
verandas or balconies (the least expensive lower-deck units have windows or portholes). All are luxuriously appointed with minibars, TVs and VCRs, direct-dial
phones, and marble bathrooms with full-size tubs. Most have queen-size beds,
although some have two twins. The staff provides 24-hour room service.

Per-person double-occupancy fares for the 1-week Society Islands cruises range
from $2,895 to $5,695 for staterooms, from $6,195 to $9,695 for suites. The 2-week
Marquesas trips cost from $6,790 to $10,390 per person for staterooms, from $12,390
to $18,390 for suites. *(Note:* You can save from $400 to $500 per person by booking
and paying for your cruise 120 days in advance.) Add about $1,000 and $2,000,
respectively, for single occupancy. Fares include all meals, wine with lunch and dinner,
soft drinks, most onboard activities, and airfare to and from Los Angeles.

For information and reservations, contact **Radisson Seven Seas Cruises,** 600 Corporate Dr., Suite 410, Fort Lauderdale, FL 33334 (☎ **800/333-3333** or 904/
776-6123 in the U.S., 54.51.00 in Papeete; www.rssc.com).

RENAISSANCE CRUISES

As we went to press, **Renaissance Cruises** was preparing to send its new 180-meter
(593-foot), 684-passenger cruise liner *R3* to Papeete. The smoke-free ship was scheduled to make 10-day voyages, four of them at Tahiti and two each at Moorea, Raiatea,
and Bora Bora.

Passengers can make use of the *R3's* sun deck, swimming pool, fitness center, well-
ness spa, casino, cabaret lounge, two bars, and four restaurants, one of them offering
an extensive buffet. Shore excursions are offered, but unlike the *Paul Gauguin,* the *R3*
doesn't have a stern platform to support onboard water sports activities.

Almost 70% of the 280 staterooms and 62 suites open to private terraces. These are
on the upper decks and are more expensive than staterooms with windows, portholes,

obstructed views, or no windows at all. No matter how much natural light gets in, if any, all units are equipped with phones, TVs, full-length mirrors (most strategically located to reflect the quarters' queen- or twin beds), and bathrooms with hair dryers.

Fares range from $4,300 to $7,300 per person double occupancy, including all meals, most activities, and round-trip airfare from Los Angeles. You can save a few bucks by booking and paying on-line.

For more information and reservations, contact **Renaissance Cruises,** 1800 Eller Dr., Suite 300, Fort Lauderdale, FL 33316 (☎ **800/525-5350;** www.renaissance-cruises.com).

THE *Haumana*

More along the lines of Blue Lagoon Cruises in Fiji (see chapter 9), the 33.5-meter (110-foot), 42-passenger catamaran *Haumana* makes 3- and 4-night cruises among Bora Bora, Raiatea, and Tahaa. It's considerably smaller and less luxurious than the other ships plying the Society Islands.

The unpretentious *Haumana* goes into shallow parts of the lagoons for swimming and snorkeling excursions, shark feeding, even breakfasting one morning while seated at tables waist deep in the Tahaa lagoon. Other activities include visits to villages and a vanilla plantation. Scuba diving can be arranged at an extra cost. On board, the crew of 14 provides handcraft demonstrations.

A main deck restaurant serves international fare, while a comfortable indoor lounge and fantail bar on the second deck supply evening entertainment and libation.

The 21 air-conditioned cabins all have large windows or portholes, queen beds, sofas or settees, minibars, TVs, VCRs, phones, and shower-only bathrooms with hair dryers. Although they have the largest windows, those along the front of the vessel are rather cramped.

The 3- and 4-night cruises cost 121,695CFP ($1,217) and 162,306CFP ($1,623) per person double occupancy, respectively, including meals, tours, and excursions. Add 50,000CFP ($500) for single occupancy.

For information or reservations, contact **Bora Bora Pearl Cruises,** B.P. 2460, Papeete (☎ **43.43.03;** fax 43.17.86).

BY CHARTERED YACHT

Boating enthusiasts can charter their own yacht—with or without skipper and crew—and knock around some of the French Polynesian islands as the wind and their own desires dictate.

The Moorings, a well-respected yacht charter company based in Florida (☎ **66.35.93;** fax 66.20.94; e-mail moorings@mail.pf), operates a fleet of sailboats based at Apooti Marina on Raiatea's northern coast. That's a few minutes' sail to Tahaa, and depending on the wind, Bora Bora and Huahine are easy blue-water trips away. Depending on the size of the boat—they range from 36 feet to 50 feet in length—and the season, weekly bare-boat rates (that is, you rent the "bare" boat without skipper or crew) range from about 9,870CFP to 40,250CFP ($987 to $4,025) per vessel. Provisions are extra. The agency will check you out to make sure you and your party can handle sailboats of these sizes; otherwise, you must pay extra for a skipper. For information and reservations, contact **The Moorings,** 19345 U.S. 19 North, Suite 402, Clearwater, FL 34624 (☎ **800/535-7289** or 727/535-1446; www.moorings.com; e-mail yacht@moorings.com).

Stardust Marine (☎ **800/634-8822** in the U.S. or 66.23.18 on Raiatea; fax 66.23.19; www.sunyachts.com; e-mail stardustraiatea@mail.pf) also has a fleet of 37- to 51-foot yachts based at Faaroa Bay on Raiatea. Its bareboat rates range from about

$2,310 to $7,210 a week per boat, depending on size and season, plus provisions, skipper, and cook if you need them.

The French-owned **Tahiti Yacht Charter,** B.P. 608, Papeete (☎ **45.04.00;** fax 45.76.00; e-mail tyc@mail.pf), has 35- to 48-foot yachts based at Papeete. It will design cruises throughout the territory, including day trips to Tetiaroa and lengthy voyages to the Tuamotus and Marquesas. So will **Archipel Croisiers,** B.P. 1160, Papetoai, Moorea (☎ **56.36.39;** fax 56.35.87; www.archipels.com; e-mail archimoo@mail.pf).

Suggested Itineraries

If You Have 1 Day

Some visitors have a 1-day layover in Tahiti between flights. If this is your case, spend at least half of it on Moorea. Head into downtown Papeete for breakfast and an early morning look at the Municipal Market. Take the 9am ferry to Moorea. Tour Moorea (including a trip to the Belvédère overlook) by rental car or scooter, or simply by riding the bus from the ferry landing to the Club Méditerranée area. Return to Papeete in the afternoon. Make a walking tour of downtown, with some shopping thrown in. In the late afternoon make your way to the Tahiti Beachcomber Parkroyal for sunset over Moorea from the hotel's Le Lotus restaurant and bar. Catch a Tahitian dance show in the evening.

If You Have 2 Days

Day 1   Take an early-morning ferry to Moorea. Drive or take a tour around the island, including the Belvédère overlook. After lunch and some beach time, have a sunset drink at the Club Bali Hai, where the views of Cook's Bay are unparalleled. Overnight on Moorea.

Day 2   Return to Papeete on an early ferry or flight and go straight to the *Marché Municipale* (Municipal Market). After breakfast make a walking tour of downtown. Have lunch, then spend the afternoon on a tour around Tahiti, either by car or with an organized tour. End the day by watching the sunset over Moorea from a hotel on the west coast, then attending a Tahitian dance show.

If You Have 7 Days

Day 1   Tour Tahiti on the first day, following the 1-day suggestions above.

Days 2, 3, and 4   Spend these 3 full days on Moorea. There's plenty to do.

Days 5 and 6   Fly to Bora Bora on the morning of your fifth day. Stay there 2 days. Be sure to tour the island and take a trip on the lagoon.

Day 7   Return to Papeete in time for your international flight.

Fast Facts: French Polynesia

American Express   The territory's one full-service representative is in Papeete. See "Fast Facts: Tahiti" in chapter 4.

Area Code   The international country code for French Polynesia is 689. There are no domestic area codes.

Business Hours   Although many shops in downtown Papeete stay open over the lunch period, general shopping and business hours are from 7:30 to 11:30am and from 2 to 5pm Monday to Friday, 8am to noon on Saturday. In addition to regular hours, most grocery stores also are open from 2 to 6pm Saturday and from 6 to 8am on Sunday.

Camera/Film   Photographic film and color-print processing are widely available but expensive. You can bring 10 rolls with you duty-free.

Clothing   Evening attire for men is usually a shirt and slacks; and for women, a long, brightly colored dress (slacks or long skirts help to keep biting sand flies away from your ankles). Topless sunbathing is the norm at most beaches. Shorts are acceptable during the day almost everywhere. Outside Papeete, the standard attire for women is the colorful wraparound sarong known in Tahitian as a *pareu,* which can be tied in a multitude of ways into dresses, blouses, or skirts.

Doctor   Highly qualified specialists practice on Tahiti, where some clinics possess state-of-the-art diagnostic and treatment equipment; nevertheless, public hospitals tend to be crowded with local residents, who get their care for free. Most visitors use private doctors or clinics. English-speaking physicians are on call by larger hotels. Each of the smaller islands has at least one infirmary (see "Fast Facts: Tahiti" and "Fast Facts: Moorea" in chapters 4 and 5). American health insurance plans are not recognized, so remember to get receipts at the time of treatment.

Drug Laws   Possession and use of dangerous drugs and narcotics are subject to heavy fines and jail terms.

Electricity   Electrical power is 220 volts, 50 cycles, and the plugs are the French kind with two round, skinny prongs. Most hotels have 110-volt outlets for shavers only, so you will need a converter and adapter plugs for your other appliances. Some hotels, especially those on the outer islands, have their own generators, so ask at the reception desk what voltage is supplied.

E-mail   You can send and receive e-mail at cafes in Papeete and Bora Bora (see "Fast Facts: Tahiti" and "Fast Facts: Bora Bora" in chapters 4 and 6), and many hotel and resort staffs will check it for you. If you bring your own computer, be aware that some modems won't recognize the dial tones here; consult your owner's manual or Internet service provider before leaving home for what to do if this happens.

Embassies/Consulates   The nearest full-service U.S. embassy is in Suva, Fiji (see chapter 10). Australia, Austria, Belgium, Chile, Denmark, Finland, Germany, Italy, Monaco, New Zealand, Norway, the Netherlands, South Korea, Sweden, and the United Kingdom have honorary consulates in Papeete. Tahiti Tourisme has their phone numbers (see "Visitor Information & Entry Requirements," above).

Emergencies   If you are in a hotel, contact the staff. Otherwise, the emergency phone number is **17** throughout the territory. See "Safety," below.

Etiquette   Even though many women go topless and wear the skimpiest of bikini bottoms at the beach, the Tahitians have a sense of propriety that you would find in any Western nation. Don't offend them by engaging in behavior that would be impermissible at home.

Firearms   All weapons except bush knives (machetes) and BB guns are prohibited, but don't try to bring either into the territory.

Gambling   Some hotels in Papeete have small gambling casinos. You can also play "Lotto," the French national lottery.

Hitchhiking   Thumbing rides is possible in the rural parts of Tahiti and on the outer islands. Women traveling alone should be extremely cautious (see "Safety," below).

Insects   There are no dangerous insects in French Polynesia. The only real nuisances are mosquitoes and tiny, nearly invisible sand flies known locally as "no-nos," which appear at dusk on most beaches here. Wear trousers or long skirts and plenty of insect repellent (especially on the feet and ankles) to ward off the no-nos. If you forget to bring insect repellent along, look for the Off or Dolmix Pic brands at the pharmacies.

Liquor Laws   Regulations about where and when you can drink are liberal, and some bars stay open until the very wee hours on weekends. Official *conventionné* restaurants and hotels pay reduced duty on imported alcoholic beverages, so they will cost less there than at local bars and nightclubs.

Mail   Airmail postage from French Polynesia to the United States and Canada is 120CFP ($1.20) for both letters and postcards. Letters usually take about a week to 10 days to reach overseas destinations in either direction.

Mailing addresses in French Polynesia consist of post office boxes *(boîtes postales* in French, or B.P. for short) but no street numbers or names.

Maps   Tahiti Tourisme distributes free maps of each island. Most useful is that of downtown Papeete. Each weekly edition of the free *Tahiti Beach Press* carries artistic island and Papeete maps. Libraire Vaima, a large bookstore in Papeete's Vaima Centre, carries several *cartes touristiques.*

Newspapers/Magazines   The *Tahiti Beach Press,* an English-language weekly tabloid devoted to news of Tahiti's tourist industry, runs features of interest to tourists and advertisements for hotels, restaurants, real estate agents, car-rental firms, and other businesses that cater to tourists and have English-speaking staffs. It is given away free by the establishments that buy ads in it. The daily newspapers, *La Dépêche de Tahiti* and *Les Nouvelles,* are in French. Le Kiosk in front of the Vaima Centre on boulevard Pomare in Papeete carries the *International Herald Tribune, Time,* and *Newsweek.*

Pets   Your pet will be placed in quarantine.

Police   The emergency number for police is **17.**

Radio/TV   French Polynesia has one government-operated AM radio station with programming in French and Tahitian. Several private AM and FM stations in Papeete almost exclusively play American and British musical numbers in English; the announcers, however, speak French. The government-owned television station broadcasts two channels entirely in French and Tahitian. The government-owned radio and TV stations can be received throughout the territory via satellite. Canal+, a cablelike broadcast channel on Tahiti and Moorea, occasionally shows movies and sporting events in English, and it usually carries *ABC News with Peter Jennings* at some point each evening. Moorea has an American-style cable system with CNN, ESPN, and HBO, all in English, and some hotels pick up ESPN and CNN's international programs (they're not the same as the channels we see in the U.S.).

Safety   French Polynesia has seen increasing property theft in recent years, including break-ins of hotel rooms and resort bungalows. Although street crimes against tourists still are rare, friends of mine who live here don't stroll off Papeete's busy boulevard Pomare after dark. For that matter, stay alert wherever you are after dusk. Women should not wander alone on deserted beaches any time, since some Polynesian men may still consider such behavior to be an invitation for instant amorous activity.

Taxes   In addition to the stiff duties imposed on most imported goods, the government levies a value-added tax (VAT) of 2% to 6% on most goods and services, including restaurant and hotel bills. This hidden levy will increase as France weans the territory off its dole. Unlike in Europe, you can't get the VAT refunded when you leave. The territory adds 8% tax to hotel bills, and the Moorea and Bora Bora communes tack on another 100CFP to 200CFP ($1 to $2) per night.

Telephone/Fax   Direct international dialing is available to all telephone and fax numbers in French Polynesia. The international country code is **689.**

International calls can be placed through your hotel, though with a surcharge, which can more than double the fee. It's less expensive to dial them directly from a post office or even a pay phone (see below). In the post offices, place your call at the desk and wait for it to come through to one of the booths across the room.

The direct-dial charge for calls to North America, Europe, Australia, and New Zealand is 135CFP ($1.35) per minute, 100CFP between midnight and 6am. Local calls on Tahiti cost 30CFP (30¢) for the first five minutes. Calls to Moorea cost about 30CFP (30¢) per minute. Calls to the other islands cost at least 100CFP ($1) a minute.

Calls within French Polynesia and to overseas can be dialed direct without going through a long-distance operator. To call overseas, dial 00, then the country code (1 for the U.S. and Canada), followed by the area code and phone number. The international operator is at 19. The emergency *(secours)* police number is 17. For directory information *(service des renseignements),* dial 12. The information operators speak English.

Public pay phones are located at all post offices and are fairly numerous elsewhere on Tahiti. They sit in large glass-and-metal booths with black lettering on a yellow background.

No pay phones will take coins. All will accept only a *télécarte,* a credit card sold at all post offices and by many shops. They come in 1,000CFP, 2,000CFP, and 5,000CFP ($10, $20, and $50) sizes. The disadvantage is that you can't just walk up and put in a coin; the advantage is that you don't have to stand there and feed the machine's voracious appetite while calling home. I buy a 1,000CFP or 2,000CFP version and keep it with me during my visit.

Time   Local time in the most visited islands is 11 hours behind Greenwich Mean Time. I find it easier to think of it as 5 hours behind U.S. Eastern Standard Time or 2 hours behind Pacific Standard Time. Translated: When it's noon Pacific Standard Time in California, it's 10am in Tahiti. When it's noon Eastern Standard Time on the U.S. East Coast, it's 5am in Tahiti. Add 1 hour to the Tahiti time during daylight saving time.

The Marquesas Islands are 30 minutes ahead of the rest of the territory.

French Polynesia is on the east side of the International Date Line; therefore, Tahiti has the same date as the U.S., the Cook Islands, and the Samoas, and is 1 day behind Australia, New Zealand, Fiji, and Tonga.

Tipping   Despite inroads made by uninformed American tourists (TIPPING IS NOT FORBIDDEN, reads a sign in one Papeete restaurant), tipping is considered contrary to the Polynesian custom of hospitality. In other words, tipping is not expected unless the service has been truly beyond the call of duty. Some hotels accept contributions to the staff Christmas fund.

Water   Tap water is consistently safe to drink only in the city of Papeete and on Bora Bora, but you can buy bottled mineral water at every grocery. Derived from a spring on Tahiti, Vaimato is the purest of the local brands, which are much less expensive than imported French waters. Well water in the Tuamotus tends to be brackish; rainwater is used there for drinking.

Weights/Measures   French Polynesia is on the metric system.

Tahiti | 4

Tahiti's status as a large and abundant island centrally located in the eastern South Pacific made it a gateway and natural base for the early European explorers. It was from Tahiti that most of the rest of the South Pacific was explored and added to the world maps in the 18th century. In later years, Papeete became a major shipping crossroads.

Vehicles of every sort now race along Papeete's waterfront and the four-lane freeway linking it to the trendy suburban district of Punaauia on the west coast. Indeed, suburbs are creeping up the mountains overlooking the city and sprawling for miles along the coast in both directions. The island is so developed and so traffic clogged that many Tahitians commute up to 2 hours in each direction on weekdays.

Located on Tahiti's northwest corner, Papeete curves around one of the South Pacific's busiest harbors. There wasn't even a village here until the 1820s, when Queen Pomare set up headquarters along the shore and merchant ships and whalers began using the harbor in preference to the less protected Matavai Bay to the east. A claptrap town of stores, bars, and billiard parlors sprang up quickly, and between 1825 and 1829 it was a veritable den of iniquity. It grew even more after the French made it their headquarters upon taking over Tahiti in 1842. A fire nearly destroyed the town in 1884, after which thatch was outlawed as a building material. Waves churned up by a cyclone did severe damage in 1906, and in 1914 two German warships shelled the harbor and sank the French navy's *Zélée*.

Papeete was well known for Quinn's, a waterfront establishment whose reputation as the quintessential South Seas bar has survived its demise. For many, the watershed in Papeete's transition from a backwater port to a modern city was not the building of the airport or the nuclear testing facility in the early 1960s; it was the tearing down of Quinn's and its replacement by modern retail stores in 1973.

Papeete's frantic pace, chic shops, busy Municipal Market, and lively mix of French, Polynesian, and Chinese cultures may invigorate you. Or you may want to leave immediately for Moorea, Bora Bora, or another island. In either case, you will have to spend at least a few hours here, since all international flights land at Faaa on the island's northwest coast. So let's make the most of this legendary and still very beautiful island.

1 Arriving & Getting Around

ARRIVING & DEPARTING

ARRIVING

All international flights arrive at **Faaa International Airport,** 7 kilometers (4 miles) west of downtown Papeete, many of them in the middle of the night. Banque de Polynésie has a currency exchange booth in the baggage area, or you can wait until you reach its airport branch in the main concourse past Customs (there's an ATM machine there, and Banque Socredo has one to the right as you exit Customs). Once you've cleared Customs, you will see a booth straight ahead staffed by **Tourisme Tahiti.** Start there for maps and other information. Group tour operators will be holding signs announcing their presence.

A snack bar to the right opens for all night flights (the upstairs cafeteria is expensive and not that good).

Unless you're on a package tour, your only choice of transportation to your hotel between 10pm and 6am will be a **taxi.** A large board mounted near the taxi area gives the official fares. From 8pm to 6am they are 1,500CFP ($15) to the hotels on the west coast; 2,500CFP ($25) to downtown. Add 100CFP ($1) for each bag.

If you arrive any other time, and are in good physical condition, you can haul your baggage across the parking lot in front of the terminal, climb the stairs to the main road, and flag down *le truck* (see "Getting Around," below).

If you're driving a rental car, take Route 1 west to the Tahiti Beachcomber Parkroyal, the Hotel Sofitel Maeva Beach Coralia, or Le Meridien Tahiti. If you're going to downtown, watch for the Route 5 signs directing you to the freeway that connects Papeete to the west coast. Take Route 1, the old road that runs along the inland side of the airport, to reach the Outrigger Hotel Tahiti.

To the right of the Air Tahiti terminal, the airport's **baggage storage room** is open Monday through Friday from 6am to 7pm, Saturday and Sunday from 6am to noon and from 1:30 to 6:30pm, and 2 hours before every international flight departs. Charges range from 395CFP ($3.95) per day for regular-size bags to 1,030CFP ($10.30) for large items such as surfboards and bicycles. On the other hand, every hotel will keep your baggage for free.

DEPARTING

Check-in time for departing international flights is 90 minutes before flight time; for domestic flights, it's 1 hour in advance. There is no airport departure tax for either international or domestic flights.

Note: There is no bank or currency exchange bureau in the departure lounge, so change your money before clearing Immigration.

Impressions

Edward called for him in a rickety trap drawn by an old mare, and they drove along a road that ran by the sea. On each side of it were plantations, coconut and vanilla; now and then they saw a great mango, its fruit yellow and red and purple among the massy green of the leaves, now and then they had a glimpse of the lagoon, smooth and blue, with here and there a tiny islet graceful with tall palms.

—W. Somerset Maugham, 1921

Tahiti

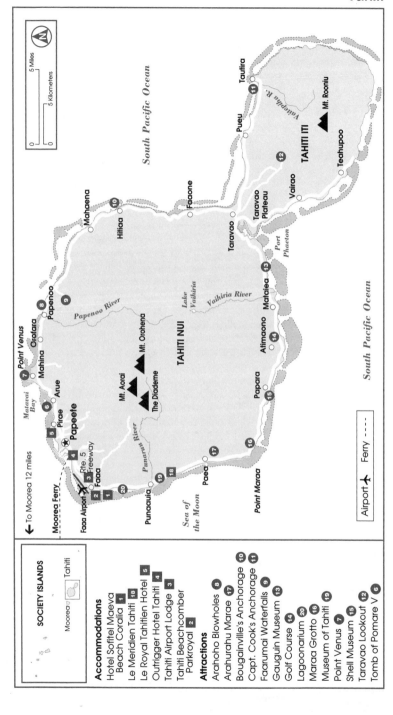

SOCIETY ISLANDS

Moorea / Tahiti

Accommodations

Hotel Sofitel Maeva Beach Coralia **1**
Le Meridien Tahiti **18**
Le Royal Tahitien Hotel **5**
Outrigger Hotel Tahiti **4**
Tahiti Airport Lodge **3**
Tahiti Beachcomber Parkroyal **2**

Attractions

Arahoho Blowholes **8**
Arahurahu Marae **17**
Bougainville's Anchorage **10**
Capt. Cook's Anchorage **11**
Faarumai Waterfalls **9**
Gauguin Museum **13**
Golf Course **14**
Lagoonarium **20**
Maraa Grotto **16**
Museum of Tahiti **19**
Point Venus **7**
Shell Museum **15**
Taravao Lookout **12**
Tomb of Pomare V **6**

Airport ✈   Ferry - - - -

TAHITI NUI

TAHITI ITI

South Pacific Ocean

Sea of the Moon

← To Moorea 12 miles

73

GETTING AROUND

Except for the Route 5 freeway between Papeete and Punaauia, the island's highway system consists primarily of a paved two-lane road running for 72 miles around Tahiti Nui and halfway down each side of Tahiti Iti. From the isthmus, a road partially lined with trees wanders up to the high, cool Plateau of Taravao, whose pastures and pines give it an air more of provincial France than of the South Pacific.

BY *LE TRUCK*

Although it may appear from the number of vehicles scurrying around Papeete that everyone owns a car or scooter, the average Tahitian gets around by *le truck.* These colorful vehicles are called trucks instead of buses because the passenger compartments are gaily painted wooden cabins mounted on the rear of flatbed trucks. Each compartment has padded benches along each side and Plexiglass windows that slide up when it's raining.

There are official bus stops *(arrêt le truck* in French), but as a practical matter, the trucks will stop for you almost anywhere, even if it means coming to a screeching halt in the middle of rush hour. These vehicles all are privately owned, and a fare won't be missed. Wave to catch the driver's eye. To get off at your destination, search around for one of the doorbell buttons mounted over or behind your head and give it a good push. Pay the driver in his cab after you have dismounted.

As disorganized as the trucks may appear, there really is a method to their madness. Most of them begin their initial runs before the crack of dawn (about 5am) from their owner's residence and proceed to the market in Papeete. Successive runs are made from the market to the end of their route and back during the course of the day. The villages or districts served by each truck are written on the sides and front of the passenger cabin.

Trucks going west line up on rue du Maréchal-Foch behind the Municipal Market. They travel along rue du Général-de-Gaulle, which becomes rue du Commandant-Destremeau and later route de-l'Ouest, the road that circles the island. There is frequent service from dawn to 10pm along this route as far as the Continent shopping center south of the Hotel Sofitel Maeva Beach Coralia. Trucks labeled Faaa, Maeva Beach, and Outuamaru will pass the airport and the Outrigger and Tahiti Beachcomber Parkroyal hotels.

Trucks going east line up in the block west of the Banque de Polynésie on boulevard Pomare, opposite Tourisme Tahiti and near the Municipal Market and rue Paul Gauguin. They proceed out of town via avenue du Prince-Hinoi, passing the Hotel Royal Tahitien cutoff on their way to Pirae, Arue, and Mahina. They run frequently from 6am to 5pm as far as the Royal Matavai Bay Hotel Resort (formerly the Hyatt Regency Tahiti), less so between 5pm and 10pm.

Long-distance trucks tend to be larger than their short-haul cousins, and their service much less frequent the farther you get from Papeete. In general, the last long-distance runs of the day leave their villages about midday for Papeete, then depart the market shortly after everyone gets off work at 5pm.

Confused? Never fear, for all you really have to do to ride *le truck* is to show up at stations near the market and look like a tourist who wants a ride to your hotel. The drivers or their assistants will find you and tell you which vehicle to get in.

Fares going west between Papeete and Maeva Beach are 120CFP ($1.20) until 6pm, 200CFP ($2) thereafter. Fares going east to Mahina are 140CFP ($1.40) during the day and 250CFP ($2.50) after 6pm. A trip to the end of the line in either direction will cost about 600CFP ($6).

Note: No truck goes completely around Tahiti, so you will have to walk across the Taravao isthmus to make a circumnavigation of the island. If you're adventurous enough to try it, go clockwise: take an early-morning eastbound long-distance truck to Taravao, walk across the isthmus, then hail a returning west coast truck to Papeete. More trucks run along the west coast than along the east, and there are more hitch-hiking possibilities in case you get stranded. Bear in mind, however, that hitchhiking is not a reliable means of transport on Tahiti, and women traveling alone or with other women should exercise extreme caution if they have to do so.

BY TAXI

Papeete has a large number of taxis, although they can be hard to find during the morning and evening rush hours, especially if it's raining. You can flag one down on the street or find them gathered at one of several stations. The largest gathering points are on boulevard Pomare near the market (☎ **42.02.92**) and at the Centre Vaima (☎ **42.98.35**). Most taxi drivers understand some English; one who speaks it fluently is Alan Foures, an American from Boston whose Tahitian wife owns **Emile's Taxi** (☎ **42.55.52**).

Taxi fares are set by the government and are posted in the main concourse at Faaa airport and on a board at the Centre Vaima taxi stand on boulevard Pomare. Few cabs have meters, so be sure that you and the driver have agreed on a fare before you get in. Note that *all fares are increased by at least 30% from 8pm to 6am.* A trip anywhere within downtown Papeete during the day will start at 800CFP ($8) and go up 120CFP ($1.20) for every kilometer after the first one. As a rule of thumb, the fare from the Papeete hotels to the airport or vice versa is about 1,500CFP ($15) during the day; from the west coast hotels to the airport, about 1,000CFP ($10). A trip to the Gauguin Museum on the south coast will cost 1,000CFP ($100) one-way. The fare for a 4-hour journey all the way around Tahiti is about 16,000CFP ($160). Drivers may charge an extra 50CFP to 100CFP (50¢ to $1) per bag of luggage.

BY RENTAL CAR

International firms on Tahiti are **Avis** (☎ **800/331-1212** or 41.93.93) and **Europcar** (☎ **800/227-7368** or 45.24.24), which is known as National Car Rental/Interent in the United States and Canada. Europcar is slightly less expensive than the others, with rates starting at 1,850CFP ($18.50) a day plus 40CFP (40¢) per kilometer, or 8,000CFP ($80) a day with unlimited kilometers. Consider the unlimited-kilometer rate if you intend to drive around the island, since the round-island road is 114 kilometers (72 miles) long, not counting side trips on Tahiti Iti.

DRIVING HINTS   In Papeete priority is given to vehicles entering an intersection from the right side. This rule does not apply on the four-lane boulevard Pomare along the waterfront, but be careful everywhere else because drivers on your right will expect you to yield the right of way at intersections where there are no stop signs or traffic signals. Outside of Papeete, priority is given to vehicles already on the round-island road.

PARKING   People park everywhere in downtown Papeete, including on the side-walks. Accordingly, finding a parking space can be difficult. Some large buildings, such as the Centre Vaima, have garages in their basements. I usually resort to the lots on the waterfront by the Moorea Ferry docks, especially in front of the Royal Papeete Hotel. The spaces are not metered, but many are reserved at night for the food wagons that gather there in the evenings (see "Dining," below). Be safe and find a space close to boulevard Pomare.

Fast Facts: Tahiti

American Express   The full-service American Express representative is **Tahiti Tours,** on rue Jeanne-d'Arc (☎ **54.02.50**), across from the Centre Vaima in downtown Papeete. The mailing address is B.P. 627, Papeete, Tahiti, French Polynesia.

Bookstores   **Librairie Vaima,** located next door to the main bookstore on the second level of the Centre Vaima (☎ **45.57.57**), has some English-language novels and a wide selection of books on French Polynesia, many of them in English and some of them rare editions. It also sells the excellent *Carte Touristique,* or Tourist Map, published by the Institut Géographique Nationale, showing geographical features (in topographical relief) and the system of roads and trails on all the Society Islands. **Le Kiosk** in front of the Centre Vaima sells the *International Herald Tribune, Time,* and *Newsweek.*

Business Hours   Although some shops stay open over the long lunch break, most businesses are open from 8 to 11:30am and 2 to 5pm, give or take 30 minutes. Saturday hours are 8 to 11:30am, although some shops in the Centre Vaima stay open Saturday afternoon. The Papeete Municipal Market is a roaring beehive from 5 to 7am on Sunday, and many of the nearby general stores are open during those hours. Except for some small groceries, most other stores are closed on Sunday.

Camera/Film   Film and 1-hour color print processing are available at several stores in downtown Papeete. One of the best is **Tahiti Photo,** in the Centre Vaima (☎ **42.97.34**), where they speak English.

Currency Exchange   **Banque de Polynésie, Banque de Tahiti,** and **Banque Socredo** all have at least one branch on boulevard Pomare and in many suburban locations where you can cash traveler's checks. They all charge a fee of at least 500CFP ($5) for each transaction. You can avoid the fee by getting cash advances against your Visa or MasterCard credit or bank cards at automatic teller machines (ATMs) at Faaa Airport and in front of the Banque Tahiti and Banque Socredo offices on boulevard Pomare in the block west of the Centre Vaima. The instructions are in French and English.

Banking hours on Tahiti generally are 8 to 11:45am and 1:30 to 4:30pm Monday through Friday. Banque de Tahiti's branch on boulevard Pomare next to the Centre Vaima is open Saturday from 8 to 11:30am.

In addition, there's a privately owned currency exchange on the waterfront at the foot of rue Paul Gauguin, next to Tourisme Tahiti, Banque Socredo, and the Immigration office. It's open 7am to 7pm Monday through Saturday, 7am to 1pm on Sunday and holidays.

Drugstores   **Pharmacie du Vaima,** on rue de Général-de-Gaulle at rue Georges La Garde behind the Centre Vaima (☎ **42.97.73**), is owned and operated by English-speaking Nguyen Ngoc-Tran, whose husband runs Pharmacie Tran on Moorea. Pharmacies rotate night duty, so ask your hotel staff to find out which one is open after dark.

E-Mail   **Tiki Soft Café,** on rue Paul Gauguin at the Rond Point de L'Est traffic circle (☎ **88.93.98**), 3 blocks inland from boulevard Pomare, has three computer terminals where you can send and receive e-mail or surf the Internet. Access costs 250CFP ($2.50) for 15 minutes, 1,000CFP ($10) for an hour. Open Monday through Friday from 7:30am to midnight, Saturday from 6pm to 2am. The owners speak English.

Emergencies Consult with your hotel staff. The emergency police telephone number is 17 (but don't expect the person on the other end of the line to speak English). The **Central Gendarmerie** is at the inland terminus of avenue Bruat (☎ **42.02.02**).

Eyeglasses Optique Vaima (☎ **42.77.52**) is in the Centre Vaima.

Hairdressers/Barbers Staffs of the beauty salons in the Hotel Sofitel Maeva Beach Coralia and the Tahiti Beachcomber Parkroyal speak English.

Hospitals Both **Clinique Cardella** (☎ **42.80.10**), on rue Anne-Marie-Javouhey, and **Clinic Paofai** (☎ **43.77.00**) on boulevard Pomare have highly trained specialists and some state-of-the-art equipment. They are open 24 hours.

Libraries The *Office Territorial D'Action Culturelle* (**Territorial Cultural Center**) on boulevard Pomare, west of downtown Papeete (☎ **42.88.50**), has a small library of mostly French books on the South Pacific and other topics. Hours are 8am to 5pm Monday through Friday, except on Wednesday when it closes at 4pm.

Post Office The main post office is on boulevard Pomare a block west of the Centre Vaima. The main desks on the second floor (take the escalators) are open from 7am to 3pm Monday through Friday, but there's also one postal clerk downstairs who is on duty from 7am to 6pm Monday through Friday, from 8 to 11am Saturday. Mail may be picked up at the *poste restante* counter on the ground floor next to the international telephone counter (it's held for a maximum of 2 weeks). The branch post office at the Faaa airport terminal is open from 6 to 10am and 1 to 4pm Monday through Friday, and from 6am to 10am on Saturday, Sunday, and holidays.

Restrooms Free public toilets are on the waterfront east of rue Paul Gauguin, but don't expect them to be clean. Use the facilities at the restaurants or hotels.

Safety Papeete has seen increasing street crime. The busy boulevard Pomare along the waterfront generally is safe, but be very careful if you wander onto the side streets after dark.

Telephone/Telex/Fax The telephone, telegraph, and telex desks on the first floor of the main post office on boulevard Pomare are open Monday through Friday from 7am to 6pm and Saturday from 8 to 11am. The desks on the second floor are open from 7am to 3pm Monday through Friday. Out of town, check with the local post office. See "Fast Facts: French Polynesia" in chapter 3 for more information about pay phones and international calls.

2 Exploring Tahiti

Tahiti is shaped like a figure eight lying on its side. The "eyes" of the eight are two extinct, eroded volcanoes joined by the flat Isthmus of Taravao. The larger western part of the island is known as Tahiti Nui ("Big Tahiti" in Tahitian), while the smaller eastern section beyond the isthmus is named Tahiti Iti ("Little Tahiti"). Together they comprise about 416 square miles, about two-thirds the size of the island of Oahu in Hawaii.

Tahiti Nui's volcano has been eroded over the eons so that now long ridges, separating deep valleys, march down from the crater's ancient rim to the coast far below. The rim itself is still intact, except on the north side where the Papenoo River has cut its way to the sea. The highest peaks, Mount Orohena (2,241 meters [7,353 ft.]) and Mount Aora (2,078 meters [6,817 ft.]), tower above Papeete. Another peak, the toothlike Mount Te Tara O Maiao, or the Diadème (1,329 meters [4,360 ft.]), can be seen from the eastern suburb of Pirae but not from downtown.

With the exception of the east coast of Tahiti Iti, where great cliffs fall into the lagoon, and a few places where the ridges end abruptly at the water's edge, the island is skirted by a flat coastal plain. Tahiti's residents live on this plain or in the valleys, or on the hills adjacent to it.

THE TOP ATTRACTIONS

Arahurahu Marae. Paea, 22.5km (14 miles) west of Papeete. No phone. Free admission. Daily 24 hours.

Arahurahu is the only *marae*—an ancient temple or meeting place—in all of Polynesia that has been fully restored, and it is maintained like a museum. This particular temple apparently had no special historical importance, but it was restored in 1954, complete with exhibit boards explaining the significance of each part. For example, the stone pens near the entrance were used to keep the pigs to be sacrificed to the gods. Arahurahu is used for the reenactment of old Polynesian ceremonies during July's *Heiva i Tahiti* celebrations.

Lagoonarium. Punaauia, 11.4km (7 miles) west of Papeete. ☎ **43.62.90.** Admission 500CFP ($5) adults, 300CFP ($3) children under 12. Daily 9am–9pm.

You don't have to be a snorkeler or diver to enjoy the deep, for this underwater viewing room is surrounded by pens containing reef sharks, sea turtles, and many colorful species of tropical fish. It's part of the Captain Bligh Restaurant and Bar (see "Dining," below), and has a terrific view of Moorea.

✪ **Marché Municipale (Municipal Market).** Papeete, between rue du 22 Septembre and rue François Cardella, 1 block inland from blvd. Pomare. No phone. Free admission. Mon–Fri 5am–6pm, Sat 5am–1pm, Sun 4–8am.

An amazing array of fruits, vegetables, fish, meat, handcrafts, and other items are sold under the big tin pavilion of Papeete's bustling public market. Unwritten rules dictate that Tahitians sell fruits and traditional vegetables, such as taro and breadfruit; Chinese sell European and Chinese vegetables; and Chinese and Europeans serve as butchers and bakers. If your stomach can handle it, look for hogs' heads hanging in the butcher stalls. The market is busiest early in the mornings, but it's like a carnival here from 5 to 7am every Sunday, when people from the outlying areas of Tahiti, and even from the other islands, arrive to sell their produce (by 8am the pickings are slim). A Tahitian string band plays during lunch at the upstairs snack bar, which purveys inexpensive island chow.

✪ **Musée de Tahiti et Ses Isles (Museum of Tahiti and Her Islands).** Punaauia, 15.1km (9 miles) west of Papeete. ☎ **58.34.76.** Admission 500CFP ($5) adults, children free. Tues–Sun 9:30am–5:30pm. Turn toward the lagoon at the Total station and follow the signs.

Set in a lagoonside coconut grove with a gorgeous view of Moorea, this ranks as one of the best museums in the South Pacific. On display is the geological history of the islands; their sea life, flora, and fauna; and the history and culture of their peoples. Exhibits are devoted to traditional weaving, tapa-cloth making, early tools, body ornaments, tattooing, fishing and horticultural techniques, religion and maraes, games and sports, warfare and arms, deaths and funerals, writers and missionaries. Most, but not all, of the display legends are translated into English.

✪ **Musée Gauguin (Gauguin Museum).** Mataiea, 51.2km (32 miles) west of Papeete. ☎ **57.10.58.** Admission 600CFP ($6) adults, 250CFP ($2.50) children. Daily 9am–5pm.

This museum-memorial to Paul Gauguin, the French artist who lived in the Mataiea district from 1891 until 1893, owns one of his minor paintings and some of his sculptures, wood carvings, engravings, and a ceramic vase. It has an active program to borrow his major works, however, and one might be on display during your visit. Otherwise, the exhibits are dedicated to his life in French Polynesia. It's best to see them clockwise, starting at the gift shop, which sells excellent reproductions of his works. The museum sits in lush **Harrison Smith Botanical Gardens,** which were started in 1919 by Harrison Smith, an American who left a career teaching physics at the Massachusetts Institute of Technology and moved to Tahiti. He died here in 1947. His gardens, which now belong to the public, have a plethora of tropical plants from around the world. Admission to the gardens is 400CFP ($4) per person. There's a snack bar.

Point Venus. Mahina, 10km (6 miles) east of Papeete. No phone. Free admission. Open 24 hours daily.

Tahiti's northernmost point, the skinny Point Venus, is where Capt. James Cook observed the transit of the planet Venus in 1769. The low, sandy peninsula covered with iron wood (casuarina) trees is about 2 kilometers from the main road. Captains Wallis, Cook, and Bligh landed here from their ships, which they anchored behind the reef in Matavai Bay offshore. Captain Cook made his observations of the transit of Venus across the sun in 1769 from a point between the black-sand beach and the meandering river cutting the peninsula in two. The beach and the parklike setting around the tall white lighthouse, which was completed in 1868 (notwithstanding the 1867 date over the door), are popular for picnics. There are a snack bar, souvenir and handcraft shop, and toilets.

Walking Tour—Papeete

Start: Tourisme Tahiti/Cruise Ship Welcome Center
Finish: Papeete Town Hall
Time: 2 hours
Best Time: Early morning or late afternoon
Worst Time: Midday, or Sunday when most establishments are closed

Begin at Tourisme Tahiti's information office and the cruise ship welcome center at the foot of rue Paul Gauguin, and stroll westward along boulevard Pomare. Opposite the tuna boat dock stands the

1. **Centre Vaima,** whose chic shops are a mecca for Papeete's French and European communities (the Municipal Market still attracts most Tahitians and Chinese). Quinn's Bar stood in the block east of the Centre Vaima, where the Noa Noa boutique is now. The Centre Vaima takes its name from the Vaima Restaurant, everyone's favorite eatery in those days, which it replaced.

Across the four-lane boulevard from the Vaima is the wooden boardwalk along:

2. **The Quay,** where cruising yachts from around the world congregate from April to September, resident boats all year. Beyond them on the other side of the harbor is **Motu Uta,** once a small natural island belonging to Queen Pomare but now home of the wharves and warehouses of Papeete's shipping port. The reef on the other side has been filled to make a breakwater and to connect Motu Uta by road to **Fare Ute,** the industrial area and French naval base to the right. The inter-island boats dock alongside the filled-in reef, and their cargoes of copra (dried coconut meat) are taken to a mill at Fare Ute, where coconut oil is extracted and later shipped overseas to be used in cosmetics.

Walk west along the waterfront past the main post office, next to which you come to:

3. **Parc Bougainville,** a shady park named for the French explorer, who found Tahiti a little too late to get credit for its discovery, and now home to an outdoor restaurant. Two naval cannons hang over the sidewalk: The one nearest the post office was on the *Seeadler,* Count von Luckner's infamous World War I German raider, which ran aground in the Cook Islands after terrifying the British and French territories of the South Pacific. The other was on the French navy's *Zélée.* Bougainville's statue stands between the guns.

On the waterfront a block farther along boulevard Pomare, at the end of avenue Bruat, stands the:

4. **Pacific Battalion Monument,** a tribute to the French Polynesians who fought with General Charles de Gaulle's Free French forces during World War II. The territory quickly went over to the free French side after the fall of France to Nazi Germany in 1940, and it permitted the Allies to build an airstrip on Bora Bora in 1942. Later, the majority of French Polynesians supported de Gaulle as president of France, and the conservative Gaullist party has been an important force in local politics ever since.

Keep going west along the waterfront to rue l'Arthémise, where you can't miss the impressive steeple of:

5. **Eglise Evangélique,** the largest Protestant church in French Polynesia. The local evangelical sect grew out of the early work by the London Missionary Society. Today the pastors are Tahitian. Sleek outrigger racing canoes are kept on the shady black sand beach across the boulevard. They can be seen cutting the harbor during lunchtime and in the late afternoons (canoe racing is Tahiti's national sport). Imbedded in the stone gateway are the twin hulls of the ***Hokule'a,*** a traditional voyaging canoe that toured the South Pacific in the 1980s, setting off a wave of Polynesian pride.

Boulevard Pomare continues west for 6 more blocks, the canoes and harbor on one side and a few remaining stately old colonial homes on the "mountain side" of the street. Near its end, on the banks of Tipaerui Stream, stands the Office Territorial d'Action Culturelle, Tahiti's cultural center and library.

It's a pleasant stroll to this quiet enclave, but we will turn around and backtrack east on boulevard Pomare to Parc Bougainville (see number 3, above), where we can take a refueling stop at **Le Parc Bougainville** (see "Dining," below). After you have recovered, cut through the park and proceed east along rue de Général-de-Gaulle. To the right as you walk back toward the Centre Vaima are the spacious grounds of:

6. **Place Tarahoi,** Papeete's governmental center, which was royal property in the old days and site of Queen Pomare's mansion, which the French used as their headquarters after 1842. Her impressive home is long gone but is replicated by the Papeete Town Hall (see below). As you face the grounds, the buildings on the right house the French government, including the High Commissioner's office and home. The modern building on the left is the Territorial Assembly. You can walk around hallways of the Assembly building during business hours. In front stands a monument to Pouvanaa a Oopa (1895–1977), a Tahitian who became a hero fighting for France in World War I and then spent the rest of his life battling for independence for his homeland. At one point in the 1960s and '70s he spent 15 years in prison in France but returned home in time to see more local autonomy granted to the territory. In fact, his fellow Tahitians promptly sent him back to Paris as a member of the French Senate.

Walking Tour—Papeete

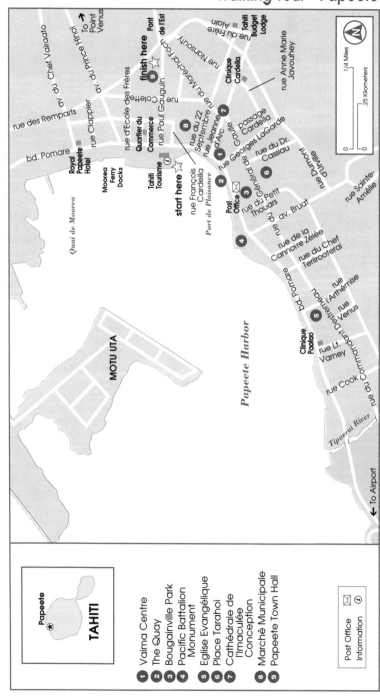

1. Vaima Centre
2. The Quay
3. Bougainville Park
4. Pacific Battalion Monument
5. Eglise Evangélique
6. Place Tarahoi
7. Cathédrale de l'Imaculée Conception
8. Marché Municipale
9. Papeete Town Hall

Post Office
Information

TAHITI
Papeete

Continue 2 more blocks along rue du Général-de-Gaulle past the rear of the Centre Vaima to Tahiti's oldest Catholic church:

7. **Cathédrale de L'Immaculée Conception,** which houses a series of paintings of the Crucifixion. It's a very cool, quiet, and comforting place to worship or just to contemplate.

Rue du Général-de-Gaulle becomes rue du Maréchal-Foch past the church, but follow it for a block until rue Colette angles off to the left. Take it to:

8. **Marché Municipale,** Papeete's Municipal Market. Take a stroll under the large tin pavilion and examine the multitude of fruits and vegetables offered for sale (see "The Top Attractions," above).

After sampling the market and the marvelous handcraft stalls along its sidewalk and upstairs, walk along rue Colette 2 more blocks to:

9. **Papeete Town Hall,** a magnificent replica of Queen Pomare's mansion, which once stood at Place Tarahoi. This impressive structure, with its wraparound veranda, captures the spirit of the colonial South Pacific. This *Hôtel de Ville* or *Fare Oire* (French and Tahitian, respectively, for town hall) was dedicated in 1990 by French President François Mitterand during an elaborate celebration. It's worth a walk up the grand entrance steps and worth catching a cool breeze from its broad balconies.

THE CIRCLE ISLAND TOUR

Known locally as the ✪ **Circle Island Tour,** a drive around Tahiti is a popular way to see the island's outlying sights, and a bit of old Polynesia away from Papeete's bustle. It takes less than a day and can be done even if you're staying on Moorea (take an early-morning ferry over and a late-afternoon boat back to Moorea).

The road around the island is 114 kilometers (72 miles) long, not counting side trips on Tahiti Iti. It's 54 kilometers (32 miles) from Papeete to Taravao along the east coast, and 60 kilometers (40 miles) back along the west coast. If your car has an odometer, reset it to zero; if not, make note of the total kilometers at the outset.

On the land side of the road are red-topped concrete **kilometer markers** *(postes kilomètres* in French, or "PK" for short), which tell the distance in kilometers between Papeete and the isthmus of Taravao. The end of each kilometer is marked with a PK. The markers give the distance from Papeete to Taravao in each direction—not the total number of kilometers around the island. The large numbers facing the ocean are the number of kilometers from Papeete; the numbers facing you as you drive along are the number of kilometers you have to go to Papeete or Taravao, depending on your direction. Distances between the PKs are referred to in tenths of kilometers; for example, PK 35.6 would be 35.6 kilometers from Papeete.

For a detailed description of the tour, buy a copy of Bengt Danielsson's *Tahiti: Circle Island Tour Guide.* French and English editions are available in the local bookstores.

If you drive yourself, avoid getting snarled in morning and evening weekday rush hours.

The North & East Coasts of Tahiti Nui

Proceeding clockwise from Papeete, you'll leave town by turning inland off Boulevard Pomare at the Hotel Prince Hinoi and following the broad **avenue du Prince-Hinoi,** the start of the round-island road.

FAUTAUA VALLEY, LOTI'S POOL & THE DIADEME   At PK 2.5, a road goes right into the steep-walled Fautaua Valley and the **Bain Loti,** or Loti's Pool. Julien Viaud, the French merchant mariner who wrote under the pen name Pierre Loti, used this pool as a setting for his novel, *The Marriage of Loti,* which recounted the love of a Frenchman for a Tahitian woman. Now part of Papeete's water-supply system, the pool is covered in concrete and is not by itself worth a side trip. From the main road you can look up the valley and see the **Diadème,** a rocky outcrop protruding like a crown from the interior ridge (I think it looks like a single worn molar sticking up from a gum). The road goes into the lower part of the valley and terminates at the beginning of a hiking trail up to the **Fautaua Waterfall,** which plunges over a cliff into a large pool 300 meters (985 feet) below. The all-day hike to the head of the valley is best done with a guide (see "Golf, Water Sports & Other Outdoor Pursuits," below).

TOMB OF POMARE V   At PK 4.7 turn left at the sign and drive a short distance to a Protestant churchyard commanding an excellent view of Matavai Bay to the right. The tomb with a Grecian urn on top was built in 1879 for Queen Pomare. Her remains were removed a few years later by her son, King Pomare V, who abdicated in return for a French pension and later died of too much drink. Now he is buried there, and tour guides like to say the urn is not an urn at all but is a liquor bottle, which makes it a monument not to Pomare V but to the cause of his death.

HOME OF JAMES NORMAN HALL   At PK 5.4, on the mountain side of the road just east of the small bridge, stands the now-overgrown home built by James Norman Hall, co-author with Charles Nordhoff of *Mutiny on the Bounty.* Nordhoff and Hall served together in World War I, moved to Tahiti to write, and produced three novels on the mutiny (also *Men Against the Sea* and *Pitcairn's Island*) and several more books about French Polynesia. Hall died in 1951 and is buried on the hill above his home. A poem he wrote is engraved on the gravestone: "Look to the Northward, stranger/Just over the hillside there/Have you in your travels seen/A land more passing fair?" The house belongs to the territorial government and may someday be a museum, but it was not open to the public during my most recent visit.

ONE TREE HILL   At PK 8, you'll come to the top of One Tree Hill, so named by Capt. James Cook because a single tree stood on this steep headland in the late 1700s. For many years it was the site of a luxury hotel, now closed. Pull into the round-about at the entrance and stop for one of Tahiti's most magnificent vistas. You'll look down on the north coast all the way from Matavai Bay to Papeete, with Moorea looming on the far horizon. If the hotel has reopened, drive in to the reception area, which sits on top of the hill, coupling this view and a chance for a refreshment break.

Impressions

The air was full of that exquisite fragrance of orange blossom and gardenia which is distilled by night under the thick foliage; there was a great silence, accentuated by the bustle of insects in the grass, and that sonorous quality, peculiar to night in Tahiti, which predisposes the listener to feel the enchanting power of music.

—Pierre Loti (Julien Viaud), 1880

❂ POINT VENUS At PK 10, turn left at Super Marché Venus Star and drive to Point Venus, Tahiti's northernmost point, where Capt. James Cook observed the transit of the planet Venus in 1769 (see "The Top Attractions," above).

After you've looked around the black sand beach and lighthouse, head back to the main road for a refreshment stop at **Chez Kennedy,** a small snack bar opposite the Point Venus turnoff. Its juicy, Australian-style hamburgers are among Tahiti's best.

OROFARA LEPER COLONY At PK 13.2 begins the entrance to Orofara Valley, which the French colonial administration made a leper colony in 1914. Leprosy once was a fairly common disease throughout Polynesia, and until then, those afflicted were sent into the hills. Today leprosy is curable with sulfa drugs, and victims can remain at home with their families.

PAPENOO VALLEY At PK 17.1, Tahiti's longest bridge crosses its longest river at the end of its largest valley at one of its largest rural villages—all named Papenoo. The river flows down to the sea through the only wall in Tahiti Nui's old volcanic crater. Four-wheel-drive vehicles go up the valley on their excursions across the island (see "Safari Expeditions," below).

ARAHOHO BLOWHOLES At PK 22, the surf pounding against the headland at Arahoho has formed overhanging shelves with holes in them. As waves crash under the shelves, water and air are forced through the holes, resulting in a geyser-like phenomenon. An overlook with free parking and toilets is west of the sharp curve.

❂ FAARUMAI WATERFALLS At PK 22.1, a sign on the right just past the blowhole marks a paved road that leads 1.3 kilometers up a small valley to the Cascades de Faarumai, Tahiti's most accessible waterfalls. Park near the stand of bamboo trees and follow the signs. Vaimahuta falls are an easy walk; Haamaremare Iti and Haamaremarerahi falls are a 45-minute climb up a more difficult trail. Vaimahuta falls plunge straight down several hundred feet from a hanging valley into a large pool. Bring insect repellent.

MAHAENA BATTLEFIELD At PK 32.5, the Tahitian rebellion came to a head on April 17, 1844, when 441 French troops charged several times and many poorly armed Tahitians dug in near the village of Mahaena. The Tahitians lost 102 men and the French, 15. It was the last set battle of the rebellion.

BOUGAINVILLE'S LANDING At PK 37.6, a plaque mounted on a rock on the northern end of the bridge at Hitiaa commemorates Bougainville's landing. The French explorer anchored just offshore when he arrived in Tahiti in 1768. The two small islands on the reef, Oputotara and Variararu, provided slim protection against the prevailing trade winds, and Bougainville lost six anchors in 10 days trying to keep his ships off the reef. Tahitians recovered one and gave it to the high chief of Bora Bora, who in turn gave it to Captain Cook in 1777.

FAATAUTIA VALLEY At PK 41.8 begins a view of Faatautia Valley, which looks so much like those in the Marquesas that in 1957 director John Huston chose it as a location for a movie version of *Typee,* Herman Melville's novelized account of his ship-jumping adventures among the Marquesans in the 1840s. The project was scrapped after another of Huston's Melville movies, *Moby Dick,* bombed at the box office. **Vaiharuru Waterfall** cascades into the uninhabited valley, which surely looks much today as it did a thousand years ago.

TARAVAO At PK 53, after passing the small-boat marina, the road climbs up onto the Isthmus of Taravao. At the top are the stone walls of Fort Taravao, which the French built in 1844 to bottle up what was left of the rebellious Tahitians on the Tahiti Iti peninsula. Germans stuck on Tahiti during World War II were interned there. It is

It came upon me little by little. I came to like the life here, with its ease and its leisure, and the people, with their good-nature and their happy smiling faces.
—W. Somerset Maugham, 1921

now used as a French army training center. The village of Taravao with its shops, suburban streets, and churches has grown up around the military post. Its snack bars are a good place for a refueling stop.

TAHITI ITI

Taravao joins the larger Tahiti Nui to its smaller Siamese twin, the peninsula of Tahiti Iti. The latter is much more sparsely populated, and paved roads dead-end about halfway down its north and its south sides. A series of cliffs plunges into the sea on Tahiti Iti's rugged east end.

TARAVAO PLATEAU   If you have to choose one of three roads on Tahiti Iti, take the one that dead-ends high up into the rolling pastures of the Taravao Plateau. It begins at the traffic signal on the north coast road to Tautira and runs up through cool pastures reminiscent of rural France, with huge trees lining the narrow paved road. From there you'll have a spectacular view of the entire isthmus and down both sides of Tahiti Nui. At more than 1,200 feet high, the plateau is blessed with a refreshing, perpetually spring-like climate.

THE NORTH COAST   The road on the north coast of Tahiti Iti goes for 18 kilometers (11 miles) to the sizable village of **Tautira,** which sits on its own little peninsula. Captain Cook anchored in the bay off Tautira on his second visit to Tahiti in 1773. His ships ran aground on the reef while their crews were partying one night. He managed to get them off but lost several anchors in the process. One of them was found in 1978 and is now on display at the Museum of Tahiti and Her Islands, which we will come to on the west side of the island.

A year after Cook landed at Tautira, two Franciscan priests were put ashore there by the *Aguila,* a Spanish ship from Peru, whose captain claimed the island for Spain. It was the third time Tahiti had been claimed for a European power. The *Aguila* returned a year later, but the priests had had enough of Tahiti and sailed back to Peru.

As far as anyone knows, Tautira's next famous visitor was Robert Louis Stevenson, who spent 2 months there in 1888 working on *The Master of Ballantrae,* a novel set not in Tahiti but in Scotland. Stevenson's mother was with him in Tautira. After she returned to London, she sent the local Protestant church a silver communion service, which is still being used today. See chapter 12 for more about Stevenson's South Pacific adventures.

THE SOUTH COAST   The picturesque road along the south coast of Tahiti Iti skirts the lagoon, passing through small settlements. Novelist Zane Grey had a deep-sea-fishing camp at PK 7.3, near the village of Toahotu from 1928 to 1930. He caught a silver marlin that was about 14 feet long and weighed more than 1,000 pounds—even after the sharks had had a meal on it while Grey was trying to get it aboard his boat. He wrote about his adventures in *Tales of Tahitian Waters.*

According to Tahitian legends, the demi-god Maui once made a rope from his sister Hina's hair and used it to slow down the sun long enough for Tahitians to finish cooking their food in their earth ovens (a lengthy process). He accomplished this feat while standing on the reef at a point 8.5 kilometers (5 miles) along the south coast road, and his footprints are still there. Beyond Maui's alleged footprints, the Bay of

Tapueraha provides the best natural harbor on Tahiti and was used as a base by a large contingent of the French navy during the aboveground nuclear tests at Moruroa atoll in the 1960s. Some of the old mooring pilings still stand just offshore.

THE SOUTH COAST OF TAHITI NUI

As you leave Taravao, heading back to Papeete along Tahiti's south coast, note the PK markers begin to decrease the nearer to Papeete you get. The road rims casuarina-ringed Port Phaeton, which cuts nearly halfway across the isthmus. Port Phaeton and the Bay of Tapueraha to the south are Tahiti's finest harbors, yet European settlement and most development have taken place on the opposite side of the island, around Papeete.

PAPAEARI   At PK 52 stands Tahiti's oldest village. Apparently the island's initial residents recognized the advantages of the south coast and its deep lagoons and harbors, for word-of-mouth history says they came through the Hotumatuu Pass in the reef and settled at Papeari sometime between A.D. 400 and 500. Robert Keable, author of *Simon Called Peter,* a best-selling novel about a disillusioned clergyman, lived here from 1924 until he died in 1928 at the age of 40. His home, now a private residence, stands at PK 55. Today Papeari is a thriving village whose residents often sell fruit and vegetables at stands along the road.

✪ THE GAUGUIN MUSEUM   At PK 51.2 is the entrance to the museum-memorial to Paul Gauguin, who lived near here from 1891 until 1893 (see "The Top Attractions," above). The museum sits in lush **Harrison Smith Botanical Gardens,** started in 1919 by American Harrison Smith. The museum and gardens are open daily from 9am to 5pm. There's a snack bar here, but your best bet is to continue west.

RESTAURANT DU MUSÉE GAUGUIN   At PK 50.5, the circle island tour buses deposit their passengers for lunch at this lagoonside restaurant, which is worth a stop just for its phenomenal view of Tahiti Iti. Owner Roger Gowan, a transplanted Englishman, offers a buffet for 2,250CFP ($22.50) per person. À la carte main courses featuring shrimp and mahimahi range from 1,800CFP to 3,200CFP ($18 to $32). Sandwiches are available for 500CFP ($5). The restaurant is open daily from noon to 3pm. For reservations, phone ☎ **57.13.80.**

VAIHIRIA RIVER   At PK 48 the main road crosses the Vaihiria River. An unpaved jeep track beside the bridge leads inland to Lake Vaihiria. At 1,500 feet above sea level, Tahiti's only lake is noted for its freshwater eels. Cliffs up to 3,000 feet tall drop to the lake on its north side.

ATIMAONO   At PK 41 begins the largest parcel of flat land on Tahiti, site of Olivier Bréaud International Golf Course, French Polynesia's only links. Irishman William Stewart started his cotton plantation here during the American Civil War. Nothing remains of the plantation, but it was Stewart who brought the first Chinese indentured servants to Tahiti.

DORENCE ATWATER'S GRAVE   At PK 36 stands a Protestant church in whose yard is buried Dorence Atwater, American consul to Tahiti after the Civil War. Atwater had been a Union Army soldier held as a prisoner of war by the Confederates. He was assigned to a Southern hospital, where he recorded the names of Union soldiers who died while in captivity. He later escaped and brought his lists to the federal government, thus proving that the Confederacy was keeping inaccurate records. His action made him a hero in the eyes of the Union Army. He later moved to the south coast of Tahiti, married the daughter of a chief of the Papara district, and at one time invested in William Stewart's cotton venture.

The Moon & Six Million

In 1891, a marginally successful Parisian painter named Paul Gauguin left behind his wife and six children and sailed to Tahiti. He wanted to devote himself to his art, free of the chains of civilization.

Instead of paradise, however, Gauguin found a world that suffered from some of the same maladies as did the one from which he fled. Poverty, sickness, and frequent disputes with church and colonial officials marked his decade in the islands. He had syphilis, a bad heart, and an addiction to opium.

Gauguin disliked Papeete and spent his first 2 years in the rural Mataiea district, on Tahiti's south coast, where a village woman asked what he was doing there. Looking for a girl, he replied. The woman immediately offered her 13-year-old daughter Tehaamana, the first of Gauguin's early-teenage Tahitian mistresses. One of them bore him a son in 1899.

Tehaamana and the others figured prominently in Gauguin's impressionistic masterpieces, which brought fame to Tahiti but did little for his own pocketbook. After 649 paintings and a colorful career, immortalized by W. Somerset Maugham in *The Moon and Sixpence,* Gauguin died penniless in 1903.

At the time of his death, apparently of a drug overdose, in the Marquesas Islands, a painting by Gauguin sold for 150 French francs. Today, on the rare occasion when one comes on the market, it fetches far in excess of $6 million.

Papara village also is home to the ***Musée de Coquillage*** (Seashell Museum). It has a collection of polished shell collages and dried sea snakes, sea-turtle shells, and crabs—many of which are for sale as well as for viewing. The museum is open Tuesday through Friday from 8am to 5pm, and Saturday and Sunday from 9am to noon and from 1 to 5pm. Admission is 300CFP ($3) for adults and 200CFP ($2) for children.

MARAA GROTTO At PK 28.5, on Tahiti's southwest corner, the road turns sharply around the base of a series of headlands, which drop precipitously to the lagoon. Deep into one of these cliffs goes the Maraa Grotto, also called the Paroa Cave. It usually has a lake inside and goes much deeper into the hill than appears at first glance. The mouth of the cave is clearly visible from the road. Park in the parking lot, not along the road.

THE WEST COAST OF TAHITI NUI

North of Maraa the road runs through the Paea and Punaauia suburbs of Papeete. The west coast is the driest part of Tahiti, and it's very popular with Europeans, Americans, and others who have built homes along the lagoon and in the hills overlooking it and Moorea. It's so populated that local officials are extending the Route 1 freeway as far south as the Punaruu River, just north of *Musée de Tahiti et Ses Isles* (Museum of Tahiti and Her Islands). But we'll stay on Route 1, the old road.

✪ ARAHURAHU MARAE At PK 22.5 a small road on the right of Magasin Laut leads to a narrow valley, on the floor of which sits the restored Arahurahu Marae (see "The Top Attractions," above). It's worth a stop here to see one of the best examples of ancient Polynesian temples and meeting places.

✪ MUSÉE DE TAHITI ET SES ISLES At PK 15.1, turn left at the gas station and follow the signs through a residential area to the lagoon and the Musée de Tahiti et Ses Isles (Museum of Tahiti and Her Islands), one of the South Pacific's best (see "The Top Attractions," above).

LAGOONARIUM   At PK 11.4, the Captain Bligh Restaurant and Bar has a terrific view of Moorea and is home to the Le Lagoonarium de Tahiti, an underwater viewing room (see "The Top Attractions," above).

The old road divides into four lanes soon after the Lagoonarium, and passes shopping centers and marinas in Punaauia. It splits just before the Hotel Sofitel Maeva Beach Coralia. The left lanes feed into the Route 5 freeway, which roars back to Papeete. The right lanes will take you along Route 1, the old road that goes past the west coast hotels and the Faaa airport before returning to town.

ORGANIZED TOURS

Several companies offer tours around the coastal road. Expect to pay about 4,000CFP ($40) for a half-day tour, 7,300CFP ($73) for all day, plus entrance fees to the museums and other attractions and lunch at the Restaurant du Musée Gauguin.

English-speaking William Leteeg of **Adventure Eagle Tours** (☎ **77.20.03**) lends his experiences growing up on the island to his commentaries. Other circle-island tour operators with English-speaking guides are **Tahiti Tours** (☎ **42.78.70**), **Tahiti Nui Travel** (☎ **42.68.03**), and **Marama Tours** (☎ **82.08.42**). They have reservations desks in several hotels.

He won't take you all the way around the island, but oceanographer and fisheries biologist Philippe Siu of **Iaora Tahiti Ecotours** (☎ **56.46.75**; fax 42.73.10; www. iaora.com; e-mail ecotours@mail.pf) offers a much more in-depth explanation of local history, flora, and fauna than you'll get on the usual tour. This "History and Culture of Tahiti" tour stops at Musée de Tahiti et Ses Isles (Museum of Tahiti and Her Islands), Arahurahu Marae, and Matavai Bay. Half-day trips cost 55,000CFP ($50) per person; full days go for 110,000CFP ($110). The latter includes lunch.

SAFARI EXPEDITIONS

So-called safari expeditions into Tahiti's interior offer a very different view of the island, and some spectacular views at that. Riding in the backs of open, four-wheel-drive vehicles, you follow narrow, unpaved roads up over the mountains from one coast to the other, usually via the breathtaking Papenoo Valley. Weather permitting (see "Readers Recommend" below), you'll ride through a water supply tunnel cut through the island's steep interior ridge, and from there down a track to Lake Vaihiria and on along Vaihiria River to the south coast. You'll stop for a refreshing swim in the chilly water. The cool temperatures at the higher elevations are refreshing.

Patrice Bordes's **Tahiti Safari Expedition** (☎ **42.14.15**) is the best. Marama Tours (☎ **83.96.50**) also is good. They charge about 5,000CFP ($50) per person for a half-day, 7,500CFP ($75) for a full day. Reservations may be made at most hotel activities desks.

It's far from inexpensive, but a spectacular way to see Tahiti's interior mountains, valleys, and waterfalls is by helicopter with **Heli-Pacific** (☎ **85.668.00**; fax 85.68.08) and **Heli-Inter Polynesia** (☎ **81.99.00**; fax 81.99.99).

Readers Recommend

Pick a Clear Day. For those booking on safari expeditions to Tahiti's interior, check the weather forecasts very closely in advance as the vendors can or will refuse to take passengers there if the weather is inclement. It might also be advisable to book with a cancellation option or penalty since a trip around the island is really not a comparable substitute.

—Lawrence R. Walz, Atlanta, Georgia

3 Golf, Water Sports & Other Outdoor Pursuits

GOLF The 18-hole, 6,950-yard **Olivier Bréaud International Golf Course,** PK 40.2, Atimaono (☎ **57.40.32**), sprawls over the site of William Stewart's cotton plantation. A clubhouse, pro shop, restaurant, bar, locker rooms, showers, swimming pool, spa pool, and driving range are on the premises. Greens fees are about 4,800CFP ($48). **Marama Tours** (☎ **83.96.50**) has an all-day golf outing for about 14,000CFP ($140) per person, including greens fees, equipment, and transportation to and from the course.

HIKING Tahiti has a number of hiking trails, such as the cross-island Papenoo Valley–Lake Vaihiria route. Another ascends to the top of Mount Aorai. None of these should be undertaken without the proper equipment and a guide. Downpours can occur in the higher altitudes, swelling the streams that most trails follow, and the nights can become bitterly cold and damp. The "rainy side" of the island can shift from one day to the next, depending on which way the wind blows. In addition, the quick-growing tropical foliage can quickly obscure a path that was easily followed a few days before. Permits are required to use some trails that cross government land.

One way to explore the interior on foot—and have a guide schooled in the island's flora, fauna, geology, and archaeology—is a hike to the Fautaua Falls with **Iaora Tahiti Ecotours** (☎ **56.46.75;** fax 42.73.10; www.iaora.com; e-mail ecotours@mail.pf). The walk follows a steep-walled gorge up the Fautaua Valley, site of Loti's Pool (see "Circle Island Tour," above). At the top of the falls, you'll see the ruins of an old French fort and the governor's mansion dating from the French-Tahitian war of 1844–46. It's a moderately strenuous hike with several wet-feet river crossings.

You can also check with Tourisme Tahiti for the names of other guides and hiking clubs (see "Visitor Information & Entry Requirements" in chapter 3).

WATER SPORTS Based at the Tahiti Beachcomber Parkroyal, **Tahiti Aquatique** (☎ **53.34.96**) offers a comprehensive list of water sports activities. Some sample prices (per person, unless otherwise indicated): scuba diving, per dive including equipment and a guide, 5,000CFP ($50); introductory dive, 5,500CFP ($55); snorkeling gear rental, 800CFP ($8); waterskiing, 2,700CFP ($27) per 15 minutes; kayak rental, 1,500CFP ($15) per hour or 3,000CFP ($30) for 3 hours; and jet-skiing, 6,000CFP ($60) for 30 minutes.

4 Shopping

THE SHOPPING SCENE

There's no shortage of things to buy in Tahiti, especially in Papeete: black pearls, both French and Tahitian fashions, and handcrafts. The selection and prices on some items may be better on Moorea.

If you just can't live without visiting a modern shopping mall, head for the **Continent Centre Commercial,** on the main road in Punaauia about a quarter-mile south of the Hotel Sofitel Maeva Beach Coralia. Here you'll find a huge supermarket, several boutiques, a snack bar with excellent hamburgers for 400CFP ($4), and a post office (open Monday through Friday from 8am to 5pm, Saturday from 8am to noon). The local **Centre Artisinant** stands across the parking lot under a teepee-shaped roof (see "Handcrafts," below).

Duty-free shopping is very limited, with French perfumes the best deal. **Duty Free Tahiti** (☎ **42.61.61**), on the street level, water side of the Centre Vaima, is the largest duty-free shop. Its specialties are Seiko, Lorus, and Cartier watches, and Givenchy, Yves St. Laurent, Chanel, and Guerlain perfumes. The **airport departure lounge** has two duty-free shops.

BLACK PEARLS

French Polynesia is the world's largest producer of cultured black pearls. In fact, so many are being produced that competition is fierce among the islands' shops, some of whom (or their agents, commissioned tour guides and bus and taxi drivers) will bombard you with sales pitches almost from the moment you arrive. Some stalls in Papeete's Municipal Market even sell pearls, but give them a miss and buy yours from an experienced, reputable dealer.

Most of the territory's pearls are grown at farms in the lagoons of the Tuamotu Archipelago east of Tahiti, with Manihi being the most productive (see chapter 6).

Pearls are cultured by implanting a small nucleus into the shell of a live oyster, which then coats it with nacre, the same lustrous substance that lines the mother-of-pearl shell. The nacre of the oysters used in French Polynesia, the *Pinctada margaritifera,* produces dark pearls that are known as "black" but whose actual color ranges from black with shades of rose or green, which are the rarest and most valuable, to slightly grayer than white. The bulk of the crop is black with bluish or brownish tints. Most range in size from 10mm to 17mm (slightly less than half an inch to slightly less than three-quarters of an inch).

Size, color, luster, lack of imperfections, and shape determine a pearl's value. No two are exactly alike, but the most valuable are the larger ones that are most symmetrical, that have few dark blemishes, and whose color is dark with the shades of a peacock showing through a bright luster. A high-quality pearl 13mm or larger will sell for $10,000 or more, but there are thousands to choose from in the $300 to $1,000 range. Some small, imperfect-but-still-lovely pearls cost much less.

National Geographic carried very informative articles on cultured pearls in its August 1985 and June 1997 issues, so dig them out of the attic before heading off to Tahiti.

With most tourists now spending minimum time on Tahiti in favor of the other islands, you may find pearl prices in Papeete to be less than on Moorea and Bora Bora. That's not always the case, so you should look in **Island Fashion Black Pearls** or **Matira Pearls** on Bora Bora before making a purchase in Papeete (see "Shopping" in chapters 5 and 6). You're also more likely to get a salesperson over there who speaks English fluently.

The city has scores of *bijouteries* (jewelry shops) carrying black pearls in a variety of settings. Most are in or around the Centre Vaima, along boulevard Pomare, and in the Quartier du Commerce, the narrow streets off boulevard Pomare between rue Paul Gauguin and rue d'école des Frères north of the Municipal Market.

Your beginning point should be the ✪ **Musée de la Perle Robert Wan,** on the rue Jeanne d'Arc side of the Centre Vaima (☎ **45.43.45**). Named for Robert Wan, the man who pioneered the local industry back in the 1960s, this museum explains the history of pearls back to antiquity, the method by which they are cultured, and the things to look for when making your selection. The museum is open Monday through Saturday from 8am to 7pm, Sunday from 9am to 7pm. Admission is 600CFP ($6) for adults, 300CFP ($3) for children. Call for a free ride from local hotels.

Adjoining the museum, **Tahiti Perles** (☎ **45.05.05**) carries only excellent-quality pearls and uses only 18-karat gold for its settings, so the prices tend to be high.

Don't Pay Full Price!

With so many black pearls flooding the market, discounting is the rule of the day throughout French Polynesia. Don't pay the price marked on a pearl or a piece of jewelry until you have politely asked for a discount.

On the second level of the Centre Vaima, **Sibani Perles Joallier** (☎ **41.36.34**) carries the jewelry line of Didier Sibani, another pioneer of the local industry. European-style elegance is the theme here and at the other Sibani outlets throughout the islands.

From the Centre Vaima, walk east along boulevard Pomare, then turn right on rue du Commandant Jean Gilbert (between Banque Socredo and Tahiti Sport) in the Quartier du Commerce. This sort of "Pearl Row" has a number of small jewelry stores specializing in pearls, and some major traders have upstairs offices here. Among the storefront shops is **Pai Moana Perles** (☎ **43.31.10**), owned by Canadian Peter Ringland and American Rick Steger, whose pearl farm at Manihi in the Tuamotus directly supplies this little shop as well as outlets on Moorea and in Hawaii. They do all of their simple but elegant jewelry designs here.

HANDCRAFTS

Economic hard times in recent years have had one salutary effect: Strapped for income, many local residents are producing a wide range of jewelry made from seashells, homemade quilts, rag dolls, needlework, and straw hats, mats, baskets, and handbags.

The most popular item by far, however, is the cotton *pareu,* or wraparound sarong, which is screened, blocked, or printed by hand in the colors of the rainbow. The same material is made into other tropical clothing and various items, such as bedspreads. Pareus are sold virtually everywhere a visitor might wander.

✪ **Papeete Municipal Market** is the place to shop. It has stalls both upstairs and on the surrounding sidewalk, where local women's associations offer a wide selection of handcrafts at reasonable prices. The market is one of the few places where you can regularly find pareus for 1,000CFP ($10), bedspreads made of the colorful tie-dyed and silk-screened pareu material, and *tivaivai,* the colorful applique quilts stitched together by Tahitian women as their great-grandmothers were shown by the early missionaries. By and large, cloth goods are sold at the sidewalk stalls; those upstairs have a broader range of shell jewelry and other items.

Several villages have *centres artisinants,* where local women display their wares. The one in Punaauia, in the Continent Centre Commercial parking lot just south of the Hotel Sofitel Maeva Beach Coralia, is the best place to look for tivaivai quilts, which sell for about 35,000CFP ($350).

For finer-quality handcrafts, such as woodcarvings from the Marquesas Islands, shell chandeliers, tapa lamp shades, or mother-of-pearl shells, try **Manuia Curios** (☎ **42.04.94**) on place Notre Dame opposite the Catholic cathedral. Manuia Curios carries some artifacts from several South Pacific countries, including some from the Sepik River area of Papua New Guinea. **Tamara Curios** (☎ **42.54.42**), on rue de Général-de-Gaulle in Fare Tony, has a wide range of quality shell jewelry, wood carvings, place mats, and local pineapple jam made with rum.

TROPICAL CLOTHING

You've arrived in Tahiti and you notice that everyone under the sun is wearing print sun dresses or flowered aloha shirts. Where do you go to get yours?

Each hotel has at least one boutique carrying tropical clothing, including pareus. The prices there reflect the heavy tourist traffic, but they aren't much worse than at the stores in Papeete. Clothing, to put it bluntly, is dear in French Polynesia.

On boulevard Pomare, stop in **Marie Ah You** (☎ **42.03.31**) and **Aloha Boutique** (☎ **42.87.52**), both in the block west of the Centre Vaima. Their selections for women are trendy and a bit expensive. In the Centre Vaima, **Anemone** (☎ **43.02.66**) has an unusual combination of quality T-shirts and chocolates.

It's a comfort to get into a pareu when one gets back from town . . . I should strongly recommend you to adopt it. It's one of the most sensible costumes I have ever come across. It's cool, convenient, and inexpensive.

—W. Somerset Maugham, 1921

Tahiti Art (☎ 42.97.43), in Fare Tony on boulevard Pomare just west of the Centre Vaima, specializes in block-printed traditional designs (as opposed to the swirls and swooshes with leaves and flowers popular on most pareus). It was block printing long before this became the most popular style throughout the South Pacific, and its designs are among the most unique in town.

5 Accommodations

If you can't get a room at the hotels I recommend below, downtown Papeete has several properties convenient to the Moorea Ferry docks. Most charge between 12,000CFP and 16,000CFP ($120 to $160) for a double room.

The **Hotel Tiare Tahiti**, B.P. 2359, Papeete (☎ 43.68.48; fax 43.68.47), an upstairs, 5-story facility on boulevard Pomare a block west of the Centre Vaima, was built in 1996 and is modern and clean. The rooms are minimally furnished, however, and can be noisy, since most face directly onto the busy boulevard (request one on the upper floors). A saving grace if you're a TV addict: The sets have CNN and ESPN in English.

The Chinese-accented **Hotel Le Mandarin**, B.P. 302, Papeete (☎ 53.33.50; fax 42.16.32; e-mail mandarin@mail.pf), enjoys a much quieter location on rue Collette opposite the Town Hall. It's popular with business types from the outer islands.

Rooms at the circular, 7-story high-rise **Hotel Pacific Kon Tiki**, B.P. 111, Papeete (☎ 43.72.82; fax 42.11.66), on boulevard Pomare opposite the Moorea Ferry Docks, are among the least expensive here—10,300CFP ($103) for a double. Rooms on the top floors have impressive sea or mountain views. A circular restaurant on top of the building is better known for its spectacular vistas than for its French and Tahitian cuisine.

In Tipaeru, a 10-minute walk west of downtown, the 1970s vintage **Matavai Hotel, Resort & Sports Centre**, B.P. 32, Papeete (☎ 42.67.76; fax 42.36.90), is a former Holiday Inn. The recently refurbished American-style rooms are clean and comfortable. The public areas have seen better days, however, and there's no Polynesian ambience afoot. Many New Zealanders on low-cost package tours stay here. The Matavai is the only hotel here which is allowed to pick you up at the airport. The "sports center" is a public recreation complex out front with tennis, squash, and other diversions.

VERY EXPENSIVE

✪ **Le Meridien Tahiti.** B.P. 380595, Tamanu 98718, Tahiti (Punaauia, 15km [9 miles] south of Papeete, 8km [5 miles] south of airport). ☎ **800/225-5843** or 47.07.07. Fax 47.07.08. www.lemeridien-tahiti.com. E-mail: sales@lemeridien-tahiti.com. 138 units, plus 12 bungalows. A/C MINIBAR TEL TV. 34,000CFP–47,400CFP ($340–$474) double; 44,900CFP–52,200CFP ($449–$522) bungalow. AE, DC, MC, V.

Near the Museum of Tahiti and Her Islands, this luxury resort opened in 1998 alongside Tahiti's only stretch of white-sand beach. It's an excellent choice—provided you don't have to get to Faaa airport to catch a flight during the weekday morning traffic jam, when the usual 15-minute ride can take up to 2 hours. The Melanesian-inspired architecture is stunning, with sway-back shingle roofs evoking the "spirit houses" of Papua New Guinea. The breezy lobby opens to a magnificent rooftop reflecting pool imaging the sky and palm trees outside. From there, a grand staircase leads down first to a mezzanine bar and then to the main restaurant beside a large, curving swimming pool. Imported sand surrounding the wade-in pool compensates for the pebbly beach and shallow lagoon here.

The best accommodations are 12 over-water bungalows with either glass-floors or steps into the lagoon from their porches, but try to get a north-facing unit since these have Moorea views. The luxuriously appointed guest rooms occupy 2-, 3- and 4-story buildings flanking the main activities area. All units here have reed-faced wardrobes; minibars and tea/coffee-making facilities hidden under TV consoles; sofas in sitting areas; and desks with good light, modem ports, and power outlets. The rooms also have balconies with views over the lagoon or the reflecting pool. On the ends of the buildings, "senior suites" add a separate bedroom and large balcony, while entry to "junior suites" is through a triangular lanai rather than from an interior hallway. Throughout, large bathrooms come equipped with tubs under windows looking into the bedroom area, separate shower stalls, and expansive teak vanities surrounding a single sink. Rooms on one floor are designated as no-smoking, and some units are equipped for disabled guests.

Dining/Diversions: Opening to the swimming pool, La Plantation proffers French-style breakfasts and gourmet dinners. Up on the mezzanine, you can grab a pre-dinner drink and listen to a pianist in L'Astrolabe bar. Lunch and afternoon snacks are available under a big thatch roof in the beachside grill known as Le Fare Te Moana. Tahitians make music every night and put on shows at least once a week, dancing on an island out in the swimming pool.

Amenities: Activities and car-rental desks, swimming pool, fitness center, water-sports program including equipment rental and scuba diving, boutiques, concierge, nightly turndown, limited room service, valet parking, baby-sitting arranged, laundry, twice daily shuttle to Papeete.

Outrigger Hotel Tahiti. B.P. 416, Papeete (1km [0.5 mile] west of downtown, 6km [3.5 miles] east of airport). ☎ **800/688-7444** or 86.48.48. Fax 86.48.40. www.outrigger.com. E-mail: reservation@outrigger.com. 250 units. A/C MINIBAR TEL TV. 27,500 CFP–65,000 CFP ($275–$650) double. AE, DC, MC, V.

An easy walk to downtown and a quick drive to the airport, this state-of-the-art hotel was built from scratch in 1998-99 on the site of the old Hotel Tahiti, whose massive thatch-roofed public areas hosted many a local soiree. The new facility is also aimed at big functions, with meeting space capable of accommodating as many as 1,000 persons at receptions. Those meeting rooms open up to a large stone terrace on the shore of the lagoon facing Moorea. The terrace—which comes equipped with sand-bordered horizon pool, water slide, and whirlpool—is the focal point here, since there's no beach, only a shoreline bulkhead. You can venture into the lagoon, however, because scuba diving, waterskiing, canoeing, sailing, and other water sports are available at the hotel's dock.

Guest rooms are in 4- and 5-story shingle-roofed hotel blocks. Except for 10 suites, which have polished wood floors and one or two bedrooms, the spacious units are all identical except for the vistas off their private balconies (rates increase from harbor to ocean to Moorea view). All have carpeted floors; a king or two twin beds; refrigerators (stocked on request); irons and boards; desks with modem ports and 110-volt power outlets; tea/coffeemakers; TVs with CNN, HBO, and a sports channel in English; and bathrooms equipped with combo tub-showers, hair dryers, and toiletries. Rooms on one floor are non-smoking, 5 are equipped for disabled quests, and 50 are Voyager Club units with their own concierge and lounge. The Hawaii-based Outrigger chain makes sure you'll find those good old American amenities—ice and vending machines—in the hallways.

Dining/Diversions: An open-kitchen restaurant serves international breakfasts and dinners, with seating either on the terrace or under the natural thatch roofs of two over-water dining rooms, one looking out toward Moorea. There's also a Chinese restaurant here. Evoking Tahiti's by-gone days, Quinn's Bar opens to the stone terrace and provides lunch, snacks, and libation to poolside sun worshippers. Locals make island music during the evenings and stage Tahitian dance shows on a platform on stilts over the lagoon.

Amenities: Boutiques, activities and car-rental desks, arts and crafts center, fitness and beauty center, business center with e-mail access, concierge, limited room service, laundry, valet parking.

✪ **Tahiti Beachcomber Parkroyal.** B.P. 6014, Faaa, Tahiti (Faaa, 8km [5 miles] west of Papeete). ☎ **800/835-7742** or 86.51.10. Fax 86.51.30. www.tahiti-resorts.com. E-mail: tahiti@parkroyal.pf. 182 units, plus 32 bungalows. A/C MINIBAR TV TEL. 31,700CFP–35,700CFP ($317–$357) double, 40,600CFP–52,400CFP ($406–$524) bungalow. AE, DC, MC, V. Take any Faaa or Maeva Beach truck.

Recent improvements and additions have kept this extraordinarily well-managed property's ranking as Tahiti's best all-around hotel. Known simply as "The Beachcomber," it sits at Tataa Point on the island's northwest corner, from whence souls supposedly leaped to the ancient Polynesian homeland in pre-Christian days. Today's guests get one of Tahiti's best views of Moorea, especially from romantic over-water bungalows which directly face the sister island. The Beachcomber was born in the 1960s as a Travelodge, so don't expect large rooms in its original wings. On the other hand, you'll have plenty of space in 60 new deluxe hotel units built in 1999 on the south end of the property. Whatever their vintage, all units here have private patios or balconies with Moorea view through the coconut palms dotting the property. And as at all Parkroyal properties, they have tea/coffee-making facilities.

The resort doesn't have a natural beach (nor is the lagoon here as clear as those on the outer islands), but bulkheads separate the sea from white imported sand. Or you can frolic in two pools, one in a large new complex sitting lagoonside before the main building (a waterfall cascades into an adjacent Jacuzzi pool here), or in another, smaller pool with water cascading over its horizon (and apparently into the lagoon). Both pools have adjacent bars dispensing libation and snacks.

Dining/Diversions: Partially over the lagoon and abutting the resort's horizon pool, the romantic Le Lotus Restaurant provides afternoon tea and gourmet lunches and dinners (see "Dining," below). In the main building, and opening to the big new pool, the Te Tiare Restaurant serves breakfast, lunch, and dinner, while a coffee shop will keep you fed in between meal times. Tahitian string bands play nightly in Le Tiare Bar, and locals stage Tahitian dance shows several nights a week from an island in the new pool.

Amenities: Tennis courts, boutique, beauty salon, tour and car-rental desks, water-sports equipment rental, Laundromat and laundry service, nightly turndown, baby-sitting arranged, valet parking.

EXPENSIVE

Hotel Sofitel Maeva Beach Coralia. B.P. 6008, Papeete, Tahiti (Punaauia, 7.5km [4 miles] west of Papeete). ☎ **800/221-4542** or 42.80.42. Fax 43.84.70. www.accor-hotels.com. 230 units. A/C MINIBAR TV TEL. 20,000CFP–25,500CFP ($200–$255) double. AE, DC, MC, V. Take any Faaa or Maeva Beach truck.

Designed like a modern version of a terraced Mayan pyramid, this high-rise building sits beside Maeva Bay and a half-moon, dark-sand beach of the same name. Built in the late 1960s and last refurbished in the early 1990s, it now is the fourth-ranked hotel here, considerably behind the Tahiti Beachcomber Parkroyal, Le Meridien Tahiti, and the Outrigger Hotel Tahiti (see above). Unfortunately the murky lagoon off the beach isn't as good for swimming and snorkeling as for anchoring numerous yachts, whose masts slice the beach's view of Moorea. The smallish, European-style rooms open to balconies; those on the upper floors on the north (or "beach") side have commanding views of Moorea, while those on the garden side look south along Tahiti's west coast.

Dining/Diversions: The open-air Restaurant L'Amiral de Bougainville, under a large thatch roof on the ground level next to a rectangular pool, serves three meals a day, while the indoor Sakura Restaurant has appropriate blond-wood, paper-wall decor for its teppanyaki-style Japanese dishes cooked by your table. Nighttime entertainment features Tahitian dance shows.

Amenities: Boutique; car rental, tour, and activities desks; swimming pool; tennis courts and pro; golf driving range; water-sports activities and equipment; laundry; baby-sitting.

MODERATE

Hotel Royal Papeete. B.P. 919, Papeete, Tahiti (bd. Pomare opposite Moorea Ferry Docks). ☎ **42.01.29.** Fax 43.79.09. 70 units. A/C TEL. 10,700CFP–12,000CFP ($107–$120) double. AE, DC, MC, V.

This somewhat shop-worn but friendly hotel is one of my bases of operations, primarily because of its proximity to the Moorea Ferry Docks and the inexpensive, mobile snack bars that gather there at night (see "Dining," below). Presiding over a cozy lobby, the friendly veteran staff is adept at helping both business and vacation travelers, many of them Americans who find the rooms here more like home than tropical (even the plumbing fixtures were made in the United States). Some have refrigerators and shower-only bathrooms, but none has tea/coffee-making facilities. Avoid rooms 221 through 227 and 321 through 327, which are subject to the weekend beat of La Cave nightclub downstairs and the whine of Papeete's diesel-powered generating plant next door.

Le Gallieni Restaurant serves the most reasonably priced cooked breakfasts in town, plus French and Continental lunches and dinners. Its cozy bar is a popular watering hole for Moorea residents waiting for the ferry.

✪ **Le Royal Tahitien Hotel.** B.P. 5001, Pirae, Tahiti (Pirae, 4km [2.5 miles] east of downtown). ☎ **818/843-6068** or 42.81.13. Fax 41.05.35. E-mail: royalres@mail.pf. 40 units. A/C TEL. 17,000CFP ($170) double. AE, DC, MC, V. Take a Mahina truck or follow av. Prince Hinoi to Total and Mobil stations opposite each other; turn left, follow lane to Maire de Pirae, then into parking lot.

One of the best values in French Polynesia, this American-owned hotel is the only moderately priced place on the island with its own beach, a stretch of deep black sand from which its suburban neighbors fish and swim. And the Australian manager and English-speaking staff are Tahiti's best when it comes to friendly, personalized service. Sitting in an expansive lawn and lush garden traversed by a small stream, a new swimming pool sports a waterfall cascading over rocks, under which is built a daytime snack bar. Your fellow guests are likely to be expatriate businesspersons living on the other islands and travelers who have made their own arrangements (few tour groups stay here).

The spacious guest rooms are in contemporary 2-story wood and stone buildings which look like an American condominium complex. They have a Scandinavian ski lodge ambiance, with Danish-style furniture and stone-like brick walls. The tropics are in abundance outside, however, for each room looks onto the lawn and gardens. The rooms have tea/coffee-making facilities.

The tropics also pervade a beachside restaurant covered by a 1937-vintage thatch ceiling. Both the restaurant and adjacent bar are popular with local businesspeople, since they are one of the few beachside establishments on Tahiti. The menu features good French cuisine—another draw. A local band plays on Friday and Saturday evenings.

INEXPENSIVE

Cost-conscious travelers, be warned: There's a huge difference in quality between French Polynesia's moderate and inexpensive accommodations. The latter are very basic, roof-over-your-head kinds of places. In fact, no establishment in the entire territory is comparable in price or quality to the inexpensive motels so common in the United States, Canada, Australia, and New Zealand. Nor will you get the same value for money as in the other South Pacific countries.

Tourisme Tahiti has a list of "non-classified" pensions, private homes, and camping facilities (see "Visitor Information & Entry Requirements" in chapter 3). If you decide to go this route, a knowledge of French will be very helpful if not essential.

It's not the cleanest place in town, but backpackers can find a dorm bed at **Tahiti Budget Lodge,** B.P. 237, Papeete (☎ **42.66.82**), on rue du Frère Alain at the end of rue Edouard Ahnne downtown, for about 2,000CFP ($20) a night. MasterCard and Visa cards accepted.

Tahiti Airport Lodge. B.P. 2580, Faaa (at P.K. 5.5 opposite Faaa Airport). ☎ **82.23.68.** Fax 82.25.00. 10 units (4 with private bathroom). 6,600CFP–7,600CFP ($66–$76) double. 1,000CFP ($10) discount for more than 1 night. Rates include breakfast, taxes, airport transfers. No credit cards.

Perched on the side of a hill in the Cité de l'Air housing development above Faaa airport, Charlie and Margarite Bredin's clean and friendly bed-and-breakfast commands a spectacular view of Moorea from its lovely, open-air guest lounge. Unfortunately you won't get this view from any of their rather dark rooms, which range from ample motel-size with king beds and private bathrooms down to tiny share-bathroom units barely big enough to accommodate a double bed. All rooms have fans and electric mosquito deterrents, and all showers dispense hot water. The house is a steep, 5-minute climb from the round-island road, but Charlie will pick you up from the airport or the bus stop in his gaudy pink pick-up truck. He will also take you on beach picnics for an extra fee. Charlie speaks English as well as French, so communication shouldn't be a problem here.

6 Dining

The island has a plethora of excellent French, Italian, and Chinese restaurants. Those recommended below are but a few of many on Tahiti; don't hesitate to strike out on your own.

MA'A TAHITI   The Tahitians have adopted many Western and Chinese dishes, but *ma'a Tahiti* (Tahitian food) remains highly popular. Like their Polynesian counterparts elsewhere, Tahitians still cook meals in an earth oven, known here as a *himaa*. Pork, chicken, fish, shellfish, leafy green vegetables such as taro leaves, and root crops such as taro and yams are wrapped in leaves, placed on a bed of heated stones, covered with more leaves and earth, and left to steam for several hours. When all is done, the earth is removed, the food unwrapped, and everyone proceeds to eat with his or her fingers. Results of the himaa are quite tasty, since the steam spreads the aroma of one ingredient to the others, and liberal use of coconut cream adds a sweet richness.

Tahiti's big resort hotels usually have at least one *tama'ara'a* (Tahitian feast) a week; phone them to see when one will be offered. They usually run about 6,500CFP ($65) a head, but most include a Tahitian dance show after the meal (see "Island Nights," below). Another good sampling is at the Sunday buffet at the Captain Bligh Restaurant and Bar (see below).

Many individual Tahitian dishes are offered by restaurants whose cuisine may otherwise be French, Italian, or Chinese. One you will see on almost every menu is *poisson cru,* French for "raw fish"; it's a Tahitian-style salad of fresh tuna or mahimahi marinated in lime juice, cucumbers, onions, and tomatoes, all served in coconut cream. (Red chilies are added to spice up a variation known as "Chinese poisson cru.") Another is local freshwater shrimp—they're grown in ponds on Moorea—sautéed and served in a sweet sauce of curry and coconut cream.

✪ LES ROULOTTES   Prices in some hotel dining rooms here can be shocking, but you don't have to spend a fortune to eat well in French Polynesia. In fact, the best food bargains in Papeete literally roll out on the Moorea Ferry docks: *les roulottes.*

These portable meal wagons have assigned spaces in the waterfront parking lots. Some owners set up charcoal grills behind their trucks and small electric generators in front to provide plenty of light for the diners, who sit on stools along either side of the vehicles. A few operate during the daytime, but most beginning arriving about 6pm. The entire waterfront soon takes on a carnival atmosphere, especially on Friday and Saturday nights.

The traditional menu includes charbroiled steaks or chicken with French fries (known, respectively, as *steak frites* and *poulet frites),* familiar Cantonese dishes, poisson cru, and *salade russe* (Russian-style potato salad tinted red by beetroot juice) for 800CFP to 1,100CFP ($8 to $11) per plate. Glassed-in display cases along the sides of some trucks hold actual examples of what's offered at each (not exactly the most appetizing exhibits, but you can just point to what you want rather than fumbling in French). But you'll find just as many trucks specializing in crepes, pizzas, couscous, and waffles *(gaufres).* So many tourists eat here that most truck owners understand some English.

Even if you don't order an entire meal at les roulottes, stop for a crepe or waffle and enjoy the scene.

SNACK BARS & FOOD COURTS   Papeete has a McDonald's, at the corner of rue de Général-de-Gaulle and rue de Dr. Cassiau behind the Centre Vaima—a Big Mac, an order of fries, and a Coke costs about 650CFP ($6.50). But locals still prefer their plethora of snack bars, which they call simply "snacks." You can get a hamburger and usually poisson cru, but their most popular item is the *casse-croûte,* a sandwich made from a crusty French baguette and ham, tuna, *roti* (roast pork), *hachis* (hamburger), lettuce, tomatoes, and cucumbers—or even spaghetti. They usually cost about 150CFP ($1.50) or less.

Another option is the **Downtown Food Court,** in the arcade of Fare Tony, the big building on boulevard Pomare on the western side of the Centre Vaima (no phone). Stalls here dispense inexpensive pastries, burgers, salads, and Chinese and European dishes. Open Monday through Friday from 6am to 3pm, Saturday 6am to 1pm.

OTHER MONEY-SAVING TIPS   You can save at regular restaurants by taking advantage of *plats du jour* (daily specials), especially at lunch, and *prix-fixe* (fixed priced) menus, sometimes called "tourist menus" by Tahiti's restaurants. These three- or four-course offerings usually are made from fresh produce direct from the market and represent a significant savings over ordering from the menu.

"Restaurants Conventionné" get breaks on the government's high duty on imported alcoholic beverages, so wine and mixed drinks in these establishments cost significantly less than elsewhere. And order *vin ordinaire* (table wine) served in a carafe. The chef buys good-quality wine in bulk and passes the savings on to you.

You can also make your own snacks or perhaps a picnic lunch to enjoy at the beach. Every village has at least one Chinese-owned grocery store *(magasin chinoise)*. In downtown Papeete, the large **Champion** supermarket is on rue de Général-de-Gaulle in the block west of the église Evangélique. On the west coast, head for the huge **Continent** supermarket south of the Hotel Sofitel Maeva Beach Coralia. Fresh sticks of French bread cost about 40CFP (40¢) everywhere, and the markets carry cheeses, deli meats, vegetables, and other sandwich makings, many imported from France.

Locally brewed Hinano beers sell for about 150CFP ($1.50) in grocery stores, versus 350CFP ($3.50) or more at the hotel bars, and bottles of decent French wine cost a fraction of restaurant prices.

VERY EXPENSIVE

✪ **Auberge du Pacifique.** PK 11.2, Punaauia (3.7km [2.2 miles] south of Hotel Sofitel Maeva Beach Coralia on the round-island road; the Paea trucks go by it during the day; take a taxi at night). ☎ **43.98.30.** Reservations recommended, especially on weekends. Main courses 2,000CFP–3,500CFP ($20–$35). AE, MC, V. Wed–Mon 11:30am–2pm and 6:30–9:30pm. FRENCH/TAHITIAN.

This lagoonside restaurant has been Tahiti's finest since 1974. Owner Jean Galopin was named a Maître Cuisinier (Master Chef) de France in 1987, in large part because of his unique blending of French and Tahitian styles of cooking. His *fafa* (chicken and taro leaves steamed in coconut milk) is in marked contrast with what comes out of a local himaa on Sunday afternoon. Jean has shared many of his techniques in a popular cookbook, *La Cuisine de Tahiti et des Iles.* The roof over his main dining room opens to reveal the twinkling stars above, while a second, air-conditioned salon sports a mural by noted local artist François Revello. Guests are welcome to visit Tahiti's only air-conditioned wine cellar and choose from among excellent French vintages. A special tourist menu features poisson cru and main courses such as a light mahimahi soufflé.

Captain Bligh Restaurant and Bar. PK 11.4, Punaauia, at the Lagoonarium (3.9km [2.3 miles] south of Hotel Sofitel Maeva Beach Coralia on the round-island road; the Paea trucks go by it during the day; take a taxi at night). ☎ **43.62.90.** Reservations recommended on weekends. Main courses 1,600CFP–3,500CFP ($16–$35). AE, MC, V. Tues–Sun 11:30am–2pm; Tues–Sat 7–9pm; bar Tues–Sat 9am–9pm. FRENCH.

One of Tahiti's most unusual restaurant settings, this large thatch-roofed building extends over the lagoon (you can toss bread crumbs to the fish swimming just over the railing), or you can stroll along a pier to a tiny man-made island and dine al fresco under the stars. The pier goes on out to the Lagoonarium, an under-water viewing room (see "The Top Attractions," above). Specialties of the house are grilled steaks and lobster plus a few other seafood dishes, such as curried shrimp and mahimahi under a creamed pepper sauce. The Captain Bligh usually stages Tahitian dance shows Friday and Saturday at 8:30pm, and has a *ma'a* Tahiti buffet Sunday at noon.

Le Belvédère. Fare Rau Ape Valley (perched high on a ridge overlooking Papeete and Moorea; transportation provided by restaurant from your hotel). ☎ **42.73.44.** Reservations required. Fixed-price meal 4,800CFP ($48) per person, including wine and ride. AE, MC, V. Thurs–Tues 11:30am–2pm and 6–9:30pm. FRENCH.

Dinner at Le Belvédère is a highlight of Tahiti for many visitors, for it has a spectacular view of the city and Moorea from its perch 2,000 feet up in the cool hills above Papeete. The restaurant provides free round-trip transportation from your hotel up the narrow, one-lane, winding, switchback road that leads to it (I don't encourage anyone to attempt this drive in a rental car). Le Belvédère's truck makes several trips for lunch or dinner. The 5pm pickup reaches the restaurant in time for a sunset cocktail. The specialty of the house is fondue bourguignonne served with six sauces. Other choices are mahimahi grilled with butter, steak in green-pepper sauce or "any way you like it," shish kebab, and chicken with wine. Unfortunately the quality of the cuisine doesn't match the view, so treat the evening as a sightseeing excursion, not as a fine dining experience.

✪ **Le Lotus.** In Tahiti Beachcomber Parkroyal, Faaa (7km [4 miles] west of Papeete). ☎ **86.51.10,** ext. 5512. Lunch salad bar 2,200CFP ($22), fixed-price lunch 3,200CFP ($32); fixed-price dinner 5,450CFP–6,950CFP ($54.50–$69.50). AE, DC, MC, V. Daily noon–2:30pm; Tues–Sat 7–9:30pm. GOURMET FRENCH.

With two round, thatch-roof dining rooms extending over the lagoon and enjoying an uninterrupted view of Moorea, Le Lotus has the best setting of any restaurant in the South Pacific. The widely spaced tables are all at the water's edge (a spotlight between the two dining rooms shines into the lagoon, attracting fish in search of a handout). The gourmet French fare and attentive but unobtrusive service more than live up to this romantic scene.

You'll have a choice at lunchtime of grazing at an extensive salad bar or picking a three-course meal (both are excellent values). Rather than ordering a la carte at dinner, you can pick from two-, three-, or four-course set meals. The chef's lightly smoked fish preceded my appetizer of salmon rolls around pumpkin pancakes with a light and delicate cream sauce. That led to a main course of fresh local shrimp and sliced vegetables surrounding a mound of couscous. From an excellent range of desserts, I

Readers Recommend

Casablanca Cocktail Restaurant. *"We stumbled upon Casablanca Cocktail Restaurant when, in the dark, we couldn't find the Beachcomber. Casablanca is very attractive, though more St. Tropez than Papeete. There are white trellises around the tables, and yachts all around. A very tolerable pop band was playing, and the food, to our astonishment, was quite superb, far and away the best we had this trip. Not surprisingly, the place was full."*

—Jan Fletcher, London, England

Author's Note: *The moderately priced Casablanca Cocktail Restaurant sits beside the docks of Marina Taina, at P.K. 9 in Punaauia (☎ 43.91.35). Highlights are Mediterranean treatments of local seafood. Wednesday usually is couscous night. In addition to pop on other evenings, classical music is featured on Tuesday, jazz on Saturday. Casablanca is open daily for lunch and dinner. Reservations are recommended.*

chose farandole, a variation of profiteroles with praline mousse. You'll have many more options, all of them terrific. The view of Moorea and the adjacent swimming pool with swim-up bar also make this an outstanding place for a long lunch, silver-service afternoon tea, or leisurely sunset cocktail.

MODERATE

L'Api'zzeria. Bd. Pomare, between rue du Chef Teriirooterai and rue l'Arthémise. ☎ **42.98.30.** Reservations not accepted. Pizzas and pastas 400CFP–1,300CFP ($4–$13); meat courses 1,500CFP–2,350CFP ($15–$23.50). MC, V. Mon–Sat 11:30am–10pm. ITALIAN.

Locals tell me you can find Papeete's best pizza at this small building sitting among a grove of trees across from the harbor. Most guests prefer tables outside under the trees rather than inside, which resembles an Elizabethan waterfront tavern accented with nautical relics such as a ship's brass compass in one corner and a large pilot wheel used as a table divider. The food, on the other hand, is definitely Italian. Both the pizzas and tender steaks are cooked in a wood-fired oven. The menu also features spaghetti, fettuccine, lasagna, steak milanese, veal in white or marsala wine sauce, and grilled homemade Italian sausage.

✪ **Les 3 Brasseurs.** Bd. Pomare, between rue Prince Hinoi and rue Clappier, opposite Moorea ferry docks. ☎ **50.60.25.** Reservations not accepted. Sandwiches and salads 700CFP–1,500CFP ($7–$15); main courses 1,150CFP–2,400CFP ($11.50–$24). MC, V. Daily 9am–1am. FRENCH.

Part of a small French chain, this sidewalk microbrewery is Papeete's trendiest pub. Local professional types of all ages love to sip the home brew at tables under a canvas awning out on the sidewalk or just inside the open-front, dark-wood tavern. The tabloid menu is all in French, but wait staffers speak enough English to explain the offerings. Easily understandable are sandwiches, salads, half a roast chicken served hot or cold, and grilled steaks, mahimahi, and tuna plain or with optional French sauces. A bit more mysterious is *jarret de porc,* smoked ham hocks served with sautéed potatoes and sauerkraut. The best deal here is the *croque brasseurs,* a ham sandwich served casserole style under melted gruyere cheese and accompanied by a glass of beer and a green salad with excellent vinaigrette dressing, all for 900CFP ($9).

✪ **Lou Pescadou.** Rue Anne-Marie Javouhey at passage Cardella (take narrow passage Cardella, a 1-block street that looks like an alley, directly behind the Centre Vaima). ☎ **43.74.26.** Reservations not accepted. Pizzas and pastas 600CFP–1,350CFP ($6–$13.50); meat courses 1,550CFP–2,550CFP ($15.50–$25.50). MC, V. Mon–Sat 11:30am–2pm and 6:30–11pm. ITALIAN.

A lively crowd of young professionals generally packs this cozy place, and they're drawn in by the ambience: red-and-white-checked tablecloths, dripping candles on each table, Ruffino bottles hanging from every nook and cranny, a backlit stained-glass window, ceiling fans circulating the aroma of garlic and oregano, shuttered windows thrown open so passersby can look in, friendly waiters running hither and yon carrying pizzas. Good, fresh, and tasty Italian fare at reasonable prices also help make it one of Papeete's most popular eateries (come prepared to wait for a table). The individual-size pizzas are cooked in a wood-fire oven range, and the pasta dishes include lasagna and spaghetti and fettuccine under tomato, carbonara, and Roquefort sauces.

INEXPENSIVE

L'Oasis du Vaima. Rue Général-de-Gaulle at rue Jeanne d'Arc (corner of Centre Vaima, opposite Cathédrale de l'Immaculée Conception). ☎ **45.45.01.** Sandwiches, burgers, quiches, small pizzas 300CFP–1,000CFP ($3–$10); meals 1,150CFP–1,700CFP ($11.50–$17). No credit cards. Mon–Sat 5am–6pm. SNACK BAR.

A Very Indecent Dance

"The young girls when ever they can collect 8 or 10 together dance a very indecent dance which they call Timorodee singing most indecent songs and useing most indecent actions in the practice of which they are brought up from their earlyest Childhood."

So wrote Capt. James Cook after seeing his first Tahitian dance show in 1769.

Before the great explorer arrived, the Tahitians would stage dancing entertainments known as *heivas* for almost any reason, from blessing the harvest to celebrating a birth. After eating meals cooked in their earth ovens, they would get out the drums and nose flutes and dance the nights away. Some of the dances involved elaborate costumes, while others were quite lasciviously and explicitly danced in the nude or seminude, which only added to Tahiti's reputation as an island of love.

The puritanical Protestant missionaries managed to get laws enacted in the early 1820s to end all dancing. Of course, strict prohibition never works, and Tahitians—including a young Queen Pomare—would sneak into the hills to do what came naturally. Only after the French took over in 1842 was dancing permitted again, and then only with severe limitations on what the dancers could do and wear. A result of these various restrictions was that most of the traditional dances performed by the Tahitians prior to 1800 were totally forgotten within a period of 100 years.

You'd never guess that Tahitians ever stopped dancing, for after tourists started coming in 1961, they went back to the old ways—or so it would seem. Today traditional dancing is a huge part of their lives—and of every visitor's itinerary. No one goes away without vivid memories of the elaborate and colorful costumes, the thundering drums, and the swinging hips of a Tahitian *tamure* in which young men and women provocatively dance around each other.

The tamure is one of several dances performed during a typical dance show. Others are the *o'tea,* in which men and women in spectacular costumes dance certain themes, such as spear throwing, fighting, or love; the *aparima,* the hand dance, which emphasizes everyday themes, such as bathing and combing one's hair; the *hivinau,* in which men and women dance in circles and exclaim *"hiri haa haa"* when they meet each other; and the *pata'uta'u,* in which the dancers beat the ground or their thighs with their open hands. It's difficult to follow the themes without understanding Tahitian, but the color and rhythms (which have been influenced by faster, double-time beats from the Cook Islands) make the dances thoroughly enjoyable—and leave little doubt as to the temptations that inspired the mutiny on the *Bounty.*

You'll find me having breakfast of a small quiche or a tasty pastry with strong French coffee at this kiosklike building on the southwest corner of Centre Vaima. In addition to dishing out ice cream and milk shakes to passersby at a sidewalk counter, it serves up a variety of goodies, from crispy casse-croûtes to two delicious plats-du-jour selections each day, on a covered dining terrace and in an air-conditioned dining room upstairs. A special treat for Papeete: You can make a light meal from the salad bar.

Le Parc Bougainville. Bd. Pomare, in Bougainville Park (beside the post office). ☎ **53.25.50.** Salads, sandwiches, burgers 300CFP–600CFP ($3–$6); meals 800CFP–1,500CFP ($8–$15). MC, V. Daily 5am–11pm. FRENCH/CANTONESE/SNACK BAR.

Outdoor dining under awnings or at umbrella tables, an English-speaking staff, and reasonable prices make this open-air cafe a good spot for a meal or light refreshment. Service can be a bit indifferent, but the wide-ranging menu offers a bit of everything: Cooked breakfasts, burgers, hot dogs, crêpes, omelets, roast chicken or steaks with French fries, and Cantonese-style noodle soups, sweet-and-sour chicken, fried rice, chow mein, and stir fries. I always enjoy bite-size shrimp under a spicy, Thai-style curry sauce. The ice cream counter serving fresh fruit juices is a refueling break during your walking tour of Papeete.

Le Retrot. Bd. Pomare, front of Centre Vaima, on waterfront. ☎ **42.86.83.** Salads 400CFP–1,200CFP ($4–$12); sandwiches and burgers 400CFP–750CFP ($4–$7.50); pizza and pastas 700CFP–1,300CFP ($7–$13); main courses 1,500CFP–2,250CFP ($14–$22.50). Daily 6am–midnight. FRENCH/ITALIAN/SNACKS.

You'll find better food elsewhere, but this Parisian-style sidewalk cafe is a popular place to grab a quick bite, a drink, or an ice cream while watching the world pass along the Quay. A diverse selection of salads, sandwiches, pizzas, and pasta gets attention from the cafe crowd. There's also a tapas bar to one side and an excellent ice cream stand on the corner. Tahitian musicians entertain on Friday and Saturday nights and at midday Sunday.

Snack Epi d'Or. Rue du Maréchal-Foch near rue Edouard-Ahnne (behind the Municipal Market). ☎ **43.07.13.** Sandwiches 180CFP–360CFP ($1.80–$3.60); pizza slices 250CFP ($2.50). No credit cards. Mon–Sat 5am–5pm, Sun 4:30am–10am. SNACK BAR.

The casse-croûtes here are the freshest and crispiest in town, for Epi d'Or bakes its own French bread. You can buy baguettes by themselves or as sandwiches, or opt for salads, Italian-style panninis, or small quiches and pizzas. There's an upstairs dining room here, but most folks grab a casse-croûte and run.

7 Island Nights

A 19th-century European merchant once wrote of the Tahitians, "Their existence was in never-ending merrymaking." In many respects this is still true, for once the sun goes down Tahitians like to make merry as much today as they did in the 1830s, and Papeete has lots of good choices for visitors who want to join in the fun.

✪ **TAHITIAN DANCE SHOWS**   As mentioned in the listings under "Accommodations," above, traditional dance shows usually are staged along with Tahitian feasts at Tahiti's two big resort hotels. Call them to find out when the feasts and dance shows are scheduled.

Another good place to catch a show is the **Captain Bligh Restaurant and Bar** (☎ **43.62.90**), which usually has them on Friday and Saturday at 8:30pm.

GAMBLING   Three small gambling casinos beckon visitors to wager at baccarat, roulette, blackjack tables, and a Chinese wheel-of-fortune game known as *pau.* They are in **Hotel Royal Papeete** (☎ **42.09.29**), **Hotel Kon Tiki Pacific** (☎ **43.72.82**), and **Hotel Prince Hinoi** (☎ **42.33.66**), all within a block of each other on boulevard Pomare, opposite the Moorea Ferry Docks. All are open daily from 2pm to 2am. Although they technically are private clubs (local residents must pay dues), overseas visitors get in free (tell the doorman you're a tourist). Dress codes are smart casual: slacks for men, dresses for women.

PUB CRAWLING   Papeete has a nightclub or watering hole to fit anyone's taste, from upscale private *(privé)* discotheques to down-and-dirty bars and dance halls where Tahitians strum on guitars while sipping on large bottles of Hinano beer (and engage in a few fisticuffs after the stroke of midnight). If you look like a tourist, you'll

Impressions

They have several negative comments on the beachcombing life in Tahiti: Not much cultural life. No intellectual stimulus. No decent library. Restaurant food is disgraceful . . . But I noticed that Saturday after Saturday they turned up at Quinn's with the most dazzling beauties on the island. When I reminded them of this they said, "Well that does compensate for the poor library."

—James A. Michener, 1951

be allowed into the private clubs. Generally, everything gets to full throttle after 9pm (except on Sunday, when most are closed). None of the clubs is inexpensive. Expect to pay 1,000CFP ($10) or more cover charge, which will include your first drink. After that, beers cost at least 500CFP ($5), with most mixed drinks in the 1,000CFP–1,500CFP ($10–$15) range.

Before you head out, stroll over to the Municipal Market, where you will find Tahitian women weaving flower crowns, traditional headgear for Papeete's female merrymakers. Buy one if you want to look the part. The Tahitians will love you for it; everyone else will think you're a silly tourist.

The **Hotel Royal Papeete** (☎ 42.01.29), on boulevard Pomare, is home to two popular nightspots: The **Tamure Hut** is one of the city's few clubs designed for visitors as well as locals. The decor evokes the earlier period when Quinn's Bar dominated Papeete's nightlife scene. Live bands crank out various styles of dance music, from Tahitian to 1950s rock-and-roll. It's open Saturday from 9pm to 3am. **La Cave** has loud Tahitian music for dancing on Friday and Saturday from 9pm to 3am. It's dark inside and popular with mahus, so one cannot always be sure at first glance of every stranger's gender.

The narrow rue des Ecoles is the heart of Papeete's mahu district, where male transvestites hang out. The **Piano Bar** (☎ 42.88.24) is the most popular of the "sexy clubs" along this street, especially for its late-night strip shows featuring female impersonators. When you've seen enough, go next door to **Lido Nightclub** (☎ 42.95.84). Both are open daily from 3pm to 3am.

5 Moorea

Most visitors to French Polynesia soon grab the ferry to Moorea, and with very good reason. Here, only 20 kilometers (12 miles) from Tahiti, is an island so stunningly beautiful that Hollywood often uses "stock shots" of its jagged mountains, deep bays, and emerald lagoons to create a South Seas setting for movies that don't even take place in French Polynesia. Although an increasing number of Moorea residents take the ferry to work in Papeete each weekday morning, and ride your bumper in their haste to get there, this still is a surprisingly peaceful island where a hint of old Polynesia coexists with modern resort hotels and fine restaurants. Compared to the noisy city across the Sea of the Moon, Moorea is a rural paradise. And it's a clean and tidy paradise, thanks to a mayor who sends out crews to pick up road-side trash.

Geologists attribute Moorea's rugged beauty to a great volcano, the northern half of which either fell into the sea or was blown away in a cataclysmic explosion, leaving the heart-shaped island we see today. The remaining rim of the old crater has eroded into the jagged peaks and spires that give the island its haunting, dinosaurlike profile. Cathedral-like Mount Mouaroa—Moorea's trademark "Shark's Tooth" or "Bali Hai Mountain"—shows up on innumerable postcards and on the 100-CFP coin. Mount Tohiea has a hole in its thumblike top, made by the legendary hero Pai when the god of thieves attempted to steal Mount Rotui in the middle of the night. Legend says Pai threw his spear from Tahiti and pierced the top of Mount Tohiea. The noise woke up Moorea's roosters, who alerted the citizenry to put a stop to the dastardly plan.

Mount Rotui stands alone in the center of the ancient crater, its black cliffs and stovepipe buttresses dropping dramatically into Cook's Bay and Opunohu Bay, two dark blue fingers cutting deep into Moorea's interior. If not the world's most gorgeous bodies of water, these mountain-shrouded bays are certainly among the most photographed.

A paved road climbs to the base of the cliffs of the crater's wall to the Belvédère overlooking both bays, Mount Rotui, and the jagged old crater rim curving off to left and right. It is one of the South Pacific's most awesome views.

An offshore coral reef around Moorea encloses a calm blue lagoon, making the island ideal for swimming, boating, snorkeling, and diving. Unlike the black sands of Tahiti, white beaches stretch for miles on Moorea.

Impressions

From Tahiti, Moorea seems to have about forty separate summits: fat thumbs of basalt, spires tipped at impossible angles, brooding domes compelling to the eye. But the peaks which can never be forgotten are the jagged saw-edges that look like the spines of some forgotten dinosaur.

—James A. Michener, 1951

There are no towns on Moorea, which adds to its charm. Most of the island's 12,000 or so residents live on its fringing coastal plain, many of them in small settlements where lush valleys meet the lagoon. Vanilla was the island's big crop early in the 20th century, and clapboard "vanilla houses" built with the profits still stand, surrounded by wide verandas trimmed with Victorian fretwork. Tourism is the base of Moorea's economy today, but vegetables, pineapples, and copra are still grown and are shipped to market in Papeete.

1 Getting Around

The ferries from Papeete land at Vaiare, a small bay 5 kilometers (3 miles) south of the airport on Moorea's east coast (see "Getting There & Getting Around" in chapter 3).

Moorea has no *"le truck"* service like Tahiti's but buses meet most ferries at Vaiare to carry passengers to their final destinations. Tell the drivers where you're going; they will show you which vehicle is going to your hotel. The trip from Vaiare to the end of the line at the Club Med, on Moorea's northwest corner, takes about 1 hour. These trucks also return to Vaiare prior to each departure, starting at the Club Med. They stop at the hotels and can be flagged down along the road elsewhere. The one-way fare is 200CFP ($2) regardless of direction or length of the ride.

BY TAXI   Moorea's taxis are owned by individuals who don't run around looking for customers. The only **taxi stands** are at the airport (☎ **56.10.18**) and Club Med (☎ **56.33.10**). The airport stand is manned daily from 6am to 6pm. The hotel desks can call one for you, or phone **Pero Taxis** (☎ **56.14.93**) or **Albert Tours** (☎ **56.13.53**). Make advance reservations for service between 6pm and 6am.

Fares are 600CFP ($6) at flag fall plus 110CFP ($1.10) per kilometer. They double from 8pm to 6am. Expect to pay about 1,700CFP ($17) one-way from the ferry or airport to the Cook's Bay area, about 3,500CFP ($35) one-way from the airport or Cook's Bay to the Club Med area, less for stops along the way. Be sure that you understand what the fare will be before you get in.

BY RENTAL CAR & SCOOTER   Avis (☎ **800/331-1212** or 56.32.68) and **Europcar** (☎ **800/227-7368** or 56.34.00) have booths at the Vaiare ferry wharf, opposite the Club Med, and elsewhere on Moorea. Europcar is the most widespread and the less expensive of the two, with daily rates starting at 2,300CFP ($23) plus 46CFP (46¢) per kilometer. Unlimited kilometer rates begin at 5,600CFP ($56) for 4 hours, 7,900CFP ($79) for 24 hours. Europcar also rents little "Fun Cars" (noisy, open-air buglike contraptions with 2 seats and 3 wheels) starting at 2,200CFP ($22) for 1 hour to 4,800CFP ($48) for 8 hours. The local firm **Albert Rent-a-Car** (☎ **56.13.53**) has unlimited-mileage rates starting at 6,000CFP ($60) for 8 hours, 7,500CFP ($75) for 24 hours. Insurance is included in all rates, but gasoline is not.

Europcar also rents scooters and mopeds starting at 4,500CFP ($45) for 4 hours, 5,500CFP ($55) for 24 hours, including gasoline, full insurance, and unlimited kilometers. Albert Rent-a-Car's scooter prices are about 1,000CFP ($10) less.

Reservations for cars and scooters are a very good idea, especially on weekends, when many Tahiti residents come to Moorea for a day or two.

BY BICYCLE   The 60-kilometer (36-mile) road around Moorea is relatively flat. The two major hills are on the west side of Cook's Bay and just behind the Hotel Sofitel Ia Ora (the latter is worth the climb, since it has a stupendous view of Tahiti). **Albert Rent-a-Car** (☎ 56.13.53) rents bicycles. They cost about 1,500CFP ($15) per day, more if you keep them overnight.

Fast Facts: Moorea

Bookstores   **Kina Maharepa** (☎ 56.22.44) in the Maharepa shopping center has English novels and magazines. **Supersonics** (☎ 56.14.96) in Le Petit Village shopping center opposite the Club Med carries some English-language magazines and newspapers.

Camera/Film   The hotel boutiques, **Kina Maharepa** (☎ 56.22.44) in the Maharepa shopping center, and **Supersonics** (☎ 56.14.96) in Le Petit Village opposite the Club Med, all sell film.

Currency Exchange   **Banque Socredo, Banque de Tahiti,** and **Banque de Polynésie** have offices in or near the Maharepa shopping center near the Hotel Bali Hai. **Banque de Polynésie** also is in Le Petit Village opposite the Club Med, and Banque Socredo has an office at Vaiare. Banque Socredo and Banque de Polynésie have ATMs at their branches. Banks are open Monday through Friday from 8am to noon and 1:30 to 4:30pm.

Doctor   **Dr. Christian Joinville** (☎ 56.32.32) has an office in Centre Noha, opposite the post office in Maharepa. He has lived on Moorea many years, speaks English fluently, and has treated many visitors, including me.

Drugstores   **Pharmacie Tran** (☎ 56.10.51) is in Maharepa. The owner, Tran Thai Thanh, is a Vietnamese refugee who speaks English. Open Monday through Friday from 7:30am to noon and 2 to 5pm; Saturday from 7:30am to noon; and Sunday and holidays from 8 to 11am. In case of emergency, knock on the door.

E-mail   There was no cyber cafe on Moorea during my last visit. Ask if your hotel will let you use its computer.

Emergencies   The telephone number for the **Gendarmerie** in Cook's Bay is **56.13.44.** Local police have offices at Pao Pao (☎ 56.13.63) and at Haapiti (☎ 56.10.84) near the Club Med.

Hairdressers/Barbers   **Harmony Coiffure** (☎ 56.18.04) is in Centre Noha in Maharepa, opposite the post office.

Hospitals   The island's **infirmary,** which has an ambulance, is at Afareaitu on the southwest coast (☎ 56.24.24).

Information   The local **Comité du Tourisme,** B.P 531, Maharepa, Moorea (☎ 56.29.09; www.moorea-tourisme.com), has an office at Le Petit Village shopping center opposite the Club Med. Hours are Tuesday through Thursday 8am to 4pm, Friday 8am to 3pm, and Saturday 8am to noon (more or less; they can change). The committee has a booth at the airport, where you can pick up maps and brochures any time.

Post Office   Moorea's main post office is in the shopping center at Maharepa. It's open Monday through Thursday 7:30am to noon and 1:30 to 3pm, Friday

7:30am to 3pm, and Saturday 7:30 to 9:30am. You place long-distance and international telephone calls at the counter. A new post office in Papetoai village will be open by the time you get here.

Taxes Moorea's municipal government adds 100CFP to 150CFP ($1 to $1.50) per night to your hotel bill. Don't complain: the money keeps the island clean.

Water Tap water on Moorea is not safe to drink, so buy bottled water at any grocery store. Some hotels filter their water; ask if it's safe before drinking from the tap.

2 Exploring Moorea

The sights of Moorea may lack great historical significance, but the physical beauty of the island makes a tour—at least of the north shore, around Cook's and Opunohu Bays—a highlight of any visit here.

As on Tahiti, the round-island road is marked every kilometer with a PK post. Distances are measured between the intersection of the airport road with the main round-island coastal road and the village of Haapiti on Moorea's opposite side. In other words, the distances indicated on the PKs increase from the airport in each direction, reaching 30 kilometers near Haapiti. They then decrease as you head back to the airport.

THE CIRCLE ISLAND TOUR

Few things give me as much pleasure as riding around Moorea, its magnificent peaks hanging over my head one minute and plunging into its two great bays the next. I've done it by bicycle, scooter, car, and foot, and I always have trouble keeping my eyes on the road, so dramatically beautiful are the surroundings.

If you're short on time, at least see Cook's and Opunohu Bays on the north shore. There are few places on earth this gorgeous.

The hotel activities desks offer tours around Moorea and up to the Belvédère lookout in the interior. **Albert Tours** (☎ **56.13.53**), **Moorea Transports** (☎ **56.12.86**), and **Billy Transports** (☎ **56.12.64**) all have half-day round-island tours including the Belvédère for about 2,500CFP ($25) per person. Albert Tours may knock off 500CFP ($5) if you book direct instead of through an agent or hotel activities desk.

The tour buses all stop at one black pearl shop or another (guess who gets a commission when you buy the pearl of your dreams!). I suggest you look at more than one establishment before making your purchase, since quality, settings, and prices vary from store to store (see "Shopping," below).

MAHAREPA Begin at the airport on Moorea's northeast corner. The airstrip is on the island's only sizable area of flat land. At one time it was a *motu,* or small island, sitting on the reef by itself. Humans and nature have since filled the lagoon except for Lake Temae, which you can see from the air if you fly to Moorea. Head west from the round-island road/airport road junction.

Temae, 1 kilometer from the junction, supplied the dancers for the Pomare dynasty's court and is still known for the quality of its performers. Herman Melville spent some time here in 1842 and saw the famous, erotic *upaupa,* which he called the "lory-lory," performed clandestinely, out of sight of the missionaries.

The relatively dry north shore between the airport and the entrance to Cook's Bay is known as **Maharepa.** The road skirts the lagoon and passes the Hotel Bali Hai and the shopping center and other businesses that have grown up around it.

Seen for the first time by European Eyes, this coast is like nothing else on our workaday planet; a landscape, rather, of some fantastic dream.
—Charles Nordhoff and James Norman Hall, 1933

✪ **COOK'S BAY**   As the road curves to the left, you enter **Cook's Bay,** the finger-like body of water virtually surrounded on three sides by the jagged peaks lining the semicircular "wall" of Moorea. **Mount Tohiea** is the large thumb with a small hole in its top made by Pai's spear. **Mount Mouaroa,** the "Shark's Tooth," is the cathedral-like mountain buttressed on its right by a serrated ridge. It comes into view as you drive farther along the bay.

Huddled along the curving beach at the head of the bay, the village of **Pao Pao** is one of Moorea's economic centers. The **Marché Municipale** (Municipal Market) is open Monday to Saturday from 5am to 5pm and Sunday from 5 to 8am. Unlike Papeete's market, this one has slim pickings. The paved road that seems to run through the school next to the bridge cuts through the valley between Cook's Bay and Opunohu Bay. Its surface soon turns to dirt, but it intersects with the main road between Opunohu Bay and the Belvédère lookout.

A small **Catholic church** sits on the shore on the west side of Cook's Bay, at 10 kilometers from the airport. Inside is a large mural artist Peter Heyman painted in 1946 and an altar decorated with mother-of-pearl. From the church, the road climbs up the side of the hill, offering some fine views, and then descends back to the lagoon's edge. Here you'll pass the University of California's **Gump Biological Research Station** and then a road leading to the **Moorea Distillery and Fruit Juice Factory** (☎ **56.22.33**), which turns the island's produce into the Rotui juices sold throughout the territory.

OPUNOHU BAY   Towering over you is jagged **Mount Rotui,** the huge green-and-black rock separating Moorea's two great bays. Unlike Cook's Bay, Opunohu is virtually devoid of development, a testament to efforts by local residents to maintain the natural beauty of their island (they have ardently resisted efforts to build a luxury resort and golf course here). As soon as the road levels out, you can look through the trees to yachts anchored in **Robinson's Cove,** one of the world's most photographed yacht anchorages. Stop here and put your camera to work.

From the cove, you can walk along the shore to ✪ **Jardin Kellum** (☎ **56.18.52**), at P.K. 17.5 on the round-island road. This extraordinary bayside botanical garden was started by the late Hank and Gladys Kellum, an American couple who once owned all the land on the east side of Opunohu Bay and well up into the valley. Hank Kellum arrived here in 1925 aboard his parent's converted lumber schooner. He soon brought Gladys from Hawaii, and they lived for 65 years in their clapboard colonial-style house, which still looks out over the bay. Today their daughter, Meremere Kellum-Ottino, will give you a personalized tour of the house and garden and explain (in French or English) the 100-plus species of tropical plants growing here. She charges 300CFP ($3) per person and is open Tuesday to Saturday, preferably in the mornings. Just show up and ring the cow bell by the road.

From the garden, the road soon curves right along a beach backed by shade trees and the valley at the head of Opunohu Bay. The beach was turned into Matavai Bay on Tahiti for the 1983 production of *The Bounty,* starring Mel Gibson and Anthony Hopkins.

THE BELVÉDÈRE LOOKOUT   After the bridge by the beach, a paved road runs up Moorea's central valley through pasture land, across which Warren Beatty and

Moorea

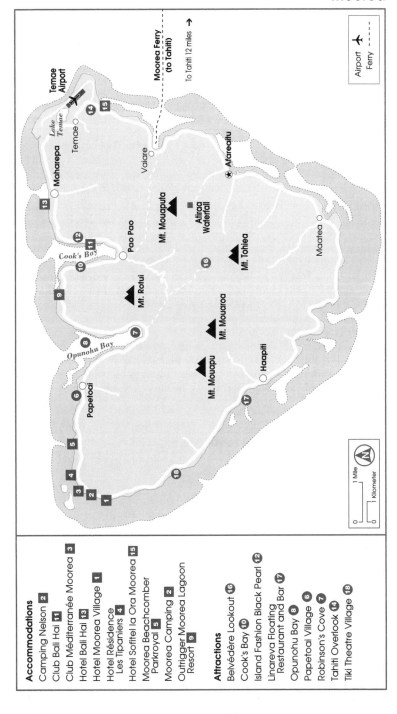

Accommodations
Camping Nelson 2
Club Bali Hai 11
Club Méditerranée Moorea 3
Hotel Bali Hai 13
Hotel Moorea Village 1
Hotel Résidence
  Les Tipaniers 4
Hotel Sofitel Ia Ora Moorea 15
Moorea Beachcomber
  Parkroyal 5
Moorea Camping 2
Outrigger Moorea Lagoon
  Resort 9

Attractions
Belvédère Lookout 16
Cook's Bay 10
Island Fashion Black Pearl 12
Linareva Floating
  Restaurant and Bar 17
Opunohu Bay 8
Papetoai Village 6
Robinson's Cove 7
Tahiti Overlook 14
Tiki Theatre Village 18

Airport ✈
Ferry ----

Moorea Ferry
(to Tahiti)
To Tahiti 12 miles →

Temae
Airport
Lake
Temae
Temae
Maharepa
Vaiare
Afareaitu
Mt. Mouaputa
Atiraa
Waterfall
Mt. Tohiea
Pao Pao
Cook's Bay
Maatea
Mt. Rotui
Mt. Mouaroa
Opunohu Bay
Haapiti
Mt. Mouapu
Papetoai

1 Mile
1 Kilometer

Annette Bening strolled in the movie "Love Affair" (the scenes with Katherine Hepburn were filmed in the white house on the hill to your right). The road then climbs steeply up the old crater wall to the restored ✪ **Titiroa Marae,** which was part of a concentration of marae and other structures. Higher up you'll pass an archery platform used for competition (archery was a sport reserved for high-ranking chiefs and was never used in warfare in Polynesia). A display in the main marae parking lot explains the history of this area. You can walk among the remains of the temples, now shaded by towering Tahitian chestnut trees which have grown up through the cobblestonelike courtyards.

The narrow road then ascends to the ✪ **Belvédère** lookout, whose awesome panorama of the valley and the bays on either side of Mount Rotui is unmatched in the South Pacific. You won't want to be without film here. There's a snack bar in the parking lot, so grab a cold drink or ice cream while you take in this remarkable vista.

HAAPITI   Back on the coastal road, the sizeable village of **Papetoai,** which has more than its share of "vanilla houses," was the retreat of the Pomare dynasty in the 1800s and the base from which Pomare I launched his successful drive to take over all of Tahiti and Moorea. It also was headquarters for the London Missionary Society's work throughout the South Pacific, and the road to the right past the new post office leads to an octagonal **Temple Protestant,** built on the site of a marae dedicated to Oro, son of the supreme Taaroa and the god of war. The original church was constructed in the 1820s, and although advertised as the oldest European building still in use in the South Pacific, the present structure dates to the late 1880s.

From Papetoai, the road runs through the Haapiti hotel district on the northwest corner and then heads south through the rural parts of Moorea. The 300-bungalow Club Med and the businesses it has generated, including Le Petit Village shopping center across the road, dominate the northwest corner of the island.

The Club Med area is your last chance to stop for refreshment before you travel the sparsely populated southern half of Moorea. There are several choices here (see "Dining," below).

Two kilometers beyond the Club, look for the **Tiki Theatre Village,** a cultural center consisting of thatch huts on the coastal side of the road. It's the only place to see what a Tahitian village looked like when Captain Cook arrived, so pull in. See "Cultural Experiences," below, for details.

When those first Europeans arrived, the lovely, mountain-backed village of **Haapiti** was home of the powerful Marama family, which was allied with the Pomares. It became a center of Catholic missionary work after the French took over the territory and is one of the few villages whose Catholic church is as large as its Protestant counterpart. Stop here and look up behind the village for a view of Mount Mouaroa from a completely different perspective.

THE SOUTH COAST   South of Haapiti, just as the road curves sharply around a headland, is a nice view of a small bay with the mountains towering overhead (there's no place to park on the headland, so stop and walk up for the view). In contrast to the more touristy north shore, the southeast and southwest coasts have retained an atmosphere of old Polynesia.

The village of **Afareaitu,** on the southwest coast, is the administrative center of Moorea, and the building that looks like a charming hotel across from the village church actually is the island's *mairie,* or town hall.

About half a kilometer (a quarter-mile) beyond the town hall, opposite an A-frame house on the shore, an unpaved road runs straight between several houses and then continues uphill to the **Atiraa Waterfall,** which plunges more than 32 meters (100 feet) down a cliff into a small pool. You can drive partway to the falls, then walk 20

Nothing on Tahiti is so majestic as what faces it across the bay, for there lies the island of Moorea. To describe it is impossible. It is a monument to the prodigal beauty of nature.

—James A. Michener, 1951

minutes up a steep, slippery, and muddy trail. Wear shoes or sandals with good traction if you make this trek, for in places the slippery trail is hacked into a steep hill; if you slip, it's a long way down to the rocks below. Villagers will be waiting at the beginning of the footpath to extract an access fee of 200CFP ($2) per person.

Beyond Afareaitu, the small bay of **Vaiare** is a beehive of activity when the ferries pull in from Papeete.

Just past the Hotel Sofitel Ia Ora, the road climbs a hill. At the top is the ✪ **Tahiti Overlook:** a magnificent view of the hotel, the green lagoon flecked with brown coral heads, the white line of the surf breaking on the reef, the deep blue of the Sea of the Moon, and all of Tahiti rising on the horizon. There's a parking area at the overlook, so stop and burn up some film.

SAFARI TOURS

Several companies offer trips in four-wheel drive vehicles through Moorea's mountainous interior. I think Alex and Gheslaine Haamatearii's ✪ **Inner Island Safari Tours** (☎ 56.20.09) is the best, since they drive up a steep, rough, one-lane track to "Magic Mountain." This 600-foot-tall grassy knob at the top of the old crater wall above Papetoai village commands a marvelous 360° view of the village, Opunohu Bay, the north coast, and the reefs offshore. On the way here, you will go through the valleys, up to the Belvédère lookout, then down to a vanilla plantation in Opunohu Valley. The guides explain the island's flora and fauna. The trip ends with a drive around Moorea's south coast and a hike up to Atiraa Waterfall for a refreshing swim (see "The South Coast," under "The Circle Island Tour," above). Alex and Gheslaine charge 4,000CFP ($40) per person for their half-day tours, 5,500CFP ($55) for a full day.

You won't go up Magic Mountain, but American Derek Grell of **Tefaarahi Safari Tours** (☎ 56.41.24) will take you to see ancient petroglyphs he has discovered on land he owns up in the highlands. Derek charges the same as Inner Island Safari Tours.

So do **Moorea Safari Tours** (☎ 56.35.80), **Moorea Transport** (☎ 56.12.86), and **Albert Tours** (☎ 56.13.53), all variations on this same theme. (Albert may give a discount if you book directly.)

Book at any hotel activities desk except the Club Med, which has its own tour.

ECO-TOURS

You can learn all about Moorea's botany, human and natural history, and ecology of its reef system by touring with marine biologist Dr. Frank Murphy of **Iaora Tahiti Ecotours** (☎ 56.46.75; fax 42.73.10; www.iaora.com; e-mail ecotours@mail.pf). A Canadian, Frank came to Moorea as director of the University of California's Gump Biological Research Station and decided to stay. His natural history tour includes stops at the station and Jardin Kellum before a climb up the Opunohu Valley to the Titiroa marae and the Belvédère. On the waterborne tour, you'll visit the reefs, where Frank will explain how coral forms and responds to environmental pressures. Either tour can be a full or half day. They cost 5,500CFP ($55) per person for half day, 11,000CFP ($110) for a full day. A minimum of six persons are required (or you must pay the fare for six persons).

CULTURAL EXPERIENCES

The best cultural experience in all of French Polynesia is at ✪ **Tiki Theatre Village,** 2 kilometers (1.2 miles) south of Club Med (☎ **56.18.97**). Built in the fashion of ancient Tahitian villages, this cultural center has old-style *fares* (houses) in which the staff demonstrates traditional tattooing; tapa making and painting; wood and stone carving; weaving; cooking; and making costumes, musical instruments, and flower crowns. There's even a "royal" house floating out on the lagoon, where they illustrate the modern art of growing black pearls.

They will even arrange a traditional beachside wedding. The bride is prepared with flowery *monoi* oil like a Tahitian princess, while the groom is tattooed (with a wash-off pen). Both wear traditional costumes.

The village is open Tuesday to Sunday from 11am to 3pm. Admission and a guided tour cost 2,000CFP ($20). A special historical show at 11am on Friday and Sunday costs 3,000CFP ($30) per person, or 4,000CFP ($40) if you need transportation from your hotel.

The village also stages a terrific evening Tahitian feast and dance show (see "Island Nights," below).

3 Dolphin Watching, Hiking, Water Sports & Other Outdoor Pursuits

Local residents have successfully fought various proposals to build a golf course on Moorea, so for the time being, stay on Tahiti if you must play. Moorea also has no public tennis courts, so pick a hotel which has them.

DOLPHIN & WHALE WATCHING   Among the many activities at the Moorea Beachcomber Parkroyal (see "Water Sports," below), by far the most popular are the ✪ **Dolphin Quest** (☎ **55.19.48**) encounters with the intelligent sea mammals. Children as young as 5 years old can wade in shallow water with the dolphins, which live in a fenced area (Dolphin Quest is dedicated to their care and conservation). Kids 12 and older can join adults in snorkeling with the mammals in deeper water. The wading excursions cost 9,500CFP ($95) for adults, 5,500CFP ($55) for children 5 to 12, while snorkeling with the dolphins costs 10,500CFP ($105) for kids and adults. Moorea Beachcomber Parkroyal guests get a 1,000CFP ($10) discount.

Equally popular are the Thursday and Sunday ✪ **Dolphin & Whale Watching** excursions led by American marine biologist Dr. Michael Poole (☎ **56.28.44**). An expert on sea mammals, Dr. Poole will take you out beyond the reef to meet some of the 150 acrobatic spinner dolphins he has identified as regular Moorea residents. In calm conditions you can don snorkeling gear and swim with them. You'll also be on the lookout for pilot whales who swim past year-round and giant humpback whales which frequent these waters from July to October. The excursions cost about 6,000CFP ($60) per person, including pick-ups at most hotel docks.

FISHING   Chris Lilley, an American who has won several sports fishing contests, takes guests onto the open ocean in search of big game on his *Tea Nui* (☎ **55.19.19** ext. 1903 or 56.15.08 at home). You can go out for half a day for about 14,000CFP ($140) per person, or charter the boat for a whole day for about 55,000CFP ($550). In keeping with South Pacific custom, you can keep the little fish you catch; he sells the big ones. Chris is based at the Moorea Beachcomber Parkroyal.

HIKING   You won't need a guide to hike from the coast road up the Opunohu Valley to the Belvédère. Up and down will take most of a day. It's a level but hot walk along the valley floor and steep approaching the lookout. Bring lots of water.

Based at Hotel-Résidence Les Tipaniers, **Tahiti Evasion** (☎ **56.48.77**) leads walks up the Opunohu Valley to the Belvédère and from Afareaitu to the Atiraa Waterfall and up Mount Tohiea. Either hike takes a full day and costs 5,000CFP ($50) per person. **Tropic Escape** (☎ and fax **56.42.49**) has guided hikes ranging from a 2-hour stroll to a waterfall to an 8-hour climb to the summit of Mount Rotui. Prices range from 3,000CFP to 5,000CFP ($30 to $50) per person. The activities center at the **Moorea Beachcomber Parkroyal** (☎ **55.19.19**) also has guided half- and full-day hikes at 3,200CFP and 4,200CFP ($32 and $42) per person, respectively.

HORSEBACK RIDING   Landlubbers can go horseback riding along the beach and into the interior with **Tiahura Ranch** (☎ **56.28.55**), west of the Club Med in Haapiti, or with **Pegasus Ranch** (☎ **56.34.11**) in Maharepa. Rates are about 3,500CFP ($35) for a 1-hour ride.

LAGOON EXCURSIONS   Based opposite the Hotel Bali Hai in Maharepa, Hiro Kelley's **Moorea Tours** (☎ **56.13.59**) has snorkeling, picnic trips to a small island, and glass-bottom boat excursions. His "motu picnic" features a leisurely ride along the north shore, past both bays, in a thatched-roof vessel equipped with two outboard motors. Guides quip humorous one-liners throughout the trip. You'll walk from the boat to the motu—a small island near Club Med—so wear shoes you don't mind getting wet. After an opportunity for guests to snorkel, the staff demonstrates coconut husking (you'll be invited to husk your own and drink its fresh milk) and prepares a sumptuous lunch of freshly grilled fish and chicken with potato salad, bread, cheese, pineapple, and libation. On other days, the staff feeds sharks while you snorkel in the lagoon (it's safe). Hiro's trips range in price from 2,500CFP ($25) for a glass-bottom boat ride to 4,800CFP ($48) for either the motu picnic (including the libation) or the shark-feeding expedition. Hiro is the son of the late Hugh Kelley, a cofounder of the Bali Hai Hotels. Call for his schedule and prices.

A variation on the motu picnic theme is a **Coconut Cookout** with Maco Roometua, a gregarious, English-speaking Tahitian based at the Hotel Sofitel Ia Ora (☎ **56.12.90** or 56.36.05 at home). Maco takes you out to a small island off Moorea's southeast coast in the *A'a Katiki Nui,* a traditional Tahitian sailing outrigger. You can snorkel (bring your own gear) and watch Maco and the staff feed the sharks. You can take a less exciting snorkel while fish and chicken grill for a picnic lunch on the beach. He usually voyages on Tuesday and Friday from 9am to 3:30pm and charges 7,500CFP ($75) a head, including lunch, soft drinks, beer, and wine. (Note: Unlike Moorea Tours, Maco combines the picnic and shark-feeding trips into one; hence, the higher price.)

SCUBA DIVING   Although Moorea's lagoon is not in the same league as those at Rangiroa and Bora Bora, its outer reef has some decent sites for viewing coral and sea life. The island's oldest diving operator is Philippe Molle's **Moorea Underwater Scuba-diving Tahiti (M.U.S.T.)** (☎ **56.17.32**), whose base is in Cook's Bay. Philippe and his instructors take divers out to the reef. On the northwest coast, the Beach-comber Parkroyal is home to **Bathy's Club Moorea** (☎ **55.19.19**, ext. 1139), while **Scubapiti Moorea** (☎ **56.30.38**) resides at Résidence Les Tipaniers. All charge about 5,500CFP ($55) for one dive, including equipment (gauges are metric). Beginner's lessons cost about 6,500CFP ($65). Bathy's Club also will take you diving with dolphins for 13,000CFP ($130).

WATER SPORTS   Most hotels have active water sports programs for their guests, such as glass-bottom boat cruises and snorkeling in, or sailing on, Moorea's beautiful lagoon. Of the resort hotels, the Sofitel Ia Ora and the Club Med have the best lagoons for water sports.

By far the most extensive array of sporting activities is at the **Moorea Beachcomber Parkroyal** (☎ **55.19.19**), whose facilities can be used by both guests and visitors willing to pay. In addition to Bathy's Club Moorea scuba diving (see above), these include parasailing (magnificent views of the bays, mountains, and reefs from up there hanging from a parachute); waterskiing; sailboarding; scooting about the lagoon and Opunohu Bay on jet skis; viewing coral and fish from Aquascope boats; walking on the lagoon bottom while wearing diving helmets; sailing on a 38-foot catamaran; viewing coral from a glass-bottom boat; line fishing; and speedboat rentals. Nonguests can also pay to use the pool, snorkeling gear, and tennis courts, and to be taken over to a small islet. Call the hotel for prices, schedules, and reservations, which are required.

4 Shopping

THE SHOPPING SCENE

Of Moorea's many boutiques and other shops, I mention those that have been in business for many years and which I have found to give good value for your money.

Every village has at least one Chinese grocery store. Chez Toa supermarket at Vaiare is by far the island's largest. The staff speaks English at Chez Are, a modern establishment on Cook's Bay in Pao Pao.

A one-stop place to shop is in front of the Club Med, where numerous stores sell pareus, T-shirts, souvenirs, and some Marquesan wood carvings. The neocolonial buildings of **Le Petit Village** shopping center anchor this area. A **Sibani Perles** outlet occupies about a third of the center (see below), while **Supersonics** (☎ **56.29.73**) carries film, watch and camera batteries, stamps, magazines, and other items; **Tahiti Parfum** (☎ **56.17.12**) sells French perfumes; and **Arts Polynésiens** purveys reproductions of Tahiti's Gauguin Museum (see separate listing below). There's also a branch of Chez Toa supermarket here.

BLACK PEARLS

Equipped with the chain's bamboo-trimmed display cases, the local branch of the upmarket **Sibani Perles** (☎ **56.14.62**) is in Le Petit Village shopping center opposite the Club Med. Near the center, **Herman Perles** (☎ **56.42.79**) is noted for the crystal and gold settings surrounding its black pearls. It also carries a collection of Marquesan wood carvings and a few duty-free perfumes.

✪ **Island Fashion Black Pearls.** Cook's Bay, 200 yards north of Cook's Bay Resort Hotel. ☎ **56.11.06.**

Ron Hall sailed from Hawaii to Tahiti with the actor Peter Fonda in 1974; Peter went home, Ron didn't. Now Ron runs this air-conditioned Moorea retail outlet, which he has decorated with old photos of Tahiti, including one of the infamous Quinn's Bar, and an original Leeteg painting of a Tahitian vahine (Ron's wife Josée was herself a championship Tahitian dancer when they met in the 1970s). In 15 minutes of "pearl school," Ron will show you the basics of picking a pearl. He also will have your selection set in a mounting of your choice, and his prices are fair. In addition to stylish pearls, Island Fashion has one of Moorea's best selections of bathing suits, aloha shirts, and T-shirts. Open Monday through Saturday from 9am to 6pm.

Pai Moana Pearls. Haapiti, opposite Club Med. ☎ **56.25.25.**

This is the Moorea outlet for the Pai Moana pearl farm owned by Canadian Peter Ringland and American Rick Steger, who also have a small shop in Papeete (see

"Shopping" in chapter 4). The sales personnel always speak English (some are expatriate Americans). Open daily from 9am to 7pm.

Teva's Moorea Perles Centre. Cook's Bay, in Aquarium de Moorea. ☎ **56.24.00.**

This shop carries some large black pearls in highly unusual settings, such as lizard-foot pendants, fashioned by the noted designer Teva Yrondi. It's also sells artistic pottery fashioned in a workshop out back. Open daily from 9:30am to noon and 2:30 to 5:30pm.

ART & ANTIQUES

Arts Polynésiens. Haapiti, in Le Petit Village opposite Club Med. ☎ **56.39.42.**

This shop represents both the Gauguin Museum on Tahiti and Moorea's Galerie A.P.I. (see below). From the museum come reproductions of Gauguin's paintings as well as such souvenir items as coasters and T-shirts bearing his works. Galerie A.P.I. supplies paintings, tapa cloth, and Marquesan wood carvings. Also for sale are paintings and ceramics by local artists. Open Monday through Saturday from 9am to noon and 2 to 6pm, Sunday from 9am to noon.

Galerie A.P.I. Haapiti, east side of Club Med. ☎ **56.13.57.**

Take the gravel road on the eastern edge of the Club Med to find Patrice Bredel's beachside art gallery and home. A long-time Moorea resident, he has exclusive rights to sell works by noted local artists François Ravello and Michelle Dallet. One museumlike room displays such artifacts as 18th-century stone carvings from the Marquesas, ancient hair decorations made of human bone, and intricately carved canoe paddles from the Austral Islands. Open Monday through Saturday from 9:30am to noon and 2:30 to 5:30pm.

Galerie de la Baie de Cook. Cook's Bay, near Club Bali Hai. ☎ **56.12.67.**

Chantel Cowan's art gallery features paintings of Polynesia by the likes of William Alister MacDonald, Peter Heyman, and Leeteg (William Edgar), plus intricate wood carvings and sennit weavings by some of the most skilled artisans still at work in French Polynesia. She also displays *Vaamotu,* a sailing canoe built in the traditional Polynesian fashion by her husband Francis Cowan, a noted student of the old ways. It's not for sale. Open daily from 9am to 6pm.

Galerie van der Heyde. Cook's Bay, 150 yards north of Cook's Bay Resort Hotel. ☎ **56.14.22.**

Dutch artist Aad van der Heyde has lived and worked on Moorea since 1964. One of his bold, impressionist paintings of a Tahitian woman was selected for French Polynesia's 100-CFP postage stamp in 1975. Aad will sell you an autographed lithograph of the painting for 8,900CFP ($89). Some of his paintings are displayed in the gallery's garden. He also has a small collection of pearls, wood carvings, tapa cloth, shell and coral jewelry, and primitive art from Papua New Guinea. Open Monday through Saturday from 8am to 5pm.

Sculpture Par Woody. Papetoai, between village and Moorea Beachcomber Parkroyal. ☎ **56.55.46.**

American Woody Howard was studying horticulture at the University of Hawaii when he came to Moorea in 1982 to work on the Hotel Bali Hai's plantation. Like so many others, he stayed. Today you can visit his lagoonside workshop and watch him carve award-winning wooden images of dolphins, fish, women, and other Polynesian wildlife. Open Monday through Saturday 8am to 5pm, if he's not off looking for his next exquisite piece of native wood.

CLOTHING & SOUVENIRS
Heimata Boutique. Pao Pao, Cook's Bay, near Municipal Market. ☎ **56.18.51.**

Seamstress Micheline Tetuanui's little shop has very reasonable prices on pareus and souvenir items, such as soap made with tiare-scented monoi oil and Hinano beer glasses. It also has a small selection of tablecloths and napkins printed with tapa designs. You may find Micheline sewing away on tropical fashions, many of them in traditional Tahitian fabrics and styles. Open Monday through Saturday from 8am to noon and 2 to 5pm.

✪ **La Maison Blanche (The White House).** Mararepa, near Hotel Bali Hai. ☎ **56.13.26.**

This whitewashed vanilla planter's house with railing enclosing a magnificent front veranda is now home to this shop carrying an array of pareus, tropical dresses, aloha shirts, bathing suits, T-shirts, shell jewelry, and other handcrafts. Prices reflect the high quality of the merchandise. Open daily from 8:30am to 5pm.

5 Accommodations

Most of Moorea's hotels and restaurants are huddled in or near Cook's Bay or in the Haapiti district on the northwest corner of the island. With the exceptions of the Hotel Bali Hai and the Sofitel Ia Ora Coralia, those in or near Cook's Bay do not have the best beaches on the island, but their views of the mountains are unsurpassed in the South Pacific. Those on the northwest corner, on the other hand, have generally fine beaches, lagoons like giant swimming pools, and unobstructed views of the sunset, but not of Moorea's mountains. The two areas are relatively far apart, so you may spend most of your time near your hotel unless you rent transportation or otherwise make a point to see the sights. An alternative is to split your stay between the two areas.

All Moorea hotels provide water sports activities, Tahitian string bands nightly and dance shows at least 1 night a week, activities desks, and laundry and baby-sitting services. Unless otherwise noted below, the resorts have swimming pools. All rooms and bungalows are equipped with ceiling fans.

Under construction between the two bays, the expensive **Outrigger Moorea Lagoon Resort,** B.P. 416, Papeete (☎ **800/688-7444** or 86.48.48; fax 86.48.40; www.outrigger.com; e-mail reservation@outrigger.com), was expected to be in operation in 2000, featuring 106 bungalows, half of them over-water.

IN COOK'S BAY
The time-share **Club Bali Hai,** B.P. 26, Maharepa, Moorea (☎ **800/282-1401** or 56.13.68; fax 56.19.22; www.balihai.hotel.com; e-mail club.balihai@mail.pf), is worth mentioning because of its incredible view of Moorea's ragged mountains across the water, a scene that epitomizes the South Pacific. Forget the rooms, which need renovation, but do come here to have a drink at the thatch-roofed bayside bar and take in the view. Tuesday happy hours at the thatch-roof bayside bar and the Friday night dance shows are popular with local residents (see "Island Nights," below).

✪ **Hotel Bali Hai Moorea.** B.P. 26, Maharepa, Moorea (between Cook's Bay and the airport). ☎ **800/282-1402** in California, 800/282-1401 in the rest of the U.S., or 56.13.59. Fax 56.19.22. www.balihaihotels.com. E-mail: balihaires@mail.pf. 63 units. A/C. 12,000 CFP–27,200 CFP ($120–$272) double. Rates are for bookings directly to hotel. AE, DC, MC, V.

Opened in 1961 by Moorea's legendary Bali Hai Boys (see box below), this aging resort lacks the modern amenities you'll find elsewhere, but it is well maintained and has old South Seas charm and friendliness that many of the newer properties lack. It's

The Bali Hai Boys

Californians Jay Carlisle, Don "Muk" McCallum, and the late Hugh Kelley gave up their budding business careers as stockbroker, lawyer, and sporting goods salesman, respectively, and in 1960 bought an old vanilla plantation on Moorea. Much to their chagrin, the vanilla boom had gone bust in the 1920s. Simply put, there was no money to be made in vanilla.

So instead of planting, they refurbished an old beachfront hotel that stood on their property. Taking a page from James A. Michener's *Tales of the South Pacific,* they renamed it the Bali Hai and opened for business in 1961. With construction of Tahiti-Faaa International Airport across the Sea of the Moon that same year, their timing couldn't have been better. With Jay managing the money, Hugh doing the building, and Muk overseeing the entertainment, they quickly had a success on their hands. Travel writers soon dubbed them the "Bali Hai Boys."

Supplies and fresh produce weren't easy to come by in those days, so they put the old vanilla plantation to work producing chickens, eggs, and milk. It was the first successful poultry and dairy operation on the island.

In addition, we can thank the Bali Hai Boys for over-water bungalows—cabins sitting on pilings over the lagoon with glass panels in their floors so that we can watch the fish swim below us. Once a novelty, their romantic invention has spread throughout French Polynesia and even to Samoa.

also considerably less expensive than most of the others, especially when booked as part of an air-hotel package, which makes it even more attractive to cost-conscious travelers.

The Bali Hai Boys created the over-water bungalow here, and piers connect 9 of them to the beach, where a large shingle-roof building housing a beachside restaurant and sunken bar stands. The other bungalows sit in a coconut grove, although a few have porches extending over a decent beach and the water. There are also beachfront and garden bungalows, some of them standing around a swimming pool with a waterfall on one end and a swim-up bar on the other. The poolside units are all air-conditioned to keep out noise from the nearby round-island road. A few long bungalows are divided into four hotel rooms, but these least-expensive units usually are reserved for package tours. Over-water and beachfront units have thatch roofs, while other units are getting longer-life shingles. All sport large, tiled shower-only baths, tile floors, small fridges, and double and single beds. Wednesday and Saturday nights see barbecues and Tahitian dance shows which are among the best here (see "Island Nights," below). Other entertainment features the likes of crab races, a long-standing Bali Hai tradition. There's also a satellite-fed TV in the bar area, where guests can watch CNN news, English movies, and live sporting events.

Dining: The dining room serves moderately priced French and American fare, including a breakfast buffet that costs about 500CFP ($5) less than at more expensive resorts. Lunch is served around the pool.

Amenities: Moorea Tours, based across the road, offers bicycle and snorkeling equipment rentals and snorkeling, picnics, and sunset cruises (see "Lagoon Excursions," above). There's a tennis court and canoes for guests to use for free, plus a swimming pool with swim-up bar. Although friendly, the staff provides few services (you'll have to pay cash in advance to have your laundry done by an independent contractor).

Hotel Sofitel la Ora Coralia. B.P. 28, Maharepa, Moorea (Temae, on the northeast coast, facing Tahiti). ☎ **800/763-4835**, 56.12.90, or 41.04.04 in Papeete. Fax 41.05.05. www. accor-hotels.com. 110 units. A/C MINIBAR TV TEL. 22,500CFP–42,500CFP ($225–$420) bungalow. AE, DC, MC, V.

On the island's northeast coast south of the airport, this resort was built in the 1960s beside one of the South Pacific's best lagoons and a long, lovely beach over which grapeleaf and casuarina trees hang. It's also the only hotel with a view of Tahiti, whose green, cloud-topped mountains seem to climb out of the horizon beyond the reef. Most of the Ia Ora's thatch-roofed bungalows stand in a long coconut grove, but 20 are over the lagoon. The over-waters and 10 deluxe beachfront models—all built in the mid-1990s—are air-conditioned and have TVs, while the rest have ceiling fans and no tubes. Five of the 10 deluxe bungalows, most of the older beachfront units, and those perched on a ridge above the trees have unobstructed views of Tahiti. Most of the over-water units, however, face the lagoon rather than Tahiti. Unfortunately, many guests have complained about the smaller beachfront bungalows dating from the 1960s, since these are not fully screened and are thus liable to be invaded by mosquitoes and other critters. If you can't afford one of the new over-water or beachfront units, you'll be better off sacrificing the view and taking one of the larger garden bungalows here.

Dining/Diversions: French dinners are served in La Perouse Restaurant, a large thatch building overlooking lily ponds. Providing breakfast, lunch, and libation, the beachside Molokai Restaurant and Bar opens to a swimming pool with water cascading over two sides, seemingly into the lagoon. Tahitians strum guitars and sing most nights, and there's a dance show once a week, usually on Saturday night.

Amenities: Guests can book water sports at a poolside shack and tours and other excursions at an activities desk in the lobby. Most activities cost extra.

ON THE NORTHWEST COAST

Club Méditerranée Moorea. B.P. 575, Papeete, Tahiti (Haapiti, on the island's northwest corner). ☎ **800/528-3100** in the U.S., 56.15.00, or 42.96.99 in Papeete. Fax 42.16.83. 350 units. 12,700CFP–15,400CFP ($127–$154) per person, including all meals with wine. AE, DC, MC, V.

One of the oldest Club Meds, this huge playground is the center of activity on the northwest corner of Moorea (17 miles from the airport). The setting is exceptional, with an azure lagoon lying between the beach and a private motu on the reef offshore, which the club's guests can use for sunbathing in the buff (the skimpiest of bottoms are required on the main beach). The club is such a world unto itself that it even marches to its own clock, set an hour earlier than Moorea's in order to give the guests extra time in the sun. You pay one price for everything, including meals with wine and a wide range of mile-a-minute activities. The only extras are drinks at the bar, scuba diving, tours of the island, and a snorkeling extravaganza to Marlon Brando's Tetiaroa atoll.

The club's 350 bungalows are a cross between traditional and colonial styles: shingled roofs, tongue-in-groove plank walls, polished hardwood floors, and brass-trimmed ceiling fans and mirrors. Each has two oversize twin beds; if you don't have a roommate, one of the same sex may be assigned. Honeymooners may prefer the quarters at the Club Med on Bora Bora, which are newer and provide more privacy (see chapter 6).

Although good, the food is better known for its substantial quantity than quality. Breakfasts and lunches are all-you-can-eat buffets and dinners are sit-down affairs. The staff performs in nightclub style several nights a week.

Hotel Moorea Village. P.O. Box 1008, Papetoai, Moorea (in Haapiti, 1km [0.6 mile] west of the Club Med). ☎ **56.10.02.** Fax 56.22.11. E-mail: mooreavillage@mail.pf. 75 bungalow.

9,000CFP–11,500 ($90–$115) double without kitchen; 16,000CFP–20,000CFP ($160–$200) double with kitchen. AE, MC, V.

One of Moorea's better values if you can do without any luxuries whatsoever, this rather basic resort attracts Americans and Europeans on low-end package tours. Its 75 bungalows are closely packed on a grassy lawn under coconut palms within walking distance of the Club Med and nearby restaurants and shops. All but 10 of the simply furnished bungalows consist of one room and a bath under a peaked thatch roof that extends out over a covered, semi-circular front porch equipped with plastic table and chairs. These units have platform double beds plus a single bed serving as a settee, two chairs and a small drink table, refrigerators and hot pots (bring your own tea and coffee), and narrow baths with skinny shower stalls and thin towels. Ten other units are larger and have kitchens. Beachside bungalows are worth the extra cost. Avoid the garden units by the noisy round-island road.

The restaurant-bar is perched on a bank next to the beach, while one side opens to a swimming pool. Breakfast, lunch, and libations are served on a long porch hanging over the sand along the lagoon side of the restaurant. Evening meals indoors emphasize both French and Chinese cooking at moderate prices. The Tahitian feast here at midday Sunday is one of the most authentic in the islands (see "Dining," below).

Hotel-Résidence Les Tipaniers. B.P. 1002, Papetoai, Moorea (in Haapiti, east of the Club Med). ☎ **800/521-7242** or 56.12.67. Fax 56.29.25. 22 bungalows. 5,500CFP ($55) double, 10,500CFP–11,500CFP ($105–$115) bungalow without kitchenette, 12,600CFP–14,600CFP ($126–$146) double with kitchenette. AE, DC, MC, V.

This pleasant place sits in a coconut grove beside the same sandy beach as the Club Med. The widely spaced bungalows stand back in the trees, which gives the small complex an open, airy atmosphere. They also are far enough from the road to be quiet. Much improved "standard superior" bungalows are replacing the comfortable if simple older units facing the beach (some of the older units left in the garden are now known as "standards"). Well worth an extra 1,000CFP ($10) a night, these larger new models have an L-shaped settee facing sliding glass doors to covered porches. Behind the settees are raised sleeping areas with queen-size beds, and behind that, fully tiled bathrooms have sizeable showers and vanity space.

To the rear of the property, other bungalows are equipped with kitchens and can sleep up to five persons. Also back there is a building housing four small hotel-style rooms equipped with twin beds (you can push them together), reading lights, and ample tiled bathrooms with showers. Okay for couples, these rooms are the least expensive yet still comfortable place to stay on Moorea. All units here have ceiling fans.

Dining: A pleasant restaurant with a deck over the beach is open from 7am to 7pm daily for breakfast, lunch, and snacks. The hotel is also home to the excellent Restaurant Les Tipaniers, which is known for its Italian fare (see "Dining," below).

Amenities: There is no swimming pool, but guests can make free use of snorkeling gear, canoes, and bicycles, or pay for kayaking, waterskiing, motu trips, and diving with Scubapiti, which is based here.

✪ **Moorea Beachcomber Parkroyal.** B.P. 1019, Papetoai, Moorea (between Papetoai and Haapiti). ☎ **800/421-0536** or 55.19.19. Fax 55.19.55. www.tahiti-resorts.com. E-mail: moorea@parkroyal.pf. 52 units, 102 bungalows. A/C MINIBAR TV TEL. 29,200CFP ($292) double; 32,300CFP–44,300CFP ($323–$443) bungalow. AE, DC, MC, V.

Although relatively isolated about 2½ kilometers (1½ miles) east of the Club Med area, Moorea's top-rated and best-managed resort has plenty to keep its house guests busy. The beach and sometimes murky lagoon here aren't Moorea's best, but the resort has the widest range of water-sports activities on the island—all of them available to nonguests (see "Dolphin Watching, Hiking, Water Sports & Other Outdoor Pursuits," above).

Most of the Beachcomber's bungalows extend partially over the water from unpainted concrete supports anchored on manmade islands (the hotel has won environmental awards for restoring the reef around these islets). They are of European construction, but mat walls and rattan furnishings lend tropical ambiance. Wood frame doors open to porches, but only small windows in the rear of each unit give ventilation (plans were afoot to air condition the bungalows). The spacious, air-conditioned hotel rooms are in a curving 2-story building; they all have patios or balconies facing the beach. All units here have tea/coffee-making facilities and bathrooms with bidets and combination tub-showers (the latter is a rarity on Moorea). About half of your fellow guests will be Americans.

Dining/Diversions: In a tropical setting under a large thatch roof, an airy dining room opening to the pool offers lunches, light dinners, and snacks continuously from 11am to 9:30pm. A much larger restaurant provides extensive breakfast buffets and is used for special functions and evening entertainment. The Tahitian weekly dance show on the beach is one of Moorea's most colorful.

Amenities: A large, airy central building with a shingle roof built at several angles houses the hotel's reception, bar, boutiques, car rental desk, and indoor activities area. It opens to a large pool area surrounded by an ample sunning deck. Services include concierge, limited room service (staff will deliver breakfast to some over-water units by canoe), laundry, massage, and baby-sitting.

HOSTELS & CAMPING

Camping Nelson et Josiane. PK 27.1, Papetoai, Moorea (in Haapiti, near the Club Med). ☎ **56.15.18.** Fax same as phone. 9 units (7 small; 2 large), 20 bunks. 700CFP ($7) per camper; 1,000CFP–1,200CFP ($10–$12) dorm bed; 2,550CFP–3,000CFP ($25.50–$30) per person small bungalow; 5,000CFP ($50) single or double per large bungalow. Lower rates for stays of more than 1 night. 2-night minimum required for camping. No credit cards.

All guests share adequate toilets, cold-water showers, and communal kitchen facilities at this campground and hostel in a beachside coconut grove about 200 yards west of the Club Med. In addition to camping space on a shadeless lawn, very basic accommodations here include small bungalows for couples, a block of 10 tiny dorm rooms (two bunks each) that looks as though it might belong in a migrant labor camp, and two other thatch-roofed hostel bungalows down the road (and still on the beach). Each of the latter has a kitchen, modern bathroom, and porch.

Moorea Camping. PK 27.5, Papetoai, Moorea (in Haapiti, west of the Club Med). ☎ **56.14.47.** Fax 56.30.22. 20 tent sites, 20 beds, 8 units, 5 bungalows. 800CFP–1,000CFP ($8–$10) per camper; 1,000CFP–1,200CFP ($10–$12) dorm bed; 2,200CFP–3,200CFP ($22–$32) per person in rooms; 4,500CFP–5,500CFP ($45–$55) single or double per bungalow. Lower rates for stays of more than 1 night. No credit cards.

You pay slightly more to camp here, but this establishment in a coconut grove has much more shade and a better beach for swimming than at Camping Nelson et Josiane (see above). A beachside pavilion covers picnic tables and a communal kitchen. Two long plywood houses—actually little more than permanent tents—contain eight rooms with foam mattresses. One bungalow can accommodate up to four persons.

6 Dining

The restaurant scene changes quickly on Moorea, but the ones I recommend below have been in business several years and offer very good value. As on Tahiti, you can save by eating at snack bars for breakfast, lunch, or an early dinner.

Tahitian Feasts

The **Tiki Theatre Village,** at P.K. 31 in Haapiti (☎ **56.18.97**), provides the most authentic Tahitian feast on the island on Tuesday, Wednesday, Friday, and Saturday nights. You watch the *himaa* being opened about dusk, then choose your fare from the goodies laid out on several buffet tables in the beachside, thatch-roof dining room. The combined feast and show cost 6,500CFP ($65). See "Cultural Experiences," above, for information about the village, and "Island Nights," below, for details about its evening show.

Most hotels stage Tahitian feasts, followed by traditional dance shows, at least one evening a week. Call to find out their schedules.

One of my favorites is the Sunday feast at **Hotel Moorea Village** (☎ **56.10.02**) in Haapiti. You can watch the dirt being removed from atop the *himaa* shortly after noon, then sit down about 1pm at long tables in the beachside dining room. The succulent food is served in the traditional Tahitian way, family-style, without silverware. (That's right. You eat with your fingers.) Dancers from a nearby village put on a short show after the feast. It's a bargain at 3,900CFP ($39) per person, which includes wine. It's a popular event with locals, some of whom hang around after the show to drink at the bar. They reportedly can become rowdy later in the afternoon.

IN COOK'S BAY

In addition to those I recommend below, the Maharepa area near the Hotel Bali Hai has several restaurants where you pay from 1,200CFP to 2,400CFP ($12 to $24) for main courses. Expatriates from France operate most of them, so expect heavy traditional French sauces over fresh local fish or New Zealand steaks. They all provide free or discounted transportation, so call for reservations.

Of these, **Le Pêcheur** (☎ **56.36.12**) has a view of the lagoon across the road to accompany its seafood specialties, and it has entertainment on Saturday evenings. Local French residents flock to **Le Cocotier** (☎ **56.12.10**), which offers a variety of nightly specials. **La Case** (☎ **56.42.95**) proffers Swiss as well as French dishes. Actually in Cook's Bay, **Caprice des Isles** (☎ **56.44.24**) occupies a large thatch-roof building made of coconut logs.

✪ **Alfredo's.** Pao Pao, near Club Bali Hai. ☎ **56.17.71.** Reservations recommended. Pizzas 1,300CFP ($13); main courses 1,250CFP–2,400CFP ($12.50–$24). MC, V. Tues–Sun 11am–2:30pm, daily 5:30–9:30pm. ITALIAN/FRENCH.

Gregarious French restaurateur Christian Boucheron, who worked at hotels in northern Virginia for 19 years, will make you feel right at home in this old building, formerly a Chinese grocery store. In fact, Christian's white patio tables with green-and-red tablecloths are usually packed, mostly with Americans and other English-speaking visitors who come here for some of the finest Italian fare in the islands (and French residents tired of their own heavily laden traditional sauces).

The wonderfully sweet tomato sauce used on pizzas and pastas is the result of adding local honey to the recipe. Start with the carpaccio, made with fresh, sashimi-quality yellowfin tuna marinated in olive oil, lime juice, and crushed garlic. In season, the big tank in the middle of the dining room holds live local lobsters.

Call for free dinner transportation from as far away as the Hotel Bali Hai (they'll pay half the taxi fare from the Sofitel Ia Ora or the Moorea Beachcomber Parkroyal). Hotel Bali Hai guests can charge meals to their rooms here.

Chez Jean-Pierre. Pao Pao, near Municipal Market. Reservations accepted. Main courses 950CFP–1,900CFP ($9.50–$19). MC, V. Mon–Tues and Thurs–Sat 11:15am–2:30pm; Thurs–Tues 6:15–9:30pm. CANTONESE.

When my body tells me to eat my vegetables, I head for this plain but clean Chinese place operated by Micheline Tetuanui (who also owns the Heimata Boutique next door) and her family. Chicken with sweet Moorea pineapple is their most popular dish, but the house specialty isn't even on the menu: a crispy whole reef fish fresh grown in a pen in the bay just outside one of the two dining rooms here. Saturday night features Tahitian-style roast pig with coconut cream. The portions are small relative to similar Chinese restaurants in the United States, and a serving of plain rice costs extra, but everything's fresh and tasty here.

Le Mahogany. Maharepa, east of Hotel Bali Hai. ☎ **56.39.73.** Reservations recommended. Snacks (lunch only) 800CFP–950CFP ($8.50–$9.50); main courses 1,100CFP–1,850CFP ($11–$18.50). DC, MC, V. Thurs–Tues 11am–2:30pm and 6–9:30pm. FRENCH/CHINESE.

French chef François Courtien spent 30 years cooking at the Hotel Bali Hai before joining Tahitian Blondine Agnia at her pleasant little dining spot next to the local gym. It's a favorite with local expatriates who appreciate value and friendly service. Polished mahogany tables, mat walls, and a window opening to a garden provide tropical ambiance.

Start with a rich and tasty avocado and shrimp cocktail or a bowl of lobster bisque which will leave a spicy pepper aftertaste on your tongue. Proceed to a daily special such as Moorea-grown shrimp with curry, garlic, or whiskey sauce, or choose from the regular offerings such as swordfish in garlic butter or salmon in basil sauce. End with a *tarte tatin,* a caramelized apple pie served with vanilla ice cream. As an alternative, the Cantonese main courses are as good as any Chinese restaurant's here. Lunchtime snacks include salads, omelets, burgers, and grilled mahimahi or steak.

Call for free transportation.

✪ **Te Honu Iti (Chez Roger).** Pao Pao, north of Municipal Market. ☎ **56.19.84.** Reservations recommended. Main courses 1,100CFP–2,900CFP ($11–$29); sandwiches and burgers 400CFP–600CFP ($4–$6). MC, V. Daily 11:30am–2pm and 6:30–10pm. CLASSICAL FRENCH/CANTONESE.

This extraordinary restaurant, usually the home of owner-chef Roger Iqual, who won the *Concours National de la Poêle d'Or* (Golden Pot Contest) in Cannes for a sea-bass concoction, burned down not long ago and was being rebuilt during my last visit. It's worth inquiring if Roger has reopened, for this scenic setting beside Cook's Bay is worthy of his cuisine.

Roger works his magic on fresh seafood, prepared in the classical French fashion but with some delightful twists, such as lightly smoking sashimi-thin slices of yellowfin tuna and serving them over a piquant potato salad. Roger's chalkboard menu often features his delicate mahimahi mousse, a local favorite. A special tourist menu lets you choose from among three main courses, plus salad, dessert, and a glass of wine, a beer, or a soft drink for 2,400CFP ($24). There's nothing pretentious here, since Te Honu Iti (The Little Turtle) started as a snack bar before Roger bought it and still has a relaxed atmosphere. It also remains a "snack" at lunch, offering sandwiches and burgers. Roger doesn't cook them, but his menu offers a selection of Cantonese dishes.

If Roger hasn't reopened here, you can find him offering the same menu, prices, and hours at **Le Pitcairn,** south of the Club Med in Haapiti (☎ **56.55.46**).

SNACK BARS IN COOK'S BAY

Le Sylesie Patisserie. Maharepa, next to the post office. ☎ **56.15.88.** Reservations not accepted. Snacks and light meals 400CFP–1,400CFP ($4–$14); breakfasts 450CFP–1,500CFP ($4.50–$15). MC, V. Daily 6:30am–6pm. PATISSERIE/SNACKS.

This largest of the Le Sylesie branches has a wider selection of pastries, crêpes, pizzas, salads, omelets, quiches, burgers, sandwiches, fruit plates, ice cream, sundaes, and other goodies than its sister in Haapiti (see below). The patio tables here are set in a cool, shady spot for a full, American-style breakfast (served all day) or tasty lunch, but you can get sunburned while eating outside in the late afternoon.

⊙ **Snack L'Ananas Bleu.** Pao Pao, opposite Club Bali Hai. ☎ **56.12.06.** Reservations not accepted. Breakfast 550CFP–1,200CFP ($5.50–$12); burgers and sandwiches 650CFP–1,000CFP ($6.50–$10); main courses 1,250CFP–1,550CFP ($12.50–$15.50). MC, V. Daily 7:30am–2:30pm. SNACK BAR/CREPES.

"Top Burger" says the roadside sign in front of Matahi Hunter's little front-porch restaurant, and indeed you can get a big juicy beef, fish, or teriyaki one accompanied by French fries here. Continental or cooked breakfasts are served all day, or you can join the French in partaking of a substantial serving of steak, beef curry, shrimp in garlic or curry sauce, or grilled fish for lunch. Ice cream, sundaes, and fruit drinks provide relief from the midday heat.

Snack Rotui. Pao Pao, west of the bridge at the head of Cook's Bay. ☎ **56.18.16.** Reservations not accepted. Sandwiches 130CFP–180CFP ($1.30–$1.80); plate lunches 500CFP ($5). No credit cards. Tues–Sun 7am–6pm. SNACK BAR.

Located on the shore of Cook's Bay, this is run by a Chinese family, and for about 400CFP ($4) you can get a casse-croûte sandwich, a soft drink, and a slice of delicious homemade cake topped with chocolate pudding. Daily plate lunches, usually a Chinese dish with rice, are prepared earlier in the day and served without refrigeration. A few tables under a roof beside the beach catch the breezes off the bay.

ON THE NORTHWEST COAST

If chef Roger Iqual hasn't reopened Te Honu Iti (Chez Roger) in Cook's Bay (see above), you should find him here at **Le Pitcairn,** south of the Club Med (☎ 56.55.46).

Restaurants come and go in La Petit Village shopping center opposite the Club Med, but the reasonably priced **Lagon Cafe** (☎ 56.39.41) has been around a while, offering breakfast, lunch, afternoon sandwiches and salads, and French cuisine at dinner. It's open daily from 7:30 to 9:30am and 11:30am to 6pm, and Monday to Saturday from 7 to 9:30pm.

Although I wasn't particularly impressed, others have enjoyed the food at **La Plantation,** opposite the Club Med (☎ 56.45.10), this area's most romantic restaurant. Soft lighting, music, and tables set on a big porch help set the scene. Pizzas come with a dozen familiar toppings, while country-style French main courses range from 1,600CFP to 2,350CFP ($16 to $23.50).

Budget travelers will find a *roulotte* or two stationed outside the Club Med each evening. See "Dining" in chapter 4 for more information about these meal wagons.

⊙ **Linareva Floating Restaurant and Bar.** Haapiti, 7km (4 miles) south of the Club Med. ☎ **56.15.35.** Reservations recommended for dinner. Main courses 1,800CFP–2,450CFP ($18–$24.50). MC, V. Daily 11:30am–5pm and 6–9pm. FRENCH SEAFOOD.

You'll pay a price to have dinner here, but Eric Lussiez's restaurant and bar is consistently Moorea's finest restaurant. It's also the most unusual: the hull of the original *Tamarii Moorea,* the first ferry to ply between Papeete and Moorea. Eric completely rebuilt the old vessel (twice, actually, for it sank at its dock due to a plumbing error after the job was finished). He outfitted the dining room with polished wood, large windows, and plenty of bright brass and other nautical decor. The menu changes with availability of local seafood such as shark and emperor fish, most expertly prepared with traditional French sauces. Tour groups stop here for lunch, when dinnertime prices are almost cut in half. Ask about discounted transportation from Haapiti-area hotels when you make your reservation.

✪ **Restaurant Les Tipaniers.** Haapiti, at Hotel-Résidence Les Tipaniers, east of the Club Med. ☎ **56.12.67.** Reservations recommended. Pasta and pizza 950CFP–1,450CFP ($9.50–$14); main courses 1,600CFP–2,250CFP ($16–$22.50). AE, DC, MC, V. Daily 7–9:15pm. ITALIAN/FRENCH.

This romantic, thatch-roofed restaurant is popular with both visitors and Moorea's permanent residents, who come here for delicious pizzas with a variety of toppings and homemade spaghetti, lasagna, tagliatelle, and gnocchi served with Bolognese, carbonara, or seafood sauce. French dishes include pepper steak and fillets of mahimahi in butter or vanilla sauce. Discounted transportation is available for guests staying at Haapiti-area hotels.

SNACK BARS ON THE NORTHWEST COAST

Le Motu Pizza Grill. Haapiti, opposite Club Med. ☎ **56.16.70.** Reservations not accepted. Burgers and sandwiches 450CFP–800CFP ($4.50–$8); pizza and pasta 950CFP–1,100CFP ($9.50–$11); main courses 1,400CFP–1,900CFP ($14–$19). MC, V. Daily 9:30am–9pm. SNACKS/ITALIAN/FRENCH.

You can get a full meal at this open-air restaurant (there is a small air-conditioned dining room open during hot weather), but it's best known for excellent sandwiches and hamburgers, including a monster-size hamburger-filled baguette. Pizzas and daily Italian pastas also are offered. Light fare includes salads, crêpes, and soft ice cream, and you can choose from a wide selection of soft drinks, beer, and wine.

Le Sylesie Patisserie. Haapiti, west of the Club Med. ☎ **56.20.45.** Sandwiches, salads, burgers 400CFP–900CFP ($4–$9); breakfasts 500CFP–1,500CFP ($5–$15). No credit cards. Daily 6:30am–5pm. SNACKS/BREAKFAST.

A sister of Le Sylesie in Maharepa (see above), this little shop serves some of the same croissants-and-coffee or full American-style breakfasts (served all day), crêpes, burgers, sandwiches, small pizzas, quiches, and pastries. The low-slung building has six tables under cover in front.

7 Island Nights

No one has gone to Moorea for its nightlife since the One Chicken Inn, its colorful version of Quinn's infamous Tahitian-style bar in Papeete, bit the dust in Pao Pao 2 decades ago. The island's evening entertainment now is limited to the hotels, with a few exceptions.

Remember that the hotels' schedules change, so do your detective work. Call ahead before striking out. Most charge 4,500CFP to 6,500CFP ($45 to $65) per person for dinner and a Tahitian dance show.

The ✪ **Tiki Theatre Village** (☎ **56.18.97**) in Haapiti, 2 kilometers (1.2 miles) west of the Club Med, stages the island's most authentic feast and dance show on Tuesday, Wednesday, Friday and Saturday. They pick you up from your hotel and deposit you on the beach for a rum punch and sunset. After the staff uncovers the earth oven, they take you on a tour of the village. A buffet of both Tahitian and Western foods is followed by an energetic, 1½-hour dance show with some of the most elaborate yet traditional costumes to be seen in French Polynesia. The performers can number more than 70 if overseas troupes are visiting the island. The dinner and show cost 6,500CFP ($65) per person, or you can come for the 9pm show for 2,500CFP

($25). Add 1,000CFP ($10) in either case for transportation. See "Cultural Experiences," above, for more about Tiki Theatre Village.

Le Pêcheur restaurant in Maharepa (☎ **56.36.12**) has live entertainment and dancing on Saturday evenings, all for the price of a meal. See "Dining," above.

Chez Billy (no phone), on the beach west of Hotel Moorea Village in Haapiti, offers a chance to dance, drink, and occasionally fight with the locals on Friday and Saturday nights. Billy kicks off at 8pm and roars on into the wee hours. Expect to pay a 1,000CFP ($10) cover charge, 350CFP ($3.50) and up for drinks.

Among the hotels, **Club Méditerranée** (☎ **56.14.09**) has nightly skits, floor shows, and other entertainment for its guests. When business is slow, it may open its doors to outsiders.

Hotel Bali Hai (☎ **56.13.59**) has a fine show at 6:30pm Wednesday, followed by a charcoal barbecue with a rack of lamb. Its Saturday night show explains Tahitian culture.

Hotel Sofitel Ia Ora (☎ **56.12.90**) usually has its main dance show at 8pm on Saturday. **Moorea Beachcomber Parkroyal** (☎ **55.19.19**) has a barbecue and Tahitian dance show twice a week, with Saturday's performed under the stars on the beach.

Hotel Moorea Village (☎ **56.10.02**) has a barbecue with a pareu fashion show on Saturdays at 7:30pm.

One of my favorite French Polynesian experiences is happy hour at the ✪ **Club Bali Hai** (☎ **56.13.68**) on Tuesday from 6 to 7pm. Many of the island's English-speaking expatriate residents show up to take advantage of half-price drinks, which usually are served at the bar by the bay. It's one of the greatest vistas in the South Pacific (you'll want to become a modern Paul Gauguin in order to capture the changing colors as the sunset paints the bay, sky, and the jagged mountains). The Club also has a happy hour starting at 5pm Friday; it's followed by a barbecue and a show by one of Moorea's top dance troupes.

6 Bora Bora & the Other Islands of French Polynesia

Many visitors to French Polynesia go on from Tahiti and Moorea to see the dramatic, tombstone-like central mountain and incredibly beautiful lagoon of Bora Bora, whose sing-song name has come to symbolize the ultimate escape from civilization. Bora Bora has become French Polynesia's most touristy island—and its most expensive. Go to Bora Bora to see its beautiful scenery, to dive and swim with the sharks in its great lagoon, and to tell everyone back home you've been here. But don't go expecting a Polynesian cultural experience.

To catch a glimpse into old Polynesia, you'll have to stop at Huahine, which many of us consider to be French Polynesia's third most beautiful island, and at Raiatea and Tahaa, which share a deep-water lagoon and are the territory's sailing center. On these islands, agriculture still far outweighs tourism. On them you'll see "the way Tahiti used to be," as they say in these parts.

If you're an avid diver, head to the low-lying atolls of the Tuamotu Archipelago, where Rangiroa offers an extraordinary amount of sea life swimming in the world's second-largest lagoon, and where Manihi provides both diving and tours of its famous black pearl farms, the territory's second-largest industry.

1 Bora Bora

Because of its fame and beauty, little Bora Bora has become a playground for the rich and occasionally the famous. It has seen an explosion of hotel construction in recent years, with piers and over-water bungalows reaching out like tentacles over its gorgeous lagoon. Indeed, some travel industry professionals think that Bora Bora is already over-built and over-priced. The island also can be packed with tourists when cruise ships anchor in its lagoon. And despite a municipal clean-up effort, it's one of the most unkempt islands here. Don't be surprised to see trash lying around the roadside and animals—especially dogs—wandering in and out of many restaurants.

Despite these negatives, you'll still appreciate why James A. Michener wrote that this half-atoll/half-mountain is the world's most beautiful island.

Lying 230 kilometers (143 miles) northwest of Tahiti, Bora Bora is one of those middle-aged islands consisting of a high center completely surrounded by a lagoon enclosed by coral reef. What makes it so beautiful is the combination of sand-fringed motus sitting on the outer reef, the multihued lagoon cutting deep bays into the central high island, and the basaltic tombstone known as Mount Otemanu towering over it all.

Be first to board the plane, for all this should be visible from the left side of the aircraft as you fly up from Papeete and descend to the island's airport on Motu Mute, a flat island on the northern edge of the barrier reef. Beyond Motu Mute the lagoon turns deep blue because it's deep enough for the U.S. Navy to have used Bora Bora as a way station during World War II. The airstrip you land on is another legacy of that war, built by the U.S. Navy as part of Operation Bobcat, during which 6,000 American sailors and soldiers were stationed on this tiny island. Bora Bora never saw combat during World War II, but it was a major refueling base on the America-to-Australia supply line.

You'll get to see the lagoon close up soon after landing, for all passengers are ferried across it from the airport, some directly to their hotels but most to **Vaitape,** the main village on the west coast, sitting opposite Teavanui Pass, the only entrance through the reef into the lagoon.

As is the case on Tahiti and Moorea, a road runs around the shoreline of Bora Bora, cutting in and out of the bays and skirting what seem like a thousand white-sand beaches lapped by the waters of the lagoon. The best of the beaches—in fact, one of the best in French Polynesia—stretches for more than 3 kilometers (2 miles) around a flat, coconut-studded peninsula known as **Matira Point.**

The island is so small that the road around it covers only 27 kilometers (17 miles) from start to finish. All the 4,500 or so Bora Borans live on a flat coastal strip that quickly gives way to the mountainous interior. The highest point on the island is the unusual slab, **Mount Otemanu** (727 meters [2,379 feet]), Bora Bora's trademark. Next to it is the more normal **Mount Pahia** (661 meters [2,165 feet]). These two mountains never quite seem the same from any two different viewpoints. Mount Otemanu can look like a tombstone from one direction, a needle from another. Because these mountains are relatively low, Bora Bora doesn't get as much rain as the taller Tahiti, Moorea, or Raiatea. Water shortages can occur, especially during the drier months from June through September (consequently, most hotels have their own desalinization facilities).

GETTING AROUND

Le trucks going to the hotels meet Air Tahiti's airport launches when they land at Vaitape. They also wait for the inter-island ferry *Ono Ono,* which docks at the Farepiti wharf, at the mouth of Faanui Bay about 1.5 kilometers (1 mile) north of the village. (See "Getting There & Getting Around" in chapter 3 for more information.) At either location, get in the truck with the name of your hotel painted on the side. Fares to the Matira Point hotel district are 300CFP ($3) from Vaitape and 500CFP ($5) from Farepiti.

Impressions

I saw it first from an airplane. On the horizon there was a speck that became a tall, blunt mountain with cliffs dropping sheer into the sea. And about the base of the mountain, narrow fingers of land shot out, forming magnificent bays, while about the whole was thrown a coral ring of absolute perfection. . . . That was Bora Bora from aloft. When you stepped upon it the dream expanded.

—James A. Michener, 1951

There is no public transportation system on Bora Bora. The larger hotels get their guests to Vaitape and back, but the frequency can vary depending on how many tourists are on the island. Some restaurants will pick up dinner guests who call for reservations.

BY RENTAL CAR, SCOOTER & BICYCLE   Avis (☎ 800/230-4898 or 67.74.34) and **Europcar** (☎ 800/227-7368 or 67.70.15) both have rental-car offices at Vaitape wharf. Avis also rents scooters, and both have bicycles. Europcar is somewhat less expensive, with cars beginning at 4,500CFP ($45) for 2 hours and 7,200CFP ($72) for 24 hours, including unlimited kilometers and insurance. So-called "Fun Cars" (two-seat motorized tricycles) rent for 5,500CFP ($55) a day. Europcar also is less expensive for mountain bikes, which range from 1,100CFP ($11) for 2 hours to 1,800CFP ($18) for all day. At Avis, scooters range from 3,400CFP ($34) for 2 hours to 6,900CFP ($69) for 24 hours.

With the exception of a short stretch on the east coast, the 27 kilometers (17 miles) of road around Bora Bora are paved. Most of it is flat, but be very cautious on the unpaved portion, which climbs a steep hill. Always drive or ride slowly and carefully and forever be on the lookout for pigs, chickens, pedestrians, and the island's ubiquitous dogs.

BY TAXI   The hotel desks will call a taxi, or phone **Otemanu Tours** (☎ 67.70.49), **Jeanine Buchin** (☎ 67.74.14), or **Jacques Isnard** (☎ 67.72.25). Fares between Vaitape and the Matira hotel district are at least 1,000CFP ($10) from 6am to 6pm, 1,500CFP ($15) from 6pm to 6am; a ride between Vaitape and Anau village on the east coast costs 5,000CFP ($50) anytime. Taxis aren't metered, so make sure you and the driver agree on a fare before setting out.

Fast Facts: Bora Bora

Baby-Sitters   The hotels will arrange English-speaking baby-sitters, or contact **Robin Teraitepo** at Chez Ben's (☎ 67.74.54).

Bookstores   **Libraire Vaite,** in the Centre Commercial Le Pahia just north of the Vaitape wharf (☎ 67.62.02), has some English-language books.

Camera/Film   **Camera Shop,** in Le Jardin Gauguin shopping center north of the Hotel Bora Bora (☎ 67.76.93), offers professional photo services and overnight processing of color print film. It also has a branch at Vaitape wharf. Some hotel boutiques will send your film here for you.

Currency Exchange   **Banque de Tahiti, Banque Socredo,** and **Banque de Polynésie** have branches in Vaitape; all are open Monday through Friday from 8 to 11:45am and from 2 to 4pm, but beyond that, each has its own business hours. Banque de Tahiti has an ATM.

Doctor & Dentist   The island's infirmary is in Vaitape (☎ 67.70.77), as are the offices of Dr. Azad Roussanaly (☎ 67.77.95). For dental service, see Dr. J. F. Macouin, in the Centre Commercial Le Pahia north of the wharf (☎ 67.70.55).

Drugstores   A pharmacy north of the town wharf in Vaitape is open Monday through Friday from 8 to noon and 3:30 to 6pm, Saturday from 8 to noon and 5 to 6pm, and Sunday from 9 to 9:30 am.

E-mail   **L'Appetisserie,** in the Centre Commercial Le Pahia just north of the Vaitape wharf (☎ 67.78.88), has a computer terminal for e-mail, which costs

Bora Bora

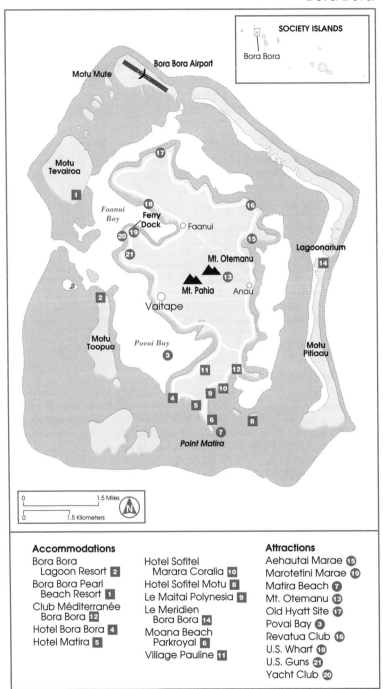

SOCIETY ISLANDS

Bora Bora

Motu Mute

Bora Bora Airport

Motu Tevairoa

Faanui Bay

Ferry Dock

○ Faanui

Lagoonarium

Mt. Otemanu

Mt. Pahia

Anau

Vaitape

Motu Toopua

Povai Bay

Motu Pitiaau

Point Matira

0   1.5 Miles
0   1.5 Kilometers

Accommodations

Bora Bora
  Lagoon Resort **2**
Bora Bora Pearl
  Beach Resort **1**
Club Méditerranée
  Bora Bora **12**
Hotel Bora Bora **4**
Hotel Matira **5**

Hotel Sofitel
  Marara Coralia **10**
Hotel Sofitel Motu **8**
Le Maitai Polynesia **9**
Le Meridien
  Bora Bora **14**
Moana Beach
  Parkroyal **6**
Village Pauline **11**

Attractions

Aehautai Marae **15**
Marotetini Marae **19**
Matira Beach **7**
Mt. Otemanu **13**
Old Hyatt Site **17**
Povai Bay **3**
Revatua Club **16**
U.S. Wharf **18**
U.S. Guns **21**
Yacht Club **20**

500CFP ($5) to send, 300CFP ($3) to receive. Surfing access time goes for 500CFP ($5) for 15 minutes, 1,000CFP ($10) for 30 minutes. See "Dining," below, for more about this pastry shop.

Information   The **Bora Bora Comité du Tourisme** (☎ and fax **67.76.36**) has an office in the large building on the north side of Vaitape wharf. It's not always staffed, but hours are posted as Monday through Friday from 7:30am to noon and 1:30 to 4pm, Saturday from 8 to 11:30am. The address is B.P. 144, Vaitape, Bora Bora.

Police   The gendarmerie is opposite the Vaitape wharf (☎ **67.70.58**).

Post Office   The post office in Vaitape is open on Monday from 8am to 3pm, Tuesday through Friday from 7:30am to 3pm, and on Saturday from 8 to 10am.

Safety   The island has experienced a rash of petty theft recently, so keep an eye on your valuables and lock your rental car.

EXPLORING BORA BORA
✪ THE CIRCLE ISLAND TOUR

Since the island is only 17 miles around, many visitors see it on bicycles (give yourself at least 4 hours), scooter, or car. Since some of those sights I mention below may not be easy to find, however, consider taking a guided sightseeing tour around the island. Alfredo Doom's **Bora Bora Tours** (☎ **67.70.28**) operates from the Hotel Bora Bora. Paul Desmet's **Otemanu Tours** (☎ **67.70.49**) has its base north of Vaitape but will pick up at the hotels. You can book them at any hotel activities desk. They both charge about 2,500CFP ($25) a person.

If you do it yourself, begin at the wharf in **Vaitape,** where there's a monument to French yachtsman Alain Gerbault, who sailed his boat around the world between 1923 and 1929 and lived to write about it (thus adding to Bora Bora's fame).

From the wharf, head south (counterclockwise) around the island. The road soon curves along the shore of **Povai Bay,** where Mounts Otemanu and Pahia tower over you. Take your time along this bay; the views are the best on Bora Bora. When you reach the area around the Bamboo House Restaurant, stop for a look back across the water at Mount Otemanu.

The road climbs the small headland, where a huge banyan tree marks the entrance to the Hotel Bora Bora on **Raititi Point,** then runs smoothly along curving **Matira Beach,** one of the South Pacific's finest. You can do some good snorkeling just off the end of the beach closest to the hotel. When the road curves sharply to the left, look for a narrow paved road to the right. This leads to **Matira Point,** the low, sandy, coconut-studded peninsula that extends out from Bora Bora's south end. Down this track about 50 yards is a **public beach** on the west side of the peninsula, opposite the Moana Beach Parkroyal. The lagoon is shallow all the way out to the reef at this point, but the bottom is smooth and sandy. When I first came to Bora Bora in 1977, I camped a week on Matira Point; the Moana Beach Parkroyal is only one of many structures in what was then a deserted coconut grove completely surrounded by unspoiled beach.

Up the east coast, you'll pass through the island's busy hotel and restaurant district before climbing a steep hill above the Club Méditerranée. A trail cuts off to the right on the north side of the hill and goes to the **Aehautai Marae,** one of several old temples on Bora Bora. This particular one has a great view of Mount Otemanu and the blue outlines of Raiatea and Tahaa islands beyond the motus on the reef.

You will go through a long stretch of coconut plantations before entering **Anau,** a typical Polynesian village with a large church, a general store, and tin-roofed houses crouched along the road. Except for a few native homes and **Club Revatua** (☎ **67.71.67**), where you can stop to refuel, the northwest coast is deserted. Here you ride through several miles of coconut plantations pockmarked by thousands of holes made by the land crabs known as *tupas*. After turning at the northernmost point, you pass a group of over-water bungalows and another group of houses, which climb the hill. Some of these are expensive condominiums; the others are part of defunct project that was to have been a Hyatt resort. Across the lagoon are Motu Mute and the airport.

Faanui Bay was used during World War II as an Allied naval base. It's not marked, but the U.S. Navy's Seabees built the concrete wharf on the north shore as a seaplane ramp. At the head of the bay, a road cuts off into the Faanui valley, from which an unmarked hiking trail leads over the saddle to Bora Bora's east coast. (You'll need a guide for this trek; ask at your hotel activities desk.)

Just beyond the main shipping wharf at the point on the south side of Faanui Bay is the restored **Marotetini Marae,** which in pre-European days was dedicated to navigators. In his novel *Hawaii,* James Michener had his fictional Polynesians leave this point to discover and settle the Hawaiian Islands. Nearby are tombs in which members of Bora Bora's former royal family are buried. If you look offshore at this point, you'll see the only pass into the lagoon. The remains of two **American guns** that guarded it stand on the hill above but are best visited on a safari tour (see below).

Near the end of your round-island tour you will enter the village of Nunue, home of **Bora Bora Cash API,** the island's large warehouse-style general store; it's the best place to shop for groceries and other supplies. As you enter Vaitape, the older, more traditional **Magasin Chin Lee** is a major gathering place for local residents. It's a good place to soak up some island culture while trimming your thirst with a cold bottle of Eau Royale. Opposite the store is the modern **Centre Commercial Le Pahia,** with a patisserie, a hairdresser, a branch of Sibani Perles, a bookstore, and other shops.

SAFARI TOURS

While the regular tours stick to the shoreline, others head into the hills in open-air four-wheel-drive vehicles for panoramic views and visits to the old U.S. Navy gun sites. The mountain roads are mere ruts in places, so you could get stuck if it has been raining. Dany Leverd's **Tupuna Four-Wheel Drive Expeditions** (☎ **67.75.06**) is the best. Book at any hotel activities desk. He charges about 6,000CFP ($60) per person.

✪ LAGOON OUTINGS

Bora Bora has one of the world's most beautiful lagoons, and getting out on it, snorkeling and swimming in it, and visiting the islands on its outer edge are absolute musts. Most lagoon tours take you out in fast outrigger canoes and include shark-feeding demonstrations (the guide feeds reef sharks while you watch from a reasonably safe distance while snorkeling). Shark-feeding is likely to be one of your most indelible memories of this island.

Some excursions go to the **Bora Bora Lagoonarium** (☎ **67.71.34**), a fenced-in underwater area off a motu near Le Meridien Bora Bora, where you can swim with (and maybe even ride) the manta rays and observe the sharks (who are on the other side of the fence here). The lagoonarium is open Sunday through Friday.

Your hotel or pension can recommend one of several guides for lagoon trips. **Marona Tours** (☎ **67.72.26**) is the most authentic. Half-day excursions cost about 5,500CFP ($55), including a picnic lunch on a motu. Book at any hotel desk.

A much drier way to see the underwater delights is in the semi-submersible vessel ***Aquascope Moana View*** (☎ **67.61.92**), which operates along the outer edges of the lagoon and along the reef outside the pass. The 50-minute voyages cost 4,000CFP ($40) for adults, 3,000CFP ($30) for children 4 to 12. The transfer boat usually leaves Vaitape wharf at 9am, 10:15am, 11:30am, 2:30pm, and 3:45pm, but call for reservations.

DIVING, FISHING & WATER SPORTS

✪ SCUBA DIVING   Certified and noncertified divers alike can swim among the coral heads, sharks, rays, eels, and some 1,000 species of colorful tropical fishes out in the lagoon here. Every resort has a scuba diving program. Both 30-minute introductory courses and one-tank lagoon dives cost about 6,000CFP ($60), while open-water and night dives are priced at 7,500CFP ($75).

Based adjacent to the Hotel Bora Bora, friendly dive operators Michel and Anne Condesse offer morning, afternoon, and evening dives from their **Bora Bora Diving Center** (☎ and fax 67.71.84; e-mail boradiving@mail.pf). They provide buoyancy compensators, fins, snorkels, wet suits, regulators, and all other equipment, which my traveling companion found to be in excellent condition (but be prepared for the metric system, since depth and pressure gauges display measurements in meters and kilograms). They also teach PADI certification courses.

You can go "diving" and not even get your head wet on a so-called **Aqua Safari** at Bora Bora Diving Center. That is, you go down in about 3 meters (10 feet) of water and walk around on the bottom while wearing nothing but your swim suit and a funny yellow helmet, sort of like deep-sea divers used to wear. Air is pumped into the helmets from the surface through a hose. These adventures cost 5,500CFP ($55). Make your reservations at least a day in advance.

TOPdive Bora Bora (☎ 67.50.50; fax 67.50.51; e-mail topdive@mail.pf) is the island's other major dive operator. It's based at the **TOPdive Resort Bora Bora,** B.P. 515, Vaitape (same phone, fax, and e-mail), a new and overpriced resort on the lagoon north of Vaitape.

SPORT FISHING   For combined sailing and fishing, American Richard Postma's **Tara Vana** (☎ 800/548-5331 or 67.77.79; www.taravana.com; e-mail taravana@ibm. com) is the world's first sail-powered luxury game fishing boat. This 50-footer is available for day trips or for overnight charters to the other Leeward Islands. Sailing or fishing costs from 80,000CFP ($800) for ½ day, 100,700CFP ($1,007) for a full day, including food but not alcoholic beverages. Among Richard's first guests were actors Dennis Quaid and Meg Ryan, and former *Baywatch* star Pamela Anderson Lee came along later.

OTHER WATER SPORTS   Every hotel has some water toys for its guests to use, and the activities desks will arrange fishing, diving, and other water sports. You don't have to stay there to use the equipment and facilities at the **Hotel Sofitel Marara Coralia** (☎ 67.70.46), but you will have to pay. These include waterskiing, sailing on Hobie Cats, paddling canoes, and getting a bird's-eye view of the lagoon while hanging below a parasail.

Based at Village Pauline (see "Accommodations," below), **Bora Bora Kayaks** (☎ 67.72.16) rents one- and two-person sea kayaks ranging from 1,000CFP ($10) for 1 hour to 4,000CFP ($40) all day. These quality boats were made in the United States and come equipped with snorkeling and fishing gear.

SHOPPING

Local artisans display their straw hats, pareus, and other handcraft items at **Bora Bora I Te Fanau Tahi** (no phone), in the large hall at the Vaitape wharf. It's always open when cruise ships are in the lagoon. The local **Tourism Committee** (☎ 67.70.10) has its offices on the waterfront side of the building and can tell you when that will be.

Tetiaroa: Marlon's Mana

Marlon Brando did more than star in the remake of *Mutiny on the Bounty* when he came to Tahiti in 1962. He fell in love with his beautiful Tahitian co-star, Tarita, who became his wife and the mother of two of his children. He also fell for Tetiaroa, an atoll 42 kilometers (25 miles) north of Tahiti and Moorea.

In the old days, this cluster of 12 flat islets surrounding an aquamarine lagoon was the playground of Tahiti's high chiefs, who frequently were joined by the *Ariori,* those traveling bands of sexually explicit entertainers and practitioners of infanticide. High-ranking women would spend months on Tetiaroa, resting in the shade to lighten their skins and gorging on starchy foods to broaden their girths. Chiefly men and women were said to possess *mana,* and the bigger the body, the more the mana.

For a time an American dentist who married into the royal family owned Tetiaroa, but it had been abandoned by the time Brando bought it in 1966. He turned one of his islets into a refuge for Tetiaroa's thousands of seabirds. He built a retreat for himself on a second islet and a small, rather rustic resort on a third.

Guests at the resort would seldom see the great actor, on whose waistline Tetiaroa worked its expansive magic. During the day he would stay at home in the shade, playing with his radios and computers. At night he would go fishing and lobstering.

A series of hurricanes almost blew his resort away in 1983, and Brando's relationship with Tahiti turned to human disaster a decade later when his son Christian shot and killed his sister's Tahitian boyfriend in Hollywood. Marlon's distraught daughter later committed suicide on Tahiti.

Ex-wife Tarita still operates the resort, which is once again a local playground, especially on weekends. You can stay there or make day trips from Papeete by Air Tahiti or by yachts based in Papeete and Moorea (contact any hotel activities desk or travel agent). For information or reservations at the resort, contact **Hotel Tetiaroa,** B.P. 2418, Papeete, Tahiti (☎ **82.63.02,** fax 85.00.51).

Art du Pacific (☎ **67.63.85**), among several shops in Le Jardin Gauguin 1½ kilometers (1 mile) north of the Hotel Bora Bora, has one of the best collections of wood carvings from the Marquesas Islands. They are expensive, but Gauguin's paintings reproduced on hair clasps, compacts, business card cases, and other small items make affordable and easily transported gifts. Open Monday through Saturday from 9am to 5:30pm.

Boutique Bora Bora (☎ **67.79.72**), opposite the ferry wharf in Vaitape, has more T-shirts and pareus than most shops here, plus wood carvings, books, calendars, curios, and a few black pearls. Open Monday through Saturday from 8am to 6pm, Sunday from 9am to 5pm.

Boutique Gauguin (☎ **67.76.67**), in a white house next to Le Jardin Gauguin 1 mile north of Hotel Bora Bora, offers a selection of handcrafts, clothing, and black pearls in addition to curio items such as ashtrays and coasters featuring the works of Paul Gauguin. Some of its pareus are particularly artistic. Hours are Monday through Saturday from 8:30am to 6pm and Sunday from 9:30am to 4:30pm.

✪ **Matira Pearls** (☎ **67.79.14**), at Matira Point, is operated by two Americans, Steve Fearon, whose family once owned a piece of the Hotel Bora Bora, and Steve Donnatin, who's been living here since 1984. Much about their air-conditioned shop will remind you of Island Fashion Black Pearls on Moorea, including their explanation of pearls. Set and loose black pearls start at $100. Unlike dealers who aim their jewelry at visitors from Europe, their customized settings are designed to emphasize the pearl, not the gold. They also have a selection of bathing suits, aloha shirts, and T-shirts. Hours are Monday through Saturday 9am to 5:30pm, Sunday 10am to 5pm.

Moana Arts (☎ **67.70.33**), virtually next to the Hotel Bora Bora, is where noted photographer Erwin Christian sells some of his dramatic works, which you will inevitably see in numerous books and on many postcards. He also has a selection of designer resort wear. Open Monday through Saturday from 9am to noon and 2 to 6pm.

Pakalola Boutique (☎ **67.71.82**), over Bora Bora Burger in Vaitape, has the island's largest selection of T-shirts, pareus, tropical clothing, wood carvings, black pearls, shell jewelry, and curios such as Hinano beer glasses. Open Monday through Saturday from 8am to 6pm.

Sibani Perles (☎ **67.72.49**), opposite Magasin Chin Lee in Vaitape, offers the designs of Didier Sibani, one of the pioneers of the black pearl industry. His elegant and pricey designs are displayed in bamboo cases. Open Monday through Saturday 9am to 5:30pm.

ACCOMMODATIONS

Bora Bora has some of the South Pacific's finest—and most expensive—resorts. In light of how many have been built in the past few years, it may also have a few too many of them for the time being. As a result, it could pay to shop around and ask for discounts during the off-season.

As I noted in chapter 1, most bungalows here don't provide a great deal of privacy. The high cost of labor and land means that a resort must have at least 40 units to be economically viable, and that most bungalows are likely to be close together. Except for the bungalows with private patios at the Hotel Bora Bora and the Bora Bora Pearl Beach Resort, and a few over-waters at the Hotel Sofitel Marara Coralia (see below), the off-shore resorts described in the Fiji chapters later in this book offer a higher level of seclusion.

It was due to open after my last visit so I wasn't able to see it, but you might find more privacy at the **Hotel Sofitel Motu,** on a small, one-hill island directly off Matira Beach. It's said to be more intimate and exclusive than the other Sofitel resorts here. Of its 30 luxuriously appointed bungalows, 20 are over-water, while the others are 10 meters (30 feet) up the hill; thus all units have views back over the lagoon to Bora Bora. Rates were slated to be 54,000CFP to 68,000CFP ($540 to $680) for a double. For information and reservations, contact the Hotel Sofitel Marara Coralia (see below), with which it is to be jointly managed.

Except at the Club Med, guests pay extra for everything except their rooms. If you're going to dine exclusively at your hotel, add about 8,000CFP ($80) per person per day for a meal plan.

Keep in mind that mosquitoes and sand flies love to feast on guests on Bora Bora's motus, so you'll want a good supply of mosquito coils and insect repellent if you opt for one of the off-shore resorts.

VERY EXPENSIVE

✪ **Bora Bora Lagoon Resort.** B.P. 175, Vaitape, Bora Bora (on Motu Toopua, 1km [0.5 mile] off Vaitape). ☎ **800/223-6800** or 60.40.00. Fax 60.40.01. www.boraboralagoonresort. orient-express.com. E-mail: bblr@mail.pf. 80 bungalows. A/C MINIBAR TV TEL. 52,000CFP–82,000CFP ($520–$820) double. Rates include full breakfast and airport transfers. AE, DC, MC, V.

Speedboats shuttle 23 times a day from Vaitape wharf to this posh Polynesian-style resort on Motu Toopua, a hilly island facing the rounded peak of Mount Pahia (not

Mount Otemanu's tombstone). The main building, under three interlocking thatch roofs, holds a reception area, bar, and gourmet restaurant. The end facing Mount Pahia actually protrudes over the lagoon. To the rear, an expansive stone deck surrounds one of French Polynesia's largest swimming pools, where you'll find another bar and restaurant.

Long piers with hand-carved railings lead to the 50 over-water bungalows, and 30 more sit ashore in tropical gardens. All of the 528-square-foot units are identical. Peaked thatch roofs cover their polished wood floors and walls, evoking a ship's cabin. Floor-to-ceiling jalousie windows on one side and doors sliding open to porches or decks on another let in light and provide some ventilation. Sofas and easy chairs with ottomans offer relaxation. Armoires hide TVs with CNN and other satellite programming. And spacious bathrooms come equipped with telephones, glass-door showers, and double sinks (which leave little space for toiletries). All units have robes, slippers, plastic reef shoes, and coffeemakers; two rooms are equipped for disabled guests. Three of the beachside bungalows—one of which has a whirlpool tub—interconnect to form suites. As luxurious as they are, the units are so close together you can overhear your neighbor's favorite TV show (not to mention certain amorous activities). And cross-ventilation could be better, since only 10 over-water and 10 garden units have air conditioners, and the lone ceiling fans have huge amounts of air to churn in the others.

Dining/Diversions: With widely spaced tables all facing the lagoon, the Otemanu dining room presents gourmet French dinners featuring fresh seafood flown in from overseas. The poolside restaurant serves grills and lighter fare all day. The main indoor bar hosts visiting musicians nightly, and Tahitians stage outdoor dance shows 2 nights a week.

Amenities: Sailboats, canoes, Windsurfers, and other equipment are parked on a white-sand beach, where an activities shack provides scuba diving, snorkeling, fishing, and other outdoor activities. A special feature here is a private, all-day picnic for just two people; you're taken to a deserted island, fed a silver-service lunch at an umbrella table standing in the lagoon, then left alone all afternoon to do whatever comes naturally. That all costs a mere 40,000CFP ($400) per couple. Other amenities include two lighted tennis courts; game room and library; fitness center; boutique; activities desk; twice-daily maid service; laundry; baby-sitting; limited room service; *New York Times Fax* delivered to rooms daily.

✪ **Bora Bora Pearl Beach Resort.** B.P. 169, Vaitape, Bora Bora (on Motu Tevairoa, 1km [0.5 mile] off Farepiti). ☎ 607/273-5012 in the U.S. or 60.52.00. Fax 60.52.22. www.spmhotels.com. E-mail: reception@borapearlbeach.pf. 80 units. A/C MINIBAR TV TEL. 46,000CFP–60,000CFP ($460–$600). AE, DC, MC, V.

Designed and built in 1998 by local interests, the Pearl Beach is the most traditionally Polynesian resort on the island. It sits beside a white sand beach out on Motu Tevairoa, the largest of the islands dotting the outer reef, and has better views of Mount Otemanu across the lagoon than does the Bora Bora Lagoon Resort to its south (see above). Free boats run between the resort and Farepiti wharf from 8am to 10pm, with bus connections on to Vaitape 5 times a day (it's a 20-minute walk if you don't catch the bus). Covered by interconnected conical thatch roofs, the open-air restaurant, main bar, and library stand on a raised earthen platform, which enhances their views down across Bora Bora's largest freshwater swimming pool to the lagoon and mountains.

Long, curving piers extend out to 50 spacious over-water bungalows, all of which are identical except for their views. The 15 "premium" units are worth paying extra for, since they are more private and enjoy unimpeded views of Bora Bora. Mat- and tapa-lined walls and split bamboo trim give all the bungalows here lots of Polynesian charm.

They all have thatch roofs, king platform beds, settees which can see duty as single beds, coffee tables over glass panels in hardwood floors, desks built into little alcoves extending out over the lagoon, TVs and minibars hidden in cabinets, tea/coffeemakers, phones with modem ports, and ceiling fans to augment the trade winds and air conditioners. Unscreened sliding doors open to large decks equipped with chaise lounges, steps down to a lagoonside platform, and a unique, private sitting area to one side. To the rear, bathrooms have tubs and separate showers, a water closet, and a sink and vanity virtually hanging out over the lagoon.

If privacy is more important that the sound of water lapping under your bungalow, consider one of the 10 beachside bungalows. Identical to the over-waters, they have the views from front porches and walled-in gardens with whirlpool tubs, sun decks, and al fresco bathrooms out back. (Another 20 garden units with no view but with their own private swimming pools were being built here.)

As at all Pearl Beach resorts, the Tahitian staff here is friendly and English-fluent, and management is sensitive to North American likes and dislikes.

Dining/Diversions: Looking out over the pool and lagoon, the main dining room offers excellent French cuisine with a Polynesian flair. A poolside bar and restaurant offers lunch, snacks, and libation. Tahitians make music nightly and stage dance shows 3 times a week. Two movies a night are shown in the conference room.

Amenities: Surrounded by a stone sundeck and a faux waterfall, the big, wade-in pool has a sand-look bottom and boasts a whirlpool on an islet out in the middle. Guests can also enjoy splashing or snorkeling in the natural sand-bottom lagoon (the beach sand is subject to erosion but dredges replenish it as needed), and pay to play with kayaks, canoes, jet skis, paddleboats, aqua bikes, and other toys. Gilles Petrie, one of French Polynesia's top dive operators, is in charge of the shop here. Land-based activities include shuffleboard, volleyball, tennis on lighted courts, and 18 holes of mini-golf. If the sun's too hot, you can retire inside and play board games, billiards, table tennis, and foosball. Other amenities are conference room, activities desk, concierge, babysitting, twice-daily maid service, limited room service, and laundry.

✪ **Hotel Bora Bora.** B.P. 1, Vaitape, Bora Bora (Matira Point, 4.4 miles from Vaitape). ☎ **800/421-1490** or 60.44.11. Fax 60.44.22. E-mail: hbbresa@mail.pf. 54 bungalows. MINIBAR TEL. 45,000CFP–75,000CFP ($450–$750). AE, DC, MC, V.

Despite stiff competition from newcomers in recent years, this has been French Polynesia's premier resort since it opened in the early 1960s. It has undergone some changes lately, with its owners—the luxury-laden Amanresorts—locking the gates to outsiders and putting an emphasis on expedient rather than laid-back Polynesian service (as a result, many veteran Tahitian staffers jumped ship to join the new Bora Bora Pearl Beach Resort). The bungalows have been completely rebuilt, too, but left alone was the thatch-roofed central building that always has been a key part of the resort's charm. It sits atop a low headland overlooking the start of magnificent Matira Beach, whose coral gardens provide some of the best snorkeling of any hotel in the territory. Down below, one of the best beach bars in the South Pacific rests right on those white sands. The entire complex faces west, presenting glorious sunsets over the lagoon and hilly Motu Toopua. (But note: no swimming pool.)

The comfortable Tahitian-style bungalows are among the palm trees on the flat shoreline on either side of the headland. On the north, some of the 15 over-water bungalows are actually perched right on the reef's edge, where coral gives way to a deep blue lagoon (snorkeling off their porches is like flying off a canyon wall). A few others enjoy views of Mount Otemanu's tombstone across Povai Bay. Most of the bungalows are smaller than those at Bora Bora Lagoon Resort, but not the hotel's huge L-shaped units known as villas. Virtual houses, the villas all have separate bedrooms, and the "garden" versions even have their own small swimming pools surrounded by rock walls for privacy. The villas and overwater bungalows all have four-poster king-size beds with romantic mosquito nets. Furnishings throughout are top of the line, with some Oriental antique pieces here and there. All units have coffeemakers, refrigerators, stereo sound systems, and oak-trimmed, claw-foot bathtubs in addition to showers. Three of the villas are air-conditioned and have Jacuzzis.

The only serious drawback here is the neighboring round-island road, which can send the noise of Bora Bora's innumerable scooters into some units at the crack of dawn. Signs at each end of the property keep intruders out, which has caused great consternation among the local populace.

Dining/Diversions: Offering a mix of Continental and Polynesian fare, the hotel's dining room overlooks the lagoon on three sides. You can have your lunch brought to the pool- and beachside bar. A second bar adjoins the restaurant, and Tahitians strum their guitars and sing there every evening, when a dress code is in effect (no shorts, tank tops, or shower sandals). Traditional dance shows occur at least 2 nights a week.

Amenities: Lighted tennis courts; water sports, including scuba diving; bicycles; boutique; convenience store; games bungalow, table tennis, and billiards; activities and car-rental desks; twice-daily maid service; laundry; baby-sitting; twice-daily shuttle to Vaitape; afternoon tea; *New York Times Fax;* free bicycles.

✪ **Hotel Sofitel Marara Coralia.** B.P. 6, Bora Bora (north of Matira Point on the east side). ☎ **800/763-4835** in the U.S. or 41.04.04 in Papeete, 67.70.46 on Bora Bora. Fax 41.05.05 or 67.74.03. www.accor-hotels.com. 64 units. A/C MINIBAR TEL. 31,000CFP–50,000CFP ($320–$500). AE, DC, MC, V.

Known locally as The Marara, this hotel may lack the traditions of the Hotel Bora Bora, but it has its own history: Italian movie producer Dino De Laurentiis built it in 1977 to house star Mia Farrow and the crew working on his box-office bomb *Hurricane*. A beehive-shaped central building houses the restaurant and bar, both of which open to a swimming pool sunken into a deck built out over Matira Beach and the lagoon. It's not as luxurious as the other major resorts here, but its bungalows aren't far behind. Of the bungalows here, 43 face a curving beach of white sand, the lagoon, and Raiatea and Tahaa on the horizon. A long pier joins another 21 over-water models to the shore. They have the largest decks of any over-water bungalows in French Polynesia, and if you can get one of them, bungalows 51, 52, 62, 63, and 64 are the most private. Every unit here is air conditioned and comes equipped with king or double beds, thick bamboo furniture, ceiling fans, coffeemakers, and ample bathrooms with walk-in showers and windows opening to the living area.

Dining/Diversions: Open on three sides to the lagoon, the restaurant features French and Chinese cuisines, with many meals served buffet style. Evening entertainment features a Tahitian string band every night and a traditional dance show, which is held once a week, usually Saturday evening.

Amenities: Swimming pool; extensive water sports, including scuba diving and parasailing; tennis court; boutique; activities and car-rental desks; twice-daily maid service; activities and car-rental desks; laundry; baby-sitting; shuttle bus to Vaitape.

Le Meridien Bora Bora. B.P. 190, Vaitape, Bora Bora (on Motu Pitiaau, 1km [0.5 mile] off Anau village). ☎ **800/225-5843** or 60.51.51. Fax 60.51.10. www.lemeridien-tahiti.com. E-mail: sales@lemeridien-tahiti.com. 100 units. A/C MINIBAR TV TEL. 62,650CFP–76,700CFP ($626.50–$767). AE, DC, MC, V.

Located on the northern tip of an atoll-like island stretching 10 kilometers (6 miles) along the southeastern side of the outer reef, Le Meridien is the most unusual of Bora Bora's new resorts. Most obvious is its architecture, for as at its sister property on Tahiti (see "Accommodations" in chapter 4), a Melanesian theme prevails here, accented by sway-back thatch roofs covering the main buildings and tribal sculptures from Papua New Guinea standing in the public areas. The terrain is different, too, since the skinny island gives access to both ocean waves crashing on the barrier reef and to a long, sandy beach beside the lagoon. The architects also created a seawater-fed, lake-like lagoon, in which you can swim if you tire of the real lagoon or the resort's small freshwater pool. The prevailing trade winds whip across this sandy islet, and a scarcity of rain means scant shade trees (you'd better love sand and sun if you stay here). And note that the hotel's launch shuttles to Anau village, which is still an expensive taxi ride to Vaitape (see "Getting Around," above).

Of the 100 identical guest units here, 85 are built over-water and are reached by long piers stretching out like pincers from the north and south ends of the beach. Only a few of them have views of Mount Otemanu, whose tombstone is seen from its narrow end out here. Standing over waist-deep water, they are primarily notable for their huge glass floors, which make it seem as if you're walking on air (maids cover the glass with carpets at evening turndown). All units here are smaller than those at Bora Bora's other resorts, however, and you could stumble over too much furniture for the space available (shins have been skinned on the pointed ends of the lengthy, canoe-shaped coffee tables). Only the 10 otherwise identical "beach" bungalows, which actually sit beside the manmade lake, are air conditioned. All units here have king beds which can be converted to twins, sofas which can sleep a third person, writing tables, rather modest decks or porches, large closets with robes, and bathrooms equipped with both tubs and showers.

Dining/Diversions: Opening to the lake, Le Tipanie dining room serves breakfast buffets and French dinners and hosts weekly Tahitian dance shows performed on a platform floating on the lake. The thatch-roof, sand-floor Le Teava provides poolside lunches and afternoon snacks. Musicians perform nightly in the canoe-shaped main bar overlooking the beach and lagoon.

Amenities: Swimming pool, boutique, pearl shop, library, game room, air-conditioned TV lounge with videos, concierge, activities desk, 24-hour room service, twice-daily maid service, *New York Times Fax* available daily. Out at the beach, snorkeling, windsurfing, and canoes are free; you'll pay for diving, lagoon excursions, and island tours.

✪ **Moana Beach Parkroyal.** B.P. 156, Vaitape, Bora Bora (east side of Matira Point). ☎ **800/346-6262** or 60.49.00. Fax 60.49.99. www.tahiti-resorts.com. E-mail: borabora@ parkroyal.pf. 41 bungalows. MINIBAR TV TEL. 53,900CFP–78,400CFP ($539–$784). AE, DC, MC, V.

This deluxe resort stands out for its 30 exquisitely crafted over-water bungalows. These were the first in which you can remove the tops of their glass coffee tables and actually feed the fish swimming in the turquoise lagoon below. A Japanese-style sliding wall separates the king-size bed from the lounge area; the bathroom has two sinks and an American-size tub; and you can bake on a private deck with steps leading down to the lagoon. Bedside tables have built-in stereo tape players. Ashore on Point Matira, 11 beachside bungalows are less enchanting, but like the over-water units, they have Raiatea and Tahaa in their lagoon views. Also beside the beach, a circular thatch-roofed building surrounding a small courtyard houses the reception area, a lounge complete with a TV equipped to play any type of videotape, and the restaurant and bar, both with outdoor seating. Canoes, sailboards, and other toys are available at the beach.

Dining/Diversions: The airy, beachside dining room offers very fine French selections, with emphasis on seafood. A Tahitian string band entertains every evening.

Amenities: Swimming pool; water sports, including scuba diving and waterskiing; activities and car-rental desks; boutique; laundry; baby-sitting; room service (delivered to over-water bungalows by canoe); twice-daily maid service.

EXPENSIVE

Club Méditerranée Bora Bora. B.P. 34, Vaitape, Bora Bora (north of Matira Point on the east side). ☎ **800/258-2633**, 60.46.04, or 42.96.99 in Papeete. Fax 42.16.83. 150 units. A/C TEL. 17,200CFP–21,800CFP ($172–$218) per person. Rates include all meals with wine and most activities. AE, DC, MC, V.

Lush tropical gardens provide the setting for this Club Med beside the northeastern end of Matira Beach. Behind it, the round-island road climbs up the interior hills, which provide a backdrop. The focus of attention is a large thatch-roofed beachside pavilion housing a reception area, bar, dining room, and nightclub. Guests pay extra for scuba diving, but all meals and a wide range of water-sports activities are included in the rates. Considering the prices elsewhere on Bora Bora, that makes the Club the best value here. There's a pool, two lighted tennis courts, an archery range, and a place to practice your golf swing. Accommodation is in a mix of stand-alone and duplex bungalows and 2-story, motel-style buildings. The air-conditioned beachfront bungalows are the preferred—and most expensive—choice here, especially for honeymooners and others seeking a degree of privacy. The rooms are comfortably if minimally furnished (their most interesting feature: lights shining up from their tile floors). If you don't have a roommate, one of the same sex may be assigned.

Hotel Matira. B.P. 31, Bora Bora (on Matira Beach, south of Hotel Bora Bora). ☎ **67.70.51** or 67.78.58. Fax 67.77.02. E-mail: matira@mail.pf. 20 units. 22,000CFP–37,000CFP ($220–$370). AE, MC, V.

The reception desk is just inside Matira Bar and Restaurant (see "Dining," below), which serves as headquarters for this collection of bungalows on and near the beach. All units have thatch roofs, timber sides, porches on the front, shower-only bathrooms, refrigerators, coffeemakers, and a double bed or two singles. The most expensive bungalows have Japanese-style sliding walls separating sleeping and living areas. Four units are on the beach adjacent to the restaurant, but these are subject to road noise. The rest are about 500 meters away on Matira Point, a much more preferable location. Ask for a discount if you book directly with the hotel.

✪ **Le Maitai Polynesia.** B.P. 505, Vaitape, Bora Bora (north of Matira Point on east side). ☎ **60.30.00.** Fax 67.66.03. E-mail: maitaibo@mail.pf. 55 units. A/C MINIBAR TV TEL. 21,000CFP ($210) double room; 28,350–37,800CFP ($283.50–$378) bungalow. AE, DC, MC, V.

Back in the early 1990s, I spoke with Pauline Youseff, who then had her Village Pauline hostel and campground on this spot (see below). Pauline looked over her prime location, right on Matira Beach between the Moana Beach Parkroyal and Sofitel Marara Coralia resorts, and promised to put up a moderately priced hotel (moderate by Bora Bora's inflated standards, that is). She moved the campground in 1996, and with help from investors taking advantage of French Polynesia's hotel-promoting tax laws, she opened this modern hotel in 1998. The round-island road runs through the property, separating the beach and bungalows from the thatch-roofed main building and hotel rooms. Wedged between the shore and a cliff, the grounds are cramped but festooned with tropical plants. The beach in front of the resort is tiny, too, but canoes and some other water sports equipment sit along a longer stretch of sand bordering the property.

The 28 medium-size, air-conditioned hotel rooms are among the best buys on Bora Bora. They occupy 2-story blocks behind the main building. Units on the upper floor have at least partial lagoon views from their balconies, but downstairs you'll be looking at the hotel's kitchen. Inside, they all have kings or two double beds, writing desks, chairs, and safes. Opaque windows swing open from the bedroom to reveal sizeable bathrooms with showers, hair dryers, some toiletries, and teak-trimmed vanities. Across the road, seven beach- and 10 over-water bungalows are virtually identical, with thatch roofs, polished wood floors, mat-lined walls, ceiling fans, porches or over-water decks, and ample bathrooms with showers. About 300 meters (328 yards) north of the property, 10 "villa suites" are actually thatch-roofed houses with separate bedrooms and kitchens with doors opening to covered porches. The villas aren't on the beach, but they are well suited for small families. You'll have to do without face towels and coffeemakers, which aren't provided here.

Dining/Diversions: In the main building, the Haere Mai dining room serves breakfast, lunch, and dinner, and several other restaurants are within an easy walk. The Manuia Bar serves libation and hosts Tahitian musicians.

Amenities: Baby-sitting, limited room service, laundry, water-sports equipment.

HOSTELS & CAMPING

It's difficult to get a reservation since local French residents love its beachside location on the peninsula leading to Matira Point, but the pension-style **Chez Nono,** B.P. 282, Vaitape, Bora Bora (☎ **67.71.38;** fax 67.74.27), has simple rooms, bungalows, and an apartment starting at 6,000CFP ($60) for a double. Expect to share a bathroom here.

Although inconveniently located near Anau village on the east coast, **Chez Stillo,** B.P. 267, Vaitape, Bora Bora (☎ **67.71.32**), has the island's only beachside campsites. They cost 1,000CFP ($10) per night per camper.

Village Pauline. B.P. 215, Vaitape, Bora Bora (0.5 mile north of Hotel Bora Bora). ☎ **67.72.16.** Fax 67.78.14. 30 tent sites, 8 dorm beds, 7 units (none with bathroom), 5 bungalows. 1,800CFP ($18) tent site; 2,500CFP ($25) dorm bed; 6,000CFP ($60) double; 9,000CFP ($90) bungalow. MC, V.

Pauline Youseff has a variety of no-frills accommodations at her very popular place, one of the better hostels in the South Pacific. It sits in tropical gardens across the road from a beach and is the only accommodation here in any price range with a view of Mount Otemanu's tombstone, albeit through towering palms. Pauline's bungalows have hot-water showers, kitchens, and front porches with tables and chairs. Budget travelers can pitch a tent in the yard, sleep in an eight-bed dormitory building, or elect a simple garden room with a window; they all share communal toilets, showers, and a kitchen. All buildings have thatched roofs. A "Fare Tourisme" books tours and excursions and rents bikes and sea kayaks.

DINING

The local *roulottes* roll out on and near Vaitape wharf after dark. See "Dining" in chapter 4 for details about the food wagons, which offer the only inexpensive meals on Bora Bora.

EXPENSIVE

✪ **Bloody Mary's Restaurant & Bar.** Matira, 1km (0.6 mile) north of Hotel Bora Bora. ☎ **67.72.86.** Reservations recommended. Lunch 900CFP–1,400CFP ($9–$14); main courses 2,400CFP–4,000CFP ($24–$40). MC, V. Mon–Sat 11am–3pm and 6:30–9:30pm. Bar Mon–Sat 10am–9:30pm. SEAFOOD/STEAKS.

You won't be far wrong if you think Bloody Mary's looks like a set for a South Seas movie, because stage hands who worked on the 1977 flop *Hurricane* stayed around to build the charming structure. Ceiling fans, colored spotlights, and stalks of dried bamboo dangle from a large thatch roof over a floor of fine white sand (it's perfectly all right to take off your shoes). The butcher-block tables are made of coconut-palm lumber, and the seats are sections of palm trunks cut into stools.

Just don't expect gourmet cuisine, for Bloody's is essentially a barbecued seafood and steak restaurant. Come here for an evening of fun, as many famous souls have done (their photos are on a board out by the road). You'll be shown the fish and beef laid out on a bed of ice. The chef will charbroil your selection and serve it with a salad, vegetables, and your choice of sauce on the side. The cozy bar here is one of the few places on Bora Bora where American expats regularly hang out. The lunch menu consists of burgers, fish and chips, and salads, which are not served at dinner. Guests get free transportation from hotels if they reserve by 5pm.

MODERATE

Bamboo House. Matira, 1.5km (1 mile) north of Hotel Bora Bora. ☎ **67.76.24.** Reservations advised. Burgers 850CFP–1,500CFP ($8–$15); main courses 1,400CFP–2,800CFP ($14–$28). AE, MC, V. Daily 11:30am–2pm and 6:30–8:30pm. FRENCH/SEAFOOD.

That's exactly what this little place is: a bamboo house, and a charming one at that. The entire building is made of varnished split bamboo, and lots of dried bamboo leaves are stacked or hung here and there to render a jungly effect. Prime tables are on a small front porch, where you can watch the passing scene on the main road. The menu depends on what seafood is caught in local waters but usually features parrot fish, tuna, and shrimp, all well prepared in French sauces. Lunch offers beef and mahimahi burgers, salads, and pastas in addition to the regular main courses. Free transportation is provided from the hotels by reservation. Like Bloody Mary's, it has a rogues' gallery of famous faces pasted on a roadside board.

La Bounty. Matira, east side in hotel district. ☎ **67.70.43.** Reservations recommended. Pizza and pasta 900CFP–1,450CFP ($9–$14.50); main courses 1,200CFP–1,950CFP ($12–$19.50). MC, V. Tues–Sun 11:30am–2pm and 6:30–9pm. FRENCH/ITALIAN.

Chef Eric Fadier has been providing the island's best pizza and other reasonably priced Italian (and French) fare under this L-shaped thatch roof since 1993. The pies make an ample meal for one person or can be shared as an appetizer. His spaghetti and tagliatelle are tasty, too, with smoked salmon, carbonara, alfredo, Neapolitan, blue cheese, or seafood sauces. Steaks and fish come under French sauces such as mustard or creamy vanilla. I was pleased with local shrimp in a whiskey sauce made piquant by thinly sliced onions. Pizzas come quickly here, but everything else is prepared to order and takes longer. It's excellent quality for the price, however, so the wait is worth it.

✪ Chez Ben's. Matira, between Hotel Bora Bora and Matira Point. ☎ **67.74.54.** Sandwiches and salads 500CFP–900CFP ($5–$9); pizzas and meals 1,000CFP–2,100CFP ($10–$21). AE, MC, V. Sun, Mon, Thurs 11am–8pm; Tues, Wed, Sat 11am–5pm. SNACK BAR/PIZZA.

Bora Bora–born Ben Teraitepo and Oklahoma-born wife Robin hold forth at this lunch, afternoon snack, and early dinner spot, under a lean-to tin roof just across the road from a shady portion of Matira Beach. Ben's fresh tuna salad sandwiches and Robin's "Italian Stuff" (pizzas and pastas) fall into the delicious category. They also serve sandwiches, unusually spicy poisson cru, tacos, and fajitas. They will even deliver. Ben and Robin will shoo the dogs and cats away if they bother you. While not inexpensive on the global scale, their prices are a fraction of what you'll pay at the nearby Hotel Bora Bora.

Matira Bar and Restaurant. In Hotel Matira, 1 mile south of Hotel Bora Bora. ☎ **67.70.51.** Reservations recommended. Main courses 1,000CFP–1,600CFP ($10–$16). AE, MC, V. Daily 7–10am, 11am–2pm, and 6–9pm. CANTONESE.

Literally hanging over the beach, this restaurant is an excellent place to have a lagoon-side lunch, sunset drink, or good Chinese meal without completely breaking the bank. The menu offers a selection of beef, pork, chicken, duck, and seafood dishes done in the Cantonese fashion, with Hakka overtones (Tahiti's first Chinese immigrants came from the Hakka region of the mainland).

Te Manuata. Matira, in hotel district opposite Magasin Temerii. ☎ **67.75.61.** Reservations recommended at dinner, accepted at lunch. Lunch 800CFP–1,500CFP ($8–$15); main courses 1,400CFP–2,100CFP ($14–$21). MC, V. Mon–Sat 11:30am–2pm and 6:30–9:30pm, Sun 7–10am. FRENCH/CHINESE.

This small, Tahitian-owned restaurant with bamboo walls and a thatch roof is a favorite with the locals, especially at lunch when a special menu (almost hidden in the back of the *carte)* offers poisson cru, sandwiches, juicy burgers, omelets, and steak or chicken with French fries. Or you can opt for a main course, most of them French treatments of seafood. As an intriguing alternative, fresh tuna is cooked with a choice of islandy vanilla, pineapple, or coconut sauces. Only breakfast is offered on Sunday.

INEXPENSIVE

L'Appetisserie. North of Vaitape wharf, in Centre Commercial le Pahia. ☎ **67.78.88.** Reservations not accepted. Pastries and sandwiches 200CFP–750CFP ($2–$7.50); meals 1,350CFP ($13.50). No credit cards. FRENCH/PASTRIES.

French pastry chef Mark André was trying to sell this popular spot during my last visit, but if he's still here, you'll get fabulous croissants, tarts, quiches, sandwiches, pizzas by the slice, or a French-style *plat du jour,* all at extraordinarily reasonable prices for the high quality. Order at the counter and the staff will deliver to tables inside the shop or umbrellas out on the shopping center sidewalk. There's a computer terminal here for checking your e-mail (see "Fast Facts: Bora Bora," above).

ISLAND NIGHTS

As on Moorea, things are really quiet on Bora Bora after dark. You may want to listen to a Tahitian band playing at sunset or watch the furious hips in a Tahitian dance show. If so, you will be limited to whatever is going on at the resorts (see "Accommodations," above, for their general entertainment schemes). Remember that schedules change; call ahead.

La Récife Discothèque (☎ 67.73.87), about 1 kilometer (0.6 mile) north of Vaitape, is the island's one nightclub, and it opens only on Fridays and Saturdays at 11pm (that's right, 11pm) and closes at 3am (or later) the following mornings. The clientele are mostly Tahitians between 18 and 24 years old, and fights have been known to break out at that late hour. Admission is 500CFP ($5), although women get in free on Friday. Beers cost at least 500CFP ($5) each.

2 Huahine

The first of the Leeward Islands northwest of Tahiti, mountainous Huahine is the third most beautiful island here, behind Moorea and Bora Bora. It's notable for its Bora Bora-like beaches and Mooreaesque bays and basaltic thumbs sticking up atop steep cliffs. It also has ancient maraes, a picturesque main town, and independent-spirited residents whose main livelihood is farming. As the least developed of the islands with luxury hotels and comfortable hostels, Huahine offers one of the territory's best opportunities to observe Polynesian life relatively unchanged by fast-paced Western civilization.

Pronounced *Wa-EE-nee* by the French and *Who-a-HEE-nay* by the Tahitians, Huahine actually is two islands enclosed by the same reef and joined by a bridge. About 4,000 people live on the two islands, and most of them earn a living growing cantaloupes and watermelons and harvesting copra for the Papeete market. Huahine was not annexed by France until 1897—more than 50 years after Tahiti was taken over—and its people are still independent in spirit. At the time the first Europeans arrived, Huahine was governed as a single chiefdom and not divided into warring tribes as were the other islands, and this spirit of unity is still strong. Pouvanaa a Oopa, the great leader of French Polynesia's independence movement, was born on Huahine.

The ancient chiefs built a series of maraes on the shores of Lake Fauna Nui, which separates the north shore from a long, motu-like peninsula, and on Matairea Hill above the lakeside village of Maeva. These have been restored and are some of the most impressive in French Polynesia.

The main village of Fare, hardly more than a row of Chinese stores opposite a wharf, is nestled alongside the lagoon on the northwest shore, opposite the main pass in the reef. When the inter-island boats put in from Papeete, Fare comes to life before the crack of dawn—or long before. Trucks and buses arrive from all over Huahine with passengers and cargo bound for the other islands. The rest of the time, however, Fare lives at the lazy, slow pace of the South Seas of old as a few people amble down its tree-lined main street and browse through the Chinese general stores facing the town wharf.

GETTING AROUND

The airport is on the peninsula paralleling the north side of the island, 3 kilometers (2 miles) from Fare. Unless you have previously reserved a rental car or are willing to walk into Fare, take your hotel minibus. At other times, **Enite's Taxi** (☎ **68.82.37**) will carry you around.

Europcar has an agency on the main road in Fare (☎ **800/227-7368** or 68.82.59). Rates start at 5,800CFP ($58) for 4 hours, 7,900CFP ($79) for 24 hours. Scooters cost 4,900CFP ($49) for 4 hours, 5,800CFP ($58) for all day and overnight. Mountain bikes run 1,100CFP ($11) for 4 hours, 1,900CFP ($19) for 24 hours. You'll pay about the same at **Avis** (☎ **800/230-4898** or 68.73.34).

Huahine's major roadways are paved, but drive very carefully on the gravel sections, especially the *traversière,* which traverses the mountains from Maroe Bay to Faie Bay on the east coast. Other than during periods of heavy rain, this road is passable but is very steep and rough; travelers have died trying to ride bicycles down it. The island's only gasoline stations are in the center of Fare.

Each district has its *le truck,* which runs into Fare at least once a day, but the schedules are highly irregular. If you take one from Fare to Parea, for example, you may not be able to get back on the same day.

FAST FACTS: HUAHINE

Currency Exchange   Banque Socredo is in Fare, on the road that parallels the main street and bypasses the waterfront. Banque de Tahiti and most other businesses are along Fare's waterfront. Both have ATMs.

Doctor   The government infirmary is in Fare (☎ **68.82.48**).

Drugstore   The pharmacist at the drugstore opposite the town wharf speaks English (☎ **68.80.90**). Open Monday through Friday from 7:30 to 11:30am and 2 to 5pm, Saturday from 7:30 to 11:30am.

E-mail   There're no e-mail connections here other than your hotel's computer.

Police   The phone number of the gendarmerie in Fare is **68.82.61.**

Post Office   The colonial-style post office is in Fare, on the bypass road opposite the Hotel Bali Hai entrance. Hours are Monday through Thursday from 7:30am to 3pm, Friday from 7am to 2pm. There are telecarte phones outside on the veranda.

Safety   Campers have reported thefts from their tents on Huahine, so don't camp.

EXPLORING HUAHINE
✪ TOURING THE MARAES

You can visit the many 16th-century maraes near the village of Maeva on your own, or your hotel can arrange a guided tour. Start east of Maeva village, where the large, reed-sided meetinghouse sits over Lake Fauna Nui. The stones sitting at the lake's edge and scattered through the adjacent coconut grove were family maraes. More than 200 stone structures have been discovered between there and Matairea Hill, which looms over Maeva, including some 40 maraes (the others were houses, paddocks, and agricultural terraces). Of six maraes and other structures on Matairea Hill, some were built as fortifications during the 1844–48 French-Tahitian war. The track up the hill can be muddy and slippery during wet weather, and the steep climb is best done in early morning or late afternoon.

A large marae that is easier to reach stands on the beach about half a mile across the bridge on the east end of Maeva. To find it, follow the left fork in the dirt road after crossing the bridge. The setting is impressive.

From the bridge you will see several stone fish traps, which were restored by Dr. Yoshiko H. Sinoto, the chairman of the anthropology department of the Bernice P. Bishop Museum in Honolulu and the man responsible for restoring many maraes throughout Polynesia. They work as well today as they did in the 16th century, trapping fish as the tide ebbs and flows in and out of the narrow passage separating the lake from the sea.

When construction began on the now defunct Hotel Bali Hai Huahine on the north side of Fare in 1973, workers discovered some old artifacts while excavating the lily ponds. Dr. Yoshiko just happened to be on the island and took charge of further excavations. During the next two years the diggers uncovered adzes, fishhooks, and ornaments that had been undisturbed for more than 1,000 years, according to radiocarbon dating of a whale bone found with the other items. So far it's the earliest evidence of habitation found in the Society Islands.

HORSEBACK RIDING, DIVING & OTHER OUTDOOR PURSUITS

La Petite Ferme ("The Little Farm," ☎ **68.82.98**), on the main road north of Fare, just before the airport turnoff, has Marquesas-bred horses that can be ridden with English or western saddles along the beach and around Lake Fauna Nui. Prices start at 5,700CFP ($57) for half a day. They also organize 2- and 3-day horseback camping trips into Huahine's interior.

Huahine Discover Tours, at the Fare wharf (☎ **68.75.45**), will take you on a photo safari into the island's mountainous interior by more modern means: a four-wheel-drive vehicle. These half-day adventures also visit a pearl farm and cost 3,500CFP ($35) per person. **Huahine Land** (☎ **68.89.21**) does the same trip for 4,000CFP ($40) per person. Book at any hotel activities desk.

Pacific Blue Adventures (☎ **68.87.21;** fax 68.80.71), the local scuba dive operator whose office is on the Fare wharf, charges 5,500CFP ($55) for a one-tank dive. The guide often feeds the sharks and pets the moray eels.

Vaipua Cruise (☎ **68.86.42**) offers all-day motu picnic trips by outrigger canoe for 5,000CFP ($50) per person.

Huahine

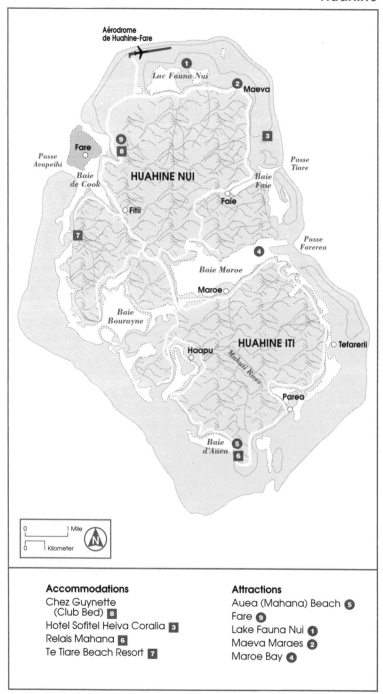

Aérodrome
de Huahine-Fare

Lac Fauna Nui

①

② **Maeva**

③

*Passe
Avapeihi*

Fare

⑨
⑧

*Baie
de Cook*

HUAHINE NUI

○**Fitii**

Faie ○

*Baie
Faie*

*Passe
Tiare*

⑦

④

*Passe
Farerea*

Baie Maroe

Maroe○

*Baie
Bourayne*

HUAHINE ITI

○**Tefarerii**

Haapu○

Mahuti River

Parea
○

*Baie
d'Aüea*

⑤
⑥

0   1 Mile
0   1 Kilometer

Ⓝ

Accommodations
Chez Guynette
  (Club Bed) **⑧**
Hotel Sofitel Heiva Coralia **③**
Relais Mahana **⑥**
Te Tiare Beach Resort **⑦**

Attractions
Auea (Mahana) Beach **⑤**
Fare **⑨**
Lake Fauna Nui **①**
Maeva Maraes **②**
Maroe Bay **④**

ACCOMMODATIONS

The former Bali Hai Huahine is closed, but plans were underway to build an Outrigger hotel on the site, just north of Fare's business district.

RESORTS

Hotel Sofitel Heiva Coralia. B.P. 38, Fare, Huahine (on Maeva Motu, 10km [6 miles] from airport). ☎ **800/763-4835**, 68.85.86, 41.04.04 in Papeete. Fax 41.05.05. www.accor-hotels. com. 24 units, plus 29 bungalows. MINIBAR TEL. 22,500CFP ($250) double room; 32,000–60,000 ($320–$600) double bungalow. AE, DC, ME, V.

Spiffed up recently, this resort sits at the end of Maeva Motu, the flat almost-island joined to the mainland by a one-lane bridge. A large, airy, thatch-roofed central building opens to adult and children's swimming pools, which are necessary here since erosion has taken away much of the white-sand beach. Still, the property enjoys views of the speckled lagoon and Huahine's green mountains beyond. Guests can engage in water sports on the lagoon or set off on jet-ski, canoe, and archaeological excursions. The spacious duplex or stand-alone bungalows are tropically furnished with bamboo chairs and tables, and they all have ceiling fans, wooden floors, coffeemakers, and bathrooms with large showers. Each has sliding doors opening to a covered porch. The pick are the six over-water models joined to the shore by a curving pier; they have glass panels for fish watching and balconies with steps to the lagoon. Although in long buildings and not as private, the rooms are as spacious and well-equipped as the bungalows.

Dining/Diversions: The dining room, known as the Omai Restaurant in honor of the Tahitian who went to London with Capt. James Cook, specializes in French cuisine and offers abundant buffets twice a week when the staff performs traditional Tahitian dances. The bar provides libation.

Amenities: Children's and adults' swimming pools, water sports equipment, scuba diving, double-hull canoe with glass bottom for lagoon excursions, air-conditioned TV-video lounge, boutique, small library, laundry, baby-sitting.

✪ **Relais Mahana.** B.P. 30, Fare, Huahine (on Avera Bay near Huahine's south end). ☎ **68.81.54.** Fax 68.85.08. 22 bungalows. 18,400CFP–20,500CFP ($184–$205). AE, DC, MC, V.

This pleasant but relatively remote property offers one of the best beach-lagoon combinations in the entire South Pacific, for it sits right on the long white beach stretching down the peninsula on Huahine's south end. A pier from the main building runs out over a giant coral head, around which fish and guests swim. The peninsula blocks the brunt of the southeast trade winds, so the lagoon is usually as smooth as glass. Just climb down off the pier and step right in or go for a ride on a paddleboat.

The family-owned Mahana has bungalows directly on the beachfront or with views of the water; all have shingle roofs, one double or two single beds, ceiling fans, bathrooms with showers (very hot water), and porches. The only drawback is that the solid walls inhibit ventilation.

Dining/Diversions: Excellent French-style meals are served in the dining room. One evening a week sees Tahitian entertainment.

Amenities: Swimming pool with bar, video lounge, Laundromat, tennis court, table tennis, rental bikes, and water-sports equipment (including kayaks, canoes, and paddleboats).

✪ **Te Tiare Beach Resort.** B.P. 36, Fare, Huahine (in Fiiti District, 20 min. by boat from Fare). ☎ **888/600-8455** or 60.60.50. Fax 60.60.51. www.spmhotels.com. E-mail: tetiarebeach@mail.pf. 40 units. A/C MINIBAR TV TEL. 26,000CFP–52,000CFP ($260–$520). AE, DC, MC, V.

Rudy Markmiller made a fortune in the overnight courier business in California and then spent more than a decade—and a sizeable chunk of his loot—building Huahine's best luxury resort, which opened in 1999. A land dispute has blocked road access, so guests are ferried here from Fare by fishing boat, which makes this seem like a remote off-shore resort. You will land at a thatch-roofed, over-water structure housing reception, lounge, bar, and dining room. A long pier connects this central complex to a westward-facing white-sand beach with gorgeous sunsets over Raiatea and Tahaa out on the horizon. The lagoon gets deep quickly here, making for excellent swimming and snorkeling over coral heads close to shore. A friendly Tahitian staff fluent in both French and English provides personalized service.

The 40 spacious bungalows all have thatch roofs; terra-cotta tile floors; remote-control TVs and air conditioners; king beds; high-quality rattan sofas, easy chairs, and writing tables; coffeemakers; walk-in dressing rooms with built-in chests of drawers; huge L-shaped decks, one half of them under thatch roofs); and enormous bathrooms equipped with tubs, separate showers, water closets, hair dryers, and robes. Steps lead into the lagoon from the decks of the 16 over-water bungalows, which have spa tubs in their bathrooms. Six other units sit beside the beach, but the 19 garden units (the least expensive here) don't have unimpeded views of the lagoon.

Dining/Diversions: The airy dining room serves excellent international fare, including theme night buffets. (You can ride the resort's launch out here for dinner if you're staying elsewhere—the last trip back is at 11pm). Local musicians perform nightly, and Tahitians arrive by boat to stage dance shows at least once a week, usually on Saturday.

Amenities: You can use canoes, paddleboats, and kayaks, or cool off in a beachside swimming pool equipped with its own bar and activities shack. There's an extra charge to go diving, sailing, fishing, picnicking on a motu, horseback riding, or touring the maraes. Waverunners and waterskiing are available but not in front of the resort. Other amenities are twice-daily maid service, laundry, babysitting, and a boutique.

HOSTELS

Chez Guynette (Club Bed). B.P. 87, Fare, Huahine (opposite the town wharf). ☎ **68.83.75.** 6 units (all with bathroom), 7 bunks. 1,400CFP–1,600CFP ($14–$16) dorm bed; 4,000CFP–4,300CFP ($40–$43) room (higher rates apply to 1-night stays). MC, V.

Marty and Moe Temahahe (wife Marty is American; Moe is Tahitian) bought this friendly place in 1999, enlarged the communal kitchen and lounge, and gave the whole place a good painting and scrubbing. A corridor runs down the center of the building to the kitchen and lounge at the rear. The simple but clean rooms and dorms flank the hallway to either side. The rooms are screened and have ceiling fans and bathrooms with cold-water showers. The dorms also have ceiling fans; they share two toilets and showers. The Temahahes offer breakfast, lunch (sandwiches, salads, poisson cru), wine, and beer out on their streetside patio.

DINING

Huahine's version of *les roulottes* gather on the Fare wharf when boats are in port. See "Dining" in chapter 4.

The best place in town for a lagoonside sunset drink is **Snack Te Manava,** at the north end of the wharf (☎ **68.89.31**), where you can also get snacks and meals.

✪ **Restaurant Tiare Tipanie.** Fare, north end between wharf and bypass road. ☎ **68.80.52.** Reservations accepted. Burgers and light meals 500CFP–1,000CFP ($5–$10); main courses 1,000CFP–1,700CFP ($10–$17); 3-course dinner 2,000CFP ($20). MC, V. Tues–Sat 11:30am–1:45pm; Mon–Sat 6–8:45pm. FRENCH.

Hélène and Phillipe Esteva's establishment on the pleasant veranda of a converted house is the pick here, offering good French fare such as poisson cru, sashimi, and steak in bordelaise sauce. Lunch features omelets, sandwiches, hamburgers, salads, and a daily plat du jour. Their special three-course dinners are a bargain.

3 Raiatea & Tahaa

The mountainous clump of land you can see on the horizon from Huahine or Bora Bora is actually two islands, Raiatea and Tahaa, which are enclosed by a single barrier reef. Cruising yachts can circumnavigate Tahaa without leaving the lagoon, and Huahine and Bora Bora are relatively easy hauls from here. Accordingly, this is one of the South Pacific's two great yacht-chartering centers. There are no beaches on either Raiatea or Tahaa, and except for sailing and cruise ship visits, tourism is not an important part of their economies, which are based on agricultural produce and, in the case of Raiatea, government salaries.

Raiatea, the largest island in the Leeward Group, is by far the more important of the two, both in terms of the past and the present. In the old days Raiatea was the religious center of all the Society Islands, including Tahiti. Polynesian mythology has it that Oro, the god of war and fertility, was born in Mount Temahani, the extinct flat-top volcano that towers over the northern part of Raiatea. Taputapuatea, on its southeast coast, was at one time the most important marae in the islands. Legend also has it that the great Polynesian voyagers who discovered and colonized Hawaii and New Zealand left from there. Archaeological discoveries have substantiated the link with Hawaii.

Today Raiatea (pop. 7,000) is still important as the economic and administrative center of the Leeward Islands. Next to Papeete, the town of Uturoa (pop. 3,500) is the largest settlement and is one of the most important transportation hubs in French Polynesia. Uturoa's waterfront has undergone a major transformation of late, with a big new cruise ship terminal and welcome center now dominating the town wharf.

Tahaa (pronounced "Tah-ah-ah") is much smaller than Raiatea in terms of land area, population (about 1,500), and the height of its terrain. It's a lovely island, with a few very small villages sitting deep in bays that cut into its hills. Other than sailors, few visitors see it, and those who do make day tours from Raiatea.

GETTING AROUND

The Raiatea airstrip is 3 kilometers (2 miles) north of Uturoa. You will have to rent a vehicle or take a taxi, for there is no regular public transportation system on Raiatea and no public transport whatsoever on Tahaa. Nor is there an airport on Tahaa.

The *Uporu* (☎ 65.67.10) runs between Uturoa and Tahaa's west coast, with departures from Uturoa Monday through Friday, usually at 6:45am, 11am, and 3pm, and Saturday at 11am. Fares are about 800CFP ($8) one-way, 1,200CFP ($12) return. Water-taxi service is available at **Apooiti Marina** (☎ 66.13.48); rides cost between 1,500CFP and 2,500CFP ($15 to $25), depending on where you're going.

There are no regular *le trucks* on Raiatea, but some leave the outlying villages for Uturoa at the crack of dawn and return in the afternoon. They gather around the market on the waterfront in the heart of town. Asking around is the only way to find out when they leave, where they go, and when (and whether) they return to Uturoa.

Avis (☎ **800/230-4898** or 66.34.35) and **Europcar** (☎ **800/227-7368** or 66.34.06) both have rental-car offices here. Prices range from 5,300CFP ($53) for 4 hours to 8,056CFP ($80.50) a day, including insurance and unlimited kilometers. Europcar also has an office on Tahaa (☎ **65.67.00**), so you can take the *Uporu* there, rent a car, and drive around the island.

There is a taxi stand near the market in Uturoa, or contact **René Guilloux** (☎ 66.31.40), **Marona Teanini** (☎ 66.34.62), or **Apia Tehope** (☎ 66.36.41). Fares are about 600CFP ($6) from the airport to town and 1,200CFP ($12) to the Hotel Hawaiki Nui.

FAST FACTS: RAIATEA & TAHAA

Bookstores   Librairie d'Uturoa (☎ 66.30.80) on the inland side of the main street, in the center of town, carries French books and magazines.

Currency Exchange   French Polynesia's three banks have offices on Uturoa's main street. **Banque Socredo** next to the municipal market has an ATM. There is no bank on Tahaa.

Drugstores   **Pharmacie de Raiatea** (☎ 66.34.44) in Uturoa carries French products.

E-mail   There're no e-mail connections here other than your hotel's computer.

Emergencies   See "Police," below.

Hospitals   Opposite the post office, the hospital at Uturoa (☎ 66.32.92) serves all the Leeward Islands. Tahaa has an infirmary at Patio (☎ 65.63.31). Private physicians and dentists practice in Uturoa; ask your hotel for a recommendation.

Information   The local tourism committee has a tourist information office in Uturoa in the new cruise ship center (☎ 66.23.33). The friendly, English-speaking staff is quite helpful. Usual hours are Monday through Friday from 8 to 11:30am and 1:30 to 4pm.

Police   The telephone number of the Uturoa gendarmerie is ☎ 66.31.07. On Tahaa, the gendarmerie is at Patio, the administrative center, on the north coast (☎ 65.64.07).

Post Office   The post and telecommunications office is in a modern building north of Uturoa on the main road (as opposed to a new road that runs along the shore of reclaimed land on the north side of town) and is open Monday through Thursday from 7:30am to 3pm, Friday from 7am to 2pm, and Saturday from 8 to 10am. There are telecarte phones outside.

EXPLORING RAIATEA & TAHAA

Highlights of a visit to Raiatea include day trips to and around Tahaa, picnics on small islands on the outer reef, canoe adventures up the Faaroa River (French Polynesia's only navigable river), and hikes into the mountains to see the *tiare apetahi,* a one-sided white flower found nowhere else on earth. Legend says that the five delicate petals are the fingers of a beautiful Polynesian girl who fell in love with a prince but couldn't marry him because of her low birth. Just before she died heartbroken in her lover's arms, she promised to give him her hand to caress each day throughout eternity. At daybreak each morning, accordingly, the five petals pop open.

✪ **TAPUTAPUATEA MARAE**   On the outskirts of Opoa village 35 kilometers (21 miles) south of Uturoa, the **Taputapuatea Marae** is one of the most sacred locations in all of Polynesia, for legend says Opoa Pass offshore was the departure point for the discovery and settlement of both Hawaii and New Zealand. The large marae on the site actually was built centuries later by the Tamatoa family of chiefs. Vying for supremacy, the Tamatoas mingled religion with politics by creating Oro, the ferocious god of war and fertility supposedly born on Mount Temehani, and by spreading his cult. It took almost 200 years, but Oro eventually became the most important god in the region. Likewise, the Tamatoas became the most powerful chiefs. They were on the verge of conquering all of the Society Islands when the missionaries arrived in 1797. With the Christians' help, Pomare I became king of Tahiti, and the great marae the

Tamatoas built for Oro was soon left to ruin, replaced by the lovely Protestant church nearby in Opoa village.

The marae was restored once in the 1960s, and the Tahiti Museum began an even more extensive rehabilitation in 1994. The museum's archaeologists have discovered human bones under some of the structures, apparently the remains of sacrifices to Oro. The marae's huge *ahu,* or raised altar of stones for the gods, is more than 50 yards long, 10 yards wide, and 3.5 yards tall. Flat rocks, used as backrests for the chiefs and priests, still stand in the courtyard in front of the ahu. The entire complex is in a coconut grove on the shore of the lagoon, opposite a pass in the reef, and legend says that bonfires on the marae guided canoes through the reef at night.

Taputapuatea is worth a visit, not only for the marae itself but for the scenery there and along the way. The road skirts the southeast coast and follows Faaroa Bay to the mouth of the river, then back out to the lagoon.

SEEING UTUROA   A stroll through Uturoa will show you what Papeete must have been like a few generations ago. A number of Chinese stores line the main street, which parallels the waterfront a block inland, but Raiatea is not the place to shop except for handcrafts made on Tahaa (check the vendors' stalls on the harbor side of the city park for pareus and handcrafts, including brassieres made of two polished coconut shells). The market on the waterfront is busiest when the inter-island boats arrive.

The road beside the gendarmerie, just north of downtown Uturoa, leads to a trail that ascends to the television towers atop 970-foot-tall **Papioi Hill.** The view from the top includes Uturoa, the reef, and the islands of Tahaa, Bora Bora, and Huahine. Another trail begins with a jeep track about 200 yards south of the bridge, at the head of Pufau Bay on the northwest coast. It leads up to the plateau atop **Mount Temehani.** The mountain itself actually is divided in two by a deep gorge.

ORGANIZED TOURS & SAFARI EXPEDITIONS   Try to avoid days when cruise ships are in port, since their passengers can monopolize all shore-based activities here.

American Bill Kolans of ✪ **Almost Paradise Tours** (☎ **66.23.64**) has lived on Raiatea since sailing his boat down from Hawaii in 1979. He leads road expeditions to Taputapuatea and other archaeological sites, and provides very informative commentary about the history and culture of the islands (his is the only such English-language tour here). His 3-hour island tour costs 4,000CFP ($40) per person.

Take your pick between **Raiatea 4x4** (☎ **66.24.16**) and **Jeep Safari Raiatea** (☎ **66.15.73**), two French-owned companies which will take you into the island's interior via four-wheel-drive Jeep. Both have two trips a day, require reservations a day in advance, and charge 5,000CFP ($50) per person.

LAGOON OUTINGS, DIVING & OTHER OUTDOOR PURSUITS

If you can put together your own group (because a minimum of four persons is required), you can take a variety of **Lagoon Excursions** and see firsthand the Raiatea-Tahaa lagoon, one of the most beautiful in French Polynesia. All trips include snorkeling, and most include picnics on tiny islets sitting on the outer reef; unlike the mainland part of Raiatea, they have beautiful white-sand beaches. Book at your hotel or call Roselyne and Andrew Brotherson at **Manava Excursions** (☎ **66.28.26**), which charges 4,000CFP ($40) per person for an all-day trip to Tahaa, including visits to a vanilla plantation and pearl farm, a picnic on a motu, and snorkeling over a coral garden. It also has a half-day boat trip up the Faaroa River and on to the Taputapuatea marae. Roselyne speaks pretty good English; Andrew's is passable.

The Moorings (☎ **66.35.93**) and **Stardust Marine** (☎ **66.23.18**), charter sailboat operators, are based on Raiatea (see "Seeing the Islands by Cruise Ship & Yacht," in Chapter 3). If a boat is available, it can be chartered on a daily basis. Arrangements for longer charters ordinarily should be made before leaving home.

Raiatea may not have beaches, but the reef and lagoon are excellent for scuba diving. Based at Apooiti Marina, **Hémisphère Sub Raiatea** (☎ **66.12.49**; fax 66.28.63) takes divers on one-tank excursions for about 5,500CFP ($55).

ACCOMMODATIONS

HOTELS

✪ **Raiatea Pearl Resort.** B.P. 43, Uturoa, Raiatea (2km [1.2 miles] south of town). ☎ **607/ 273-5012** or 66.20.23. Fax 66.20.20. www.spmhotels.com. E-mail: h.raiateapearl@mail.pf. 32 units. MINIBAR TV TEL. 14,000CFP ($140) double room, 18,000CFP–32,000CFP ($180–$320) double bungalow. AE, DC, MC, V.

Formerly known as the Hotel Hawaiki Nui, and before that as the Hotel Bali Hai Raiatea, the island's best hotel sits on a narrow site wedged between the road and lagoon. The friendly and helpful staff speaks English, but the ambiance is definitely French. Like everywhere else on Raiatea, there is no beach, but eight over-water bungalows extend out over the clifflike reef face. The other bungalows, some of which have two units under their thatch roofs, are either along the seawall or in the gardens beyond. The least expensive units here are hotel rooms, which have the same amenities as the bungalows. A pier extends out to a dock from which you can climb into the water and get the sensation of flying as you snorkel along the face of the reef.

Dining: Opening to a lagoonside pool, the dining room offers excellent French cuisine.

Amenities: Facilities include tennis courts, snorkeling gear, table tennis, and an activities desk that will arrange scuba diving, and lagoon and historical tours.

✪ **Sunset Beach Motel.** B.P. 397, Uturoa, Raiatea (in Apooiti, 5km [3 miles] northwest of Uturoa). ☎ **66.33.47.** Fax 66.33.08. E-mail: sunsetbeach@mail.pf. 21 bungalows, 25 campsites. TV. 8,000CFP ($80) double bungalow; 1,100CFP ($11) per person campsite. MC, V.

One of the best values in French Polynesia for guests wanting to do their own cooking, this property occupies a coconut grove on a skinny peninsula sticking out west of the airport. The bungalows sit in a row just off a palm-draped beach. The lagoon here is very shallow, but the beach enjoys a gorgeous westward view toward Bora Bora. The lagoon excursion companies pick up their guests off a long pier that stretches to deep water (guests can paddle canoes or water-ski from it). Although of European construction rather than Polynesian, the modern bungalows are spacious, are comfortably furnished, and have fully equipped kitchens and TVs with the local French-language channels. Each has a large front porch with lagoon view. Solar panels provide hot water for cleaning and showering. Part of the grove is set aside for campers, who have their own building with toilets, showers, and kitchen. Manager-owner Eliane Boubée and her son Moana both speak English.

HOSTELS & CAMPING

Pension Manava. B.P. 559, Uturoa, Raiatea (6km [3.5 miles] south of town). ☎ **66.28.26.** 4 bungalows (all with bathroom), 2 units (none with bathroom). 4,000CFP ($40) double room; 6,000CFP ($60) bungalow with kitchen; 5,000CFP ($50) bungalow without kitchen. No credit cards.

Roselyne and Andrew Brotherson rent two rooms in their house and have four simple bungalows in their gardens, across the road from the lagoon. Both rooms share a bathroom and the Brotherson's kitchen. The bungalows have corrugated tin roofs, louvered windows, double and single beds, and large baths with hot-water showers. Two also have kitchens. Roselyne will cook breakfast and provide free dinner transportation to town on request.

Peter's Place. Avera, Raiatea (6km [3.7 miles] south of Uturoa). ☎ **66.20.01.** 8 units. 1,200CFP–1,400CFP ($12–$14) per person in units; 800CFP ($8) campsite per person (higher rates for stays of 1 night). No credit cards.

Backpackers will find a home in Peter Brotherson's simple and basic rooms in a plywood building, or they can pitch a tent in his expansive front yard across the road from the lagoon. Everyone shares communal toilets, hot-water showers, and a kitchen under its own thatch-line tin roof. Peter organizes tours to the marae and hiking expeditions to a plantation and waterfall in a valley behind his place. Guests get free use of canoes.

DINING

Raiatea's version of Papeete's *les roulottes* congregate after dark at the market in the middle of Uturoa's business district. They stay open past midnight on Friday and Saturday.

Club House. Apooiti Marina, 4.5km (3 miles) north of Uturoa. ☎ **66.11.66.** Reservations recommended for dinner. Snacks 650CFP–1,250CFP ($6.50–$12.50); main courses 1,200CFP–2,600CFP ($12–$26). MC, V. Daily 9am–2pm and 5–10:30pm. FRENCH/ITALIAN.

You'll find yachties sipping cold brews under this big, L-shaped Polynesian-style building next to the boats moored in Apooiti Marina, the local base for The Moorings charter company. An outrigger canoe hanging from the ceiling and lights inside bamboo Tahitian fish traps help set a romantic mood for seafood and steaks in French sauces, or Italian-style pastas. A mixture of seafood in a rich creamy tomato sauce over spaghetti didn't disappoint. A snack menu offers salads and omelets, or you can order simple grilled chicken served with French fries. Chicken cooked in Coca-Cola is also offered, but your guess is as good as mine as to what that tastes like.

Restaurant Moana. Main street, Uturoa (upstairs in Léogite Building, opposite market). ☎ **66.35.33.** Reservations recommended weekend evenings. Main courses 900CFP–1,800CFP ($9–$18). AE, MC, V. Tues–Sun 10:30am–1:30pm and 6:30–9:30pm. CHINESE.

Proprietor Alphonse Léogite lived in the United States for 15 years before returning home to Raiatea and opening this excellent establishment in Uturoa's business district. He uses chrome chairs, potted plants, and linen tablecloths to set an urbane ambiance for good Chinese cuisine. Most items on the menu will be familiar, but you can ask for sea cucumber steamed with ginger and served with pork and vegetables. If that's not on hand, try seafood prepared with shredded taro. The restaurant undergoes a metamorphosis and becomes Le Zenith discothèque at 10pm on Friday, Saturday, and Sunday.

Snack Moemoea. Waterfront, Uturoa (in Toporo Building). ☎ **66.39.84.** Sandwiches 300CFP–550CFP ($3–$5.50); main courses 1,100CFP–1,600CFP ($11–$16). No credit cards. Mon–Fri 6am–5pm, Sat 6am–2pm. SNACKS/FRENCH/CHINESE.

While there are several snack bars open for breakfast and lunch near the Uturoa market, this is far and away the most pleasant of the lot. The old corner storefront has tables both outside on the sidewalk and inside on the ground floor or on a mezzanine platform. The menu includes casse-croûte sandwiches and fine hamburgers, excellent poisson cru, grilled fish, and steaks.

ISLAND NIGHTS

Except for string bands playing each evening at the Raiatea Pearl Resort (see "Accommodations," above), only weekend nights come alive in Uturoa, and that's only because **Restaurant Moana** (☎ 66.35.33) turns itself into Le Zenith discotheque at 10pm on Fridays and Saturdays. Cover charges are 1,000CFP ($10), drinks cost 500CFP ($5) and up. See "Dining," above.

4 Rangiroa

The largest and most often visited of the great chain of atolls known as the Tuamotu Archipelago, Rangiroa lies 312 kilometers (194 miles) northeast of Tahiti. It consists of a ring of low, skinny islets enclosing a tadpole-shaped lagoon more than 46 miles long and 14 miles wide. That's wide enough so that when you stand on one side of the lagoon, you cannot see the other. In fact, the entire island of Tahiti could be placed in Rangiroa's lagoon, with room left over.

The islets are so low—never more than 10 feet above sea level, not including the height of the coconut palms growing all over them—that ships can't see them until they're a few miles away. For this reason, Rangiroa and its sisters in the Tuamotus are also known as the Dangerous Archipelago. Hundreds of yachts and ships have been wrecked on these reefs, either unable to see them until it was too late or dragged ashore by tricky currents.

Rangiroa has two navigable passes into its interior lagoon, and currents of up to 6 knots race through them as the tides first fill the lagoon and then empty it during their never-ending cycle. Even at slack tide, watching the coral rocks pass a few feet under your yacht is a tense experience. Once inside the lagoon, however, you anchor in a huge bathtub whose crystal-clear water is stocked with an incredible amount and variety of sea life (including a multitude of large sharks and manta rays).

Most visitors come to Rangiroa primarily for the territory's best scuba diving and snorkeling. Others venture across the lagoon to Rangiroa's islets, where they can literally get away from civilization at a very remote resort.

GETTING AROUND

Rangiroa's airstrip and most of its hotels and pensions lie on a perfectly flat, 7-mile-long island on the north side of the lagoon. The airport is about equidistant from the village of Avatoru on the west end and Tiputa Pass on the east. The hotels and pensions send buses or vans to meet their guests.

Europcar (☎ 800/227-7368 or 96.08.28) has an agency near Avatoru and a desk at the Kia Ora Village (see "Accommodations," below). Open-air "Fun Cars" (the most you'll need here) range from 2,500CFP ($25) for 1 hour to 5,000CFP ($50) for half a day (as long as you'll need to see the islet). Scooters range from 2,500CFP ($25) for 1 hour to 5,500CFP ($55) for all day. Bicycles cost 500CFP ($5) for half a day.

For a taxi, call **Rangi Tour Service** (☎ 96.03.28).

FAST FACTS: RANGIROA

Currency Exchange   Banque de Tahiti has a branch in Avatoru. It's open Monday through Wednesday from 8 to 11:30am and 2 to 4pm, Thursday from 1:30 to 4pm, and Friday from 8 to 11:30am and 1:30 to 4pm.

E-mail   There're no e-mail connections here other than your hotel's computer.

Hospitals   There are infirmaries at Avatoru (☎ 96.03.75) and across the pass at Tiputa (☎ 96.03.96).

Photographic Needs   For film, check the boutique at the Hotel Kia Ora Village. You won't get overnight processing here.

Post Office   The small post office in Avatoru is open Monday through Thursday from 7am to 3pm, Friday 7am to 2pm. There's a telecarte phone outside.

Water   Except at Kia Ora Village, the tap water is brackish. Don't drink it.

LAGOON EXCURSIONS & SCUBA DIVING

Except for walks around Avatoru and Tiputa, typical Tuamotuan villages with white-washed churches and stone walls lining the main streets, plan on either doing nothing or enjoying the fantastic lagoon. The hotels and pensions either have or can arrange **lagoon excursions** by boat. One favorite destination is the so-called *Lagon Bleu* (Blue Lagoon), an area of colorful corals and plentiful sea life. These are not inexpensive—plan on paying 10,000CFP ($100) or more for a full day's outing.

The best **scuba diving** here is from December to March, when huge hammerhead sharks gather off Tiputa Pass for their mating season, and when the manta rays look for mates between July and October. You can see gray and black-tipped sharks all year. But be aware that dives here are deeper and longer when compared to American standards, so bring your own buddy and be prepared to stretch the limits of the dive tables in order to see the magnificent sea life. Divers must be certified in advance and bring their medical certificates.

Any of the hotels or pensions can arrange scuba dives. My traveling companion went with **Raie Manta Club** (☎ **96.04.80**), which operates from the Hotel Kia Ora Village and from a base near Avatoru. All equipment is included in the price, but she was issued a leaky buoyancy compensator and a regulator without depth or pressure gauges, so bring your own if you can. Also, inflatable boats are used, so there'll be no shade. (Frankly, the Manihi Pearl Beach Resort has much better boats and equipment; see below.) Both Raie Manta and **Rangiroa Paradive** (☎ **96.05.55**), another operator based at Chez Glorine pension at Tiputa Pass, charge about 5,500CFP ($55) per dive, including all equipment.

ACCOMMODATIONS

Kia Ora Sauvage. B.P. 4607, Papeete, Tahiti (hotel is 1-hour boat ride from airport). ☎ **96.02.22**, or 800/763-4845. Fax 96.02.02. 5 bungalows. 34,000CFP ($340) double. Meals 7,000CFP ($70) per person per day. AE, DC, MC, V.

This outpost offers one of the South Pacific's most remote Robinson Crusoe–like escapes. Guests are transferred daily by a 1-hour speedboat ride from Hotel Kia Ora Village, which manages this retreat. Once there, you will find a thatched main building, where the Tahitian staff cooks up the day's catch, often caught during the guests' lagoon excursions. Accommodations are in five comfortable bungalows built entirely of native materials. They have their own modern bathrooms. Round-trip boat transfers cost 7,500CFP ($75) per person.

Kia Ora Village. B.P. 4607, Papeete, Tahiti (3km [2 miles] east of airport, near east end of island). ☎ **96.02.22**, or 800/763-4835. Fax 96.02.20. 58 units. A/C MINIBAR. 20,000CFP–51,000CFP ($200–$510) double. Meals 7,000CFP ($70) per person per day. AE, DC, MC, V.

This romantic establishment has been Rangiroa's premier hotel for more than 2 decades, and it has gotten better in recent years. Its thatch-roofed buildings look like a Polynesian village set in a coconut grove directly on the lagoon. The Japanese owners (they're the Coca-Cola distributors in Tokyo) have built a big new thatch roof over a main building housing reception and activities desks, a games room, and day-use

At Rangiroa you pick up a hundred natives with pigs, guitars, breadfruit and babies. They sleep on deck, right outside your bunk, and some of them sing all night.
                                                                    —James A. Michener, 1951

facilities for guests coming and going from Kia Ora Sauvage (see above). Guests here are mainly European and Japanese couples, plus some American divers.

White sand has been hauled over from the ocean side of the island, but the beach still is a bit rocky; however, a long pier reaches out into deep water for excellent swimming and snorkeling. Ten bungalows sit over the reef and share the sunsets. Recent additions include 2-story beachside bungalows with air conditioned bedrooms downstairs and up, and 1-story models with only the downstairs bedroom. All these additions have whirlpool tubs set in their partially covered front decks. Some of the much smaller original bungalows have been left as less expensive "garden" models. All units have modern bathrooms, refrigerators that can be stocked on request, ceiling fans, and sliding doors to decks or porches.

Dining/Diversions: A beachside open-air dining room serves primarily French fare (you'll need to buy the meal plan here), and a bar sitting over the lagoon provides spectacular sunsets. Local villagers stage Tahitian dance shows once a week, but otherwise there's no nighttime diversions here.

Amenities: A wide range of water sports equipment and activities is available, including a wild ride in snorkeling gear on the riptide through Tiputa Pass. Guests pay about 13,000CFP ($130) each for all-day lagoon excursions to the famous "Pink Sands" and "Blue Lagoon" (both are on opposite side of the lagoon, an hour's boat ride away). The hotel also arranges much less expensive tours to Avatoru and boat trips to Tiputa village across the pass. Rental bikes and scooters are available from Europcar on the premises.

Raira Lagoon Hotel & Restaurant. B.P. 87, Avatoru, Rangiroa (5 minutes from airport). ☎ **96.04.23.** Fax 96.05.86. www.rairalagon.com. E-mail: rairalag@mail.pf. 10 bungalows. 11,000CFP ($110) per person. Rates include all meals. AE, MC, V.

The pick of Rangiroa's pensions, this pleasant establishment has basic but comfortable thatch-roofed bungalows equipped with ceiling fans, tiled baths with cold-water showers, reading lights, and front porches with chairs. A lagoonside thatch pavilion has a bar and restaurant serving French food (many guests are French residents of Tahiti). The hotel has Fun Cars, scooters, and bikes to rent.

5 Manihi

Known for its black pearl farms, Manihi lies 520 kilometers (312 miles) northeast of Tahiti in the Tuamotus. Although not nearly as large or as deep as Rangiroa's, its clear lagoon is a better place to dive among colorful tropical fish, as opposed to the multitudinous rays and sharks which make diving at Rangiroa so exciting. Tairapa Pass, the main entry into the lagoon, is wider and deeper than those at Ranigroa, but it has a strong enough current to make "riding the rip" snorkeling trips a highlight here.

French Polynesia's pearl farming industry started here in the late 1960s, and the farms seem to sit atop every coral head dotting the lagoon. Most of the workers stay in Turipaoa, the only village here.

Gilles Petrie's **Manihi Blue Nui Dive Center,** based at the Manihi Pearl Beach Resort, the only hotel here (see below), is the best in French Polynesia, with top-of-the-line equipment and hard-topped boats with ladders. It charges about 6,000CFP ($60) per dive, and it teaches certification courses.

ACCOMMODATIONS & DINING

✪ **Manihi Pearl Beach Resort.** B.P. 2460, Papeete, Tahiti. ☎ **607/273-5012,** 43.16.10 for reservations, or 96.42.73. Fax 43.17.86 for reservations or 96.42.72. www.spmhotels.com. E-mail: manihipearlbeach@mail.pf. 41 units. MINIBAR TEL. 28,000CFP–46,000CFP ($280–$460) double. Meals 8,400CFP ($84) per person per day. AE, DC, MC. V.

You'll be as remote as you can get in French Polynesia at this comfortable and friendly resort, the only one on Manihi. Only it and the airstrip occupy a motu on the western end of the lagoon. Like at Rangiroa, the beach here is more pebbly than sandy, so most guests sun themselves on little islets equipped with palm trees and chaise lounges, or on a faux beach beside a lagoonside horizon pool.

The prevailing trade winds can generate a choppy lagoon under the 19 over-water bungalows here. Both the over-water and beachside units have mat-lined walls, natural wood floors, ceiling fans hanging from thatch roofs, king-size beds, writing tables, stocked refrigerators, coffeemakers, ample shower-only bathrooms, and covered porches with two recliners. Beachfront units also have hammocks strung between two palm trees out front, and their bathrooms are outdoors under thatch roofs and behind high wooden walls.

Most guests here are American couples, to whom the English-speaking Tahitian staff renders excellent service.

Dining/Diversions: A big A-frame thatch roof covers the dining area, which serves often exceptional and always good French fare. Tahitians do their dances twice a week. A thatch-roof bar adjacent to the pool is cozy and conducive to meeting your fellow guests.

Amenities: Games room with library and videos, pearl shop, boutique, and Manihi Blue Dive Center (see above). In addition to diving, activities include swimming, snorkeling (you can ride the rip tide through the pass), canoeing, visiting pearl farms and the village, lagoon and deep-sea fishing, spending a day on a deserted motu, cruising at sunset, billiards, and board games.

Rarotonga & the Cook Islands

7

Perhaps it's the rugged beauty, rivaling that of the more famous Tahiti. Maybe it's the warmth and friendliness of a proud Polynesian people who love to talk about their islands, and do so in English. It could be the old South Seas charm of a small island nation whose little capital is like Papeete was a very long time ago. Whatever the reason, there are few old South Pacific hands who aren't absolutely enraptured with Rarotonga and the other Cook Islands. As soon as you get there, you'll see why the local tourist authority wasn't far wrong in calling the country "Heaven on Earth."

The Cook Islanders have more than beautiful islands in common with the people of French Polynesia, some 900 kilometers (550 miles) to the east. They share with the Tahitians about 60% of their native language, and their lifestyles and religions were similar in the old days. Like many Tahitians, they have a keen interest in their eastern Polynesian past, but they are better at showing it off, at explaining to visitors both the old ways and the new.

They also enjoy having a good time, and this lust for happiness very quickly rubs off on visitors. With tourism their primary industry, the Cook Islanders offer a surprising lot to do in their very small islands, from swimming in the lagoon to climbing to the top of the rocky outcrop known as "The Needle" to crawling from one charming pub to another. Indeed, no other place in the South Pacific has so much to see and do in so small a space.

And you don't have to spend a fortune once you get here, for the Cook Islands are at least 40% less expensive than Tahiti and French Polynesia.

1 The Cook Islands Today

Rarotonga and the other 14 Cook Islands are tiny specks scattered between Tahiti and Samoa in an ocean area about a third the size of the continental United States, yet all together they comprise only 93 square miles of land. Rarotonga is by far the largest, with 26 of those square miles, yet it is only 32 kilometers (20 miles) around. A microcosm of modern Polynesia, Rarotonga has enough island activities to satisfy almost anyone, whether it's snorkeling, shopping, sightseeing, scuba diving, or several other pastimes. Its cultural tours are the best in the South Pacific.

THE NATURAL ENVIRONMENT   The Cook Islands are divided both geographically and politically into a Southern and a Northern Group. Most of the nine islands of the Southern Group, including Rarotonga, are volcanic, with lush mountains or hills. The islands of the remote Northern Group, except Nassau, are typical atolls, with circles of reef and low coral islands enclosing central lagoons. The sandy soil and scarce rainfall support coconut palms, scrub bush, and a handful of people. Although they can be reached by air, the remote Northern Group receives few visitors.

   Rarotonga, the only high, mountainous island, is in many ways a miniature Tahiti: It has jagged peaks and steep valleys surrounded by a flat coastal plain, white sandy beaches, an azure lagoon, and a reef extending about a quarter of a mile offshore. In most places the shoreline consists of a slightly raised sandy bar backed by a swampy depression, which then gives rise to the valleys and mountains. Before the coming of missionaries in 1823, Rarotongans lived on the raised ground beyond the swampy flats, which they used for growing taro and other wet-footed crops. They built a remarkable road, actually paved in part with stones, from village to village almost around the island. That "back road" still exists, although the paved round-island road now runs near the shore. The area between the two roads appears to be bush but is in fact heavily cultivated with a plethora of crops and fruit trees.

   While Rarotonga masquerades as a small version of Tahiti, **Aitutaki** plays the role of Bora Bora in the Cook Islands. Although lacking the spectacular mountains that Bora Bora has, little Aitutaki is nearly surrounded by a large, shallow lagoon whose multi-hued beauty and abundant sea life rival those of its French Polynesian counterpart and make this charming, atoll-framed outpost the second most-visited of the Cooks.

   The vegetation of the southern islands is typically tropical: The mountains and hills are covered with native brush, while the valley floors and flat coastal plains are studded with coconut and banana plantations and a wide range of flowering trees and shrubs.

GOVERNMENT   The Cook Islands have a Westminster-style parliament with 25 elected members led by a prime minister. Parliament meets twice a year, in February and March and from July to September. There is also a House of Ariki (hereditary chiefs), which advises the government on matters of traditional custom and land tenure. Each island has an elected Island Council and a Chief Administrative Officer, who is appointed by the prime minister.

THE ECONOMY   The economy is based on tourism and agriculture, mainly tropical fruit and fruit juices. Some revenue is derived from the Cook Islands' status as a tax-free haven. Without overseas aid, cash sent home by islanders living abroad, and the money earned from tourism, however, the country would be in serious financial trouble. In fact, it ran into a great deal of difficulty in the mid-1990s when the debt-ridden government failed to back its local currency with adequate New Zealand dollars, thus rendering the local money worthless. When foreign lending organizations forced the government to mend its ways (see "History 101," below), expenditures were drastically reduced and more than half of all government workers were fired. Before the cutbacks, more than 3,300 islanders—almost 20% of the total population—were civil servants. Overseas traders now insist on being paid in New Zealand dollars, which

---

Impressions

If I could vacation on only one Pacific island I would choose Rarotonga. It's as beautiful as Tahiti, much quieter, much stuffier and the food is even worse. But the climate is better and the natives are less deteriorated.

                                                                    —James A. Michener, 1951

is why your credit card statement will refer to Avarua as being in New Zealand. Many Cook Islanders pulled up stakes and left for New Zealand, resulting in a decrease in the islands' population.

2 History 101

Legend says that the first Polynesians arrived in the Cook Islands by canoe from the islands of modern-day French Polynesia about A.D. 1200, although anthropologists think the first of them may have come much earlier. In any event, they discovered the Cook Islands as part of the great Polynesian migrations that settled all of the South Pacific long before the Spanish explorer Alvaro de Mendaña laid the first European eyes on any of the Cook Islands when he discovered Pukapuka in 1595.

The Spanish at that time were more interested in getting from Peru to the riches of Manila than in general exploration. Thus, except for Rakahanga, which was discovered by Pedro Fernández de Quirós during a voyage along the same general route in 1606, the islands did not appear on European maps for another 170 years.

And then, as happened in so many South Pacific island groups, along came Capt. James Cook, who stumbled onto some of the islands during his voyages in 1773 and 1777; he named them the Hervey Islands. In 1824 the name was changed to the Cook Islands by the Russian cartographer John von Krusenstern.

Captain Cook sailed around the Southern Group but missed Rarotonga, which apparently was visited first by the mutineers of H.M.S. *Bounty,* under Fletcher Christian. There is no official record of the visit, but oral history on Rarotonga has it that a great ship arrived offshore about the time of the mutiny. A Cook Islander visited the ship and was given some oranges, the seeds of which became the foundation for the island's citrus industry.

When the first Europeans arrived, the local Polynesians were governed by feudal chiefs, who owned all the land within their jurisdictions and held life-and-death power over their subjects. Like other Polynesians, they believed in a hierarchy of gods and spirits, among them Tangaroa, whose well-endowed carved image is now a leading handcraft item.

MORE MISSIONARIES   The man who claimed to have discovered Rarotonga was the same man who brought Christianity to the Cook Islands, the Rev. John Williams of the London Missionary Society. Williams had come from London to Tahiti in 1818 as a missionary, and he soon set up a base of operations on Raiatea in the Society Islands, from which he intended to spread Christianity throughout the South Pacific. He

Dateline

- **A.D. 1200** First Polynesians arrive.
- **1595** Mendaña discovers Pukapuka.
- **1606** De Quirós finds Rakahanga.
- **1773–77** Capt. James Cook discovers more islands, names them the Hervey Islands.
- **1789** Capt. Bligh finds Aitutaki shortly before mutiny on the *Bounty.*
- **1790** *Bounty* mutineers probably visit Rarotonga.
- **1814** American sandalwood trader discovers Rarotonga.
- **1821** Tahitian missionaries convert Aitutaki to Christianity.
- **1823** Rev. John Williams rediscovers Rarotonga, lands missionaries.
- **1824** Missionaries divide Rarotonga into five villages.
- **1863** William Marsters starts unique family with three wives on Palmerston Island.
- **1888** Residents on Manihiki trick French warship into turning away; Britain declares protectorate.
- **1901** Cook Islands included in boundaries of newly independent New Zealand.
- **1942** U.S. troops build airstrip on Aitutaki.
- **1965** Cook Islands become independent in association with New Zealand. Sir Albert Henry elected first prime minister.
- **1974** Queen Elizabeth II dedicates new Rarotonga International Airport. Islands opened to tourists.

continues

- 1978 Sir Albert Henry indicted, stripped of knighthood.
- 1989 Geoffrey Henry, Sir Albert's cousin, becomes prime minister.
- 1990 Rarotonga gets television.
- 1992 Rarotonga hosts South Pacific Arts Festival, adding public buildings and infrastructure.
- 1994 Sheraton Hotel project goes bust.
- 1995 Cook Islands dollar becomes virtually worthless in New Zealand.
- 1996 International lenders force reduction in number and pay of civil servants; economy nosedives.
- 1999 Sir Geoffrey Henry loses parliamentary majority, steps down as prime minister.

set his sights on the Hervey Islands after a canoeload of Polynesians from there was blown by a storm to Raiatea. They were receptive to Williams's teachings and asked that missionaries be sent to the Herveys.

In 1821 Williams went to Sydney and on the way dropped two teachers at Aitutaki. One of them was a Tahitian named Papeiha. By the time Williams returned two years later, Papeiha had converted the entire island. Pleased with this success, Williams and a new missionary named Charles Pitman headed off in search of Rarotonga. It took a few weeks, during which Williams stopped at Mangaia, Mauke, Mitiaro, and Atiu, but he eventually found it in July 1823. Until the day he died years later in a cannibal's oven in Vanuatu, Williams insisted he had discovered Rarotonga—never mind the inconvenient fact that the *Bounty* mutineers were there or that an American sandalwood trader almost certainly stopped on the island in 1814.

Williams, Pitman, and Papeiha were joined in 1824 by Aaron Buzacott, another missionary. Pitman soon left for the village of Ngatangiia on the east coast, Papeiha went to Arorangi in the west, and Buzacott took over in Avarua in the north. Williams spent most of the next 4 years using forced native labor to build a new ship, *The Messenger of Peace,* and eventually sailed it west in search of new islands and more converts.

Meanwhile, the missionaries quickly converted the Cook Islanders. They overcame the powerful feudal chiefs, known as *ariki,* whose titles but not their power have been handed down to their present-day heirs. On Rarotonga, the missionaries divided the island into five villages and split the land into rectangular parcels, one for each family. Choice parcels were set aside for the church buildings and rectories. Rarotongans moved down from the high ground near their gardens and became seaside dwellers for the first time.

The religion the missionaries taught was rock-ribbed and puritanical. They blamed the misdeeds of the people for every misfortune, from the epidemics of Western diseases that came with the arrival of more Europeans to the hurricanes that destroyed crops. They preached against sexual permissiveness and cut off the hair of wayward women. The Rarotongans took it all in stride. Whenever the missionaries would shear a woman's locks, she would appear in public wearing a crown of flowers and continue on her merry way. For the most part, however, the transition to Christianity was easy, since in their old religion the Rarotongans, like most Polynesians, believed in a single, all-powerful Tangaroa, who ruled over lesser gods.

Out of the seeds planted by Williams and the London Missionary Society grew the present-day Cook Islands Christian Church, to which about 60% of all Cook Islanders belong. The churches, many of them built by the missionaries in the 19th century, are the center of life in every village, and the Takamoa College bible school that the missionaries established in 1837 still exists in Avarua. The Cook Islands Christian Church still owns the land under its buildings; the churches of other denominations sit on leased property.

COMING OF THE KIWIS It was almost inevitable that the Cook Islands would be caught up in the wave of colonial expansion that swept across the South Pacific in

All in the Family

The missionaries weren't the only Englishmen to have a lasting impact on the Cook Islands.

In 1863 a farmhand from Gloucester named William Marsters accepted the job as caretaker of tiny, uninhabited Palmerston Island, an atoll sitting all by itself northwest of Rarotonga. He took his Cook Islander wife and her sister with him. They were joined by a Portuguese sailor and his wife, who was a first cousin of Mrs. Marsters.

The Portuguese sailor skipped the island within a year, leaving his wife behind. Marsters then declared himself a minister of the Anglican church and married himself to both his wife's sister and to her first cousin.

Marsters proceeded to start three families, one with each of his three wives. Within 25 years he had 17 children and 54 grandchildren. He divided the island into three parts, one for each clan, which he designated the "head," "tail," and "middle" families. He prohibited marriages within a clan (in a twist of logic, he apparently thought sleeping with your half-brother or half-sister apparently wasn't incest).

Obviously there was a lot of marrying outside the clans, for today there are uncounted thousands of Marsters in the Cook Islands and New Zealand. All trace their roots to Palmerston Atoll, although only 50 or so live there.

William Marsters died in 1899 at the age of 78. He is buried on Palmerston near his finely crafted homestead.

the late 1800s. The French, who had established Tahiti as a protectorate, wanted to expand their influence west, and in 1888 a French warship was sent to Manihiki in the Northern Group of the Cooks. The locals quickly sewed together a British Union Jack and ran it up a pole. The French ship turned away. Shortly thereafter the British declared a protectorate over the Cook Islands, and the Union Jack went up officially.

The islands were small and unproductive, and in 1901 Britain gladly acceded to a request from New Zealand's Prime Minister, Richard Seddon, to include the Cook Islands within the boundaries of his newly independent country. In addition to engineering the transfer, Seddon is best remembered in the Cook Islands for his vehement hatred of the Chinese. He instituted the policy that has effectively barred the Chinese—and most other Asians, for that matter—from the Cook Islands to this day.

Otherwise, New Zealand, itself a former colony, was never interested in becoming a colonial power, and the Kiwis never did much to exploit—or develop—the Cook Islands or Western Samoa (over which they exercised a League of Nations trusteeship from the end of World War I until 1962). For all practical purposes, the Cook Islands remained a South Seas backwater for the 72 years of New Zealand rule, with a brief interlude during World War II when U.S. troops built and manned an airstrip on Aitutaki.

SIR ALBERT GETS THE BOOT   The situation began to change after 1965, when the Cook Islands became self-governing in association with New Zealand. Under this arrangement, New Zealand provides for the national defense needs of the islands and renders substantial financial aid. There is an official New Zealand "representative" in Avarua, not an ambassador or consul. For all practical purposes, the Cook Islands are independent, although the paper ties with New Zealand deprive them of a seat in the United Nations. The Cook Islanders hold New Zealand citizenship, which means they can live there. New Zealanders, on the other hand, are not citizens of the Cook Islands.

The first prime minister of the newly independent government was Sir Albert Henry, one of the South Pacific's most colorful modern characters. He ruled for a controversial 13 years, during which the Cook Islands were put back on the map.

That came in 1974. Using aid from New Zealand, which wanted to provide an independent source of revenue for its former colony, the government enlarged Rarotonga's airport. Queen Elizabeth II was on hand for the new strip's grand opening. Three years later The Rarotongan Beach Resort opened, and the Cook Islands became an international destination.

Sir Albert ruled until the national elections in 1978. Even though his party won a majority, he and it were indicted for bribery. Allegedly, government funds had been used to pay for charter flights that ferried his party's voters home from New Zealand on election day. The chief justice of the High Court agreed, and Sir Albert and his party were booted out of power. Queen Elizabeth then stripped him of his knighthood. He remained highly popular with his supporters, however, and many Cook Islanders still refer to him as "Sir Albert." When he died in 1981, his body was taken around Rarotonga on the back of a pickup truck, the road lined with mourners.

MORE MONEY, NO MONEY Sir Albert was succeeded by Dr. Tom Davis, who had worked in the United States for the National Aeronautics and Space Administration until returning home. To avoid a repetition of the scandal that caught Sir Albert, he added a seat in Parliament for voters living overseas. The constitution also was amended to include a bill of rights. Davis ruled until 1987, when his own party deposed him in favor of Dr. Pupuke Robati.

The premiership returned to Henry hands in 1989 with the victory of Sir Geoffrey Henry, Sir Albert's cousin. Sir Geoffrey's tenure has been marked by scandal, first when a long-planned and almost-completed Sheraton Hotel project was caught up in a Mafia scandal in Italy. Although there has been talk about reviving the project, the hotel's unfinished buildings stand hauntingly like ancient ruins-in-the-making. Sir Geoffrey also allowed too much Cook Islands currency to be printed, which left it valueless outside the country, and he caught severe criticism for signing letters guaranteeing billions of dollars in loans that the Cook Islands didn't make and can never repay. His government also doubled the government workforce, from some 2,000 employees to more than 3,600—nearly 60% of the total employment here.

International lending organizations cracked the whip in 1996, forcing the debt-strapped government to cut expenses by laying off more than half of the bloated civil service and seriously cutting the salaries of those who remained on the government payroll. Many axed civil servants and other islanders left the country for New Zealand and Australia (the population dropped from an estimated 22,400 to 16,500 between 1995 and 1999). After a close election in 1999, which he apparently had won, Henry stepped aside when members of his own Cook Islands Party switched to the opposition.

3 The Islanders

POPULATION About half of the 16,500 or so people who live in the Cook Islands reside on Rarotonga, and of these, about 4,000 live on the north coast in Avarua, the only town in the country. Some 80% to 85% of the entire population is pure Polynesian. In culture, language, and physical appearance, this great majority is closely akin to both the Tahitians and the Maoris of New Zealand. Only on Pukapuka and Nassau atolls to the far northwest, where the residents are more like the Samoans, is the cultural heritage significantly different.

Impressions

People here honor the Sabbath even more virtuously than Scottish Highlanders, but they also honor Tangaroa, ancient god of fertility, whose well-endowed figure appears on their own one-dollar coin.

—Lawrence Millman, 1990

COOK ISLANDS CULTURE Modern Cook Islanders have maintained much of the old Polynesian way of life, including the warmth, friendliness, and generosity that characterize Polynesians everywhere. Like their ancestors, they put great emphasis on family life. Within the extended family it's share and share alike, and no one ever goes without a meal or a roof over his or her head. In fact, they may be generous to a fault, since many of the small grocery stores they run reputedly stay on the verge of bankruptcy.

Although not a matriarchy, Cook Islands culture places great responsibility on the wife and mother. The early missionaries divided all land into rectangular plots (reserving choice parcels for themselves and their church buildings, of course), and women are in charge of the section upon which their families live. They decide which crops and fruit trees to plant, they collect the money for household expenses, and, acting collectively and within the churches, they decide how the village will be run. The land cannot be sold, only leased, and when the mother dies, it passes jointly to her children. Since many women prefer to build simple homes so as not to set off squabbles among their offspring when they pass away, most houses provide basic shelter and are not constructed with an eye to increasing value. In fact, when a woman dies, the house occasionally is left vacant by succeeding generations.

The burial vaults you will see in many front yards are the final resting places of the mothers who built the houses. Their coffins are sealed in concrete vaults both for sanitary reasons and because to shovel dirt on a woman's dead body is to treat her like an animal. (Likewise, striking a woman is the quickest way for a Cook Islands man to wind up in prison.) The survivors care only for the graves of persons they knew in life, which explains the many overgrown vaults. Eventually, when no one remembers their occupants, the tops of the old vaults will be removed and the ground plowed for a new crop.

Cook Islanders have also retained that old Polynesian tradition known as "island time." The clock moves more slowly here, as it does in other South Pacific Islands. Everything will get done in due course, not necessarily now. So service is often slow by Western standards, but why hurry? You're on vacation.

In addition to those who are pure Polynesian, a significant minority are of mixed European-Polynesian descent. There are also a number of New Zealanders, Australians, Americans, and Europeans, most of whom live on Rarotonga and seem to move to the beat of "island time," too. There are very few Chinese or other Asians in the Cook Islands—thus the relative scarcity of Asian cuisine here.

4 Language

Nearly everyone speaks English, the official language. All signs and notices are written in it. The everyday language for most people, however, is Cook Islands Maori, a Polynesian language similar to Tahitian and New Zealand Maori. A little knowledge of it is helpful, particularly since nearly all place-names are Maori.

Cook Islands Maori has eight consonants and five vowels. The vowels are pronounced in the Roman fashion: *ah, ay, ee, oh, oo* instead of *a, e, i, o, u* as in English. The consonants used are *k, m, n, p, r, t,* and *v.* These are pronounced much as they are in English. There also is *ng,* which is pronounced as the *ng* in "ring." The language is written phonetically; that is, every letter is pronounced. If there are three vowels in a row, each is sounded. The name of Mangaia Island, for example, is pronounced "Mahn-gah-*ee*-ah."

More than likely, Cook Islanders will speak English to all Europeans, but here are some helpful expressions with suggested pronunciations.

English	Maori	Pronunciation
hello	kia orana	kee-ah oh-rah-znah
good-bye	aere ra	ah-*ay*-ray rah
thank you	meitaki	may-ee-*tah*-kee
how are you?	peea koe	*pay*-ay-ah *ko*-ay
yes	ae	*ah*-ay
no	kare	*kah*-ray
good luck	kia manuia	*kee*-ah mah-*nu*-ee-ah
European person	Papa'a	pah-*pah*-ah
wrap-around sarong	pareu	*pah*-ree-oo
keep out	tapu	*tah*-poo
small island	motu	*moh*-too

5 Visitor Information & Entry Requirements

VISITOR INFORMATION

The helpful staff at the **Cook Islands Tourism Corporation** will provide information upon request. The address is P.O. Box 14, Rarotonga, Cook Islands (☎ **29-435;** fax 21-435; www.cook-islands.com; e-mail tourism@cookislands.gov.ck). The main office and visitors center is just west of the traffic circle in the heart of Avarua. Other offices are:

North America: 5757 W. Century Blvd., Suite 660, Los Angeles, CA 90045-6407 (☎ **888/994-COOKS** or 310/641-5621; fax 310/338-0708; e-mail cooks@ itr-aps.com).

New Zealand: 1/127 Symonds St. (P.O. Box 37391), Parnell, Auckland (☎ **09/ 366-1199;** fax 09/309-1876).

Australia: P.O. Box H95, Hurlstone Park, NSW 2193 (☎ **02/9955-0446;** fax 02/9955-0447; e-mail cookislands@altus.speednet.com.au).

Germany: Dirkenstr. 40, 1020 Berlin (☎ **30/23-17628;** fax 30/238-17641).

France: 13 rue d'Alembert, 3800 Grenoble (☎ **476/904-163;** fax 476/182-931).

Belgium: rue Americaine 27, 1050 Brussels (☎ **2/538-2930;** fax 2/538-2885).

You can also get information from the **Tourism Council of the South Pacific** (see "Visitor Information & Entry Requirements" in chapter 2).

Once you get to Rarotonga, visit the Cook Islands Tourism Corporation office and pick up brochures and other current information. The office should have copies of *What's On In The Cook Islands,* the *Cook Islands Sun,* and *Jasons Passport Cook Islands,* three free tourist publications with facts, advertisements, and excellent maps of the islands. The daily newspaper, the *Cook Islands News,* carries radio and TV schedules, weather forecasts, shipping information, and advertisements for island nights and other entertainment.

The New Zealand & U.S. Dollars

At this writing, NZ$1 = approximately $.60, the rate of exchange used to calculate the U.S. dollar prices given in this chapter. This rate may change by the time you visit, so use the following table only as a guide.

NZ$	US$	NZ$	US$
.25	.15	15	9.00
.50	.30	20	12.00
.75	.45	25	15.00
1	.60	30	18.00
2	1.20	35	21.00
3	1.80	40	24.00
4	2.40	45	27.00
5	3.00	50	30.00
6	3.60	75	45.00
7	4.20	100	60.00
8	4.80	125	75.00
9	5.40	150	90.00
10	6.00	200	120.00

If you're heading to the outer islands, check the bookstores for Elliott Smith's guidebook, *Cook Islands Companion*. It's out of date but still has useful information.

ENTRY REQUIREMENTS

Visas are not required for visitors, who can stay for 31 days if they have valid passports, onward or return air tickets (they will be examined at the immigration desk upon arrival), and sufficient funds. Extensions are granted on a month-to-month basis for up to 5 months beyond the initial 31-day visa upon application to the Immigration Department near the airport in Avarua. Visitors intending to stay more than 6 months must apply from their home country to the **Principal Immigration Officer,** Ministry of Labour and Commerce, P.O. Box 61, Rarotonga, Cook Islands.

Customs allowances are 2 liters of spirits or wine, 200 cigarettes or 50 cigars, and NZ$250 ($150) in other goods. Arriving passengers can purchase items from the duty-free shop and change money before clearing Immigration. Firearms, ammunition, and indecent materials are prohibited. So are live animals, including pets (they will be placed in quarantine until you leave the country). Personal effects are not subject to duty. All food and other agricultural products must be declared and will be inspected.

6 Money

The New Zealand dollar is the medium of exchange. Occasionally you will see colorful local notes and unusual coins, such as the triangular $2 piece and the famous Tangaroa dollar. The latter bears the likeness of Tangaroa—well-defined private part and all—on one side and Queen Elizabeth II on the other (the Queen reportedly was not at all pleased about sharing the coin with Tangaroa in all his glory). Both New Zealand and Cook Islands currencies have the same values, but the local currency cannot be exchanged outside the islands.

At the time of this writing, the New Zealand dollar was worth about US70¢, give or take a few cents. The exchange rate is carried in the business sections of most daily newspapers. You also can find the present rate by clicking through the financial section of the *Washington Post* newspaper's Worldwide Web site at **www.washington-post.com.**

HOW TO GET LOCAL CURRENCY **Westpac Bank** has its main office west of the traffic circle on the main road in Avarua. It's open Monday through Friday from 9am to 3pm, Saturday from 9 to 11am. Westpac does not charge a fee to cash traveler's checks.

ANZ Bank is at the rear of the first-floor shopping arcade in the C.I.D.C. House, the large modern structure west of the traffic circle in Avarua (it has wooden stairs ascending in front). It's open Monday through Thursday from 9am to 3pm, Friday from 9am to 4pm. ANZ Bank charges NZ$2 ($1.20) per traveler's check transaction regardless of the amount.

Note: **There are no ATMs in the Cook Islands.** You can get cash advances against your MasterCard and Visa cards, but you'll have to visit the banks during business hours.

If you're going to Aitutaki or another outer island, you can use your credit cards at the larger hotels and some restaurants, but not elsewhere. Accordingly, carry cash or small-denomination traveler's checks, which can be cashed at the post offices.

CREDIT CARDS American Express, MasterCard, and Visa are widely accepted by hotels and restaurants on Rarotonga and Aitutaki, Diners Club less so.

7 When to Go

THE CLIMATE
The islands of the Southern Group, which are about as far south of the equator as the Hawaiian Islands are north, have a very pleasant tropical climate. Even during the summer months of January and February, the high temperatures on Rarotonga average a comfortable 29°C (84°F), and the southeast trade winds usually moderate even the hottest day. The average high drops to 25°C (77°F) during the winter months, from June to August, and the ends of Antarctic cold fronts can bring a few downright chilly nights during those months. It's a good idea to bring a light sweater or jacket for evening wear anytime of the year.

December through April is both the cyclone (hurricane) and rainy season. There always is a chance that a cyclone will wander along during these months, but most of the rain comes in short, heavy cloudbursts that are followed by sunshine. Rain clouds usually hang around Rarotonga's mountain peaks, even during the dry season, from June to August.

In short, there is no bad time weatherwise to visit the Cook Islands, although the "shoulder" months of April, May, September, and October usually provide the best combination of sunshine and warmth.

HOLIDAYS & SEASONS
Legal holidays are New Year's Day, Anzac (Memorial) Day (April 25), Good Friday, Easter Monday, the Queen's Birthday (in June), Gospel Day (July 26 on Rarotonga only), Constitution Day (August 4), Christmas Day, and Boxing Day (December 26).

The busiest season is from late June through August when New Zealanders and Australians escape their own winters. Make your hotel reservations early for these months. Many Cook Islanders live in New Zealand and come home for Christmas; you can easily get a room, but airline seats are hard to come by during that holiday season.

The Cook Islands Calendar of Events

February
- **Arts & Crafts Exhibition.** Original paintings, wood and shell carvings, and coral stone sculptures are featured at this annual show. Second week in February.

April
- ✪ **Dancer of the Year Contest.** Features one of the South Pacific's great traditional dance competitions; villages from all over the country send their young people to Rarotonga to compete for the coveted Dancers of the Year award. Last week in April.
- **Anzac Day.** Cook Islanders killed in the two World Wars are honored with parades and church services. April 25.

August
- ✪ **Constitution Week/Cultural Festival Week.** Honoring the attainment of self-government on August 4, 1965, this biggest Cook Islands celebration is highlighted by a weeklong Polynesian dance contest. The dancing is at its purest and most energetic as each village's team vies for the title of best in the country. There are also parades and sporting events. Begins last Friday in July and runs for 10 days.

September
- **Cook Islands Art Exhibition Week.** Works of local artists and sculptors are displayed at a variety of exhibitions. Second week in September.

October
- **Cook Islands Fashion Week.** Local fashions and accessories are featured at various displays and shows. Third week in October.
- **Gospel Day.** Honors the arrival of the first missionaries and features outdoor religious plays known as *nuku.* Last Sunday in October.

November
- **Round Rarotonga Road Run.** Marathoners race completely around Rarotonga—all 32 kilometers (20 miles) of it. First week in November.
- **Tiare Floral Week.** Shops and offices are ablaze with fresh arrangements, each leading up to a grand finale parade of flower-covered floats. Fourth week of November.

8 Getting There & Getting Around

GETTING THERE

Air New Zealand has a near monopoly on flights to and from the Cook Islands. It flies from Los Angeles to Rarotonga, via either Tahiti or Honolulu. It also has weekly service to Rarotonga from Tahiti and Fiji on its Coral Route, and it has several flights a week between Auckland and Rarotonga. **Canada 3000** operates charter flights between Vancouver and Rarotonga from November through March. For more information, see "Getting There" in chapter 2.

ARRIVING   The small terminal at Rarotonga International Airport, the country's only gateway, is 2.2 kilometers (1.3 miles) west of Avarua. Westpac Bank's terminal office is open 1 hour before and after all international flights; it has windows both inside and outside the departure lounge. Small shops in the departure lounge sell handcrafts, liquor, cigarettes, and stamps. Arriving passengers can purchase duty-free items before clearing Immigration. Air New Zealand and the other airlines have their Rarotonga offices in the terminal.

Transportation from the airport to all the hotels and hostels is by **Raro Tours** bus (☎ **25-325**), which costs NZ$10 to NZ$13 ($6 to $8) per person, depending on how far you're going. In general, taxi fares are NZ$2 ($1.50) per kilometer. See "By Taxi," below.

DEPARTING **Raro Tours** (☎ **25-325**) begins picking up departing passengers about 2 hours before each international flight. Your hotel or guesthouse will reserve a seat for you and tell you when it will arrive at your accommodation. A **departure tax** of NZ$25 ($15) for adults and NZ$12.50 ($7.50) for children between the ages of 2 and 12 is payable in New Zealand or Cook Islands currency. You can pay this in advance at Westpac Bank in Avarua, or prior to clearing immigration at Westpac's airport booth. No tax is imposed for domestic departures.

GETTING AROUND

BY PLANE **Air Rarotonga** (☎ **22-888;** e-mail bookings@airraro.co.ck) has three flights a day (except Sunday) to Aitutaki and one a day to Atiu, Mauke, Mangaia, and Mitiaro. Regular round-trip fares are about NZ$326 ($195.50) to Aitutaki, the most visited island, slightly less to the others in the Southern Group. You can save with Air Rarotonga's off-peak fares, which can be as little as NZ$218 ($131) round-trip to Aitutaki (you must buy your ticket in Rarotonga and fly on the early morning or late afternoon flights).

Air Rarotonga will also book hotels and most activities on the other islands free of charge. You can save as much as NZ$100 ($60) by buying a package of airfare and accommodations.

Don't forget to reconfirm your return flight.

BY BUS When people say "catch the bus" on Rarotonga, they mean the **Cook's Island Bus** (☎ **25-512**), which actually are two buses which leave the Cook's Corner shopping center in Avarua once an hour going clockwise and counter-clockwise around the island, respectively. The have "Cook's Passenger Transport" painted on their sides and run Monday through Friday from 7am to 4pm and Saturday from 8am to 1pm, with less frequent, one-bus evening service Monday through Saturday. The two buses each take 50 minutes to circle the island, arriving back in Avarua in time to start another trip. Get a schedule at the Cook's Corner bus stop or from the Cook Islands Tourism Corporation, or ask your hotel receptionist when a bus will pass. Elsewhere, just wave to get on board. Regardless of the length of the ride, daytime fares are NZ$2.50 ($1.50) one-way, NZ$4 ($2.40) round-trip. You can buy one-day passes for NZ$6 ($3.50) or 10-ride tickets for NZ$17 ($10). The buses cost NZ$4 ($2.40) at night.

Impressions

For my taste, there are few approaches anywhere on this planet more exhilarating than when your plane sweeps down out of the clouds and, suddenly, miraculously, you see the lush green mountains of Rarotonga rising out of the sea like a landscape from a child-hood fairy tale, like a lost world.

—Lawrence Millman, 1990

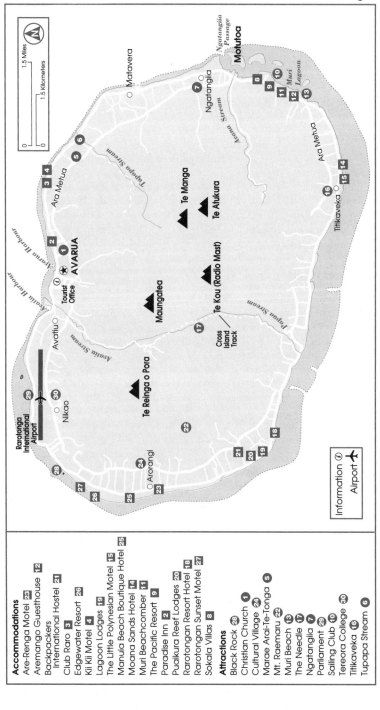

Rarotonga

Motutoa

Ngatangiia Passage

Mataivi

7 Ngatangiia

8
9 10
11
12 13

Muri Lagoon

Aviima Stream

Ara Metua

Te Manga

Te Atukura

14
15 16 Titikaveka

3 4
5 6

Ara Metua

Tupapa Stream

2
1 AVARUA

Avatiu Harbour

Avatiu Stream

ⓘ Tourist Office

Avatiu

Papua Stream

Te Kou (Radio Mast)

Maungatea

17

Cross Island Track

Te Reinga o Pora

22

18

21
20 19

Rarotonga International Airport

29
30
Nikao

28
27
26 25

24 Arorangi
23

Information ⓘ
Airport ✈

Accommodations
Are-Renga Motel 23
Aremango Guesthouse 12
Backpackers
International Hostel 21
Club Raro 3
Edgewater Resort 26
Kii Kii Motel 4
Lagoon Lodges 19
The Little Polynesian Motel 15
Manuia Beach Boutique Hotel 25
Moana Sands Hotel 14
Muri Beachcomber 11
The Pacific Resort 9
Paradise Inn 2
Puaikura Reef Lodges 20
Rarotongan Resort Hotel 18
Rarotongan Sunset Motel 27
Sokala Villas 8

Attractions
Black Rock 28
Christian Church 1
Cultural Village 24
Marae Arai-Te-Tonga 5
Mt. Raemaru 22
Muri Beach 13
The Needle 17
Ngatangiia 7
Parliament 29
Sailing Club 30
Tereora College 16
Titikaveka 15
Tupapa Stream 6

169

BY RENTAL CAR & SCOOTER   I usually rent a car or Jeep from Winton Pickering and the gang at **Budget Rent-A-Car** (☎ **800/527-0700** or 20-895; e-mail rentals@budget.co.ck), whose vehicles are consistently clean and in excellent condition. The main Budget office is in Avarua a block off the main road (behind Ronnie's Bar & Restaurant), or you can rent at a booth west of the traffic circle and at desks at the Edgewater Resort Hotel and Rarotongan Resort Hotel. Cars start at NZ$62 ($37) per day with unlimited kilometers. You will be responsible for the first NZ$1,000 ($700) of any damage. Budget provides free delivery and drop-off at the hotels or airport.

The other firms here are **Avis** (☎ **21-901** or 800/331-1212); **Tipani Rentals** (☎ **22-327** or 22-328); and **Rarotonga Rentals** (☎ **22-326**). In addition, some hotels have cars for rent.

Cook Islanders are as likely to travel by motorbike or scooter as they are by car. **Polynesian Bike Hire Ltd.** (☎ **20-895**) and **Tipani Rentals** (☎ **22-327**) both rent them on a daily or weekly basis. Rates start about NZ$25 ($15) per day. Polynesian Bike Hire Ltd. and Budget Rent-A-Car share offices (see above).

Visitors are required to have a valid Cook Islands **driver's license** before operating any motorized vehicle. To get one, go to Police Headquarters (on the main road just west of the Avarua traffic circle), present your valid overseas license, and pay NZ$10 ($6). It's valid for the same class of vehicles covered by your home-country license. If you want to rent a motorbike or scooter and you aren't licensed to drive them at home, you will have to take a driving test and pay an additional NZ$5 ($3). All drivers must be at least 21 years old. (The laminated license with your photo makes a nice souvenir.) The license desk is open Monday through Friday from 8am to 3pm, Saturday and Sunday from 8am to noon.

Driving is on the left side of the road. The speed limit is 50kmph (30 m.p.h.) in the countryside and 25kmph (15 m.p.h.) in Avarua and the villages. Gasoline (petrol) is available from service stations in Avarua and at some village shops. During my recent visit, petrol cost about NZ$1 (70¢) a liter, or about $2.60 for an American-size gallon. The road around the island is paved but somewhat rough, and drivers must be on the alert at all times for dogs, chickens, potholes, and pigs.

BY BICYCLE   There are no hills on the round-island road, so touring by bicycle (or "push bikes," as they're called here) is a pleasure. Several hotels have bicycles available for their guests to use. **Polynesian Bike Hire Ltd.** (☎ **20-895**), **Tipani Rentals** (☎ **22-327**), and **Terekira Bike Rentals** (☎ **20-331**) have them for NZ$8 ($5) per day. The latter is at Muri Beach.

BY TAXI   There are a number of cars and minibuses scurrying around Rarotonga with "taxi" signs on top. Service is available daily from 7am to midnight and whenever international flights arrive. As a rule of thumb, taxi fares should be about NZ$3 ($1.80) per kilometer, but the drivers are free to set their rates at will. Negotiate a fare before you get in. To call a taxi, phone either **A's Taxi** (☎ **27-021**), **Ngatangiia Taxi** (☎ **22-238**), **BK Taxi** (☎ **20-019**), or **Muri Beach Taxi** (☎ **21-625**).

BY SHIP   "Adventures in Paradise," the 1950s television series, may have glorified the South Pacific "copra schooners" that plied the South Seas trading corned beef and printed cotton for copra, but today's ships operating in the Cook Islands keep erratic schedules. To put it bluntly, you can't count on getting anywhere by ship these days. If you want to see whether any are running, and you don't really care when you get home, check in with the Harbour Office at the wharf in Avatiu. The daily *Cook Islands News* prints the local shipping schedules each morning.

Distances

Here are some distances from the traffic circle in Avarua.

Going East (Clockwise)	Km	Miles
Club Raro	2.4	1.5
Kii Kii Motel	2.8	1.7
Sokala Villas	10.4	6.4
Sailing Club/Pacific Resort	10.7	6.6
Muri Beachcomber	10.9	6.7
Aremango Guesthouse	11.2	6.9
Little Polynesia Motel	14.1	8.7
Moana Sands Hotel	14.3	8.8

Going West (Counterclockwise)s	Km	Miles
Airport terminal	2.2	1.3
Parliament	3.2	2.0
Golf course	5.1	3.1
Rarotongan Sunset Motel	6.3	3.9
Edgewater Resort	6.8	4.2
Dive Rarotonga	7.2	4.4
Manuia Beach Boutique Hotel	8.0	4.8
Are-Renga Motel	8.5	5.2
Puaikura Reef Lodges	11.5	7.1
Lagoon Lodges	13.1	8.0
The Rarotongan Resort	13.5	8.3
Sheraton hotel project	15.0	9.2

Fast Facts: Rarotonga

American Express   There is no American Express representative in the Cook Islands. See "Visitor Information & Entry Requirements" and "Money" in Chapter 2 for how to report lost or stolen American Express credit cards or traveler's checks. The local banks may be able to assist you in reporting lost checks.

Area Code   The international country code for the Cook Islands is **682.**

Baby-Sitters   Contact your hotel reception desk.

Baggage Storage   There are 12 storage lockers just outside the arrivals concourse at the airport. Cost is NZ$3 ($1.80). Most hotels and motels will keep your bags for free.

Bookstores   Bounty Bookshop (☎ **22-660**), in the high-rise C.I.D.B. Building in Avarua, and the **Cook Islands Trading Corporation (C.I.T.C.)** (☎ **22-000**), on the waterfront, both sell paperback novels, maps of Rarotonga and Aitutaki, and books about the Cook Islands and the South Pacific in general. The Bounty Bookshop carries the international editions of *Time* and *Newsweek,* the latter incorporated into the *Bulletin,* an Australian newsmagazine.

Business Hours   Most shops on Rarotonga are open Monday through Friday from 8am to 4pm and Saturday from 8am to noon. Some small grocery stores in the villages are open in the evenings and for limited hours on Sunday.

Camera/Film   A reasonable selection of color-print film is available at many shops in Avarua. One-hour processing of color-print film is available at

Cocophoto, in the C.I.T.C. shopping center in Avarua (☎ **22-000**). Color slides are sent to New Zealand for processing.

Clothing   Dress in the Cook Islands is informal. Shorts of respectable length (that is, not of the short-short variety) are worn during the day by both men and women, but beach attire should stay at the beach. Nude or topless sunbathing is not permitted anywhere (although some European tourists do it anyway). The colorful wraparound pareu is popular with local women. Evenings from May to September can be cool, so trousers, skirts, light jackets, sweaters, or wraps are in order after dark. The only neckties to be seen are at church on Sunday.

Crime   See "Safety," below.

Currency Exchange   See "Visitor Information & Entry Requirements" and "Money," above.

Dentist   Ask at your hotel desk for the name of a private practitioner, or go to the Tupapa Outpatient Clinic on the east end of Avarua, where hours are Monday through Friday from 8am to 4pm.

Doctor   **Dr. Wolfgang Losacker** has a private practice in the Banana Court shops at the traffic circle in Avarua (☎ **23-306**). His office hours are Monday through Friday from 10am to 1pm. Also see "Hospitals," below.

Drug Laws   Dangerous drugs and narcotics are illegal; possession can land you in a very unpleasant jail for a very long time.

Drugstores   **C.I.T.C. Pharmacy** (☎ **29-292**), in the C.I.T.C. shopping center west of the traffic circle, dispenses prescription medications and carries toiletries. The clinics on the outer islands have a limited supply of prescription medications.

Electricity   Electricity is 230 volts, 50 cycles, so converters are necessary in order to operate American appliances. The plugs, like those of New Zealand and Australia, have two-angled prongs, so an adapter will also be needed. If your appliances or the table lamps in your room don't work, check to see whether the switch on the wall outlet is turned on.

E-mail   **Cook Islands Post** (see "Post Office," below) and **Telekom Cook Islands** (see "Telephone & Fax," below) both have Internet computer terminals. (Telekom is less crowded and is air conditioned.) Access at both ranges from NZ$1.75 ($1.05) for 5 minutes to NZ$10.50 ($6.30) for 30 minutes. **Pacific Computers** (☎ **20-727**), east of the traffic circle in Avarua, charges NZ50¢ (30¢) per minute for access, NZ$2 ($1.20) for off-line e-mail sending.

Embassies/Consulates   No foreign government maintains an embassy or consulate in the Cook Islands. In case of a problem, seek advice from the travel facilitation and consular officer in the Ministry of Foreign Affairs (☎ **20-507**). The New Zealand government has a representative, whose office is at the traffic circle in Avarua. The U.S. embassy in Wellington, New Zealand, has jurisdiction.

Emergencies   The emergency number for the police is **999;** for an ambulance or the hospital, **998;** for fire, **996.** The nonemergency police number is **22-499.**

Eyeglasses   Go to **Cook Islands Optics** (☎ **26-604**), in the Mana Court shopping center west of the traffic circle.

Firearms   Don't even think about it—they're illegal.

Gambling   There are no gambling casinos in the Cook Islands, but you can bet on the Australian and New Zealand lotteries at the C.I.T.C. shopping center.

Hairdressers/Barbers   Paradise Hair & Beauty, in Panama between Avarua and the airport (☎ **22-774**), is a full-service beauty salon.

Hitchhiking   It's not illegal, but hitchhiking is frowned upon by the government.

Hospitals   The hospital (☎ **22-664,** or **998** in case of emergency) is located behind the golf course. For minor problems, go to the **Tupapa Outpatient Clinic** on the east end of Avarua; it's open Monday through Friday from 8am to 4pm.

Insects   There are no poisonous insects in the Cook Islands. Mosquitoes are plentiful, especially during the summer months and in the inland areas, so bring a good repellent. Mosquito coils can be bought at most village shops.

Laundry/Dry Cleaning   Snowbird Laundry & Dry Cleaners has 1-day laundry and dry cleaning service at its main plant in Arorangi (☎ **20-952**) and at a small laundry behind the Empire Theatre building in Avarua (☎ **21-952**). They will wash, dry, and fold a load for NZ$9 ($5.50), and will pick up and deliver if you or your hotel staff call in advance.

Libraries   The **Cook Islands Library and Museum,** in Avarua near the Cook Islands Christian Church (☎ **26-468**), is open Monday through Friday from 9am to 1pm, Saturday 9:30am to 1pm, with additional hours on Tuesday from 4 to 8pm. The library has a fine collection of works on the South Pacific, including many hard-to-find books. It costs NZ$25 ($15) to join, with NZ$15 ($9) refundable at the end of your visit.

Liquor Laws   The legal drinking age is 18. Bottled liquor, beer, and wine are available from several stores; the largest is **The Bond,** opposite Avatiu Harbour. Bars and nightclubs close promptly at midnight Saturday. The hotel bars can sell alcoholic beverages to their guests all day Sunday, and the restaurants can resume service on Sunday at 6pm.

Maps   The best readily available maps of the islands are in the tourist publications, *Jasons Passport Cook Islands, What's On In The Cook Islands,* and the *Cook Islands Sun.* Get copies at Cook Islands Tourism Corporation office or at most hotels. **Bounty Bookshop** (☎ **22-660**) sells somewhat out-of-date topographic maps prepared by the New Zealand surveyor general (see "Bookstores," above).

Newspapers/Magazines   The *Cook Islands News,* published Monday through Saturday, contains local, regional, and world news; radio and TV schedules; shipping schedules; a weather map for the South Pacific; and notices of local events, including advertisements for "island nights" at the hotels. It even has two comic strips. Copies are available at the Bounty Bookshop and the large Cook Islands Trading Corporation (C.I.T.C.) store in the center of Avarua. You can read the news on its Web site at *www.cinews.co.ck.*

Police   See "Emergencies," above.

Post Office   Cook Islands Post (☎ **29-940**) is located at the traffic circle in Avarua (it's not officially called the "post office" because the government privatized its operations as part of the recent austerity program). Hours are Monday through Friday 8am to 4pm, Saturday 8am to noon. There's a branch office opposite Titikaveka College on Rarotonga's south coast, which is open Monday through Friday from 8am to noon and 1 to 3:30pm. Each of the other islands has a post office. The international airmail rate for letters to North America is NZ$1.05 (63¢); postcards and airgrams are NZ85¢ (51¢). There is no mail delivery, so all addresses include a post office box.

Radio/TV   Rarotonga has one AM and one FM radio station; both broadcast Polynesian and Western music, and most programming is in English. One TV channel broadcasts news, sports, and entertainment daily from 6 to 11pm.

Safety   The streets here are safe. Property thefts can occur, so don't leave valuables in your hotel room or your belongings untended elsewhere.

Taxes   The government imposes a 12½% value-added tax (VAT), which is included in the price of most goods and services. You should ask if the VAT is included in the rates quoted by the hotels and hostels, or whether it will be added to your bill when you leave. The departure tax on international flights is NZ$25 ($15).

Telephone/Fax   Direct dialed calls can be made into the Cook Islands from most parts of the world. The country code is **682.**

International telephone calls and fax messages can be made or sent from most hotels or from **Telecom Cook Islands,** on the street between the Cook Islands Trading Corp. and the Cook's Corner shopping centers in Avarua (☎ **26-171**). The Telecom office is open 24 hours daily.

It will cost more to call home from the Cook Islands than anywhere else in the South Pacific: NZ$3.50 ($2.10) a minute to North America and Europe, somewhat less to Australia and New Zealand. There's an additional charge of NZ$8.50 ($5) for operator assistance. If the operator does assist, pay after the call is completed (by MasterCard or Visa credit cards if your bill is NZ$20 [$14] or more).

You can dial international calls from phonecard public phones at Telekom, the Cook Islands Trading Corp. (C.I.T.C.), and outside most post offices. Buy the phonecards from Telekom, C.I.T.C., or at the post offices. Merely insert the card in the phone and dial the local or international number; a digital readout tells you how much money you have left during the call and will warn you when to put in a fresh card. You can also buy "Kia Orana" prepaid calling cards which can be used from any phone by dialing 147, your personal identification (PIN) number, and the number you wish to call.

Some long-distance carriers have access numbers their customers can dial from within the Cook Islands to have international calls billed to their credit or prepaid cards, including **AT&T** (☎ **09111**) and **MCI** (☎ **09121**). You'll pay the regular local call charges on top of the international rates if you dial them from your hotel room.

Dial **010** for local directory assistance, **015** for international calls, and **020** for calls to the outer islands. Emergency numbers are listed under "Emergencies," above.

Time   Local time is 10 hours behind Greenwich Mean Time. Translated, that's 2 hours behind California during standard time, 3 hours behind during daylight saving time. The Cook Islands are on the east side of the International Date Line, which puts them in the same day as the U.S. and a day behind New Zealand and Australia.

Tipping   Tipping is considered contrary to the Polynesian way of life and is frowned upon.

Water   Generally, the water on Rarotonga is safe to drink from the tap, although it is not treated and can become slightly muddy after periods of heavy rain. Many hotels have their own filtration systems. If in doubt, boil it in the electric "jug" in your hotel room. The tap water on Aitutaki is not safe to drink.

Weights/Measures   The Cook Islands are on the metric system.

9 Exploring Rarotonga

The Cook Islands' capital can be seen on foot, since this picturesque little South Seas town winds for only a mile or so along the curving waterfront between its two harbors. Virtually every sight and most of the shops sit along or just off the main around-the-island road, which for this mile serves as Main Street.

A STROLL AROUND AVARUA

Let's start at the traffic circle in the heart of town at the old harbor, which is both the beginning and end of the round-island road. The rusty carcass on the reef offshore belonged to the **S.S. Maitai,** a trading ship that went aground here in 1916. To the west, the low-slung building with a large veranda houses a restaurant, several shops, and the **Banana Court Bar,** once one of the South Pacific's most famous drinking holes. The building actually began life as a hotel.

From the traffic circle, walk east. On your right is **Vanwil's,** one of the few remaining old South Seas–style trading stores. Its dark, dusty shelves carry everything from fishhooks to flashlights to fresh vegetables. About 200 yards farther on the main road stands its present-day counterpart, the modern **Beachcomber Ltd.** This pearl and handcraft shop occupies a coral-block building erected in 1843 as a school for missionary children. The local legislative council met here from 1888 to 1901, but by 1968 it was condemned as unsafe. It sat roofless and weed-infested until owners Joan Rolls and David Gragg beautifully renovated it in 1992.

In a shady parklike setting across the road stands **Taputapuatea,** the restored "palace" of Queen Makea Takau Ariki. Don't enter the grounds without permission, for they are tabu to us commoners. Queen Makea is long dead, but when she was around in the 19th century, the palace reputedly was a lively place.

Facing the palace grounds across the road running inland is the tall, white **Cook Islands Christian Church,** which was built in 1855. Just to the left of the main entrance is the grave of Albert Henry, the late prime minister. A bust of Sir Albert sits atop the grave, complete with shell lei, crown, and his reading glasses. Robert Dean Frisbie, the American-born writer and colorful South Seas character, is buried in the inland corner of the graveyard, next to the road. (See "Recommended Books" in the appendix.)

To the right, near the end of the road, is the **Cook Islands Library and Museum** (☎ **26-468**). The museum is small but worth a visit. It has excellent examples of Cook Islands handcrafts; a canoe from Pukapuka built in the old style, with planks lashed together; the island's first printing press (brought to Rarotonga by the London Missionary Society in the 1830s and used until the 1950s by the government printing office); and the bell and compass from the *Yankee,* a world-famous yacht that in 1964 wrecked on the reef behind the Beachcomber, where its forlorn skeleton rusted away for 30 years. No admission fee is charged, but there is a box for donations. The library and museum are open Monday through Friday 9am to 1pm, Saturday 9:30am to 1pm, and Tuesday 4 to 8pm. Admission is NZ$2 ($1.20).

Farther up the inland road past the **Avarua School** stands **Takamoa Theological College,** opened in 1842 by the London Missionary Society. The original **Takamoa Mission House** still sits on the campus.

Now walk a block along the street in front of the library and museum to the **Sir Geoffrey Henry National Cultural Centre** (also known as *Te Puna Korero),* the country's showplace built in time for the 1992 South Pacific Festival of the Arts. The large green building houses the Civic Auditorium, while the long yellow structures contain government offices as well as the **National Museum** and **National Library**

(☎ 20-725). Exhibits at the National Museum feature contemporary and replicated examples of ancient crafts. The museum is open Monday through Friday from 9am to 4pm. Admission is by donation. The library is open when school is in session, Monday and Wednesday from noon to 8pm and Tuesday, Thursday, and Saturday from 9am to 4pm.

Opposite the national museum is the **Tupapa Sports Ground.** Like other South Pacific islanders formerly under New Zealand or Australian rule, the Cook Islanders take their rugby seriously. Although much of the action has shifted to the stadium at Tereora College behind the airport, Tupapa may still see a brawl or two on Saturday afternoons.

Now walk back to the main road, turn left at the Paradise Inn, and head to downtown. You can take a break at one of the restaurants or snack bars along the way. From the traffic circle west is a lovely stroll, either by the storefronts or along the seafront promenade known as **Te Ara Maire Nui.** At the west end of town, stroll through **Punanga Nui Market,** where vendors sell clothing and souvenirs (see "Shopping," below), and food stalls offer take-away food that you can munch at picnic tables under the shade of casuarinas whispering in the wind (see "Dining," below).

We end our tour at **Avatiu Harbour,** which is Rarotonga's commercial port (the small anchorage at Avarua is strictly a small-boat refuge). **Rob's Paradise Bar,** under a large thatch cabana at the harbor, is the perfect place to recover with ice-cold refreshment.

THE CIRCLE ISLAND TOUR

Traveling completely around Rarotonga and seeing the sights should take about 4 hours—with the help of a motor (allow a full day if you go by bicycle). Let's travel in a clockwise direction from Avarua.

THE NORTH COAST

About 1 kilometer past the Kii Kii Motel, signs mark a small dirt road to the right. It leads to the **Marae Arai-Te-Tonga,** one of the most sacred spots on the island. Before the coming of Europeans, these stone structures formed a *koutu,* or royal court. The investiture of high chiefs took place here amid much pomp and circumstance; also, offerings to the gods and the "first fruits" of each season were brought here and presented to the local *ariki,* or chief. The basalt investiture pillar, the major remaining structure, stands slightly offset from a rectangular platform about 12 feet long, 7 feet wide, and 8 inches high. Such temples, or maraes, still are considered sacred by some Cook Islanders, so don't walk on them.

The ancient Ara Metua road crosses by Arai-Te-Tonga and leads south a few yards to a small marae on the banks of **Tupapa Stream.** A trail follows the stream up to the peaks of Mounts Te Ikurangi, Te Manga, and Te Atukura, but these are difficult climbs; it's advisable to make them only with a local guide.

THE EAST COAST

Back on the main road, **Matavera** village begins about 2 kilometers (1¼ miles) beyond Tupapa Stream. Notable for the picturesque Cook Islands Christian Church and graveyard on the mountain side of the road, it's worth a stop for a photograph before continuing on to historic **Ngatangiia** village. Legend has it that a fleet of canoes left Ngatangiia sometime around A.D. 1350 and sailed off to colonize New Zealand, departing from a point across the road from where the Cook Islands Christian Church now stands in the center of the village. Offshore is **Ngatangiia Passage,** between the mainland and **Motutapu,** a low island, through which the canoes left on their voyage.

★ Frommer's Favorite Cook Islands Experiences

Cultural Touring. One of my fondest South Pacific memories was exploring Rarotonga with the entertaining and highly informative Exham Wichman. He told me much of what this chapter has to say about the Cook Islanders' lifestyle. Exham has retired from the tour business, replaced by the terrific Cook Islands Cultural Village, Pa's wonderful nature walks, and Hugh Henry's Circle Island Historical Tour. Together, they make Rarotonga the best cultural experience of any island in the South Pacific.

Cook Islands Dancing. I never visit the Cook Islands without watching the hips swing at a traditional dance show. Take my word for it: Had the crew of H.M.S. *Bounty* seen the dancing on Rarotonga instead of Tahiti, even Captain Bligh might have stayed behind.

Pub Crawling. Like the Cook Islanders, I still crawl home from their lively pubs after a long night of partying on Fridays. The French could learn much about *joie de vivre* from the fun-loving Cook Islanders.

Experiencing Aitutaki. Although physically not as awe-inspiring as Bora Bora over in French Polynesia, the Cooks' second-most-visited island still has a friendliness that is disappearing in some more visited parts of the South Pacific.

Ngatangiia also had its day in the sun in the early 1800s, when it was the headquarters of Charles Pitman, the missionary who came with the Rev. John Williams and later translated *Pilgrim's Progress* into Cook Islands Maori. Unlike many of his fellow missionaries, Pitman carefully avoided becoming involved in local politics or business, and he objected strongly when Williams forced the Cook Islanders to build the Messenger of Peace. The **courthouse** across from the church was the first one built in the Cook Islands.

The shore at Ngatangiia, with three small islands sitting on the reef beyond the lagoon, is one of the most beautiful parts of Rarotonga. An old **stone fish trap** is visible underwater between the beach and the islands. Such traps were quite common throughout eastern Polynesia: Fish were caught inside as the tide ebbed and flowed through Ngatangiia Passage.

THE SOUTH COAST

South of Ngatangiia begins magnificent **Muri Beach,** whose white sands stretch for 14 kilometers (8 miles) around the southeast corner of Rarotonga. Sailboats glide across the crystal-clear lagoon, the island's best for boating. A fine place to enjoy the beach and go for a swim in the lagoon is the **Rarotonga Sailing Club,** or you can stop for lunch or a snack at **Maire Nui Gardens & Cafe** just before The Little Polynesian hotel (see "Dining," below).

The Cook Islands Christian Church in the village of **Titikaveka** was built in 1841 of coral blocks hand-cut from the reef almost a mile away and carried to the building site. The lagoon at Titikaveka is the deepest on the island and the best for snorkeling.

Above the village, a part of the mountain is preserved in its natural state by the ★ **Takitumu Conservation Area** (☎ **29-906;** e-mail kakerori@tca.co.ck). Call in advance or stop in at the Titikaveka post office for information about guided tours of the forest. The area is the only home of the unique and endangered kakerori *(pomarea dimidiata),* a sparrow-size yellowish bird native to Rarotonga. The conservation program has raised the kakerori population from 29 in 1989 to more than 130 today.

I have hunted long for this sanctuary. Now that I have found it, I have no intention, and certainly no desire, ever to leave it again.
—Robert Dean Frisbie, 1928

From Titikaveka, the road runs along the south coast and passes another old stone fish trap just inside **Avaavaroa Passage,** and the late Albert Henry's white beachside home. **Mount Te Rua Manga,** the rock spire also known as "The Needle," can be seen clearly from the main road between Liana's Restaurant and The Rarotongan Beach Resort. You also will pass what looks like a modern ruin; it's the site of the aborted and highly controversial Sheraton Hotel.

THE WEST COAST

The road turns at The Rarotongan Resort and heads up the west coast to the low white walls of **Arorangi,** the coastal community founded as a peacemaking "Gospel Village" by the missionary Aaron Buzacott when a dispute over land boundaries broke out in 1828. Arorangi replaced the old inland village, Puaikura, where the Tahitian missionary Papeiha went to teach Christianity after he had converted all of Aitutaki. Papeiha is buried in the yard of Arorangi's Cook Islands Christian Church, which was built in 1849. According to Polynesian legend, the canoes that left Ngatangiia in the 1300s stopped in Arorangi before heading off west to New Zealand. There is no reef passage near Arorangi, but the story enables the people on both sides of Rarotonga to claim credit for colonizing New Zealand.

The flat-topped mountain behind Arorangi is **Mount Raemaru.** Another legend says that mighty warriors from Aitutaki, which had no mountain, stole the top of Raemaru and took it home with them. There is a steep and somewhat dangerous trail to the top of Mount Raemaru.

The area north of Arorangi is well developed with hotels, restaurants, and shops. The shore just before the golf course is known as **Black Rock** because of the volcanic outcrop standing sentinel in the lagoon offshore. According to ancient Maori belief, the souls of the dead bid farewell to Rarotonga from this point before journeying to the fatherland, which the Cook Islanders called Avaiki.

There are two ways to proceed after passing the golf course. The main road continues around the west end of the **airport** runway (be careful; there are more road accidents on this sharp curve than anywhere else on Rarotonga). The New Zealand government built the original airstrip during World War II. It was enlarged in the early 1970s to handle jumbo jets, and Queen Elizabeth II officially opened the new strip, which was renamed Rarotonga International Airport, on July 29, 1974. The **Parliament Building** is located on the shore about halfway along the length of the runway. Parliament meets from February to March and from July to September. Visitors can observe the proceedings from the gallery. The **cemetery** along the road just before town is the final resting place of cancer patients who came to Rarotonga in the 1970s to see Milan Brych, a controversial specialist who claimed to have discovered a cure. When Dr. Tom Davis became prime minister, he kicked Brych out of the country.

The other way to return to Avarua from Black Rock is to turn right on the first paved road past the golf course and then left at the dead-end intersection onto the Ara Metua, or "back road," as the section running from Black Rock to town is called. About halfway to town is **Tereora College,** established as a mission school in 1865. An international stadium was built on the college campus for the 1985 South Pacific

Mini Games held on Rarotonga and is now the site of rock 'em, sock 'em rugby games on Saturday afternoons from June through August.

The short ride back to town concludes the circle island tour.

ORGANIZED TOURS

Some local tour operators and the Cook Islands Cultural Village (see "Cultural Experiences," below), will take you around the island while explaining the cultural and historical aspects of Rarotonga. Book at any hotel activities desk. You can do it independently by car or motorbike, but you'll miss the informative commentary.

✪ **Raro Safari Tours** (☎ **23-629** or 22-627) is the best way to see the island's mountainous interior without hiking. In fact, you'll get better views down over the reef and the sea from these four-wheel-drive vehicles than you will on foot. The open-air trucks go up the Avatiu Valley on some unbelievably narrow tracks. Guides give often humorous commentary about the native flora and its uses, about ancient legends, and about what life was like in the old days when Rarotongans lived up in the valleys instead of along the coast. The 3½-hour tours go daily at 9am and 1:30pm and cost NZ$45 ($27) per person.

FLIGHTSEEING

Another way to see Rarotonga is by plane. **Air Rarotonga** (☎ **22-888**) offers 20-minute sightseeing flights around the island for NZ$155 ($93) per person. Flights can be arranged at the customers' choice of time if two or more people fly. Try to go early in the morning before the clouds have built up over the mountains.

10 Cultural Experiences

Given their use of English and their pride in their culture, the Cook Islanders themselves offer a magnificent glimpse into the lifestyle of eastern Polynesia. They are more than happy to answer questions put to them sincerely by inquisitive visitors. Some of them also do it for money, albeit in a low-key fashion, by offering some of the finest learning experiences in the South Pacific. Unless you sit on the beach and do nothing, you won't go home from the Cook Islands without knowing something about Polynesian culture, both of yesteryear and the present.

✪ **COOK ISLANDS CULTURAL VILLAGE**   Plan an early visit to the **Cook Islands Cultural Village** (☎ **21-314**), on the back road in Arorangi, for it will enable you to understand what you will see during the rest of your stay here. The village consists of thatch huts featuring different aspects of life, such as the making of crafts, cooking, and even dancing. Guests are guided through the huts and then enjoy a lunch of island-style foods, music, and dancing. The tour begins at 10am, Monday through Friday. Cost for the entire morning and lunch is NZ$43 ($26), or NZ$39 ($23.50) if you provide your own transportation to and from the village. The Cultural Village also does its own half-day circle island historical tour; it costs NZ$25 ($15) and includes lunch and the village tour. A full day combining the village tour, lunch, and a trip around the island costs NZ$60 ($42).

✪ **PA'S NATURE WALKS**   While the cultural tours provide commentary on the history, lifestyles, and plants grown for domestic use, a blond, dreadlocked Cook Islander named **Pa** leads mountain and nature walks into the interior. Along the way he points out various wild plants, such as vanilla, candle nuts, mountain orchids, and the shampoo plant, and their everyday and medicinal uses in the days before corned beef and pharmacies. Either Pa's Cross-Island Mountain Trek or Pa's Nature Walk costs NZ$45 ($27) for adults, NZ$20 ($12) for children under 12. Wear good walking or running shoes and bring a bathing suit (for a dip in an ancient pool once used by warriors). The nature walk takes 3½ hours. See "Fishing, Hiking, Diving & Other Outdoor Pursuits," below, for information about the cross-island hike. Reserve at any hotel activities desk, or call ☎ **21-079**. You can also book at The Pearl Factory west of the traffic circle.

PIRI PURUTO II   To learn everything you ever wanted to know about the various uses of the coconut palm in old Polynesia, including a lengthy demonstration of old-time fire starting, catch a **Piri Puruto II Show.** Dressed in a loincloth and cap made of fibers from the top of a palm, Piri scales one of the tallest trees around and throws down several coconuts and various other materials for his fire-starting demonstration. He then whacks open the nuts with a bush knife and gives everyone a taste (the texture and flavor change with the age of each coconut). Piri appears at the Moana Sands Hotel at 5pm Tuesday. He also puts on a performance and a traditional Cook Islands meal at Piri's Place, his lagoonside home on the South Shore east of The Rarotongan Beach Resort, on Thursday at 5pm, when you can watch the show for NZ$12 ($7.20), have the meal but no show for NZ$20 ($12), or both for NZ$35 ($21). Call ☎ **20-309** for reservations. Piri also has a Sunday feast (see "Dining," below).

GOING TO CHURCH   Nearly everyone in the Cook Islands puts on his or her finest white straw hat and goes to church on Sunday morning. Many visitors join them, for even though most sermons are in Maori, the magnificent harmony of Polynesian voices in full song will not soon be forgotten. Families have been worshipping together in the same pews for generations, but the ushers are accustomed to finding seats for tourists. Cook Islanders wear their finest to church, including neckties, but visitors can wear smart casual attire.

Sunday morning services at Rarotongan village churches usually begin at 10am; buses leave the hotels at 9:30am. Reserve at the activities desk, or just show up at any church on the island.

11 Fishing, Hiking, Diving & Other Outdoor Pursuits

With tourism as its main business, Rarotonga has enough sporting and other outdoor activities to occupy the time of anyone who decides to crawl out of a beach chair and move the muscles. A few activities, such as Pa's Mountain Trek, are mentioned above in "Cultural Experiences."

BOATING & SAILING   **Captain Tama's AquaSports** (☎ **27-350**) at the Pacific Resort on Muri Beach, where the lagoon offshore is the island's best spot for swimming, snorkeling, and boating, rents a variety of water sports equipment, including beach kayaks, sailboats, Windsurfers, canoes, and snorkeling gear. Rental rates range from NZ$7 ($4.20) for an hour's use of a kayak to NZ$35 ($21) to rent a sailboat for a day. You can get unlimited use by buying an Aquapass for NZ$59 ($24.50) for the first day, NZ$30 ($18) for each additional day. Aqua Sports is open daily from 9am to 5:30pm.

FISHING   There have been some world-class catches of skipjack tuna (bonito), mahimahi, blue marlin, wahoo, and barracuda in Cook Islands waters. If the sea is calm enough for them to leave Rarotonga's relatively unprotected harbors, charter boats start deep-sea fishing as soon as they clear the reef. Several boat owners will take you out, but Elgin and Sharon Tetachuk's **Seafari Charters** (☎ **20-328**) and Wayne Barclay and Jenny Sorensen's **Pacific Marine Charters** (☎ **21-237**) have ship-to-shore radios and safety equipment. They charge NZ$95 ($57) per person for half a day's fishing, one of the lowest rates in the South Pacific. They like to have a day's notice, which you probably can give in person at the **Cook Islands Game Fishing Club** (☎ **21-419**), whose clubhouse is beside the lagoon 1 kilometer (0.6 mile) east of the traffic circle. Whether you fish or not, you'll be welcome to have snacks and drinks at the club while taking in the view and swapping a few tall tales.

Don't expect to keep your catch; fresh fish are expensive here and will be sold by the boat operator. Bring a camera.

GOLF   Visitors are welcome to take their shots at the radio towers and guy wires that create unusual obstacles on the 9 holes of **Rarotonga Golf Club** (☎ **27-360**). The course was once located on what is now the International Airport; club members had to move it when the runway was expanded. It now lies under Rarotonga's radio station antennae—balls that hit a tower or wire can be replayed. Greens fees are NZ$12 ($7). Rental equipment and drinks are available in the clubhouse. The club is open Monday through Saturday from 8am until dark.

HIKING   There are a number of hiking trails on Rarotonga, but the most popular by far is the ✪ **Cross-Island Track** from Avarua to the south coast. It begins in the Avatiu valley and follows the stream high up to the base of Mount Te Rua Manga ("The Needle"). It's a very steep and often slippery climb, but the trail is well marked. Hundreds of visitors make the trek each year, many of them on **Pa's Cross-Island Mountain Trek** (see "Cultural Experiences," above). The walks cost about NZ$45 ($27) per person. For do-it-yourselfers, Cook Islands Tourism Corporation distributes a brochure detailing the cross-island and other hikes, and it has helpful brochures published by the Cook Islands Natural Heritage Project, which explain what you will see.

LAGOON EXCURSIONS   **Captain Tama's Aquasports** (☎ **27-350**), at the Pacific Resort, has glass-bottom boat excursions on Muri Lagoon which include fish-feeding, snorkeling, and lunch on one of the small offshore islands. Captain Tama charges NZ$40 ($24).

Perhaps the ultimate glass-bottom boat cruise here is aboard the semi-submersible **Reef Sub** (☎ **25-837**), which departs from The Pacific Resort at 10am and 2pm for 2-hour voyages around Muri Lagoon. Fare is NZ$35 ($21) per person.

SCUBA DIVING   Rarotonga's lagoon is only 4 to 10 feet deep, but depths easily reach 100 feet outside the reef, and a drop-off starts at 80 feet and descends to more than 12,000 feet. There are canyons, caves, tunnels, and many varieties of coral. Visibility usually is in the 100- to 200-feet range. Two wrecks—a 100-foot fishing boat and a 150-foot cargo ship—sit in depths of 80 feet and 60 feet, respectively. Best of all for dollar-conscious travelers, the diving fees here are the lowest in the South Pacific.

Owner Barry Hill of **Dive Rarotonga** (☎ **21-873;** fax 21-837; e-mail jbateman@tumanu.co.ck), and his humorous mate Eric Bateman (of Tumanu Tropical Restaurant and Bar; see "Dining," below), make two dive trips daily. They charge NZ$45 ($27) per dive including tank, air, weight belt, and boat; or NZ$55 ($33) including all equipment. Their office is roadside in Arorangi.

Greg Wilson of **Cook Island Divers,** P.O. Box 1002, Rarotonga (☎ **22-483;** fax 22-484; www.cidivers.co.ck; e-mail gwilson@cidivers.co.ck), operates out of his house in Arorangi (watch for the roadside signs) and from the Mana Court Dive Shop in Avarua. He charges NZ$65 ($39) for a one-tank dive, including all equipment, and teaches 4-day PADI and NAUI courses for NZ$475 ($285).

At Muri Beach, Graham and Christine McDonald of **Pacific Divers** (☎ and fax **22-450;** www.pacificdivers.co.ck; e-mail dive@pacificdivers.co.ck) charge NZ$60 ($36) a dive, but two-tank dives for NZ$100 ($60) are their specialty. They also teach full PADI certification courses for NZ$450 ($270), or a 3-hour resort course for NZ$60 ($36).

SWIMMING & SNORKELING   Obviously, getting into the water has to have high priority during a visit to the South Pacific, and Rarotonga is certainly no exception. The lagoon is deep enough for snorkeling off most hotels at high tide, but you'll do better walking on the west coast reef when the tide's out. Only in Titikaveka on the south coast is the lagoon deep enough for snorkeling at low tide, specifically off the Fruits of Rarotonga shop (see "Shopping," below), which will safe-keep your bag while you snorkel, and off The Little Polynesian and Moana Sands Hotel (see "Accommodations," below). Muri Lagoon off the Pacific Resort is the best spot for boating, but the best snorkeling is just off the motu opposite the Muri Beachcomber.

Most hotels have snorkels, fins, and masks for their guests to use for free. You can rent them from the **Edgewater Resort** (☎ 25-435), or from **Dive Rarotonga** (☎ 21-873) on the west coast, or from **Captain Tama's AquaSports** (☎ 27-350) at the Pacific Resort on Muri Beach. Cost is NZ$7 ($4.20) a day.

TENNIS   The **Edgewater Resort** (☎ 25-435) has four lighted, beachside Astro Grass courts, where pro Malcolm Kajer gives private lessons for NZ$30 ($18) per hour. You can rent court time here for NZ$15 ($9) a hour (Edgewater guests can play free). Racquet rentals and balls are available.

Nonguests can play on the hard courts at **The Rarotongan Beach Resort** (☎ 25-800) for NZ$10 ($6) a hour.

12 Shopping

Thanks to the New Zealand dollar being valued less than its U.S. counterpart, Rarotonga offers some relatively good bargains for those of us carrying American bucks, especially on black pearls, native handcrafts, and tropical clothing. For the most part, you can do your shopping during your visit to Avarua, for most stores line the town's waterfront on either side of the traffic circle. Some stick to one particular item, but many carry a variety of pearls, handcrafts, and clothing.

THE SHOPPING SCENE

Manihiki and Penrhyn atolls in the Northern Group of the Cook Islands produce a fair number of **black pearls** (they actually come in a variety of colors). A hurricane damaged the crops there in the late 1990s, however, so some pearls are now imported from French Polynesia. Accordingly, you could find a few top-quality orbs here—and in U.S. dollar terms, they should be somewhat less expensive than in Tahiti. You'll be offered pearls at small shops and even by street vendors, but stick to dealers who are members of the local Pearl Guild.

I strongly encourage anyone interested in buying black pearls in the South Pacific to do some research beforehand, perhaps starting with excellent articles in the August 1985 and June 1997 issues of *National Geographic*. Also see "Shopping" in chapter 4.

Cook Islanders may not produce island **handcrafts** in the same volume as Tongans (see "Shopping" in chapter 14), but there is a fine assortment to choose from here, especially items made on the outer islands. Particularly good if not inexpensive buys are the delicately woven *rito* (white straw hats) the women wear to church on Sunday and the fine Samoan-style straw mats from Pukapuka in the Northern Group. Carvings from wood are plentiful, as is jewelry made from shell, mother-of-pearl, and pink coral. The most popular wood carvings are small totems representing the exhibitionist Tangaroa—they may be more appropriate for the nightstand than the coffee table.

The craze for block-printed, tie-dyed, and silkscreened **tropical clothing** swept from Tahiti to Rarotonga, where local artisans make colorful cotton pareus, shirts, blouses, dresses, swim wear, beach apparel, and other items. Some of their works are more artistically creative than those in French Polynesia, especially one-of-a-kind pareus and women's apparel.

For years the Cook Islands government has earned a considerable portion of its revenue from the sale of its **stamps** to collectors and dealers overseas. The **Philatelic Bureau,** next to Cook Islands Post, at the traffic circle in Avarua, issues between three and six new stamps a year. All are highly artistic and feature birds, shells, fish, flowers, and historical events and people, including the British royal family. For whatever reason—perhaps the remoteness of the islands or the beauty of the stamps—they are popular worldwide.

Unless otherwise noted, business hours are Monday through Friday 8am to 4pm, Saturday 8am to noon.

SHOPPING A TO Z

✪ **Beachcomber, Ltd.** Avarua, east of traffic circle. ☎ **21-939.**

This upscale establishment is worth a stop just to see the beautiful renovation of its 1843-vintage coral-block school house (see "A Stroll Around Avarua," above). Owners Joan Rolls and husband David Gragg completely gutted the old structure and turned it into Rarotonga's most picturesque shop. They have an excellent selection of black pearls, either loose or in exquisite settings designed and produced in their atelier behind the store. Traditional Polynesian designs minutely carved on pearls are unique to the Beachcomber. Also out back, a glassblower produces artistically gorgeous vases and other items. They also sell some of the best handcrafts available, including wood carvings, excellent black and pink coral jewelry, and exquisite *rito* hats. One section is devoted to paintings and other works by local artists, whose numbers include Joan herself.

The **Pearl Hut,** in the Village Shops across the road, is a small branch of the Beachcomber, and there is another outlet in The Rarotongan Beach Resort.

✪ **Bergman & Sons (The Pearl Shop).** Avarua, in Cook's Corner. ☎ **21-902.**

Mike and Marge Bergman and sons Trevor and Ben helped to pioneer the pearl industry in the Cook Islands, and their shop is the place to see Rarotonga's largest selection of natural and cultured pearls, whether loose or incorporated into jewelry. Both they and Beachcomber Ltd. carry small pearls still attached to their gold-trimmed shells and sold as necklaces.

The **Pearl Factory,** at the traffic circle next to the Banana Court (☎ **21-901**) is a Bergman & Sons outlet.

✪ **Island Crafts.** Avarua, in Centrepoint Building. ☎ **20-919.**

A must stop, this large shop is located on the main street, next to Westpac Bank. It has Rarotonga's largest selection of handcrafts—some from other parts of the South Pacific—and a wide selection of carved wooden Tangaroa tikis in various sizes. You can even buy a 9-karat gold pendant of the well-endowed god. The shop carries some black pearls, especially set as pendants and earrings.

Joyce Peyroux Garments. Arorangi. ☎ **20-205.**

The island's largest tropical clothing manufacturer and retailer, Mrs. Peyroux has her factory outlet on the ocean side of the road in Arorangi and her shops in the C.I.D.C. Building in the middle of Avarua (☎ **20-558**).

Kenwall Gallery/Manu Manea Fashions. Avarua, west of traffic circle. ☎ **25-527.**

This shop has women's wear, including some silkscreened items. The company's factory and showroom east of the traffic circle is worth a look. They will alter their stock dresses for free or, for a reasonable price, make one for you from scratch. The Kenwall Gallery part of the shop sells art supplies and the works of local artists such as Nga Vakapora, who paints sea life using water colors and acrylics on tapa cloth.

✪ **Maui Pearls.** Avarua, west of traffic circle next to Mana Court. ☎ **26-064.**

Cook Islander Paka Worthington attended American University in Washington, D.C. He obviously stopped at the shops owned by his friends Ron Hall on Moorea and Steve Fearon on Bora Bora (see "Shopping" in chapters 5 and 6), for this outlet bears a lot of similarities with those fine stores. Instead of teaching "pearl school," however, Paka lets a computer program explain all about the orbs. Specialties here are tension-set designs (where tension instead of a hole secures the pearl in place) and enhancers, which let you clip the pearl and setting on any chain or even a white pearl necklace.

The Perfume Factory. Avarua, on the back road between the harbors. ☎ **22-690.**

John Abbott's factory produces delightful perfumes, soaps, body oils, and after-shave lotions made of local gardenia, jasmine, aloe vera, and coconut oils. He also makes coffee, coconut, and vanilla liqueurs, some of them in souvenir bottles which replicate the Tangaroa tiki.

Perfumes of Rarotonga. Avarua, in Village Shops east of traffic circle. ☎ **26-238.**

Travis Moore, an American who married a Cook Islander, produces a selection of perfumes, soaps, and lotions that are on display here. You can also taste real coffee and coffee liqueurs.

Punanga Nui Market. Avatiu Harbour. No phone.

The vendor stalls in this waterfront municipal market are the best places to look for tie-dyed bedspreads and tablecloths. They also have good prices on T-shirts, although some may be Chinese-made cottons that will shrink (buy a size larger than you usually wear). Saturday morning is market day here and the best time to shop.

✪ **TAV Ltd.** Avarua, on second road inland behind Ronnie's Bar & Restaurant. ☎ **21-802.**

Check out Ellena Tavioni's workshop for one of the island's best selections of block-printed swim wear, sun-dresses, and other items for men, women, and children. Ellena pioneered block printing here, and she exports her clothing to the United States, Europe, the United Kingdom, and the high-end boutiques in Fiji. Here she has Rarotonga's best selection in this lovely style. Her workshop will alter items for free or will make them for you from scratch.

13 Accommodations

Rarotonga may be a small island, but it's blessed with a wide range of accommodations. While all are comfortable, this is not the place to come for super-deluxe resorts like those in French Polynesia and Fiji. Most of the properties are small, owner-operated motels, whose friendly, hands-on management makes up for their lack of luxury. They call themselves "motels" because they're modeled after the typical New Zealand motel, in which each room has a small but quite complete kitchen, which compensates for the lack of restaurants on the premises. Whether motel or hotel, rooms in all except some of the least expensive establishments have electric "jugs" for making tea and coffee.

Accommodation here is grouped in three areas: the southeast, on or near **Muri Beach;** the **west coast,** especially near Arorangi; and in or near the town of **Avarua.** The southeast coast boasts the marvelous Muri Beach and a lagoon that's wider, deeper, and better for snorkeling and sailing. The prevailing southeast trade winds, however, can make this area chilly during the austral winter months of June through August. By the same token, these same winds provide nature's air-conditioning during the warmer summer months. You get glorious sunsets on the west coast, which the mountains shield from the prevailing trade winds, thus making it somewhat drier than Muri Beach—and hotter during the summer months of December to March. Much of the west coast beach has been eroded by recent storms, and the lagoon tends to be very shallow, especially at low tide. The hotels in or near Avarua are close to shops and restaurants, but the north coast is rocky, and its lagoons are perpetually shallow. Keep these factors in mind when making your choice.

Unless noted otherwise, every hotel or motel sits in a tropical garden complete with coconut palms and flowering plants.

The government's 12½% **value added tax** may be included in the rates quoted below; ask to make sure.

HOTELS AT MURI BEACH

The Little Polynesian. P.O. Box 366, Rarotonga (Titikaveka, 14.1km [8.5 miles] from Avarua). ☎ **24-280.** Fax 21-585. E-mail: littlepoly@beach.co.ck. 9 units. MINIBAR. NZ$175–NZ$215 ($105–$129). AE, DC, MC, V.

Reminiscent of the small hotels on Moorea or Bora Bora but without the restaurant and bar, this establishment has an idyllic coconut grove location right on the beach and some of the deeper waters of Muri Lagoon. Owners/sisters Jeannine Peyroux and Dorice Reid have eight duplex units in four cottages, plus a "honeymoon" bungalow standing by itself beside the beach (it's not all that private, since other guests can walk right past its windows). Each unit has a king-size bed, ceiling fan in case the trades die down, and cooking facilities. The honeymoon bungalow also has its own veranda overlooking the beach. There's a small swimming pool surrounded by a rock ledge. Guests can use kayaks free, and motor bike hires are available.

Moana Sands Hotel. P.O. Box 1007, Rarotonga (Muri Beach, 14.3km [8.6 miles] from Avarua). ☎ **26-189.** Fax 22-189. E-mail: beach@moanasands.co.ck. 12 units, 3 houses. NZ$179 ($107.50) double, NZ$379 ($227.50) house. AE, DC, MC, V.

Right on the beach at the deepest part of Muri Lagoon, this 2-story motel-like structure has six rooms upstairs and six on the ground level. Each has a balcony or patio facing the lagoon, ceiling fan, cane table and chairs, tiled shower-only bathroom, bright flower-print drapes and spreads, and Pullman kitchen with microwave oven. Some have single beds in addition to queens; others have only a queen-size bed. The houses here are about .5 kilometers (¼ mile) west of the hotel. One of these hexagonal structures sits right on the beach; the other two sit just behind it. They have 3 bedrooms, 2 bathrooms, full kitchens, phones, and big porches.

A small dining room provides breakfasts (brought to your room if you wish) and two- or three-course fixed menu dinners (eaten dinner party-style by the beach if weather permits). No lunch is served, but guests have access to the dining room and "honesty" bar at all times. The guest lounge has a small library, games, and other distractions for children. Snorkeling equipment, kayaks, and sailboats are provided on-site.

✪ **Muri Beachcomber.** P.O. Box 379, Rarotonga (Muri Beach, 10.9km [6.5 miles] from Avarua). ☎ **21-022.** Fax 21-323. www.beachcomber.co.ck. E-mail: muri@beachcomber.co.ck. 18 units, 3 houses. A/C TV TEL (in houses only). NZ$195 ($117) double, NZ$280 ($168) house. AE, DC, MC, V.

One of my favorites here, this friendly motel sits right on Muri Beach and a short walk to The Pacific Resort, the Rarotonga Sailing Club, and The Flame Tree and Emil's restaurants, which more than makes up for its lack of on-site dining room and activities. Spotlights illuminate the tropical foliage of the grounds at night, and the rising moon over the lagoon is a sight to see. One of two New Zealander couples who own the place—Helen and Peter Kemp or Lynley and Bill Tillick—is always on hand to lend assistance and advice.

Ten of their one-bedroom, full-kitchen units are in five duplex buildings built of brown timber but with yellow peaked roofs evoking the tropics. They form two courtyards opening to the beach. Better suited for singles or couples, these spacious units have French doors which open from both living- and bedrooms to covered verandas with coffee tables and comfortable lawn chairs. Children under 12 are allowed only in the larger family units standing away from the beach but next to the swimming pool, making it easy for parents to keep an eye on the kids from their shady, similarly appointed verandas. Some of Rarotonga's best accommodations, the three deluxe "Watergarden Villas" have stucco exteriors and huge wraparound verandas, which make them look like traditional coral-block colonial houses. Although they are behind and across a lily pond from the beachside units, they are more private and better equipped, with air-conditioned bedrooms, ceiling fans over both bedrooms and living areas, telephones, TVs and VCRs, microwaves and coffee plungers in their kitchens, and daily newspapers delivered to their verandas.

The Kemps and Tillicks rent cars and scooters, and their guest laundry—in its own little pondside chalet—has a telephone for making free local calls. A tourist-friendly grocery store and a butcher shop are nearby.

The Pacific Resort & Villas. P.O. Box 790, Rarotonga (Muri Beach, 10.7km [6.4 miles] from Avarua). ☎ **20-427.** Fax 21-427. www.pacificresort.com. E-mail: thomas@pacificresort.co.ck. 46 units, 7 houses. MINIBAR (houses only) TV (villas only) TEL. NZ$273–NZ$403 ($164–$242) double; NZ$532–NZ$571 ($319–$342) villa. AE, DC, MC, V.

Although it needs some maintenance, especially in its public areas, this resort sitting in a coconut grove alongside the island's best beach and lagoon comes closest of any Rarotonga property to capturing the appearance and ambiance of French Polynesia's small resorts. The luxurious seaside "villas" have two bedrooms, private entertainment areas, full kitchens, laundry facilities, minibars, and TVs with video players. Much less inviting, the one- or two-bedroom motel-like units have a kitchenette in addition to ceiling fans, modern bathroom with shower, wicker furnishings, and its own patio or balcony. At best they are medium sized, however, and the wicker furniture in some is too big for the space available. Most units are in two-story buildings on either side of a tropical garden complete with a stream crossed by two foot bridges. More bungalow-like, the beachside and beachfront suites give the impression of having your own cottage.

Dining/Diversions: The Barefoot Bistro Bar right on the beach offers breakfast, lunch, and snacks all day. In the same building, Sandals Restaurant serves breakfast and dinner at its open-air perch beside a stream. Island Night here usually is Friday (see "Island Nights" below).

Amenities: Swimming pool, volleyball court, children's playground, boutique, activities desk, guest laundry, rental cars and bikes, baby-sitting. Captain Tama's AquaSports on premises rents water sports equipment and teaches sailing and windsurfing.

Sokala Villas. P.O. Box 82, Rarotonga (Muri Beach, 10.4km [6.25 miles] from Avarua). ☎ **29-200.** Fax 21-222. www.sokala.com. E-mail: villas@sokala.co.ck. 7 bungalows. TEL. NZ$295–NZ$440 ($177–$264) double. MC, V. No children under 12.

This unusual property sits in a small beachside casuarina-and-palm grove facing Motutapu islet across Ngatangiia Channel. Much of the thick vegetation has been left intact, obscuring the lagoon views but adding touches such as palms growing through the decks and tin roofs of some bungalows. Built entirely of New Zealand pine, they seem more like mountain cabins than tropical island retreats, with half-round log exteriors and knotty interior walls. Four two-story units have sleeping lofts opening to their own decks. The single-floor cabins have a separate bedroom. All have decks facing the beach, and five have their own little swimming pools. Each unit has a full kitchen equipped with microwave oven. Privacy is sparse, however, since the cabins are packed together on this small parcel of land.

No children under 12 need apply.

There is no restaurant, but The Flame Tree (see "Dining," below) is next door, and The Pacific Resort and Emil's Cafe are short walks away. Services include laundry and morning papers delivered to each unit. Guests can use outrigger canoes.

HOTELS ON THE WEST COAST

Are-Renga Motel. P.O. Box 223, Rarotonga (Arorangi village). ☎ **20-050.** Fax 29-223. 20 units (18 with private bathroom). NZ$40 ($24) double. No credit cards.

This good budget choice is located in the village of Arorangi and is popular with Canadian travelers. The entire property enjoys a beautiful view of the mountains, and a path leads to the beach through a churchyard across the road. The Estall family run a basic but clean establishment, and their units make up for a complete lack of frills with ample space. Nine units are in a newer, motel-like block at the rear of the property. An older building has six units in which the bedroom is separated from the living-cooking area by a curtain; the three upstairs apartments share a large veranda, while a patio does double duty for the three downstairs. All units have kitchen facilities. In addition, a small house has three bedrooms; house guests share communal showers, toilets, kitchen facilities, lounge, and spacious veranda. Low-budget travelers can share a room in the house for NZ$15 ($9) each.

Edgewater Resort. P.O. Box 121, Rarotonga (Arorangi, 6.8km [4 miles] from Avarua). ☎ **25-435.** Fax 25-475. www.edgewater.co.ck. E-mail: stay@edgewater.co.ck. 182 units. A/C TV TEL. NZ$210–NZ$390 ($126–$234) double. AE, MC, V.

In number of rooms, the Edgewater is the island's largest resort, and like The Rarotongan Beach Resort (see below), it is often full of visitors on package tours. Although it's on a relatively small parcel of land—just four beachside acres—thick tropical foliage helps make the grounds seem less crowded. One of its two-story motel-style blocks of rooms was originally built as a clinic by the controversial cancer specialist Milan Brych, who was kicked out of the country in the 1970s after making a lot of money but curing no cancer. Several more concrete block structures have been added. Each room has a bougainvillea-draped patio or balcony. Rooms in the 400 and 500 blocks are closest to the beach and farthest from the restaurant/bar/swimming pool, which can be crowded and noisy when the house is full. The more expensive beachside executive suites are even farther removed, on the other side of the tennis courts, which places them among Rarotonga's most luxurious accommodations.

Dining/Diversions: Opening to the pool, the Edgewater Brasserie serves three ordinary meals a day at moderate prices (this hotel has had a history of being unable to retain good chefs). The Spaghetti House on the main road isn't much better. Entertainment features a buffet and Cook Islands dance show two nights a week, usually Tuesday and Saturday (one of the island's best troupes usually dances here on Saturday).

Amenities: Facilities include tennis courts with professional (guests get a free lesson), a Laundromat, video rentals, boutiques, and activities and car-rental desks.

Rocks along the shoreline have been pushed back to create a small beach overlooked by the pool and expansive patio space for sunning and sitting.

✪ **Lagoon Lodges.** P.O. Box 45, Rarotonga (on southwest corner, near The Rarotongan Beach Resort, 13.1km [7.8 miles] from Avarua). ☎ **800/528-1234** or 22-020. Fax 22-021. E-mail: des@lagoon.co.ck. 21 bungalows, 1 house. NZ$135–NZ$180 ($81–$108) bungalows; NZ$425 ($255) house for up to 7 persons. AE, MC, V.

Those who agree with me that bungalow living is the way to go in the South Pacific will find it at these lodges, which are within an easy walk of The Rarotongan Beach Resort. Owners/managers Des and Cassey Eggelton have studio-, one-, and two-bedroom units. Their recently added two-story units have big decks facing the lagoon and two upstairs bedrooms. All units have bathrooms with showers, ceiling fans, kitchenettes, dining tables, and spacious porches. Even though some are duplex, there is a feeling of privacy. They also have one real house: a three-bedroom villa with its own enormous veranda and private swimming pool, all set on a quarter of an acre of land. Guests can breakfast on a terrace whose architecture will remind you of Santa Fe (it's also the venue for popular Sunday night barbecues). Other meals may soon be offered, too. The tropical gardens contain a swimming pool, grass tennis court, and barbecue area, and the beach is just across the road. There's a guest laundry here.

✪ **Manuia Beach Boutique Hotel.** P.O. Box 700, Rarotonga (Arorangi, 8km [5 miles] from Avarua). ☎ **22-461.** Fax 22-464. www.manuia.co.ck. E-mail: rooms@manuia.co.ck. 20 units. TEL. NZ$215–NZ$295 ($129–$177) double. AE, MC, V.

This little establishment had been closed after experiencing financial difficulties, but it's back on line serving an adult clientele (no children under age 12 are accepted as guests). The 20 rooms are in 10 duplex bungalows set rather close together on a narrow rectangle of beachfront land. Tropical foliage helps give the garden units some semblance of privacy, but the more expensive beachfront units definitely are the choice here. Ceiling fans send breezes down over cool, white tile floors in all units, and sliding glass doors lead to semi-private wooden verandas. Angled shower stalls in one corner and lavatories in another maximize space in rather small bathrooms. The beachfront units have king-size beds and a view of the reef across a kidney-shaped swimming pool. Garden units have a queen and a single bed. None of the rooms have kitchens, but you can amble down to the Right on the Beach Bar and dig holes in its white-sand floor while enjoying a bistro-style meal under a low-slung thatch roof (food service is provided daily from 7:30am to 9:30pm). Services by the friendly staff are limited to laundry and arranging island activities. Guests can play with canoes, and snorkeling gear is available.

Puaikura Reef Lodges. P.O. Box 397, Rarotonga (southeast corner of island, 11.5km [6.9 miles] from Avarua). ☎ **23-537.** Fax 21-537. E-mail: accommodation@puaikura.co.ck. 12 units. TEL. NZ$113 ($68) double. MC, V.

This comfortable motel's units are situated in two 1-story buildings facing a grassy lawn, swimming pool, and barbecue area across the road from one of Rarotonga's sandiest stretches of beach. Half the units have a separate bedroom, and all have a double bed and two singles, tile bathroom with shower, clock radio, ceiling fan, kitchen, and patio with table and chairs. Rental cars and scooters are available, and a shady park with covered picnic tables is across the road along the beach.

The Rarotongan Beach Resort. P.O. Box 103, Rarotonga (southwest corner of the island, 13km [8 miles] from Avarua). ☎ **25-800.** Fax 25-799. www.rarotongan.co.ck. E-mail: info@rarotongan.co.ck. 151 units. A/C TEL. NZ$240–NZ$375 ($144–$225) double. AE, DC, MC, V.

After years of neglect by the government, which built it in 1977, Rarotonga's flagship hotel has received some much needed attention from its new owner, Tata Crocombe, a Cook Islander who graduated from Harvard Business School. There's still some work to be done, but the resort is superbly situated by the beach on the island's southwest corner.

The choice units here are 30 "beachfront deluxe" units, which are staggered to give the feel of individual bungalows. They have bathrooms with outdoor-feel showers, and their sliding front doors open to stone patios. The other guest quarters here are in nine 2-story buildings linked to the central complex by covered walkways. About two-thirds of these motel-style rooms face the beach and are air-conditioned (albeit by some noisy units). The less expensive garden models don't have the view and are cooled by ceiling fans. All rooms are accented by varnished natural wood and have a double bed and a single serving as a settee, a tiled bathroom with shower, and either a patio or balcony.

Dining/Diversions/Amenities: A shingle-roofed, island-style central building houses the reception and activities and car-rental desks, boutique, pearl shop, meeting rooms, and an open-kitchen restaurant and tropical bar beside rock-lined swimming pool with waterfall. Like most along Rarotonga's west coast, the beach here has seen some erosion, but a poolside stone patio and a large lagoonside deck are available for sunbathing or sipping drinks from the bar, and two hard-surface tennis courts beckon both guests and nonguests. A water sports desk provides plenty of playthings (outsiders can rent them, too), and Cook Islanders provide nightly entertainment, including twice-weekly dance shows.

✪ **The Rarotongan Sunset.** P.O. Box 377, Rarotonga (Arorangi, 6.3km [3.8 miles] from Avarua). ☎ **28-028.** Fax 28-026. E-mail: welcome@rarosunset.co.ck. 19 units. TV TEL. NZ$185–NZ$205 ($111–$123) double, NZ$345 ($207) suite. Rates include breakfast. AE, DC, MC, V.

Nicholas Reeves' and Deborah Manley's little place has come a long way since I spent my first night ever on Rarotonga here in the mid-1980s. Back then the units were furnished like a New Zealand motel, but today tropical chairs and tables make them look like they belong in the South Seas, not in Auckland. They recently turned four of their beachfront units into three air-conditioned suites; one has a bedroom, and the others are deluxe studio apartments. They and the older units have ceiling fans, a well-designed and -equipped kitchen, and separate bedroom. Net curtains double as mosquito netting across the sliding glass fronts at night. Dense tropical foliage provides privacy on this closely packed property, but it also means that only the beachfront units have lagoon views from their verandas. Set away from the beach, an odd-shaped swimming pool has a bridge over it, with a shallow end for children; and the adjacent "Bird Cage Bar" has colorful wooden parrots suspended from its peaked ceiling. House guests have breakfast by the pool, and they and outsiders alike can attend lively Sunday evening poolside barbecues. Rental cars and bikes are available. This is a very popular choice, so book early.

HOTELS IN OR NEAR AVARUA

Often the lowest-priced property offered as part of package tours, **Club Raro** (☎ 22-415), 2.4 kilometers (1.4 miles) east of Avarua, leaves much to be desired. The lagoon shore here is so rocky that it doesn't qualify as a beach. Lined up on either side of a main complex, the motel-style rooms (no cooking facilities) can be noisy. On the other hand, it does have popular Island Night buffets and dance shows (see "Island Nights," below).

✪ **Kii Kii Motel.** P.O. Box 68, Rarotonga (2.8km [1.6 miles] east of Avarua). ☎ **21-937.** Fax 22-937. E-mail: relax@kiikiimotel.co.ck. 20 units. TV TEL. NZ$84–NZ$143 ($50.50–$86) double. AE, DC, MC, V.

Harry and Pauline Napa's motel is one of Rarotonga's better bargains if you don't need a great beach. They have six units facing the lagoon, six units facing the swimming pool, eight older units with separate bedrooms, and four budget rooms. All are spacious, are spotlessly maintained, and have full kitchens. The pool helps compensate for the absence of sand on the beach. The lower-priced budget rooms have the same amount of space as the newer units but do not have phones or TVs. There is no restaurant or bar on the premises, but Club Raro is virtually next door. Ask about lower rates during the off-season.

Paradise Inn. P.O. Box 674, Rarotonga (Avarua, east of traffic circle). ☎ **20-544.** Fax 22-544. www.cookpages.com/paradiseinn. E-mail: paradise@gatepoly.co.ck. 16 units. NZ$47–NZ$99 ($28–$59.50) double. AE, MC, V.

Owner Diane Haworth liked vacationing at Rarotonga's most unusual accommodation so much that she bought it and moved here permanently. Until being converted into this inn-like hotel in 1986, this warehouse-size pink building was a dance hall. Most rooms have Pullman kitchens, lavatories, large glass doors opening out to a narrow walkway alongside the hotel, and spiral staircases leading to sleeping lofts with double beds. Two small budget rooms lack the lofts and have only single beds downstairs. One family unit is more like an apartment. The common areas at the rear of the building are split level, with an honesty bar and patio next to the rocky lagoon shore and an open-air lounge with a TV and VCR upstairs. Except for this common area, there are no grounds; the building occupies almost all the hotel's land.

HOSTELS

Aremango Guesthouse. P.O. Box 714, Rarotonga (Muri Beach, 11.2km [6.9 miles] east of Avarua). ☎ **24-362.** 10 units (none with bathroom). NZ$33 ($20) double. No credit cards.

The Tairea family constructed this modern, peaked-roof building specifically with backpackers in mind. A central hallway runs between the relatively spacious rooms, which have ceiling fans, screened windows, and two or three single beds which couples can push together to make a double. The communal kitchen is large enough so that everyone gets a cupboard, and the shared bathrooms have hot-water showers and are fully tiled (as are all the floors here). Guests can congregate in an indoor lounge, but most prefer the side porch with tables and chairs, the yard with lounge furniture under coconut palms, or Muri Beach, just a short walk away.

Backpackers' International Hostel. P.O. Box 878, Rarotonga (Arorangi, 12km [7.4 miles] from Avarua). ☎ **21-848.** Fax 21-847. E-mail: annabill@backpackers.co.ck. 20 units (none with bathroom), 15 dorm beds. NZ$13–NZ$18 ($8–$11) per person in rooms; NZ$16.50 ($10) dorm bed. Higher rates for first 3 nights. MC, V.

Bill Bates and family have been so successful with the backpackers' hostel, a block from the beach, that they have constructed a building to hold 20 simple rooms, all of which share toilets and showers. The upstairs part of their existing building is a dormitory with 15 beds. The open-air downstairs has a TV lounge and communal kitchen. Breakfasts are available, and there's a weekly Cook Islands–style feast. Airport transfers cost NZ$2 ($1.40) each way.

Vara's Beach House. P.O. Box 434, Rarotonga (Muri Beach, 11km [6.8 miles] east of Avarua). ☎ **21-156.** Fax 22-619. www.varas.co.ck. E-mail: backpack@varas.co.ck. 15 units (3 with bathroom), 2 cabins (both with bathroom), 36 dorm beds. NZ$42 ($25) double room; NZ$18 ($11) dorm bed. MC, V (plus 4%).

The liveliest backpacker retreat here, Vara's is often jammed with as many as 70 young travelers. Only a few can stay in the 5 rooms and 2 small cabins down at the beach house, which really is on Muri Beach, but everyone does their sunning, swimming, snorkeling, and hanging down there. The other rooms and bunks are in three more houses across the road and up the hill. Each of them has a communal kitchen, lounge, and veranda with ocean view. All rooms here have two to four single beds, and more are in hallways and even dining rooms. Guests get free use of canoes and washing machines and can pay for scooters, snorkeling gear, and e-mail access.

14 Dining

If you sampled the fare at French Polynesia's fine restaurants, then you may be disappointed in the Cook Islands. Most of the cuisine here is cooked to old-fashioned New Zealand tastes, which means the chefs go easy with the spices. By and large, fresh ingredients are limited to local fruits and vegetables. Aitutaki supplies some lobster and lagoon fishes, but most of the fresh (as opposed to frozen) seafood on Rarotonga will be tuna caught outside the reef—and even that may be unavailable if the weather has kept the local fishing boats in port. The island also occasionally may lack some imported ingredients such as butter and flour if a supply ship is late arriving. You'll get good, substantial meals here, but don't expect gourmet quality anywhere except The Flame Tree (see listing below).

Like the hotels above, I have arranged the restaurants by geographic location: Muri Beach, the west coast, and in or near Avarua town.

○ ISLAND FEASTS   Like their counterparts throughout Polynesia, in pre-European days the Cook Islanders cooked all their food in an earth oven—known here as an *umu*—and they still do for special occasions. The food *(umukai)* is as finger-licking good today as it was hundreds of years ago, although it's now eaten with knives and forks rather than fingers during "Island Nights" at Rarotonga's hotels, which include Cook Island dance shows (see "Island Nights," below). The hotels provide a wide assortment of salads and cold cuts for those who are not particularly fond of taro, arrowroot, and *ika mata* (the local version of poisson cru—fish marinated in lime juice and mixed with coconut milk and raw vegetables).

Get a schedule of island nights from Cook Islands Tourism Corporation. Also check the daily *Cook Islands News* (especially the Thursday and Friday editions) or with the hotels to find out when the feasts are on. The buffets cost about NZ$35 ($24.50), and reservations are essential at all the establishments. Some of them may charge a small admission to the dance show if you don't have dinner.

In addition to his coconut tree-climbing exhibitions (see "Cultural Experiences," above), **Piri Puruto II** (☎ **20-309**) stages Piri's Umukai Picnic every Sunday at 11am at Piri's Place, his lagoonside home on the south coast, east of The Rarotongan Beach Resort. Cost is NZ$35 ($21), which includes the meal and his coconut show.

Piri gets mostly tourists, but the Sunday night beachside barbecue at **Ati's Bungalows,** in Arorangi (☎ **21-546**), also draws locals who appreciate fine *umukai* in addition to grilled steaks, chicken, and lamb chops. Ati's feast begins at 6pm and costs NZ$20 ($12) per person, plus NZ$4 ($2.50) for transportation to and from Arorangi. Reservations are essential.

FOOD STALLS   Just as *les roulottes* offer some of the best food bargains in Papeete (see "Dining" in chapter 4), Rarotonga has its own version of these popular food trucks. Here they are the **food stalls** in Punanga Nui Market, near Avatiu Harbour. The best of the lot is **Moana Takeaways,** offering everything from cold coconuts to slake a thirst to seafood platters to placate late-night hunger pangs. Prices range from

NZ$3.50 to NZ$12.50 ($2 to $7.50). Most caravans are open Monday through Saturday from 9am to 6pm, and some stay open Monday through Thursday until 9pm, Friday until 2am, and Saturday until midnight. Guess where everyone goes after crawling the pubs on Friday night.

AT MURI BEACH

Emil's Cafe. Muri Beach, between The Pacific Resort and Muri Beachcomber. ☎ **28-967.** Reservations not accepted. Sandwiches and burgers NZ$3–NZ$5 ($1.80–$3); main courses NZ$10–NZ$15 ($6–$9). No credit cards. Mon–Sat 10am–9pm, Sun 5–10pm. REGIONAL.

Order at what looks like a carryout counter at Emil Cowan's clean little restaurant in a roadside storefront. Sandwiches, burgers, scones, donuts, ice cream, and main courses are offered all day, either to take away or to eat in at a few tables inside or on the front veranda. The mains consist of fried steak, chicken, or fish served with French fries and a helping of salad. Fattening, yes, but it's also the least expensive fare on Muri Beach.

✪ **The Flame Tree.** Muri Beach, near The Pacific Resort (10.5km [6.3 miles] from Avarua). ☎ **25-123.** Reservations required. Main courses NZ$17.50–NZ$27.50 ($10.50–$16.50). AE, MC, V. Daily 6:30–9:30pm. INTERNATIONAL.

Yachtie-turned-restaurateur Sue Curruthers likes "interesting food," and she serves it here at one of the South Pacific's top restaurants, within walking distance of The Muri Beachcomber, The Pacific Resort, and Sokala Villas. Calling on the cuisines of her native Kenya and other countries Sue visited during her extensive voyages before landing on Rarotonga, she whips together a wide range of selections, all displayed on a chalkboard menu, such as an absolutely delightful fish served under coconut, chili, and peanut sauce. I particularly enjoyed one of her nightly specials: fresh parrot fish breaded, fried, and served over rice and under a mound of taro-top spinach sweetly cooked in coconut sauce. These and other recipes are in Sue's *The Flame Tree Cookbook,* available here and at bookstores in Avarua. Smoking is allowed only at outside seating, not inside the converted house.

✪ **Maire Nui Gardens & Cafe.** Muri Beach, opposite The Little Polynesian. ☎ **22-796.** Reservations not accepted. Most items NZ$8.50–NZ$12 ($5–$7). No credit cards. Mon–Fri 8am–5pm, Sat 9am–5pm, Sun noon–5pm. SALADS/SANDWICHES.

You won't appreciate Hinano MacQuarie's sophisticated cafe from the road, but wait until you walk around the thatch-roof building (which would elevate any hotel here) to the big veranda and its terrific vista of the green mountains rising beyond her flowery botanical gardens. It's the perfect spot to break a round-island tour, or stop in for breakfast, a light lunch, an afternoon snack, a fruit smoothie, or a cup of espresso, cappuccino, or fresh mint tea. Fried eggs and toast are Hinano's only breakfast offerings, but you'll have more choices from her lunch-and-afternoon blackboard menu. If it's offered, her naturally sweet pawpaw (papaya) and smoked chicken salad served with focaccia bread is an unforgettable winner.

ON THE WEST COAST

✪ **Alberto's Steakhouse.** Arorangi, near Edgewater Resort. ☎ **23-597.** Reservations accepted. Main courses NZ$14–NZ$29.50 ($8.50–$17.50); 3-course special NZ$21.50 ($13). MC, V. Daily 6–9pm (bar opens 5:30pm). STEAKS/SEAFOOD.

A New Zealander living on Rarotonga once said she appreciated the sacrifices of the Kiwis at home, since all their country's top-grade beef is exported rather than consumed at home. Some of these tender steaks end up here at Alberto and Vira Bachman's roadside restaurant, where exposed dark beams, potted plants, and tables with candles help set a romantic scene. I opted for their value-priced special: a thin but tasty rump steak with salad bar, garlic bread, and dessert. A big blackboard announces fresh local lobster in lemon butter and other nightly specials, including char-grilled tuna, wahoo, and mahimahi when available. Otherwise, Swiss-born Alberto serves fish such as blue cod pan-fried with sauces. Pastas also are on the menu, including fettuccine Alberto (seafood in a white wine sauce). Quality wines are available by the glass here.

Kaena Restaurant and Bar. Arorangi, near The Rarotongan Beach Resort. ☎ **25-433.** Reservations accepted. Main courses NZ$12.50–NZ$28 ($7.50–$17). AE, DC, MC, V. Daily 6–10pm. REGIONAL.

In business since 1982, Tauei and Lynne Solomon's little place offers convenient dining for guests of the nearby Rarotongan Resort, Lagoon Lodges, and Puaikura Reef Lodges. The Kaena shares a building with a mom-and-pop grocery; don't be misled by the outside appearance, for the restaurant is quite charmingly decorated. You can dine inside or in an enclosed verandalike room with flowering vines growing under the tin roof. Main courses include charbroiled steaks either plain or with sauce, chicken in fruit or coconut sauce, and seafood selections.

Tumanu Tropical Restaurant & Bar. Arorangi, near Edgewater Resort. ☎ **20-501.** Reservations recommended. Main courses NZ$18–NZ$27 ($11–$16). AE, MC, V. Daily 6–10pm; bar open to midnight. REGIONAL.

With its low-slung roof and lush outdoor gardens, this is the only restaurant and bar on Rarotonga that genuinely looks like it belongs in the South Seas. Julie and Eric Bateman's cozy place has subdued lighting inside, foreign flags hanging on split bamboo walls, and various paraphernalia stuck around the bar area, including old license plates from as far away as Texas, Oregon, Iowa, and Alaska. Colorful tablecloths help spice up otherwise plain dining room furniture. The menu is heavy on seafood served braised or fried, but you can also get baked chicken or steaks in pepper or mushroom sauce. A special vegetarian platter comes with fruit salad, vegetables, and cheese omelet. A caution is in order: The humor can get raunchy at Eric's lively bar. Eric spends the day diving, so stop by and leave your name on the reservation sheet just inside the entry.

Vaima Restaurant & Bar. Takitimu, 1km (0.6 mile) east of The Rarotongan Beach Resort. ☎ **26-123.** Reservations recommended. Snacks NZ$4–NZ$10 ($2.50–$6); main courses NZ$16.50–NZ$24 ($10–$14.50). MC, V. Daily 11:30am–5pm and 6:30–10pm. INTERNATIONAL.

Hikers coming off the Cross Island Track often step right into this bamboo-clad beachside restaurant, which offers cold drinks and bar snacks such as Chinese spring rolls and spicy Indian samosas all afternoon. At dinner, talented chef and co-owner Mata Young takes over, offering a wide range of exciting tastes. Her menu features the likes of spicy Thai-style chicken and pan-fried, grilled, or Cajun-style parrot fish, or you can choose from her daily blackboard specials such as Indian beef vindaloo (which she will prepare mild as well as fiery, thank goodness). The bamboo walls of the main dining room feature works by local artists (they're for sale). There are four tables on a veranda facing the beach, and picnic tables out by the sand.

IN AVARUA

Blue Note Café. Avarua, at the traffic circle. ☎ **23-236.** Breakfast NZ$3–NZ$12.50 ($2–$7.50); sandwiches, salads, and burgers NZ$5–NZ$8.50 ($3.50–$6); meals NZ$10.50–NZ$12.50 ($6.50–$7). MC, V. Daily 7am–6pm. SNACK BAR/REGIONAL.

A fine place to take a town break and watch the traffic along the waterfront, this open-air snack bar occupies one end of the veranda of the Banana Court building. Breakfast is served all day, as are cappuccino, fruit smoothies, homemade ice cream, milk shakes, and other refreshments. Sandwiches and big burgers are made to order for lunch, or you can choose a daily special such as pasta or curry.

✪ **The Cafe.** Avarua, east of traffic circle. Reservations not accepted. Sandwiches and salads NZ$6–NZ$9.50 ($3.50–$5.50). No credit cards. Mon–Fri 8am–4pm, Sat 9am–2pm. SALADS/SANDWICHES/SNACKS.

This urbane cafe, which would grace Auckland's trendy Parnell district, is the best place to grab a pastry and a cup of cappuccino or espresso before striking out on your tour of Avarua. And when you've finished your walk, you can retire here and select from daily specials such as veggie quiche, pan-seared tuna over a Greek salad, or a pannini-style sandwich (pastrami, eggplant, and mustard is nicely piquant). Lots of natural wood and big canvas patio umbrellas hung from the ceiling create an out-doorsy ambience. Half of the building is devoted to upscale housewares and gourmet foodstuffs. You can even buy quality cigars here.

Cook's Corner Cafe. Avarua, in Cook's Corner. ☎ **22-345.** Burgers and sandwiches NZ$2.50–NZ$8 ($1.50–$5); meals and breakfasts NZ$6–NZ$12.50 ($3.50–$7.50). No credit cards. Mon–Fri 7am–3:30pm, Sat 7am–noon. SNACK BAR.

You will find me having a cooked breakfast and reading the *Cook Island News* at Maureen Young's little sidewalk cafe, where everyone waits for the bus (it begins its runs here). She serves breakfast all day plus snacks, morning and afternoon teas, and light lunches, which include the likes of curry, fish and chips, and spicy roast chicken. They are purchased at a counter and eaten on the covered sidewalk of the small shopping center.

Mama's Cafe. Avarua, west of traffic circle next to Foodland. ☎ **23-378.** Sandwiches and pastries NZ$2–NZ$5.50 ($1.20–$3.50); meals NZ$5.50–NZ$7.50 ($3.50–$4.50). No credit cards. Mon–Fri 8am–3pm, Sat 8am–noon. SNACK BAR.

Look for Mama's clean cafeteria-style cafe next to the big Foodland grocery store. Walk along the cafeteria line and choose from a variety of snacks in the cold or hot cabinets. Then, if you can find one vacant, eat at one of the plastic tables in the airy indoors seating area or outside on a narrow patio. Best thing here: milk shakes from the ice cream bar at the front. Served after noon, meals include fried rice, curries, and Chinese-style stir fries.

Portofino Restaurant. Avarua, east of traffic circle. ☎ **26-480.** Reservations recommended. Pizzas NZ$11.25 ($6.50); main courses NZ$15–NZ$32.50 ($9–$19.50); pasta dinner special NZ$17.50 ($10.50). AE, MC, V. Mon–Sat 6:30–9:30pm. ITALIAN.

This cozy old clapboard store dressed up with a cross between Mediterranean and Polynesian decor is the best place in town for pizza or pasta. An open-air pavilion to one side makes room for a few fresh-air tables. Spaghetti or penne is served with Neapolitan, bolognese, Florentine, or Alfredo sauces, either as a heavy appetizer or as a main course. Tender charbroiled New Zealand–bred steaks are cooked plain or under chili, garlic, or pepper sauce. Daily specials feature such tempting dishes as a seafood lasagna with fish, crabmeat, and smoked mussels. A money-saving feature here is an all-you-can-eat pasta dinner. Pizzas and pastas are available to carry out.

Stair Case Restaurant & Bar. Avarua, east of traffic circle, over Top Shape Health & Fitness. ☎ **22.254.** Reservations accepted. Main courses NZ$12–NZ$16 ($7–$9.50); steak specials NZ$10 ($6). MC, V. Wed–Fri 6:30–9pm (bar open Fri to 2am). REGIONAL.

Although the setting here is not as scenic as at Trader Jack's (see below), this upstairs dining room does have a view of seaside palms spotlighted at night. Mat walls, cane furniture, plants, varnished wood, and soft lighting enhance a relaxed, tropical ambiance that draws more local residents than visitors. A blackboard menu offers a few

Cook Islands Dancing

No one should miss an "island night" Polynesian dance show on Rarotonga, for Cook Islanders are justly famous for their dancing. A New Zealander once told me in jest that all Cook Islanders are deaf because they grow up 3 feet from a drum whose beats you can hear from 3 miles away.

The hip-swinging tamure is very much like that in Tahiti, except it tends to be faster (which I found hard to believe the first time I saw it) and even more suggestive (which I had even more trouble believing). The costumes generally aren't as colorful as those in Tahiti, but are more likely to be made in the traditional fashion, using natural materials as opposed to dyed synthetic fabrics.

Even though the dance shows at the hotels are tailored for tourists, the participants go at it with an enthusiasm that is too seldom seen in the French Polynesian hotel shows these days. Dancing is the thing to do in the Cook Islands, and it shows every time the drums start their tattoo.

Unadulterated Cook Islands dancing is best seen during the annual Dance Week in April or during the Constitution Week celebrations in late July and early August.

In the absence of one of these celebrations, make do with a show or two at the hotels. There will be at least one performance every night except Sunday. A little detective work is required, but you'll easily find out where the next island night is being staged. Ask at your hotel tour desks or Cook Islands Tourism Corporation, which publishes a night-by-night listing of current evening entertainment and prices. Another source is the daily *Cook Islands News*. Most feasts and shows will set you back about NZ$30 to NZ$40 ($18 to $24).

---

steaks and fresh fish dishes, but the winners here are the budget-priced nightly steak specials; mine was grilled to perfection and served with a fresh, tasty potato salad. There's usually a Cook Island dance show here on Thursday, and the Stair Case turns into a very popular disco at 10pm on Friday (see "Island Nights," below).

✪ **Trader Jack's Bar & Grill.** Avarua, waterfront at traffic circle. ☎ **26-464.** Reservations recommended at dinner. Lunch NZ$11–NZ$18 ($6.50–$11); main courses NZ$18–NZ$28 ($11–$16.50). AE, DC, MC, V. Mon–Sat noon–2pm and 6–10pm, Sun 6–9pm. Bar Mon–Thurs and Sat 11am–midnight, Fri 11am–2am, Sun 6–9pm. REGIONAL.

You won't be on Rarotonga long before you hear about New Zealander "Trader Jack" Cooper's. One of Rarotonga's few restaurants actually beside the water, it's popular with local business and professional folk. The place usually is packed at happy hour Monday through Thursday and all of Friday and Saturday nights. Floor-to-ceiling windows on three sides open to the water, giving nearly everyone in the large bar, split-level dining area, and long lagoonside deck a view of the harbor, the reef, and the sea and sunsets beyond. A regular printed menu plays second fiddle to the fresh chalkboard specials, which depend on local produce and are among the best food served on the island. Snacks are offered from 3 to 6pm. Veteran pianist Garth Young is on the keyboard Sunday through Tuesday nights, and other fine musicians entertain the rest of the week.

15 Island Nights

Cook Islanders are some of the most fun-loving folks you will meet in the South Pacific, and you can easily catch their spirit. Every evening except Sunday seems to be a party night, especially Friday, when the pubs stay open until 2am (they close promptly when the Sabbath strikes at Saturday midnight). And like their Tahitian cousins, the infectious sound of the traditional drums starts everyone dancing.

PUB CRAWLING

When Rarotongans aren't dancing in a show, they seem to be dancing with each other at one or more of the most colorful bars in the South Pacific. No one ever explained to me why they call their tour-de-pubs a crawl. I assume it's because crawling is one method of travel after a few too many of the locally brewed Cook's Lagers.

All you have to do is walk along the Avarua waterfront east of the traffic circle after 10pm Friday; you'll hear the bands playing and can check out the crowds for yourself.

For the less rowdy among us, the Friday night crawl begins (and for many folks it ends) at ✪ **Trader Jack's Bar & Grill** (☎ 26-464) at Avarua's old harbor, where the town's affluent movers and shakers start boozing after work. Pianist Garth Young appears at Jack's from Sunday through Tuesday, while bands take the stage other nights.

After 10pm on Friday, you can wander over to the **Stair Case Restaurant & Bar** (☎ 22-254), east of the traffic circle, for rock-and-roll music and dancing. Younger Cook Islanders stop at **Metua's Cafe** (☎ 2-850), in Brown's Arcade near the traffic circle.

After the bewitching hour of 2am Saturday morning, many crawlers head to the food stalls at Punanga Nui Market and Avatiu Harbour.

16 A Side Trip to Aitutaki

The farther away visitors get from the South Pacific's international airports, the more likely you are to find an island and a way of life that have escaped relatively unscathed by the coming of Western ways—remnants of "old" Polynesia. This is certainly true of Aitutaki, the most frequently visited of the outer Cook Islands.

Lying 225 kilometers (140 miles) north of Rarotonga, Aitutaki is often referred to as "the Bora Bora of the Cook Islands" because it consists of a small, hilly island at the apex of a triangular barrier reef dotted with skinny flat islands. This reef necklace encloses one of the South Pacific's most beautiful lagoons, which appears at the end of the flight up from Rarotonga as a turquoise carpet spread on the deep blue sea. The view from the air is memorable.

The central island, only 8 square miles in area, is dotted with the coconut, pineapple, banana, and tapioca plantations that are worked by most of the island's 2,500 residents. A few Aitutakians make their living at the island's hotels, but the land and the lagoon still provide most of their income. Aitutaki is a major supplier of produce and seafood to Rarotonga. Much of the fresh reef fish and lobsters consumed at Rarotonga's restaurants are harvested here.

The administrative center, most of the shops, and the main wharf are on the west side of the island at **Arutanga** village, where a narrow, shallow passage comes through the reef. Trading boats cannot get through the pass and must remain offshore while cargo and passengers are ferried to land on barges. A network of mostly unpaved roads fans out from Arutanga to **Viapai** and **Tautu** villages on the east side, and to the airport on a flat hook at the northern end of the island.

The uninhabited coconut-studded small islands out on the reef have white-sand beaches on their lagoon sides and pounding surf on the other; they're perfect for picnics and snorkeling expeditions, which are Aitutaki's prime attractions.

A LITTLE HISTORY   Legend says that in the beginning Aitutaki was completely flat, but then its warriors sailed to Rarotonga and stole the top of Mount Raemaru.

At last I came to Maungapu, the highest point on Aitutaki. At 407 feet high, Maungapu is no Everest, but it offered me a view that, I submit, could not have been improved upon by Everest itself.

—Lawrence Millman, 1990

Pitched battles were fought on the way home, and parts of the mountain fell into the sea: Black Rock, on Rarotonga's northwest point; Rapota and Moturakau islands, in the south of Aitutaki's lagoon; and the black rocks along Aitutaki's west coast. In the end, the Aitutakian warriors were victorious, and the top of Raemaru is now **Mount Maungapu,** the highest point on Aitutaki at 407 feet. There's a walking trail to the top (see "Boating, Golf, Hiking & Scuba Diving," below).

According to another legend, the first Polynesians to reach Aitutaki came in through **Ootu Pass,** between the airport and **Akitua** island, site of the Aitutaki Lagoon Resort. They were led by the mighty warrior and navigator Ru, who brought four wives, four brothers, and a crew of 20 young virgins from either Tubuai or Raiatea (the legend varies as to which one) in what is now French Polynesia. Akitua island, where they landed, originally was named Urituaorukitemoana, which means "where Ru turned his back on the sea."

The first European to visit Aitutaki was Capt. William Bligh, who discovered it in 1789 a few weeks before he was set adrift in Tonga by the mutinous crew of H.M.S. *Bounty.* Just south of the post office in Arutanga is the **Cook Islands Christian Church,** the country's oldest, built in 1839 of coral and limestone. The monument in front is to John Williams, the exploring missionary who came to Aitutaki in October 1821, and to Papeiha, the Tahitian teacher who came with him and stayed for 2 years, during which he converted the entire island. Papeiha then went to Rarotonga and helped the missionaries do the same thing there. The interior of the church is unusual in that the altar is on one side rather than at one end. Worshippers from each village sit together during services, but visitors can take any vacancy during services at 10am on Sunday. An anchor suspended from the ceiling is a symbol of hope being a sure and steadfast anchor, as in Hebrews 6:19.

The volcanic part of Aitutaki is joined to the reef on the island's north end, and it was here that the American forces—with considerable help from the local residents—built the large airstrip during World War II. About 1,000 Americans were stationed at the strip, which was used as a refueling stop on the route between North America and New Zealand. Many present-day Aitutakians reportedly are the children and grand-children of those American sailors. The war ended before the Americans could complete a navigable channel from Arutanga to deep water. Today all cargo must be unloaded offshore and brought to the wharf by barge.

The late Sir Albert Henry was born and raised on Aitutaki, and the divided road to the wharf is named for him and his wife Elizabeth (one lane for Sir Albert and one lane for Lady Elizabeth).

GETTING THERE

Air Rarotonga (☎ **22-888** on Rarotonga, 31-888 on Aitutaki) has several 50-minute flights a day from Monday through Saturday to and from Aitutaki. Regular round-trip fare is about NZ$326 ($195.50), but this drops to NZ$218 ($131) if you fly during off-peak times such as early morning or late afternoon. Air Rarotonga also has day trips to Aitutaki for about NZ$349 ($209.50), which includes round-trip air fare and a lagoon excursion with a barbecue lunch.

Air-hotel packages to Aitutaki can vary in price but always represent a savings over do-it-yourself arrangements, so check with Air Rarotonga or the travel agents in Avarua to see whether they have deals. **Island Hopper Vacations** (☎ 22-026), **Hugh Henry & Associates** (☎ 25-320), and **Stars Travel** (☎ 23-669) specialize in outer-island trips.

Since Aitutaki's airport sits on the northeast corner of the island, you should fly over the lagoon on the approach; you're likely to see more of the island from the left side of the aircraft.

GETTING AROUND

The airport is about 7 kilometers (4 miles) from most hotels and guest houses. The airline provides airport transfers for NZ$5 ($3) each way. The minibuses pick up passengers from the hotels prior to departing flights. Ask the hotel desk to reconfirm your return to Rarotonga; otherwise, the bus won't stop for you. Air Rarotonga's office is in Ureia village just north of Arutanga (☎ 31-888).

There is no public transportation system on Aitutaki.

All hotels and guest houses can arrange car, scooter, and bike rentals, or you can call **Rino's Rentals** (☎ 31-197) or **Swiss Rentals** (☎ 31-600), both north of Arutanga. Scooters go for NZ$20 ($12) a day, bikes for NZ$5 ($3) a day, cars for NZ$60 ($36) a day, and Jeeps for NZ$80 ($48) a day.

FAST FACTS: AITUTAKI

Currency Exchange   Except at the hotels and guest houses, don't rely on credit cards or traveler's checks. Westpac Bank's small agency here is only open Wednesdays from 9:30am to 3pm, and only small denomination checks can be cashed at the post office in Arutanga Monday through Thursday from 8am to 3pm, Friday from 8am to 1pm.

Dentist/Doctor   See "Hospitals," below.

Drugstores   Some prescription drugs are available at the island's hospital near Arutanga. There is no private pharmacy on Aitutaki.

Emergencies   In case of emergency, contact your hotel staff. The police station is in Arutanga.

Hospitals   Medical and dental treatment are available at the island's hospital near Arutanga.

Post Office   The post office at Arutanga is open Monday through Friday 8am to 4pm.

Radio/Television   The national radio stations can be received here, and a small privately owned TV station broadcasts CNN, ESPN, and ABC News from the U.S.

Safety   The police station is in Arutanga. See "Fast Facts: Rarotonga" earlier in this chapter for general warnings and precautions.

Telegrams/Fax   The communications counter at the post office is open Monday through Friday from 8am to 4pm. It does not accept credit cards.

Visitor Information   Cook Islands Tourism Corporation does not have an office on Aitutaki, so stop at its visitor center in Rarotonga before coming here—and bring at least one of the tourist publications which has a current map of Aitutaki.

Water   Don't drink the tap water on Aitutaki unless you are sure it comes from a rainwater catchment. Ask first.

EXPLORING AITUTAKI

This is a very small island, perfect for seeing via scooter or bicycle. I describe the main attractions in the introduction to this section and in "A Little History," above, and they're all easy to find if you've brought a map with you from Rarotonga. The Aitutaki Lagoon Resort offers guided sightseeing expeditions with **Nane & Chloe Tours**

(☎ **31-248**), or you can go with Mike Henry's **Island Tours** (☎ **31-339**) for NZ$26 ($15.50) per person.

There's not much to buy up here, but one place worth exploring is **Aitutaki Hand-craft** (☎ **31-127**), south of the airport on the road to the Aitutaki Lagoon Resort. This actually is the home of Phil Low, an accomplished wood-carver. He works in his garage and shows off his wildlife, Tangaroas, ukuleles, and other works inside his and wife Jan's home. One of them is usually around daily from 8am to 5pm.

✪ LAGOON EXCURSIONS

The biggest attraction on Aitutaki is a day on the lagoon and one of the small islands out on the reef. The "standard" day trip begins at 9am and ends about 4pm. The boats spend the morning cruising and fishing on the lagoon. Midday is spent on one of the reef islands, where guests swim, snorkel, and sun while the crew cooks the day's catch and the local vegetables. The itinerary changes from day to day depending on the weather and the guests' desires.

A common destination is **Tapuaetai,** or "One Foot" Island, and its adjacent sandbar known as Nude Island (for its lack of foliage, not clothes). According to Teina Bishop, who runs one of the lagoon excursions, this tiny motu got its name when an ancient chief prohibited his subjects from fishing there on pain of death. One day the chief and his warriors saw two people fishing on the reef and gave chase. The two were a man and his young son. They ran onto the island, the boy carefully stepping in his father's footprints as they crossed the beach. The son then hid in the top of a coconut tree. The chief found the father, who said he was the only person fishing on the reef. After a search proved fruitless, the chief decided it must have been rocks he and his men saw on the reef. He then killed the father. Ever since, the island has been known as Tapuaetai (in the local dialect, *tapuae* means footprint, and *tai* is one).

Those dark things that look like cucumbers dotting the bottom of the lagoon, by the way, are bêches-de-mer (sea slugs). Along with sandalwood, they brought many traders to the South Pacific during the 19th century because both brought high prices in China. Sea slugs are harmless—except in China, where they are considered to be an aphrodisiac.

Your hotel can book an excursion for you any day except Sunday with Teina Bishop and his **Bishop's Lagoon Cruises** (☎ **31-009;** fax 31-493; e-mail bishopcruz@ aitutaki.net.ck). In addition to his all-day outings, Teina offers sunset barbecue cruises. He charges NZ$50 ($30) per person for the all-day excursions. There are no lagoon cruises on Sunday, but Teina will take you snorkeling at 1pm for NZ$30 ($18) per person.

If you come on an Air Rarotonga day trip (see "Getting There," above), you'll cruise on a larger but slower boat equipped with a bar and toilet.

The boats have canopies, but bring a hat and plenty of sunscreen. The sun on the lagoon can blister even under a canopy.

BOATING, GOLF, HIKING & SCUBA DIVING

BOATING   You can rent Hobie Cats and kayaks at **Samade** (☎ **31-526**), on the lagoon north of the Aitutaki Lagoon Resort. Instead of going to the resort at the Y intersection, follow the dirt track to the west. There's a snack bar on the premises. It's open daily. Call for prices.

GOLF   Golfers who missed hitting the radio antennae and guy wires on the Raro-tonga course can try again at the nine-hole course at the Aitutaki Golf Club, on the north end of the island between the airport and the sea. Balls hit onto the runway used to be playable, but broken clubs and increasing air traffic put an end to that. You can rent equipment at the clubhouse. The club has neither a phone nor regular hours, but the hotels and guest houses can arrange rentals and a tee-off time. Members are more likely to volunteer to mow the greens between May and August than during the wetter summer months.

HIKING   Hikers can take a trail to the top of Mount Maungapu, Aitutaki's highest point at 124 meters (410 feet). It begins about a mile north of the former Rapae Cottage Hotel (a well-known and often-used local landmark), across from the Paradise Cove Guest House. The trail starts under the power lines and follows them uphill for about a mile. The tall grass is sharp and can be soaked after a rain, but the track is usually well tramped and should be easy to follow. Nevertheless, wear trousers. The view from the top includes all of Aitutaki and its lagoon. Sunrise and sunset are the best times.

SCUBA DIVING   Divers can contact Neil Mitchell of **Aitutaki Scuba,** P.O. Box 40, Aitutaki (☎ **31-103; fax 31-310;** e-mail scuba@aitutaki.net.ck), for underwater adventure over the edge of the reef. Neil operates from his home just south of the former Rapae Cottage Hotel. He charges NZ$60 ($36) per one-tank dive, or NZ$70 ($42) including equipment, and will teach a 4-day PADI and NAUI certification course for NZ$475 ($285). Neil also can tell you how to go deep-sea fishing.

ACCOMMODATIONS

✪ **Aitutaki Lagoon Resort.** P.O. Box 99, Aitutaki (on Akitua Island, 2km [1.2 miles] south of airport, 9km [5.4 miles] from Arutanga). ☎ **20-234** for reservations or 31-201. Fax 23-234 for reservations or 31-202. E-mail: hotel@aitutakiresort.co.ck or akitua@aitutaki.net.ck. 30 bungalows. A/C MINIBAR TEL. NZ$305–NZ$665 ($183–$399) double. AE, DC, MC, V.

Although pricey, this is the best all-around resort in the Cook Islands, a scattering of individual bungalows around a central building on the beach. It's reached by foot bridge across Ootu Passage to Akitua, a sandy islet south of the airport. The ocean surf breaks on one side of Akitua; on the other, the magnificent lagoon laps a white-sand beach, off which a channel has been dredged deep enough for swimming.

The choice—and most expensive—units here are deluxe beachfront bungalows which have raised sleeping areas behind sofa-equipped lounges opening through sliding, wooden louvered doors to lagoonside decks. Their modern bathrooms have double sinks and bidets. Although close together, remodeled versions of the older bungalows have solid walls on one side, which affords privacy at the expense of ventilation (air conditioners and ceiling fans calm the heat, but they operate only when you're in your room). Cane chairs and dinette tables sit before front walls of glass, which let in lots of light, and cafe doors swing open to dressing areas just off each unit's dated but adequate shower-only bathroom. The least expensive units here are some of the original bungalows which have been spruced up but not renovated; these have big window walls on two sides, which provide ventilation at the expense of privacy. Every bungalow here is air conditioned and has a wet bar, refrigerator, and coffeemaker but no cooking facilities.

Dining/Diversions: Excellent international fare is provided in the large central building, which opens to the lagoon and a swimming pool. Another bar by the beach offers lunch and daytime snacks. Local entertainers strum and sing each evening, and 1 night a week usually sees an island dance show after dinner.

Amenities: Boutique, tour desk, water sports equipment, lounge with satellite-fed TV, nightly turndown, baby-sitting, laundry, limited room service (to deluxe bungalows only). Rental scooters are available on premises.

Aitutaki Lodges. P.O. Box 70, Aitutaki (east side of island, between Vaipai and Tautu villages). ☎ **31-334.** Fax 31-333. E-mail: aitlodge@aitutaki.net.ck. Rates include breakfast. 6 bungalows. MINIBAR. NZ$192 ($115) double. AE, MC, V.

Located on the east side of the island within a 10-minute drive of Arutanga village, Wayne and Aileen Blake's immaculate A-frame-style bungalows are set into a hillside sloping to the edge of the lagoon. Quiet and private, each has a queen-size and single bed, bathroom with a shower, ceiling fan, dinette booth, full kitchen including a stocked minibar, and porch offering spectacular views across the lagoon to the islands and the reef. The water in front of the hotel is too shallow for swimming, but Wayne or daughter Anita will customize lagoon cruises to fit his guests' desires. The Blakes will serve meals in a small thatch-roofed dining room and bar, from which guests have a grand view down a lawn to the lagoon.

Maina Sunset Motel. P.O. Box 34, Aitutaki (on west coast, 6km [3.7 miles] from airport, 1km [0.6 mile] south of Arutanga). ☎ **31-511.** Fax 31-611. 12 units, 1 apt. NZ$145–NZ$160 ($87–96) double, NZ$170 ($102) apt. AE, DC, MC, V.

Tauei and Lynn Solomon, owners of the Kaena Restaurant on Rarotonga, built this little motel on one of the prettiest stretches of beach on the island—but unfortunately they then fouled a fine view of Maina Island and glorious sunsets by constructing an unattractive pier out into the shallow lagoon. Their 1-story, New Zealand-style motel units are built around a courtyard with small pool. Four of the units have full kitchens and separate bedrooms; the others are like motel rooms with kitchens. All have verandas facing the pool, ceiling fans, and jalousie windows to permit ample cross-ventilation. A beachside dining room provides local-style breakfasts and dinners at moderate prices. The Solomons installed their own supply of drinkable tap water.

Paradise Cove Guest House. P.O. Box 64, Aitutaki (1.5km [1 mile] north of former Rapae Cottage Hotel). ☎ **31-218.** Fax 31-456 or 31-293. 5 units (none with private bathroom), 6 bungalows. NZ$35 ($21) double room; NZ$50 ($30) double hut. MC, V.

In a gorgeous beachside setting, the almost tentlike, very basic bungalows here are the only accommodations in the Cook Islands constructed of thatch and other natural materials. Low-slung thatch roofs cover just enough space for a bed and small refrigerator. They have electric lights and are fully screened. The rooms are in a European-style house that has a communal kitchen and large lounge. All guests share toilets and cold-water showers.

Rino's Beach Bungalows. P.O. Box 140, Aitutaki (Ureia Village, on west coast 0.5km [0.25] mile] north of Arutanga). ☎ **31-197.** Fax 31-559. 4 units, 4 apts (all with private bathroom). NZ$85 ($51) double room; NZ$125 ($75) beachfront apartment. MC, V.

These clean, comfortable New Zealand-style rooms and duplex apartments sit beside the beach in Ureia village, about halfway between Arutanga and the former Rapae Cottage Hotel. The more expensive apartments open directly to decks by the beach, while the standard rooms are in 2-story buildings just behind them. All units have kitchenettes, coffeemakers, table fans, and walls of wood paneling and concrete blocks painted white, although some flowered fabrics lend an islandy touch.

Sunny Beach Lodge. P.O. Box 94, Aitutaki (Ureia Village, on west coast 0.7km [0.4 mile] north of Arutanga). ☎ and fax **31-446.** 4 units. TV. NZ$80 ($48) double. No credit cards.

A palm grove sits between the beach and this modern, clean, and comfortable motel-style building. Entry to the spacious, U-shaped rooms is off a long porch equipped with plastic chairs. All four units have double and single beds, dinette tables and chairs, full kitchens, and shower-only bathrooms. End units with big jalousie windows on the sides are preferable.

Viakoa Units. Amuri, Aitutaki (on west coast 1.5km [1 mile] north of Arutanga). ☎ and fax **31-145.** 7 units (all with private bathroom). NZ$50 ($30) double. No credit cards.

Although separated from the beach by a palm-shaded yard, the basic but clean units here are a good choice for penny-conscious backpacking couples who want a hot shower, a double bed, and more space that they'll get at the Paradise Cove Guest House (see above). Built motel-fashion in two parallel wings, the rooms also have kitchens, dining tables, ceiling fans, and screened louvered windows.

DINING

The Crusher Bar. Amuri (west coast, 1.5km [1 mile] north of former Rapae Cottage Hotel). ☎ **31-283.** Reservations required. Main courses NZ$16–NZ$18 ($9.50–$11). MC, V. Sat–Thurs 7:30–11pm; bar open Sat–Thurs 6:30pm–midnight. REGIONAL.

Along with English-born wife Lesley, owner Teariki "Ricky" Devon makes this one of the most charming South Seas restaurant-bars I have ever been in. An entertainer who made his mark in Australia and Europe, Ricky brought Lesley and their children home to Aitutaki a few years ago and named this old-fashioned, thatch-roofed spot after the gravel-maker at the rock quarry not far away. Dinners consist of a salad bar and local fish and New Zealand steaks. Thursday is Island Night here, with a Cook Island dance show before a buffet. Saturday sees a "backpacker's special" meal for NZ$12.50 ($7.50), and Sunday is roast night for NZ$18 ($11).

When enough guests are on hand, Ricky and whomever he can round up take to the stage and entertain the rest of the night. "Ricky isn't a bar owner," said one guest, "He's a first-rate blues musician." You'll soon forget the food, but you will long remember the music.

Kuramoo Takeaways. Ureia Village, on west coast 0.5km (0.25 mile north of Arutanga). ☎ **31-604.** Reservations not accepted. Hot dogs and burgers NZ$1.50–NZ$5.50 (90¢–$3.50); meals NZ$7–NZ$16 ($4–$9.50). No credit cards.

Order at the carry-out window cut into this bright blue building, then settle in at one of the plastic tables under a thatch lean-to roof. Burgers come Antipodean-style (with slaw and a slice of beetroot), and the simple meals feature local produce (octopus is fried and served with French fries and a salad) or tender New Zealand beef (the grilled steaks bring the locals here). For dessert have a banana or pineapple fritter with ice cream. No beer or wine are served.

Ralphie's Bar & Grill. Amuri, on west coast opposite former Rapae Cottage Hotel. ☎ **31-418.** Reservations required for dinner. Lunches NZ$7.50–NZ$10.50 ($4.50–$6.50); main courses NZ$17.50–NZ$21 ($10.50–$12.50). MC, V. Sun–Thurs 10am–9pm, Fri 10am–2am, Sat 10am–midnight. REGIONAL.

Andrew and Moyra McBirney offer a variety of fare. To one side, they serve fish and chips, salads, and other light items at a counter. You can take it away or eat at picnic tables under tin or thatch roofs. Dinners served inside their modern octagonal building with shingle roof feature daily specials from a blackboard menu, usually fresh seafood and a mixture of grills.

ISLAND NIGHTS

Other than whatever is going on at the Aitutaki Lagoon Resort (see "Accommodations," above), evening entertainment during the week consists of having dinner and listening to music (live or recorded) at **The Crusher Bar** (☎ 31-283; see "Dining," above). As I said above, this is one of the most charming South Seas bars I have ever been in.

Island Night feasts and dance shows usually take place Thursday at The Crusher Bar; Friday at **Ralphie's Bar & Grill** (☎ 31-418; see "Dining," above); and Saturday at the Aitutaki Lagoon Resort.

Introducing Fiji

8

If there is one thing every visitor remembers about Fiji, it's the enormous friendliness of the Fijian people. You'll see why as soon as you get off the plane, clear Customs and Immigration, and are greeted by a procession of smiling faces, all of them exclaiming an enthusiastic *"Bula!"* That one word—"health" in Fijian—expresses the warmest and most heartfelt welcome you'll receive anywhere.

This relatively large and diverse country's great variety will also be immediately evident, for the taxi drivers who whisk you to your hotel are not Fijians of Melanesian heritage, but Indians whose ancestors migrated to Fiji to escape the shackles of poverty in places like Calcutta and Madras. Now slightly less than half the population, these "Fiji Indians" have played major roles in making their country the most prosperous of the independent South Pacific island nations.

The great variety continues to impress as you go around the islands, for in addition to Fiji's cultural mix, you'll find gorgeous white-sand beaches bordered by curving coconut palms, azure lagoons and colorful reefs offering some of the world's best scuba diving and snorkeling, green mountains sweeping to the sea, and a warm climate in which to enjoy it all.

For budget-conscious travelers, Fiji is an affordable paradise. Its wide variety of accommodations ranges from deluxe resorts nestled in tropical gardens beside the beach to down-to-basics hostels catering to the young and the young-at-heart. It has a number of charming and inexpensive small hotels and the largest and finest collection of remote, Robinson Crusoe–like offshore resorts in the entire South Pacific—if not the world. Regardless of where you stay, you are in for a memorable time. The Fijians will see to that.

1 Fiji Today

From their strategic position in the southwestern Pacific some 3,200 miles southwest of Honolulu and 1,960 miles northeast of Sydney, Fiji is the transportation and economic hub of the South Pacific islands. **Nadi International Airport** is the main connection point for flights going to the other island countries, and Fiji's capital city, **Suva,** is one of the region's prime shipping ports.

The archipelago forms a horseshoe around the reef-strewn **Koro Sea,** a body of water shallow enough for much of it to have been dry land during the last Ice Age some 18,000 years ago. There are more than 300 bits of land ranging in size from **Viti Levu** ("Big Fiji"), which

There is no part of Fiji which is not civilized, although bush natives prefer a more naked kind of life.

—James A. Michener, 1951

is 10 times the size of Tahiti, to tiny atolls that barely break the surface of the sea. With a total land area of 7,022 square miles, Fiji is slightly smaller than the state of New Jersey. Viti Levu has 4,171 of those square miles, giving it more dry land than all the islands of French Polynesia put together.

Viti Levu and **Vanua Levu,** the second-largest island, lie on the western edge of Fiji. The **Great Sea Reef** arches offshore between them and encloses a huge lagoon dotted with beautiful islands. Many scuba divers think of the coral reefs in this lagoon, the **Astrolabe Reef** south of Viti Levu, and the **Rainbow Reef** between Vanua Levu and Taveuni as the closest places on earth—or below it—to paradise.

GOVERNMENT When the British granted independence to its former colony in 1970, they left Fiji with a constitution which set up a parliamentary democracy and left control of most land with the majority Fijians, while giving the Indians a chance to gain political power. Indians outnumbered the indigenous Fijians by the mid-1980s, however, and in coalition with some of the more liberal Fijians, they gained the upper political hand in parliamentary elections of 1987. Their new government lasted just 1 month until the Fijian-dominated army stormed into parliament and staged the region's first military coup. When the Commonwealth suspended Fiji's membership, the Fijian-led interim government declared the country to be the officially independent Republic of the Fiji Islands. In 1990 it promulgated a constitution giving the country a Fijian president and a parliament in which Fijians were guaranteed a majority and thus control of the government. This arrangement lasted until 1998, when the country adopted a new, fairer constitution which created a 65-member parliament made of up of 19 Fijian, 17 Indian, 3 general electors (anyone who's not a Fijian or Indian), 1 Rotuman, and 25 open seats. This led the way to the country's first Indian prime minister being elected in 1999 (see "History 101," below).

THE ECONOMY Fiji is the most self-sufficient of the South Pacific island countries. Tourism is its largest and most profitable industry; in fact, Fiji is the tourism Goliath among South Pacific island nations, getting twice as many visitors each year as French Polynesia, its nearest rival.

Sugar is still a close second to tourism. Grown primarily by Indian farmers, the cane is milled by the Fiji Sugar Company, a government-owned corporation. The cane is harvested between June and November and processed at five sugar mills, one each in Lautoka, Ba, Tavua, Rakiraki, and Labasa. The one at Lautoka is the largest crushing mill in the Southern Hemisphere. The Rakiraki mill produces for domestic consumption; the rest is exported. There is no refining mill here, so most of the sugar served in Fiji is brown, not white.

The Emperor Gold Mine on northern Viti Levu makes an important contribution, as do copra, timber, garments, furniture, coffee (you'll get a rich, strong brew throughout the country), and other consumer goods produced by small manufacturers (the Colgate toothpaste you buy in Fiji is made here). Fiji also is a major transshipment point for goods destined for other South Pacific island countries.

Despite its relative prosperity, however, Fiji has a persistent problem with unemployment. More than half the population is under the age of 25, and there just aren't enough jobs being created for the youngsters coming into the work force. A marked increase in burglaries and other property crimes has been linked to this lack of jobs.

Fiji also saw corruption grow during the post-coup years, with the National Bank of Fiji almost failing because of bad loans made to political cronies, among others. The country's foreign reserves dropped precipitously, forcing a devaluation of the Fiji dollar to about US50¢ (it had been on a virtual par with the U.S. dollar prior to the 1987 coups).

2 History 101

The Dutch navigator Abel Tasman sighted some of the Fiji Islands in 1642 and 1643, and Capt. James Cook visited one of the southernmost islands in 1774, but Capt. William Bligh was the first European to sail through and plot the group. After the mutiny on the *Bounty* in April 1789, Bligh and his loyal crew sailed their longboat through Fiji on their way to safety in Indonesia. They passed Ovalau and sailed between Viti Levu and Vanua Levu. Large Fijian *druas* (speedy war canoes) gave chase near the Yasawas, but with some furious paddling, the help of a fortuitous squall, and the good luck to pass through a break in the Great Sea Reef, Bligh and his ship escaped to the open ocean. The druas turned back.

Bligh's rough, handmade charts were amazingly accurate and shed the first European light on Fiji. For a while, Fiji was known as the Bligh Islands, and the passage between Viti Levu and Vanua Levu still is named Bligh Water.

The Tongans warned the Europeans who made their way west across the South Pacific about Fiji's ferocious cannibals, and the reports by Bligh and others of reef-strewn waters only added to the dangerous reputation of the islands. Consequently, European penetration into Fiji was limited for many years to beach bums and convicts who escaped from the British penal colonies in Australia. There was a sandalwood rush between 1804 and 1813. Other traders arrived in the 1820s in search of *bêche-de-mer* (sea cucumber). This trade continued until the 1850s and had a lasting impact on Fiji, since along with the traders came guns and whisky.

CAKOBAU RISES The traders and settlers established the first European-style town in Fiji at Levuka on Ovalau in the early 1820s, but for many years the real power lay on Bau, a tiny island just off the east coast of Viti Levu (you'll fly over it between Suva and Levuka). With the help of Swedish mercenary Charlie Savage, who supplied the guns, High Chief Tanoa of Bau defeated several much larger confederations and extended his control over most of western Fiji. Bau's influence grew even more under Tanoa's son and successor, Cakobau. Monopolizing the *bêche-de-mer* trade and waging almost constant war against his rivals, this

Dateline

- **1500 B.C.** Polynesians arrive from the west.
- **500 B.C.** Melanesians settle in Fiji, push Polynesians eastward.
- **A.D. 1300–1600** Polynesians, especially Tongans, invade from the east.
- **1643** Abel Tasman sights some islands in Fiji.
- **1774** Capt. James Cook visits Vatoa.
- **1789** After mutiny on the *Bounty,* Capt. William Bligh navigates his long-boat through Fiji, is nearly captured by a war canoe.
- **1804** Sandalwood rush begins on Vanua Levu.
- **1808** Swedish mercenary Charlie Savage arrives at Bau, supplies guns to Chief Tanoa in successful wars to conquer western Fiji.
- **1813** Charlie Savage is killed; sandalwood era ends.
- **1822** European settlement begins at Levuka.
- **1835** Methodist missionaries settle on Lekeba in Lau Group.
- **1840** United States Exploring Expedition under Capt. John Wilkes explores Fiji and charts waters.
- **1848** Prince Enele Ma'afu exerts Tongan control over eastern Fiji from outpost in Lau Group.
- **1849** U.S. Consul John Brown Williams' home burned and looted during July 4th celebrations; he blames Cakobau.

continues

- **1851** American warship arrives, demands Cakobau pay $5,000 for Williams' losses.
- **1853** Cakobau installed as high chief of Bau, highest post in Fiji.
- **1854** Cakobau converts to Christianity.
- **1855** American claims against Cakobau grow to $40,000; U.S. warship arrives, claims some islands as mortgage.
- **1858** Cakobau offers to cede Fiji to Britain for $40,000.
- **1860** John Brown Williams dies, his claims still unsettled.
- **1862** Britain rejects Cakobau's offer.
- **1867** Unrest grows; Europeans crown Cakobau as King of Bau; Rev. Thomas Baker eaten.
- **1868** Polynesia Company buys Suva in exchange for paying Cakobau's debts.
- **1871** Europeans form central government at Levuka, make Cakobau king of Fiji.
- **1874** Cakobau's government collapses; he and other chiefs cede Fiji to Britain without price tag.
- **1875** Measles kills one-fourth of all Fijians; Sir Arthur Gordon becomes first governor.
- **1879** First Indians arrive as indentured laborers.
- **1882** Capital moved from Levuka to Suva.
- **1916** Recruitment of indentured Indians ends.
- **1917** German Raider Count Felix von Luckner captured at Wakaya.
- **1917–18** Fijian soldiers support Allies in World War I.
- **1942–45** Fijians serve as scouts with Allied units in

continues

devious chief rose to the height of power during the 1840s. He never did control all the islands, however, for Enele Ma'afu, a member of Tonga's royal family, moved to the Lau Group in 1848 and quickly exerted Tongan control over eastern Fiji. Ma'afu brought along Wesleyan missionaries from Tonga and gave them a foothold in Fiji.

Although Cakobau ruled much of western Fiji as a virtual despot, the chiefs under him continued to be powerful enough at the local level to make his control tenuous. The lesser chiefs, especially those in the mountains, also saw the Wesleyan missionaries as a threat to their power, and most of them refused to convert or even to allow the missionaries to establish outposts in their villages. (The Rev. Thomas Baker was killed and eaten during an attempt to convert the Viti Levu highlanders in 1867.)

CAKOBAU FALLS Cakobau's slide from power is usually dated from the Fourth of July 1849, when John Brown Williams, the American consul, celebrated the birth of his own nation. A cannon went off and started a fire that burned Williams's house. The Fijians retrieved his belongings from the burning building and kept them. Williams blamed Cakobau and demanded $5,000 in damages. Within 2 years an American warship showed up and demanded that Cakobau pay up. Other incidents followed, and American claims against the chief totaled more than $40,000 by 1855. Another American man-of-war arrived that year and claimed several islands in lieu of payment; the U.S. never followed up, but the ship forced Cakobau to sign a promissory note due in 2 years. In the late 1850s, with Ma'afu and his confederation of chiefs gaining power, and disorder growing in western Fiji, Cakobau offered to cede the islands to Great Britain if Queen Victoria would pay the Americans. The British pondered his offer for 4 years before turning him down.

Cakobau worked a better deal when the Polynesia Company, an Australian planting and commercial enterprise, came to Fiji looking for suitable land after the price of cotton skyrocketed during the American Civil War. Instead of offering his entire kingdom, Cakobau this time tendered only 200,000 acres of it. The Polynesia Company accepted, paid off the American claims, and in 1870 landed Australian settlers on 23,000 acres of its land on Viti Levu, near a Fijian village known as Suva. The land was unsuitable for cotton and the climate too wet for sugar, so the speculators sold their property to the government, which moved the capital there from Levuka in 1882.

FIJI BECOMES BRITISH   The Polynesia Company's settlers were just a few of the several thousands of European planters who came to Fiji in the 1860s and early 1870s. They bought land for plantations from the Fijians, sometimes fraudulently and often for whiskey and guns. Claims and counterclaims to land ownership followed, and with no legal mechanism to settle the disputes, Fiji was swept to the brink of race war. Some Europeans living in Levuka clamored for a national government; others advocated turning the islands over to a colonial power. Things came to a head in 1870, when the bottom fell out of cotton prices, hurricanes destroyed the crops, and anarchy threatened. Within a year the Europeans established a national government at Levuka and named Cakobau king of Fiji. The situation continued to deteriorate, however, and 3 years later Cakobau was forced to cede the islands to Great Britain. This time there was no price tag attached, and the British accepted. The deed of cession was signed on October 10, 1874, at Nasovi village near Levuka.

Britain sent Sir Arthur Gordon as the new colony's first governor. As the Americans were later to do in their part of Samoa, he allowed the Fijian chiefs to govern their villages and districts as they had done before (they were not, however, allowed to engage in tribal warfare) and to advise him through a Great Council of Chiefs. He declared that native Fijian lands could not be sold, only leased. That decision has to this day helped to protect the Fijians, their land, and their customs, but it has led to bitter animosity on the part of the land-deprived Indians.

In order to protect the native Fijians from being exploited, Gordon prohibited their being used as laborers (not that many of them had the slightest inclination to work for someone else). When the planters decided in the early 1870s to switch from profitless cotton to sugarcane, he convinced them to import indentured servants from India. The first 463 East Indians arrived on May 14, 1879 (see "Fiji's Indians," below).

THE COUNT CONFOUNDED   Following Gordon's example, the British governed "Fiji for the Fijians"—and the European planters, of course—leaving the Indians to struggle for their civil rights. The government exercised jurisdiction over all Europeans in the colony and assigned district officers (the "D.O.s" of British colonial lore) to administer various geographic areas.

As usual there was a large gulf between the appointed civil servants sent from Britain and the locals. An example occurred in 1917 when Count Felix von Luckner arrived at Wakaya Island off eastern Viti Levu in search of a replacement for his infamous World War I German

World War II; failure of Indians to volunteer angers Fijians.

- **1956** First Legislative Council established with Ratu Sir Lala Sukuna as speaker.
- **1966** Fijian-dominated Alliance Party wins first elections.
- **1969** Key compromises pave way for constitution and independence. Provision guarantees Fijian land ownership.
- **1970** Fiji becomes independent; Alliance party leader Ratu Sir Kamisese Mara chosen first prime minister.
- **1987** Fijian-Indian coalition wins majority, names Dr. Timoci Bavadra as prime minister with Indian-majority cabinet; Col. Sitiveni Rabuka leads two bloodless military coups, installs interim government. Most Sunday activities banned outside hotels.
- **1991** New constitution guaranteeing Fijian majority is promulgated. Sunday ban eased.
- **1992** Rabuka's party wins election; he becomes prime minister.
- **1994** Second election cuts Rabuka's majority; he retains power in coalition with mixed-race general electors.
- **1995** Rabuka appoints constitutional review commission.
- **1996** Sunday ban repealed.
- **1998** Parliament adopts new constitution with 25 "open" seats holding balance of power.
- **1999** Labor union leader Mahendra Chaudhry is elected as Fiji's first Indian prime minister.

raider, the *Seeadler,* which had gone aground in the Cook Islands. A local constable became suspicious of the armed foreigners and notified the district police inspector. Only Europeans—not Fijians or Indians—could use firearms, so the inspector took a band of unarmed Fijians to Wakaya in a small cattle trading boat. Thinking he was up against a much larger armed force, von Luckner unwittingly surrendered.

PREPARING FOR INDEPENDENCE   One of the highest-ranking Fijian chiefs, Ratu Sir Lala Sukuna, rose to prominence after World War I. (Like *tui* in Polynesian, *ratu* means "chief" in Fijian.) Born of the chiefly lineage of both Bau and the Lau Islands in eastern Fiji, Ratu Sukuna was educated at Oxford, served in World War I, and worked his way up through the colonial bureaucracy to the post of chairman of the Native Land Trust Board. Although dealing in that position primarily with disputes over land and chiefly titles, he used it as a platform to educate his people and to lay the foundation for the independent state of Fiji. As much as anyone, he was the father of modern, independent Fiji.

After the attack on Pearl Harbor began the Pacific war in 1941, the Allies first rushed to Fiji's defense in the face of the Japanese advance across the Pacific, then turned the islands into a vast training base. The airstrip at Nadi was built during this period, and several coastal gun emplacements can still be seen.

Heeding Ratu Sukuna's call to arms (and more than a little prodding from their village chiefs), thousands of Fijians volunteered to fight and did so with great distinction as scouts and infantrymen in the Solomon Islands campaigns. Their knowledge of tropical jungles and their skill at the ambush made them much feared by the Japanese. The Fijians were, said one war correspondent, "death with velvet gloves."

The war also had an unfortunate side: Although many Indians at first volunteered to join, they also demanded pay equal to the European members of the Fiji Military Forces. When the colonial administrators refused, the Indians disbanded their platoon. Their military contribution was one officer and 70 enlisted men of a reserve transport section, and they were promised they would not have to go overseas. Many Fijians to this day begrudge the Indians for not doing more to aid the war effort.

THE BRITS QUIT   Ratu Sukuna continued to push the colony toward independence until his death in 1958, and although Fiji made halting steps in that direction during the 1960s, the road was rocky. The Indians by then were highly organized, in both political parties and trade unions, and they objected to a constitution that would institutionalize Fijian control of the government and Fijian ownership of most of the new nation's land. Key compromises were made in 1969, however, and on October 10, 1970—exactly 96 years after Cakobau signed the Deed of Cession—the Dominion of Fiji became an independent member of the British Commonwealth of Nations.

Under the 1970 constitution, Fiji had a Westminster-style Parliament consisting of an elected House of Representatives and a Senate composed of Fijian chiefs. For the first 17 years of independence, the Fijians maintained a majority—albeit a tenuous one—in the House of Representatives and control of the government under the leadership of Ratu Sir Kamisese Mara, the country's first prime minister.

Then, in a general election held in April 1987, a coalition of Indians and liberal Fijians voted Ratu Mara and his Alliance party out of power. Dr. Timoci Bavadra, a Fijian, took over as prime minister, but his cabinet was composed of more Indians than Fijians. Hard feelings immediately flared between some Fijians and Indians.

RAMBO STAGES A COUP   Within little more than a month of the election, members of the predominantly Fijian army stormed into Parliament and arrested Dr. Bavadra and his cabinet. It was the South Pacific's first military coup, and although peaceful, it took nearly everyone by complete surprise.

The coup leader was Col. Sitiveni Rabuka (pronounced "Rambuka"), whom local wags quickly nicknamed Rambo. A Sandhurst-trained career soldier, the 38-year-old Rabuka was third in command of the army. A Fijian of non-chiefly lineage and a lay preacher in the Methodist church, he immediately became a hero to his "commoner" fellow Fijians, who saw him as saving them from the Indians and preserving their land rights from a government dominated by Indians, who at the time slightly outnumbered the Fijians.

Rabuka at first installed a caretaker government, retaining Ratu Sir Penaia Ganilau as governor-general and Ratu Mara as prime minister. In September 1987, after the British Commonwealth suspended Fiji's membership, he staged another bloodless coup. A few weeks later he abrogated the 1970 constitution, declared Fiji an independent republic, and set up a new interim government with Ratu Ganilau as president, Ratu Mara as prime minister, and himself as minister of home affairs and army commander. At the urging of Methodist ministers, who are a powerful political force here, he also instituted a tough ban on all Sunday business except at the country's hotels (it was quickly relaxed so taxis and buses could take Fijians to church).

The government instituted pay cuts and price hikes in 1987 after the Fijian dollar fell sharply on world currency markets. Coupled with the coups, the economic problems led to thousands of Indians—especially professionals, such as doctors, lawyers, accountants, and schoolteachers—fleeing the country.

Dr. Bavadra was released shortly after the coups. He died of natural causes in 1989. Ratu Ganilau died in 1994 and was succeeded as president by Ratu Mara.

Rabuka's interim government ruled until 1990, when it promulgated a new constitution guaranteeing Fijians a parliamentary majority—and rankling the Indians. His pro-Fijian party won the initial election, but he barely hung onto power in fresh elections in 1994 by forming a coalition with the European, Chinese, and mixed-race general-elector parliamentarians. Although some of his more conservative backers advocated sending all Fiji Indians back to India, Rabuka took a more moderate stance. Despite opposition by the preachers, for example, he got Parliament to lift the Sunday ban in 1996.

INDIANS MAKE A COMEBACK   Rabuka also appointed a three-person Constitutional Review Commission, which proposed a new constitution, which parliament adopted in 1998. It created a parliamentary house of 65 seats, with 19 held by Fijians, 17 by Indians, 3 by general-electors, 1 by a Rotuman, and 25 open to all races.

A year later, with support from many Fijians who were disgruntled with their own leaders because of the country's poor economy, rising crime, and deteriorating roads, labor union leader Mahendra Chaudhry's party won an outright majority of parliament, and he become Fiji's first Indian prime minister. Chaudhry had been minister of finance in the Bavadra government toppled by Rabuka's coup in 1987.

Chaudhry quickly appointed several well-known Fijians to his cabinet, including President Mara's daughter as minister of tourism. For his part, the revered Ratu Mara encouraged his fellow Fijians to support the new administration. As we went to press, Chaudhry was working to shore up Fiji's economy, and there had been no hint of another Fijian-led coup.

3 The Islanders

Fiji's population officially was 775,077 in 1996, the last time a census was taken. Indigenous Fijians made up 51%, Indians 43%, and other races—mostly Chinese, Polynesians, and Europeans—the other 6%. Although the overall population has been rising slightly, thanks to a high Fijian birth rate, the country has lost about 5,000 Indians annually since the 1987 military coups.

It's difficult to imagine peoples of two more contrasting cultures living side by side. "Fijians generally perceive Indians as mean and stingy, crafty and demanding to the extent of being considered greedy, inconsiderate and grasping, uncooperative, egotistic, and calculating," writes Professor Asesela Ravuvu of the University of the South Pacific. On the other hand, he says, Indians see Fijians as "jungalis," still living on the land, which they will not sell, poor, backward, naive, and foolish.

Given that these attitudes are not likely to change any time soon, it is remarkable that Fijians and Indians actually manage to coexist. Politically correct Americans may take offense at some things they could hear said in Fiji, since racial distinctions are a fact of life here.

From a visitor's standpoint, the famously friendly Fijians give the country its laid-back South Seas charm while at the same time providing relatively good service at the hotels. Although a few of the industrious Indians can be aggravating at times, they make Fiji an easy country to visit by providing excellent maintenance of facilities and efficient and inexpensive services, such as transportation.

Regardless of his or her race, the 1998 constitution officially makes everyone here a "Fiji Islander."

THE FIJIANS

When meeting and talking to the smiling Fijians, it's difficult to imagine that less than a century ago their ancestors were among the world's most ferocious cannibals. Today the only vestiges of this past are the four-pronged wooden cannibal forks sold in any handcraft shop (they make interesting conversation pieces when used at home to serve hors d'oeuvres). Yet in the early 1800s, the Fijians were so fierce that Europeans were slow to settle in the islands for fear of literally being turned into a meal—perhaps even being eaten alive. More than 100 white-skinned individuals ended up with their skulls smashed and their bodies baked in an earth oven. "One man actually stood by my side and ate the very eyes out of a roasted skull he had, saying, 'Venaca, venaca,' that is, very good," wrote William Speiden, the purser on the U.S. exploring expedition that charted Fiji in 1840.

Cannibalism was an important ritualistic institution among the early Fijians, the indigenous Melanesian people who came from the west and began settling in Fiji around 500 B.C. Over time they replaced the Polynesians, whose ancestors had arrived some 1,000 years beforehand, but not before adopting much of Polynesian culture and intermarrying enough to give many Fijians lighter skin than that of most other Melanesians, especially in the islands of eastern Fiji near the Polynesian Kingdom of Tonga. (This is less the case in the west and among the hill dwellers, whose ancestors had less contact with Polynesians in ancient times.) Similar differences occur in terms of culture. For example, while Melanesians traditionally pick their chiefs by popular consensus, Fijian chiefs hold titles by heredity, in the Polynesian fashion.

FIJIAN SOCIETY

Ancient Fijian society was organized by tribes, each with its own language, and subdivided into clans of specialists, such as canoe builders, fishermen, and farmers. Powerful

---

Impressions

Many of the missionaries were eaten, leading an irreverent planter to suggest that they triumphed by infiltration.

—James A. Michener, 1951

A Bowl of Grog

Known as *kava* elsewhere in the South Pacific, the slightly narcotic drink Fijians call *yaqona* ("yong-gona") rivals the potent Fiji Bitter beer as the national drink. You likely will have half a coconut shell full of "grog" offered—if not shoved in your face—beginning at your hotel's reception desk. Fiji has more "grog shops" than bars.

And thanks to the promotion of kavalactone, the active ingredient, as a health-food answer to stress and insomnia in the U.S. and elsewhere, growing the root has become an important part of the economy here and elsewhere in the South Pacific. Its price nearly doubled between 1996 and 1999. (But note that some kava tablets sold in American health food stores don't have enough kavalactone to give you the same drowsy effect you'll get from a bowl of grog over here.)

Yaqona plays an important ceremonial role in Fijian life. No significant occasion takes place without yaqona, and a *sevusevu* (welcoming) ceremony usually is held for tour groups visiting Fijian villages. Mats are placed on the floor, the participants gather around in a circle, and the yaqona roots are mixed with water and strained through coconut husks into a large carved wooden bowl, called a *tanoa*.

The ranking chief sits next to the tanoa during the welcoming ceremony. He extends in the direction of the guest of honor a cowrie shell attached to one leg of the bowl by a cord of woven coconut fiber. It's extremely impolite to cross the plane of the cord once it has been extended.

The guest of honor (in this case your tour guide) then offers a gift to the village (a kilogram or two of dried grog roots will do these days) and makes a speech explaining the purpose of his visit. The chief then passes the first cup of yaqona to the guest of honor, who claps once, takes the cup in both hands, and gulps down the entire cup of sawdust-tasting liquid in one swallow. Everyone else then claps three times.

Next, each chief drinks a cup, clapping once before bolting it down. Again, everyone else claps three times after each cup is drained. Except for the clapping and formal speeches, everyone remains silent throughout the ceremony, a tradition easily understood considering kava's numbing effect on the lips and tongue.

---

chiefs ruled each tribe and constantly warred with their neighbors, usually with brutal vengeance. Captured enemy children were hung by the feet from the rigging of the winners' canoes, and new buildings sometimes were consecrated by burying live adult prisoners in holes dug for the support posts. The ultimate insult, however, was to eat the enemy's flesh. Victorious chiefs were even said to cook and nibble on the fingers or tongues of the vanquished, relishing each bite while the victims watched in agony.

Fijians wouldn't dream of doing anything like that today, of course, but they have managed to retain much of their old lifestyle and customs, including their hereditary system of chiefs and social status. Most Fijians still live in small villages along the coast and riverbanks or in the hills, and you will see many traditional thatch *bures,* or houses, scattered in the countryside away from the main roads. Members of each tribe cultivate and grow food crops in small "bush gardens" on plots of communally owned native land assigned to their families. More than 80% of the land in Fiji is owned by Fijians.

A majority of Fijians are Methodists today, their forebears having been converted by puritanical Wesleyan missionaries who came to the islands in the 19th century. A backer of Prime Minister Rabuka and a strong advocate of Fiji's Sunday Ban, the Methodist Church is a powerful political force in the country.

A hundred years of prodding by the British have failed to make the Fijians see why
they should work for money.
   It is doubtful if anyone but an Indian can dislike Fijians. . . . They are one of the
happiest peoples on earth and laugh constantly. Their joy in things is infectious; they
love practical jokes, and in warfare they are without fear.
                                                                    —James A. Michener, 1951

FIJIAN CULTURE

THE TABUA   The highest symbol of respect among Fijians is the tooth of the sperm whale, known as a *tabua* (pronounced "tambua"). Like large mother-of-pearl shells used in other parts of Melanesia, tabuas in ancient times played a role similar to money in modern society and still have various ceremonial uses. They are presented to chiefs as a sign of respect, given as gifts to arrange marriages, offered to friends to show sympathy after the death of a family member, and used as a means to seal a contract or other agreement. The value of each tabua is judged by its thickness and length, and some of the older ones are smooth with wear. It is illegal to export a tabua out of Fiji, and even if you did, the international conventions on endangered species make it illegal to bring them into the U.S. and most other Western countries.

FIRE WALKING   Legend says that a Fijian god once repaid a favor to a warrior on Beqa island by giving him the ability to walk unharmed on fire. His descendants, all members of the Sawau tribe on Beqa, still walk across stones heated to white-hot by a bonfire—but usually for the entertainment of tourists at the hotels rather than for a particular religious purpose.

Traditionally, the participants—all male—had to abstain from women and coconuts for 2 weeks before the ceremony. If they partook of either, they would suffer burns to their feet. Naturally a priest (some would call him a "witch doctor") would recite certain incantations to make sure the coals were hot and the gods were at bay and not angry enough to scorch the soles.

Today's fire walking is a bit touristy but still worth seeing. If you don't believe the stones are hot, go ahead and touch one of them—but do it gingerly.

Some Indians in Fiji engage in fire walking, but it's strictly for religious purposes.

ETIQUETTE   Fijian villages are easy to visit, but remember that to the people who live in them, the entire village is home, not just the individual houses. In your native land, you wouldn't walk into a stranger's living room without being invited, so find someone and ask permission before traipsing into a Fijian village. The Fijians are highly accommodating people, and it's unlikely they will say no; in fact, they may ask you to stay for a meal or perhaps stage a small yaqona ceremony in your honor. They are very tied to tradition, however, so do your part and ask first.

If you are invited to stay or eat in the village, a small gift to the chief is appropriate. The gift should be given to the chief or highest-ranking person present to accept it. Sometimes it helps to explain that it is a gift to the village and not payment for services rendered, especially if it's money you're giving.

Only chiefs are allowed to wear hats and sunglasses in Fijian villages, so it's good manners for visitors to take theirs off. Shoulders are covered at all times. Fijians go barefoot and walk slightly stooped in their bures. Men sit cross-legged on the floor; women sit with their legs to the side. They don't point at one another with hands, fingers, or feet, nor do they touch each other's heads or hair. They greet each other and strangers with a big smile and a sincere "Bula."

The question of what to do with these clever Indians of Fiji is the most acute problem in the Pacific today. Within ten years it will become a world concern.

—James A. Michener, 1951

FIJI'S INDIANS

The Fiji Indians' version of America's *Mayflower* was the *Leonidas,* a labor transport ship that arrived at Levuka from Calcutta on May 14, 1879, and landed 463 indentured servants destined to work the sugarcane fields.

As more than 60,000 Indians would do over the next 37 years, these first immigrants signed agreements *(girmits,* they called them) requiring that they work in Fiji for 5 years; they would be free to return to India after 5 more years. Most of them labored in the cane fields for the initial term of their girmits, living in "coolie lines" of squalid shacks hardly better than the poverty-stricken conditions most left behind in India. After the initial 5 years, however, they were free to seek work on their own. Many leased small plots of land from the Fijians and began planting sugarcane or raising cattle on their own. To this day most of Fiji's sugar crop, the country's most important agricultural export, is produced on small leased plots rather than on large plantations. Other Indians went into business in the growing cities and towns and, joined in the early 1900s by an influx of business-oriented Indians, thereby founded Fiji's modern merchant and professional classes.

Of the immigrants who came from India between 1879 and 1916, when the indenturing system ended, some 85% were Hindus, 14% were Muslims, and the remaining 1% were Sikhs and Christians. Fiji offered these adventurers far more opportunities than they would have had in caste-controlled India. In fact, the caste system was scrapped very quickly by the Hindus in Fiji, and, for the most part, the violent relations between Hindus and Muslims that racked India were put aside on the islands.

Life for the Indians was so much better in Fiji than it would have been in India that only a small minority of them went home after their girmits expired. They tended then—as now—to live in the towns and villages, and in the "Sugar Belt" along the north and west coasts of Viti Levu and Vanua Levu. Hindu and Sikh temples and Muslim mosques abound in these areas, and places such as Ba and Tavua look like small towns on the Indian subcontinent. On the southern coasts and in the mountains, however, the population is overwhelmingly Fijian.

4 Languages

Fiji has three official languages. To greatly oversimplify the situation, the Fijians speak Fijian, the Indians speak Hindi, and they speak English to each other. Schoolchildren are taught in their native language until they are proficient in English, which thereafter is the medium of instruction. This means that English-speaking visitors will have little trouble getting around and enjoying the country.

There is one problem for the uninitiated, however: the unusual pronunciation of Fijian names. For instance, Cakobau is pronounced "Thak-*om*-bau." There are many other names of people and places that are equally or even more confusing.

FIJIAN

As is the case throughout Melanesia, many native languages are spoken in the islands of Fiji, some of them similar, others quite different. Fijians still speak a variety of dialects in their villages, but the official form of Fijian—and the version taught in the schools—is based on the language of Bau, the small island that came to dominate western Fiji during the 19th century.

Fijian is similar to the Polynesian languages spoken in Tahiti, the Cook Islands, Samoa, and Tonga in that it uses vowel sounds similar to those in Latin, French, Italian, and Spanish: *a* as in b*a*d, *e* as in s*a*y, *i* as in b*ee*, *o* as in g*o*, and *u* as in kanga*roo*.

Some Fijian consonants, however, sound very much different from their counterparts in English, Latin, or any other language. In devising a written form of Fijian, the early Wesleyan missionaries decided to use some familiar Roman consonants in unfamiliar ways. It would have been easier for English speakers to read Fijian had the missionaries used a combination of consonants—*th,* for example—for the Fijian sounds. Their main purpose, however, was to teach Fijians to read and write their own language. Since the Fijians separate all consonant sounds with vowels, writing two consonants together only confused them.

Accordingly, the missionaries came up with the following usage: *b* sounds like *mb* (as in reme*mb*er), *c* sounds like *th* (as in *th*at), *d* sounds like *nd* (as in Su*nd*ay), *g* sounds like *ng* (as in si*ng*er), and *q* sounds like *ng* + *g* (as in fi*ng*er).

Here are some Fijian names with their unusual pronunciations:

Ba	mBah	**Labasa**	Lam-*ba*-sa
Bau	mBau	**Mamanuca**	Ma-ma-*nu*-tha
Beqa	*mBeng*-ga	**Nadi**	*Nan*-di
Buca	*mBu*-tha	**Tabua**	*Tam*-bua
Cakobau	Thack-*om*-bau	**Toberua**	Tom-*bay*-rua
Korotogo	Ko-ro-*ton*-go	**Tubakula**	Toom-ba-*ku*-la

You are likely to hear these Fijian terms used during your stay:

English	Fijian	Pronunciation
hello	bula	boo-lah
hello (formal)	ni sa bula	nee sahm boo-lah
good morning	ni sa yadra	nee sah yand-rah
good night	ni sa moce	nee sah mo-thay
thank you	vinaka	vee-nah-kah
thank you very much	vinaka vaka levu	vee-nah-kah vah-ka lay-voo
house/bungalow	bure	boo-ray
tapa cloth	masi	mah-see
sarong	sulu	sue-loo

If you want to know more Fijian, look for A. J. Schutz's little book *Say It in Fijian* (Pacific Publications, Sydney), available at many bookstores and hotel boutiques.

5 Planning a Trip to Fiji

Given the size and diversity of the country, any trip to Fiji requires careful planning to avoid disappointment. You could spend your entire vacation in Nadi, and while the tourism industry provides a host of activities to keep you busy, you will miss the best parts of Fiji. After all, this is a country of more than 300 gorgeous islands, and not to experience more than one is a mistake. By and large, the main island of Viti Levu does not have the best beaches in Fiji, and where it does have good sands, the reef offshore is more walkable than swimmable, especially at low tide. In other words, look beyond Nadi for good beaches and the best diving.

The Fiji Islands

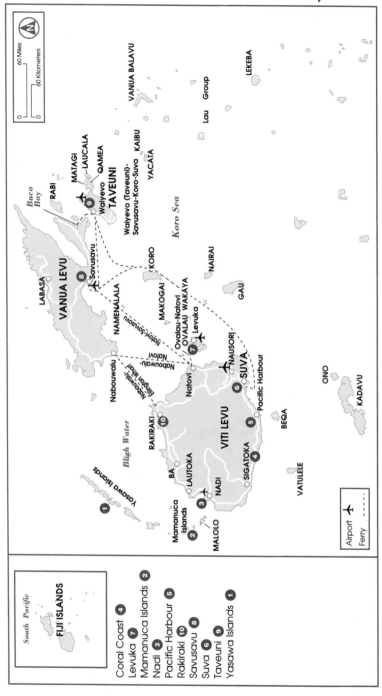

Coral Coast ④
Levuka ⑦
Mamanuca Islands ②
Nadi ③
Pacific Harbour ⑤
Rakiraki ⑩
Savusavu ⑧
Suva ⑥
Taveuni ⑨
Yasawa Islands ①

FIJI'S REGIONS IN BRIEF

From a tourist's standpoint, Fiji is divided into several regions, each with its own special characteristics and appeal. Here's what each has to offer.

ON THE ISLAND OF VITI LEVU

NADI Most visitors arrive at Nadi International Airport, a modern facility located among sugarcane fields on Viti Levu's dry western side. Known collectively as **Nadi,** this area is the focal point of much of Fiji's tourism industry, and it's where most tourists on package deals spend their time. There are a variety of hotels between the airport and hot, dusty, predominantly Indian **Nadi Town,** whose main industry is tourism and where duty-free, souvenir, and handcraft merchants wait to part you from your dollars. None of the airport hotels is on the beach, and even at the Sheraton Fiji and Sheraton Royal Denarau Resort, the area's two large resorts, coastal mangrove forests make the beaches gray and the water offshore murky. There are many things to do in Nadi, but knowledgeable visitors with more than 1 or 2 days to spend in Fiji will consider it a transit stopover on the way to someplace else.

THE CORAL COAST The **Queen's Road** runs around the south coast of Viti Levu through the **Coral Coast,** the first resort area in Fiji. Here you'll find comfortable hotels, luxury resorts, and fire-walking Fijians, but the beaches lead into very shallow lagoons, and most visitors staying on the "The Coast" these days primarily are tourists on packages. It's still a good choice for anyone who wants on-the-beach resort living while being able to see conveniently some of the country. Offshore, the island of **Vatulele** has one of the world's finest small resorts. Farther south, **Kadavu** and its Astrolabe Reef hail scuba divers.

PACIFIC HARBOUR About 30 miles west of Suva, Pacific Harbour was developed in the early 1970s as a resort complete with golf course, private residences, shopping center, cultural center, and seaside hotel. Since this area is in Viti Levu's rain belt, the project never reached its full potential. Today Pacific Harbour is known primarily for excellent deep sea fishing and the South Pacific's finest golf course. It's also the jumping-off point for the **Beqa Lagoon,** which attracts divers from around the planet.

NORTHERN VITI LEVU An alternative driving route to Suva, the **King's Road** runs from Lautoka through the Sugar Belt of northern Viti Levu, passing through the predominantly Indian towns of Ba and Tavua to **Rakiraki,** a Fijian village near the island's northernmost point and site of one of the country's few remaining colonial-era hotels. Jagged green mountains lend a gorgeous backdrop to the shoreline along the Rakiraki coast. Offshore, **Nananu-I-Ra Island** beckons backpackers.

All of the King's Road except about 50km (31 miles) through the central mountains is paved. East of Rakiraki, it turns into deep, mountain-bounded **Viti Levu Bay,** one of the most beautiful parts of Fiji. From the head of the bay, the road then twists and turns its way through the mountains, following the Wainbuka River until it emerges near the east coast at Korovou. A left turn there takes you to Natovi Wharf; and a right, to Suva. In other words, it's possible to drive or take buses all the way around Viti Levu via the Queen's and King's Roads.

SUVA The Queen's Road goes on to **Suva** (pop. 85,000), Fiji's busy capital and one of the South Pacific's most cosmopolitan cities. Steamy Suva houses a fascinating mix of atmospheres and cultures. Remnants of Fiji's century as a British possession and the presence of so many Indians give the town a certain air of the colonial "Raj"—as if this were Agra or Bombay, not the boundary between Polynesia and Melanesia. On the other hand, Suva has modern high-rise buildings and lives at as fast a pace as will be found in the South Pacific west of Tahiti—no surprise since in many respects it's the bustling economic center of the region. The streets are filled with a melting-pot blend of Indians, Chinese, Fijians, other South Pacific islanders, "Europeans" (a term used in Fiji to mean persons of white skin regardless of geographic origin), and individuals of mixed race.

JUST OFF VITI LEVU

LEVUKA & OVALAU   From Suva, it's an easy excursion to the picturesque island of **Ovalau** and its historic town of **Levuka,** which has changed little in appearance since its days as a boisterous whaling port and the first capital of a united Fiji in the 1800s. Few places in the South Pacific have retained their frontier facade as has this living museum. You can also visit an old-time Fijian village here, carefully constructed to look like the old days.

THE MAMANUCA ISLANDS   Beckoning offshore, the **Mamanuca Islands** offer day cruises from Nadi and several offshore resorts of various sizes appealing to a broad spectrum, from swinging singles to quieter couples and families. Generally speaking, they are in the driest part of Fiji, which means sunshine most of the time. Some are flat atolls so small you can walk around them in 5 minutes. Others are on hilly, grassy islands reminiscent of the Virgin Islands in the Caribbean. They are relatively close together, and most offer excursions to the others. They also are close to Nadi, so you don't have to spend much extra money or time to get there.

THE YASAWA ISLANDS   Other visitors join up with **Blue Lagoon Cruises** at its base in **Lautoka,** Fiji's second-largest city and its prime sugar-milling center. The cruises spend several days or a week in the **Yasawas,** a chain of gorgeous and unspoiled islands shooting off north of the Mamanucas. Like Moorea and Bora Bora in French Polynesia, the Yasawas are often used as movie sets. Two versions of *The Blue Lagoon* were filmed here, the latest starring Brooke Shields as the castaway schoolgirl. The Yasawas have two deluxe resorts and several establishments catering to backpackers.

NORTHERN FIJI

Vanua Levu, Taveuni, and their nearby islands are known locally as "The North" since they comprise Fiji's Northern Province. Over on Vanua Levu, Fiji's second largest island, a little town with the exotic name **Savusavu** lies nestled in one of the region's most protected deep-water bays. Savusavu and the "Garden Isle" of **Taveuni** are throwbacks to the old South Pacific, a land of copra plantations and small Fijian villages tucked away in the bush. Travelers looking for a do-it-yourself soft adventure trip into the past can take a local bus across Vanua Levu to Savusavu and a ferry on to Taveuni. Both Savusavu and Taveuni have excellent places to stay, and there are fine resorts off Vanua Levu and near Taveuni's north coast on **Matagi, Qamea,** and **Laucala.**

STAYING AT ONE OF FIJI'S OFFSHORE RESORTS

Fiji has one of the world's finest collections of offshore resorts, small establishments with islands all to themselves. They all have lovely beach settings and modern facilities, and without exception they are excellent places to get away from it all. The major drawback of any offshore resort, however, is that you've done just that. You won't see much of Fiji while you're basking in the sun on a tiny rock some 25 miles offshore. Consider them for what they have to offer, but not as bases from which to explore the country. I have included the offshore resorts in the following chapters along with the nearest large island. If you decide to stay at one of them, I suggest you read all these chapters before making your choice of resort.

Read over carefully what I've said about the owners and managers, and especially the styles with which they run their operations. For example, if you don't enjoy getting to know your fellow guests at sometimes raucous dinner parties, you might not like Vatulele or Turtle Island resorts, but you might love The Wakaya Club or Yasawa Island Resort. If you like a large resort with a lively, Club Med-like ambience, you might prefer Mana Island and Plantation resorts. Many other resorts offer peace, quiet, and few fellow guests. If you want to feel like a houseguest at a rich person's private island, look no farther than Fiji Forbes' Laucala Island. If you are taking the kids, Jean-Michel Cousteau Fiji Island Resort and Matagi Island are two of the best small family resorts in the South Pacific, while nearby Qamea Beach Club doesn't allow kids under 13 years old. Choose carefully!

DIVING IN FIJI
Fiji is justly famous among divers as being the "Soft Coral Capital of the World" because of its enormous number and variety of colorful soft corals. These species grow well where moderate to heavy currents keep them fed. In turn, the corals attract a host of fish. As one example, more than 35 species of angelfish and butterfly fish swim in these waters.

Several of Fiji's most popular dive destinations are in Northern Fiji, especially the colorful **Rainbow Reef** and **Great White Wall,** both on Vanua Levu's barrier reef but within a few miles of Taveuni. The Great White Wall is covered from between 75 feet and 200 feet deep with pale lavender corals, which appear almost snow-white under water. Near Qamea and Matagi, off Taveuni, are the appropriately named **Purple Wall,** a straight drop from 30 to 80 feet, and Mariah's Cove, a small wall as colorful as the Rainbow Reef. Also in the north, **Magic Mountain** on the Namena barrier reef around Moody's Namena has hard corals on top and soft ones on the sides, which attract an enormous number of small fish and their predators.

Another popular site is **Beqa Lagoon,** easily reached by boat from Pacific Harbour, about 30 miles west of Suva. The soft corals in Beqa's **Frigate Passage** seem to fall over one another, and **Side Streets** has unusual orange coral.

The relatively undeveloped island of Kadavu is surrounded by the famous **Astrolabe Reef,** where holes in the coral attract volumes of fish and other sea life.

Even the heavily visited **Mamanuca Islands** off Nadi have their share of good sites, including **The Pinnacle,** a coral head rising 60 feet from the lagoon floor, and a W-shaped protrusion from the outer reef. A drawback for some divers is that they don't have the Mamanuca sites all to themselves.

All but a few resorts in Fiji have dive operations on site, as will be pointed out in the following chapters. Many of them have contacts in North America.

THE BACKPACKERS' TRAIL
Fiji is the most popular destination in the South Pacific for backpackers. The country is the least expensive of the island countries, and it offers a wide range of hostel accommodation, including establishments operated by Fijian villagers. After one night in a Nadi hostel, backpackers will have no trouble picking up the scent of the trail. In general, here's how it goes:

Popular side trips from Nadi are to Mana Island and Beachcomber Island Resort, both in the nearby Mamanucas, and longer excursions to Tavewa and Waya islands in the Yasawas. Mana and the Yasawas have become increasingly popular in recent years, since they offer basic accommodation in or near Fijian villages.

For those with limited time, the usual circuit from Nadi swings around the Coral Coast to Suva. The city is interesting, but as a backpackers' destination, it pales in comparison to Levuka on Ovalau, reached by daily bus-ferry. There are no beaches on Ovalau, but you can stay on Leleuvia, a tiny islet between Ovalau and Viti Levu.

If you have more time, you can fly or catch ferries from Suva to Savusavu and Taveuni.

Another route from Nadi heads to the north side of Viti Levu and Nananu-I-Ra, an island off Rakiraki that is equipped with basic accommodation (take your own food) and occasionally a shortage of water. After a few days on the lovely beaches there, you take the ferry from Ellington Wharf to Nabouwalu on Vanua Levu, where you connect by bus to Labasa and on to Savusavu. From there, a bus-ferry combination goes to Taveuni. From Taveuni, you can get a ferry to Suva.

Suggested Itineraries

These are *suggested* itineraries. I have designed them primarily with sightseeing in mind. Since Fiji is a relatively large country with much to see and do, your actual itinerary obviously will depend on your particular interests—water sports or cultural tours, lounging on a beach or sightseeing.

Many people stop in Fiji for a few days on their way to or from Australia or New Zealand. If you're one of them, don't cut your visit too short. Give yourself at least enough time to learn something about the islands and their peoples.

If your ambition is to rest on a tropical beach and not do much else, choose an off-shore resort rather than staying on the "mainland" of Viti Levu. Frankly, their beaches are better than what you will find on the big island.

The usual circuit goes something like this: Nadi; Coral Coast; Suva; day trip to Levuka, Taveuni, or Savusavu; return to Nadi. An option in the dry season (May to September) is to drive from Nadi to Suva on the King's Road around northern Viti Levu, overnighting in Rakiraki, then return to Nadi via the Queen's Road.

If You Have 1 Day
Visit your hotel desk early to see what's happening. If nothing out of the ordinary catches your eye, spend the morning touring the Mamanuca Islands on the *Island Express.* Have lunch in Nadi Town, quickly shop for handcrafts, then take the open-air local bus to Lautoka. The bus stops at the market, so look there first for handcrafts. Stroll around the business district, including the duty-free shops. During the evening, take in a *meke,* the traditional Fijian feast and dance, at one of the Nadi hotels. (If shopping doesn't appeal, spend the entire day at a resort in the Mamanucas.)

If You Have 3 Days
Unless you can afford a room at the Sheratons, which are on Denaru Beach (see "Accommodations" in the chapter on Nadi and Viti Levu), consider staying 1 night in Nadi and then moving to the Coral Coast. You'll be on the beach and closer to Suva.
Day 1   Take a day cruise to one of the Mamanuca resorts, where you can snorkel, swim, play with the water toys, and have lunch.
Day 2   Take a day trip to Suva, which usually includes stops at the cultural center at Pacific Harbour. Do your handcraft shopping in Suva, and don't miss the Fiji Museum.
Day 3   Take a land excursion from Nadi, such as the Nausori Highlands.

If You Have 7 Days (Blue Lagoon Cruise)
Days 1–4   Take a Blue Lagoon Cruise through the Yasawa Islands. You will see a *meke* and eat Fijian food, so on night four (back in Nadi), eat curry.
Day 5   Now that you're rested up, drive to Suva. Tour the town, including the Fiji Museum. Do your handcraft shopping. Overnight in Suva.
Day 6   Take a day trip to Levuka, Fiji's first capital.

> ## ⚙ Frommer's Favorite Fiji Experiences
>
> **Cruising.** One of my more pleasant tasks is to visit the offshore resorts in the lovely Mamanuca Islands; the best part is getting there on one of the cruise boats operating out of Nadi. I once had the flu on a Blue Lagoon Cruise and still loved it.
>
> **Meeting the People.** The Fijians are justly renowned for their friendliness to strangers, and the Indians are as well-educated and informed as anyone in the South Pacific. Together, these two peoples make for fascinating conversations at every turn.
>
> **Touring Levuka.** Having grown up in Edenton, which still looks very much like it did as North Carolina's colonial capital in the 1700s, I feel almost nostalgic in Levuka, which hasn't changed much since it played the same role in Fiji.
>
> **Exploring the North.** The old South Pacific of copra plantation and trading boat days still lives in Savusavu and Taveuni. True, it rains more up there in Fiji's "North," but that makes the steep hills lushly green. The diving and snorkeling here are absolutely world class.
>
> **Relaxing at an Offshore Resort.** Nothing relaxes me more than running sand between my toes at one of Fiji's small get-away-from-it-all resorts. I am particularly fond of those in lush Northern Fiji, such as Matagi, Qamea, and Moody's Namenalala.

Day 7 Morning flight back to Nadi, followed by a day of rest or one of the tours described in the chapter on Nadi and Viti Levu.

If You Have 7 Days (No Cruise)
Day 1 Do what I recommend above for a 1-day visit. Overnight in Nadi.
Day 2 Make your way by bus, taxi, or rental car to the Coral Coast. Overnight on the coast.
Day 3 Proceed on to Suva in the morning; tour the town and the Fiji Museum. Overnight in Suva.
Day 4 Take a day trip to Levuka, Fiji's first capital.
Days 5–7 Fly to Taveuni and spend the remainder of your holiday seeing the main island and relaxing at an offshore resort.
Day 7 Return to Nadi. If you have time, take one of the tours mentioned in the chapter on Nadi and Viti Levu.

If You Have 7 Days & Want to Do Whirlwind Sightseeing
I actually did this 7-day whirlwind swing around Fiji once, so I know it can be done. You won't have much time to do other than sightsee.
Day 1 Catch an early-morning flight from Nadi to Savusavu. Tour the town in the morning; spend the afternoon swimming and relaxing. Overnight in Savusavu.
Day 2 Morning flight to Taveuni (about 20 minutes). Tour the island and have lunch; then overnight on Taveuni or at one of the resorts on Matagi, Qamea, or Laucala.
Day 3 Morning flight to Suva. Tour the city. Overnight in Suva.
Day 4 Day trip to Levuka. Overnight in Suva.
Day 5 Drive the Coral Coast, stopping off at Pacific Harbour Cultural Centre and Marketplace. Overnight on the Coral Coast.
Day 6 Spend the morning resting on the Coral Coast, then drive to Nadi.
Day 7 Take the *Island Express* tour of the Mamanucas during the morning. Shop in Nadi Town or Lautoka during the afternoon.

If You Have 2 Weeks

Days 1–4   Take one of Blue Lagoon Cruises' short trips through the Yasawa Islands.

Day 5   Drive the Coral Coast, stopping off at the Pacific Harbour Cultural Centre. Overnight on the Coral Coast.

Day 6   Spend the morning resting on the Coral Coast, then drive to Suva (plan to arrive before dark).

Day 7   Tour Suva, including the Fiji Museum. Do your handcraft shopping.

Day 8   Take a day trip to Levuka, Fiji's first capital.

Day 9   Fly to Taveuni on a morning Air Fiji flight. Tour the island and overnight there or at Matagi, Qamea, or Laucala offshore resorts.

Day 10   Spend the day at leisure.

Day 11   Take a morning flight to Savusavu. Tour the town and overnight there.

Day 12   Spend the day at leisure.

Day 13   Fly to Nadi and overnight there.

Day 14   Take one of the Nadi tours mentioned and complete any unfinished handcraft shopping.

6 Visitor Information & Entry Requirements

VISITOR INFORMATION

The **Fiji Visitors Bureau,** G.P.O. Box 92, Suva, Fiji Islands (☎ **0800/721721** from within Fiji or **302433;** fax 300970 or 302751; www.bulafiji.com or www.bulafiji-americas.com; e-mail info@fijifvb.gov.fj), provides maps, brochures, and other materials from the bureau's head office in a restored colonial house at the corner of Thomson and Scott Streets in the heart of Suva. It also has small office in the international arrivals concourse at Nadi International Airport (☎ **722433**), which is open for all arriving flights.

The bureau's award-winning Web site (www.bulafiji.com) is a trove of up-to-date information (local weather and currency exchange rates for the entire South Pacific, for example) and is linked to the home pages of the country's airlines, tour operators, attractions, and hotels. It also has a directory of e-mail addresses. Its alternative Web site (www.bulafiji-americas.com) also features money-saving special deals and package tours just for the North Americans.

Other "FVB" offices are:

United States and Canada: 5777 West Century Blvd., Suite 220, Los Angeles, CA 90045 (☎ **800/932-3454** or 310/568-1616; fax 310/670-2318; e-mail fiji@primenet.com).

Australia: Level 12, St. Martins Tower, 31 Market St., Sydney, NSW 2000 (☎ **02/9264-3399;** fax 02/9264-3060; e-mail fijiau@ozemail.com.au).

New Zealand: 48 High St., 5th Floor (P.O. Box 1179), Auckland (☎ **09/373-2133;** fax 09/309-4720; e-mail office@fijinz.co.nz).

Japan: Noa Building, 14th Floor, 3–5, 2 Chome, Azabuudai, Minato-Ku, Tokyo 106 (☎ **03/3587-2038;** fax 03/3587-2563; e-mail fijijp@magical.egg.or.jp).

Korea: Room 808, Paiknam Bldg., 188–3 I-ka, Ulchiro Chung-ku, 100–191 Seoul (☎ **2/773-8559;** fax 2/752-6921; e-mail fijikr@hotmail.com).

The bureau also has marketing representatives in:

Belgium: rue Americain 27, B-1050 Brussels (☎ **2/538-2930;** fax 2/538-2885; e-mail 101516.1527@compuserve.com).

France: 13 rue d-Alembert, F-38000 Grenoble (☎ **76/700-617;** fax 76/700-918; e-mail 100772.1160@compuserve.com).

Germany: Petersburger Strasse 94, 10247 Berlin (☎ **30/4225-6026;** fax 30/ 4225-6287; e-mail 100762.3614@compuserve.com).

United Kingdom: 34 Hyde Park Gate, London SW7 5BN (☎ **171/584-3661;** fax 171/584-2838; e-mail fijirepuk@compuserve.com).

You can also get information in advance from the **Tourism Council of the South Pacific** (see "Visitor Information & Entry Requirements" in chapter 2).

Other Web sites worth exploring include **www.fijivillage.com** and **www.fijilive. com**, both of which have current news, weather, and sports.

Before you leave Nadi International Airport, drop in on the Fiji Visitors Bureau office and pick up a copy of *Spotlight on Nadi* and *Fiji Magic,* two informative publications aimed at the tourist market. They will tell you what is going on during your visit. The bureau also distributes pamphlets with information about budget travel in Fiji; it lists all of the hostels.

If you have a TV in your room, you can tune in to the **Visitor Information Network (VIN),** an advertiser-supported channel.

Warning: When you see "Tourist Information Centre" in Nadi or elsewhere, it more than likely will be a travel agent or tour operator, whose staff invariably will steer you to their products. The only official, nonprofit tourist information centers are operated by the Fiji Visitors Bureau, at the Suva and Nadi locations given above.

ENTRY REQUIREMENTS

Visitor permits good for stays of up to 4 months are issued upon arrival to citizens of the United States; all Commonwealth countries; most European, South American, and South Pacific island nations; and Mexico, Japan, Israel, Pakistan, South Korea, Thailand, Tunisia, and Turkey. You must have a valid passport, onward or return airline tickets, and enough money or proof of finances to support yourself during your stay.

Citizens of all other countries must apply for visas in advance from the Fiji embassies or consulates. In the United States, contact the **Embassy of Fiji,** 2233 Wisconsin Ave., Suite 240, NW, Washington, D.C. 20007 (☎ **202/337-8320;** fax 202/ 337-1996). Other Fiji embassies or high commissions are in Ottawa, Canada; Canberra, Australia; Wellington, New Zealand; London, England; Brussels, Belgium; Jakarta, Indonesia; Tokyo, Japan; Kuala Lumpur, Malaysia; Port Moresby, Papua New Guinea; or Seoul, South Korea. Check your local phone book.

Persons wishing to remain longer must apply for extensions from the Immigration Department, whose primary offices are at the Nadi International Airport terminal (☎ **722454**) and in the Labour Department building on Victoria Parade in downtown Suva (☎ **211775**).

Vaccinations are not required unless you have been in a yellow fever or cholera area shortly before arriving in Fiji.

Customs allowances are 500 cigarettes; 2 liters of liquor, beer, or wine; and F$50 ($35) worth of other goods in addition to personal belongings. Pornography is prohibited. Firearms and nonprescription narcotic drugs are strictly prohibited and subject to heavy fines and jail terms. Pets will be quarantined. Any fresh fruits and vegetables must be declared and are subject to inspection and fumigation.

7 Money

The national currency is the Fiji dollar, which is divided into 100 cents and trades independently on the foreign exchange markets. The Fiji dollar is abbreviated "FID" by the banks and airlines, but I use **F$** in this chapter. Some hotels and resorts quote their rates in U.S. dollars, indicated here by **US$.**

The Fiji & U.S. Dollars

At this writing, F$1 = approximately US50¢, the rate of exchange used to calculate the U.S. dollar prices given in the Fiji chapters. This rate may change by the time you visit, so use the following table only as a guide.

F$	US$	F$	US$
.25	.13	15.00	7.50
.50	.25	20.00	10.00
.75	.38	25.00	12.50
1.00	.50	30.00	15.00
2.00	1.00	35.00	17.50
3.00	1.50	40.00	20.00
4.00	2.00	45.00	22.50
5.00	2.50	50.00	25.00
6.00	3.00	75.00	37.50
7.00	3.50	100.00	50.00
8.00	4.00	125.00	62.50
9.00	4.50	150.00	75.00
10.00	5.00	200.00	100.00

As we went to press, the Fiji dollar was worth about US50¢ to US55¢. The exchange rate is not published in American newspapers, but someone at the Fiji Visitors Bureau offices usually knows the approximate value. Also, the FVB's Worldwide Web site (see "Visitor Information & Entry Requirements," above) is linked to up-to-date currency exchange tables on the financial pages of the *Washington Post's* Web site (www.washingtonpost.com).

Like their islander counterparts elsewhere in the South Pacific, Fijians may take offense if you try to haggle over a price. On the other hand, many Fiji Indian merchants will expect you to do just that (see "Shopping in Nadi" in chapter 9).

HOW TO GET LOCAL CURRENCY   An **ANZ Bank** branch in the international arrivals concourse at Nadi International Airport is open 24 hours a day, 7 days a week. It charges a F$2 ($1) fee for each transaction over F$100 ($50), F$1 (50¢) if under that amount. Neither ANZ's other branches nor any other bank charges such a fee. There's an ATM on the wall outside the branch, where you can draw Fijian currency using your MasterCard or Visa cards.

ANZ Bank, Westpac Bank, National Bank of Fiji, and **Bank of Baroda** all have offices throughout the country where currency and traveler's checks can be exchanged. **Bank of Hawaii** has offices in Nadi Town and Suva (its operations are more American than the others, which subscribe to Australian and New Zealand banking practices). Bank of Hawaii and ANZ Bank both have ATMs at their Nadi and Suva branches. Banking hours nationwide are Monday through Thursday from 9:30am to 3pm and Friday from 9:30am to 4pm. You can also cash traveler's checks at **Thomas Cook Travel Service** offices in Nadi Town and Suva. See the "Fast Facts" sections in chapters 9, 10, and 11 for specific currency exchange locations.

ANZ Bank, Westpac Bank, and Bank of Hawaii will make cash advances against MasterCard and Visa credit cards. All the banks can arrange international transfers of funds.

CREDIT CARDS   American Express, MasterCard, and Visa are widely accepted by the hotels, car-rental firms, travel and tour companies, duty-free shops, and some restaurants. Don't count on using a Diners Club card outside the hotels.

8 When to Go

THE CLIMATE

During most of the year, the prevailing southeast trade winds temper Fiji's warm, humid, tropical climate. Average high temperatures range from 83°F (28°C) during the austral winter (June to September) to 88°F (31°C) during the summer months (December to March). Evenings are in the warm and comfortable 70s (21°C to 28°C) throughout the year.

The islands receive the most rain during the austral summer, but the amount depends on which side of each island the measurement is taken. The north and west coasts tend to be drier (and warmer), and the east and south coasts wetter (and somewhat cooler but more humid). Nadi, on the west side of Viti Levu, gets considerably less rain than does Suva, on the southeast side (some 200 inches a year). Consequently, most of Fiji's resorts are on the western side of Viti Levu. Even during the wetter months, however, periods of intense tropical sunshine usually follow the rain showers.

Fiji is in the heart of the South Pacific cyclone belt and receives its share of hurricanes between November and April. Fiji's Meteorological Service is excellent at tracking hurricanes and issuing timely warnings, and the local travel industry is very adept at preparing for them. I've been through the excitement of a few Fiji cyclones, and I never let the thought of one keep me from returning every chance I get.

EVENTS

Unlike the other South Pacific island countries, there are no grand national festivals here. The annual **Hibiscus Festival,** held in Suva during the first week of August, features a plethora of events, including traditional dance shows, parades, and the Hibiscus Ball. A similar **Bula Festival** is held in Nadi during the middle of July.

A colorful military ceremony marks the **changing of the guard** at Government House in Suva during the first week of each month.

Local Hindus celebrate **Deepawali,** which is their way of pronouncing *Diwali,* or the Hindu "Festival of Lights," in late October or early November, when they light their houses with oil lamps and candles.

The country has many one-time festivals and events. For a list, contact the Fiji Visitors Bureau (see "Visitor Information & Entry Requirements," above).

HOLIDAYS

Banks, government offices, and most private businesses are closed for New Year's Day, Good Friday, Easter Saturday, Easter Monday, National Youth Day (second Friday in March), Ratu Sukuna Day (May 30 or Monday closest thereto), Queen Elizabeth's Birthday (the Monday closest to June 14), The Prophet Mohammed's Birthday (a Monday in mid-July), Constitution Day (last Monday in July), Fiji Day (the Monday closest to October 10), Deepawali (late October or early November), Christmas Day, and December 26 (for Boxing Day).

Banks take an additional holiday on the first Monday in August, and some businesses may also close for various Hindu and Muslim holy days.

9 Getting There & Getting Around

GETTING THERE

Air New Zealand, Air Pacific, Canadian International Airlines/Air Canada, Canada 3000, and Qantas Airways fly to Fiji from North America. Air New Zealand, Air Pacific, Ansett Airlines, Polynesian Airlines, Qantas Airways, Royal Tongan Airlines,

Solomon Airlines, Air Nauru, and Air Calin (the international airline of New Caledonia) have regional services from Australia and New Zealand to Fiji as well as among the South Pacific islands. See "Getting There" in chapter 2 for details.

ARRIVING & DEPARTING

ARRIVING AT NADI   Most international flights arrive at and depart from **Nadi International Airport,** about 11 kilometers (7 miles) north of Nadi Town. A few flights arrive from Auckland, Samoa, and Tonga at Nausori Airport, some 12 miles from Suva on the opposite side of the island. Both airports are used for domestic flights. They are the only lighted airstrips in the country, which means you don't fly domestically after dark. Since many international flights arrive during the night, at least a 1-night stay-over in Nadi likely will be necessary before leaving for another island.

Arriving passengers may purchase duty-free items at two shops in the baggage claim area before clearing Customs (imported liquor is expensive in Fiji, so if you drink, don't hesitate to buy two bottles).

A large sign on the wall behind the Immigration counters lists all the hotels in the Nadi area, their present room rates, and the taxi fares to get to them.

After clearing Customs, you emerge onto an open-air concourse lined on both sides by airline offices, travel and tour companies, car-rental firms, and a 24-hour-a-day branch of the **ANZ Bank** (see "Money," above).

The **Fiji Visitors Bureau** has an office just to the left, and the friendly staff will give advice, supply information, and even make a hotel reservation for the cost of the phone call. Ask them for a map of Fiji and copies of *Spotlight on Nadi* and *Fiji Magic.* Brochures from every hotel and activity in Fiji are on display. The bureau's airport office is open during regular business hours (see "Fast Facts: Fiji," below) and for at least an hour after the arrival of all major international flights.

Touts for the inexpensive hotels will be milling about, offering free transportation to their establishments. The larger hotels will also have transportation available for their guests.

Taxis will be lined up to the right outside the concourse (see "Getting Around," below, for fares to the hotels).

Local buses to Nadi and Lautoka pass the airport on the Queen's Road every day; walk straight out of the concourse, across the parking lot, and through the gate to the road. Driving in Fiji is on the left, so buses heading for Nadi and its hotels stop on the opposite side, next to Raffles' Gateway Hotel; those going to Lautoka stop on the airport side of the road. You will see the covered bus stands. See "Getting Around Nadi" in chapter 9 for details.

The Nadi domestic terminal and the international check-in counters are to the right of the arrival concourse as you exit Customs (or to the left if you are arriving from the main road). An inexpensive **snack bar** can be found between the two terminals.

The Left Luggage counter at the far end of the departures concourse provides **baggage storage** for F\$3 to F\$6 (\$2 to \$4) a day, depending on the size. The counter is open 24 hours every day. The hotels all have baggage-storage rooms and will keep your extra stuff for free.

A **post office,** in a separate building across the entry road from the main terminal, is open Monday through Friday from 8am to 4pm.

ARRIVING AT SUVA   Suva is served by **Nausori Airport,** on the flat plains of the Rewa River delta about 12 miles from downtown. The small terminal has a snack bar but few other amenities. Taxis between Nausori and downtown Suva cost about F\$17 (\$8.50) each way.

DEPARTING   Passengers leaving the country must pay a **departure tax** of F$20 ($10)—in Fiji currency—at a desk to the right of the check-in counters at Nadi or at a small desk at Nausori Airport (check in first at either airport, since you get your boarding pass stamped). There is no departure tax for domestic flights.

Nadi Airport has a modern, air-conditioned international departure lounge with a currency exchange counter, snack bar, showers, and the largest duty-free shops in the South Pacific. Duty-free prices, however, are higher here than you'll pay elsewhere in the country, and there is no bargaining.

Nausori Airport near Suva has a small duty-free shop in its departure lounge. Some of Air Pacific's flights bound from Nadi to Western Samoa first stop at Nausori, where you will get off and clear Immigration before continuing to Apia.

GETTING AROUND

Fiji has an extensive and reliable transportation network of airlines, rental cars, taxis, ferries, and both long-distance and local buses. This section deals primarily with getting from one island or major area to another; see the "Getting Around" sections in the next chapters for details on transportation within the local areas.

BY PLANE & HELICOPTER

As noted above, only the Nadi and Nausori airports are lighted, so you won't be landing elsewhere in Fiji after dark.

Air Fiji (☎ **888/354-3454** or 722521 in Nadi, 313666 in Suva; www.airfiji.net; e-mail airjiji@is.com.fj) and **Sunflower Airlines** (☎ **800/707-FIJI** in the U.S. or 723016 in Nadi, 315755 in Suva; www.fiji.to; e-mail sunflowerfiji@is.com.fj) both fly from Nadi to the tourist destinations. Air Fiji has one morning and one afternoon flight between Suva and Levuka, making possible a day trip to the old capital (see "Levuka & Ovalau" in chapter 10). Air Fiji's main office is on Victoria Parade in Suva, opposite FINTEL. It also has an office in the international concourse at Nadi International Airport.

From Nadi, one-way **fares** on both Air Fiji and Sunflower Airlines are F$44 ($22) to Malololailai Island (Plantation Island and Musket Cove resorts); F$56 ($28) to Mana Island; F$103 ($51.50) to Suva; F$155 ($77.50) to Savusavu; and F$191 ($95.50) to Taveuni.

Air Fiji's **"Discover Fiji Pass"** permits visitors to fly on any four of its flights during a 30-day period for US$236. It must be purchased outside Fiji, and restrictions apply.

Air Fiji and Sunflower flights from Nadi to Taveuni stop in Savusavu going and coming, so don't let an uninformed travel agent book you back to Nadi or Suva in order to get from Taveuni to Savusavu (it has been known to happen).

Turtle Airways (☎ **722988;** www.bulafiji.com/airlines/turtlair) flies small seaplanes from Nadi Bay to the offshore resorts. Fares are about F$200 ($100) per person. You can charter one of its planes for F$890 ($445) an hour. You can also fly out to Northern Fiji via **Charter Pacific** (☎ **850430;** e-mail hotspring@is.com.fj), which is based in Savusavu.

Island Hoppers (☎ **720140;** www.helicopters.com.fj; e-mail islandhoppers@is.com.fj) will whisk you out to the Mamanucas in one of its helicopters. One-way fares are F$178 ($89) to the southern islands, F$133 ($66.50) to Treasure Island Resort.

Baggage allowances may be 10 kilograms (22 lb.) instead of the 20 kilograms (44 lb.) allowed on international flights. Check with the airlines to avoid showing up with too much luggage.

Remember to **reconfirm** your domestic return flights as soon as possible after arriving at your destination, and to check in when the airlines tell you to (the planes sometimes arrive and depart a few minutes early).

By Rental Car

Rental cars are relatively expensive in Fiji. Each company has its own pricing policy, with frequent discounts, special deals, and some give-and-take bargaining over long-term and long-distance use. All major companies, and a few not so major, have offices in the commercial concourse at Nadi International Airport, so it's easy to shop around. Most are open 7 days a week, some for 24 hours a day. Give careful consideration to how many kilometers you will drive; it's 197 kilometers (118 miles) from Nadi Airport to Suva, so an unlimited kilometer rate could work to your advantage.

Avis (☎ **800/331-1212** in the U.S. or 722233 in Nadi; e-mail aviscarsfj@is.com. fj) has more than 50% of the business here, and for good reason: the Toyota dealer is the local agent, so it has the newest and best maintained fleet. Rates start at F$66 ($33) a day plus F44¢ (22¢) per kilometer, or F$110 ($55) a day with unlimited kilometers. Add another F$20 ($10) a day for liability insurance coverage. In addition to the office at Nadi Airport, Avis can be found in Suva (☎ **313833**), in Korolevu on the Coral Coast (☎ **530176**), at Nausori Airport (☎ **478936**), and at several hotels.

Thrifty Car Rental (☎ **800/367-2277** in the U.S. or 722935 in Nadi), which is handled in Fiji by Rosie The Travel Service, is next best, with rates and cars comparable to Avis's.

Budget Rent-A-Car (☎ **800/527-0700** in U.S. or 722735 in Nadi) also has an agency here.

Khan's Rental Cars (☎ **790617**), the largest local company, is affiliated with Network Rentals of Australia. Other local operators include **Roxy Rentals** (☎ **722763**), **Satellite Rentals** (☎ **721957**), **Central Rent-A-Car** (☎ **722711**), and **Sharmas Rent-A-Car** (☎ **701055**), but be sure to "kick the tires"—in other words, check their cars thoroughly before renting from them.

Even though your home **insurance** policy may cover any damages that occur in Fiji, you must pay out of your own pocket and file a claim when you get home. Since that can be an enormous hassle, I strongly recommend local coverage when you rent a car. Give close attention to the insurance offered, however, for it may not cover damages that occur off the paved roads. Some policies even require you to pay the first F$500 ($250) or more of damages in any event.

All renters must be at least 21 years old, and a few companies require them to be at least 25.

DRIVING RULES   Your valid home driver's license will be honored in Fiji. *Driving is on the left-hand side of the road,* not on the right as in North America and Europe. **Seat belts** are mandatory. **Speed limits** are 80kmph (48 m.p.h.) on the open road and 50kmph (30 m.p.h.) in the towns and built-up areas.

Driving under the influence of alcohol or other drugs is a criminal offense in Fiji, and the police frequently throw up road blocks and administer Breathalyzer tests to all drivers.

You must **stop for pedestrians** in all marked crosswalks.

Most **roads** in Fiji are narrow, poorly maintained, and often crooked. Not all drivers are well-trained, experienced, or skilled, and some of them (including bus drivers) go much too fast for the conditions. Consequently, **drive defensively** at all times. **Always be alert** for potholes, landslides, hairpin curves, and various stray animals (cows and horses a very real danger, especially at night). Frankly, I try not to drive in Fiji after dark.

Also watch out for speed bumps known in Fiji as **road humps;** many villages have them, and most are poorly marked with small black and white roadside posts. You will be upon them before you see them. They are large enough to do serious damage to the bottom of your car, which no local rental insurance covers.

The Queen's Road is paved between Suva and Lautoka, and the King's Road is sealed except for a 30-mile stretch through the central mountains. Most other roads, including the unpaved portion of the King's Road, can be impassable during periods of heavy rain. Be very careful when coming down a hill on an unpaved road, as cars can easily skid on loose dirt and gravel.

Gasoline (petrol) is readily available, even on Sunday, at Shell, Mobil, and BP service stations in all the main towns. When I was there it was selling for F98¢ (49¢) a liter, or about $1.86 for an American-size gallon.

For information about road maps, see "Maps" under "Fast Facts: Fiji," below.

BY BUS

Buses are plentiful and inexpensive in Fiji, and it's possible to go all the way around Viti Levu on them. I did it recently by taking the Queen's Coach from Nadi to Suva one morning, an express to Rakiraki the next afternoon, then another express to Lautoka and a local back to Nadi.

Fiji Express (☎ 722811 in Nadi, 312287 in Suva) is the only air-conditioned "tourist class" express bus operating between Suva and Nadi Airport. It begins its two daily runs at the Centra Suva hotel at 8am and 3:30pm. It stops at the major hotels along the Queen's Road before arriving at Nadi about 12:30pm and 7pm, respectively. The one return trip begins at 1:30pm, with arrival in Suva about 6pm. Fares run up to F$27 ($13.50), depending on how far you go. Book at any hotel tour desk or the UTC office at Nadi Airport.

Sunset Express (☎ 720266 in Nadi, 322811 in Suva) has air-conditioned buses running twice a day between Lautoka and Suva, with stops at Nadi Airport and Sigatoka. These usually leave Nadi Airport daily at 9:45am and 3:45pm, with arrival in Suva at 1:15 and 7:15pm. The return trips depart Suva at 8:45am and 4pm, getting back to Nadi Airport at 12:30 and 7:50pm. The Nadi–Suva fare is F$12 ($6). Sunset Express has an office on the second floor of the Nadi Airport arrivals concourse.

Pacific Transport Ltd. (☎ 700044 in Nadi, 304366 in Suva) has several express and local buses between Lautoka and Suva from Monday through Saturday via the Queen's Road. They all stop at the domestic terminal at Nadi Airport and the markets at Nadi Town, Sigatoka, and Navua. The Fiji Visitors Bureau usually has schedules at its offices. The express buses take about 4 hours between Nadi and Suva, compared to 5 hours on the local "stages." All these buses cater to local residents, do not take reservations, and have no air-conditioning. The Nadi-to-Suva fare is about F$8 ($4), express or local.

Sunbeam Transport Ltd. (☎ 662822 in Lautoka, 382122 in Suva), **Reliance Transport Bus Service** (☎ 663059 in Lautoka, 382296 in Suva), and **Akbar Buses Ltd.** (☎ 694760 in Rakiraki) have express and local service between Lautoka and Suva via the King's Road. The Fiji Visitors Bureau may have their schedules. If not, ask around the local markets. The Lautoka–Suva fare is about F$10 ($5).

Fume-belching **local buses** use the produce markets as their terminals, but they'll stop anywhere if you signal the driver from the side of the road. While more and more modern models are being used, the older buses have side windows made of canvas panels that are rolled down during inclement weather (they usually fly out the sides and flap in the wind like great skirts).

Impressions ————————————————————————————————

The buses in Fiji are like mobile balconies, with no glass in their windows.

—John Dyson, 1982

Buses run every few minutes along the Queen's Road between Lautoka and Nadi Town, passing the airport and most of the hotels and restaurants along the way (see "Getting Around Nadi" in chapter 9).

A system of **mini-vans** scoot along between the Nadi market and Rodwell Road, just around the corner from the Suva Municipal Market. These vehicles are not regulated by the government and should be considered unsafe.

BY TAXI

Taxis are as abundant in Fiji as taxi meters are scarce outside of Suva. Some of the Nadi Airport taxi drivers have allegedly taken advantage of naive tourists, so make sure to settle on a fare to your destination before setting out. Some will complain about short fares and will badger you for more business later on during your stay; politely ignore these entreaties. In Suva, make sure the meter is turned on, if the taxi has one. See the distance chart for approximate taxi fares for destinations between Nadi Airport and Suva.

In Nadi and on the Coral Coast, you will see the same taxi drivers stationed outside your hotel every day. Usually they are paid on a salaried rather than a fare basis, so they may be willing to spend more time than usual showing you around.

Not to be confused with unlicensed minibuses, **"share taxis"** or "rolling taxis"—those not otherwise occupied—will pick up passengers at bus stops and charge the bus fare. They are particularly good value on long-distance trips. A taxi from Suva, for example, will stop by the Nadi Town market and pick up a load of passengers at the bus fare rather than drive back to the capital empty. Ask around the local market bus stops if share taxis are available. You'll meet some wonderful Fijians that way.

The following are distances from Nadi International Airport via the Queen's Road. The taxi fares are approximate; use the amounts given for guidance and bargaining.

From Nadi Airport to:	Km	Miles	Approx. Taxi Fare
Tanoa/Mocambo Hotels	1.3	.8	F$2.50 ($1.25)
Skylodge Hotel	3.3	2.0	F$3.00 ($1.50)
Dominion/Sandalwood Inn	5.2	3.1	F$4.00 ($2.00)
Sheratons/Denarau Island	15.0	9.3	F$16.50 ($8.25)
Nadi Town	9.0	5.4	F$6.00 ($3.00)
Fijian Resort	60.0	36.0	F$40.00 ($20.00)
Sigatoka	70.0	42.0	F$45.00 ($22.50)
The Reef Resort	78.0	46.8	F$50.00 ($25.00)
Hideaway Resort	92.0	55.2	F$50.00 ($25.00)
The Naviti	97.0	58.2	F$60.00 ($30.00)
The Warwick Fiji	104.0	62.4	F$60.00 ($30.00)
Pacific Harbour	148.0	88.8	F$85.00 ($42.50)
Suva	197.0	118.2	F$110.00 ($55.00)

BY FERRY

As an alternative to flying, you can take one of the ferries which run between the main islands. The schedules change frequently depending on the weather and the condition of the ships, so call the operators for the latest information. Double all one-way fares for round-trips.

The newest and most comfortable ship is the *Adi Savusavu,* operated by **Beachcomber Cruises** (☎ 661500 in Lautoka, 307889 in Suva). It runs between Suva and Savusavu three times a week, with extensions to Taveuni once a week. Both first- and economy class cabins are air conditioned and have airline-style seats. The ship takes about 11 hours to steam between Suva and Savusavu, often an overnight voyage. Fares from Suva to Savusavu are about F$47 ($23.50) for first class, F$38 ($19) for economy, slightly more to Taveuni. You can book passage in the Suva booking office in Suite 8, Epworth House, Nina Street.

Consort Shipping Lines (☎ 302877 in Suva) has roll-on, roll-off ferry service between Suva, Koro, Savusavu, and Taveuni twice a week. One-way deck-class fares from Suva are about F$28 ($19.50) to Savusavu, and F$37 ($18.50) to Taveuni. The company's main ticketing office is in the Dominion Arcade behind the Fiji Visitor's Bureau in downtown Suva.

Patterson Brothers Shipping Co. Ltd. (☎ 315644 in Suva, 661173 in Lautoka) operates a combination of buses and ferries from Nadi and Suva to Labasa on Vanua Levu. The Nadi route goes by bus to Ellington Wharf on northern Viti Levu, then by ferry to Nabouwalu on Vanua Levu, and by bus to Labasa. From Labasa you can catch a local bus across the mountains to Savusavu, but it makes for a long, grueling trip). The Suva-Labasa route goes by Natovi Wharf on eastern Viti Levu. One-way fare on these routes is about F$35 ($17.50) per adult. The company also connects Suva to Ovalau via Natovi Wharf. That fare is about F$24 ($12). Patterson Brothers main ticketing office is in Suite ½, Epworth House, Nina Street, Suva.

Emosi's Express Shipping (☎ 313366 in Suva, 440057 in Levuka) provides service between Suva, Levuka, and the backpacker's resort on Leleuvia Island (which this company owns). One-way Suva–Leleuvia fare is F$20 ($10). One-way Suva–Levuka costs F$25 ($12.50). Emosi's office is on Gordon Street in Suva, just uphill from Victoria Parade.

Fast Facts: Fiji

The following facts apply to Fiji generally. For more specific information, see the "Fast Facts" in the following chapters.

American Express   The full-service representative, **Tapa International Ltd.,** has offices in Nadi and Suva. See "Fast Facts" in chapters 9 and 10 for details.

Area Code   The international country code for Fiji is **679.** There are no area codes within Fiji.

Business Hours   Stores generally are open Monday through Friday from 8am to 4:30pm, although many close for lunch from 1 to 2pm, and some stay open until 5:30pm. Saturday hours are from 8:30am to noon in town, but many suburban stores stay open until 6pm and even 8pm. Shops in many hotels stay open until 9pm everyday. Government office hours are Monday through Thursday from 8am to 1pm and 2 to 4:30pm, Friday from 8am to 1pm and 2 to 4pm.

Camera/Film   **Caines Photofast,** the largest processor of Kodak films, has shops in the main towns.

Climate   See "When to Go," earlier in this chapter.

Clothing   Modest dress is the order of the day, particularly in the villages. As a rule, don't leave the hotel swimming pool or the beach in bathing suits or other skimpy attire. If you want to run around half naked, go to Tahiti where the French think it's all right. The Fijians do not. Do not enter a Fijian village wearing a hat or with your shoulders uncovered.

For their part, Fijian men and women wear *sulus,* the same wraparound skirts known as pareus in Tahiti and the Cook Islands and lavalavas in the Samoas. Fijian women wear *chambas,* or hip-length blouses, over their sulus. Many Indian women prefer to wear colorful saris, six-foot lengths of cloth wrapped and pleated around the body.

Crime   See "Safety," below.

Currency Exchange   See "Money," above.

Doctor   Medical and dental care in Fiji is not up to the standards common in the industrialized world. The hospitals tend to be overcrowded and understaffed. Most hotels have private physicians on call or can refer one. Doctors are listed at the beginning of the White Pages section of the Fiji telephone directory under the heading "Medical Practitioners." See "Fast Facts" in the following chapters for specific doctors.

Drug Laws   One drive past the Suva Gaol will convince you not to smuggle narcotics or dangerous drugs into Fiji.

Drugstores   The main towns have reasonably well-stocked drugstores. Their medicines are likely to be from Australia or New Zealand. The large Morris Hedstrom department stores throughout Fiji carry a wide range of toiletries, including Coppertone, Colgate, and many other brands familiar to Americans. See "Fast Facts" in the following chapters for specific locations.

Electricity   Electric current in Fiji is 240 volts, 50 cycles. Many hotels have converters for 110-volt shavers, but these are not suitable for hair dryers. The plugs are the angled two-prong types used in Australia and New Zealand. Outlets have separate on-off switches mounted next to them.

E-mail   Many hotels and resorts will send and receive e-mail for their guests. Cafes in Nadi, Lautoka, and Suva have computer terminals with Internet access, as does Telekom Fiji (the local phone company) in Suva (see "Fast Facts" in chapters 9 and 10).

Embassies/Consulates   The **U.S. Embassy** is at 31 Loftus St., Suva (☎ 314466). Major diplomatic missions in Suva are: **Australia,** 37 Princes Rd. (☎ 382211); **New Zealand,** 10th Floor, Reserve Bank of Fiji Bldg., Pratt Street (☎ 311422); **United Kingdom,** Victoria House, 47 Gladstone Rd. (☎ 311033); **Japan,** 2nd Floor, Dominion House, Thomson St. (☎ 302122); **France,** 1st Floor, Dominion House, Thomson St. (☎ 312233); **People's Republic of China,** 147 Queen Elizabeth Dr. (☎ 311833); and **South Korea,** Vanua House, 8th Floor, Victoria Parade (☎ 300977). Others include **Papua New Guinea** (☎ 304244); **Malaysia** (☎ 312166); **Marshall Islands** (☎ 387899); **Federated States of Micronesia** (☎ 304180); **Nauru** (☎ 313566); and **Tuvulu** (☎ 301355).

Emergencies   The emergency telephone number for police, fire, and ambulance is **000** throughout Fiji.

Firearms   They are illegal in Fiji, and persons found with them could be fined severely and sentenced to jail.

Gambling   There are no casinos in Fiji, but you can play Tattslotto and a newspaper numbers game known as "Fiji Sixes."

Hitchhiking   Local residents seldom hitchhike, so the custom is not widespread. Women traveling alone should never hitchhike.

Insects   Fiji has no dangerous insects, and its plentiful mosquitoes do not carry malaria. The only dangerous animal is the bolo, a venomous snake that is docile and rarely seen.

Liquor Laws   The legal drinking age is 18. Both beer and spirits are produced locally and are considerably less expensive than imported brands, which are taxed heavily. If you drink quality brands of liquor, bring some with you. Fiji Bitter and Fiji Gold are the local beers. Fiji Bitter served in a bottle is known as a "Stubbie." Fiji Gold is a much lighter lager than Fiji Bitter. Most bars also sell Budweiser from the U.S. and most Australian and New Zealand beers. Bartenders here are taught to keep your mug full and your pockets empty—that is, they keep pouring and bringing you new beers until you tell them emphatically to stop.

Maps   Most hotel gift shops sell maps of Fiji. *Spotlight on Nadi* contains an excellent map of the country; get copies at the Fiji Visitors Bureau.

Newspapers/Magazines   Two national newspapers are published in English: the *Fiji Times* and the *Daily Post.* Both are tabloids and appear Monday through Saturday mornings (and Sunday for the *Daily Post).* They carry the latest major stories from overseas. The international editions of *Time* and *Newsweek* (the latter in the rear of *The Bulletin,* an Australian newsmagazine) and the leading Australian and New Zealand daily newspapers are available at some bookstores and hotel shops. The latter usually are several days old before they reach Fiji. Two magazines cover South Pacific regional news: the excellent *Islands Business International* and *Pacific Islands Monthly,* both published in Suva. *The Review* is a monthly magazine concentrating on Fiji business and politics.

Pets   You will need advance permission to bring any animal into Fiji; if not, your pet will be quarantined.

Police   The emergency phone number is **000** throughout Fiji. See "Safety," below.

Post Office   All the main towns have post offices operated by **Fiji Post,** and there is a branch at Nadi International Airport across the entry road from the terminal. Airmail connections between Fiji and North America are fairly rapid, but allow at least a week for delivery. Surface mail can take 2 months or more to reach the U.S. mainland. Airmail rates are F23¢ (12¢) for postcards and airgrams, and F63¢ (32¢) for letters. Post offices are open Monday through Friday from 8am to 4pm. Mail will move faster if you use the country's official name—Fiji Islands—on all envelopes and packages sent there.

Radio/TV   The Fijian government operates three nationwide radio networks whose frequencies depend on the location of the relay transmitters. Radio Fiji 1 carries programming in Fijian. Radio Fiji 2 is Hindi. Radio Fiji Gold broadcasts in English and sounds very much like a popular-music station in Western countries. Radio Fiji 1 and Radio Fiji Gold both carry news bulletins on the hour, and full world, regional, and local news reports and weather bulletins daily at 7am and 6pm. English-language FM stations can be heard in Suva and Nadi.

Fiji has one broadcast TV channel, which can be received around Suva, Nadi, and Lautoka around the clock. Financial news from the CNBC cable network is broadcast starting at 6am Tuesday through Saturday, and programs from Australian television are aired during the off-hours. The local news comes on about 6pm daily, usually followed by world news from Australian TV. The published schedules, carried in the two newspapers, are more or less reliable, but programs don't start crisply on the hour as they do in the U.S. Some hotels have Sky TV, a pay system which airs live sports via ESPN during the afternoons.

Safety   Fiji has experienced a serious increase in property crime in recent years ("Petty theft is a national pastime," says one local resident), and armed robberies have become more frequent. A tourist's chances of being robbed or assaulted in Fiji are lower than in the centers of most large American cities, but caution is advised. Stick to the main streets after dark, and take a taxi back to your hotel if you're out late at night. Some of the smaller hotels in Suva lock their front doors at 11pm, and the large resorts have checkpoints to monitor who comes and who goes. Do not leave valuables in your hotel room or unattended elsewhere, including rental cars and tour buses.

Women should not wander alone on deserted beaches and should be extremely cautious about accepting an offer to have a few beers outside a bar or to be given a late-night lift back to their hotel or hostel.

Taxes   Fiji imposes a 10% value added tax (VAT) on most goods and services. Businesses technically are required to include the tax in the prices they charge. These are known as "VAT Inclusive Prices," or VIP for short. A few still add it like a sales tax, however, and hoteliers need not include it in the rates they quote outside Fiji. Accordingly, be sure to ask whether a hotel room rate or other price includes the VAT.

Visitors leaving the country by air must pay a departure tax of F$20 ($10) in Fiji currency.

Telephone/Fax   International calls can be dialed directly into Fiji from most areas of the world. The international country code is **679.**

The international long-distance carriers have access numbers their customers can call from within Fiji to reach their international networks: **AT&T** (☎ **00-48-901001**); **MCI** (☎ **00-48-901002**); **Sprint** (☎ **00-48-901003**); **Hawaii Telecom** (☎ **00-48-901004**); and **Teleglobe Canada** (☎ **00-48-901005**). These numbers can be dialed toll free from any phonecard public phone (see below). MCI prepaid calling cards are the least expensive way to call the U.S.

International phone, telegram, and fax service also is available at all post offices and at **Fiji International Telecommunications Ltd. (FINTEL),** a colonial-style building on Victoria Parade in downtown Suva. See "Fast Facts: Suva" in chapter 10 for details.

The numbers for **directory assistance** in Fiji are **011** for domestic information, **022** for international numbers.

Pay phones are located at all post offices and many other locations. You can make local, domestic long-distance ("trunk"), or international calls without operator assistance from any of them.

Pay phones accept only Fiji Telecom **phonecards,** not coins. Post offices and many shops (including the gift shops in the Nadi Airport terminal) sell phonecards in denominations up to F$50 ($25). Lift the receiver and slip the card into the slot, picture side up. A digital readout will tell you how much money you have left on the card at all times during your call. Calls to the U.S. cost about F$3 ($1.50) a minute when dialed directly. You *cannot* use your AT&T or other phone company credit cards from a phonecard phone.

You can also purchase a **TeleCard** from the post offices and many shops. These pre-paid cards can be used from any telephone in Fiji, not just pay phones.

To call outside Fiji, dial **05** first, then the country code and phone number. No prefix is required for domestic long distance calls.

Most post offices provide fax service.

Time   Local time in Fiji is 12 hours ahead of Greenwich Mean Time from March 1 to October 31. Daylight saving time is in effect from November 1 to February 28, when local time is 13 hours ahead of GMT. Although the 180°

meridian passes through Taveuni, all of Fiji is west of the International Date Line, so it's 1 day ahead of the U.S. and shares the same day with Australia and New Zealand. Translated: When it's 5am on Tuesday in Fiji, it's noon on Monday in New York and 9am on Monday in Los Angeles.

Tipping Tipping is discouraged throughout Fiji unless truly exceptional service has been rendered. That's not to say the porter won't give you that where's-my-money look once he figures out you're an American.

Water Except during periods of continuous heavy rain, the tap water in the main towns and at the resorts is safe to drink. Bottled "Fiji" spring water is widely available at shops and hotels.

Weights/Measures Fiji is on the metric system.

Nadi & Viti Levu 9

Although you won't see much of the real Fiji if you spend your entire vacation in Nadi, this area has more activities to keep you busy than any other part of the country. That's because Nadi's international airport and warm, dry climate have made it the country's main tourist hub.

Nadi is the fastest growing area of Fiji, with new homes, department stores, and shopping centers popping up all along the 9 kilometers (5.4 miles) of the traffic-heavy Queen's Road between the airport and **Nadi Town,** a 7-block strip lined with a plethora of duty-free, handcraft, souvenir, and other shops. The predominantly Indian town has seen some improvement in recent years. The main drag has been spruced up with planter boxes along the sidewalks, big stores now offer fixed prices and polite clerks, and restaurants provide some of the finest dining in the South Pacific.

But Nadi is just the gateway to the more charming parts—and the much better beaches—of the main island of Viti Levu and the rest of the country. From here, it's an easy 33-kilometer (20-mile) trip to **Lautoka,** Fiji's second largest city, which offers a genteel contrast to tourist-oriented Nadi Town. It's also easy to hop over to the pleasant resorts out in the little **Mamanuca Islands,** which have the beaches and clear lagoons the mainland lacks. Farther out, the even more beautiful and less developed **Yasawa Islands** are the target of the low-key Blue Lagoon Cruises, one of the finest such operations in the world.

South of Nadi along the Queen's Road, the **Coral Coast** has widely spaced resorts with gorgeous scenery and Fijian villages in between. On the Queen's Road between the Coral Coast and Suva, **Pacific Harbour** has great golfing, fishing, and especially diving in the Beqa Lagoon. Or you can go the other way around, along the King's Road from Lautoka through the waving sugar cane fields of **Northern Viti Levu,** where **Rakiraki** beckons with its charming colonial-era hotel.

1 Getting Around Nadi

All of Fiji's major international and local **car-rental** firms have offices in the international arrival concourse of Nadi International Airport.

Taxis gather outside the arrival concourse at the airport and are stationed at the larger hotels. Ask the reception desk to call you one. The aggressive drivers will find you in Nadi Town. Cabs operated by **Tavarus Taxis & Tours,** opposite the Dominion International Hotel

Impressions

The air smelled of blossoms and moistened earth; the hotel maids, who looked and dressed rather like Africans, were singing in the corridors. Most surprising of all, the neatness and tranquillity extended to the town outside the front door, and the country-side at the back. The hotel did not seem to be an island built for foreigners in a sea of squalor.

—Ronald Wright, 1986

(☎ 724125), are all radio-dispatched and air conditioned, which most others here are not.

Local buses ply the Queen's Road between the markets in Nadi Town and Lautoka, leaving each hour on the hour and on the half-hour between 6am and 8pm Monday through Saturday. The buses destined for Votualevu pass the Tanoa International and Fiji Mocambo hotels. Pay when you board. Tell the driver where you're going; he'll tell you how much to pay. Fares vary according to the length of the trip, but F50¢ (25¢) will get you around the Nadi area, and F$1.20 (60¢) will take you from the airport to Lautoka.

A cream-and-blue **Denarau Island bus** is the only one between Nadi Town and the Sheraton resorts, running every 30 minutes daily from 6:30am to 6:30pm. It does not go up the Queen's Road to the airport. One-way fare is F42¢ (21¢).

For more information, including approximate taxi fares in the Nadi area, see "Getting There & Getting Around" in chapter 8.

Fast Facts: Nadi

The following facts apply specifically to Nadi and Lautoka. For more information, see "Fast Facts: Fiji" in chapter 8.

American Express Tapa International Ltd. (☎ 722100 or 722325) has full American Express services at its office in the arrival concourse of Nadi International Airport. The address is P.O. Box 9240, Nadi Airport, Fiji Islands. Open Monday through Friday from 8:30am to 4:30pm and Saturday from 9am to noon.

Bookstores "Bookshops" here are actually stationery stores. Hotel boutiques are the best places to buy novels, magazines, and books about Fiji.

Camera/Film Caines Photofast has a film and 1-hour processing shop on Queen's Road in Nadi Town (☎ 701608). Most of the hotel gift shops also sell film and 1-day processing.

Currency Exchange Bank of Hawaii, ANZ Bank, Westpac Bank, National Bank of Fiji, and **Baroda Bank** all have offices on the Queen's Road in Nadi Town and in Lautoka. Bank of Hawaii and ANZ Bank have ATMs. ANZ Bank has a branch at Nadi International Airport which is open 24 hours a day, and a small office in the Sheraton Fiji which is open Monday through Friday from 7am to 1pm and 2 to 3pm, Saturday from 8am to 1pm. **Thomas Cook Travel Service** has a currency exchange office on the Queen's Road in Nadi Town next to the Mobil Station; it's open Monday through Friday from 8:30am to 5pm, Saturday from 8:30am to noon.

Dentist Ask your hotel staff to recommend a dentist in private practice.

Nadi

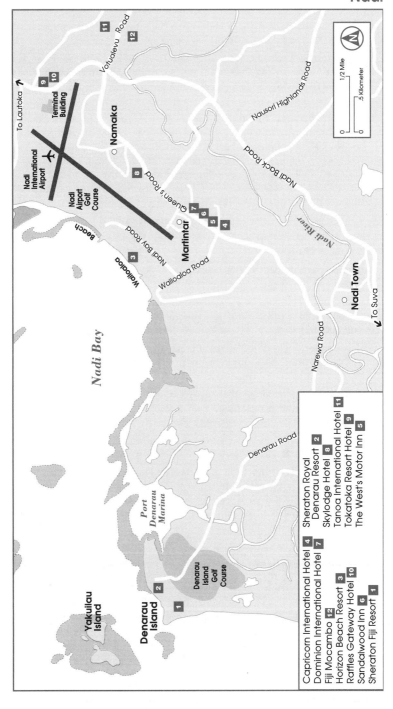

Nadi International Airport
Terminal Building
To Lautoka ↗
Nadi Airport Golf Course
Namaka ○
Votualevu Road
Nausori Highlands Road
Nadi Back Road
Queen's Road
Martintar ○
Wailoaloa Road
Beach
Wailoaloa
Nadi Bay
Nadi River
Narewa Road
Nadi Town ○
To Suva ↙
Denarau Road
Port Denarau Marina
Denarau Island Golf Course
Denarau Island
Yakuilau Island

9 10   **11 12**   **8**   **7 6 5 4**   **3**   **2 1**

1/2 Mile
.5 Kilometer

Capricorn International Hotel **4**
Dominion International Hotel **7**
Fiji Mocambo **12**
Horizon Beach Resort **3**
Raffles Gateway Hotel **10**
Sandalwood Inn **6**
Sheraton Fiji Resort **1**
Sheraton Royal Denarau Resort **2**
Skylodge Hotel **8**
Tanoa International Hotel **11**
Tokatoka Resort Hotel **9**
The West's Motor Inn **5**

Doctor   Dr. Ram Raju, 2 Lodhia St., Nadi Town (☎ **701769** or 976333 mobile) has treated many visitors, including me.

Drugstores   There are three drugstores on Queen's Road in Nadi Town. **Budget Pharmacy** (☎ **700064**) is the best stocked. For toiletries go to one of the **Morris Hedstrom** department stores on the Queen's Road, in both Nadi Town and Namaka.

E-mail   Bedarra Booking Office, on the Queen's Road in Martintar (☎ **725130**), has computer terminals for e-mail and Web surfing. Rates are F40¢ (20¢) a minute or F$10 ($5) for 30 minutes. The e-mail address is bedarra@is.com.fj. Open Monday through Saturday 9am to 6pm. In Lautoka, **The Last Call** restaurant, at Tui Street and Marine Drive (☎ **650525**), charges F44¢ (22¢) a minute plus F50¢ (25¢) for each page printed. Open Monday through Thursday 9am to 9pm, Friday 9am to 11pm, Saturday noon to 11pm.

Emergencies   The emergency telephone number is **000.**

Eyeglasses   Try **Opticare,** 54 Naviti St. (near Vakabale Street and the market), Lautoka (☎ **663337**).

Hairdressers/Barbers   Several hotels have hairdressers. Angie Vuki in the Dominion International was trained in Australia (☎ **722255,** ext. 2021).

Hospitals   The government-operated **Lautoka Hospital** (☎ **663337**) is the region's main facility. There is a government medical clinic in Nadi Town (☎ **700362**).

Information   The **Fiji Visitors Bureau** (☎ **722433**) has an office in the arrivals concourse of Nadi International Airport. Other so-called Tourist Information Centres in reality are travel agents or tour operators.

Laundry/Dry Cleaning   **Prabhat Steam Laundry** (☎ **723061**), on Northern Press Road between the airport and Nadi Town, has 1-day laundry and dry-cleaning service.

Police   The Fiji Police have stations at Nadi Town (☎ **700222**) and at the airport terminal (☎ **722222**).

Post Office   The Nadi Town post office, on Hospital Road near the south end of the market, is open Monday through Friday 7:30am to 5pm, Saturday 8 to 11am. It has a well-stocked stationery store in the lobby. A small airport branch across the main entry road from the terminal (go through the gates and turn left) is open Monday through Friday 8am to 4pm.

2 Sightseeing, Cultural Tours & a Side Trip to Lautoka

Most Coral Coast and Pacific Harbour tours and activities are available from Nadi, since the operators provide transportation. Accordingly, I have included all activities available from Nadi in this and the following sections. It can take 1 hour and more to reach the Coral Coast, 2 to get to Pacific Harbour, so be prepared for some long days.

All but a few hotels have tour desks that can make reservations or arrangements for all the activities mentioned below, and the reception-desk staffs of the others will do so. Like travel agents, the activities desks get a percentage of the proceeds; their services cost you nothing extra. Round-trip bus transportation from the Nadi area hotels is included in the price of the tours and outings; a bus will usually pick you up within

Viti Levu & Ovalau

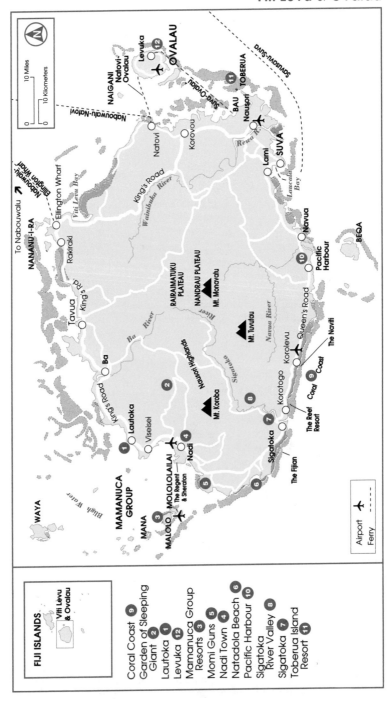

239

30 minutes of the scheduled departure time. Children under 12 years of age pay half fare on most of the activities.

The major tour operators are **United Touring Fiji (UTC)** (☎ 722811), **Road Tours of Fiji** (☎ 722935), and **Sun Tours of Fiji** (☎ 722666). They have decades of experience, their vehicles are clean and air conditioned, and their staffs are knowledgeable.

Pick up copies of *Spotlight on Nadi* and *Fiji Magic,* which give up-to-date, detailed information (the latter has four full pages of small type devoted just to tours and cruises from Nadi).

SIGHTSEEING TOURS

Several companies operate tours on air-conditioned buses to various destinations near Nadi and on the Coral Coast, and to Suva. Their rates are about the same, but some shopping around could pay off. Talk to more than one hotel activities desk; since most desks are operated by the tour companies, they understandably will steer you to their trips. Here are some of the key sightseeing tours.

✪ **THE CORAL COAST RAILWAY**   The *Fijian Princess* (☎ 520434), a restored sugarcane locomotive, pulls passengers from Shangri-La's Fijian Resort on the Coral Coast to lovely Natadola Beach, where you swim (bring your own towel) and have lunch at a restaurant on the beach. Occasionally there's an evening run to Sigatoka that includes cocktails, and a Fijian dance show. These outings cost about F$80 ($40) from the Nadi hotels and F$70 ($35) from those on the Coral Coast, including lunch.

Once at Natadola Beach, you can take a sailboat ride out to **Robinson Crusoe Island** for swimming, snorkeling, and a Fijian-style picnic lunch on the beach. These excursions cost F$69 ($34.50) per person. Waterskiing is extra. The boat runs Tuesday through Friday and on Sunday.

FLIGHTSEEING & BALLOONING   Island Hoppers Fiji (☎ 720410) and **Turtle Airways** (☎ 722389) offer sightseeing flights over Denarau Island, Nadi Bay, the Mamanucas, and Vuda Point north of Nadi. The flights cost about F$150 ($75) per person. You can float from the Nausori Highlands out over the plains around Nadi Bay with **Paradise Balloons** (☎ 721011) for F$265 ($132.50) per person.

✪ **GARDEN OF THE SLEEPING GIANT**   This lovely, 50-acre orchid range was started in 1977 by the late Raymond Burr, star of TV's *Perry Mason* and *Ironside* shows, to house his private collection of tropical orchids (he once also owned Naitoba, a small island in the Lau Group). There's much more here than orchids, however, and the guides will describe a variety of local plants and their uses, from birds of paradise to water lilies. You can get here on a tour or on your own by rental car or taxi. Look for the sign at Wailoko Road off the Queen's Road between Nadi and Lautoka. It's open Monday through Saturday from 9am to 5pm. Entrance fees are F$9.90 ($4.95) for adults, F$4.90 ($2.45) for children, including guided tour and fruit drink. Burr's former home in the hills overlooking Saweni Bay north of Nadi is now owned by Don and Aileen Burness, who have a collection of Fijian artifacts. Call them for information about touring the home (☎ 662206).

NADI AREA   Several companies have half-day tours of the Nadi area, including the Nadi Town market, an Indian sugarcane farm, a Fijian village, a Muslim mosque and Hindu temple, and the orchid range at Garden of the Sleeping Giant (see above). Another version of this tour goes to Lautoka instead of Nadi Town, with a stop at the Garden of the Sleeping Giant on the way. Many of these tours include **Viseisei Village,** on the Queen's Road about halfway between Nadi and Lautoka. One legend says the first Fijians settled here, but today it's a typical, fairly prosperous Fijian village, with some very modern houses and some shacks of concrete block and tin, a small

---

Dreaded Degei

The tour guides like to point out that Viseisei village between Nadi and Lautoka is where the great canoe *Kaunitoni* came out of the west and deposited the first Fijians some 3,000 years ago. From there, the legend goes, they dispersed all over the islands. The yarn is helped by the local district name Vuda, which means "our origin" in Fijian, and Viseisei, which means "to scatter."

Although it's clear today that the Fijians did indeed migrate from the west, no one knows for sure whether they landed at Viseisei, for like all Pacific Islanders, the Fijians had no written language until the missionaries arrived in the mid-19th century.

The most common oral legend has the great chiefs Lutunasobasoba and Degei arriving in the *Kaunitoni* on the northwest coast of Viti Levu. From there they moved inland along the Nakauvadra Range in Northern Viti Levu. Lutunasobasoba died on this trip, but Degei lived on to become a combination man, ancestor, and spirit—and an angry spirit at that, for he is blamed for causing wars and a great flood that washed the Fijians to all parts of the islands.

The dreaded Degei supposedly still inhabits a mysterious cave in the mountains above Rakiraki, but no one is about to go in there to find out.

---

handcraft shop, and the usual road humps that bring traffic to a crawl. These trips usually cost about F$45 ($22.50).

NAUSORI HIGHLANDS   Several road tours go through the sugarcane fields to the steep, grass-covered hills of the Nausori Highlands, a cool 2,500 feet above Nadi. There are some fine vistas from up there, including many out to sea. These tours also include visits to Fijian villages and Muslim mosques. Cost is about F$35 ($17.50) per adult.

SIGATOKA HIGHLANDS   For a variation of the Sigatoka Valley trip, this one goes up the valley and then on forestry roads across the steep hills of the scenic Nausori Highlands to Nadi. The full-day trip includes information about Fiji's pre-European history. Price is about F$75 ($37.50), including lunch in a Fijian village.

SIGATOKA VALLEY & KULA ECO PARK   Another full-day tour goes to the town of Sigatoka on the Coral Coast and the meandering river and fertile valley of the same name. The valley has so many market gardens that it is known as "Fiji's Salad Bowl." The tour usually includes a stop at **Nadroga,** a small village in the valley where Fijians still make pottery in the traditional way of their ancestors. There also will be time for lunch and some shopping in Sigatoka. **Kula Eco Park,** opposite the Outrigger Reef Fiji Resort on the Coral Coast, has a collection of tropical birds, whose collective feathers have the colors of a rainbow, and an aquarium stocked with examples of local sea life. You can visit Kula Bird Park (☎ **500505**) on your own. It's open daily 10am to 4:30pm. Admission is F$11 ($5.50) for adults, free for children under 13.

SUVA DAY TOUR   The three major tour companies all have buses leaving Nadi about 8am Monday through Saturday for the 4-hour drive to Suva, picking up passengers at the Coral Coast hotels and stopping for a tour of Pacific Harbour Cultural Centre (see "Pacific Harbour," below). Guests have lunch on their own in Suva, then are escorted on a guided tour of the city. The buses leave Suva about 4pm for the return trip. You'll pay about F$70 ($35.50) per person from Nadi, less from the Coral Coast hotels. See chapter 10 for information about the capital.

CULTURAL TOURS

Although several tours include brief visits to Fijian villages, these trips give a more in-depth look at Fijian culture.

NAVUA RIVER TOUR   This full-day trip goes by bus to Navua, a rice-growing town near the mouth of the Navua River on Viti Levu's south coast. Guests then travel by outrigger canoe past waterfalls and through forests to Namuamua, a Fijian village that puts on a yaqona ceremony, a lunch of local-style foods, and a traditional dance show. Price is about F$105 ($52.50) from the Nadi hotels, less from those on the Coral Coast. UTC calls this its Jewel of Fiji tour; others call it Namuamua Inland Tour. A variation includes a ride on a *bilibili* bamboo raft down the river (see "River Rafting" under "Boating, Golf, Hiking & Other Outdoor Pursuits," below).

WATERFALLS & CAVES   Two of the most informative outings are the waterfall and cave tours offered by ✪ **Adventures in Paradise** (☎ **520833**), on the Coral Coast opposite the Outrigger Reef Fiji Resort. Led by energetic Fijian Rusi Brown, the waterfall tour goes to Biausevu village in the Korolevu Valley. A tour bus takes you to the village, where you'll be welcomed at a traditional yaqona ceremony. Then comes a 30-minute hike along a rocky stream to the falls, with Rusi explaining the local fauna on the way. A picnic lunch is served at the falls, which plunge straight over a cliff into a swimming hole. The sometimes slippery trail fords the stream seven times, so wear canvas shoes or a pair of strap-on sandals for the hike, and a bathing suit and towel if you want to take a very cool and refreshing dip after the sweaty hike.

On Rusi's other excursion, you'll spend 45 minutes inside the Naihehe Cave, which was used as a fortress by Fiji's last cannibal tribe, and then return via a bilibili raft on the Sigatoka River (the cave is an hour's drive up the Sigatoka Valley). A yaqona ceremony will welcome you to the village, and you'll have a picnic lunch before the raft ride.

Rusi charges F$89 ($44.50) per person for the waterfall tour, F$109 ($54.50) for the cave trip, including lunch and transfers. Subtract F$10 ($5) if he picks you up at a Coral Coast hotel. Book at any hotel activities desk.

At least one tour company in Nadi has day trips by boat up the winding Sigatoka River and its flat valley. The cruises stop for visits to the ancient Tavuni Hill Fort, demonstrations of pottery making, a kava welcoming ceremony, and a Fijian feast. The boats then go down river to the Sigatoka Sand Dunes (see "The Coral Coast," below).

A SIDE TRIP TO LAUTOKA

Most visitors stay in Nadi and come to Lautoka, Fiji's second-largest town (pop. 30,000) and second major seaport, to board Blue Lagoon Cruises or the boats heading to Beachcomber and Treasure Island Resorts and to the Yasawa Islands. Those who do spend a few hours looking around this pleasant town of broad avenues and shady sidewalks are greeted by towering royal palms marching in a long, orderly row down the middle of **Vitogo Parade,** the main drag running from the harbor into the heart of town.

The duty-free shops and other stores along Vitogo Parade mark the boundary of Lautoka's business district; behind them are several blocks of stores and the lively **Lautoka Market,** which doubles as the bus station and is second in size only to Suva's Municipal Market. Handcraft stalls at the front of the market offer a variety of goods, especially when cruise ships are in port. Shady residential streets trail off beyond the playing fields of **Churchill Park** on the other side of Vitogo Parade. The Hare Krishnas have their most important temple in the South Pacific on Tavewa Avenue.

Tourism may rule Nadi, but sugar is king in Lautoka. The **Fiji Sugar Corporation's** huge mill was built in 1903 and is one of the largest crushing operations in the southern hemisphere. If you pass the industrial port, you'll also see a mountain of wood chips ready for export; the chips are a prime product of the country's pine plantations.

GETTING THERE   Local buses leave the market in Nadi Town every half hour for the Lautoka Market from Monday through Saturday between 6am and 8pm. The fare is no more than F$1.20 (60¢), depending on where you get on. The one-way taxi fare to Lautoka is about F$20 ($10) from Nadi.

If you're driving yourself from Nadi, you will come to two traffic circles on the outskirts of Lautoka. Take the second exit off the first one and the first exit off the second. That will take you directly to the post office and the southern end of Vitogo Parade.

WHERE TO STAY IN LAUTOKA   If you do elect to stay in Lautoka, the town's best digs are at the **Waterfront Hotel,** P.O. Box 4653, Lautoka (☎ **800/521-7242** or 664777; fax 665870; e-mail waterfronthotl@is.com.fj), a modern facility on Marine Drive, diagonally across the park at the south end of Vitogo Parade. Equipped with phones, quiet air conditioners, and televisions with satellite programming, its 47 rooms range from F$106 to F$128 ($73 to $89.50) double. The large dining room with harbor view is best known for its businesspeople's lunches and evening theme buffets, but snacks are served all day by the swimming pool. American Express, Diners Club, MasterCard, and Visa cards are accepted.

You can get a simple but clean room or dorm bed at **Cathay Hotel,** P.O. Box 239, Lautoka (☎ **660566;** fax 660136; www.fiji4less.com.fj; e-mail cathay@is.com.fj). This white, 2-story concrete structure on shady Tavewa Avenue a block inland from Vitogo Parade has a pool, TV lounge, bar, and dining room offering simple fare. Some of its 38 rooms have ceiling fans instead of air conditioners, but the price depends entirely on the size of the room, not the condition of its air. Room rates range from F$29 to F$47 ($19.50 to $23.50) double. Dorm beds go for F$9.50 ($4.75), with a F$1 (50¢) discount for YHA members. The Cathay takes American Express, Diners Club, MasterCard, and Visa cards.

WHERE TO DINE IN LAUTOKA   ✪ **The Last Call,** on the waterfront at Tui Street and Marine Drive (☎ **650525**), is the pick here. Father-son owners Flaviano and Ivan Pisoni, who moved here from Milan, Italy, offer Italian-style salads, sandwiches made with real Italian bread, snacks such as spicy bruschetta, and pizzas with a range of toppings (chili prawns will set your mouth afire). Their only main courses are various sauces served in bowls over macaroni, spaghetti, and fusilli, just like in the old country. Or you can simply take a break here on your shopping excursion for a genuine espresso, cappuccino, or latte, or perhaps a fresh fruit smoothie or a cooling gelato-style ice cream cone. Snacks and pizzas cost F$3.50 to F$8 ($1.75 to $4), while pastas will set you back F$10 to F$13 ($5 to $6.50). The Last Call is open Monday through Thursday from 9am to 9pm, Friday from 9am to 11pm, Saturday from noon to 11pm, and Sunday from 5 to 9pm. MasterCard and Visa cards are accepted.

3 Island Escapes from Nadi

The Great Sea Reef off northwest Viti Levu in effect encloses a huge lagoon whose usually calm waters surround the nearby Mamanuca and Yasawa island groups with speckled shades of yellow, green, and blue as the sea changes from shallow to deep. It's a fine place to escape to a small island for a least a day. Most of the excursions mentioned below depart from **Port Denarau,** the marina facility on Denarau Island. Bus transportation from the Nadi area hotels is included in their prices. Book at your hotel activities desk.

Aqualand (☎ **750500**) is a group of buildings on a tiny islet with little vegetation but lots of sand and a surrounding lagoon (it's not nearly as popular as Beachcomber Day Cruises; see below). Water sports enthusiasts can pay to play all day at a wide variety of activities, such as scuba diving, waterskiing, windsurfing, parasailing, and scooting around on small craft. Round-trip transfers on a fast catamaran (just 15 minutes to the island) cost F$59 ($29.50) for a half day, F$79 ($39.50) for a full day, including lunch and nonmotorized activities. Children pay half fare. A pass for motorized activities such as waterskiing costs F$80 ($40) per person. You can pay separately for the activities and order snacks à la carte once you get there. There is no overnight accommodation at Aqualand.

☉ Beachcomber Day Cruises (☎ **661500**) sail from both Port Denarau and Lautoka to youth-oriented Beachcomber Island Resort (see "Resorts Offshore from Nadi," below). Adults pay F$60 ($30) for bus transportation, the cruise, and an all-you-can-eat buffet lunch on Beachcomber Island, or F$69 ($34.50) for all that plus unlimited soft drinks and use of snorkeling gear. Add F$16 ($8) from the Coral Coast. Otherwise, snorkeling gear and activities cost extra. It's a fine way to join the young folks frolicking in the sun without having to stay overnight. A few tops have been known to drop at Beachcomber, so if the sight of a woman's unclothed breasts offends, think twice before signing up for this one. Transfers are made from Port Denarau via a speedy catamaran or from Lautoka on the *Tui Tai,* a much slower sailboat.

Captain Cook Cruises (☎ **701823**) uses the *Ra Marama,* a 110-foot square-rigged brigantine built in Singapore during the 1950s and once the official yacht of Fiji's colonial governors-general, for day cruises out to Tivua Island, an uninhabited 4-acre islet in the Mamanucas. The sail takes 1 hour each way. A traditional Fijian welcoming ceremony greets guests at the island, where they can swim, snorkel, and canoe over 500 acres of surrounding coral gardens (or see the colors from a glass-bottom boat). Drinks on board the *Ra Marama* and a barbecue lunch on the beach are included in the F$73 ($36.50) per person cost.

Malamala Island (☎ **702433**) is a 6-acre islet studded with palm trees and circled with white-sand beaches. The only inhabitants will be you and your fellow passengers, who will use Malamala's only building, a thatch bure, for a barbecue lunch. Guests are taken to the island on the glass-bottom boat *Tropic Sea.* The F$69 ($34.50) price includes lunch, drinks, and coral viewing.

Malololailai Island, 9 miles offshore, can be visited by plane as well as on a day cruise via the **Malolo Cat** (☎ **720774**), a speedy catamaran used to transport guests between Port Denarau and the island. The *Malolo Cat* charges F$49 ($24.50) per person. **Sunflower Airlines** (☎ **723016**) has frequent flights from Nadi Airport to the little gravel strip separating Plantation Island and Musket Cove. Sunflower's special excursion round-trip fare is F$55 ($26.50). Both trips include free use of some facilities at Plantation Island and Musket Cove, but you pay for motorized water sports such as parasailing and waterskiing. Once on Malololailai, you can hang out at either resort, shop at Louis and Georgie Czukelter's **Art Gallery** on the hill above Musket Cove (no phone), and dine at **Anandas Restaurant and Bar** (☎ **722333**) by the airstrip. Book at the restaurant to play the island's short nine-hole golf course; fees are F$15 ($7.50).

South Sea Cruises (☎ **750500**) runs the fast, diesel-powered catamaran *Tiger IV* three times a day through the Mamanucas. It primarily serves as a ferry for visitors who have too much luggage to fly to the Mamanucas. It departs on its 3-hour loops from Port Denarau daily at 9am, 12:15pm, and 3:15pm. You can ride along and sightsee through the islands for F$45 ($22.50) per person, but you won't be able to luxuriate on any beaches, as the boat stops at each resort only long enough to put off and pick up passengers and their luggage. On the other hand, you can take the morning voyage, get off at **Mana Island Resort** or **Castaway Island Resort** (see "Resorts Offshore from Nadi," below), have a buffet lunch, swim and sunbathe, and catch the afternoon boat back to Denarau Island. The Mana and Castaway excursions cost F$85 ($42.50) and F$95 ($47.50), respectively, including buffet lunch.

Seafari Cruise is what South Sea Cruises (☎ 750500) calls its rent-a-boat service at Port Denarau. You design your own cruise to the Mamanuca Group, such as picnicking at a deserted beach or picking your own snorkeling spots. Prices depend on the size of the boat. The largest can hold up to 20 passengers.

4 Blue Lagoon Cruises

Started with a converted American crash vessel in the 1950s, ✪ **Blue Lagoon Cruises** are so popular with Australians, New Zealanders, and a growing number of Americans, Canadians, and Europeans that they're usually booked solid more than 2 months in advance of each daily departure from Lautoka.

Two of Blue Lagoon's vessels are 126-foot-long ships capable of carrying 54 passengers in 22 air-conditioned cabins. Two others, the 181-foot-long *Yasawa Princess* and the 155-foot-long *Nanuya Princess,* carry up to 66 passengers in 33 staterooms. The newest vessel, the sleek, 185-foot *Mystique Princess,* looks as if she should belong to a Greek shipping magnate, and her 35 staterooms do indeed approach tycoon standards.

The ships make cruises ranging from 2 to 6 nights through the Yasawas. They all depart Lautoka (the *Mystique Princess* will pick you up in the Mamanuca Islands) in time to arrive in the Yasawas for a welcoming cocktail party and dinner on board. They then proceed to explore the islands, stopping in little bays for snorkeling, picnics or lovo feasts on sandy beaches, and visits with the Yasawans in their villages. The ships anchor in peaceful coves at night, and even when they cruise from island to island, the water is usually so calm that only incurable landlubbers get seasick.

Rates range from F$705 to F$2,209 ($358 to $1,105) per person double occupancy per cruise, including all meals, activities, and taxes. Singles pay a hefty supplement, but there are reduced fares for children.

For reservations or information, contact a travel agent or **Blue Lagoon Cruises,** P.O. Box 54, Lautoka (☎ 661622 or 661268; fax 664098; www.bluelagooncruises. com; e-mail blc@is.com.fj).

5 Boating, Golf, Hiking & Other Outdoor Pursuits

The Nadi area has a host of sporting and outdoor activities to suit almost every interest. Most of these are near Nadi, but some require a boat trip to the Mamanuca Islands or a bus ride to other locations on Viti Levu. See "Resorts Offshore from Nadi," below, for more information about what the islands have to offer. The Sheraton resorts on Denarau Island both have water sports equipment and activities.

FISHING   The two Sheraton hotels and all the resorts in the Mamanucas offer sports fishing as a pay-extra activity for their guests. On the mainland, **South Sea Cruises** (☎ 750500) has a fleet of fishing boats and guides based at Port Denarau. Offshore, that same company operates under the name **Pleasure Marine** (same phone), with boats at Musket Cove Resort and Mana Island Resort. **Bay Cruises** (☎ 722676) also has fishing boats available.

GOLF & TENNIS   The 18-hole, 7,150-yard, par-72 resort course of **Denarau Golf & Racquet Club** (☎ 750477) occupies most of Denarau Island, with the club house opposite the Sheraton resorts. It has a restaurant serving breakfast, lunch, and dinner at moderate prices, a bar, and locker rooms with showers. Greens fees are F$85 ($42.50) for guests of the two big resorts and F$90 ($45) for those of us who can't afford to stay there. The course is open daily from 7am to dark.

The club's four all-weather courts and six Wimbledon-standard grass courts are operated by Peter Burwash International. The unlighted grass courts are open daily from 7am to dark, while the lighted hard courts stay open until 10pm. Guests of the Sheratons pay F$12 ($6) an hour; everyone else pays F$20 ($10). Lessons are available. Proper tennis attire is required.

The **Fiji Mocambo Hotel** (☎ 722000) has a short, nine-hole executive course, and the hotel tour desks can arrange for you to play at the 18-hole **Nadi Airport Golf Club** (☎ 722148) near Newtown Beach, behind the airport. The latter is a 5,882-yard, par-70 course which isn't particularly challenging, but the setting, on the shores of Nadi Bay, is attractive.

The South Pacific's best course is at **Pacific Harbour** (☎ 450022), in Deuba near Suva, some 89 miles from Nadi (see "Pacific Harbour," below).

HIKING An arm of Rosie The Travel Service (☎ 722755), **Adventures Fiji** offers trekkers (as hikers are known in these parts) the chance to make a 1-day walk some 2,000 feet up into the Nausori Highlands above Nadi. I found this walk to be strenuous (you have to be under 45 to sign up unless you're in good physical condition) but fascinating. Wear walking shoes with excellent traction and that you don't mind getting wet, for the sandy trail goes into and out of steep valleys and crosses streams. Also wear sunscreen, for most of this walk is through grasslands with no shade. We had a long midday break in a Fijian village, where we shared a local-style lunch sitting cross-legged in a simple Fijian home, then took a 45-minute side excursion up a narrow valley to a waterfall. Cost is F$62.50 ($31.25) per person. The company also has 4-, 6- and 10-day hikes across central Viti Levu ranging in price from F$478 to F$1,155 ($239 to $577.50), including transfers, guide, accommodation, and meals provided by Fijian villagers along the way.

JET BOATS For a thrill-a-minute carnival ride afloat, **Shotover Jet Fiji** (☎ 750400) will take you twisting and turning through the mangrove-lined creeks behind Denarau Island. This is the company that pioneered jet-boating on the Shotover River in New Zealand, and its speedy "Big Red" boats go roaring around these Fijian waterways. Heart-stopping 360-degree turns are guaranteed to get the adrenaline flowing and the clothes wet. The half-hour rides depart every 30 minutes daily from Port Denarau. A shuttle connects the nearby Sheraton and Regent; there are scheduled pickups from other Nadi area hotels, so call for reservations. Price is F$69 ($34.50) for adults and F$25 ($12.50) for children.

✪ **RIVER RAFTING** Travel videos and brochures seem always to feature tourists lazily floating down a Fijian river on a raft made of bamboo poles lashed together. In the old days, mountain-dwelling Fijians really did use *bilibilis*—long, flimsy bamboo rafts—to float their crops down river to market. They would discard the rafts and walk home. Today you can ride your own bilibili down the Navua River, between Pacific Harbour and Suva. Several companies have cultural tours up the river to picturesque Namuamua village (see "Cultural Tours," above), but **Discover Fiji Tours** (☎ 722811 in Nadi or 450180 on the Coral Coast) not only takes you upriver by motorized canoe, it brings you back on a bilibili. The river itself is a scenic delight as it cuts a gorge through the foothills. Depending on how much it has rained recently, you'll have a few gentle rapids to negotiate, and you'll stop for dips in waterfalls tumbling right into the river. Wear swim suit and sandals, but bring a sarong to wear in the village, where you'll be welcomed at a yagona ceremony. Namuamua is much like any other modern Fijian village with tin roofs on plywood or concrete block houses, but it has glorious mountain views from a fork in the river.

These full-day trips cost about F$95 ($47.50) from the Nadi hotels, F$88 to F$92 ($44 to $46) from the Coral Coast. Children pay about half fare.

Rivers Fiji (☎ **800/346-6277** in the U.S. or 450147 in Pacific Harbour; fax 450148; www.riversfiji.com; e-mail riversfiji@is.com.fj) uses modern inflatable rafts and kayaks for white-water trips through the Upper Navua River Gorge and the Wainikoroiluva (or "Luva") River, a tributary of the Navua. Inflatable kayaks are used on the Luva, which can have Class II rapids depending on how much it has rained lately. These are long day trips but worth it for rafting and kayak fans. The Luva kayak adventures cost F$175 ($87.50) from Nadi, F$160 ($80) from the Coral Coast and Suva. Rafting on the Upper Navua costs F$190 ($95) from Nadi, F$180 ($90) from the Coral Coast and Suva. They don't go every day, and 24 hours advance reservations are required, so call ahead for more information.

SAILING   **Captain Cook Cruises** (☎ **701823**, fax 702045) has regularly scheduled, 4-day, 3-night "sailing safaris" to Waya Island in the Yasawas on the square-rigged, 108-foot *Spirit of the Pacific.* You actually stay ashore in thatch bures beside an otherwise deserted beach. You'll share communal toilets and showers. Days are spent examining Fijian gardens, boating over to a deserted island, visiting a village for a *meki* island feast and dance show, and lots of swimming and snorkeling. Cost is F$495 ($225.50) per person, including meals and activities.

✪ *Whale's Tale* (☎ **722455,** fax 720134), a luxury, 100-foot auxiliary sailboat owned by American Paul Myers, takes no more than 12 guests on day cruises from Port Denarau through the Mamanucas. The F$160 ($120) per person cost may seem steep, but it includes a continental breakfast with champagne on departure; a buffet lunch prepared on board; and all beverages, including beer, wine, and liquor, and sunset cocktails. The *Whale's Tale* also is available for charters ranging from 1 day in the Mamanucas to 3 days and 2 nights in the Yasawas. Rates depend on the length of trip.

South Sea Cruises (☎ **750500**) has day sails aboard the M. V. *Seaspray,* an 83-foot schooner that starred in the 1960s TV series *Adventures in Paradise.* These cost F$160 ($80) per person, including morning tea, lunch, beer, wine, and soft drinks.

Because of Fiji's reef-strewn waters, the government will not permit strictly "bareboat" yacht charters, but you can rent both boat and skipper or local guide for extended cruises through the islands. **Fiji Yacht Charters,** Private Bag 0352, Nadi Airport (☎ **662215;** fax 662633; www.fijiyachting.com; e-mail musketcovefiji@is.com.fj), acts as an agent for several boats based at Musket Cove Resort in the Mamanucas. These include the *Dulcinea,* a 55-foot ketch, and the *Hobo,* a 37-footer. They and other vessels have day cruises for F$80 ($40) an hour and are available for longer cruises. Musket Cove's marina is a mecca for cruising yachts such as these, some of whose skippers hang around and take charters for a living.

SCUBA DIVING & SNORKELING   Dive operators in the Nadi area include **Tropical Divers Fiji** (☎ 750777, ext. 189) at the Sheraton Fiji Resort; **South Sea Divers** (☎ 701455) at Sheraton Royale Denarau Resort; **Inner Space Adventures** (☎ 723883) at Newtown on Wailoaloa Beach; and the American firm **Aqua-Trek** in Nadi Town opposite the Mobil Station and at Mana Island Resort in the Mamunucas (☎ 702413 or 800/541-4334 in the U.S.). All have dive guides and teach courses. Prices are about F$110 ($55) for a two-tank dive.

Resorts in the Mamanuca Islands all have dive operations (see "Resorts Offshore from Nadi," below).

The marina at Port Denarau is home base for 2 live-aboard dive boats, both of which offer cruises among Fiji's reefs.

The more far-ranging is the ***Princess II,*** P.O. Box 9082, Nadi Airport (☎ **800/ 576-7327** or 725116; fax 725220 in Fiji or 303/417-0557 in the U.S.; E-mail: princessii@is.com.fj or princessii@south-seas-adventures.com), which is owned and operated by Keith and Selwyn Douglas, relatives of the Matagi Island Douglases (see "Resorts Off Taveuni" in chapter 11). This 85-foot luxury vessel goes to all the way to the colorful reefs off Taveuni, with dives off northern Viti Levu, Wakaya, and Namena along the way. It can accommodate 12 divers in 6 cabins, each with its own air-conditioning unit. The main lounge has a bar, sound system, and video players, and there's a darkroom on board. Rates range from U.S. $1,200 per person for a 4-night cruise to U.S. $2,600 for a 9-nighter, including meals and diving.

The ***Fiji Aggressor,*** a 106-foot, 16-passenger live-aboard catamaran based in Lautoka, makes weekly voyages through the Mamanuca and Yasawa islands. This luxurious vessel is equipped with E-6 photo lab, video, and high-speed canopied dive boat. You'll dive at least twice a day for 5½ days out of the week. Rates are US$2,295 per person, including accommodations, meals, snacks, and unlimited diving, but not equipment. For information and reservations, contact **Live/Dive Pacific,** 74–5588 Pawai Place, Bldg. F, Kailua-Kona, HI 96740 (☎ **800/344-5662** or 808/329-8182 in Hawaii; fax 808/329-2628; www.pac-aggressor.com; e-mail 102162.2335@ compuserv.com).

6 Shopping in Nadi

Bargaining is not considered polite when dealing with Fijians. And although the better stores have gotten away from the practice, bargaining is quite acceptable when dealing with most Indian merchants. They will start high, you will start low, and somewhere in between will be found a mutually agreeable price. I usually knock 40% off the asking price as an initial counter-offer and then suffer the merchants' indignant snickers, secure in the knowledge that they aren't about to kick me out of the store. After all, the fun has just begun.

Caution: Fijians normally are extremely friendly people, but beware of so-called **sword sellers.** These are Fijian men who carry bags under their arms and approach you on the street. "Where you from, States?" will be their opening line, followed quickly by "What's your name?" If you respond, they will quickly inscribe your name on a sloppily carved wooden sword carried in the bag. They expect you to buy the sword, whether you want it or not. They are especially numerous in Suva, but they likely will come up to you in Nadi, too. The Fiji government discourages this practice but has had only limited success in stopping it. The easiest way to avoid this scam is to not tell any stranger your name.

DUTY-FREE SHOPPING   Fiji has the most developed duty-free shopping industry in the South Pacific, as will be very obvious when you walk along the main thoroughfare in Nadi Town. One shop after another offers brand-name perfume, jewelry, watches, electronic equipment, cameras, liquor, cigarettes, and a plethora of other items.

The Fiji government charges a flat 10% import tax on merchandise brought into the country, so except for the shops in the airport departure lounge, the stores aren't exactly "duty free." Accordingly, check around carefully before leaving home if you are thinking of buying an expensive watch or camera. You likely will find better prices and selections at the larger-volume dealers at home, especially in the United States, Canada, Australia, and New Zealand. Find the item at home first so that you can compare the price in Fiji.

Also compare the models offered in the duty-free shops with those available at home. Those sold in Fiji may not be the latest editions.

If you decide to make a purchase, follow this advice from the Fiji National Duty Free Merchants Association: Request receipts accurately describing your purchases. Make sure all guarantee and warranty cards are properly completed and stamped by the merchant. Examine all items before making payment. If you later find that the item is not what you expected, return to the shop immediately with the item and your receipt. As a general rule, purchases are not returnable and deposits are not refundable.

Personally, I pay for my duty-free purchases by credit card. That way, if something goes wrong after I'm back home, I can call for help from the large financial institution that issued my card.

To avoid the hassles of bargaining, visit **Jack's Handicrafts, Prouds,** and **Tappoo,** the largest and most reputable merchants. They have well-stocked shops on Queen's Road in Nadi Town as well as in the shopping arcades of the larger hotels in Nadi and on the Coral Coast. They also are in Sigatoka and downtown Suva. Jack's Handicrafts' upstairs rooms have clothing and leather goods. Tappoo carries a broad range of merchandise, including electronics, cameras, and sporting goods. Prouds concentrates more on jewelry, perfumes, and watches.

If you missed anything, you'll get one last chance at the huge shops in the departure lounge at Nadi airport.

HANDCRAFTS   Fijians produce a wide variety of handcrafts, such as carved *tanoa* (kava) bowls, war clubs, and cannibal forks; woven baskets and mats; pottery (which has seen a renaissance of late); and *masi* (tapa cloth). Although generally not of the quality of those produced in Tonga, they are made in prolific quantities. Be careful when buying some wood carvings, however, for many of today's items are machine-made, and many smaller items are imported from Asia. Only with masi can you be sure of getting a genuine Fijian handcraft.

On the other hand, virtually every shop now sells some very fine face masks and *nguzunguzus* ("noozoo noozoos"), the inlaid canoe prows carved in Solomon Islands, and some primitive art from Papua New Guinea. (Although you will see plenty hanging in the shops, the Fijians never carved masks in the old days.)

If you're going to Suva, wait until you've visited **Wolf's Boutique** (the top handcraft store in the country) and the **Government Handicraft Centre.** There you will see some of the best items, all of them authentic, and get a firm idea of the going prices. See chapter 10 for details.

The largest and best-stocked shop on Queen's Road is ✪ **Jack's Handicrafts** (☎ 700744), opposite the Morris Hedstrom department store. It has a wide selection of handcrafts, jewelry, T-shirts, clothing, and paintings by local artists. The prices are reasonable and the staff helpful rather than pushy. The Chefs restaurant complex is on premises (see "Dining in Nadi," below). Jack's Handicrafts also has an outlet in the shopping arcade of the Sheraton Fiji Resort (☎ 701777) and in Sigatoka (☎ 500810).

Other places to look are **Nadi Handicraft Center** (☎ 702357), opposite the Bank of Hawaii on the other side of Queen's Road, and **Nad's Handicrafts** (☎ 703588), near the north end of town. Nadi Handicraft Center has an upstairs room carrying clothing, leather goods, jewelry, and black pearls from Tahiti. Nad's usually has the best selection of Fijian pottery.

In the Sheraton Royale arcade on Denarau Island, **Sogo Fiji** (☎ **750000,** ext. 2317) has an excellent selection of handcrafts, including some from Solomon Islands and Papua New Guinea (the Sogo Fiji outlet on Queen's Road in Nadi Town doesn't carry handcrafts). The Sheraton's shops are open daily 9am to 9pm.

Nadi Handicraft Market (no phone) is a collection of stalls on the Queen's Road near the south end of Nadi Town. The best are operated by Fijian women who sell baskets and other goods woven of pandanus.

If you're going that way, check out the handcraft stalls in the **Lautoka Market** for shells and shell jewelry, mats, straw hats and purses, grass skirts, and tapa cloth. The wood carvings tend to be a bit touristy, since the stalls do most of their business on days when cruise ships put into Lautoka.

TROPICAL CLOTHING   Although not of the quality in other South Pacific countries, colorful tie-dyed clothing and sulus are for sale at most of the hotel boutiques and in the shops along Queen's Road in Nadi Town. **Sogo Fiji** carries up-market designer dresses and beachwear at its stores on Queen's Road in Nadi Town (☎ 701604), in Sigatoka, and on Victoria Parade in Suva. **Tiki Togs** is the country's largest producer of resort wear; it has shops in most major hotels and on Victoria Parade in Suva.

For the most unusual items, ✪ **Michoutouchkine Creations,** in the shopping arcade of the Sheraton Fiji Resort (☎ 750518), has the creations of Nicolai Michoutouchkine and Aloi Pilioki, the noted Vanuatu artists whose squiggly swirls distinguish each of their shirts, blouses, pants suits, and beach towels.

7 Accommodations in Nadi

Most Nadi area hotels are on or near the Queen's Road, either near the airport or in the suburban area known as **Martintar** between the airport and Nadi Town. Except for backpacker-oriented hostels in Newtown on Wailoaloa Beach, none of these establishments is on a beach, and even if they were, runoff from the mountains, hills, cane fields, and coastal mangrove swamps perpetually leaves **Nadi Bay** murky, sometimes for several miles offshore.

About 7km (4.3 miles) to the west of Nadi Town, pancake-flat **Denarau Island** is home to a huge real estate project known in its entirety as Denarau Island Resort. It includes the two Sheraton hotels and an adjacent 164-room condo development, an 18-hole golf course, Port Denarau marina where most of the area's cruises are based, and room for four more hotels and numerous residential lots. Another 150-room hotel and a 150-unit time share development were in the works as we went to press. Denarau is only technically an island, for a narrow, winding creek through a mangrove forest is all that separates it from the mainland. If you stay on Denarau, you will have to take a taxi to get anywhere else after 6:30pm, when the only bus stops running between there and Nadi Town. See "Getting There & Getting Around" in chapter 8 for taxi fares.

Fiji's other big resort, the 400-room **Shangri-La's Fijian Resort,** 45 minutes south of Nadi (see "The Coral Coast," below), has a whiter beach and clearer lagoon than those at Denarau, but it lacks the convenience of having so many activities on its doorstep.

Some of the **room rates** quoted below and elsewhere in these chapters on Fiji are "inclusive of VAT," meaning that the government's 10% value added tax (VAT) is included; for others, the VAT will be added to your bill when you check out. Ask the hotels if the VAT is included.

IN THE AIRPORT AREA

✪ **Fiji Mocambo.** P.O. Box 9195, Nadi Airport (Votualevu Rd., 1 mile south of airport). ☎ **800/942-5050** or 722000. Fax 720324. E-mail: mocambo@is.com.fj. 127 units. A/C TV TEL. F$198–F$264 ($99–$132) double. AE, DC, MC, V.

From their perch atop a hill south of the airport, each of the Mocambo's spacious rooms has its own patio or balcony overlooking the hotel's lush gardens, the surrounding cane fields, and the sea or mountains beyond. The views are an advantage over its rival, the nearby Tanoa International Hotel (see below). The "superior" rooms on the top floor have peaked ceilings that give them the feel of individual bungalows; some of their bathrooms also come equipped with separate tubs and large, walk-in showers.

Covered walkways lead downhill to the open-air Coffee Garden Restaurant, under a lean-to roof and a huge poinciana tree that also shades part of the deck surrounding a large swimming pool. Except during dinner hours, it's open around the clock for snacks and full meals. Dinners are served in both the Marau Alcove, a fine-dining room, and in the main lounge, which has live music and is a popular spot for dancing after 9pm (the music can be heard in some rooms; don't hesitate to ask for another if it bothers you). You won't hear the noise from an air-conditioned karaoke bar, which is open daily from 10pm to 6am.

The Mocambo also has lighted tennis courts and a short, nine-hole golf course, plus a beauty salon, business center, and shopping arcade. Room service is available 24 hours a day.

Raffle's Gateway Hotel. P.O. Box 9891, Nadi Airport (Queen's Rd., directly opposite airport). ☎ **722444.** Fax 720620. E-mail: gaby@is.com.fj. 93 units. A/C TV TEL. F$96.50–F$160.50 ($48–$80) double. AE, DC, MC, V.

Along with the more modern and entertaining Tokatoka Resort Hotel next door, this older property (no connection to Singapore's famous Raffles Hotel) is Nadi's most convenient place to wait for a flight at the airport just across Queen's Road. And as at the Tokatoka, you can slip down a water slide into a swimming pool, this one shaped like a figure **8.** A plantation theme dominates the property, with the main building somewhat reminiscent of a colonial planter's home. Medium-size rooms are in 2-story buildings on either side of a courtyard and a second, older swimming pool with its own thatch-roof bar. The rooms are modest but nicely appointed with coconut wood furniture. The more expensive units have sitting areas. All units have shower-only bathrooms. The roadside main building houses a restaurant and 24-hour coffee shop (room service is available around the clock, too).

Tanoa International Hotel. P.O. Box 9203, Nadi Airport (Votualevu Rd., 1½ mile south of airport). ☎ **800/835-7742** or 720277. Fax 720191. E-mail: tanoahotels@is.com.fj. 135 units. A/C MINIBAR TV TEL. F$180–F$220 ($90–$110) double. AE, DC, MC, V.

This well-managed hotel is the Fiji Mocambo's chief rival as Nadi's top airport hotel. You walk into a bright public area with reception, tour desk, comfortable bar and lounge with nightly entertainment, indoor-outdoor restaurant specializing in reasonably priced theme-night buffets, air-conditioned coffee shop open 24 hours a day, beauty parlor, small clothing emporium, and well-stocked gift shop. These all open onto a lush garden with swimming pool, beside which a big tin roof covers varnished wood tables and chairs for dining or relaxing.

Thatch-covered walkways link the public building to medium-size, motel-style guest rooms in white, 2-story blocks. Most rooms have cool tile floors, bright spreads, tropical furniture, coffeemakers, a double and a single bed, combination tub-shower bathrooms, and balconies or patios. Two one-bedroom suites are among Nadi's finest hotel rooms and are often taken by local dignitaries. A special facility is a guest Laundromat. Services include baby-sitting, laundry and dry cleaning, and 24-hour room service.

Tokatoka Resort Hotel. P.O. Box 9305, Nadi Airport (Queen's Rd. opposite airport). ☎ **720222.** Fax 720400. E-mail: tokatokaresort@is.com.fj. 112 units. A/C TV TEL. F$130–F$286 ($65–$143). AE, DC, MC, V.

The highlight at this modern complex is an unusual swimming pool-restaurant-bar at the rear of the property, which makes the Tokatoka a favorite of families with children. The youngsters can play to their heart's content on an S-shaped water slide streaming down into the angular pool, which is partially under the same steel-beam- and brick-supported roof covering the restaurant and bar. Indeed, this is the best place in Nadi to kill time while waiting for a flight home. You'll also find Nadi's most varied mix of accommodations here, from hotel rooms to two-bedroom villas, all of them equipped with cooking facilities and tropical-style furniture (some of it a bit well-used in the older units). Open 24 hours a day, the Harvesters' Restaurant serves snacks all the time plus blackboard dinner specials. Weekends also see moderately priced dinner buffets, which are served daily during busy periods. A jazz group plays every evening from an island in the pool. There's a tour desk, grocery store, boutique, beauty salon, and guest laundry here. Some units are equipped for disabled guests.

DENARAU ISLAND

✪ **Sheraton Fiji Resort.** P.O. Box 9761, Nadi (Denarau Island, 7km [4.3 miles] west of Nadi Town). ☎ **800/325-3535** or 750777. Fax 750818. 292 units, plus 82 condos. A/C MINIBAR TV TEL. F$485–F$660 ($242.50–$330) double, F$450–F$1,400 ($225–$700) condo. AE, DC, MC, V.

This 1987-vintage property is the most luxurious of Fiji's three big resorts. A fountain flows through a series of pools running down the center of its airy, off-white grand foyer, which opens to a large rectangular swimming pool and the beach beyond. With the lawn-type umbrella tables of a cafe on one side and a series of glass-enclosed boutiques and shops on the other, the lobby is strongly reminiscent of a shopping mall back home (it does indeed have some very fine shops) and contrasts sharply with the dark-wood, handcraft-accented public areas of Sheraton Royal Denarau Resort next door. In other words, this Sheraton could be put down in any tropical resort location, not necessarily in the South Seas.

Nevertheless, its bright, spacious, and tropically decorated rooms have ocean views, private terraces or balconies, two queen-size beds or one king-size bed, ceiling fans for days when the air-conditioning is unnecessary, and the usual fridge and tea/coffee-making facilities found in this part of the world. The resort also manages the 82 adjacent condos known as the "Sheraton Villas." Built in 1999 around a courtyard, one end of which opens to a beachside swimming pool and bar, these are Nadi's best digs. They come in various sizes ranging from a single room to three-bedrooms and are appointed with all the comforts of home, including full kitchens and washers and dryers.

Dining/Diversions: Three bars and four food outlets (none of them inexpensive) include the dressy Ports O' Call and the relaxed Verandah, where enormous buffets feature a different international cuisine each night. Fijians strum their guitars and sing island songs every evening. Planters Bar is a dimly lit pub with disco dancing after 9pm.

Amenities: Shopping arcade with bank and several boutiques; fitness center; sailboats, Windsurfers, and paddleboats; private island across the lagoon where guests can swim, snorkel, and sunbathe; activities desk; concierge; laundry; baby-sitting; children's program and playground; 24-hour room service; business services; free "Bula Bus" shuttle to Sheraton Royal Denarau Resort and golf club.

✪ **Sheraton Royal Denarau Resort.** P.O. Box 9018, Nadi Airport (Denarau Island, 7km [4.3 miles] west of Nadi Town). ☎ **800/325-3535** or 750000. Fax 750259. 273 units. A/C MINIBAR TV TEL. F$365–F$860 ($182.50–$430) double. AE, DC, MC, V.

Formerly The Regent of Fiji, this venerable hotel has been one of the finest in the South Pacific since 1972, and it has considerably more Fijian charm than the Sheraton Fiji Resort, its newer and more modern sibling next door. Covered by a peaked wooden roof, a dark, breezy foyer opens to an irregular-shaped pool with thatch-covered, swim-up bar on one end (something the Sheraton Fiji's rectangular pool lacks). A grassy berm, built after cyclones damaged the beach, separates the pool from the gray beach.

Like those at the Sheraton Fiji, the rooms here are in a series of 2-story, motel-style blocks grouped in "villages" surrounded by thick, lush tropical gardens and linked by covered walkways to the central building. With lots of varnished wood trim, the spacious units are equipped with twin or double beds, large bathrooms with separate tubs and showers, dressing areas with twin vanities, refrigerators, radios, tea/coffee-making facilities, and private patios or balconies. TVs can be supplied on demand for a fee. The furnishings are made of rattan or bamboo and are accented by tapa cloth and exposed timbers.

Dining/Diversions: The five restaurants here, none of them inexpensive, have barbecue buffets several nights a week and a Fijian feast with fire-walking once a week. Boasting fine and relatively expensive Japanese cuisine, **Hamacho Restaurant** (☎ **750177**) sits on the Sheraton Fiji end of the property. There's another Hamacho branch on the Queen's Road in Martintar (☎ **720252**). Reservations are essential at either Hamacho.

Amenities: Swimming pool with swim-up bar; shopping arcade with several boutiques; bank; beauty salon; games room; pitch-and-putt golf course; sailboats, Windsurfers, paddleboats; private island across the lagoon where guests can swim, snorkel, and sunbathe; tour desk; concierge; laundry; baby-sitting; children's program and playground; 24-hour room service; business services; free "Bula Bus" shuttle to Sheraton Fiji Resort and golf club.

IN THE MARTINTAR AREA

Capricorn International Hotel. P.O. Box 9043, Nadi Airport (Queen's Rd. at Wailoaloa Rd., 5.2km [3.3] miles south of airport). ☎ **720088.** Fax 720522. E-mail: capricorn@is.com.fj. 62 units. A/C TV TEL. F$75–F$95 ($37.50–$45) double. AE, DC, MC, V.

You won't enjoy luxuries at this simple motel-style place, but you will get a clean room and a very firm mattress—both trademarks here and at its equally spotless sister in Suva, the Capricorn Apartment Hotel (see "Accommodations in Suva" in chapter 10). The smallish rooms here are simply furnished with blonde wood desks, wicker chairs and coffee tables, double and single beds, coffeemakers, and fridges. Tops are rooms with balconies or patios overlooking a lush tropical courtyard, whose pool has a small rock waterfall flowing into it. These more spacious units have glass shower stalls with doors, while the others have French-style showers, which can result in wet tile floors. Other poolside rooms have sliding doors opening to walkways. Least expensive are standard rooms, entered from the rear but with window walls overlooking the courtyard. A thatch-covered walkway connects the rooms to a open-air building with Indian restaurant, bar, activities desk, and gift shop. This often is the lowest priced Nadi property offered on package tours.

Dominion International Hotel. P.O. Box 9178, Nadi Airport (Queen's Rd., 5.1km [3.1] miles south of airport). ☎ **800/448-8355** or 722255. Fax 720187. www.dominion-international.com. E-mail: dominion@is.com.fj. 85 units. A/C TEL. F$115–F$155 ($57.50–$77.50) double. AE, DC, MC, V.

The aging but well-maintained Dominion is one of the few establishments in Fiji at which you can park a car right next to your door or the stairs leading to your room. The rooms are in two white, 3-story buildings flanking a tropical garden surrounding a swimming pool. A central building with restaurant and bar sits at the Queen's Road end, completing the hotel's U shape. The motel-style rooms have white tile floors, tub-shower bathrooms, and glass doors sliding onto patios or bougainvillea-draped balconies. All rooms have a queen and twin bed plus two chairs and a coffee table in one corner. A few are equipped for disabled guests.

A dining room under a dark, Fijian-style roof extracts a reasonable price for rather plain fare. Also on the premises are a tour desk, gift shop, hairdresser, and nine-hole putting course.

Sandalwood Inn. P.O. Box 9454, Nadi Airport (Martintar, near Queen's Rd., 5.3km [3.2] miles south of airport). ☎ **800/448-8355** or 722044. Fax 720103. E-mail: sandalwood@is.com.fj. 49 units (44 with private bathroom). A/C TEL. F$32 ($16) double without bathroom; F$38–F$70 ($19–$35) double with bathroom. AE, DC, MC, V.

"Clean and comfortable at a sensible price," is the appropriate motto at John and Ana Birch's establishment, which makes it especially popular with New Zealanders (John's a Kiwi; Ana is a friendly Fijian). The original buildings here have seen better days, and when their lease expires in 2001, John and Ana probably will move their entire operation to a more modern complex called the Sandalwood Lodge, about 200 yards away on the same side road as their original property. Even if they haven't completely moved, the lodge's 24 New Zealand-style motel units are highly preferable to the old rooms. They have kitchenettes and surround a nicely landscaped lawn with swimming pool. Meanwhile, the top floor of their old 2-story, concrete building houses spacious, air-conditioned rooms with telephones and large windows opening to balconies upstairs.

The ground level holds a restaurant, small bar, and lounge. An older, 1-story building on the opposite side of a swimming pool has smaller, non-air-conditioned rooms, some with their own small bathrooms, others sharing two toilets and two showers.

✪ **Skylodge Hotel.** P.O. Box 9222, Nadi Airport (Namaka, on Queen's Rd., 3.3km [2 miles] south of airport). ☎ **800/448-8355** or 722200. Fax 724330. E-mail: skylodge@is.com.fj. 53 units. A/C TV TEL. F$104 ($52) double without kitchen, F$131 ($65.50) double with kitchen. AE, DC, MC, V.

The eclectic Skylodge was built as a crew base for Qantas Airways in the early 1960s, but it has been remodeled and upgraded over the years and is very good value today. The more desirable rooms are in four-unit bungalows scattered through 11 acres of lawns and tropical trees; some have cooking facilities. The other rooms in the original wooden lodge are spacious and have tiled bathrooms with combination tub-showers. Some of these are next to the bar and swimming pool, beside which you can dine outdoors under a steel roof.

The restaurant and lounge are in a low, thatch-accented central building adjacent to the swimming pool. The restaurant offers well-prepared European, Fijian, and Indian dishes at moderate prices. Dining is inside or alfresco at the side of the pool. You can play pitch-and-putt golf outdoors or darts and billiards inside. The friendly, veteran staff provides valet laundry and limited room service, and there's a coin-operated laundry for do-it-yourselfers. A bonus: you can watch CNN International and ESPN sports in your room.

The West's Motor Inn. P.O. Box 10097, Nadi Airport (Queen's Rd., 2.1 miles south of airport). ☎ **720044.** Fax 720071. E-mail: westmotorinn@is.com.fj. 62 units (all with private bathroom). A/C TV TEL. F$99–F$129 ($49.50–64.50) double. AE, DC, MC, V.

Despite a name conjuring up images of a motel, this gay-friendly establishment is more like an inn. Lending charm, a courtyard swimming pool partially wraps around—and is shaded by—an ancient mango tree. The rooms are comfortably furnished, although their shower-only bathrooms are cramped. Most have wooden louvered windows and doors which swing open to this vista, either directly to the courtyard or to balconies above. All of the rooms have ceiling fans and tea/coffee-making facilities. You might get a less expensive local rate for the smaller rooms in the rear, but they have no view. A cafe and bar area with white tile floors opens to the pool and tree, and there's a gift shop and activities desk here. The cafe turns into a lively piano bar at night (see "Island Nights in Nadi," below).

HOSTELS

Touts bombard backpackers arriving at Nadi airport with offers of cheap accommodation, for this area has a host of hostels, all of them in fierce competition with each other. When I first came here in 1977, I stayed at the **Sunseekers Hotel,** on Narewa Road across the bridge from Nadi Town (☎ **700400;** fax 702047). It's still in business, but a much better choice is the Fijian-run **Sunview Motel and Hostel,** P.O. Box 9103, Nadi Airport (☎ **724994** or 724933; fax 721533), on Gray Road off the Queen's Road behind the Bounty Restaurant in Martintar. A dorm bed there costs F$12 ($6), including breakfast. But why not stay at the beach?

Horizon Beach Resort. P.O. Box 1401, Nadi (on Wasawasa Rd., Newtown Beach, 1.5km [1 mile] west of Queen's Rd.). ☎ **722832.** Fax 720662. 13 units (all with private bathroom), 15 dorm beds. F$30–F$40 ($15 to $20) double room, F$10 ($5) dorm bed. Dorm rates include breakfast. AE, MC, V.

In Newtown Beach, a compound of suburban homes and budget hostels, this 2-story clapboard house sits across an open lot from Wailoaloa Beach. It's is owned by the family of Gopi Chand, a retired government health inspector, and they keep it spotless. Representing excellent value for the money, the rooms are spacious and have their own bathrooms with hot-water showers. Six of them are air-conditioned. The dorm beds are in two rooms, one with 10 bunks, the other with five. There's an open-air restaurant-bar serving good, inexpensive meals and cold beers. Guests here represent various nationalities and ages. Inner Space Adventures scuba diving base is across the street.

8 Dining in Nadi

While you will see Fijian-style dishes on many menus, invariably they will have at least one Indian curry. Most curries in Fiji are prepared on the mild side, but you can ask for it extra spicy and get it so hot you can't eat it. Curries are easy to figure out from the menu: lamb, goat, beef, chicken, vegetarian. If in doubt, ask the waiter or waitress. *Roti* is the round, heavily leaden bread normally used to pick up your food (it is a hybrid of the round breads of India and Pakistan). *Puri* is a soft, puffy bread, while *papadam* is round, crispy, and chiplike.

The entire meal may come on a round steel plate, with the curries, condiments, and rice in their own dishes arranged on the larger plate. The authentic method of dining is to dump the rice in the middle of the plate, add the smaller portions around it, then mix them all together.

You'll find the local **McDonald's** on the Queen's Road about 1 kilometer (0.6 mile) north of Nadi Town. A Big Mac, medium fries, and a Coke combo costs about F$5.65 ($2.85), but the most interesting items are the vegetable McNuggets and the McVegetable burger, a tasty fried vegetable curry patty.

IN THE AIRPORT AREA

Maharaja Restaurant. Queen's Rd., in K. Nataly & Sons Building near Skylodge Hotel. ☎ **722962.** Reservations not accepted. Main courses F$6–F$12 ($3–$6). MC, V. Mon–Sat 9am–10pm, Sun 7–10pm. INDIAN/EUROPEAN/CHINESE.

Traditional Feasts

Like most South Pacific islanders, the Fijians in pre-European days steamed their food in an earth oven, known here as a *lovo*. They would use their fingers to eat the huge feasts *(mekes)* that emerged, then settle down to watch traditional dancing and perhaps polish off a few cups of yaqona.

The ingredients of a lovo meal are *buaka* (pig), *doa* (chicken), *ika* (fish), *mana* (lobster), *moci* (river shrimp), *kai* (freshwater mussels), and various vegetables, such as dense *dalo* (taro root), spinach-like *rourou* (taro leaves), and *lumi* (seaweed). Most dishes are cooked in sweet *lolo* (coconut milk). The most plentiful fish is the *walu*, or Spanish mackerel.

Fijians also make delicious *kokoda* ("ko-kon-da"), their version of fresh fish marinated in lime juice and mixed with fresh vegetables and coconut milk. Another Fijian specialty is *palusami,* a rich combination of corned beef or fish baked in banana leaves or foil with onions, taro leaves, and coconut milk.

Several Nadi hotels have mekes on their schedule of weekly events. The foods are cooked in a lovo on the hotel grounds and served buffet style, often beside the swimming pool if weather permits. Traditional Fijian dance shows follow the meals. *Spotlight on Nadi* and *Fiji Magic* both list the schedules, or phone the hotels to find out.

This somewhat cramped storefront establishment is the best place in Nadi to sample authentic curries in a more refined setting than you'll get at other so-called curry houses. They are well seasoned here, either mild, medium, or so hot you'll want to grab a fire extinguisher. There's a selection of European dishes, which lean toward plain but hearty grilled steaks, fish, and pork and lamb chops. You can also order Chinese dishes prepared in the Cantonese style.

DENARAU ISLAND

The Wet Mongoose Bar & Grill. Port Denarau Marina. ☎ **926460.** Reservations recommended for dinner. Main courses F$12–F$32 ($6–$16). AE, MC, V. Daily 8am–2:30pm and 5–11pm. STEAKS/SEAFOOD.

This sister of Cardo's in Suva (see "Dining in Suva" in chapter 10) occupies a colonial-style building beside the narrow muddy waterway at Port Denarau. Choice tables are on the wraparound porch, which catches the breeze and offers a view across the water and cane fields to the green mountains rising beyond. This vista is especially gorgeous on a moonlit night, but bring insect repellent. You can avoid the mossies (and sacrifice the view) inside the air-conditioned, nonsmoking dining room. Owner Cardo is known throughout Fiji for providing quality char-grilled steaks and fish, and they're his best offerings here. A reasonable rendition of veal parmigiana is the best of a few Italian choices. Daily specials could include kabob-style shrimps under a very spicy chili and garlic sauce. This is a pleasant spot to relax after a cruise or a hair-raising ride on a Shotover Jet, and it's an inexpensive escape from the high-priced Sheraton dining rooms. Ask about transportation from the Sheratons when you make your reservations.

IN THE MARTINTAR AREA

✪ **The Bounty Restaurant.** Queen's Rd., Martintar. ☎ **720840.** Reservations accepted. Breakfast F$4.50–F$10 ($2.25–$5); lunch F$2.50–F$10 ($1.25–$5); main courses F$14–F$20 ($7–$10). AE, MC, V. Daily 9am–10pm. INTERNATIONAL/FIJIAN.

Brian and Veronika Smith always offer a daily Fijian special, usually including excellent palusami, at this friendly storefront restaurant. You can get the best hamburger in town here, or order a cooked breakfast anytime. The regular menu stars grilled steaks that are just as tender but cost less than half as much as those out at the Sheraton resorts. The Bounty Special is a sweet combination of grilled chicken, onions, green peppers, and pineapple simmered in wine and served in a hollowed-out pineapple. Candles and subdued lighting add a romantic atmosphere to the dining area. Back in a corner, a TV above a small bar and two New Zealand–style drinking tables makes this the nearest thing in Fiji to a sports pub (American games come on live in the mornings and afternoons out here). A separate room has two billiard tables. You'll find a mixed clientele of tourists, resident expatriates, Air Pacific pilots, and parliamentarians back at the bar, where Brian pumps the coldest draft beers in the Southern Hemisphere.

IN NADI TOWN

✪ **Chefs The Restaurant.** Sangayam Road (behind Jack's Handicrafts). ☎ **703131.** Reservations advised. Main courses F$20–F$40 ($10–$20). AE, DC, MC, V. Mon–Sat 11am–2pm and 6–10pm. INTERNATIONAL.

Chef Eugene Gomes, who left the Sheraton Fiji to open the dining complex at Jack's Handicrafts (see The Edge and The Corner, below), shows off his culinary skill here in one of the South Pacific's handful of exquisite restaurants. A large, Sphinx-like rock wall with waterfall and an aqua-and-coral color scheme dominate this modern, urban-style dining room. The service is extraordinarily attentive, and the cuisine very well presented. You won't soon forget the staff's rolling a trolley to your table loaded with monstrous wooden salt and pepper shakers. The changing menu varies with the season. You may find wonderful pan-fried *paka o paka* (snapper) under a sweet brown apple sauce, or king prawns perfectly char-grilled and served with a salad of Boston lettuce and a slightly Roqueforty dressing. Eugene also has grilled beef tenderloin and rack of lamb to satisfy his Australian and New Zealand patrons. Guests of both Sheratons can charge their bills here to their rooms.

The Corner. Queen's Rd. (opposite Jack's Handicrafts). Reservations not accepted. ☎ **703131.** Sandwiches, burgers, and hot dogs F$2.50–F$6.50 ($1.25–$3.25); meals F$5.50–F$10 ($2.75–$5). AE, DC, MC, V. Mon–Sat 8am–10pm. CAFETERIA.

One of chef Eugene Gomes' operations, this pleasant cafeteria has an ice cream bar at the entrance offering tropical fruit selections in freshly baked cones. The cafeteria menu is varied: pastries and coffee (get your latte here), hot dogs and hamburgers, sandwiches and salads, roast chicken, and fish and chips. Most meals are Cantonese stir-fries, but a highlight here is a creamy Thai curry chicken that shows off chef Eugene Gomes's international experience with the Sheraton chain. At night the menu turns to tandoori-style Indian meals.

Daikoku. Queen's Rd. (near the bridge). ☎ **703622.** Reservations recommended weekends and holidays. Sushi F$5–F$7 ($2.50–$3.50); main courses F$18–F$48 ($9–24). AE, DC, MC, V. Mon–Sat 11:30am–2pm and 6–10pm; Sun 6–10pm. JAPANESE.

There are three dining areas at this fine restaurant, whose walls and ceilings are made of imported Japanese pine burned slightly to accent the grain. You can elect either the sushi bar, which uses only the freshest salmon, tuna, and lobster; the teppanyaki room, where the chef will stir-fry vegetables, shrimp, chicken, or extraordinarily tender beef as you watch; or the main dining room, which offers sukiyaki, udon, and other traditional Japanese dishes. You can pay a bundle here, but you'll get top-flight Nipponese cuisine.

✪ **The Edge.** Sagayam Rd. (behind Jack's Handicrafts). ☎ **703131.** Reservations not accepted. Salads, sandwiches, burgers F$7.50 ($3.75); main courses F$10–F$15 ($5–$7.50). AE, DC, MC, V. Mon–Sat 9am–10pm. INTERNATIONAL.

The third dining establishment of chef Eugene Gomes, this air-conditioned cafe is a more comfortable, sophisticated version of The Corner. It has an ice cream bar, a variety of hamburgers, and many of the same Asian stir-fries and Thai curry chicken offered at The Corner, but here they are served at your table. The dinner menu features a few simple but tasty selections, such as seafood lasagna, chicken enchiladas, and stir-fried beef. Cool and casual, The Edge is a fine place to take a shopping break over a cup of cappuccino, espresso, or herbal tea.

Mama's Pizza Inn. Queen's Rd., Nadi Town, opposite Mobil Station. ☎ **701221.** Reservations not accepted. Pizzas F$6.50–F$23 ($3.75–$11.50); pastas F$6.50 ($3.75). MC, V. Mon–Sat 10am–11pm, Sun 10am–11pm. ITALIAN.

Travelers in need of a tomato sauce fix can follow the aroma of garlic to Robin O'Donnell's cozy establishment. Robin is a Fiji-born European, but her pizzas are worthy of an Italian upbringing. They range from a small plain model to a large deluxe version with all the toppings. She also has spaghetti (with both meat and vegetarian tomato sauce), lasagna, and fresh salads. Order at what looks like a bar in a drinking establishment and take your meal at one of the picnic-style tables. There's a suburban Mama's with the same menu, prices, and hours in the Colonial Plaza shopping mall on the Queen's Road in Namaka (☎ 720922).

DINNER CRUISES

You can dine out on the lagoon on a **Starlight Dinner Cruise,** offered by Captain Cook Cruises (☎ 701823). The boat departs from Port Denarau daily at 5:30pm and returns at 8:30pm. You'll have a choice of three main courses such as steak or a whole coral trout on a sizzling platter. Fijians serenade you with island music. The cruise cost F$75 ($37.50) per person, including the meal, champagne (you pay extra for wine and other drinks), and transportation from Nadi-area hotels.

9 Island Nights in Nadi

The large hotels usually have something going on every night. As noted in "Dining in Nadi," above, this may be a special meal followed by a Fijian meke dance show. They also frequently have live entertainment in their bars during the cocktail hour. Check the *Spotlight on Nadi* and *Fiji Magic* tourist publication for what's happening.

Unlike the fast, hip-swinging, suggestive dancing of Tahiti and the Cook Islands, Fijians follow the custom of the Samoas and Tonga, with gentle movements taking second place to the harmony of their voices. Only in the spear-waving war dances do you see much action. Nevertheless, taking in a meke is a popular way to spend at least one evening in Nadi.

The most popular watering hole here is ✪ **The Bounty Restaurant,** on the Queen's Road in Martintar (☎ 720840), which draws many expatriate residents to its sports TV and icy draft beer (see "Dining in Nadi," above).

For live music, head to the main dining room and bar in the **Fiji Mocambo Hotel** (☎ 722000), where one of Fiji's top rock bands plays for dancing after 9pm Tuesday through Saturday. The cafe at **The West's Motor Inn,** on the Queen's Road in Martintar (☎ 720044) becomes a pleasant, gay-friendly piano bar from Monday to Saturday. See "Accommodations in Nadi," above.

10 Resorts Offshore from Nadi

As I pointed out in chapter 8, offshore resorts are great places to relax or engage in romance or water sports, but they are not in themselves bases from which to explore the country.

Making Your Choice

Although I've placed reviews of Fiji's offshore resorts in the sections devoted to their jumping-off points, you'll want to consider *all* of them carefully before making a selection. In addition to reading about the resorts reviewed below, also see The Wakaya Club and Toberua Island Resort in chapter 10; and Moody's Namena, Fiji Forbes' Laucala Island, Qamea Beach Resort, and Matagi Island Resort in chapter 11.

Most of the resorts off Nadi are in the Mamanuca Islands, a chain of small flat atolls and hilly islands ranging from 8 kilometers to 32 kilometers (4 miles to 20 miles) west of Nadi. Others are in the Yasawas, a similar but much less developed chain as much as 100 kilometers (60 miles) northwest of Nadi. Another is on Vatulele, a flat, raised coral island 48 kilometers (30 miles) south of Viti Levu but serviced from Nadi Airport.

Lt. Charles Wilkes, commander of the U.S. exploring expedition that charted Fiji in 1840, said the Yasawas reminded him of "a string of blue beads lying along the horizon," and they haven't changed much over the intervening century and a half. Fijians still live in small villages huddled among the curving coconut palms beside some of the South Pacific's most awesomely beautiful beaches.

The climate on all these islands is semiarid. Coupled with their proximity to Nadi Airport, this consistent sunshine made the Mamanuca Islands the first in Fiji to be opened to tourists back in the early 1960s. They still are very popular with Australians and New Zealanders on 1- or 2-week holidays. The younger resorts in the Yasawas and on Vatulele fall into the super-expensive, super-deluxe category.

Unless food is included in the room rates, expect to pay about F$80 ($40) per person a day for all three meals.

GETTING THERE   The resorts arrange transfers for their guests (reservations are required out here), so you'll probably do as you're told. How much it costs depends on whether you take a boat or fly.

The **South Sea Cruises** (☎ 750500) provides ferry service from Port Denarau to most of the Mamanuca resorts three times daily on the speedy catamaran *Tiger IV.* One-way fares are F$41 ($20.50). You'll have to transfer to Tokoriki Island Resort from Mana Island by speedboat.

Beachcomber Island Resort is served by the fast catamaran *Drodrolagi* from Denarau Island and the much slower sailing ship *Tui Tai* from Lautoka (☎ 661500 for both).

Another fast catamaran, the *Malolo Cat* (☎ 720774) runs from Denarau to Plantation Island and Musket Cove resorts on Malololailai Island. Round trips cost F$75 ($37.50) per person.

The quickest and easiest way to the islands is via **Sunflower Airlines** (☎ 723016) and **Air Fiji** (☎ 722521), which fly several times a day from Nadi Airport to both Mana Island and Malololailai, home of Plantation and Musket Cove resorts (see "Getting There & Getting Around" in chapter 8). It's much more expensive, but **Island Hoppers** (☎ 720140) flies its helicopters to Plantation, Musket Cove, Mana Island, Treasure Island, Tokoriki, and Castaway Island resorts, and **Turtle Airways** (☎ 722988) provides chartered seaplane service to most of the islands. **Pleasure Marine** (☎ 750500) provides water-taxi service to the islands from Port Denarau.

VERY EXPENSIVE

✪ **Turtle Island.** P.O. Box 9317, Nadi Airport (Nanuya Levu Island, 80km [50 miles] north of Nadi, a 30-min. seaplane ride). ☎ **800/826-3083** or 722921. Fax 720007. www.

turtlefiji.com. E-mail: usa@turtlefiji.com or turtle@is.com.fj. 14 bungalows. MINIBAR. US$1,088 per couple. Rates include meals, drinks, and all activities, including game fishing and 1 scuba dive per day. Round-trip seaplane transfers US$740 per couple. 6-night stay required. AE, DE, MC, V.

San Franciscan Richard Evanson graduated from Harvard Business School, made a bundle in cable television, got divorced, ran away to Fiji, and in 1972 bought Nanuya Levu, one of the few privately owned islands in the Yasawas. Growing lonely and bored, he decided to build a small resort on his hilly, 500-acre retreat. By 1980 he had completed three bures. Then a Hollywood producer leased the entire island as a set for the second version of *The Blue Lagoon,* starring the then-teenage Brooke Shields. Clocks were set ahead 1 hour to maximize daylight, and the resort still operates on "Turtle Time," an hour ahead of the rest of Fiji. The movie's most familiar scenes were shot on Devil's Beach, one of Nanuya Levu's dozen gorgeous little stretches of sand wedged between rocky headlands (guests can retire in private to the likes of "Honeymoon" and "Nudy" beaches).

The resort itself sits on idyllic, half-moon-shaped Dolphin Beach, beside a nearly landlocked body of water Richard has dubbed the "Blue Lagoon." The beachside central building is not as impressive as at Fiji's other high-end resorts, but it's comfortable and charming nevertheless. Beside it, ceiling fans whirl under the sprawling branches of a *baka* tree, which shades an outdoor dining and entertainment area. The beach turns into a sand bar at low tide, but you can swim and snorkel then off a long pier over the blue lagoon. Other activities include canoeing, kayaking, diving, fishing, horseback riding, hiking the island's 13 kilometers (8 miles) of trails, visiting other islands, and sunset cruising. Everything is included in the rates except Hawaiian-style therapeutic massage.

The widely spaced bungalows stand on the beach to either side of the central complex. A dozen bures have two-person spa tubs embedded in the hardwood floors of their enormous bedrooms. Separate sitting areas have sofas, wet bars, coffeemakers, and remote-controlled CD players. Much of the furniture is constructed of tree limbs, including writing tables and four-poster king-size beds equipped with mosquito netting. Bathrooms have walk-in showers with his-and-her heads, his-and-her toilets, and his-and-her lavatories, plus robes, slippers, hair dryers, and hand-milled toiletries. Front porches have lily ponds on one side and queen-size beds under a roof on the other. The other two bungalows are more modest (no spa tubs), but one of these, on a headland with a 360° view of the lagoon and surrounding islands, is the most private of all. Every unit has its own kayaks and a hammock strung between shade trees by the beach.

Only couples are accepted here except during certain family weeks in July and at Christmas. The resort no longer adheres to a mixed-sex couples only rule (i.e., no gay and lesbian couples); now any "loving couple" is welcome.

Dining/Diversions: Supplied by the resort's own garden, the kitchen serves excellent quality meals dinner-party fashion at a long, polished table in the beachside dining room. (This style of dining, practiced here and at Vatulele Island Resort, is a major difference from other deluxe resorts such as The Wakaya Club and Yasawa Island Resort, where guests are left more to themselves.) If they don't want company, however, couples can dine alone on the beach or on a pontoon floating on the lagoon.

Impressions

Every resort seemed to have a platoon of insanely friendly Fijians.

—Scott L. Malcolmson, 1990

Once a week all guests have dinner at the top of a 150-meter (500-foot) high peak with a panoramic vista. Staff members strum guitars and sing island songs during cocktail hour and after dinner. Fashion shows and Fijian mekes are staged some evenings.

Amenities: Wide range of water sports activities and equipment, including scuba diving and deep-sea fishing; boutique; laundry; evening turndown; limited room service; massage.

✪ **Vatulele Island Resort.** P.O. Box 9936, Nadi Airport (Vatulele Island, 50km [30 miles] south of Viti Levu, a 30-min. flight from Nadi). ☎ **800/828-9146** or 720300. Fax 720062. www.vatulele.com. E-mail: vatulele@is.com.fj. 18 bungalows. MINIBAR. US$968 double. Rates includes room, food, bar, all activities except sport fishing and scuba diving. 4-night minimum stay required. Round-trip transfers US$308 per person (free with stays of 8 nights or longer). AE, DC, MC, V.

When Australian TV producer Henry Crawford (*A Town like Alice*) and Fiji-born hotel manager Martin Livingston (formerly of Turtle Island Lodge, above) both turned 40 in the late 1980s, they decided to build the ultimate hideaway resort. They chose a 1-kilometer-long (0.5-mile) beach on Vatulele, a relatively flat island off the Coral Coast known for its unique red prawns (that is, shrimp that are red while alive, not just after being cooked). With an eye on the environment, they cleared just enough thick native brush to build 18 spacious bures and a central dining room-bar-lounge complex. Each bure faces the beach but is separated from its companions by lots of privacy-providing foliage and distance. In a fascinating blend of Santa Fe and Fijian native architectural styles, the bures and main building have thick adobe walls supporting tall Fijian thatch roofs. Each L-shaped bure has a lounge and raised sleeping areas under one roof, plus another roof covering an enormous bathroom that can be entered both from the bed/dressing area and from a private, hammock-swung patio. Each unit has a king-size bed with mosquito net suspended from the rafters.

Although benchlike seats in the lounge of each bure can double as beds for children, kids under 12 are allowed only during certain weeks, usually coinciding with Australian school holidays.

Dining/Diversions: Most meals here are dinner parties inside the main building, or weather permitting, on the adjacent patio. You can dine anytime and anyplace you want, however, including in your bure, out on the beach, or in "The Folly," a cabana sitting all by itself on a headland at one end of the beach. You can even take a picnic lunch to a private beach or out to a tiny nearby islet. Although staff members play guitars and sing island songs, the nightly dinner parties *are* the entertainment at Vatulele, and they can go into the wee hours.

Amenities: A library with 2,000 volumes; scuba diving; deep sea fishing; wide array of nonmotorized water sports equipment; tiny private island for secluded picnics; all-weather tennis court; limited room service (raise a flag on the beach in front of your bure to order a drink); evening turndown; laundry.

Yasawa Island Resort. P.O. Box 10128, Nadi Airport (Yasawa Island, 100km [60 miles] north of Nadi, 35 min. by charter flight). ☎ **722266.** Fax 724456. www.yasawaislandresort.com. E-mail: yasawa@is.com.fj. 16 units. A/C MINIBAR TEL. US$450 double, US$825 double honeymoon bungalow. Rates include room and all meals and nonmotorized water sports but no drinks. Round-trip transfers US$240 per person. AE, DC, MC, V.

This informal resort sits in a small indentation among steep cliffs lining the west coast of skinny, relatively dry Yasawa Island, northernmost of the chain. It had fallen on hard times, but owners Garth and Denise Downey have it back up and going strong. They also have priced it well below Turtle and Vatulele, even though their bungalows are just as big, their food is just as good, and they have a swimming pool, which the others don't. After arriving at a private dirt airstrip that reaches from shore to shore (one end actually goes uphill), you'll be handed a fruit punch and driven to the resort in an air-conditioned van. There you'll find an airy octagonal main building whose tall, thatch-covered tin roof is held up by umbrella-like beams. Sitting next to a pool fed by chlorinated seawater, it holds a spacious dining area and bar. The Great Sea Reef is far enough offshore that surf slaps against shelves of black rock just off a nearby beach of deep white sand.

The large, air-conditioned guest bures come in two types. Most are long, 1,000-square-foot rectangular models with thatch roofs over white stucco walls (the style makes this resort physically reminiscent of Vatulele Island Resort). On one end of each bure, a row of potted tropical plants separates a raised sleeping area from a spacious living room with bar, table and chairs, divans built into a wall, and two ceiling fans. On the other, a bathroom has toiletries, a hair dryer, Japanese-style robes, and a large shower with his-and-her heads. There's no shower curtain, so you can watch yourself cavort in the mirrors above two sinks across the room. A door leads from the shower to a private sunbathing patio. There's also a separate dressing area and walk-in closet equipped with iron and board. A few other one- and two-bedroom models are less appealing but are better arranged for families and have fine views from the side of the hill backing the property. Far more expensive (double the usual rate), the remote, extremely private "Lomolagi" honeymoon bure has its own beach.

Activities included in the rates are tennis, croquet, fishing, snorkeling, sailing, hiking to a lookout with a 360° panoramic view, village visits, and picnics and shelling expeditions to deserted beaches. Guests pay extra for scuba diving and deep-sea fishing. Children under 12 are not allowed here.

Dining/Diversions: Excellent cuisine features local seafood such as lobster and "pretty ladies" (reef crabs). Guests are offered at least one meat and one seafood course for dinner. They all dine together for twice-weekly Fijian-style lovos, but otherwise they can choose their own spacious seating arrangements. Staff members play string instruments during cocktail hour and dinner, and nearby villagers come over to serenade.

Amenities: Tennis and croquet court; pool; Windsurfers; laundry; evening turn-down; massage.

EXPENSIVE

✪ **Castaway Island Resort.** Private Mail Bag, Nadi Airport (Qalito Island, 21km [13 miles] off Nadi). ☎ **800/888-0120** or 661233. Fax 665753. E-mail: castawayfiji@is.com.fj. 66 units. MINIBAR. F$445–F$515 ($222.50–$257.50) double. Rates include breakfast buffet. AE, DC, MC, V.

Built in the mid-1960s of logs and thatch, without the use of heavy equipment, Castaway maintains its rustic, Fijian-style charm despite many improvements over the years. The central activities building, perched on a point with white beaches on either side, still has a thatch roof, and the ceilings of the bures are still lined with genuine tapa cloth. Fijian staff members mingle freely with guests, who can join them at their church on Sunday.

Although the guest bures sit relatively close together in a coconut grove, their roofs sweep low enough to provide some privacy. Each unit has a queen-size bed (don't expect a firm mattress), two settees that can double as beds for children, and rattan table and chairs.

Dining/Diversions: In addition to the central lounge-dining-bar building, a beachside water sports shack has a "Sundowner Bar" upstairs, appropriately facing west toward the Great Sea Reef. Guests dine in the central building, usually at umbrella tables on a stone beachside patio, or grab a wood-fired pizza at the Sundowner Bar. Sydney restaurateur Geoff Shaw, who owns Castaway, makes sure the food is good and substantial. Staff members entertain with Fijian songs.

Amenities: Facilities include a swimming pool, tennis court, games room, medical center with nurse, well-stocked boutique, children's playroom, nursery, and massage bure with an outdoor rock shower. The resort has a wide variety of water sports, including scuba diving, parasailing, and jet- and waterskiing. Guests pay extra for most motorized sports. For children, the staff provides a wide range of activities, from learning Fijian to sack races.

Musket Cove Resort. Private Mail Bag, Nadi Airport (Malololailai Island, 14km [9 miles] off Nadi). ☎ **800/521-7242** or 722371. Fax 720378. www.musketcovefiji.com. E-mail: musketcove@is.com.fj. 6 units, 30 bungalows, 6 villas. A/C TEL (rooms only). F$180–F$220 ($90–$110) double room; F$280–F$396 ($140–$198) bungalow; F$395–F$480 ($197.50–$240) villa. AE, DC, MC, V.

One of three Australians who own Malololailai Island, Dick Smith founded this retreat in 1977. Built of native materials and decorated accordingly, but considerably spiffed up since then, the older bures sit in a row across a coconut grove from the beach. They have full kitchens (there are two small groceries on the island). Newer, larger models are closer to the beach and have separate bedrooms and much larger baths than their older siblings; they have toasters but no cooking facilities. Still newer units sit beside a manmade lagoon and are the largest and most expensive bungalows here. Most expensive of all are 6 luxury villas, which have a living room, full kitchen, and master bedroom downstairs and two bedrooms upstairs (each bedroom has its own private bathroom). On the bottom end, six air-conditioned hotel rooms are over an office building toward the rear of the property. They have king-size beds, settees, chairs, phones, coffeemakers, cozy but attractive shower-only bathrooms, and doorways opening to a porch wrapping around the building.

Dining/Diversions: Dick's Place is the pleasant open-air bar and restaurant next to the swimming pool and a large flame tree (poinciana) that bursts into bloom around Christmas. There's another cafe and a grocery store next to Musket Cove's modern marina, where cruising yachties call from June to September. The yachties also congregate at the "$2.50 Bar," under a thatch roof out on a tiny manmade island reached by the marina's pontoons. Musket Cove hosts the annual Fiji Regatta Week in September, when it's the starting line for the yacht race from Musket Cove to Port Vila (Vanuatu).

Amenities: Several boats are available for day sailing (see "Boating, Golf, Hiking & Other Outdoor Pursuits," above). Although a broad mud bank appears here at low tide, Dick dredged out a swimming beach area when he built the marina. It has Hobie Cats, Windsurfers, and rowboats. For a fee, guests can go scuba diving, rent boats, and make excursions to other islands.

Tokoriki Island Resort. P.O. Box 10547, Nadi Airport (Tokoriki Island, 32km [20 miles] off Nadi). ☎ **661999.** Fax 665295. E-mail: tokoriki@is.com.fj. 27 bungalows. A/C. F$315–F$440 ($157.50–$220) double. AE, DC, MC, V.

The farthest away from Nadi of the Mamanuca resorts, this sunny property sits beside a wide beach stretching 1½km (1 mile) along the western shore of hilly Tokoriki Island—thus rendering unimpeded sunset views. Tokoriki is a 15-minute speedboat ride from Mana Island, or you can get here by helicopter or seaplane. Sun lovers will be quite at home here, since the relatively dry location means a scarcity of tall palms and other sources of beachside shade. So will swimmers and snorkelers, for once you get past rock shelves along the shoreline, the sand slopes gradually into a safe lagoon with colorful coral gardens protected by a barrier reef.

The resort itself sits on a flat shelf of land backed by a steep hill (a 4km [2½-mile] hiking trail leads up to the ridgeline). Bungalows lined up along the beach flank the huge central building here. With thatch covering their peaked tin roofs, most of these spacious units have sleeping areas separated from lounges by a divider. The lounge areas have chairs, coffee tables, two single beds serving as settees, and wet bars in one corner. Sliding doors open from them to covered porches looking across grassy lawns to the beach. "Deluxe" bungalows have spacious bathrooms with outdoor showers behind rock walls, while "standard" units have walk-in showers indoors. At the far end of the property, 3 honeymoon bures are perched up on a hillside, insuring privacy and lagoon views from their decks. The honeymoon models and some of the standard bungalows are air conditioned. All have ceiling fans, refrigerators, and coffeemakers.

Dining/Diversions: A central thatch-topped bar divides the long central building into lounge and dining areas. The latter opens to a swimming pool, and guests can take their excellent meals alfresco during fair weather.

Amenities: You pay extra for scuba diving, but a wide range of other water sports activities is included in the room rates.

Treasure Island Resort. P.O. Box 2210, Lautoka (Eluvuka Island, 19km [12 miles] off Lautoka). ☎ **666999.** Fax 669955. www.treasure.com.fj. E-mail: treasureisland@is.com.fj. 67 units. A/C MINIBAR. F$395 ($197.50) double. AE, DC, MC, V.

Treasure Island occupies a tiny atoll that barely breaks the surface of the vast lagoon, about an hour's boat ride from the port town of Lautoka. It's geared to couples and families rather than to the sometimes-raucous singles who frequent its neighbor, the Beachcomber Island Resort.

Treasure's 33 duplex bungalows hold 66 rooms. Recently refurbished, they have wood-paneled walls, bright furniture, built-in vanities, shower-only bathrooms, and three single beds, one of which serves as a settee. Each bungalow has a porch facing the emerald lagoon and white beach that encircles the island (a sandy stroll of 20 minutes or less brings you back to your starting point). A series of pathways through tropical shrubs joins the bures, several playgrounds for both adults and children, and swimming and spa pools set off by a row of red hibiscus from an airy central activities building.

Dining: Three tasty meals a day are served in Treasure Island's pleasant à la carte dining room.

Amenities: Water sports include kayaking, parasailing, windsurfing, and scuba diving. Guests pay for motorized activities and to visit Beachcomber Island Resort. Adults and kids can surf the Internet and collect e-mail on a computer terminal in the main building. Guests can use two guest laundries; you pay for your detergent, but the machines are free.

MODERATE

✪ **Beachcomber Island Resort.** P.O. Box 364, Lautoka (Tai Island, 19km [12 miles] off Lautoka). ☎ **800/521-7242** or 661500. Fax 664496. E-mail: beachcomber@is.com.fj. 84 dorm beds, 14 "lodge" units (none with bathroom), 20 bures (all with bathroom). F$69 ($34.50) dorm bed; F$220 ($110) double lodge; F$300 ($150) double bure. Rates include all meals. AE, DC, MC, V.

Back in 1963, Fiji-born Dan Costello bought an old Colonial Sugar Refining Company tugboat, converted it into a day cruiser, and started carrying tourists on day trips out to a little atoll known then as Tai Island. The visitors liked it so much that some of them didn't want to leave. Recognizing the market, Costello built a few rustic bures, built a dining area and bar, and gave the little dot of sand and palm trees a new name: Beachcomber Island.

Today it still packs in the young and young-at-heart on a "deserted" island—deserted, that is, except for other like-minded souls in search of fun, members of the opposite sex, and a relatively inexpensive vacation (considering the three all-you-can-eat meals a day included in the rates). The youngest-at-heart cram into an 84-bunk, coed dormitory. If you want more room, you can have or share a semiprivate lodge (they have communal toilets and showers). And if you want your own bure with private bathroom, you can have that, too—just don't expect luxury. Three "family" bures can sleep up to 6 persons, but they share outdoor showers. Rates also include snorkeling gear, coral viewing in glass-bottom boats, volleyball, and minigolf; you pay extra for sailboats, canoes, windsurfing, scuba diving, waterskiing, and fishing trips.

Mana Island Resort. P.O. Box 610, Lautoka (Mana Island, 32km [20 miles] off Nadi). ☎ **650423.** Fax 650788. E-mail: mana@is.com.fj. 32 units, 128 bungalows. A/C TEL. F$260–F$500 ($130–$225) double. Rates include buffet breakfast. AE, DC, MC, V.

The largest resort off Nadi, this lively, Japanese-owned property attracts Japanese singles and honeymooners, plus Australian and New Zealand couples and families. Since it has the only pier big enough to land the inter-island ferries, Mana is a popular day-trip destination from Nadi (see "Island Escapes from Nadi," above). Seaplanes, planes, and helicopters land here, and Pleasure Marine has its water taxi base at Mana, so both day trippers and guests have a wide choice of ways to get here. The complex sits on a flat saddle between two hills and two beaches, which means guests have a calm place to swim and snorkel whichever way the wind is blowing.

Accommodation is in bungalows of European construction with Fijian-shaped tile roofs; standard units have been around a long time, but new deluxe models on the beach are by far the choice here. A block of 32 more modern hotel rooms faces the beach; entry is via rear walkways with lashed log railings. The rooms and deluxe bungalows are air conditioned. The older bungalows have ceiling fans but still can be quite warm at midday.

Guests can dine either on European-style fare in a large central building that also has a bar, lounge, and nightclub, or at another beachside restaurant serving seafood and steaks. There's a wide range of water sports activities, with guests paying to use the motorized toys. **Aqua-Trek,** an American firm, has one of its Fiji scuba-diving operations here (☎ **800/541-4334** or 702413; www.aquatrek.com).

Plantation Island Resort. P.O. Box 9176, Nadi Airport (Malololailai Island, 14km [9 miles] off Nadi). ☎ **669333.** Fax 669200. E-mail: plantation@is.com.fj. 41 units, 75 bungalows. A/C TEL. F$190 ($95) double room; F$285–F$445 ($142.50–$222.50) bungalow. AE, DC, MC, V.

One of the oldest, largest, and most diverse of the offshore resorts, Plantation attracts Australian couples and families, and day trippers from Nadi, giving it a Club Med–style atmosphere of nonstop activity. It sits on the western end of Malololailai island, which boasts one of the South Pacific's most picturesque palm-draped beaches. The resort has four types of accommodations: duplex bures suitable for singles or couples, two-bedroom bungalows suitable for families, and bright hotel rooms in a 2-story building next to the beach. All units have phones, but only the hotel rooms are air conditioned. My personal choice is one of the spacious duplex bures with two ceiling fans. A large central building beside the beach has a bar, dance floor, lounge area, coffee shop, and restaurant. Guests can also wander over to Ananda's, a barbecue-oriented restaurant near the airport, or to Musket Cove for a meal. Facilities include a freshwater swimming pool, tennis courts, a beach, and free nonpowered water sports. Waterskiing, parasailing, scuba diving, and coral viewing are possibilities. There's also a children's playroom with a full-time baby-sitter.

HOSTELS

Not only rich folks go offshore from Nadi. In the Mamanucas, **Ratu Kini's Village** on Mana Island welcomes young backpackers to stay in dormitories or simple houses for F$35 ($17.50) per person a day in dorms, F$73 to F$85 ($36.50 to $42.50) per house, including all meals. Round trip transfers cost F$60 ($30) per person. Guests are not allowed to use the facilities at Mana Island Resort, however. Book at Ratu Kini's office on the upper level of the Nadi airport arrivals concourse (☎ 723333). If you book at a hostel, make sure you ask for **Ratu Kini's village** (he's the friendly chief).

In the Yasawas, favorite backpacker destinations are **David's Place** and **Coral View Resort** (once known as Uncle Robert's), both beside a long, gorgeous beach on Taweva Island in sight of Turtle Island Resort. Both charge F$77 ($38.50) for a simple, Fijian-style bure; F$35 ($17.50) for a dorm bed; F$27 ($13.50) for a camp site (all including meals). Transfers take 1½ to 2 hours each way and cost F$100 ($50) round-trip. David's also has trips to the famous Sawa-I-Lau Caves, featured in the *Blue Lagoon* movies. Most Nadi hostels will make reservations, or you can book David's Place through **David Travel Service,** P.O. Box 10520, Nadi Airport (☎ **721820;** fax 663939), on the second floor of Nadi airport's arrivals concourse building. Coral View Resort also has an office up there (☎ **724244**) and in Lautoka (☎ **669312;** fax 669316). You also can book Coral View at the **Cathay Hotel** in Lautoka (☎ **660566**).

Two scuba diving bases on Waya Island in the Yasawas also are popular with back-packers: **Wagalailai** (☎ **724364**) and the German-operated **Octopus Club Fiji** (☎ **666337** in Lautoka). Accommodation is in rooms with shared toilets and showers. Octopus Club is a little more upscale, and both their Fijian-style bures have showers and toilets. Octopus Club charges F$98 ($68.50) for two people, including breakfast and dinner. Both are in Fijian villages, so you will have a chance to soak up some culture while there. Both charge about F$35 ($17.50) per person for camping, F$100 ($50) in bures, including all meals.

11 The Coral Coast

Long before big jets began bringing loads of visitors to Fiji, many affluent local residents built cottages on the dry southwestern shore of Viti Levu as sunny retreats from the frequent rain and high humidity of Suva. When visitors started arriving in big numbers during the early 1960s, resorts sprang up among the cottages almost overnight, and promoters gave a new, more appealing name to the 50-kilometer (30-mile) stretch of beaches and reef on either side of the town of Sigatoka: the Coral Coast.

The appellation was apt, for coral reefs jut out like wide shelves from the white beaches that run between mountain ridges all along this picturesque coastline. In most spots the lagoon just reaches snorkeling depth at high tide, and when the water retreats you can put on your aqua sports or a pair of old running shoes and walk out nearly to the surf pounding on the outer edge of the shelf.

Frankly, the Coral Coast is now overshadowed by other parts of Fiji. Its large hotels host groups of tourists. Nevertheless, it does have some dramatic scenery, and it's a central location from which to see both the Suva and Nadi "sides" of Viti Levu.

GETTING THERE: THE QUEEN'S ROAD

Visitors reach the Coral Coast from Nadi International Airport by taxi, bus, or rental car along the Queen's Road (see "Getting There & Getting Around" in chapter 8).

After a sharp right turn at the south end of Nadi Town, the highway runs well inland, first through sugarcane fields undulating in the wind and then past acre after acre of pine trees planted in orderly rows, part of Fiji's national forestry program. The blue-green mountains lie off to the left; the deep-blue sea occasionally comes into view off to the right.

Momi Bay & Natadola Beach

The Old Queen's Road branches off toward the coast and Momi Bay, 16 kilometers (10 miles) south of Nadi Town. This graded dirt road leads to the **Momi Guns,** the World War II naval batteries now maintained as a historical park by the National Trust of Fiji. To make this side trip, turn at the Momi intersection and follow the dirt road for 5 kilometers (3 miles) through the cane fields to a school, then turn right and drive another 4 kilometers (2½ miles) to the concrete bunkers. They command a splendid view over the water to the west. The park has toilets and drinking water.

Maro Road branches off the Queen's Road 35 kilometers (21 miles) south of Nadi and runs down to ✪ **Natadola Beach,** one of the prettiest in Fiji. A sign for Tuva Indian School marks Maro Road, which runs westward between a mosque Gosai & Sons store. Turn right on Maro Road and right again at the first intersection almost immediately after leaving the Queen's Road. This dirt track leads another 8 kilometers (5 miles) to a T-intersection. Turn left, cross a one-lane railroad bridge, and you'll arrive at the beach. Natadola has a grassy, parklike area all along it. A break in the reef allows some surf to break here, especially on the south end. Here you'll find **Natadola Beach Resort** (☎ 721000), a small, Mediterranean-style hotel with a dining room and bar in a shady courtyard. The *Fijian Princess,* a refurbished train which comes here from Shangri-La's Fijian Resort daily (see "Sightseeing, Cultural Tours & a Side Trip to Lautoka," above), stops just outside the hotel, which has changing rooms and welcomes daytime guests for lunch.

Sigatoka Sand Dunes National Park

The pine forests on either side of the Queen's Road soon give way to rolling fields of mission grass before the sea suddenly emerges at a viewpoint above Shangri-La's Fijian Resort on Yanuca Island. After you pass the resort, watch on the right for the visitor center for **Sigatoka Sand Dunes National Park** (☎ 520343). Fiji's first national park protects high sand hills that extend for several miles. About two-thirds of them are stabilized with grass, but some along the shore are still shifting sand (the surf crashing on them is dangerous). Ancient burial grounds and pieces of pottery dating from 5 B.C. to A.D. 240 have been found among the dunes, but be warned: Removing them is against the law. Exhibits in the visitor center explain the dunes and their history. Rangers are on duty daily from 7am to sunset. Admission to the visitor center is free, but you'll pay F$5 ($2.50) to actually visit the dunes. Call ahead for a guided tour, which costs F$3 ($1.50) per person. (*Note:* You must go to the visitor center before visiting the dunes, which are not accessible from "Club Masa" about 1 kilometer [0.5 mile] toward Sigatoka.)

Sigatoka Town

About 3 kilometers (2 miles) from the park visitor center, the Queen's Road enters **Sigatoka** (pop. 2,000), a quiet, predominantly Indian town perched along the west bank of the **Sigatoka River,** Fiji's longest waterway. The broad, muddy river lies on one side of the main street; on the other is a row of duty-free and other shops. The river is crossed by the new Melrose Bridge, named in honor of Fiji's winning the Melrose Cup at the Hong Kong rugby matches in 1997.

While here, you can do some serious shopping at **Jack's Handicrafts** and **Sigatoka Handicraft Centre,** both on the main street facing the river. **Prouds** and **Tappoo** also have large stores on the waterfront, as does **Sogo Fiji,** purveyor of up-market resort- and beachwear. The street between Morris Hedstrom department store and Westpac Bank will take you to the active **Sigatoka Municipal Market.**

WHERE TO DINE IN SIGATOKA   Next to Jack's Handicrafts, Roshni and Jean-Pierre Gerber's clean but not air-conditioned **Le Cafe** (☎ **520668**) offers a mixed menu of sandwiches, salads, curries, spaghetti, pizzas, fish and chips, banana fritters, and other snacks. Prices range from F\$5.50 to \$F12 (\$2.75 to \$6). No credit cards. Le Cafe is open Monday through Saturday from 8am to 5pm. The Gerbers—she's from Fiji, he's a Swiss chef—serve dinners at Le Cafe on the Queen's Road opposite the Outrigger Reef Fiji Resort (see "Dining," below).

SIGATOKA VALLEY

From Sigatoka, you can go inland along the west bank of the meandering river, flanked on both sides by a patchwork of flat green fields of vegetables that give the **Sigatoka Valley** its nickname: "Fiji's Salad Bowl." The pavement ends about 1 kilometer (0.5 mile) from the town; after that, the road surface is poorly graded and covered with loose stones.

The residents of **Lawai** village at 1.6 kilometers (1 mile) from town offer Fijian handcrafts for sale. Two kilometers (1.2 miles) farther on, a small dirt track branches off to the left and runs down a hill to **Nakabuta,** the "Pottery Village," where the residents make and sell authentic Fijian pottery. This art has seen a renaissance of late, and you will find bowls, plates, and other items in handcraft shops elsewhere. Tour buses from Nadi and the Coral Coast stop there most days.

If you're not subject to vertigo, you can look forward to driving past Nakabuta: the road climbs steeply along a narrow ridge commanding panoramic views across the large Sigatoka Valley with its quiltlike fields to the right and much smaller, more rugged ravine to the left. It then winds its way down to the valley floor and the **Sigatoka Agricultural Research Station,** on whose shady grounds some tour groups stop for picnic lunches. The road climbs into the interior and eventually to Ba on the northwest coast; it intersects the **Nausori Highlands** road leading back to Nadi, but it can be rough or even washed out during periods of heavy rain. Unless they have a four-wheel-drive vehicle or are on an organized tour with a guide, most visitors turn around at the research station and head back to Sigatoka.

TAVUNI HILL FORTIFICATION

A sign on the east end of the old Sigatoka River bridge in town (turn right at the stoplight) points left to the **Tavuni Hill Fortification,** built by an exiled Tongan chief as a safe haven from the ferocious Fijian hill tribes living up the valley. Those highlanders fought constant wars with the coastal Fijians, and they were the last to give up cannibalism and convert to Christianity. When they rebelled against the Deed of Cession to Great Britain in 1875, the colonial administration sent a force of 1,000 men up the Sigatoka River. They destroyed all the hill forts lining the river, including Tavuni. Today the fort is a Fiji Heritage Project open to the public. There's a reception bure, with toilets and a refreshment stand, which has brochures and exhibits. Admission is F\$6 (\$3) for adults and F\$3 (\$1.50) for children.

GETTING AROUND THE CORAL COAST

The larger hotels have car-rental desks as well as taxis hanging around their main entrances. Express buses between Nadi and Suva stop at Shangri-La's Fijian Resort, the Outrigger Reef Fiji Resort, the Hideaway Resort, The Naviti, and The Warwick Fiji. Local buses ply the Queen's Road and will stop for anyone who flags them down. See "Getting There & Getting Around" in chapter 8 for more information.

FAST FACTS: THE CORAL COAST

The following information applies to Sigatoka and the Coral Coast. If you don't see an item here, see "Fast Facts: Nadi" earlier in this chapter or "Fast Facts: Fiji" in chapter 8.

Camera/Film   Caines Photofast has a shop on Market Road in Sigatoka (☎ 500877). Most hotel boutiques sell color print film and provide 1-day processing.

Currency Exchange   ANZ Bank, Westpac Bank, and **National Bank of Fiji** have branches on the riverfront in Sigatoka. The hotel desks will cash traveler's checks.

Drugstores   Patel Pharmacy (☎ 500213) is on Market Road in Sigatoka.

E-mail   Adventures in Paradise, on the Queen's Road adjacent to the Outrigger Reef Fiji Resort (☎ 520833), has computer terminals for e-mail and Web surfing.

Emergencies   The emergency phone number for police, fire, and ambulance is **000.**

Hospitals   Government-run **Sigatoka Hospital** (☎ 500455) can handle minor problems.

Police   The emergency number is **000.** The Fiji Police has posts at Sigatoka (☎ 500222) and at Korolevu (**530322**).

Post Office   Post offices are in Sigatoka and Korolevu.

Telephone/Telegrams/Fax   You can make long-distance telephone calls and send telegrams and faxes at the post offices in Sigatoka and Korolevu. Coral Coast telephone numbers are listed under "Sigatoka" in the Fiji phone directory.

WHAT TO SEE & DO

The hotel reception or tour desk can make reservations for many of the activities mentioned in the Nadi sections in this chapter. These include tours of the Sigatoka Valley and day trips to Pacific Harbour and Suva. You may have to pay more for Nadi-based activities such as cruises and island excursions than if you were staying on the west coast. On the other hand, you are closer to Coral Coast activities, such as the *Fijian Princess* railroad trips to Natadola Beach (☎ 520434), the cave and waterfall tours offered by **Adventures in Paradise** (☎ 520833), and the rafting trips on the Navua River. The **Kula Eco Park** is just east of the Outrigger Reef Fiji Resort (☎ 500505).

From here you can easily take advantage of the golf, fishing, and diving at Pacific Harbour (see "Pacific Harbour," below) and see the sights in Suva (see chapter 10).

If you have children in tow, you can take them to the amusement park at **The Naviti** resort (see "Accommodations," below).

WATER SPORTS & OTHER OUTDOOR ACTIVITIES   Most hotels have abundant sports facilities for their guests (see "Accommodations," below).

Pro Dive Fiji, P.O. Box 123, Korolevu (☎ 530199; fax 5303000; e-mail: prodivefiji@is.com.fj), provides scuba diving for the Coral Coast hotels. One-tank dives cost about F$55 ($27.50), F$75 ($37.50) with full equipment rental. You can take an introductory lesson or a PADI certification course. Book at any hotel activities desk.

SHOPPING   The larger hotels have shopping arcades with duty-free shops and clothing and handcraft boutiques, and Fiji's major handcraft and duty-free dealers have stores in Sigatoka (see "Sigatoka Town," above). Prices at relaxed ✪ **Baravi Handicrafts** (☎ 520364), in Vatukarasa village 13 kilometers (8 miles) east of Sigatoka, are somewhat less than you'll find at the larger stores, and it has a snack bar offering excellent coffee made from Fijian-grown beans. The owners actively promote Fijian handcraft-making and buy direct from village artisans. Open Monday through Saturday 7:30am to 6pm, Sunday 8:30am to 5pm. Vatukarasa also has two roadside stalls where you might find an unusual seashell. On the Queen's Road in the hotel district, **Korotogo Souvenir Centre** (☎ **520118**), opposite the Outrigger Reef Fiji Resort, has fixed prices on its merchandise.

ACCOMMODATIONS

The venerable Reef Resort, the longtime anchor of an enclave of hotels and restaurants 8 kilometers (5 miles) east of Sigatoka, has been replaced by the modern, 255-room **Outrigger Reef Fiji Resort** (☎ **800/688-7444** or 500044; fax 520074; www. outrigger.com). The new facility was under construction during my visit. From what I could see then, you'll find a fine resort. A huge swimming pool complex compensates for a poor beach in front of the property. There's plenty of room here for a nine-hole golf course and horseback riding. Even if you don't stay here, it's a major landmark on the Coral Coast.

VERY EXPENSIVE

✪ **Shangri-La's Fijian Resort.** Private Mail Bag NAPO353, Nadi Airport (Yanuca Island, 60km [36 miles] from Nadi Airport, 10km [6 miles] west of Sigatoka). ☎ **520155** or 800/ 942-5050. Fax 520402. www.shangri-la.com. E-mail: fijianresort@is.com.fj. 432 units, 4 bungalows. A/C TEL. F$325–F$680 ($162.50–$340) double; F$820–F$950 ($410–$475) bungalow. AE, DC, MC, V.

Fiji's largest hotel, this resort occupies all 105 acres of flat Yanuca Island, which is joined to the mainland by a short, one-lane causeway. The ocean side of Yanuca is lined with a coral-colored sand beach that is superior to those at the two Sheratons on Denarau Island near Nadi. Covered walkways wander through thick tropical foliage to link the hotel blocks to two main restaurant-and-bar buildings, both adjacent to swimming pools, shady lawns, and beaches. Blue road signs point the way, for it's easy to miss a turn in this sprawling complex. The Fijian is so spread out that a shuttle constantly runs around the property, and a mobile bar operates along the beach. Fijian artisans weave baskets and mats, carve war clubs, and string shell jewelry in a handcraft demonstration area near the hotel's entrance, a large bure surrounded by breadfruit trees. Near the reception desk, a bas-relief depicts scenes of Fijian village life.

The Fijian's spacious rooms, all equipped with comfortable lounge furniture and colorful flower-print spreads, occupy 2- and 3-story buildings. All of them are on the shore of the island, so each room has a view of the lagoon and sea from its own private balcony or patio. Each has a refrigerator, tea/coffee-making facilities, radio, piped-in music, and spacious shower-only bathrooms. A few beachside bungalows can sleep up to six persons.

Dining/Diversions: The Fijian's four restaurants have something for everyone's taste, if not necessarily for everyone's pocketbook, and seven bars are ready to quench any thirst. Evening entertainment features buffet dinners followed by fire walking, traditional Fiji dancing, theme nights, and karaoke.

Amenities: Two swimming pools; five tennis courts (three lighted); games room; TV lounges; library book exchange; beauty salon; boutiques; guest Laundromat; scuba diving, snorkeling, deep-sea fishing, parasailing, jet-skiing, and other water sports, most for a fee; nine-hole executive golf course; bowling green; gymnasium; bicycle rental; business center; concierge; tour desk; 24-hour room service; baby-sitting; and children's programs.

MODERATE

✪ **Hideaway Resort.** P.O. Box 233, Sigatoka (Queen's Rd., 92km [55 miles] from Nadi Airport, 21km [13 miles] east of Sigatoka). ☎ **500177.** Fax 520025. E-mail: hideaway@is.com.fj. 100 units. A/C TV. F$190–F$265 ($95–$132.50) bungalow; F$355 ($177.50) family unit. Rates include full breakfast. AE, DC, MC, V.

Brothers Robert and Kelvin Wade bought this beachside property in the 1980s and have been enlarging and improving it ever since. During their early years it was famous as a young persons' hangout, with a large dormitory and mile-a-minute entertainment. The dormitory belongs to history now, but the Hideaway still attracts an active clientele of all ages, both married and single.

The Wades have added accommodations laterally along their narrow strip of land between the Queen's Road and the beach. Near the main building, their 16 original, A-frame bungalows have been brought up to speed. Most of their other units are in modern, duplex bungalows with tropical furnishings and shower-only bathrooms equipped with hair dryers, but the crown jewels here are new "deluxe villas" at the far, private end of the property. With pastel stucco walls, trim of local timber antiqued with mud, curved dividers separating sleeping areas from vanities, and blue-tile outdoor showers, they are like smaller and much less expensive versions of the bungalows at the super-expensive Vatulele Island Resort (see "Resorts Offshore from Nadi," above). A few larger family units here can sleep up to five persons. All bungalows here are adding air-conditioning; in the meantime, ask for it if it matters.

The Wades' most noticeable recent addition is their beachside swimming pool with waterfall, water slide, and special area for training scuba divers. The main building with dining, bar, and entertainment areas opens to this vista, especially appealing at night when underwater lights illuminate the pool and a flame shoots from the top of the water slide. Meals are plain European, Fijian, and Indian fare and feature buffets, barbecues, and Fijian lovos several nights a week. A band provides nightly entertainment and disco dancing in the main lounge. A host of activities includes tennis, horseback tours, trips to the mountains and waterfalls, snorkeling, scuba diving, windsurfing, glass-bottom boat rides, minigolf, kayaking, Fijian fish-drives, and onsite games such as crab races. There's a fitness center under its own thatch roof where you can catch the news on CNN while pumping iron.

The Naviti. P.O. Box 29, Korolevu (Queen's Rd., 97km [58 miles] from Nadi Airport, 26km [16 miles] east of Sigatoka). ☎ **800/448-8355** or 530444. Fax 530099. E-mail: naviti@is. com.fj. 140 units. A/C MINIBAR TV TEL. F$216–F$258 ($108–$129) double. AE, DC, MC, V.

A sister of The Warwick Fiji (see below), this resort attracts mainly Australian and New Zealand families by its extensive children's activities, including a small amusement park with a carousel, Ferris wheel, and other rides. There's even an ice cream parlor where adults or kids can get cones all day. The resort sits on 40 acres of coconut palms waving in the trade wind beside a lovely beach and very shallow lagoon, in which guests can wade to an islet offshore. That's plenty of room not only for the amusement park but also for a nine-hole golf course, five lighted tennis courts, and playgrounds.

Double-deck covered walkways join 2-story concrete block buildings, which hold some of Fiji's more attractive hotel rooms (bathrooms have both tubs and walk-in showers), to a central facility, where Fijian-shaped shingle roofs cover a 24-hour coffee shop, a candlelit restaurant for fine dining, a games room, shops, and a large lounge where a band plays for dancing Sunday through Wednesday. There's also a Laundromat and tour and car-rental desks. Activities include scuba diving, deep-sea fishing, coral viewing, sunset cruises, and horseback and donkey riding along the beach and to a waterfall.

The Warwick Fiji. P.O. Box 100, Korolevu (104km [62 miles] from Nadi Airport, 32km [20 miles] east of Sigatoka). ☎ **800/448-8355** or 530555. Fax 530010. Fax 520010. E-mail: warwick@is.com.fj. 250 units. A/C MINIBAR TV TEL. F$260–F$450 ($130–$225) double. AE, DC, MC, V.

Sitting on a lovely palm-fringed beach, this complex appears to be little different from other tropical resorts when seen from the road. The interior of the central building, however, clearly reflects a legacy of distinctive architecture from its origins as the Hyatt Regency Fiji. A sweeping roof supported by natural wood beams covers a wide reception and lobby area bordered on either end by huge carved murals depicting Capt. James Cook's discovery of Fiji in 1779. Tall windows across the rear look out through towering palms to the sea. A curving staircase descends from the center of the lobby into a large square well, giving access to the dining and recreation areas on the beach level. A lounge and cafe open to one of two swimming pools here, this one bordered by palms and a sprawling poinciana tree but in need of replacement (the second, newer pool is much preferable). The Warwick's comfortable, medium-size rooms are in 2- and 3-story blocks that flank the central building. Each room has its own balcony or patio with a view of the sea or the tropical gardens surrounding the complex. There are standard rooms and somewhat better-appointed "Warwick Club" models. The most expensive units directly face the lagoon from the ends of the buildings.

The sand-floored Wicked Walu, under a thatch roof on a tiny island offshore, features seafood selections and is the choice dining spot here. The casual, open-air Cafe Korolevu has a wide variety of cuisine for breakfast, lunch, and dinner. Overlooking the lagoon, Pappagallo offers Italian fare in a romantic setting.

Services include valet laundry, baby-sitting, business services, and massage. There are two swimming pools with bars, water sports equipment, tennis and squash courts, volleyball, jogging paths, horseback riding, sports and fitness center, tour desks, beauty salon, and boutiques.

INEXPENSIVE

Bedarra House. P.O. Box 1213, Sigatoka (78km [47 miles] from Nadi Airport, 8km [5 miles] east of Sigatoka). ☎ and fax **520166.** E-mail: bedarrahouse@is.com.fj. 13 units. A/C. F$132–F$170 ($66–$82.50). AE, DC, MC, V.

More like an inn than a hotel, the Bedarra House began life as a private home with bedrooms on either end of a great, 2-story-tall central hall, which opened to a veranda overlooking a swimming pool and, through the trees, the lagoon across the Queen's Road. Today a square bar and lounge furniture occupy the central room, and a romantic restaurant has taken over the veranda (see "Dining," below). Upstairs, another veranda wraps around the house. Inside the house, guests can opt for two-bedroom suites capable of sleeping up to four persons, or hotel-style rooms equipped with double beds. These may someday be air conditioned; in the meantime, fans kick up a breeze. Out back, a two-room bure can accommodate four persons. And to the side of the house, a 2-story motel block was under construction during my visit; it will hold eight air-conditioned rooms, three of them with cooking facilities. Shower-only bathrooms are common throughout.

HOSTELS

✪ **The Beachouse.** P.O. Box 68, Korolevu (105km [65 miles] from Nadi Airport, 37km [23 miles] east of Sigatoka). ☎ **0800/530530** toll-free in Fiji or 530500. Fax 530400. E-mail: beachouse@is.com.fj. 8 units (none with private bathroom), 40 dorm beds. F$38.50 ($19.25) double, F$16.50 ($8.25) dorm bed, F$8.80 ($4.40) per person camping. MC, V.

Andrew Waldken-Brown, a European who was born in Fiji, and his Australian wife, Jessica, have turned his family's old beachside vacation cottage into one of the South Pacific's best backpacker resorts. The beach here is one of the finest on the Coral Coast, and guests get free use of canoes, paddle boards, and bikes.

Built in the old South Seas style of tin roof, clapboard sides, and big windows with push-out, prop-up shutters, the charming cottage serves as lounge, bar, and dining room, where guests (but not outsiders) can order inexpensive meals. On the other hand, Andrew and Jessica built their airy dorms from scratch and gave them the ultimate in luxuries—at least as far as backpackers are concerned. Downstairs is divided into quadrangles, each with its own ceiling fan. The five beds in each section all have reading lights. Upstairs is aimed at couples, with partitions separating roomettes with double beds and ceiling fans, but the walls don't reach the ceiling, so you can be easily overheard. All windows here are screened, but the upstairs beds have mosquito nets to add romance. All guests, including campers who can pitch their tents in the spacious grounds, share clean toilets and a modern communal kitchen.

Tubakula Beach Bungalows. P.O. Box 2, Sigatoka (Queen's Rd., 79km [49 miles] from Nadi Airport, 13km [7 miles] east of Sigatoka). ☎ **500097.** Fax 340236. www.fiji4less.com.fj. E-mail: cathy@is.com.fj. 23 bungalows (all with bathroom), 24 dorm beds. F$13.50 ($6.75) dorm bed; F$50–F$86 ($25–$43) bungalow. AE, DC, MC, V.

If you want to be closer to the action around the Outrigger Reef Fiji Resort than at The Beachouse, this establishment (whose name is pronounced "*Toomb*-a-koola") sits almost next door in a beachside coconut grove. It appeals to anyone who wants a dorm bunk or a basic bungalow with kitchen but none of the usual hotel facilities. The bungalows are A-frame cottages with simple furnishings. Downstairs has a lounge, kitchen, bathroom, and bedroom; upstairs is a sleeping loft. Each unit can sleep six persons, so sharing one represents good value. The most expensive bungalows have been refurbished and are on the beach. The dorms are in European-style houses. No more than four beds are in any one room, and guests share communal kitchens, showers, and toilets. There's a swimming pool and a mini-mart selling beer, soft drinks, and basic groceries.

DINING

Many Coral Coast hotels have special nights, such as meke feasts of Fijian foods cooked in a lovo, served buffet style, and followed by traditional dancing. The specifics, including prices, are given in the tourist publication *Fiji Magic.*

More than likely the advent of the 255-room Outrigger Reef Fiji Resort will result in a covey of restaurants along the Queen's Road just outside its gates.

Bedarra House. Queen's Rd., Korotogo, west of the Outrigger Reef Fiji Resort. ☎ **500476.** Reservations recommended. Main courses F$13–F$19 ($6.50–$9.50). AE, DC, MC, V. Daily 7am–10pm. INTERNATIONAL.

Overlooking a lush tropical garden surrounding a swimming pool, the veranda of the innlike Bedarra House (see "Accommodations," above) is the most romantic place to dine here. The menu offers an uninspired but varied selection, including tender steaks under peppercorn or red wine sauce, fresh local fish pan-fried with lemon caper sauce, crumbed veal slices topped with asparagus, a vegetarian pasta, and a spicy version of spaghetti carbonara. You can also try Fijian dishes such as palusami and *ika vakalolo* (fish steamed in coconut milk). Stop in for breakfast, lunch, and afternoon Devonshire tea.

Le Cafe. Queen's Rd., Korotogo, opposite the Outrigger Reef Fiji Resort. ☎ **520877.** Reservations accepted. Pizzas and main courses F$5.50–F$14.50 ($2.75–$7.25). No credit cards. Mon–Sat 5–10pm. INTERNATIONAL.

After they've served breakfast and lunch at Le Cafe in Sigatoka (see "Where to Dine in Sigatoka," above), Roshni and Jean-Pierre Gerber turn their attention to this little establishment, where they display their culinary skills in a variety of tastes: fish and chips, Indian curries, Italian pastas and some of Fiji's best pizzas, chicken cordon bleu, fresh fish fillet with drawn lemon butter sauce, pepper or garlic steak, garlic prawns, or local lobster with mornay sauce. I ordered pork medallions in a piquant mushroom sauce, but the excellent eggplant parmesan served as a vegetable made me yearn for more of Roshni's and Jean-Pierre's Italian offerings. Top it off with their special banana or pineapple fritters, fried in a light, tempuralike batter.

✪ **Vilisite's Seafood Restaurant.** Queen's Rd., Korolevu, between The Warwick and The Naviti. ☎ **530054.** Reservations required. Lunch F$2–F$13 ($1–$6.50); full dinners F$20–F$35 ($10–$17.50). MC, V. Daily 8am–10pm. SEAFOOD.

Vilisite (sounds like "Felicity"), a friendly Fijian who lived in Australia, operates one of the few places in Fiji where you can dine right by the lagoon's edge. Come in time for a sunset drink and bring a camera, for the westward view from her veranda down the Coral Coast belongs on a postcard. Her extraordinarily well-prepared cuisine is predominantly fresh local seafood—fish, shrimp, lobster, octopus—in curry, garlic, and butter, or coconut milk (the Fijian way). She offers only five items on the dinner menu, and they are all full meals. If these won't do, she will adjust for individual tastes or diets. At dinner, kids can choose from the regular lunch menu, which features sandwiches, hamburgers, chop suey, curry, and very good fish and chips. Vilisite will arrange rides for dinner parties of four or more from as far away as the Outrigger Reef Fiji Resort, but be sure to ask about the cost. If you dine at only one restaurant in Fiji, have a meal here. You won't soon forget the view or this extraordinarily friendly Fijian, who certainly knows how to cook.

ISLAND NIGHTS ON THE CORAL COAST

Coral Coast night life centers around the hotels and whatever Fiji meke shows they are sponsoring. The famous **Fijian fire walkers** from Beqa, an island off the south coast (remember, it's pronounced "Mbengga," not "Beck-a"), parade across the steaming stones to the incantations of "witch doctors" at various hotels on the Coral Coast and at Nadi. The **Warwick Fiji** (☎ 530010), **The Naviti** (☎ 530444), and the **Hideaway Resort** (☎ 500177) usually sponsor a fire-walking show at least once a week. Call the hotels or check the *Fiji Magic* for times. Admission is about F$10 ($5) per person.

12 Pacific Harbour

Although it never really took off, Pacific Harbour was begun in the early 1970s as a recreation-oriented, luxury residential community and resort (translated: a real estate development). Today Pacific Harbour is noted primarily for its excellent golf course, great deep-sea fishing, and diving in the beautiful Beqa Lagoon offshore.

Sitting on the Queen's Road, the **Cultural Centre & Market Place of Fiji** went into receivership a few years ago and appears shopworn. Designed to serve both tourists and residents of the real estate development, the Marketplace consists of colonial-style clapboard buildings joined by covered walkways. In addition to the grocery store, you can wander through its boutiques and handcraft shops (open Monday through Saturday from 9am to 5pm), and poke through a small museum. The Cultural Centre wasn't operating during my visit. If it has reopened, it will be worth a visit if you're interested in Fijian culture. And don't miss the **Dance Theatre of Fiji,** dedicated to preserving ancient dances and rituals, if it has resumed performances. Call ☎ 450177 to see if it's open again.

GETTING THERE & GETTING AROUND

Pacific Harbour is on the Queen's Road, 30 kilometers (50 miles) west of Suva. All buses plying between Nadi and Suva stop at the Centra Resort Pacific Harbour, where you'll also find taxis waiting in the parking lot. See "Getting There & Getting Around" in chapter 8 for more information.

FISHING, GOLF & SCUBA DIVING

FISHING   The waters off southern Viti Levu are renowned for their big game fish, especially when the tuna and mahimahi are running from January to May and when big wahoos pass by in June and July. The women's world records for wahoo and travelli were set here.

Several boats are based here, including **Baywater Charters** (☎ 450573; fax 450606), which will tailor an excursion to your liking—be it going for the big ones offshore or trolling for smaller but exciting catch inshore. Fishing costs about F$500 ($250) for half a day, F$900 ($450) for a full day (the boat is equipped with sleeping quarters and showers, so longer trips are possible). It's also available for picnic trips over to Beqa, or for sunset cruises.

Between Pacific Harbour and Suva, the **Ocean Pacific Club,** P.O. Box 3229, Lami Town (☎ 303252; fax 300732), also caters to anyone who is serious about fishing. The Club has a fleet of boats, comfortable accommodations, a restaurant, and a bar.

GOLF   One of the South Pacific's finest, the course at **Centra Resort Pacific Harbour** (☎ 450048) is the centerpiece of the planned resort community on the north side of the Queen's Road, opposite the resort hotel. The club house needs serious refurbishment, but the 18-hole, par-72 course designed by Robert Trent Jones, Jr., is worth playing despite the heat, humidity, and frequent rain here. Some of the fairways cross lakes; others cut their way through narrow valleys surrounded by jungle-clad hills. Visitors are welcome to use the links: greens fees are F$30 ($15). A full range of equipment can be rented at the pro shop.

SCUBA DIVING & SNORKELING   San Francisco–based **Aqua-Trek** (☎ 800/541-4334 or 450324; fax 450324; www.aquatrek.com) has expeditions to Beqa Lagoon, a 30-minute boat ride across an open water channel from the Central Resort Pacific Harbour. Divers pay F$150 ($75) for a two-tank dive. Aqua-Trek also teaches resort and a full range of PADI courses.

Other operators here are **Tropical Expeditions** (☎ 450188; fax 450426) and **Dive Connections** (☎ 450541; fax 450539).

ACCOMMODATIONS

Centra Resort Pacific Harbour. P.O. Box 144, Pacific Harbour (142km [88 miles] from Nadi Airport, 48km [30 miles] west of Suva). ☎ **800/835-7742** or 450022. Fax 450262. E-mail: centrapacharb@is.com.fj. 83 units. A/C MINIBAR TV TEL. F$143 ($71.50) double. AE, DC, MC, V.

Built in the early 1970s and formerly known as the Pacific Harbour International Hotel, Golf, and Country Club, this beachside hotel attracts primarily divers, fishers, and serious golfers. The complex sits beside a long gray-sand surf beach with a terrific view of Beqa across the channel. You enter an open lobby upstairs, where there's a restaurant, bar, and gift shop. Steps lead down to a kid's club play area, an irregular-shaped pool, and the beach. The spacious hotel-style rooms are in 2-story wings to either side. They all have tile floors, a queen or two double beds, coffeemakers, irons and boards, tub-shower bathrooms with hair dryers, and doors opening to balconies or patios facing the sea.

DINING

Oasis Restaurant. Queen's Rd., in Pacific Harbour Marketplace. ☎ **450617.** Reservations accepted. Snacks, sandwiches, and lunch F$4.50–F$15 ($2.25–$7.50); main courses F$14–F$24 ($7–$12). MC, V. Daily 10am–3pm and 6–10pm. REGIONAL.

Owned by English expatriates Monica Vine and Colin Head, this airy dining room with widely spaced tables makes an excellent pit stop if you're driving between Nadi and Suva. Their house specialty is authentic London-style fish and chips, often using flaky red snapper fresh from the sea. You can get tasty burgers, sandwiches, salads, curries, omelets, and English-style breakfasts all day. Evening sees a blackboard dinner menu with the likes of pan-fried mahimahi, perhaps caught by one of the charter boat skippers having a cold one and throwing darts at Colin's friendly corner bar.

13 Northern Viti Levu

Few travelers will be disappointed by the scenic wonders on the northern side of Viti Levu. Cane fields climb hilly valleys to towering green mountain ridges. Cowpokes round up cattle on vast ranches. A stunning bay is bounded by dramatic cliffs and spires. A narrow mountain road winds along the rushing Wainibuka River, once called the "Banana Highway" because in pre-road days Fijians used it to float their crops down to Suva on disposable bilibili rafts made of bamboo. A relatively dry climate beckons anyone who wants to catch a few rays.

GETTING THERE: THE KING'S ROAD

The only way to get here is via the **King's Road,** which runs for 290 kilometers (180 miles) from Nadi Airport around the island's northern side to Suva—93 kilometers (57½ miles) longer than the Queen's Road to the south. All but about 50 kilometers (31 miles) of the King's Road (the stretch along the Wainibuka River Valley through the central mountains) is paved. Since the unsealed portion is slow going, most visitors who drive the King's Road spend at least a night in **Rakiraki,** on Viti Levu's northern point, about halfway between Nadi and Suva.

Scheduled local and express buses run the entire length of the King's Road, as do unscheduled share taxis (see "Getting Around" in chapter 8). From the Nadi side, the buses depart from the Lautoka Market. The Rakiraki Hotel and the backpacker's resorts on Nananu-I-Ra Island provide their guests with transport from Nadi (see "Accommodations," below).

The King's Road officially begins at Lautoka. To reach it by car from Nadi, follow the Queen's Road north and take the second exits off both traffic circles in Lautoka.

BA & TAVUA

From Lautoka, the King's Road first crosses a fertile plain and then ascends into hills dotted with cattle ranches before dropping to the coast and entering the gorgeous **Ba Valley,** Fiji's most productive sugar-growing area. With some 65,000 residents, most of them Indians, this valley of steep hills is second only to Suva in both population and economic importance. Many of the country's most successful Indian-owned businesses are headquartered in the town of **Ba,** a prosperous farming community on the banks of the muddy Ba River. Indeed, while most Fiji towns have the air of the British Raj or Australia, the commercial center of Ba is a mirror image of many towns in India. Ba has one of Fiji's five sugar mills. Gravel roads twisting off from town into the valley offer some spectacular vistas. One of these roads follows a tributary into the central highlands and then along the Sigatoka River down to the Coral Coast. You can explore the Ba Valley roads in a rental car, but take the cross-island route only if you have a four-wheel-drive vehicle and a good map.

From Ba, the King's Road continues to **Tavua,** another predominantly Indian sugar town backed by its own much smaller valley reaching up to the mountains.

RAKIRAKI

The enchanting peaks of the Nakauvadra Range keep getting closer to the sea as you proceed eastward toward Rakiraki. Legend says the mountains are home to Degei, the prolific spiritual leader who arrived with the first Fijians and later populated the country. As the flat land is squeezed between foothills and sea, cane fields give way to the grasslands and mesas of the 17,000-acre Yaqara Estate, Fiji's largest cattle ranch. Offshore, conelike islands begin to dot the aquamarine lagoon.

Although everyone calls this area Rakiraki, the chief commercial town actually is **Vaileka,** about 1 kilometer (0.5 mile) off the King's Road. Just before you reach the well-marked junction, look on the right for the **Grave of Udre Udre.** Legend says the stones at the base of the tombstone represent every one of the 900 men this renowned cannibal chief had for dinner.

Vaileka itself is home to the **Penang Mill,** the only sugar mill in Fiji producing solely for domestic consumption. There also is a nine-hole **Penang Golf Course** near the mill, which visitors may play (arrange at the Rakiraki Hotel; see "Accommodations," below).

Rakiraki itself is a Fijian village (with the usual car-destroying road humps) on the King's Road, about 1 kilometer (0.5 mile) past the Vaileka junction. It's home of the *Tui Ra,* the high Fijian chief of Ra district, which encompasses all of northern Viti Levu. He likes to stroll over to the Rakiraki Hotel, on the village's eastern boundary.

After the village, a paved road leads to **Ellington Wharf,** jumping-off point for **Nananu-I-Ra,** a semiarid island about 15 minutes offshore, which has a good moderately priced resort and four backpackers' retreats (see "Accommodations," below). A ferry leaves Ellington Wharf for Nabouwalu on Vanua Levu every day except Sunday.

RAKIRAKI TO SUVA

From Ellington Wharf, the King's Road rounds the island's north point into **Viti Levu Bay,** whose surrounding mountains topped with basaltic cliffs, thumbs, and spires give it a tropical splendor similar to Moorea's. About 15 kilometers (9.3 miles) from Rakiraki stands **St. Francis Xavier Church,** home of the unique *Naiserelagi,* or Black Christ mural painted by artist Jean Charlot in 1963. From the head of the bay, the road begins to climb through rice paddies and more cattle country to the head of the winding **Wainibuka River.** This "Banana Highway" is a major tributary of the mighty Rewa River that eventually flows into the sea through a broad, flat delta northeast of Suva. The cool, often cloudy highlands of the Wainibuka Valley is old Fiji, a land of few Indians and many traditional Fijian villages perched on the slopes along the river. If you're driving, be careful on the many switchback curves above the river. There are no shoulders to pull off on, and you suddenly come upon several one-lane wooden bridges that can be icy slick during frequent rains. And watch out for the huge buses that regularly ply this route, taking up the entire road as they rumble along at breakneck speeds.

You leave the Wainibuka and enter the dairy-farming region of eastern Fiji, source of the country's fresh milk and cheeses (be alert for cows on the road!). The small town of **Korovou,** 107 kilometers (66 miles) from Rakiraki, is the major junction in these parts. Turn right for Nausori and Suva at the dead end (a left turn will take you to Natovi Wharf).

From Korovou, the King's Road goes directly south for 25 kilometers (15½ miles) until it joins the **Rewa River,** now a meandering coastal stream. You soon come to bustling Nausori, the delta's main town. Turn right and cross the steel-girdered bridge to reach Suva.

ACCOMMODATIONS

Hilly, anvil-shaped Nananu-I-Ra, a 15-minute boat ride from Ellington Wharf, has long been popular as a sunny retreat for local Europeans who own beach cottages there (the island is all freehold land). Today young backpackers like to stop off for a few days here on their way by bus and ferry from Nadi to Savusavu and Taveuni. All that sunshine has a price, for Nananu-I-Ra is semiarid between May and September, when water shortages can occur. Accordingly, backpackers usually bring extra drinking water as well as their own groceries.

Of the backpackers' resorts, European-managed **Kon Tiki Island Lodge,** P.O. Box 340, Rakiraki (☎ **694290**), on the island's isolated western end, and **Charlie's Place,** P.O. Box 407, Rakiraki (☎ **694676**), near the other two on the more developed south end, are less restrained. **Betham's Beach Cottages,** P.O. Box 5, Rakiraki (☎ and fax **694132**), and **Nananu Beach Cottages,** P.O. Box 140, Rakiraki (☎ **694633**), have more the flavor of a relaxing but polite visit to grandma's (translated: no loud parties or topless sunbathing). All have dorm beds for about F$16.50 ($8.25) per person and cottages ranging from about F$40 to F$70 ($20 to $35) single or double. Express minibuses run daily from Nadi to Ellington Wharf for about F$25 ($12.50) per person. Boat transfers from the wharf are F$18 ($9). These properties all promote heavily at Nadi's inexpensive hotels and hostels, so you will have no trouble getting the full details.

✪ **Rakiraki Hotel.** P.O. Box 31, Rakiraki (Rakiraki village, on King's Rd., 1.5 miles east of Vaileka, 82 miles from Nadi Airport). ☎ **800/448-8355** or 694101. Fax 694545. E-mail: tanoahotels@is.com.fj. 46 units. A/C TEL. F$79–F$99 ($39.50–$49.50) unit; F$15 ($7.50) dorm bed. AE, DC, MC, V.

This venerable place is one of the few remaining colonial-era hotels in Fiji, and that means lots of charm unhurried by the pace of modern tourism. The two clapboard roadside buildings were built as guesthouses when American soldiers were stationed nearby during World War II. One houses a tongue-and-groove paneled bar and dining room, where guests enjoy home-cooked meals. The other has an old-fashioned hall down the middle with five rooms to either side. Two are air conditioned, the others have ceiling fans, and all have private baths. Two of these rooms have four beds each, which are rented on a dormitory basis.

Out in the back yard, three modern 2-story motel blocks have 36 rooms outfitted to international standards, with quiet air-conditioning units, phones, and tiled shower-only bathrooms. These rooms flank a pool, tennis court, games area under a thatch roof, and championship-caliber bowling green. Behind all is an extensive garden full of tropical fruits and vegetables, which the chef raids daily.

The friendly staff will arrange excursions to Vaileka and to Fijian villages, horseback riding, golfing, scuba diving, and treks into the highlands.

Suva & Levuka

This chapter could easily be called "A Tale of Two Capitals," for Suva and Levuka are the present and former seats of Fiji's government. Today they are as different as night and day. Modern Suva has become a vibrant, sophisticated little city whose young professionals take advantage of good restaurants, bars, and nightclubs. Meanwhile, never-changing Levuka remains a charming example of what South Pacific towns were like in the 1870s.

Neither the likelihood of frequent showers nor an occasional deluge should discourage you from visiting Suva, though if you're looking for a beachfront resort, this is not the place to base yourself. Grab your umbrella and wander along its broad avenues lined with grand public buildings, across its orderly parks and parade grounds left over from the British Empire, and through its narrow side streets crowded with Fijians, Indians, Chinese, Europeans, Polynesians, and people of various other ancestries.

Suva sprawls over a hilly, 10-square-mile peninsula jutting like a thumb from southeastern Viti Levu. To the east lies windswept **Laucala Bay** and to the west, Suva's busy harbor and the suburbs of **Lami Town** and **Walu Bay.** Jungle-draped mountains rise to heights of more than 1,200 meters (4,000 feet) on the "mainland" to the north, high enough to condense moisture from the prevailing southeast trade winds and create the damp climate that cloaks the city in lush green foliage all year round.

Suva was a typical Fijian village in 1870, when the Polynesia Company sent a group of Australians to settle the land it bought in exchange for paying Chief Cakobau's foreign debts. The Aussies established a camp on the flat, swampy, mosquito-infested banks of **Nubukalou Creek,** on the western shore of the peninsula. When they failed to grow first cotton and then sugar, speculators obtained the land and in 1875 convinced the new British colonial administration to move the capital from Levuka in 1882.

The business heart of the city still sits near Nubukalou Creek, and visitors can see most of the city's sights and find most of its shops, interesting restaurants, and lively nightspots along historic **Victoria Parade,** the main drag.

On the beautiful island of Ovalau some 20 miles east of Viti Levu, the old town of Levuka still looks very much as it did during its heydays before the government moved to Suva. Levuka makes a wonderful day trip from Suva—or longer if you don't need accommodations with modern amenities.

1 Getting There & Getting Around

GETTING TO SUVA

Suva is served by **Nausori Airport** 12 miles northeast of downtown near the Rewa River town of Nausori. Taxis between there and Suva cost F$17 ($8.50) each way. You can also get here via bus from Nadi. See "Getting There & Getting Around" in chapter 8 for more information.

If you're driving from the Nadi side, don't leave without a good map of Suva, whose maze of streets can be confusing, especially at night (I try never to drive in Suva after dark). If you can find it in a Nadi or Lautoka bookstore, the best map is *Suva and Lami Town* (No. FSM-1), published by the Fiji Department of Lands & Surveys.

GETTING AROUND SUVA

Hundreds of **taxis** prowl the streets of Suva. Licensed taxis have meters, but occasionally a driver without one will claim to be a "private car" or "limousine." Official fares are F50¢ (35¢) at the flag fall and F$1 (70¢) for each kilometer, but you will have to negotiate anything over 10 kilometers (6.2 miles). Make sure the driver drops the flag. The main **taxi stand** is on Central Street, behind the Air Pacific office in the CML Building on Victoria Parade (☎ 312266), and on Victoria Parade at Sukuna Park (no phone). I have been very satisfied with **Black Arrow Taxis** (☎ 300541 or 300139 in Suva, 477071 in Nausori) and **Nausori Taxi & Bus Service** (☎ 477583 in Nausori, or 304178 in Suva), which is based at the Centra Suva parking lot. Other taxis gather at the Suva Municipal Market.

Local **buses** fan out from the municipal market from before daybreak to midnight Monday through Saturday (they have limited schedules on Sunday). The fares vary but should be no more than F60¢ (30¢) to most destinations in and around Suva. The excellent *Suva City and Lami Town* map mentioned above shows the bus routes by color-coding the streets.

See "Getting There & Getting Around " in chapter 8 for the phone numbers of the major **car-rental** firms.

Fast Facts: Suva

The following facts apply to Suva. If you don't see an item here, see "Fast Facts: Fiji" in chapter 8.

American Express **Tapa International Ltd.** (☎ 302333) has an office on the 4th floor of the ANZ House, 25 Victoria Parade. Hours are Monday through Friday from 8:30am to 5pm, Saturday from 9am to noon. Personal check cashing is available only from 9:30am to 3pm weekdays, since you have to take your approved check to the ANZ Bank downstairs. The mailing address is G.P.O. Box 654, Suva.

Bookstores **Dominion Book Centre,** in Dominion Arcade on Thomson Street behind the Fiji Visitors Bureau ☎ 304334), has the latest newsmagazines, local and Australian newspapers, and books on the South Pacific. The *Fiji Times,* 177 Victoria Parade (☎ 304111), sells maps and books, including Albert J. Schütz's *Suva: A History and Guide* (Sydney, Pacific Publications, 1978), to which I am indebted for much of the walking tour in this chapter.

Currency Exchange **Bank of Hawaii, Westpac Bank, ANZ Bank, National Bank of Fiji,** and **Bank of Baroda** have offices on Victoria Parade, south of the

Fiji Visitors Bureau. ANZ and Bank of Hawaii both have ATMs. **Thomas Cook Travel Service,** on Victoria Parade near the Fiji Visitors Bureau (☎ **301603**), cashes traveler's checks Monday through Friday from 8:30am to 5pm and Saturday from 8:30am to noon.

Dentist   Ask your hotel staff for a recommendation.

Doctor   Most expatriate residents go to the private **Gordon Street Medical Centre,** 98–100 Gordon St. (☎ **313355**). It's open 24 hours a day. The clinic has Fiji's only recompression chamber facility.

Drugstores   Gordon Street Medical Centre (see "Doctor," above) has a pharmacy.

E-mail   Republic of Cappuccino, in the Dolphins Food Court, Victoria Parade at Loftus Street (☎ **300333**), has Internet terminals (see "Dining in Suva," below). Open Monday through Friday 7am to 11pm, Saturday 8am to 11pm, Sunday 10am to 7pm. **Telecom Fiji** has less noisy terminals at its customer service office in Ganilau House, on Scott Street (Victoria Parade extended) at Edward Street (☎ **210335**). Open Monday through Thursday 8am to 4:30pm, Friday 8am to 4pm. Both charge F22¢ (11¢) a minute for access.

Embassies/Consulates   See "Fast Facts: Fiji" in chapter 8.

Emergencies   Phone **000.**

Eyeglasses   Two companies sell complete lines of eyewear, including contact lenses: **Jekishan & Jekishan,** Epworth House, Victoria Parade (☎ **311002**); and **Asgar & Co. Ltd.,** Queensland Insurance Centre, Victoria Parade (☎ **300433**).

Hairdressers/Barbers   Cut Above Salon, Honson Arcade, Thomson Street, next to Canadian Airlines International (☎ **304553**).

Hospitals   Colonial War Memorial Hospital, end of Ratu Mara Road at Brown Street, is the public hospital, but see "Doctor," above, for a private clinic.

Information   The **Fiji Visitors Bureau** (☎ **302433**) has its headquarters in a restored colonial house at the corner of Thomson and Scott Streets, in the heart of Suva. It's open Monday through Thursday from 8am to 4:30pm, Friday from 8am to 4pm, and Saturday from 8am to noon.

Laundry and Dry Cleaning   White & Brite Selfservice Laundry, 177 Meade Rd. (☎ **384333**), in the Nabua suburb, has coin-operated washers and dryers; it's a F$6 ($4.20) round-trip taxi ride from downtown. **Flagstaff Laundry & Drycleaners,** 62 Bau St. (☎ **301214**), has full 1-day service.

Libraries   Suva City Library on Victoria Parade (☎ **313433**) has a small collection of books on the South Pacific. It's open Monday, Tuesday, Thursday, and Friday from 9:30am to 6pm; Wednesday from noon to 6pm; and Saturday from 9am to 1pm. The library at the University of the South Pacific (☎ **313900**) has one of the largest collections in the South Pacific. The university is on Laucala Bay Road.

Maps   The Fiji Visitors Bureau has maps (see "Information," above). The excellent *Suva and Lami Town* is published by the **Department of Lands & Surveys,** whose main sales office is in the Government Buildings on Victoria Parade (☎ **211395**).

Photographic Needs   Caines Photofast, corner of Victoria Parade and Pratt Street (☎ **313211**), sells a wide range of film and provides 1-hour processing of color-print film.

Police   Fiji Police's **Central Station** is on Joske Street, between Pratt and Gordon Streets (☎ 311222).

Post Office   Fiji Post's **General Post Office** is on Thomson Street, opposite the Fiji Visitor's Bureau. It's open Monday through Friday from 8am to 4:30pm, Saturday from 9am to noon.

Rest Rooms   Sukuna Park, on Victoria Parade, has attended (and therefore reasonably clean) public restrooms, on the side next to McDonald's. You must pay F24¢ (12¢) to use the toilets, or F61¢ (31¢) for a shower.

Safety   The busy blocks along Victoria Parade are relatively safe during the evenings, but the same cannot be said for the rest of Suva. Don't wander off Victoria Parade after dark on foot; take a taxi. See "Safety" in "Fast Facts: Fiji" in chapter 8.

Telephone/Telegrams/Fax   The easiest way to call overseas is with a pre-paid phonecard (see "Fast Facts: Fiji" in chapter 8). International phone, telegram, fax, and telex service is provided by **Fiji International Telecommunications Ltd. (FINTEL)** at its colonial-style building on Victoria Parade. It's open Monday through Saturday from 8am to 8pm. You may reverse the charges or pay cash. Stand by for a short wait if paying cash, for the operator will place your call and ring you when the connection is made. A typical station-to-station call from Fiji to the U.S. will cost F$2.67 ($1.34) per minute. Person-to-person calls cost extra.

Edward Street next to the General Post office has several phonecard public telephones.

2 Exploring Suva

While you could easily spend several days poking around the capital, most visitors come here for only a day, usually on one of the guided tours from Nadi or the Coral Coast. That's enough time to see the city's highlights, particularly if you make the walking tour described below.

The easiest way to see the residential suburbs as well as downtown Suva is on a guided tour. **United Touring Fiji (UTC),** which has a tour desk in the lobby of the Centra Suva (☎ 312287), charges F$30 ($15) per person for the 2-hour tour.

THE TOP ATTRACTIONS

✪ **Fiji Museum.** In Thurston Gardens, Ratu Cakobau Rd. off Victoria Parade. ☎ **315944.** Admission F$3.30 ($1.65), free for school-age children. Guided tours F$2.50 ($1.25). Mon–Thurs 9:30am–4:30pm, Fri 9:30am–4pm, Sat–Sun 1–4:30pm.

You'll see a marvelous collection of war clubs, cannibal forks, tanoa bowls, shell jewelry, and other Fijian relics here in one of the South Pacific's finest museums. Although some artifacts were damaged by Suva's humidity while they were hidden away during World War II, much remains. Later additions include the rudder and other relics of H.M.S. *Bounty,* burned and sunk at Pitcairn Island by Fletcher Christian and the other mutineers in 1789 but recovered by the National Geographic Society in the 1950s. Exhibits in the rear of the building explain Fiji's history.

Parliament of Fiji. Battery Rd., off Vuya Rd. ☎ **305811.** Free admission. Mon–Fri 8am–1pm and 2–4:30pm.

Sitting on a ridge about 1 kilometer (0.6 miles) southeast of downtown, Fiji's new parliament building resides under a modern shingle-covered version of a traditional Fijian roof. Large tapa cloth banners hang in the chamber, in which both houses meet. There are no organized tours, but you can watch the debates from the visitors gallery, or just

The English, with a mania for wrong decisions in Fiji, built their capital at Suva, smack in the middle of the heaviest rainfall . . . Yet Suva is a superb tropical city.
—James A. Michener, 1951

stroll along the outside walkways and peer in through floor-to-ceiling windows. The entry is on Battery Road, which runs off Vuya Road, which in turn makes an arc uphill from Ratu Sukuna Road off Queen Elizabeth Drive. It's about 1 kilometer (0.6 mile) uphill from Queen Elizabeth Drive, but the easiest way to get here is by taxi. Call the main number or check with the Fiji Visitors Bureau to find out when parliament meets.

Suva Municipal Market. Usher St. at Rodwell Rd. No phone. Free admission . Mon–Fri 5am–6pm, Sat 5am–1pm.

A vast array of tropical produce is offered for sale at Suva's main supply of food, the largest and most lively market in the South Pacific. If they aren't too busy, the merchants will appreciate your interest and answer your questions about the names and uses of the various fruits and vegetables. The market teems on Saturday morning, when, it seems, the entire population of Suva shows up to shop and select television programs for the weekend's viewing. Few sights say as much about urban life in the modern South Pacific as does that of a Fijian carrying home in one hand a bunch of taro roots tied together with pandanus, and in the other a collection of rented video-cassettes stuffed into a plastic bag. The bus station is behind the market on Rodwell Road; on the other side of this busy street is the **Suva Flea Market,** where other vendors sell mostly clothing and a few handcrafts.

Walking Tour—Suva

Start: The Triangle.
Finish: Government House.
Time: 2½ hours.
Best Time: Early morning or late afternoon.
Worst Time: Midday, or Saturday afternoon and Sunday, when the market and shops are closed and downtown is deserted.

Begin at the four-way intersection of Victoria Parade, Renwick Road, and Thomson and Central Streets. This little island in the middle of heavy traffic is:

1. **The Triangle.** Now the center of Suva, in the late 1800s this spot was a lagoon fed by a stream that flowed along what is now Pratt Street. A marker in the park commemorates Suva's becoming the capital, the arrival of Fiji's first missionaries, the first public land sales, and Fiji's becoming a colony. Three of the four dates are slightly wrong. From The Triangle, head north on Thomson Street, bearing right between the Fiji Visitors Bureau and the old Garrick Hotel (now the Sichuan Pavilion Restaurant), whose wrought-iron balconies recall a more genteel but non-air-conditioned era.

Continue on Thomson Street past the Morris Hedstrom department store to:

2. **Nubukalou Creek.** The Polynesia Company's settlers made camp beside this stream and presumably drank from it. A sign on the bridge warns against eating fish from it today—with good reason, as you will see and smell. Morris Hedstrom's picturesque covered walkway along the south bank gives the creek its

nickname: The Venice of Fiji. Across the bridge, smiling Fijian women wait under a flame tree in a shady little park to offer grass skirts and other handcraft items for sale. Pass to the left of them for now, and head down narrow:

3. **Cumming Street.** This area, also on reclaimed land, was home of the Suva market until the 1940s. Cumming Street was lined with saloons, yaqona "grog" shops, and curry houses known as "lodges." It became a tourist-oriented shopping mecca when World War II Allied servicemen created a market for curios. When import taxes were lifted from electronic equipment and cameras in the 1960s, Cumming Street merchants quickly added the plethora of duty-free items you'll find there today.

When you've finished browsing, return to Thomson Street, turn right and then left on Usher Street, which takes you past the intersection at Rodwell Road and Scott Street to the:

4. **J Municipal Market,** a beehive of activity, especially on Saturday mornings (see "The Top Attractions," above). Big ships from overseas and small boats from the other islands dock at Princes Wharf and Kings Wharf beyond the market on Usher Street.

We will head south along wide Stinson Parade back across Nubukalou Creek and along the edge of Suva's waterfront to Edward Street and the gray tin roofs of the:

5. **Municipal Curio and Handicraft Centre.** In yet another bit of cultural diversity, you can haggle over the price of handcrafts at stalls run by Indians but not at those operated by Fijians. Wait until you have visited Wolf's Boutique and the Government Handicraft Centre, however, before making a purchase (see "Shopping in Suva," below).

Continue on Stinson Parade past Central Street. The gray concrete building on the corner is the YWCA. When you get there, cut diagonally under the palms and flame trees across:

6. **Sukuna Park,** named for Ratu Sir Lala Sukuna, founding father of independent Fiji. This shady waterfront park is a favorite brown-bag lunch spot for Suva's office workers. On the west side is the harbor and on the east, Victoria Parade. For many years only a row of flame trees separated this broad avenue from the harbor, but the shallows have been filled and the land extended into the harbor by the width of a city block. The large, nondescript auditorium standing south of the park is the Suva Civic Centre.

Head south on the seaward side of Victoria Parade, pass the cream-colored colonial-style headquarters of FINTEL, the country's electronic link to the world, to:

7. **Suva Town Hall,** a picturesque old building with an intricate, ornamental wrought-iron portico and a sign proclaiming it now to be the Ming Palace Restaurant. Built as an auditorium in the early 1900s and named Queen Victoria Memorial Hall, this lovely structure later was used as the Suva Town Hall (city offices are now in a modern building adjacent to the Civic Centre on the waterfront). The stage still stands at the rear of the restaurant.

At this point you can take a shopping break at the Government Handicraft Centre, in the rear of Ratu Sukuna House, the tall office building across Victoria Parade at the corner of MacArthur Street (see "Shopping in Suva," below).

Afterwards, continue south on Victoria Parade until you come to the:

8. **Suva City Library.** The American industrialist and philanthropist Andrew Carnegie gave Fiji £1,500 sterling to build this structure. The central portion of the colonnaded building opened in 1909 with an initial collection of 4,200 books. The wings were added in 1929. Books on Fiji and the South Pacific are

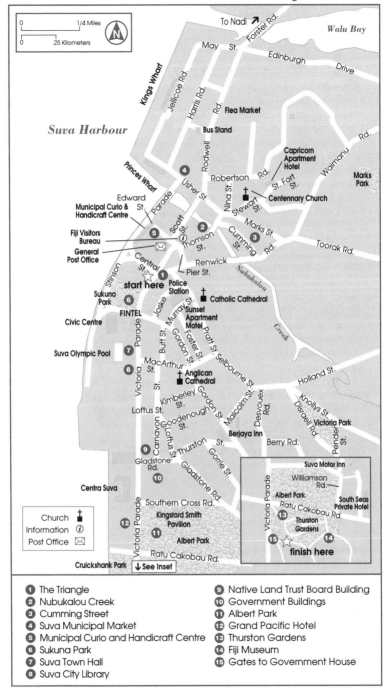

Suva Harbour

Walu Bay

To Nadi ↗

0 ___ 1/4 Miles
0 ___ .25 Kilometers

Kings Wharf

Princes Wharf

May St.
Forster Rd.
Edinburgh
Drive

Jellicoe Rd.
Harris Rd.
Rd.
Flea Market
Bus Stand
Rodwell

Usher St.
Robertson Rd.
St. Fort St.

Capricorn Apartment Hotel

Waimanu Rd.

Marks Park

Edward St.
Parade
Scott St.
Nina St.
Stewart St.
✝ **Centennary Church**

Marks St.

Municipal Curio & Handicraft Centre

Fiji Visitors Bureau
Thomson St.
Cumming Rd.
❸

Toorak Rd.

General Post Office
⑤
ⓘ
✉
❷

Central St.
Stinson
Renwick
Pier St.
Nubukalou

Creek

start here
❶
Police Station
✝ **Catholic Cathedral**

Sukuna Park
❻

FINTEL
Joske
Murray St.
Sunset Apartment Motel

Civic Centre

Butt St.
Foster St.
Pratt St.
Selbourne St.

Suva Olympic Pool
❼

Gordon St.
MacArthur St.
❽
Victoria St.
✝ **Anglican Cathedral**

Holland St.

Kimberley St.
Gordon St.
Malcolm St.
Desvoeux Rd.

Loftus St.
Goodenough St.
Knollys St.
Disraeli Rd.
Victoria Park

Carnavon St.
Loftus St.
Thurston St.
Berjaya Inn
Berry Rd.
Pender St.

❾
Gladstone Rd.
Gladstone Rd.
Gorrie St.

Centra Suva
❿

Southern Cross Rd.
Suva Motor Inn
Williamson Rd.

Church ✝
Information ⓘ
Post Office ✉

Kingsford Smith Pavilion
⑫
Victoria Parade
⑪
Albert Park

Victoria Parade
Albert Park
Ratu Cakobau Rd.
South Seas Private Hotel
⑬
Thurston Gardens
⑮ ☆
⑭
finish here

Cruickshank Park
↓ **See Inset**
Ratu Cakobau Rd.

❶ The Triangle
❷ Nubukalou Creek
❸ Cumming Street
❹ Suva Municipal Market
⑤ Municipal Curio and Handicraft Centre
❻ Sukuna Park
❼ Suva Town Hall
❽ Suva City Library
❾ Native Land Trust Board Building
❿ Government Buildings
⑪ Albert Park
⑫ Grand Pacific Hotel
⑬ Thurston Gardens
⑭ Fiji Museum
⑮ Gates to Government House

shelved to the left of the main entrance. (See "Fast Facts: Suva," above, for the library's hours.)

Keep going along Victoria Parade past Loftus Street to the corner of Gladstone Road, where sits the:

9. **Native Land Trust Board Building.** This site is known locally as Naiqaqi (The Crusher) because a sugar-crushing mill sat here during Suva's brief and unsuccessful career as a cane-growing area in the 1870s. A small statue of Ratu Sukuna stands in front of the modern office building that now occupies the site. Ratu Sukuna served as chairman of the Native Land Trust Board, whose main job is to collect and distribute rents on the 80% of the country that is owned by the Fijians.

Across Gladstone Road you can't miss the imposing gray edifice and clock tower of the:

10. **Government Buildings.** Erected between 1937 and 1939 (they look much older), these British-style gray stone buildings house the High Court, the prime minister's office, and several government ministries. Parliament met here until 1987, when Colonel Rabuka and gang marched in and arrested its leaders (it now meets in a new complex on Ratu Sukuna Road in the Muanikau suburb). The clock tower is known as "Fiji's Big Ben." When it works, it chimes every 15 minutes from 6am to midnight.

Now walk past the large open field on the south side of the building, which is:

11. **Albert Park,** named for Queen Victoria's consort, Prince Albert. The pavilion opposite the Government Buildings, however, is named for Charles Kingsford Smith, the Australian aviator and first person to fly across the Pacific. Smith was unaware that a row of palm trees stretched across the middle of Albert Park, his intended landing place. A local radio operator figured out Smith's predicament, and the colonial governor ordered the trees cut down immediately. The resulting "runway" across Albert Park was barely long enough, but Smith managed to stop his plane within a few feet of its end on June 6, 1928.

Opposite the park on Victoria Parade stands the:

12. **Grand Pacific Hotel,** which has been the subject of a long-delayed restoration. The Union Steamship Company built the Grand Pacific in 1914 to house its transpacific passengers during their stopovers in Fiji. The idea was to make them think they had never gone ashore, for rooms in the "GPH" were designed like first-class staterooms, complete with saltwater bathrooms and plumbing fixtures identical to those on an ocean liner. All rooms were on the second floor, and guests could step outside on a 15-foot-wide veranda overlooking the harbor and walk completely around the building—as if they were walking on the "deck." When members of the British royal family visited Fiji, they stood atop the wrought-iron portico, the "bow" of the Grand Pacific, and addressed their subjects massed across Victoria Parade in Albert Park.

Continue south on Victoria Parade to the corner of Ratu Cakobau Road, and enter:

13. **Thurston Gardens.** Originally known as the Botanical Gardens, this cool, English-like park is named for its founder, the amateur botanist Sir John Bates Thurston, who started the gardens in 1881. Henry Marks, scion of a family who owned a local trading company, presented the drinking fountain in 1914. After G. J. Marks, a relative and lord mayor of Suva, was drowned that same year in the sinking of the S.S. *Empress* in the St. Lawrence River in Canada, the Marks family erected the bandstand in his memory. Children can climb aboard the stationary *Thurston Express,* a narrow-gauge locomotive once used to pull harvested cane to the crushing mill.

My Word!

Before the Government Buildings on Victoria Parade were erected between 1937 and 1939, the land under them was a swampy area called Naiqaqi, or Crusher, for the sugar mill that operated from 1873 to 1875 where the Native Lands Trust Board Building now stands. Naiqaqi was populated by shacks, some of them houses of ill-repute.

Local residents tell of a sailor who often visited the shacks while his ship was in port. He left Suva in 1931 for a long voyage, carrying with him fond memories of Naiqaqi—and, in particular, of one of its residents, a beautiful young woman named Annie.

The sailor's next visit to Suva came in 1940. Instead of a swamp, he found an imposing gray stone building standing where the old, familiar shacks had been.

"My word," he exclaimed upon seeing the great new structures, "Annie has done well!"

Walk to the southeast corner of the gardens, where you will find the fascinating:

14. ✪ **Fiji Museum,** where you can see relics and artifacts of Fiji's history (see "The Top Attractions," above). After touring the complex, take a break at the museum's cafe, under a lean-to roof on one side of the main building; it serves soft drinks, snacks, and curries.

Backtrack through the gardens to Victoria Parade and head south again until, just past the manicured greens of the Suva Bowling Club on the harbor, you arrive at the big iron gates of:

15. Government House, the home of Fiji's president (or governor-general, if Fiji has rejoined the Commonwealth), which is guarded like Buckingham Palace by two spit-and-polish, sulu-clad Fijian soldiers. The original house, built in 1882 as the residence of the colonial governor, was struck by lightning and burned to the ground in 1921. The present rambling mansion was completed in 1928 and opened with great fanfare. It is closed to the public, but a colorful military ceremony marks the changing of the guard during the first week of each month. Ask the Fiji Visitors Bureau whether a ceremony will take place while you're there.

From this point, Victoria Parade becomes Queen Elizabeth Drive, which skirts the peninsula to Laucala Bay. With homes and gardens on one side and the lagoon on the other, it's a lovely walk or drive. The manicured residential area in the rolling hills behind Government House is known as The Domain; an enclave of British civil servants in colonial times, it now is home to the Fiji parliament, government officials, diplomats, and affluent private citizens.

3 Golf, Tennis & Other Outdoor Pursuits

Suva is no Nadi when it comes to recreation, but many city folk are avid golfers and tennis players. There are no beaches in or near the city.

GOLF & TENNIS   Most serious golfers head to the fine course at Pacific Harbour, 30 miles west of Suva (see "Pacific Harbour" in chapter 9). Here in town, the less challenging 18-hole course of the **Fiji Golf Club** (☎ 382872) lies along Rifle Range Road, on the eastern side of the peninsula. Contact the club's secretary for more information or to schedule a tee-off time.

Suva has lighted, hard-surface **public tennis courts** in Albert Park on Victoria Parade and in Victoria Park on Disraeli Road. Telephone **313428** to make a reservation.

RIVER TRIPS   Wilderness Ethnic Adventures Fiji (☎ **315730**) operates a full-day trip on the Navua River west of Suva. A bus or car picks you up at 8am for a 2-hour drive through fields, forests, and villages to the upper reaches of the river. You then spend the rest of day canoeing down the river, navigating over cascades in the hills, and then meandering through rice paddies in the flat valley below. A bus or car brings you back to Suva from the river's mouth 39 kilometers (23 miles) west of the city on the Queen's Road. Cost for the full day, including lunch beside the river, is F$69 ($34.50) per person.

SCUBA DIVING   Scubahire Ltd., 75 Marine Dr., Lami Town (☎ **361088;** fax 361047; e-mail diveconn@is.com.fj), takes snorkelers along on a variety of scuba-diving expeditions from its base at the Tradewinds Hotel, about 4 miles west of town on the Bay of Islands. Most dives on the reefs in the immediate Suva area take half a day, but the company also has full-day trips to the gorgeous, unspoiled Beqa lagoon from an auxiliary base at Pacific Harbour. Two-tank Beqa dives cost F$130 ($65) and snorkelers pay F$45 ($22.50), including equipment and lunch. Scubahire teaches a full range of PADI courses, and it offers free accommodation to backpackers who go diving.

SWIMMING   To the rear of the Old Town Hall on Victoria Parade, the **Suva Olympic Pool** is open to all comers Monday through Friday from 10am to 6pm, Saturday and Sunday from 8am to 6pm during the winter months (April through September); in summer (October through March), it's open Monday through Friday from 9am to 7pm, Saturday and Sunday from 6am to 7pm. Admission is F$1.10 (55¢) for adults and F55¢ (28¢) for children. Lockers rent for F22¢ (11¢) plus a refundable F$2 ($1) key deposit.

4 Shopping in Suva

If you took the walking tour of Suva, you already have a good idea of where to shop for handcrafts and duty-free merchandise. Most of the city's best shops are along **Victoria Parade** and on **Cumming Street.** The largest and most reliable merchants are **Jack's Handicrafts,** at Thomson and Pier streets opposite the Fiji Visitors Bureau; **Prouds,** at the Triangle near the Fiji Visitors Bureau and at the corner of Thomson and Cumming Streets; and **Tappoo,** which has a large store at the corner of Thomson and Usher Streets. The prices are fixed in these stores, but bargaining is the order of the day in Suva's so-called duty-free shops. Before you buy at the small stores, read the discussion of duty-free shopping in "Shopping in Nadi," in chapter 9.

Suva has some fine tropical clothing outlets, several of them on Victoria Parade near the Regal Theatre. **Tiki Togs,** which specializes in bright colors, has a shop at 199 Victoria Parade and another at 38 Thomson Street. The up-market resort- and beachwear specialist **Sogo Fiji** is on Victoria Parade opposite the theatre.

Stamp collectors will find colorful first-day covers from Fiji and other South Pacific island countries at the **Philatelic Bureau,** on the first floor of the General Post Office. It's open Monday through Thursday from 8am to 1pm and 2 to 4pm, Friday to 3:30pm. American Express, Diners Club, MasterCard, and VISA cards are accepted.

Warning: Suva is crawling with the **sword sellers** I warned you about under "Shopping in Nadi" in chapter 9. The government requires these scam artists to stay in Thurston Park near the Fiji Museum, but you could be approached anywhere. Avoid them!

HANDCRAFTS

Government Handicraft Centre. Corner of Victoria Parade and MacArthur St., in rear of Ratu Sukuna House. ☎ **211306.**

Before buying Fijian handcrafts elsewhere, you should browse through the merchandise here. The center was founded in 1974 to continue and promote Fiji's handcrafts. Special attention is given to rural artisans who cannot easily market their works. Although Wolf's Boutique (see below) has the highest quality merchandise, you will see fine wood carvings, woven goods, pottery, and tapa cloth, and you will learn from the fixed prices just how much the really good items are worth. The Fijian staff is friendly and helpful. Open Monday through Thursday from 8am to 4:30pm, Friday from 8am to 4pm and Saturday from 8am to 12:30pm.

Municipal Curio and Handicraft Centre. Municipal Car Park, Stinson Parade, on the waterfront. ☎ **313433.**

Having checked out the government center, you can visit these stalls and bargain with the Indian merchants (but not with the Fijians) from a position of knowledge, if not strength. Be careful, however, for some of the work here is mass produced and aimed at cruise ship passengers who have only a few hours in Fiji to do their shopping. Hours are Monday through Thursday from 8am to 4:30pm, Friday from 8am to 4pm and Saturday from 9am to noon.

✪ **Wolf's Boutique.** Thomson St., opposite Fiji Visitors Bureau. ☎ **302320.**

Wolf Walter and Emele Naivaurua have the highest quality handcrafts, not only from Fiji but from other South Pacific island countries as well, including some excellent *nguzunguzus* (inlaid canoe prows) from the Solomon Islands. Prices for Fijian-carved war clubs and figurines are very reasonable for the excellent quality. Look also for straw hats, baskets, and mats; tapa cloth; shell jewelry; and works by local artists. Open Monday through Friday from 9am to 5:30pm, Saturday from 9am to 1pm.

5 Accommodations in Suva

MODERATE

Centra Suva. P.O. Box 1357, Suva (Victoria Parade, opposite Government Buildings). ☎ **800/835-7742** or 301600. Fax 300251. 130 units. A/C MINIBAR TEL. F$225 ($112.50) double. AE, DC, MC, V.

Formerly the Suva Travelodge, this recently refurbished and upgraded hotel is the city's unofficial gathering place. The waterfront location couldn't be better: Suva Harbour laps one side, the stately Government Buildings sit across Victoria Parade on the other, and the business district is a 3-block walk away.

The balconies or patios of the Australian-style rooms look out from 2-story buildings onto a tropical garden and a boomerang-shaped swimming pool by the water's edge. Despite being brightened and freshened recently, the guest rooms have no cross-ventilation, which means they can become musty in Suva's heat and humidity. They all come equipped with two double beds or a queen and sleeper sofa; European-style writing desks and glass coffee tables; coffeemakers; irons and boards; and bathrooms with combination tub-showers, hair dryers, and marble-look vanities. The Centra has no-smoking rooms, and one unit is equipped for disabled guests.

The central building has a very pleasant restaurant featuring an open kitchen, and a bar with comfortable chairs and a view through floor-to-ceiling windows to the pool and harbor. Poolside barbecues on Sunday afternoons are popular with locals. Facilities include an activities desk and conference rooms.

Raffles Tradewinds Hotel. P.O. Box 3377, Lami Town (Queen's Rd. at Bay of Islands, a 10-min. drive west of Suva, 40 min. west of Nausori Airport). ☎ **362471.** Fax 361464. E-mail: tradewinds@is.com.fj. 110 units. A/C TV TEL. F$96–F$146 ($48–$73) double. AE, DC, MC, V.

If you don't mind being on the outskirts of town, this hotel offers a location right on the picturesque Bay of Islands, Suva's main yacht harbor. In fact, international cruising yachts tie up right alongside the hotel's bulkhead. Comfortable rooms are in two waterfront wings on either side of the main building. Those on the Suva side are smaller and have angled balconies, while those on the Nadi side are larger and have balconies facing directly to the bay. About half of the rooms have TVs.

Opening to the bay, a bar, lounge, and restaurant dispensing very good food have marble tile floors so bright they almost reflect the boats and islands outside. Patrons can also stroll across a gangplank to dine on a covered barge moored to the dock. Facilities include a small bayside pool, tour desk, and large conference center across the Queen's Road. There's entertainment most evenings and 24-hour room service.

INEXPENSIVE

Best Western Berjaya Inn. P.O. Box 112, Suva (corner of Gordon and Malcolm Sts.). ☎ **800/528-1234** or 312300. Fax 301300. E-mail: berjaya@is.com.fj. 48 units. A/C MINIBAR TV TEL. F$134–F$146 ($67–$73) double. AE, DC, MC, V.

Even sans balcony, you will have a commanding view over Suva, the harbor, and the south coast of Viti Levu from this curving, 8-story building. That's the main reason to stay here, for despite recent renovations, this hotel still shows its age. All the smallish rooms face the harbor; even though the rates for the rooms are the same for each floor, the "deluxe" models on the sixth, seventh, and eighth floors have the best views and whisper-quiet air conditioners (you'll get more noisy window units in the "standard" rooms on the lower levels). The neighborhood is residential, yet the hotel is a mere 3-block walk from the shops on Victoria Parade (but for safety reasons, don't do this stroll after dark).

A Malaysian restaurant shares a room on the building's second floor with a bar that features music Monday through Saturday nights. The lobby has a coffee shop with patio seating open from 7am to 11pm. Facilities include a swimming pool (unfortunately on the shady side of the building), beauty salon, and tour desk. There's 24-hour room service.

✪ **Capricorn Apartment Hotel.** P.O. Box 1261, Suva (top end of St. Fort St.). ☎ **303732.** Fax 303069. 34 units. A/C TV TEL. F$85–F$115 ($42.50–$57.50). AE, DC, MC, V.

Although it's a steep, 2-block walk uphill from Cumming Street, Mulchand Patel's place is popular with Australians and New Zealanders who like to do their own cooking. The 3-story, L-shaped building looks out on Suva Harbour and down the mountainous coast. Private balconies off each apartment share the view, as does a pear-shaped swimming pool on the Capricorn's grounds. Except for cane and wicker chairs and coffee tables, furniture in the older, inexpensive units is on the plain side, but the mattresses here are new and among the firmest in Fiji. Mulchand and son Mukesh make sure these roomy efficiencies are kept spotless. A dozen modern, condolike units are luxuriously furnished and much better outfitted than the older apartments. They are the more expensive units here and are on a par with any accommodation in Suva. Each unit has an air conditioner, although windows on both sides of the building let the cooling trade winds blow through.

Continental breakfasts are served on the premises (the upstairs converts into a bar at dusk), and the reception staff will sell you canned goods from its small on-premises store or have "Dial-A-Meal" deliver to your room. The maids will wash, dry, and fold your laundry for F$12 ($6) per load.

✪ **Homestay Suva.** P.O. Box 16172, Suva (on Prince's Rd. in Tamavua suburb). ☎ **370395.** Fax 370947. www.bulafiji.com/homestay. E-mail: homestaysuva@is.com.fj. 5 units (all with private bathroom). A/C. F$115–F$130 ($57.50–$115). Rates include full breakfast. AE, MC, V.

One of the few genuine bed-and-breakfasts in the South Pacific islands, Bruce and Lesley Phillip's gorgeous home sits atop a ridge in the expensive Tamavua suburb. The view from up here is stunning, for their expansive covered veranda looks out over a ridgetop swimming pool, across a steep valley, down to Walu Bay, and along the south coast of Viti Levu.

Their choice room is appropriately named Harbor View, for it also looks out over this vista (it's their most expensive choice, too). Another upstairs room, the Nukulau, looks eastward across Laucala Bay and out to little Nukulau Island sitting on the far-off reef. Three more rooms on the main floor lack a view, but every room here is quite comfortably furnished with a mix of tropical and traditional pieces. You get thick, fluffy towels and other luxurious amenities. Lesley serves extensive breakfasts on the veranda, and she will prepare moderately priced gourmet dinners on request (many guests here are business types, including women traveling alone, and Lesley's dinners often turn into full-fledged parties).

New Zealanders by birth, Bruce and Lesley settled here in the mid-1970s after wandering the world and chartering a sailboat in the Caribbean. Call them for directions if you're driving, or take a taxi from downtown for F$3 ($1.50). Bruce and Lesley charge small fees to take you on a Friday evening harbor cruise and to Nukulau Island for a Sunday picnic.

Suva Motor Inn. P.O. Box 2500, Government Bldgs., Suva (corner of Mitchell and Gorrie Sts.). ☎ **313973.** Fax 300381. E-mail: suvamotorinn@is.com.fj. 36 units, 9 apts. A/C TV TEL. F$100 ($50) double, F$170 ($85) apt. AE, DC, MC, V.

In much better condition than the Best Western Berjaya and closer to downtown than the Raffles Tradewinds, this modern 3-story hotel is very popular with business travelers who can't afford the Centra Suva, and it's a good family bet, too. Just uphill from Albert Park near the Government Buildings, the hotel is a pleasant hoof to the business district (at least during the safe daylight hours).

Built in 1996, the L-shaped structure bends around a lush tropical courtyard with a 2-level swimming pool with a whirlpool and a water slide. Opening to this vista, a small restaurant provides Japanese teppanyaki-style cuisine as well as international meals, and a bar attracts the business types after work. Accommodation is in studios and two-bedroom apartments. The studios are fully air conditioned, but only the master bedrooms of the apartments are cooled. All units are equipped with desks and modem-port phones, and tropical cane-and-wicker furniture helps soften the somewhat austere white walls and white tile floors. Apartments have full kitchens; studios have refrigerators, toasters, coffeemakers, and microwave ovens. All units have spacious bathrooms. There's a guest laundry, and the staff will assist in arranging activities and excursions.

HOSTELS

South Seas Private Hotel. P.O. Box 2086, Government Bldgs., Suva (Williamson Rd. off Ratu Cakobau Rd., behind Albert Park). ☎ **312296.** Fax 340236. www.fiji4less.com.fj. E-mail: cathay@is.com.fj. 42 dorm beds, 34 units (1 with bathroom). F$18.50 ($9.25) double room without bathroom; F$25 ($12.50) double room with bathroom; F$9.50 ($4.75) dorm bed. No credit cards.

This large barracks-like wooden structure with a long sun room across the front (it can get hot in the afternoons) could be cleaner, but it's a friendly establishment and usually is packed with young people on the go. It has dormitories, basic rooms, a rudimentary communal kitchen, a TV lounge, and laundry facilities. Bed linen is provided, but bring your own towel or pay a F$3 ($1.50) deposit to use one of theirs. There's a F$5 ($2.50) refundable key deposit, too. Showers have both hot and cold water. The rooms have fans, but they operate only from 4pm to 7am.

6 Dining in Suva

For fine dining, check out the Suva edition of **Chefs, The Restaurant,** which was due to open in the Jack's Handicraft building at the corner of Thomson and Pier Streets opposite the Fiji Visitors Bureau. Chef Eugene Gomes was planning to install local versions of The Edge and The Corner here, too. Phone numbers were not available as we went to press.

There's also a branch of Nadi's fine **Daikoku** Japanese restaurant, in the FNPF Plaza building on Victoria Parade at Loftus Street (☎ **308968**). It has the same menu as the original, but the prices are less expensive. Open Monday through Saturday noon to 2:30pm and 6 to 10pm. Reservations are recommended.

See "Dining in Nadi" in chapter 9 for more information about these restaurants.

EUROPEAN RESTAURANTS

Cardo's. Regal Lane, off Victoria Parade behind McDonald's. ☎ **314330.** Reservations recommended. Main courses F$12–F$32 ($6–16). AE, MC, V. Mon–Fri noon–2:30pm; daily 5–10pm. STEAKS/SEAFOOD.

You can clog your arteries with cholesterol at this hip upstairs steakhouse, or you can opt for chicken or fresh fish singed over the charcoal grill. Among its non-grilled items, the menu offers prawns served with a broth in a cast iron pot, Cajun-style chicken, spaghetti with eggplant, and a tasty veal parmigiana. Many of the town's young professionals will be here, enjoying both the food and a relaxed, sophisticated atmosphere enhanced by progressive jazz from the sound system. The decor is a modern version of art deco, with forest green walls and curving dividers separating knotty pine, picnic-style tables along big window walls looking over a parking lot to the harbor.

JJ's Bar & Grill. 9–10 Gordon St., just off Victoria Parade behind National Bank of Fiji. ☎ **305005.** Reservations recommended. Sandwiches and main courses F$8–F$23.50 ($4–$11.75). AE, MC, V. Mon–Wed 11:30am–3pm and 5:30–11pm, Thurs–Fri 11am–3pm and 5:30pm–midnight, Sat 5:30pm–midnight. INTERNATIONAL.

The food is secondary to being seen at this lively bistro, known locally as the "American Pub." The blonde wood decor and bar on one end of the room will remind us Yanks of many such trendy joints at home. In fact, it's operated by Virginia Blake, a Fiji native who lived for many years in New York City. The wide-ranging menu offers tastes from around the globe, but I found the Caesar salad to be a poor imitation of the real thing, and the fettuccine with chicken, snow peas, and mushrooms in a white wine sauce to be nearly unpalatable. You'll have a good time here, but approach it like you would any pub at home. Enjoy the cold beer but order the burgers, steaks, or daily seafood specials.

✪ **Old Mill Cottage.** 47–49 Carnavon St., near corner of Loftus St. ☎ **312134.** Reservations not accepted. Breakfasts F$3–F$5 ($1.50–$2.50); meals F$4–F$7 ($2–$3.50). No credit cards. Mon–Fri 7am–6pm, Sat 7am–5pm. FIJIAN/INDIAN/EUROPEAN.

One of the few remaining late 19th-century homes left in Suva's diplomatic-government section, these adjoining two-room clapboard cottages are one of the best places in the South Pacific to get consistently good home cooking. You'll find a cafeteria-like serving counter between the two structures. Order there from a selection of daily specials such as Fijian palusami, mild Indian curries, or European-style mustard-baked chicken with real mashed potatoes and peas. Diplomats (the U.S. Embassy is out the back door) and government executives pack the place at midday. Hurry and get here, for this is a high-rent district, and these charming old cottages may someday give way to a high-rise office tower. Saturday's menu is geared toward Fijian seafood dishes.

Tiko's Floating Restaurant and Steakhouse. Stinson Parade at Sukuna Park. ☎ **313626.** Reservations recommended. Main courses F$7–F$31 ($3.50–$15.50). AE, DC, MC, V. Mon–Fri noon–2pm; Mon–Sat 6–10pm. SEAFOOD/STEAKS.

Locals like to take out-of-town guests to dinner at this floating restaurant, which served time years ago with Blue Lagoon Cruises. Hopefully they don't lean to seasickness, for the old craft does tend to roll a bit when freighters kick up a wake going in and out of the harbor. Your best bets here are the nightly seafood specials, such as *walu* (Spanish mackerel) and *pakapaka* (snapper). It's not the best in town, but the fish is fresh, the service is attentive, and a terrific jazz musician-singer usually provides dinner music—all of which makes for a pleasant night out.

INDIAN RESTAURANTS

✪ **Ashiyana.** Victoria Parade, in Old Town Hall. ☎ **313000.** Reservations recommended on weekends. Main courses F$4.50–F$12.50 ($2.25–$6.25). AE, MC, V. Mon–Fri 11:30am–2:30pm and 6–10pm, Sat–Sun 6–9:30pm. INDIAN.

In contrast to the run-of-the-mill, home-style curries served throughout Fiji, this little restaurant specializes in authentic dishes from all over the subcontinent. You can choose fiery vegetable curries from southern India, tasty tandoori lamb from the Punjab, filling basmati rice dishes from the Himalayas, or that old British Raj standby, *roghan josh* (lamb simmered in yogurt and tomato). They're not so spicy as to turn away the expatriates who love this place, but they will let you know this is real Indian food. Sharing is in order, since dishes are served in copper pots over warming candles. Feel free to dispense with forks and pick up your food with pieces of delightful naan or roti bread (use your right hand only, as is the custom in India and Pakistan).

✪ **Hare Krishna Restaurant.** 16 Pratt St. ☎ **314154.** Reservations not accepted. Curries F$1.20–F$7.50 (60¢–$3.75). No credit cards. Dining room Mon–Sat 11am–2:30pm; downstairs snack bar Mon–Thurs 9am–8pm, Fri 9am–9pm, Sat 9am–3:30pm. VEGETARIAN INDIAN.

This very popular restaurant specializes in a wide range of vegetarian curries—eggplant, cabbage, potatoes and peas, okra, and papaya, to name a few—each seasoned delicately and differently from the others. Interesting pastries, breads, side dishes, and salads (such as cucumbers and carrots in yogurt) cool off the fire set by some of the curries. If you can't decide what to order, check the items on display in a cafeteria-like steam table near the entrance to the second-floor dining room, or get the all-you-can-eat *thali* sampler and try a little of everything—it's the most expensive item on the menu and will tingle your taste buds. Downstairs has an excellent yogurt and ice cream bar; climb the spiral stairs to reach the dining rooms. The Hare Krishnas allow no alcoholic beverages or smoking.

CHINESE RESTAURANTS

Lantern Palace. 10 Pratt St. ☎ **314633.** Reservations recommended. Main courses F$5–F$10 ($2.50–$5). AE, DC, MC, V. Mon–Sat 11:30am–2:30pm and 5–10pm, Sun 6–10pm. CANTONESE.

This typical Cantonese restaurant occupies a storefront on the same block of Pratt Street as the Hare Krishna Restaurant. It has the usual assortment of Chinese letters on the wall and lanterns hanging overhead, but the tables are draped with white linen cloths that contribute to a quiet, upscale atmosphere. You can choose from a wide range of excellent Cantonese dishes. Try the honey chicken.

Ming Palace. Victoria Parade in Old Town Hall. ☎ **315111.** Reservations recommended. Main courses F$8–F$12 ($4–$6). AE, MC, V. Mon–Sat 11:30am–2pm and 6–10pm, Sun 5–10pm. CANTONESE.

The owners here completely refurbished the auditorium of the Old Town Hall, which we passed during our walking tour of Suva. A huge Chinese dragon and bird now hang above the stage, and lanterns dangle from long poles reaching down from the high, arch-supported ceiling. Screens separate the tables to help keep you from feeling as if you're dining in a meeting place, and the service is attentive and efficient. The lunchtime buffet is a good value.

AN ITALIAN RESTAURANT

Pizza Hut. 207 Victoria Parade, at MacArthur St. ☎ **311825.** Reservations recommended on weekends. Pizzas F$6–F$22 ($3–$11); pastas F$6–F$7 ($3–$3.50). AE, DC, MC, V. Mon–Fri noon–2:30pm and 5–10pm, Sat noon–10:30pm, Sun 5–10pm. PIZZA/PASTA.

This is not related to the American chain by either quality or ownership (the proprietor of the Pizza Hut, the Bad Dog Cafe, O'Reilly's, and a nightclub in this corner building is Irishman Liam Hindle). Nevertheless, it still has reasonably good pizza and pasta. Pies range from small and plain ones to large ones with prawns. Also on the menu: salads, spaghetti, and lasagna. You can dine in a cozy, brick-accented dining room or eat and drink in a comfy bar while listening to the music of blues stars whose photos hang on the walls.

SNACK BARS, FOOD COURTS & COFFEE SHOPS

The modern and clean ✪ **Dolphins Food Court,** in the high-rise FNPC Place building on Victoria Parade at Loftus Street (☎ **307811**), has stalls offering good European, Chinese, and Indian fare at prices ranging from F$3 to F$6 ($1.50 to $3), plus ice cream and other goodies. The vegetarian Hare Krishna Restaurant (see above) has an outlet here. Most stalls are open daily from 11am to 10pm, although some take a break from 3 to 5pm. It's the place to which everyone heads on Sunday, when most other snack bars are closed. It will remind you of the food courts at most shopping malls back home.

If you're hankering for a Big Mac, you'll find the local **McDonald's** on Victoria Parade at the northern edge of Sukuna Park.

Palm Court Bistro. Victoria Parade, in the Palm Court Arcade, Queensland Insurance Centre. ☎ **304662.** Breakfasts F$5.50–F$6.50 ($2.75–$3.25); sandwiches, meat pies, burgers, fish and chips F$2–F$4.50 ($1–$2.25). No credit cards. Mon–Fri 7am–6pm, Sat 7am–3pm. SNACK BAR.

You can partake of excellent cooked or continental breakfasts (served all day) and a variety of other snacks and light meals at this walk-up carryout in the open-air center of the Palm Court Arcade. Order at the counter and then eat at plastic tables under cover, or go sit in the shade of the namesake palm in the middle of the arcade.

✪ **Republic of Cappuccino.** Victoria Parade at Loftus St., in FNPF Place building. ☎ **300333.** Coffee F$2.50–F$3.50 ($1.25–$1.75), pastries and quiche F$1–F$4.50 (50¢–$2.25). No credit cards. Mon–Fri 7am–11pm, Sat 8am–11pm, Sun 10am–7pm. COFFEE BAR.

"The Rock" to trendy locals, this Starbucks-style coffee shop (the American chain hasn't arrived yet) occupies the triangular corner of FNPF Place, on the Victoria Parade side of Dolphins Food Court. You can listen to recorded jazz while drinking your latte or cappuccino and eating your brownie, cake, or quiche at the tall tables by the big storefront windows. You can get your e-mail here, too (see "Fast Facts: Suva," above).

8 Island Nights in Suva

Fijian-style meke feast-and-dance nights are scarce in Suva. The **Centra Suva, Victoria Parade** (☎ **301600**), usually has one a week. Otherwise, nocturnal activities in Suva revolve around going to the movies and then hitting the bars—until the wee hours on Friday, the biggest night out.

Movies are a big deal here, especially the first-run flicks playing at ✪ **Village 6 Cinemas,** on Scott Street at Nubukalou Creek, a modern, American-style emporium with six screens and a large games arcade upstairs. Check the daily *Fiji Times* or *Daily Post* for what's playing and show times. Tickets cost F$4 ($2), and you can pig out on popcorn, candy, and soft drinks. Locals flock here on Sunday afternoon, when these plush, air-conditioned theaters offer a comfortable escape from Suva's daytime heat and humidity.

After a nighttime movie, locals head for their favorite bars. Blues and jazz fans gravitate to **Birdland,** a basement pub at 6 Carnavon Street, east of Loftus Street (☎ **303833**), which has live music Thursday through Saturday nights. A few doors down Carnavon Street, the waiters and bouncers wear cowboy hats and other western garb at **The Barn,** where you can line dance to tunes by country-and-western bands (☎ **307845**). **Trap's Bar,** 305 Victoria Parade, 2 blocks south of the Pizza Hut (☎ **312922**), is another popular watering hole where you're not likely to witness a fight. A band usually plays in the back room on weekends.

O'Reilly's, on Macarthur Street just off Victoria Parade (☎ **312968**), is an Irish-style pub serving Guinness stout and sports on TVs (as the bouncers on Macarthur Street will attest, it can get a bit rough, depending on who's winning the rugby matches).

Victoria Parade has a number of loud discotheques frequented by the young, noisy crowd. Just walk along; you'll hear them.

8 Resorts Offshore from Suva

Although you can get there from Nadi, Suva is the usual jumping-off point to two small offshore resorts, including one of the most expensive in Fiji. One is on Toberua, a tiny atoll off Viti Levu's east coast. The other is on Wakaya, in the Lomaiviti (Central Fiji) group of islands, where Count Felix von Luckner was captured in 1917.

✪ **Toberua Island Resort.** P.O. Box 567, Suva (Toberua Island, 12 miles off Viti Levu). ☎ **302356** in Suva or 472777 on island. Fax 472888. www.toberua.com. E-mail: toberua@is.com.fj. 14 bungalows. MINIBAR. US$245 double. Transfers US$26 per person from Nakelo landing, near Nausori Airport. Meals US$55 per person per day. AE, DC, MC, V.

Reached by a 1-hour taxi-and-boat trip from Suva, this resort on a tiny palm-dotted, beach-encircled atoll was built in 1968 and has lots of South Seas charm you don't get in many newer properties. The island is too flat to draw moisture from the sky; there-fore, it isn't in the "rain belt" created by the mountains behind Suva. Guests enjoy such an easygoing lifestyle that they are warned to take at least 4 days to slow down and grow accustomed to the pace. Actually, there's plenty to do: sunbathe, swim, snorkel, dive or become certified to dive, collect shells, sail, windsurf, visit nearby Fijian villages and uninhabited islands (including one with a protected booby colony), fish in the lagoon, or play a round of "reef golf"—which is exactly what it sounds like: holes and fairways are out on the reef at low tide. Anyone who gets "bure fever" after a few days on this small atoll can charter the *Adi Toberua*, a cross between a cabin cruiser and a comfortable houseboat, for trips to nearby destinations such as Levuka. Rates are about US$300 per day for boat, skipper, and meals. The boat can sleep three guests.

Toberua's large, Fijian-style bures were constructed of native materials back when huge coconut logs were used as beams to hold up their bamboo-plaited ceilings. Thatch accents and rattan furniture add to the charm. Each has a front and a lagoon-side porch (where you can have dinner) and a modern bathroom with indoor and out-door entrances. They have minibars, but forget telephones and TVs out here.

Dining/Diversions: The waterside dining room features excellent cuisine, with an emphasis on fresh seafood. Meal plans are required, since there is no other place to eat. A separate bar with easy chairs on its front porch is a popular gathering spot. Fijians strum guitars and sing at night.

Amenities: Saltwater swimming pool; sailboats, Windsurfers, fishing equipment for free; excursions, fishing trips, and scuba diving cost extra. Laundry, baby-sitting, mas-sage, golf.

✪ **The Wakaya Club.** P.O. Box 15424, Suva (Wakaya Island, Lomaiviti Group). ☎ **800/828-3454** or 440128. Fax 440406. www.wakaya.com. E-mail: info@wakaya.com. 9 units. MINIBAR. US$1,255 double. Rates include meals, bar, all activities except deep-sea fishing and scuba-diving courses. Round-trip transfers US$780 from Nadi, US$390 from Suva. AE, DC, MC, V.

A 20-minute flight away by private plane from Nausori Airport, 50 minutes from Nadi, this super-deluxe facility belongs to Canadian entrepreneur David Gilmour, who acquired the island in the 1970s. He had an interest in the Pacific Harbour devel-opment back then; as he did there, Gilmour has sold off pieces of Wakaya for deluxe getaway homes. For small fortunes you can rent these villas, including Gilmore's own Japanese-influenced mansion high on a ridge overlooking the resort (his is the largest private residence in Fiji).

Wakaya is an uplifted, tilted coral atoll with cliffs falling into the sea on its western side and beaches along the north and east. There are still relics of a Fijian fort on the cliffs; a chief and all his men once leaped to their deaths from there rather than be roasted by a rival tribe. The spot is known as Chieftain's Leap. More recent notable events have included visits by actress Cheryl Ladd (who poses—without being identified—on Wakaya's brochure) and supermodel Christie Brinkley, who brought along her daughter and nanny but not then-husband Billy Joel. In fact, Hollywood and Beverly Hills types feel right at home in Wakaya's 1,500-square-foot, deluxe rectangular bungalows. On one end they have large living rooms with wet bars. Separate entrances off spacious decks lead to bedrooms with built-in desks and mon-strous closets. Bathrooms on the far end have oversized tubs, separate shower stalls, three sinks each, toilets, and bidets. Crabtree and Evelyn toiletries are imported from England.

Compared to Vatulele, Turtle Island, and other deluxe resorts, where a party atmos-phere often prevails, the management and excellent and unobtrusive Fijian staff here leave the guests alone.

Dining/Diversions: The food is of gourmet quality and outstandingly presented. Guests dine in a huge thatch-roofed beachside building or outside, either on a patio or under two gazebo-like shelters on a deck surrounding a swimming pool with its own waterfall.

Amenities: Nine-hole golf course, tennis and croquet courts, sailing, fishing, scuba diving. Laundry services and anything else you need. Management leaves most guest contact to a highly efficient, unobtrusive Fijian staff.

9 Levuka & Ovalau

You may think you've slipped into the Twilight Zone as you stroll down historic Beach Street in Levuka, Fiji's first capital on the ruggedly beautiful island of Ovalau. Everything here seems to be from a century earlier: ramshackle dry-goods stores with false fronts, clapboard houses with tin roofs to keep them dry and shaded verandas to keep them cool, and round clocks in the baroque tower of Sacred Heart Catholic Church. Where the regular streets end, "step streets" climb to more houses up near the base of the jagged cliffs towering over the town.

Not that Levuka hasn't changed at all since its 19th-century days as one of the South Pacific's most notorious seaports. All but one of the 50 or more hotels and saloons that dispensed rum and other pleasures disappeared long ago. The sole survivor—the Royal Hotel—is now a quiet, family-run establishment. The fist-fighting whalers and drifting beach bums went the way of the square-rigged ships that once crowded the blue-green harbor beyond the row of glistening ficus trees and park benches along Beach Street. Gone, too, are the pioneering merchants and copra planters who established Levuka as Fiji's first European-style town in the 1830s and who for years carried guns to protect themselves from its ruffians.

But Levuka still looks much the same as it did in 1882, when the colonial administration moved to Suva. The 1,200-foot-tall walls of basalt, which caused the demise of Levuka by preventing expansion, create a soaring backdrop that puts Ovalau in the big leagues of dramatic tropical beauty.

Despite its history, beauty, and extremely hospitable residents, Levuka is relatively off the beaten tourist track. The volcano that created Ovalau has eroded into such rugged formations that it has very little flat land and no decent beach; therefore, the island has not attracted resort or hotel development. All of Levuka's accommodations fall into the low-budget, basic category. But this is a great place to meet people and learn about Fiji's history and culture.

GETTING THERE & GETTING AROUND

GETTING THERE   Air Fiji (☎ **888/354-3454** in the U.S., 313666 in Suva, or 722251 in Nadi) has early-morning and late-afternoon flights to Ovalau's unpaved airstrip at Bureta, on the island's west coast. The excursion fare from Suva is F$63 ($31.50) round-trip. The strip is not lighted and rainy weather or delays can cause the one late afternoon flight to be canceled. If you're on a day trip, therefore, bring your toothbrush and a change of clothes just in case (if the flight doesn't come, Air Fiji will put you up at the Royal Hotel; see below). Levuka is halfway around Ovalau on the east coast. An unpaved road circles the island along its shoreline and makes the bus ride from airport to town a sightseeing excursion in its own right. Airport bus transfers cost F$3.60 ($1.80) each way.

Ovalau Tours & Transportation, P.O. Box 149, Levuka, Ovalau (☎ **440611;** fax 440405; www.ecotoursfiji.com; e-mail mtb@soholidays.com), has day trips from Suva to Levuka. Its history version includes morning tea, lunch, and a guided walking tour of Levuka. A cultural heritage tour will take you to Devokula village (see "Attractions

Beyond Levuka," below), where you'll have a traditional Fijian meal. Both tours cost F$214 ($107) per person, including round-trip airfare. Ovalau Tours & Transportation also offers 2-night packages.

More adventurous souls can watch Ovalau's jagged green peaks go by from one of the **ferries** that run between Viti Levu and Levuka. Most boats land on the northwest coast, a 30-minute bus or taxi ride from Levuka.

For more information, see "Getting There & Getting Around" in chapter 8.

GETTING AROUND   Levuka is a small town, and your feet can get you to most places in 25 minutes.

For **taxis,** call **Vuniba Taxis** (☎ 440322), **Levuka Taxis** (☎ 440147), or **B. Murgan Transport Co.** (☎ 440180). Fares are F$1 (50¢) in town plus F50¢ (39¢) per kilometer thereafter; F$17 ($8.50) to the airport; F$25 ($12.50) to Lovoni; and F$50 ($25) around Ovalau. Be sure you and the driver agree on a fare before departing.

Local **buses** depart for the outlying villages from Beach Street about four times a day. They don't run after dark, so make sure you find out from the driver when—and whether—he returns to Levuka at the end of the day. Fares should be no more than F$1.50 (75¢). Buses to Lovoni leave at 7:30am, noon, and 5pm. They leave Lovoni for Levuka at 6:30am, 8:30am, and 5pm.

Ovalau Watersports, behind Ovalau Tours & Transportation on Beach Street next to the Community Centre, (☎ 440611), rents bicycles.

FAST FACTS: LEVUKA

The following facts apply to Levuka and Ovalau. If you don't see an item here, look in "Fast Facts: Fiji" in chapter 8.

Currency Exchange   **Westpac Bank** and **National Bank of Fiji** have offices near the Levuka Community Centre (old Morris Hedstrom store). Hours are Monday through Thursday from 9:30am to 3pm and Friday from 9:30am to 3:30pm.

Emergencies   The emergency phone number is **000.**

Hospitals   The government maintains a small hospital in Levuka (☎ 440105).

Information   The best source is **Ovalau Tours & Transportation** ☎ 440611), on Beach Street (see "Guided Tours," below).

Libraries   The Community Center has a small library. You pay a F$5 ($2.50) registration fee to use the library, and you make a refundable F$10 ($5) deposit to check out books.

Police   The Fiji Police station is opposite the Masonic Lodge (☎ 440222).

Post Office   The post office is on the waterfront near the Community Centre. Open Monday through Friday from 8am to 1pm and 2 to 4pm.

Safety   Levuka and Ovalau are safe to visit, but don't leave your valuables unattended.

Telephone/Telegrams/Fax   There are only two phonecard public phones in town: at the post office and in the Royal Hotel. Place long-distance and international calls at the post office.

EXPLORING LEVUKA
A STROLL AROUND TOWN

You can walk through Levuka in about 2 hours. Begin at the **Levuka Community Centre,** across the street from the Air Fiji office, which occupies the quaint old **Morris Hedstrom** store built by Levukans Percy Morris and Maynard Hedstrom in 1878. The trading company they founded, now one of the South Pacific's largest department store chains, pulled out of Levuka entirely a century later. The company donated the

Impressions

There appeared to be a rowdy devil-may-care sort of look about the whole of them; and the great part of the day, and the night too, seemed to be spent in tippling in public house bars. I dare say that of the row of houses that make Levuka, fully half are hotels or public houses. The amount of gin and water which is consumed must be amazing, for the bars are always crowded, and the representatives of white civilization always at it.

—Robert Philip, 1872

dilapidated structure to the National Trust of Fiji. The Levuka Historical and Cultural Society raised money throughout the country to restore it and install a small branch of the Fiji Museum, a public library, a meeting hall, a crafts and recreational center, and a small garden. The furniture is made of timbers salvaged from the rotting floor. Mrs. Dora Patterson, matriarch of the Patterson Brothers Shipping Company family, donated the museum's waterside garden; she could oversee the project from her colonial-style mansion on the hill above Levuka. From the Community Centre head south.

NASOVA & THE DEED OF CESSION   South of the museum, the post office stands at the entrance to the **Queens Wharf.** The drinking fountain in front marks the site of a carrier-pigeon service that linked Suva and Levuka in the late 1800s. The Queens Wharf is one of Fiji's four ports of entry (Suva, Lautoka, and Savusavu are the others), but along with domestic cargo, it now handles primarily exports from the Pacific Fishing Company's **tuna cannery,** established by a Japanese firm in 1964. You can follow your nose to the cannery in the industrial buildings south of the pier.

Keep going to **Nasova,** a village on the shore of the little bay about half a mile south of the cannery. Chief Cakobau signed the deed that ceded Fiji to Great Britain here. The site is now marked by three stones in the center of a grassy park at the water's edge. Plaques commemorate the signing ceremony on October 10, 1874; Fiji's independence exactly 96 years later; and the 1974 centennial celebration of the Deed of Cession. A Fijian-style thatch meeting house stands across the road.

South of Nasova, the **Old Levuka Cemetery** is tended to perfection by prison inmates. Tombstones bear the names of many Europeans who settled here in the 19th century—and some who met their demise without settling down first.

BEACH STREET   Backtrack to the weathered storefronts of Levuka's 3-block-long business district along **Beach Street.** Saloons no longer line Beach Street; instead, the Indian- and Chinese-owned stores now dispense a variety of dry goods and groceries. On the horizon beyond the ficus trees and park benches lie the smoky-blue outlines of Wakaya, Makogai, and other members of the Lomaiviti ("Central Fiji") group of islands. The green cliffs still reach skyward behind the stores, hemming in Levuka and its narrow valley. Walk along the waterfront, and don't hesitate to stick your head into the dry-goods stores.

After the last store stands the **Church of the Sacred Heart,** a wooden building fronted by a baroque stone tower. It was built by the Marist Brothers who came to Levuka in 1858. In case you missed the number of chimes marking the time, the clock in the tower strikes once on the hour—and again, for good measure, 1 minute later. Across Beach Street stands a **World War I monument** to the Fijian members of the Fiji Labour Corps who were killed assisting the British in Europe.

Walk on across Totoga Creek to low **Niukaubi Hill,** on top of which is another World War I monument, this one to Levukans of English ancestry who died fighting as British soldiers in that conflict. Parliament House and the Supreme Court building sat on this little knoll before the capital was moved to Suva. They had a nice view across the town, the waterfront, and the reef and islands offshore. At the bottom of the hill is the **Levuka Club,** a colonial-era drinking establishment.

Keep going north on Beach Street, which soon passes the 1904-vintage Anglican church before arriving in the original Fijian village known as **Levuka.** The Tui Levuka who lived here befriended the early European settlers. Later, Chief Cakobau worshipped in the Methodist church built on the south side of the creek in 1869. John Brown Williams, the American consul, is buried in the village's Old Cemetery near the church. (Remember, good manners dictate that you have permission before entering a Fijian village.)

To the north, **Gun Rock** towers over Levuka village. In order to show the chiefs just how much firepower it packed, a British warship in 1849 used this steep headland for target practice. Beach Street now runs under the overhang of Gun Rock, where the Marist Brothers said their first mass. There was no road then, only a shingly beach where the sea had worn away the base of the cliff.

INLAND   Beyond Gun Rock lies the village of **Vagadaci,** where the Duke of York—later King George V—and his brother, the Duke of Clarence, once played cricket (the field is now covered by a housing project), but I usually turn around at Gun Rock and return to the first street inland south of the hospital. It leads to the **199 steps** that climb Mission Hill from the Methodist church to the collection of buildings that comprise **Delana Methodist School.** For the energetic, the view from the 199th step is worth the climb.

From the church, cut down Chapel Hill Road and Langham Street past the Royal, the South Pacific's oldest operating hotel. Keep going south along the banks of Togoga Creek to the Roman-style **Polynesia Masonic Lodge,** which was founded in 1875. The **Town Hall,** next door, was built in 1898 in honor of Queen Victoria's 50 years on the British throne; it still houses most of Levuka's city offices. The nearby **Ovalau Club** is the oldest drinking club in the South Pacific, a reminder of the social clubs where the Old Boys of the British Empire gathered to escape the heat, drink gin, and play snooker (billiards). The Ovalau Club today has a racially diverse membership that welcomes clean-cut visitors from overseas. Behind the lodge, club, and Town Hall, **Nasau Park** provides the town's rugby and cricket field, bowling green, and tennis courts.

Now head uphill along the creek until you get to the lovely white Victorian buildings with broad verandas of **Levuka Public School,** Fiji's first educational institution (opened in 1879) and still one of its best. A row of mango and sweet-smelling frangipani trees shade the sidewalk known as Bath Road between the school and the rushing creek. Walk up Bath Road, which soon turns into a "step street" as it climbs to a waterfall and concrete-lined swimming hole known as The Bath. Cool off at this refreshing spot before heading back down the steps to Beach Street.

ATTRACTIONS BEYOND LEVUKA

✪ **Devokula Village,** about 13 kilometers (8 miles) northwest of Levuka, captures what Fijian hamlets looked like before the coming of plywood and tin. Under the leadership of the informative Jeremaia Tukutukai, who acts as chief and tour guide here, local residents have reconstructed a traditional village from scratch using all natural materials. It's best seen on a tour with Ovalau Tours & Travel (see "Guided Tours," below). The tours cost F$30 ($15) and include a traditional yaqona welcoming ceremony, a feast of all-native foods from the earth oven (you won't get tea or coffee here), a tour of the village, and a meke dance show. The villagers dress in old-time costumes during the tour. Devokula even has accommodation in small thatch bures (you'll sleep on a mattress of straw and use tapa cloth as a blanket). Guests share a communal kitchen and rudimentary toilets (the commodes are the only bow to modern conveniences here). Cost is F$77.50 ($38.75) per person in bures, F$55 ($27.50) in a dormitory, including all meals. Book and pay in advance at Ovalau Tours & Travel.

St. John's College, in the village of Cawaci north of Levuka, was founded by the Marist Brothers in 1884, primarily to educate the sons of ranking Fijian chiefs. The school sits on the grounds of **St. John's Church,** a Gothic Revival building typical of Catholic missions in the South Pacific. On a bluff overlooking the sea, the **Bishop's Tomb** holds the remains of Dr. Julian Vidal, the first Catholic bishop of Fiji.

Yavu, south of Levuka, is a hilltop overlooking the sea where, according to legend, a newly arrived chief lit a fire, which caught the attention of a chief who was already here. The two met at Yavu and agreed that one would be chief of the interior, while the other would rule the coastline. They placed two sacred stones at the spot to mark their agreement. The hilltop isn't marked, so go there with a guide (see "Guided Tours," below).

Lovoni, a picturesque Fijian village in the crater of Ovalau's extinct volcano, was the home of ferocious warriors who stormed down to the coast and attacked Levuka on several occasions. Chief Cakobau settled that problem by luring them into town to talk peace; instead, he captured them all and deported them to other parts of Fiji. Today's Lovonians have seen so many travelers wandering around their village that most are adept at pleasantly smiling while ignoring you. The houses are of wood with corrugated iron roofs.

Waitovu, about a 50-minute walk north of town (look for its mosque), has the nearest waterfall to town. Ask permission, and ask the residents to show the way. You can dive into the top pool from the rocks above.

Rukuruku village on the northwest shore has a waterfall and Ovalau's sole swimming beach.

GUIDED TOURS

Ovalau Tours & Transportation, on Beach Street next to the Community Centre (☎ **440611;** fax 440405; www.ecotoursfiji.com; e-mail: mtb@soholidays.com), has a variety of guided tours of both the town and island. An informative, 2-hour walking tour of Levuka costs F$10 ($5), while excursions to either St. John's College north of town, or to Yavu and the sacred stones, costs F$20 ($10). Day trips to Devokula Village (see above) cost $30 ($15) per person, including transportation from town, traditional feast, tour of the village, and meke dance show.

Book in advance with Ovalau Tours & Transportation or at the Royal Hotel (see below) for **Epi's Inland Tour,** a full-day outing on which you hike up across the peaks and down to Lovoni village (see "Attractions Beyond Levuka," above). It's a 4-hour hike, including a strenuous 2-hour climb over the mountains. You get to ride back to Levuka after a welcoming ceremony, a Fijian lunch, and a swim in the village's icy stream. Your guide will explain the Fijian way of life, including uses of the plants you'll pass on the trail. These trips cost F$20 ($10).

OFFSHORE ISLANDS

Leleuvia Island, P.O. Box 50, Levuka (☎ **301584** in Suva), a tiny atoll between Viti Levu and Ovalau, is one of the more popular backpacker retreats. Guests stay in a mix of dormitories, thatch bures, and European cottages. They can sunbathe (topless if desired) on the islet's gorgeous beaches and swim and snorkel over some lovely reefs. A small shop sells beer and some groceries, and the staff prepares Chinese meals served buffet-style. Rates, including three meals, are F$12 ($6) for a dorm bed, F$15 ($7.50) per person in bures without bathrooms, and F$30 (F$15) single, F$50 ($25) double in European cottages with bathroom, and F$8 ($4) per person for campsite (bring your own tent). Transportation is by Emosi's Express Shipping (see "Getting There & Getting Around" in chapter 8).

Caqueli Island (pronounced Than-*kay*-lee) also has camping and primitive bures. Owned by the local Methodist church, it's more peaceful and a lot more restrained than Leleuvia (keep your tops on, ladies). Rates are F$28 ($14) per person in bures, F$25 ($12.50) in dorms, and F$20 ($10) camping, including meals. Book at the Royal Hotel (☎ **440024**).

Lost Island, or Yanuca Taitai, is large enough for bush walks ("hikes" in American English) by guests who go for the day. It's run by villagers who prepare lovo-style lunches on a beach, provided five or more guests attend. Inquire at Ovalau Tours & Transportation (☎ **440611**) at least a day in advance.

DIVING, SNORKELING & KAYAKING

Ovalau Watersports, P.O. Box 149, Levuka, Ovalau (☎ **440611**; fax 440405; www.owlfiji.com; e-mail dive@owlfiji.com), at Ovalau Tours & Transportation on Beach Street next to the Community Centre, offers scuba diving, teaches PADI courses, and has kayak tours. Operators Nobi and Andrea Dehm are German natives who have lived and dived in Fiji since the late 1980s. They have discovered several shipwrecks in and near Levuka, but their dive sites also include choice soft-coral spots on the Wakaya Reef. Two-tank dives cost F$120 ($60), including tanks and weights. Full gear rents for F$20 ($10) per day. Snorkeling trips cost F$30 ($15) including gear. Ask for kayak prices.

ACCOMMODATIONS IN LEVUKA

Ovalau Tours & Transportation, P.O. Box 149, Levuka, Ovalau (☎ **440611**; fax 440405; www.ecotoursfiji.com; e-mail mtb@soholidays.com), puts guests up in the **Sailors' Home,** a restored colonial-era clapboard house on a hill overlooking the harbor. Two of its three spacious bedrooms have the view from windows whose tropical-style shutters fold out. The house has two bathrooms with showers, a full kitchen, and a dining room. It costs F$99 ($49.50) double, F$16.50 ($8.25) for each additional person.

Mavida Guest House. P.O. Box 4, Levuka, Ovalau (Beach St.). ☎ **440477.** 5 units (none with private bathroom), 21 dorm beds. F$12–F$15 ($6–$7.50) per person in rooms, F$8 (F$4) dorm bed. Rates include cooked breakfast. No credit cards.

Rosie Patterson of the Patterson Brothers Shipping family owns these two late 19th-century clapboard cottages, both of which have charming, enclosed veranda rooms with long rows of double-hung windows facing the lagoon across Beach Street. There's a covered patio between them for lounging. One house has private rooms, some with antique beds whose mosquito nets sweep down from seven-foot-tall headboards. The other has 21 beds jammed into every possible position in its rooms, none of them private. All guests share bathrooms and a communal kitchen. Dinners are available at a very reasonable F$6 ($3) per person.

Old Capitol Inn II. P.O. Box 90, Levuka, Ovalau (Beach St.). ☎ **440013.** 9 bunks, 6 units (none with bathroom). F$12 ($6) single, F$24 ($12) double; F$8 ($4) dorm bed. Rates include cooked breakfast. No credit cards.

This simple clapboard house on Beach Street is popular with backpackers, who congregate in the pleasant sun room facing the lagoon across Beach Street. Equipped with a double or two single beds, the rooms all flank a central hallway leading to a communal kitchen, bathroom, and showers.

Ovalau Resort. P.O. Box 113, Levuka, Ovalau (3km [2 miles] north of town). ☎ **440329.** Fax 440019. 5 bungalows. F$99 ($49.50) double. No credit cards.

This basic bungalow-style accommodation sits in a coconut grove beside Ovalau's only beach, albeit a rocky one. It has five bungalows with kitchens. There's nothing tropical about them, being constructed and furnished in a New Zealand style. There's a swimming pool to make up for lack of swimming at the beach. A charming restaurant-bar offering ordinary Western and Indian fare occupies an old whaler's cottage on the property.

✪ **Royal Hotel.** P.O. Box 47, Levuka, Ovalau (Beach St.). ☎ **440024.** Fax 440174. E-mail: royal@is.com.fj. 21 units (all with private bathroom). F$33 ($16.50) double; F$55–F$77 ($27.50–$38.50) per cottage. No credit cards.

This ancient establishment rates a star not for its accommodation but as an attraction, for even if you don't stay at the South Pacific's oldest operating hotel, have a look at its public rooms. It was built about 1852 and "modernized" in the 1890s (except for stringing an electric light to each room and installing toilets and showers, little has been done to it since). Not much imagination is required to picture W. Somerset Maugham or Robert Louis Stevenson relaxing in the comfortable rattan chairs of the Royal's charming lounge, slowly sipping gin-and-tonics at its polished bar, or playing a game of snooker at its antique billiard table. One of Levuka's fine old families, the Ashleys, has run the Royal for more than half a century with such attentive care that it seems more like a pension full of antiques than a hotel. The 14 rooms in the original building are very basic, with two cot-like single beds, a shower stall, and toilet. In contrast, four Western-style cottages between the old structure and Beach Road were built in 1998 and have more modern amenities (they are the pick of Levuka's lodgings). Two of the hotel's three older but still comfortable cottages are the island's only air-conditioned digs. The Ashleys serve three meals a day in the dining room, but book in advance.

DINING IN LEVUKA

Cafe Levuka. Beach St., middle of town. No phone. Reservations not accepted. Breakfast F$3–F$6 ($1.50–$3), sandwiches F$2.50–F$6 ($1.25–$3), dinners F$4.50–F$10 ($2.25–$5). No credit cards. Mon–Sat 8am–2pm and 6–9pm. REGIONAL.

This little storefront cafe is the only place in town to get rid of the hunger pangs after you've missed breakfast to catch the morning flight from Suva. The "California special" breakfast includes muesli (the antipodean name for granola), yogurt, fresh fruit, juice, and coffee. Both locals and visitors head for the Whale's Tale (see below) for lunch and dinner.

Whale's Tale Restaurant. Beach St., middle of town. ☎ **440235.** Reservations not accepted. Breakfast F$4.50–F$6 ($2.25–$3); sandwiches and snacks F$3.50–F$6.50 ($1.75–F$3.25); dinner F$6–F$12.50 ($3–$6.25). No credit cards. Mon–Sat 11am–3pm and 5–8pm. REGIONAL.

Australian Julia Ditrich, daughter Liza, and Fijian partner Susana Rakala renovated one of Beach Street's old storefronts and opened this cramped but pleasant place. You can get a late breakfast or a lunch of sandwiches, burgers, omelets, quiches, and daily specials. At night they put cloths on the tables and offer three-course meals from a chalkboard menu, which always includes a vegetarian selection.

11 Northern Fiji

The pristine islands of Northern Fiji are what the old South Seas are all about. Compared to relatively developed Viti Levu, Vanua Levu and Taveuni take us back to the old days of copra planters, of Fijians living in small villages in the hills or beside crystal-clear lagoons.

The rolling plains of northern Vanua Levu, the country's second-largest island, are devoted to sugarcane and are of little interest to anyone who has visited Nadi. But on Vanua Levu's south side, rugged mountains drop to coconut plantations, to an old trading town with the sing-song name Savusavu, and to villages where smiling people go about life at the ageless pace of tropical islands everywhere. And on Taveuni, Fiji's lush "Garden Isle," with the country's largest population of indigenous plants and animals, things are even more like they used to be.

The north is where visitors come to experience the natural wonders of Fiji—to "eco-tour" in today's vogue terminology. It's also where they come for some of the world's best scuba diving, for the strong currents in and around the Somosomo Strait between Vanua Levu and Taveuni feed a vast collection of colorful soft corals. Other South Pacific locations have more abundant sea life, but Northern Fiji is unsurpassed for coral viewing. Diving here is at its best from late May through October, when visibility reaches 120 feet and more. Because of the strong currents, however, dives to the outer reefs can be strenuous any time of the year.

1 Savusavu

A spine of volcanic mountains runs lengthwise down the center of Vanua Levu, trapping moisture from the prevailing southeast trade winds and giving the rolling hills and deltas of the north shore an ideal climate for growing sugarcane. Consequently, the area around the predominantly Indian town of **Labasa** is one of Fiji's prime sugar-producing regions.

On the south coast, the usually cloud-topped mountains quickly give way to narrow, well-watered coastal plains, ideal for copra plantations. Until the Great Depression of the 1930s, copra production made picturesque **Savusavu** a thriving European settlement. Savusavu is Vanua Levu's major sightseeing attraction, primarily because of its volcanic hot springs and magnificent scenic harbor—a bay so large and well protected by surrounding mountains that the U.S. Navy chose it as a possible "hurricane hole" for the Pacific Fleet during World War II.

By now I was drowsy; the warm air blowing freely through the windowless bus brought smells of flowers, damp earth, and copra-drying fires, that seemed to blend and thicken as the day lengthened and colours became enriched.
—Ronald Wright, 1986

The town of Savusavu sits snugly behind a small island in the southeastern corner of Savusavu Bay. The paved Cross-Island Road from Labasa runs along the eastern shore, through town, and out to **Lesiaceva Point** at the end of a peninsula forming the southern side of the bay and protecting it from the Koro Sea. The **Hibiscus Highway** starts at Savusavu and cuts south across the hilly peninsula to the airport before continuing along the south shore to Buca Bay. This rough road is neither a highway nor lined with hibiscus (cows grazing beneath the palms ate them all), but it does run along a picturesque, island-dotted lagoon through the heart of Vanua Levu's copra region. The coastal plain here primarily is a raised limestone shelf, which means that the reef is shallow and that the beaches pale in comparison to the magnificent white sands on Taveuni (see section 3, below).

Vanua Levu's southern coast has Fiji's largest concentration of freehold land, which Americans have been buying in recent years. Consequently, you're likely to meet more "Yanks" here than in any other part of Fiji.

GETTING THERE
Air Fiji and **Sunflower Airlines** fly from both Nadi and Suva to Savusavu. Their flights between Nadi and Taveuni usually stop here briefly in each direction. The tiny Savusavu airport is on Vanua Levu's south coast. The hotels send buses to meet guests who have reservations. You can also fly here via **Charter Pacific** (☎ 850430; e-mail hotspringshotel@is.com.fj), which is based in Savusavu.

Adventurous travelers can make a 2-day trip all the way from Viti Levu to Taveuni without flying. First comes a bus-ferry trip from Suva or Nadi to Nabouwalu on Vanua Levu. From there, buses connect to Savusavu via the Cross-Island Road, a sightseeing excursion in its own right. From Savusavu, a bus goes to Buca Bay on Vanua Levu's eastern end, where a small ferry crosses the Somosomo Strait to Waiyevo on Taveuni.

See "Getting There & Getting Around" in chapter 8 for more information.

GETTING AROUND
Some 30 **taxis**—an incredible number for such a small place—gather by the market in Savusavu when not hauling passengers. **Hot Springs Taxis** (☎ 850226) are radio dispatched. The cars of **Shiu Taxis** (☎ 850624) are in reasonably good condition. Fares from Savusavu are F$2 ($1) to the airport, F$5 ($2.50) to Namale Resort, and F$5 ($2.50) to the Cousteau Fiji Islands Resort on Lesiaceva Point.

Avis (☎ 800/230-4898 or 850911), **Budget** (☎ 800/527-0700 or 850700), **Thrifty** (☎ 800/367-2277 or 850256), and **Kahn's** (☎ 850580) have car-rental agencies in Savusavu. If you rent a car on Vanua Levu, bear in mind that even the few paved roads can be washed out during heavy rains, and that gasoline stations exist only in Labasa and Savusavu.

Local buses fan out from the Savusavu market to various points on the island. Most of them make three or four runs a day to outlying destinations, but ask the drivers when they will return to town. The longest runs should cost no more than F$6 ($4), with local routes in the F55¢ to F$1 (28¢ to 50¢) range.

You can rent **mountain bikes** from **Eco Divers-Tours** (☎ **850122**), in the Copra Shed in town. They cost F$10 ($5) for half a day, F$20 ($10) for a full day.

FAST FACTS: SAVUSAVU

The following facts apply to Savusavu. If you don't see an item here, check the Fast Facts in chapter 8.

Currency Exchange   **Westpac Bank, ANZ Bank,** and **National Bank of Fiji** have offices on the main street.

Dentist   See "Hospital" below.

Doctor   The nearest private practitioners are in Labasa.

Drugstores   See "Hospital" below.

Emergencies   Phone **000.**

Information   Visitor information is posted on the walls of the Copra Shed on the main street.

Hospitals   The government hospital (☎ **850800**) is east of town in the government compound.

Police   The police station (☎ **850222**) is east of town.

Post Office   The post office is on the main street near the east of the downtown commercial district. Open Monday through Friday 8am to 1pm and 2 to 5pm.

Safety   Savusavu generally is a safe place to visit, but don't tempt the mortals. Keep an eye on your personal property.

Telephone/Telegrams   Go to the post office. There's a phonecard public phone in the Copra Shed. **Eco Divers-Tours** in the Copra Shed (☎ **850122**) has fax and other business services.

EXPLORING SAVUSAVU

For practical purposes, there is only one street in Savusavu, and that runs along the shore for about a mile. The modern **Copra Shed,** an old warehouse that has been turned into modern shops and a cafe, stands about midway along the shore. It and the **market** are the centers of activity.

Highlights of a stroll along the bay-hugging avenue are the gorgeous scenery and the volcanic **hot springs.** Steam from underground rises eerily from the rocky beach on the west end of town, and you can see more white clouds floating up from the ground between the sports field and the school, both behind the Shell station. A concrete pot has been built to make a natural stove in which local residents place meals to cook slowly all day. Overlooking the springs and bay, the **Savusavu Hot Springs Hotel** has great views (see "Accommodations," below).

Curly and Liz Carswell of ❂ **Eco Divers-Tours,** P.O. Box 264, Savusavu (☎ **800/ 599-5507** or 850122; fax 850344; www.bulafiji.com/ecodiver; e-mail ecodivers@is. com.fj), whose office is in the Copra Shed, arrange not only diving (see below) but accommodation and excursions on Vanua Levu. Originally from New Zealand, Curly and Liz have lived in Savusavu for many years and are now Fiji citizens. They have put their knowledge of the area to work on a series of tours and excursions. One goes to Naidi village, on the Hibiscus Highway, for a look at traditional Fijian lifestyles, while another takes you to a copra and beef plantation, where you can see the modern-day version of the old South Seas coconut plantation. Either of these costs F$20 ($10) per person. Another trip goes to Waisali Rainforest Reserve, a 116-hectare (290-acre) national forest up in the central mountains; the trip includes a visit to a waterfall. It costs F$40 ($20). They have a full-day tour to Labasa for F$90 ($45) per person.

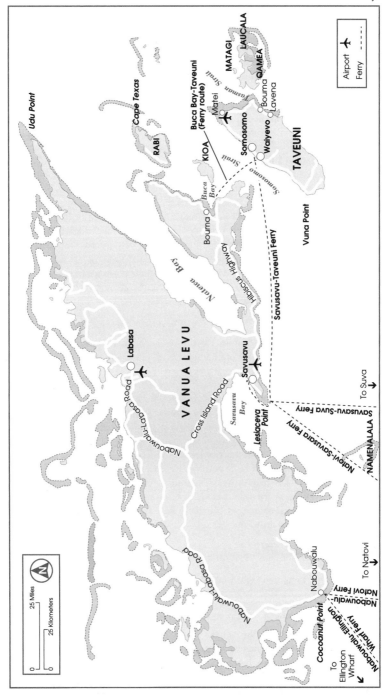

Udu Point

Cape Texas

RABI

MATAGI
LAUCALA
QAMEA

Bouma
Lavena

Matei

Buca Bay-Taveuni
(Ferry route)

KIOA

Somosomo
Waiyevo

TAVEUNI

Tasman Strait

Somosomo Strait

Vuna Point

Buca Bay

Bouma

Natewa Bay

Hibiscus Highway

Savusavu-Taveuni Ferry

VANUA LEVU

Labasa

Nabouwalu-Labasa Road

Cross Island Road

Savusavu

Savusavu Bay

Lesiaceva Point

To Suva →

Savusavu-Suva Ferry

Natovi-Savusavu Ferry

NAMENALALA

Nabouwalu-Labasa Road

Nabouwalu

To Natovi →

Nabouwalu-Natovi Ferry

Coconut Point

Nabouwalu-Ellington Wharf Ferry

To Ellington Wharf ↓

Airport ✈
Ferry ----

N

25 Miles
0

25 Kilometers
0

DIVING, KAYAKING & OTHER WATER SPORTS

Most of the resorts have complete diving facilities, as noted in "Accommodations," below. A very long boat ride is required to dive on the Rainbow Reef and Great White wall, which are more easily reached from Taveuni (see below). But that's not to say that there aren't plenty of colorful reefs near here, including the wonderful barrier formation nearly encircling Moody's Namena (see "A Resort of Savusvau," below).

Your one-stop shop here is the environmentally conscious **Eco Divers-Tours,** P.O. Box 264, Savusavu (☎ **800/599-5507** or 850122; fax 850344; www.bulafiji.com/ecodiver; e-mail ecodivers@is.com.fj), in the Copra Shed. In addition to their land-based excursions (see "Exploring Savusavu," above), Curly and Liz Carswell offer diving, kayak rentals and trips, and sailboat rentals. Two-tank dives cost F$118 ($59), with a third dive of the day for F$76 ($38). They use many of the same buoyed sites as the Jean-Michel Cousteau Fiji Island Resort. Full equipment rental is available, and they teach PADI certification courses. Snorkeling trips to colorful reefs offshore start at F$15 ($7.50) per person if four or more people go. The price goes up to F$25 ($12.50) per person for only two people. For kayakers, they offer six-day paddling excursions to Fijian villages along the northern and western coasts of Savusavu Bay. You'll stay in the villages and dine with the villagers, so consider these to be "soft adventure" excursions. The trips cost F$700 ($350) per person, based on groups of six paddlers. You can rent the single- and double ocean kayaks when they aren't on expedition, starting at F$10 ($5) and F$15 ($7.50), respectively, for 1 hour. The Carswells will also arrange waterskiing.

Day- and sunset trips are available on the *Monki,* a 50-foot sailboat based here. Contact the Savusavu Hot Springs Hotel (see "Accommodations," below). Day sails cost F$15 ($7.50) per person, including a picnic lunch; sunset cruises go for F$25 ($12.50) per person, including cocktails.

You can also contact the Savusavu Hot Springs Hotel (see "Accommodations," below) for deep-sea fishing, which costs US$400 for half a day, US$600 for a full day.

The gray-sand beaches around Savusavu aren't the reason to come here. The nearest beach to town is a shady stretch on Lesiaceva Point just outside the Jean-Michel Cousteau Fiji Islands Resort, about 5 kilometers (3 miles) west of town, which is the end of the line for west-bound buses leaving Savusavu market. There also is a half-moon beach at Naidi Bay, an extinct volcanic crater, just west of Namale Resort on the Hibiscus Highway. The road skirts the bay, but the beach is not easy to see. Take a taxi or ask the bus driver to let you off at Naidi Bay—not Naidi village or nearby Namale Resort. The bar and restaurant at Namale Resort are not open to walk-in customers, so bring something to drink and eat.

ACCOMMODATIONS
RESORTS

✪ **Jean-Michel Cousteau Fiji Islands Resort.** Post Office, Savusavu (Lesiaceva Point, 5km [3 miles] west of town). ☎ **800/246-3454** or 850188. Fax 850340. www.jmcfir.com. E-mail: jmcfir@aol.com. 25 units. MINIBAR. US$405–US$625. Rates include meals, airport transfers, and all activities except scuba diving. AE, MC, V.

This joint venture between the deluxe Post Ranch Inn of Big Sur, California, and Jean-Michel Cousteau, son of the late Jacques Cousteau, looks like an old-time Fijian village set in a flat palm grove beside the bay on Lesiaceva Point. This "environmentally correct" resort is one of the best places in the South Pacific to bring young children, since kids under 9 years old are *required* to participate in a "Bula Camp" educational activities program that will keep them busy during most of their waking moments.

The compulsory programs cost F$77 ($38.50) per child per day, including all their food and activities plus a nanny for each family.

The large, comfortable bures are built to one side of two central buildings, in which reception and the resort's bar are under a large roof built like a chief's bure. The dining room is covered by a taller and more impressive roof constructed to resemble a priest's bure. These two areas, joined for the convenience of guests, sit next to a deck-surrounded swimming pool just steps from one of the best beaches in the area. The luxurious thatch-roof bures have ceiling fans to augment the natural breezes flowing through floor-to-ceiling wooden jalousie windows that make up the front and rear walls. Most have king beds with wicker headboards, bent-rattan recliners with ottomans, desks, wardrobes trimmed with reeds, coffeemakers, porches strung with hammocks, and spacious bathrooms with dual sinks, biodegradable soaps and toiletries, and showers and toilets in a separate room. Some newer, split-level units are more spacious and better equipped for families, with two day beds in addition to the regular king.

Amenities: There is a host of water sports activities available here, including snorkeling, kayaking, and sailing, but the emphasis is on environmentally oriented activities such as visits to rain- and mangrove forests. An on-site marine biologist gives lectures and leads bird-watching expeditions and visits to Fijian villages. Scuba diving is with guides skilled in marine biology. The resort has a custom-built dive boat capable of reaching the famous Namena Reef, which surrounds Moody's Namena (see "A Resort off Savusavu," below), in about 1 hour. There's also a swimming pool, children's program (see above), restaurant, and bar.

✪ **Namale Resort.** P.O. Box 244, Savusavu (Hibiscus Highway, 7 miles east of town). ☎ **800/727-3454** or 850435. Fax 850400 or 619/535-6385 in the U.S. www.namalefiji. com. E-mail: namale@aol.com. 10 units. MINIBAR. US$575–US$675. Rates include meals, bar, and all activities except scuba diving. AE, MC, V.

Owned by toothy American motivational author and speaker Anthony Robbins, who spends about 2 months a year here and often closes the resort to outsiders while he uses it to conduct his seminars, this luxury hotel sits on a narrow headland jutting out into Naidi Bay. The rest of the property has been a working copra plantation since the 1860s, when an Englishman bought it from the local chief for 10 guns. Sitting on the headland, the main building has a soaring thatch Fijian-style bure, which covers the bar, dining area, and library.

The thatch-roof guest bures are widely scattered in the blooming tropical gardens surrounding the main building, thus affording honeymoon-like privacy if not a setting directly on the beach (this area has been geologically uplifted, so all buildings are on a shelf 10 feet to 20 feet above sea level). The stars here are 4 honeymoon bures, personally designed by Robbins' wife, Becky, with lots of romance and comfort in mind. Their four-poster bamboo beds are stacked high with down-filled pillows, or the two of you can curl up on over-size recliners while looking out your big glass doors to the lagoon beyond your private deck fringed with palms and frangipani. Steps lead down to bathrooms with whirlpool tubs, separate showers with indoor and outdoor entrances, thick towels and robes, and their own ceiling fans. The six older bures are less spectacular, but they are attractively appointed with rosewood floors, rattan furniture, and tropical spreads and drapes. Although the windows in all units are screened, the staff drops romantic mosquito nets over the beds at turndown. No smoking is allowed in the bures.

Dining: Reflecting Robbins' culinary likes, the chef prepares vegetarian as well as fish and meat dishes. Guests can dine inside the main building, but most meals are taken on a deck commanding an excellent view from the point jutting out into the bay.

Amenities: Facilities here include a swimming pool, a tennis court, an air-conditioned gym (Robbins is an avid body-builder), basketball and volleyball courts, a wide range of water sports equipment, and a fully equipped dive shop with instructor.

✪ **Savusavu Hot Springs Hotel.** P.O. Box 208, Savusavu (in town). ☎ **850195.** Fax 850430. E-mail: hotspringshotel@is.com.fj. 48 units, 24 dorm beds. A/C TEL. F$80–F$125 ($40–$62.50) double, F$20 ($10) dorm bed. AE, DC, MC, V.

Once a Travelodge, this 3-story hotel overlooking Savusavu Bay has been completely renovated by Tim and Lorna Eden, who were born and bred in Fiji (he's a former Air Pacific pilot; she's related to the Douglases of Matagi Island Resort off Taveuni). The structure sits on a hill in town, and its motel-style rooms take advantage of the view by having sliding glass doors opening to balconies. All motel-style with combination tub-shower bathrooms, units on the third and fourth floors are air conditioned and have phones; less expensive rooms on the second floor are equipped with ceiling fans and lack phones. Six rooms have four dorm beds each.

The tile-floored lobby, seafood restaurant, and bar open to a partially above-ground pool, which also shares the great view. There's a TV lounge, small gym, and library for guests to use, plus a boutique and beauty salon. This isn't a fancy establishment, but it's clean, comfortable, friendly, and very good value. There should be an e-mail computer terminal by the time you arrive.

HOSTELS

David's Budget Savusavu Holiday House. P.O. Box 65, Savusavu (in town behind Shell station). ☎ **850216** or 850149. 6 units (none with private bathroom), 8 dorm beds. F$19 ($9.50) double, F$9.30 ($4.65) dorm bed, F$6 ($3) per person camping. Rates include tax and breakfast. No credit cards.

Former Savusavu Mayor David Lal has clean and totally unpretentious rooms with table fans, two nightstands, coffee tables, and screened windows. Guests share the communal kitchen, toilets, and showers. The dormitory is in a separate building, and guests can pitch their tents in the yard. David will arrange pig hunts and guided hikes. If the house and dorm are full, you can pitch a tent in the yard. Airport transfers are free for stays of 5 days or longer, and you get a 10% discount and free laundry if you stay a week or more.

DINING

Savusavu may someday have some fine restaurants outside its resorts, but for now the choices are extremely limited. There are a few basic Chinese joints and curry shops scattered among the shops in the business district.

In the Copra Shed, **Captain's Cafe** (☎ 850511) is a pleasant place for an outdoor meal, with seating inside or outside on a deck over the bay. The name and nautical decor may be misleading, however, for when I was there only fish and chips came from the briny deep. Other offerings were sandwiches, burgers, side salads, garlic bread, and reasonably good pizzas. Fish, burgers, and sandwiches cost from F$3 to F$5.50 ($1.50 to $2.75). The pies range from F$6 to F$20 ($3 to $10). Open Monday through Saturday from 8am to 8:30pm.

ISLAND NIGHTS IN SAVUSAVU

The expensive resorts provide nightly entertainment for their guests. Otherwise, there's not much going on in Savusavu after dark. Visitors are welcome at the **Planter's Club** (☎ 850233) in a clapboard building near the west end of town. This friendly holdover from the colonial era has a snooker pool table and a pleasant bar. It's open Monday to Saturday from 10am to 10pm. Closed Christmas and Good Friday. Admission is free (bona fide visitors are asked to sign in). **Savusavu Yacht Club** (no phone), a favorite expatriate gathering spot in the Copra Shed, also welcomes visitors. It's open Monday through Saturday from noon to 10pm and Sunday from 10am to 10pm.

2 A Resort off Savusavu

Back in the 1970s, Pennsylvanians Tom and Joan Moody (she pronounces her name "Joanne") opened a small, isolated resort in Panama's San Blas Islands, catering to serious scuba divers and others who just wanted a total escape. Terrorists attacked their peaceful outpost in 1981, however, shooting and nearly killing Tom and tying Joan up. Fortunately, Tom survived, but they soon sold out and left Panama. After searching the South Pacific, they settled on dragon-shaped Namenalala, little more than a rocky ridge protruding from the Koro Sea about 20 miles south of Vanua Levu and covered with dense native forest and bush. The huge Namena barrier reef sweeps down from Vanua Levu and creates a gorgeous lagoon in which Tom can indulge his passion for diving. The Moodys have designated most of Namenalala as a nature preserve in order to protect a large colony of boobies that nest on the island, and sea turtles that climb onto the beaches to lay their eggs from November through February. In other words, the setting is remote and interesting. So is their unique little resort:

✪ **Moody's Namena.** Private Mail Bag, Savusavu. ☎ 813764. Fax 812366. www. bulafiji.com/moodys.htm. E-mail: moodysnamena@is.com.fj. 6 units. US$172 per person. Rates include meals, nonalcoholic beverages, wine at dinner, all activities except scuba diving. MC, V. Closed Feb–Mar.

The Moodys perched all but one of their comfortable bungalows up on the ridge so that each has a commanding view of the ocean but not of one another. Each of the hexagonal structures resembles a treehouse; in fact, the huge trunk of a tree grows right through the balcony surrounding one of the bures. Surely this was how Robinson Crusoe would have preferred to live. A lack of fresh ground water adds to the effect. The "his and her" toilets in each bungalow are flushed with seawater, and rainwater takes care of drinking and bathing. The entire walls of the bungalows slide back to render both views and cooling breezes, so you will sleep under a mosquito net. Instead of treading sandy paths among palm trees, you climb rocky pathways along the wooded ridge to the central building, where the Moodys provide excellent meals and ice upon which to pour the booze you bought at the duty-free store. They serve wine with dinner and can sell beer and wine at their cost, but they do not have a liquor license. After 1 day in their care, these hardships matter not at all.

Lazing on the beaches, hiking, kayaking, swimming, snorkeling, deep sea fishing, and scuba diving among the colorful reefs and sea turtles are the main activities here. Tom does not teach scuba diving, so you must be certified in advance.

The Moodys will have you brought out from Savusavu on a fast fishing boat, a voyage of 1½ hours, or arrange to charter a Turtle Island Airways' seaplane for the 1-hour flight from Nadi. The one-way fare is F$264 ($132) per person.

3 Taveuni

Cigar-shaped Taveuni, Fiji's third-largest island, lies just 4 miles from Vanua Levu's eastern peninsula across the Somosomo Strait, one of the world's most famous scuba-diving spots. Although the island is only 6 miles wide, a volcanic ridge down Taveuni's

They passed the kava cups around and drank deep of the milky, slightly stupefying grog. They chatted quietly under the starlight. They laughed, one would propose a song, and then they would break into chorus after chorus, in perfect harmony, of some of the great Fijian folk songs, songs that told of sagas of long ago and far away, and always of war and peace, of love, and of triumph over disaster.

—Simon Winchester, 1990

40-kilometer (25-mile) length soars to more than 1,200 meters (4,000 feet), blocking the southeast trade winds and pouring as much as 30 feet of rain a year on the mountaintops and the island's rugged eastern side. Consequently, Taveuni's 9,000 residents (three-quarters of them Fijians) live in a string of villages along the gently sloping, less rainy but still lush western side. They own some of the country's most fertile and well-watered soil—hence Taveuni's nickname: "The Garden Isle."

Thanks to limited land clearance and the absence of the mongoose found in such profusion on the cane-growing islands, Taveuni still has all the plants and animals indigenous to Fiji, including the unique Fiji fruit bat, the Taveuni silktail bird, land crabs, and some species of palm that have only recently been identified. The **Ravilevu Nature Preserve** on the east coast and the **Taveuni Forest Preserve** in the middle of the island are designed to protect these rare creatures.

Taveuni's most famous sight is **Lake Tagimaucia,** home of the rare tagimaucia flower that bears red blooms with white centers. A shallow lake whose sides are ringed with mud flats and thick vegetation, it sits among the clouds in a volcanic crater at an altitude of more than 800 meters (2,700 feet).

Bouma Falls are among Fiji's finest and most accessible, and the area around them is now an environmental park. Past Bouma at the end of the road, a coastal hiking track begins at **Lavena** village and runs through the Ravilevu Nature Reserve.

Fiji's last governor-general and first republican president, the late Ratu Sir Penaia Ganilau, called Taveuni's **Somosomo** village his home, thus making it Fiji's most "chiefly" village. A big meeting house here is the prime gathering place of Fiji's Great Council of Chiefs.

The main village of **Waiyevo** sits halfway down the west coast. A kilometer (0.5 mile) south, a brass plaque marks the **180th Meridian** of longitude. This would have been the international date line were it not for its slicing of the Aleutians and Fiji in two and for Tonga's wish to be on the same day as Australia. The village of **Waikiki** sports both a "Meridian Cinema" and a lovely 19th-century Catholic mission built to reward a French missionary for helping the locals defeat a band of invading Tongans.

In stark contrast to the rest of unspoiled Taveuni, the paved roads, uninhabited condominiums, and often shaggy golf course of **Soqulu Plantation** south of Waikiki stand as a reminder that not all real estate developments work. A few expatriates have homes here, but the project never really got off the ground in the 1980s.

Off Taveuni's northeastern end are the small, rugged islands of **Qamea, Matagi,** and **Laucala,** homes of three very fine offshore resorts.

GETTING THERE & GETTING AROUND

Both **Air Fiji** and **Sunflower Airlines** fly to Taveuni from Nadi, and Air Fiji has non-stop service from Nausori Airport near Suva. Taveuni's airport is at its northern tip. The hotels send buses or hire taxis to pick up their guests.

The ferries land—and most commerce takes place—at Waiyevo. The **Patterson Brothers Shipping Company's** *Yabula* ferry (☎ 850161 in Savusavu) runs across the

Somosomo Strait between Waiyevo and Buca Bay on Vanua Levu. A bus connects Savusavu to the ferry wharf at Buca Bay.

For more information, see "Getting There & Getting Around" in chapter 8.

Taxis don't regularly ply the roads. The only taxi stand is outside Lesuma Supermarket in Waiyevo. Your hotel staff can hail one within a few minutes, or you can call ☎ **880705,** 880442, or 880424. Negotiate for a round-trip price if you're going out into the villages and having the driver wait for you. None of the taxis have meters, but the fare from the airport to Navakoca (Qamea) Landing should be about F$12 ($6); to Dive Taveuni, F$2 ($1); to Waiyevo, F$15 ($7.50); and to Bouma, F$18 ($9). Taxis will take you anywhere and back for about F$15 ($7.50) an hour.

Local **buses** fan out from Waiyevo to the outlying villages about three times a day from Monday through Saturday. For example, one of them leaves Waiyevo for Bouma at 8:30am, 12:15pm, and 4:30pm. The one-way fare to Bouma is no more than F$2 ($1). Contact **Pacific Transport** (☎ **880278**) opposite Kaba's Supermarket in Nagara, the predominantly Indian village next to Somosomo.

Budget (☎ **800/527-0700** or 880233), in Kaba's Supermarket, Nagara, rents jeeps and sedans. The island's only road is paved between Waiyevo and the airport, but elsewhere it's rough, winding, narrow, and at places carved into sheer cliffs above the sea. Also, many local drivers—including bus drivers—roar along at top speed. There can be very little room to get off the road to avoid them. If you want to risk your life, rent a car. I hire a taxi and driver.

FAST FACTS: TAVEUNI

The following facts apply to Taveuni. If you don't see an item here, see "Fast Facts: Fiji" in chapter 8.

Currency Exchange   **National Bank of Fiji** has an office at Waiyevo (☎ **880433**), but it won't make cash advances against your credit or bank card. The hotels will cash traveler's checks.

Doctor   See "Hospital" below.

Emergencies   Phone **000.**

Hospitals   The government hospital (☎ **880222**) is in the government compound in the hills above Waiyevo. To get there, go uphill on the road opposite the Garden Island Resort, then take the right fork.

Police   The police station (☎ **880222**) is in the government compound.

Post Office   It's in the government compound (see "Hospital," above).

Safety   Taveuni is relatively safe, but exercise caution if out late at night.

Telephone/Telegrams   See "Post Office," above. There are phonecard public phones at the market in Waiyevo, opposite the Garden Island Resort (see "Accommodations," below), and at Bhula Bhai Store in Matei.

FISHING, HIKING, DIVING & OTHER OUTDOOR PURSUITS

The hotels and resorts can arrange sightseeing tours to all of the sights mentioned in the introduction to this section, but tourism here is devoted to outdoor activities.

FISHING   New Zealander Geoffrey Amos of **Matei Game Fishing** (☎ **880371**) will take you deep-sea fishing on his 36-foot *Lucky Strike,* based opposite Maravu Plantation Resort (see "Accommodations," below). Call for rates and reservations.

HIKING   One attraction on everyone's list is the ✪ **Bouma Falls,** in the Bouma Environmental Tourism Project on Taveuni's northeastern end, 18 kilometers (11 miles) from the airport, 37 kilometers (23 miles) from Waiyevo. The government of New Zealand provided funds for the village of Bouma to build trails to the three levels of the falls. It's a flat, 15-minute walk along a road bed from the visitor center to the lower falls, which plunge some 180 meters (600 feet) into a broad pool. From there, a trail climbs sharply to a lookout with a fine view of Qamea and as far offshore as the Kaibu and Naitoba islands east of Taveuni. The trail then enters a rain forest to a second falls, which are not as impressive as the lower cascade. Hikers must ford slippery rocks across a swift-flowing creek while holding onto a rope (a sign says BEST WAIT FOR FLOOD—it means don't cross during a flood). This 30-minute muddy climb can be made in shower sandals, but be careful of your footing. A more difficult track ascends to yet a third falls, but I've never followed it, and people who did have told me it wasn't worth the effort. Another trail, the **Vidawa Forest Walk,** leads to historic hill fortifications and more great views. Guides lead full day treks through the Vidawa Forest on Friday, but you'll need to book at your hotel activities desk or call the visitor center (☎ **880390**) at least a day in advance. The guided treks cost F$60 ($30) per person, including transfers to the park, juice, lunch, and afternoon tea. The park is open daily from 8am to 5pm. Admission is F$5 ($2.50) per person. See "Getting Around," above, for information about how to get here.

At the end of the road past Bouma, the village of Lavena is on one of Taveuni's best beaches. From there, the **Lavena Coastal Walk** runs for 5 kilometers (3 miles) along the coast, then climbs to **Wainibau Falls.** The last 20 minutes or so of this track are spent walking up a creek bed, which can be flooded during heavy rains. The creek water is safe to drink, but you might want to bring your own supplies. Admission to the village and walking track is F$5 ($2.50) per person.

Another track leads to **Lake Tagimaucia,** home of the famous flower that blooms from the end of September to the end of December. This crater lake is surrounded by mud flats and filled with floating vegetation. Beginning at Somosomo village, the hike to the lake takes about 8 hours round-trip. The trail is often muddy and slippery, and given the usual cloud cover hanging over the mountains by mid-morning, you're not likely to see much when you reach the top. Only hikers who are in shape should make this full-day trek, and then only with a guide. An alternative is to take a four-wheel-drive vehicle up Des Voeux Peak for a look down at the lake. The drive is best done early in the morning when the mountain is less likely to be shrouded in clouds. The Garden Island Resort (see "Accommodations," below) will make arrangements for a guide or vehicle.

SAILING   American Paul Negro will take one couple at a time around the islands on his 45-foot luxury catamaran *Nabuk,* which he has based in Taveuni after sailing out from California. A 3-night minimum cruise is required, at US$980 per couple, including meals. Seven-night cruises cost US$6,860. You'll get the owner's quarters, with queen-size bed and "head" equipped with freshwater shower.

۞ SCUBA DIVING   The swift currents of the Somosomo Strait feed the soft corals on the Rainbow Reef and the White Wall between Taveuni and Vanua Levu, making them two of the world's most colorful and famous scuba-diving sites. The Rainbow Reef is only 4 miles off Waiyevo, so the Garden Island Resort is the closest dive base, with Dive Taveuni second closest. In addition to the operators mentioned here, Matagi, Qamea, and Fiji Forbes resorts off Taveuni (see below) specialize in diving equally great locations off Taveuni's eastern end.

Because of the strong currents, dives on Taveuni's most famous sites must be timed according to the tides. Accordingly, you can't count on making the dives you want if the tides are wrong when you're here. A very good friend of mine spent 10 days in the area and never did get to the Rainbow Reef.

The closest operator to the Rainbow Reef and Great White Wall, both a 20-minute boat ride across the Somosomo Strait from Waiyevo, is **Aqua-Trek** (☎ **800/541-4334** or 880286; fax 880288 or 415/398-0479 in the U.S.; www.aquatrek.com; e-mail garden@is.com.fj or info@Aqua-Trek.com), part of an American dive company which owns the Garden Island Resort (see "Accommodations," below). This 5-star PADI operation has full equipment rental, E-6 film processing, and NITROX, and teaches courses from beginner to dive master. Aqua-Trek's prices start at US$82 for a two-dive excursion. PADI learn-to-dive courses cost US$330.

A bit farther away but still in range is ✪ **Dive Taveuni Resort** (see "Accommodations," below), where Ric Cammick runs two dives a day to the Rainbow Reef, White Wall, and other spots around Taveuni at a cost of US$95 a day. Bring your own regulators, wet suits, masks, fins, and snorkels. He supplies the weight belts, backpacks, and tanks.

At Beverly Camping (near the airport, Dive Taveuni Resort, and Maravu Plantation Resort), Tania de Hoon of **Aquaventure Taveuni** (☎ and fax 880381; www. aquaventure.org; e-mail aquaventure@is.com.fj) charges F$115 ($57.50) for a two-tank dive, with discounts for three or more dives. Weather permitting, Tania dives the Rainbow Reef every day. She teaches PADI open-water courses for F$478 ($239).

SWIMMING, SNORKELING & KAYAKING   Since Taveuni is a relatively new island in geological terms, it doesn't have a great number of good swimming beaches. But the few it has are first-rate. The best is at Lavena village at the far end of the north shore road (see "Hiking," above). More convenient places to swim and snorkel are **Prince Charles Beach** and the lovely, tree-draped **Beverly Beach,** both south of the airport.

But beware: The waters off Taveuni are notorious for sharks, so don't swim out to the edge of the reef.

Aqua-Trek (see "Scuba Diving," above) has snorkeling trips to Korolevu, a rocky islet off Waiyevo, for F$20 ($10) per person, plus F$11 ($5.50) for gear rental. The company will even take you snorkeling out to the Rainbow Reef, but book these trips well in advance.

One of the most popular things to do on Taveuni is to rent a kayak and paddle out to the three little rocky islets sitting off the north shore, near the airport. The reefs here are great to snorkel over, provided that kelp from the nearby seaweed farms isn't drifting by. You can land on the islands for a picnic. **Coconut Grove Beachfront Cottages & Restaurant** (☎ **880328**), opposite the airport, rents two-person ocean kayaks for F$30 ($15) half day, F$55 ($27.50) all day. Owner Ronna Goldstein will prepare a picnic lunch if you give her advance notice. You can also rent kayaks at **Beverly Campground** (☎ **880381**), from where Kenny Madden leads paddling excursions.

At Waiyevo, the **Garden Island Resort** (see "Accommodations," below) rents kayaks for F$11 ($5.50) an hour or F$44 ($22) per day. From there, you can paddle out to Korolevu, a rocky islet off Waiyevo.

The Garden Island Resort (see "Accommodations," below) can arrange trips out to **Korolevu,** a rocky island in the Somosomo Strait off Waiyevo.

ACCOMMODATIONS
RESORTS

Dive Taveuni Resort. Postal Agency Matei, Taveuni (1.5km [1 mile] south of airport). ☎ **880441.** Fax 880466. www.divetaveuni.com. E-mail: divetaveuni@divetavenuni.com. 7 units. A/C MINIBAR. US$249–US$295 per person. Rates include meals.

New Zealanders Ric and Do Cammick, who helped pioneer scuba diving here, have seven bungalows dotting the lawn surrounding their home, which commands a magnificent view of Somosomo Strait from a bluff high above the water. Their property is directly across the road from Maravu Plantation Resort (see below). You can sip a drink from the bar while taking in the view from the veranda of a central building, which also houses a dining room providing hearty meals. Six of the units here are hexagonal bungalows with side wall windows letting in the view and the breeze (plans were to air condition all units, but ask to make sure). The most stunning view of all is from the spacious deck of the honeymoon bure—or you can sit up and take in the vista from its king-size bed, or even from its outdoor shower. One deluxe unit has a separate bedroom. All units have outdoor showers, ceiling fans, and minibars. There's a swimming pool out on the lawn.

✪ **Garden Island Resort.** P.O. Box 1, Waiyevo, Taveuni (Waiyevo village, 7 miles south of airport). ☎ **880286.** Fax 880288. www.aquatrek.com. E-mail: garden@is.com.fj. 28 units, 8 dorm beds. A/C TEL. US$84 double room, US$15 dorm bed. AE, MC, V.

Built as a Travelodge motel in the 1960s, this hotel has been renovated by its owners, the San Francisco–based dive company Aqua-Trek, which has its Taveuni base here. Most of the guests here are divers, since this is the closest hotel to the White Wall and Rainbow Reef, but the friendly staff and managers welcome everyone. The motel-style rooms have queen and single beds, tropical-style chairs and desks, refrigerators, coffeemakers, balconies or patios facing the Somosomo Strait, and bathrooms with combo tubs-showers. All but the two rooms used as dormitories are air conditioned (the dorms have ceiling fans).

Opening to a strait-side swimming pool (there's no beach here), the dining room serves meals, which always include vegetarian selections, at reasonable prices. Guests and outsiders can rent kayaks and go on snorkeling trips to Korolevu islet offshore and even to the Rainbow Reef (book well in advance for this excursion). Fijians play island music in the evenings and stage a meke once a week.

Maravu Plantation Resort. Post Office, Matei, Taveuni (1km [0.5 mile] south of airport). ☎ **888/234-5447** or 880555. Fax 880600. www.maravu.com. E-mail: maravu@is.com.fj. 10 units. US$130–US$164 per person double occupancy. Rates include meals and airport transfers. AE, DC, MC, V.

Although it has its own beach across the road (it's a short walk downhill), this unusual retreat really is set among the palms of a working copra plantation (with some cocoa, coffee, and vanilla thrown in for diversification). The bures are laid out among grounds carefully planted with bananas, papayas, and a plethora of ginger plants and wild orchids brought down from the mountains. There's a sandy beach in a coconut grove across the road (a 5-minute walk), but this plantation setting means the property can get warm and humid during the day. Built like old-fashion planter's houses rather than Fijian bures, the guest bures have thatch-covered tin roofs and reed or mat accents to lend a tropical ambiance. You'll also have hardwood floors, a fridge, tea/coffee-making facilities, mosquito nets over your bed, a ceiling fan to kick up a breeze, and a front porch for lazing. Three units have outdoor showers surrounded by private sundecks behind rock walls.

Dining: Serving fine food, the dining room is under the high thatch roof and looks out to the lawns and a swimming pool surrounded by an expansive deck. Nonguests should call ahead for dinner reservations.

Amenities: There's a boat for fishing excursions and overnight camping trips to other islands, and mountain bikes for exploring Taveuni. Owner Jochen Kiess, a former German lawyer, and will require you to sign a legal release before engaging in any activities.

HOSTELS

Don't forget the dormitory at the Garden Island Resort (see above).

Tovu Tovu Resort. Postal Agency, Matei, Taveuni (0.5 mile east of airport). ☎ **880560.** Fax 880722. 4 bungalows, 8 dorm beds. F$65–F$75 ($32.50–$37.50) bungalow, F$15 ($7.50) dorm bed. AE, MC, V.

Spread out over a lawn across the road from the lagoon, Alan Petersen's simple bungalows have front porches, reed exterior walls, Linoleum-covered floors, standing fans, and bathrooms with hot-water showers. Two of them also have cooking facilities. The dorm building sits on a hill, but a fine sea view from up there is your compensation for not being closer to the beach. The Vunibokoi Restaurant is here (see "Dining," below).

COTTAGE RENTALS

In addition to Taveuni's resorts, hostel, and campgrounds, visitors can rent modern cottages complete with kitchens from three Americans who live near the airport. This is a gorgeous area, with views through the palms of the island-studded sea. Maravu Plantation Resort, Dive Taveuni, and Tovu Tovu Resort are all nearby, and it's easy to rent canoes and kayaks to visit the offshore islets.

Ronna Goldstein of **Coconut Grove Beachfront Cottages & Restaurant** (☎ and fax **880328;** www.coconutgrovefiji.com; e-mail coconutgrove@is.com.fj) has two bures set above a beach next to her restaurant, which is named for her hometown in Florida (see "Dining," below). With its interior walls made of rough-hewn mango timber, her "Mango" cottage sits by itself and has a terrific view from its front porch. Its bathroom opens to an outdoor shower, and it has a small kitchen. The Mango bure costs US$95 a day. Actually in front of but below the restaurant, Ronna's smaller "Papaya" bure lacks a kitchen but still has a sea view. It goes for US$75 a night. Inside and actually behind the restaurant, her "Guava" room has a king- and two twin beds, a ceiling fan, and its own bathroom with shower. It costs US$55 a night. She accepts MasterCard and Visa credit cards. Ronna's property slopes down to a beach.

Audrey Brown of **Audrey's By the Sea** (☎ **880039**) has a Western-style, hexagonal bungalow next to her own home on 14 acres of tropical gardens. The cottage has a kitchenette, a separate bedroom, and a bathroom with hot-water shower. Audrey charges F$105 ($52.50) a night but does not accept credit cards.

The mailing address of both is Postal Agency Matei, Taveuni.

CAMPING

You'll get a fabulous view from **Todranisiga,** Postal Agency, Matei, Taveuni (☎ and fax **8880381**), about 0.5 km (0.25 mile) south of the airport, where owner May Goulding has four large "permanent" tents sitting on a lawn overlooking the Somosomo Strait. There are great sunsets from up here, too ("Todranisiga" means "Blaze of Sun" in Fijian). May is a native of Fiji and a hospitality industry veteran, having spent 18 years helping manage Toberua Island Resort off Suva (see "Resorts Offshore from Suva" in chapter 10). Her tents have white sand foundations, big screened windows, and double-size inflatable beds. Guests share showers, toilets, and a kitchen. Guests pay F$12.50 per ($6.25) person. No credit cards.

Campers who like to sleep by the sea can find a beautiful (if not insect-free) site at **Beverly Campground** (☎ 880381), on Beverly Beach about 1.5 kilometers (1 mile) south of the airport (Maravu Plantation Resort's beach is next door). Large trees completely shade the sites and hang over portions of the lagoon-lapped shore. The ground has flushing toilets, cold-water showers, and a rudimentary beachside kitchen. Per person rates are F$10 ($5) in the bures or for a site with rental tent, F$6 ($3) for a tent site if you bring the tent. The campground rents kayaks.

Lisi's Camping (☎ **880194**) nearby has two bures made of leaves and tent sites in the large lawn surrounding Lisi's home, in which backpackers and campers can share the toilets, cold-water showers, and kitchen. The property is across the road from a beach. Rates there are F$25 ($12.50) for the bures, F$10 ($5) per person for camping. Bring your own tent. Meals are available.

DINING

The following places won't serve you gourmet fare, but their views and friendly hosts will make for a pleasant dining experience.

Beginning opposite the airport, **Coconut Grove Beachfront Cottages & Restaurant** (☎ **880328**), is where American Ronna Goldstein and Gracie, her friendly Doberman, hold fort. Ronna offers a variety of local seafood dishes, Thai and Fijian curries (try the fish), and homemade pastas. She serves breakfast and lunch (salads, soups, burgers, sandwiches, and grilled lamb chops). Dining is on Ronna's front porch, which has a great view of the little islands off Taveuni, making it a fine place to wait for a flight. Order some of Ronna's banana bread for breakfast. Main courses range from F$10 to F$19 ($5 to $9.50). Open daily from 8am to 5pm and 6 to 9pm, but dinner reservations are required by 4pm. Ronna accepts MasterCard and Visa credit cards. She closes the restaurant from mid-January to mid-April.

Walking east along the road, **Audrey's Sweet Somethings** (☎ **880039**) really isn't a restaurant but American Audrey Brown's front porch. Audrey is known as Taveuni's best baker, and she offers her pastries, cakes, and Fiji coffees for F$6 ($3) per serving. Open daily from 10am to 6pm. Audrey takes no credit cards.

Walk a little farther along the road and you'll come to **Vunibokoi Restaurant,** on the front porch of the main house at Alan Petersen's Tovu Tovu Resort (☎ **880560**). Here you can get breakfast, lunch, or dinner, with a blackboard menu featuring good Fijian and Western fare. Main courses run F$6.50 to F$15 ($3.25 to $7.50). Open daily from 8am to 2pm and 6 to 9pm. American Express, MasterCard, and Visa cards accepted.

In Waiyevo just south of the Garden Island Resort (see "Accommodations," above), the **Cannibal Cafe** (☎ **880382**) is a great place to sit and have a cold beer under a thatch roof beside the Somosomo Strait. The food is plain local fare—curry, chop suey, fish and chips—at F$4 to F$5.50 ($2 to $2.75) a plate. Go through Wathi Pokee Restaurant to reach the cafe. Open Monday through Saturday 7:30am to 8pm, Sunday 11am to 8pm. No credit cards.

4 Resorts Offshore from Taveuni

The northern end of Taveuni gives way to a chain of small, rugged islands that are as beautiful as any in Fiji. Their steep, jungle-clad hills drop to rocky shorelines in most places, but here and there little shelves of land and narrow valleys are bordered by beautiful beaches. The sheltered waters between the islands cover colorful reefs, making the area a hotbed of scuba diving and snorkeling. Except for a few Fijian villages and the three resorts that follow, these little gems are undeveloped and unspoiled.

Fiji Forbes' Laucala Island. P.O. Box 9952, Nadi Airport (Laucala Island, 25 min. by boat from Taveuni). ☎ **719/379-3263** in the U.S. or 880077. Fax 880099 or 719/379-3266 in U.S. E-mail: mpacheco@forbes.com. 7 bungalows. A/C (bedrooms only) MINIBAR TEL. US$2,495 per person per week. Rates include room, food, bar, all activities except scuba-diving instruction. No credit cards on island; must be prepaid. Minimum 4-night stay required. Transfers US$255 per person round-trip.

The late publisher Malcolm S. Forbes, Sr., bought 3,000-acre Laucala Island in 1974 and grew to love it so much that his ashes are buried there. Guests can visit the crypt, use the swimming pool outside his hilltop home, and enjoy the stunning, 360° view of Laucala and surrounding islands and reefs. Laucala is a plantation worked by Fijians who live in a modern village Forbes built for them. In fact, the ambiance here is more like being a plantation house guest than a customer at a resort. The 1920s clapboard planter's home serves as a gathering place for guests, who live in comfortable one- or two-bedroom bungalows scattered in a coconut grove beside a beach.

Dining/Diversions: Staff members prepare breakfasts in the bungalows' kitchens. Lunches are served picnic-style at various points (such as a ridge top retreat overlooking the islands or a unique tree house perched above its own private beach). Dinners are taken in the plantation home.

Amenities: There are no planned activities; guests are on their own to use a wide range of playthings, such as fishing boats and canoes. They can go scuba diving and on hiking and bird-watching expeditions. Swimming pool, tennis court, gift shop, wide range of water sports, laundry, baby-sitting, nightly turndown.

✪ **Matagi Island Resort.** P.O. Box 83, Waiyevo, Taveuni (Matagi Island, 20 min. by boat from Taveuni). ☎ **888/MATANGI** or 880260. Fax 880274. www.matagiisland.com. E-mail: matagiisland@is.com.fj. 12 units. MINIBAR. US$140–US$244 per person. Rates include all meals, nonalcoholic beverages, and all excursions and activities except scuba diving, water-skiing, and sport fishing. Round-trip transfers from Taveuni airport US$40 per person. AE, DC, MC, V.

It's unfortunate that geography places this resort next to last in my coverage of Fiji, for Matagi is one of the best values in the South Pacific—which is one reason it's also one of the most popular (book *early*, for it's usually full). Another reason is owners Noel and Flo Douglas. Of English-Fijian descent, Flo's family owns all of hilly, 260-acre Matagi, a horseshoe-shaped remnant of a volcanic cone, where in 1987 they built their resort in a beachside coconut grove on the western shore (gorgeous sunset views of Qamea and Taveuni). At first they catered to low-budget Australian divers, but as their business grew, their clientele shifted to a mix of diving and non-diving Americans, plus a few Australians and Europeans. For divers who bring their children, the Douglases send the grown-ups out in the boats for two morning dives, while the staff keeps the kids busy building sand castles on the shady beach. This arrangement makes Matagi one of the South Pacific's top family resorts. But by the same token, honeymooners can escape to two romantic bures 20 feet up in the air, one of them actually in a shady Pacific almond tree, or can be taken to a half-moon beach in aptly named Horseshoe Bay for a secluded picnic. Other nondiving activities include hiking, kayaking, bird watching, sailing, and windsurfing.

Except for the honeymoon bures, Matagi's bungalows are round, in the Polynesian-influenced style of eastern Fiji. Umbrellalike spokes radiating from hand-hewn central poles support reed-lined conical roofs. Reed dividers separate sitting areas with single bed-settees from sleeping areas to the rear of the units. Although somewhat small, the tiled shower-only bathrooms are adequate. All of the units are furnished in island styles and have round, thatch-roof front porches. One bure is equipped for disabled guests. They don't have phones, but there's a phonecard unit outside the office.

Dining/Diversions: Guests dine in a new central building under a 60-foot high conical thatch roof. The menus are limited, but the staff will cater to all tastes on request. Staff members entertain at night.

Amenities: World-famous scuba diving (for which guests pay extra); E-6 film processing on site; wide range of water sports equipment; laundry; baby-sitting; nightly turndown; massage.

✪ **Qamea Beach Resort.** P.O. Matei, Taveuni (Qamea Island, 15 minutes by boat from Taveuni). ☎ **800/392-8213** or 880220. Fax 880092. www.qamea.com. E-mail:

qamea@is.com.fj. 12 units. MINIBAR. US$520–US$600 double. Rates include meals, airport transfers, nonmotorized water sports. AE, DC, MC, V. No children under 13.

This is another property I regret coming to last, for American Jo Kloss has some of the most stunning bures and main building of any resort in Fiji, and the value-for-dollar here is excellent. In the proverbial coconut grove, this entire property shows remarkable attention to American-style comfort and Fijian detail. Qamea's centerpiece is a soaring, 52-foot-high priest's bure supported by two huge tree trunks. Rope made of coconut fiber and some well-disguised nuts and bolts hold the poles and sweeping thatch roof together. Orange light from kerosene lanterns hung high under the roof lends incredibly romantic charm at twilight, when you wash your bare feet in giant clam shells and then sit on the surrounding veranda to sip cocktails and recap your days of scuba diving, snorkeling, visiting Fijian villages, trekking to the Bouma Falls on Taveuni, or doing absolutely nothing except sleeping in your own hammock.

You will relive the old South Seas days and nights in my favorite of all Fijian bures. If I were to build a set for a South Seas movie, it would feature these bungalows covered by a foot-thick layer Fijian thatch. Spacious and rectangular, they have old-fashioned screen doors leading out to a porch complete with hammocks strung between two posts. Reed-lined, each bure is large enough to swallow the king-size bed, two over-size bamboo sitting chairs, a coffee table, and several other pieces of island-style furniture exquisitely handcrafted by the staff. If you need more space, a new split-level villa has a living room, separate room with a king-size bed draped with a mosquito net, a huge bathroom with separate tub and shower, and a front porch with lagoon view.

While Matagi gets its share of children, nearby Qamea is aimed at couples, accepting no children under 13 years old.

Dining/Diversions: Gourmet-quality meals are served in the big central bure, as is silver-service afternoon tea. The staff entertains several nights a week, including a Fijian meke dance show. Three tables are set aside for honeymooners to dine in relative privacy.

Amenities: Swimming pool; snorkeling gear, Hobie Cats, canoes for free; guests pay extra for scuba dives and lessons. Laundry, turndown.

Samoa 12

The scenic 19-mile drive from Faleolo Airport into the historic capital of Apia provides a fitting introduction to Samoa. Here in this cultural storehouse, which until 1997 was officially known as Western Samoa, the old Polynesian lifestyle known as *fa'a Samoa*—The Samoan Way—remains very much alive and well. On one side of the road lies an aquamarine lagoon; on the other, coconut plantations climb gentle slopes to the volcanic ridge along the middle of Upolu, the main island. Along the shore sit hundreds of Samoan *fales* (houses), their big turtle-shaped roofs resting on poles, their sides open to the breeze and to the view of passersby. Their grass carefully trimmed and their borders marked with boulders painted white, expansive village lawns make the entire route seem like an unending park. Samoans wrapped in *lavalavas* shower under outdoor faucets and sit together in their fales. Only the dim glow of television screens coming from beneath tin roofs rather than thatch remind us that a century has passed since Robert Louis Stevenson lived, wrote, and died here in Samoa.

Even the town of Apia harkens back to those bygone South Seas days. While landfills have extended the shoreline, government highrises now stand on the waterfront, and traffic lights blink at several corners, many old white clapboard buildings still sleep along Beach Road, just as they did when Stevenson stepped ashore here in 1889. Compared with the hustle and bustle of Papeete in French Polynesia, or with the congestion and tuna canneries of Pago Pago in nearby American Samoa, life in Apia is slow and easy.

If you go with an eye to exploring the culture as well as visiting some of the South Pacific's most beautiful and undeveloped beaches, Samoa will enchant you just as it did Stevenson, W. Somerset Maugham, and Margaret Mead, all of whom found plenty here to write home about.

Advice: Although American ways have made a serious impact in neighboring American Samoa (see chapter 13), the people there share fa'a Samoa with their relatives here in Samoa. Much of the background information in this chapter, therefore, applies equally to both countries. American Samoa suffers a serious lack of accommodation, while Samoa is blessed with comfortable and charming hotels and two first-class beach resorts. Even if you plan to visit American Samoa, I recommend you stay here and treat American Samoa as a day trip from Apia.

1 Samoa Today

The Samoa Islands, which include independent Samoa and the territory of American Samoa, stretch for some 480 kilometers (300 miles) across the central South Pacific, some 2,000 kilometers (1,200 miles) west of Tahiti and 4,000 kilometers (2,600 miles) southwest of Hawaii. Samoa has the nine western islands; the others are in American Samoa.

Independent Samoa's nine islands have a land area of 2,800 square kilometers (1,090 square miles), two-thirds of which are on **Savai'i,** the largest Polynesian island outside Hawaii and New Zealand. A series of volcanoes on a line running roughly east to west formed **Upolu,** which is about 63 kilometers (39 miles) long and 21 kilometers (13 miles) wide, or about the size of Tahiti. Although it's considerably smaller than Savai'i, 21 kilometers (13 miles) to the west, some 75% of Samoa's population lives on Upolu. On the other hand, Savai'i in many ways is the most "old Polynesia" of any island covered in this book; there are no towns there, and the villagers live very much by fa'a Samoa.

Apolima and **Manono,** the tops of two small volcanoes, sit in the Apolima Strait between the two main islands. Locals like to claim that James A. Michener was inspired by Apolima and Manono to create the mysteriously romantic island of "Bali Ha'i" in his *Tales of the South Pacific.* Michener once said in a television interview, however, that he got the idea from a cloud-draped island off Espiritu Santo in Vanuatu, where he spent much of World War II.

GEOGRAPHY   With few exceptions, all of the Samoa Islands are high and volcanic, lush, and well watered. Geologically they are younger than the islands in French Polynesia—volcanoes on Savai'i erupted as recently as 1911. Consequently, the islands are fringed with coral reefs that have had time to enclose few deep lagoons; the surf pounds directly on black volcanic rocks in many places. In others there are small bays with some of the most picturesque beaches in the South Pacific.

GOVERNMENT   An independent nation since 1962, Samoa is ruled by a Parliament made up of 47 members, of whom 45 are *matais,* or chiefs. Only matais could vote for candidates for these seats until 1991, when universal suffrage was enacted. The other two members are elected by non-Samoans living in the country. There are two political parties: the Human Rights Protection party and the Christian Democratic party.

The titular head of state is Malietoa Tanumafili II, one of Samoa's four paramount chiefs and a descendant of the Malietoa who sided with the Germans in 1887–89 during the lead-up to western Samoa's becoming a German colony in 1890 (see "History 101," below). Malietoa Tanumafili II will hold the job for life, which in effect makes Samoa a constitutional monarchy. Under the constitution, Parliament will choose his successor from among Samoa's four paramount chiefs. That person will serve not for life but for a term of 5 years.

THE ECONOMY   Samoa exports copra (dried coconut meat), coconut cream, kava, fresh fish, and beer (try a German-style Vailima brew while you're here). There is some light manufacturing, including cigarettes, but the industrial sector is in its infancy. Furthermore, the country's exclusive fishing zone is one of the smallest in the Pacific. Only foreign aid and remittances sent home by Samoans living in American Samoa or overseas keep the country out of bankruptcy.

As a consequence, Samoa's currency (the *tala)* remains seriously devalued. Local hotels, car-rental firms, and some tour operators quote their rates in U.S. dollars to avoid the "price shocks" if their prices were quoted in local currency. Although high by local standards, most prices here are among the least expensive in the South Pacific for travelers using U.S. dollars.

A majority of the work force is employed by the government. Even in those jobs, wages are so low that several thousand Samoans regularly live and work in the much more prosperous American Samoa.

2 History 101

Archaeologists believe that Polynesians settled in the Samoan Islands about 3,000 years ago from Southeast Asia. Their great migration halted here for some 1,000 years before voyagers went on to colonize the Marquesas, Society, and other island groups farther east in the great triangle known today as Polynesia. Thus the Samoas are known as the "Cradle of Polynesia."

The universe known by the early Samoans included Tonga and Fiji, to which they regularly journeyed, often waging war. Tongan invaders ruled the Samoas for some 300 years between A.D. 950 and A.D. 1250.

The first European to see the Samoas was Dutchman Jacob Roggeveen, who in 1722 sighted the Manu'a Islands in what is now American Samoa. After visiting Tahiti in 1768, the Frenchman Antoine de Bougainville sailed through the Samoas and named them the Navigator Islands because of the natives he saw in canoes chasing tuna far offshore. The first Europeans to land in Samoa were part of a French expedition under Jean La Pérouse in 1787. They came ashore on the north coast of Tutuila in American Samoa and were promptly attacked by Samoan warriors. Twelve members of the landing party and 39 Samoans were killed during the skirmish.

To the Samoans, the great ships with their white sails seemed to have come through the slit that separated the sky from the sea, and they named the strange people sailing them *papalagi*, "sky busters." Shortened to *palagi*, the name now means any Westerner with white skin.

The Rev. John Williams, who roamed the South Pacific in *The Messenger of Peace*, discovering islands and preaching the Gospel, landed the first missionaries in Samoa in 1830. Shortly afterward came traders— including John Williams, Jr., the missionary's son. European-style settlements soon grew up at Apia on Upolu and on the shores of Pago Pago Harbor on Tutuila. By the late 1850s German businessmen had established large copra plantations on Upolu. When steamships started plying the route between San Francisco and Sydney in the 1870s, American businessmen cast an eye on Pago Pago. The U.S. Navy negotiated a treaty with the chiefs of Tutuila in 1872 to permit the U.S. to use Pago Pago as a coaling station. The U.S.

Dateline

- **3,000 B.C.** Polynesians arrive from the west, settle the Samoa Islands.
- **2,000 B.C.** Samoans venture south and west, colonize Tonga, Marquesas, Society, and other island groups.
- **A.D. 950** Tongans invade, conquer Samoans, and rule until 1250.
- **1722** Dutch explorer Jacob Roggeveen is first European to sight the Samoan Islands.
- **1768** After finding Tahiti, de Bougainville sails through the Samoas but does not land; names them the Navigator Islands.
- **1787** Thirty-nine Samoans and 12 members of French exploring team under Jean La Pérouse killed during skirmish at Massacre Bay on Tutuila in American Samoa.
- **1830** Rev. John Williams lands first missionaries at Leone on Tutuila, American Samoa. European-style settlements soon established at Apia and Pago Pago.
- **1850s** Germans start plantations on Upolu.
- **1872** American Navy negotiates treaty with Tutuila chiefs for American coaling station at Pago Pago.
- **1887** German residents on Upolu stage a coup, set off an argument between U.S., Britain, and Germany.
- **1888** Ousted chief Mataafa leads bloody rebellion at Apia but loses to German-backed chief Malietoa.

continues

- **1889** Warships arrive at Apia to back claims of Western powers; hurricane sinks four, drives two aground, kills 146 sailors. Treaty of Berlin is negotiated and signed. Robert Louis Stevenson settles in Apia.
- **1890** Treaty goes into effect giving Samoa to Germany, Eastern Samoa to U.S., free hand in Tonga to Britain.
- **1894** Robert Louis Stevenson dies at Vailima, his home above Apia; is buried at end of the "Road of the Loving Hearts."
- **1900** Germany officially establishes colony of Samoa, raises its flag at Apia. U.S. negotiates treaty with Tutuila chiefs to cede their island; U.S. flag raised at Pago Pago.
- **1905** Chief of Manu'a finally cedes his islands to the U.S., completing American possession of Eastern Samoa.
- **1914** New Zealand expeditionary force seizes Samoa from Germany at outbreak of World War I, confiscates German lands.
- **1920** League of Nations establishes New Zealand trusteeship over Samoa.
- **1929** New Zealand constables put down Mau rebellion, killing nine Samoans. U.S. Senate ratifies treaties of 1900 and 1905 turning Eastern Samoa over to U.S.
- **1942–45** Allied troops use both Samoas as training bases for World War II battles in central and southwestern Pacific. Aggie Grey starts her hot dog and hamburger business in Apia.
- **1949** New Zealand creates local legislative assembly in Apia, grants Samoa limited internal self-government.
- **1951** U.S. government transfers administration of

continues

Congress never ratified this document, but it served to keep the Germans from penetrating into Eastern Samoa, as present-day American Samoa was then known.

THE GERMANS TAKE OVER   Meanwhile, German, British, and Americans jockeyed for position among the rival Samoan chiefs on Upolu, with the Germans gaining the upper hand when they staged a coup in 1887, backed up (unofficially) by German naval gunboats. They governed through Malietoa, one of the island's four paramount chiefs, who had thrown in his lot with them. One of his rivals, Mataafa, lost a bloody rebellion in 1888, during which heads were taken in Samoan style. Mataafa subsequently was exiled to the German Marshall Islands.

Continuing unrest turned into a major international incident—fiasco is a better word—when the U.S., Britain, and Germany all sent warships to Apia. Seven vessels arrived, anchored in the small and relatively unprotected harbor, and proceeded to stare down each other's gun barrels. It was March 16, 1889, near the end of the hurricane season. When one of the monster storms blew up unexpectedly, only the captain of the British warship *Calliope* got his ship under way. It was the sole vessel to escape. In all, four ships were sunk, two others were washed ashore, and 146 lives were lost despite heroic efforts by the Samoans on Upolu, who stopped their feuding long enough to pull the survivors through the roaring surf. Of the three American warships present, the *Trenton* and the *Vandalia* were sunk, and the *Nipsic* was beached. Another beached ship, the Germans' *Adler,* rested half-exposed until the reef was covered by landfill 70 years later. (A newspaper story of the time is mounted in the lounge of Aggie Grey's Hotel in Apia.)

Cooler heads prevailed after the disaster, and in December 1889 an agreement was signed in Berlin under which Germany was given Samoa, the U.S. was handed the seven islands to the east, and Britain was left to do what it pleased in Tonga (it created a protectorate). After many years of turmoil, the two Samoas were split apart and swept into the colonial system.

The German flag was raised in Apia on March 1, 1900, after which several stern governors sent more of Mataafa's followers and other resisters into exile. Malietoa remained as the chosen chief, and the Germans residing in Samoa proceeded to make fortunes from their huge, orderly copra plantations.

A KIWI BACKWATER   German rule came to an abrupt end with the outbreak of World War I in 1914, when New Zealand sent an expeditionary force to Apia and the German governor surrendered without a fight. The Germans in Samoa were interned for the duration of the war, and their huge land holdings were confiscated. The plantations are still owned by the Samoa Trust Estates Corporation (WSTEC), a government body whose name you will see all over the country.

New Zealand remained in charge until 1962, first as warlord, then after World War I as trustee, initially under the League of Nations and then under the United Nations. The New Zealand administrators did relatively little in the islands except keep the lid on unrest, at which they were generally successful. In 1929, however, the Mau Movement under Tupua Tamasese Lealofi III created an uprising. The movement was crushed when the New Zealand constables fired on Tamasese and a crowd of his followers gathered outside the government building in Apia, killing him and eight others.

Twenty years later, after opposition to colonialism flared up in the United Nations, a Legislative Assembly of matais was established to exercise a limited degree of internal self-government. A constitution was drafted in 1960, and the people approved it and their own independence a year later by referendum (the only time until 1991 that all Samoans could vote). On January 1, 1962, Samoa became the first South Pacific colony to regain its independence from the Western powers.

American Samoa from Navy to Interior Department.
- **1960** Samoans vote for independence, draft a constitution.
- **1961** *Reader's Digest* criticizes American Samoa as "America's Shame in the South Seas." U.S. aid starts flowing to Pago Pago.
- **1962** Samoa becomes first South Pacific colony to gain independence.
- **1977** American Samoans choose first locally elected governor.
- **1990** First of two hurricanes devastate crops, destroy roads.
- **1991** Second hurricane hits; universal suffrage comes to Samoa after 30 years of only chiefs voting for Parliament.

For most of its life as a colony and trusteeship territory, Samoa remained in the backwaters of the South Pacific. Only during World War II did it appear on the world stage, and then solely as a training base for thousands of Allied servicemen on their way to fight the Japanese in the islands farther west and north. Tourism increased after the big jets started landing at Pago Pago in the early 1960s, but significant numbers of visitors started arriving only after Faleolo Airport was upgraded to handle large aircraft in the 1980s.

3 The Samoan People

About 110,000 people live in Samoa, the vast majority of them full-blooded Samoans. They are the second-largest group of pure Polynesians in the world, behind only the Maoris of New Zealand.

Although divided politically in their home islands, the people of both Samoas share the same culture, heritage, and, in many cases, family lineage. Despite the inroads that Western influences have made—especially in American Samoa—they are a proud people who fiercely protect their old ways.

"Catch the bird but watch for the wave" is an old Samoan proverb that expresses the basically cautious approach followed in the islands. This conservative attitude is perhaps responsible for the extraordinary degree to which Samoans have preserved fa'a Samoa while adapting it to the modern world. Even in American Samoa, where most of the old turtle-shaped thatch fales have been replaced with structures of plywood and tin, the firmament of the Samoan way lies just under the trappings of the territory's commercialized surface.

The Teller of Tales

The salvage crews were still working on the hulks of the British, American, and German warships sunk in Apia's harbor by a hurricane in 1889 when a thin, tubercular writer arrived from Scotland.

Not yet 40 years old, Robert Louis Stevenson was already famous—and wealthy—for such novels as *Treasure Island* and *Dr. Jekyll and Mr. Hyde.* He arrived in Samoa after traveling across the United States and a good part of the South Pacific in search of a climate more suitable to his ravaged lungs. With him were his wife, Fanny (an American divorcée 11 years his senior), his stepmother, and his stepson. His mother joined them later.

Stevenson intended to remain in Apia for only a few weeks while he caught up on a series of newspaper columns he was writing. He and his entourage stayed to build a mansion known as Vailima up on the slopes of Mount Vaea, overlooking Apia, where he lived lavishly and wrote more than 750,000 published words. He learned the Samoan language and translated into it "The Bottle Imp," his story about a genie. It was the first work of fiction translated into Samoan.

Stevenson loved Samoa, and the Samoans loved him. Great orators and story-tellers in their own right, they called him Tusitala, the "Teller of Tales."

On December 3, 1894, almost 5 years to the day after he arrived in Apia, Stevenson was writing a story about a son who had escaped a death sentence handed down by his own father and had sailed away to join his lover. Leaving the couple embraced, Stevenson stopped to answer letters, play some cards, and fix dinner. While preparing mayonnaise on his back porch, he suddenly clasped his hands to his head and collapsed. He died not of tuberculosis but of a cerebral hemorrhage.

More than 200 grieving Samoans hacked a "Road of the Loving Hearts" up Mount Vaea to a little knoll below the summit, where they placed him in a grave with a perpetual view overlooking Vailima, the mountains, the town, the reef, and the sea he loved. Carved on his grave is his famous requiem:

This be the verse you grave for me:
Here he lies where he longed to be;
Home is the sailor, home from the sea,
And the hunter home from the hill.

THE AIGA

The foundation of Samoan society is the extended family unit, or *aiga* (pronounced "ah-eeng-ah"); unlike the Western family, it can include thousands of relatives and in-laws. In this basically communal system, everything is owned collectively by the aiga; the individual has a right to use that property but does not personally own it. As stated in a briefing paper prepared for the government of American Samoa by the Pacific Basin Development Council, "the attitude toward property is: if you need something which you don't have, there is always someone else who has what you need." This notion is at odds with Western concepts of private ownership, and visitors may notice the difference directly when a camera or other item left unattended suddenly disappears.

At the head of each of more than 10,000 aigas is a matai ("mah-tie"), a chief who is responsible for the welfare of each member of the clan. Although the title of matai

---

Impressions ────────────────────────────────

How impossible it would be for us, with our notions of so-called civilization and style, to exist in our northern city suburbs with open spaces for walls and the camouflage of the night our only privacy. Yet here it seemed the most natural thing in the world, a picture of harmony and a vivid example of what they call fa'a Samoa, the Samoan Way.
—John Dyson, 1982

---

usually follows bloodlines, the family can choose another person—man or woman—if the incumbent proves incapable of handling the job. The matai settles family disputes, parcels out the family's land, and sees that everyone has enough to eat and a roof over his or her head.

Strictly speaking, all money earned by a member of an aiga is turned over to the matai, to be used in the best interest of the entire clan. Accordingly, the system has been threatened as more and more young Samoans move to the U.S. or New Zealand, earn wages in their own right, and spend them as they see fit. Nevertheless, the system is still remarkably intact in both Samoas. Even in Samoan outposts in Hawaii, California, Texas, and Auckland (which collectively have a larger Samoan population than do the islands), the people still rally around their aiga, and matais play an important role in daily life.

As is true throughout the South Pacific, land ownership is a touchy subject. About 11% of the land here is freehold, which Samoan citizens can buy and sell. The rest is communal land held by the aigas, not by individuals. Non-Samoans can lease freehold and communal property, but they cannot buy it.

ORGANIZATION & RITUAL

Above the aiga, Samoan life is ruled by a hierarchy of matais known in English as high talking chiefs, high chiefs, and paramount chiefs, in ascending order of importance. The high talking chiefs do just that: talk on behalf of the high chiefs, usually expressing themselves in great oratorical flourishes in a formal version of Samoan reserved for use among the chiefs. The high chiefs are senior matais at the village or district level, and the paramount chiefs can rule over entire island groups. The chiefly symbol, worn over the shoulder, is a short broom resembling a horse's tail.

The conduct and relations between chiefs are governed by strict rules of protocol. Nowhere is ritual more obvious or observed than during a kava (pronounced '*ava* in Samoan) ceremony. This slightly narcotic brew is made by crushing the roots of the pepper plant *Piper methysticum* (see "A Bowl of Grog" in chapter 8). In the old days the roots were chewed and spit into the bowl by the virgin daughter of a chief. That method of kava preparation has disappeared in the face of modern notions of disease control. Coconut shells are scooped into a large wooden bowl of the gray liquid (which tastes of sawdust) and passed around. Each participant holds out the cup, spills a little on the mats covering the floor, and says *"Manuia"* ("Good health") before gulping it down. It's all a show of respect to host and honored guest. Kava works on the lips like Novocain, which must do wonders for the conversation that follows.

Although some Samoans can become unruly after imbibing too much of potions containing not kava but alcohol, the showing of respect permeates their life. They are by tradition extremely polite to guests, so much so that some of them tend to answer in the affirmative all questions posed by a stranger. The Samoans are not lying when they answer wrongly; they are merely being polite. Accordingly, visitors who really need information should avoid asking questions that call for a yes or no answer.

Impressions

All life is to be seen on the stage of the Samoan fale. In the evening, when television sets as well as electric lights are switched on, the scene is surreal.

—Ron Hall, 1991

MISSIONARIES & MINISTERS

Like other Polynesians, the Samoans in pre-European days worshipped a hierarchy of gods under one supreme being, whom they called Le Tagaloa. When the London Missionary Society's Rev. John Williams arrived in 1830, he found the Samoans willing to convert to the Christian God. Williams and his Tahitian teachers brought a strict, puritanical Christianity. His legacy can be seen both in the large white churches that dominate every settlement in both Samoas and in the fervor with which the Samoans practice religion today.

The majority of Samoans are members of the Congregational Christian church, a Protestant denomination that grew out of the London Missionary Society's work. Samoa almost closes down on Sunday, and even in more Westernized American Samoa things come to a crawl on the Sabbath. Swimming is tolerated in both countries only at the hotels and, after church, at beaches frequented by overseas visitors.

Christianity has become an integral part of fa'a Samoa, and every day about 6:30pm each village observes *sa,* 10 minutes of devotional time during which everyone goes inside to pray, read Scripture, and perhaps sing hymns. A gong (usually an empty acetylene tank hung from a tree) will be struck, once to announce it's time to get ready, a second time to announce the beginning of sa, and a third time to announce that all's clear. It is permissible to drive on the main road during sa, but it's not all right to turn off into a village or to walk around.

Even if you can't understand the sermon, the sound of Samoans singing hymns in harmony makes going to church a rewarding experience.

MISS MEAD STUDIES SAMOAN SEX

Despite their ready acceptance of much of the missionaries' teaching, the Samoans no more took to heart their puritanical sexual mores than did any other group of Polynesians. In 1928 anthropologist Margaret Mead published her famous *Coming of Age in Samoa,* which was based on her research in American Samoa. She described the Samoans as a peaceable people who showed no guilt in connection with ample sex during adolescence, a view that was in keeping with practices of Polynesian societies elsewhere. Some 55 years later, New Zealand anthropologist Derek Freeman published *Margaret Mead and Samoa: The Making and Unmaking of an Anthropological Myth,* in which he took issue with Mead's conclusions and argued instead that Samoans are jealous, violent, and not above committing rape. The truth may lie somewhere in between.

The Samoans share with other Polynesians the practice of raising some boys as girls, especially in families short of household help. These young boys dress as girls, do a girl's chores around the home, and often grow up to be transvestites. They are known in Samoan as *fa'afafines.*

RULES OF CONDUCT

You should be aware of several other customs of this conservative society. A briefing paper prepared by the Pacific Basin Development Council for the American Samoan Office of Tourism gives some guidelines that may be helpful.

- In a Samoan home don't talk to people while standing, and don't eat while walking around a village.
- Avoid stretching your legs straight out in front of you while sitting. If you can't fold them beneath you, then pull one of the floor mats over them.
- If you are driving through a village and spot a group of middle-aged or elderly men sitting around a fale with their legs folded, it's probably a gathering of matais to discuss business. It's polite not to drive past the meeting place. If going past on foot, don't carry a load on your shoulders or an open umbrella (even if several of Pago Pago's 200 inches (500cm) of annual rainfall are pouring on you).
- If you arrive at a Samoan home during a prayer session, wait outside until the family is finished with its devotions. If you are already inside, you will be expected to share in the service. If you go to church, don't wear flowers.
- If you are invited to participate in a kava ceremony, hold the cup out in front of you, spill a few drops on the mat, say "Manuia," and take a sip. In Samoa you do not bolt down the entire cup in one gulp as you would in Fiji; instead, save a little to pour on the floor before handing back the empty cup. And remember, this is a solemn occasion—not a few rounds at the local bar.
- Whenever possible, consult Samoans about appropriate behavior and practices. They will appreciate your interest in fa'a Samoa and will take great pleasure in explaining their unique way of life.

To those guidelines, I would add: Don't wear bathing suits, short shorts, halter tops, or other skimpy clothing away from the beach or hotel swimming pool. Although shorts of respectable length are worn by an increasing number of young Samoan men and women in Apia and Pago Pago, it is considered very bad form for a Samoan to display his or her traditional tattoos, which cover many of them from knee to waist. Even though Samoan women went bare-breasted before the coming of Christianity, that is definitely forbidden today. Traditional Samoan dress is a wrap-around *lavalava* (sarong) which reaches below the knee on men and to the ankles on women.

Finally, should you be invited to stay overnight in a Samoan home, let them know at the beginning how long you will stay. Upon leaving, it's customary to give a small gift known as a *mea alofa*. This can be money—between $5 and $10 a day per person—but make sure your hosts understand it is a gift, not a payment.

Most Samoan villages charge small "custom fees" to visitors who want to use their beaches or swim under their waterfalls. These usually are a dollar or two and are paid by local residents from other villages as well as by tourists.

In all cases, remember that almost everything and every place in the Samoas is owned by an aiga, and it's polite to ask permission of the nearby matai before crossing the property, using the beach, or visiting the waterfall. They will appreciate your courtesy in doing so.

Impressions

Imagine an island with the most perfect climate in the world, tropical yet almost always cooled by a breeze from the sea. No malaria or other fevers. No dangerous snakes or insects. Fish for the catching, and fruits for the plucking. And an earth and sky and sea of immortal loveliness. What more could civilization give?
—Rupert Brooke, 1914

4 The Samoan Language

Although English is an official language in both countries and is widely spoken, Samoan shares equal billing and is used by most people for everyday conversation. It is a Polynesian language somewhat similar to Tahitian, Tongan, and Cook Islands Maori, but with some important differences.

The vowels are pronounced not as in English (*ay, ee, eye, oh,* and *you*) but in the Roman fashion: *ah, ay, ee, oh,* and *oo* (as in kanga*roo*). All vowels are sounded, even if several of them appear next to each other. The village of Nu'uuli in American Samoa, for example, is pronounced New-u-u-lee. The apostrophe that appears between the vowels indicates a glottal stop—a slight pause similar to the tiny break between "Oh-oh!" in English. The consonants *f, g, l, m, n, p, s, t,* and *v* are pronounced as in English with one major exception: the letter *g* is pronounced like "ng." Therefore, *aiga* is pronounced "ah-eeng-ah." Pago Pago is pronounced "Pango Pango" as in "pong."

Here are some words that may help you win friends and influence your hosts.

English	Samoan	Pronunciation
hello	talofa	tah-*low*-fah
welcome	afio mai	ah-*fee*-oh my
good-bye	tofa	tow-*fah*
good luck	manuia	mah-*new*-yah
please	fa'amolemole	fah-ah-*moly*-moly
man	tamaloa	tah-mah-*low*-ah
woman	fafine	fah-*fini*
transvestite	fa'afafine	fah-fah-*fini*
thank you	fa'afetai	fah-*fee*-tie
kava bowl	tanoa	tah-*no*-ah
good	lelei	lay-*lay*
bad	leaga	lay-*ang*-ah
happy/feast	fiafia	fee-ah-*fee*-ah
house	fale	fah-*lay*
wraparound skirt	lavalava	lava-lava
dollar	tala	tah-*lah*
cent	sene	say-nay
high chief	ali'i	ah-*lee*-ee
small island	motu	mo-*too*
white person	palagi	pah-lahng-ee

Many words in Samoan—as in most modern Polynesian languages—have European roots. Take the word for corned beef, *pisupo* (pee-SOO-poh). The first Western canned food to reach Samoa was pea soup. Pisupo, the Samoan version of pea soup, was adopted as the word for corned beef, which also came in cans. It was and still is much more popular than pea soup.

5 Visitor Information & Entry Requirements

VISITOR INFORMATION

The friendly staff of the **Samoa Visitors Bureau,** P.O. Box 2272, Apia, Samoa (☎ **20-878;** fax 20-886; www.samoa.co.nz; e-mail samoa@samoa.net), have free brochures and other publications available at their office in a handsome Samoan fale on the harbor side of Beach Road east of the Town Clock. They also sell an excellent map of

Samoa. The bureau's hours are Monday through Friday from 8am to noon and from 1 to 4:30pm, Saturday from 8am to 12:30pm.

The visitors bureau has offices in:

United States: 1800 112th Ave. NE, Suite 220E, Bellevue, WA 90884-2938 (☎ **425/688-8513;** fax 425/688-8514; e-mail sdsi@compuserve.com).

Australia: P.O. Box 361, Minto Mall, Minto, NSW 2566 (☎ **02/9324-5050;** fax 02/9824-5678; e-mail samoa@ozemail.com.au).

New Zealand: Level 1, Samoa House, 283 Karangahape Rd. (P.O. Box 68423), Newton, Auckland (☎ **09/379-6138;** fax 09/379-8154; e-mail samoa@samoa.co.nz).

You can also get information in advance from the **Tourism Council of the South Pacific** (see "Visitor Information & Entry Requirements" in chapter 2).

The bell captain's desk at Aggie Grey's Hotel (see "Accommodations," below) also has brochures and other information.

ENTRY REQUIREMENTS

No **visa** or entry permit is required for visitors who intend to stay 30 days or less and who have a valid passport, a return or ongoing airline ticket, and a place to stay in Samoa. As a practical matter, however, your passport will be stamped for the length of stay you request, up to 30 days or the date of your flight out, whichever is earlier. Those who wish to stay longer must apply, prior to arrival, to the Immigration Office, Government of Samoa, P.O. Box 1861, Apia, Samoa (☎ **20-291**).

Vaccinations are not necessary unless you're arriving within 6 days of being in an infected area.

Customs exemptions for visitors are 200 cigarettes, either a 26-ounce or a 40-ounce bottle of liquor, and their personal effects. Firearms, ammunition, illegal drugs, and indecent publications are prohibited—so leave your *Playboy* magazine in Pago Pago. Plants, live animals, or products of that nature, including fruits, seeds, and soil, will be confiscated unless you have obtained prior permission from the Samoa government's Department of Agriculture and Forest.

6 Money

Samoa uses the *tala* (the Samoans' way of saying "dollar"), which is broken down into 100 *sene* ("cents"). Although most people will refer to them as dollars and cents when speaking to visitors, you can avoid potential confusion by making sure they mean dollars and not talas. The official abbreviation for the currency is SAT, but I have used **S$** in this chapter. Samoa's major hotels and most car-rental firms quote their prices in U.S. dollars. Their U.S. dollar prices are given in this chapter as **US$.**

At press time the **exchange rate** was about S$3 for each US$1 (that is, S$1 equals US33¢). The rate is not published in major newspapers, but net browsers can find it on the financial pages of the *Washington Post* newspaper's Worldwide Web site *(www.washingtonpost.com).*

Since the tala is worthless outside Samoa (and that includes American Samoa), you won't be able to buy any before arriving here. Remember, too, to change your talas back to another currency before leaving Samoa.

HOW TO GET LOCAL CURRENCY   The **ANZ Bank, Pacific Commercial Bank,** and **National Bank of Samoa** have offices on Beach Road in Apia. ANZ Bank is open Monday through Wednesday 9am to 3pm, Thursday and Friday 8:30am to 3pm. Pacific Commercial Bank's main office is open Monday through Friday 8:30am to 3pm. National Bank of Samoa is open Monday through Friday from 9am to 3pm, and its small agency near the new market also is open Saturday from 8:30am to

The Tala & U.S. Dollar

At this writing, S$1 = approximately US33¢, the rate of exchange used to calculate the U.S. dollar prices given in this chapter. This rate may change by the time you visit, so use the following table only as a guide.

S$	US$	S$	US$
.25	.08	15.00	5.00
.50	.17	20.00	6.67
.75	.25	25.00	8.25
1.00	.33	30.00	10.00
2.00	.67	35.00	11.55
3.00	1.00	40.00	13.20
4.00	1.32	45.00	14.85
5.00	1.65	50.00	16.50
6.00	2.00	75.00	25.00
7.00	2.31	100.00	33.00
8.00	2.64	125.00	41.25
9.00	3.00	150.00	50.00
10.00	3.33	200.00	67.00

12:30pm. No bank fees are charged to exchange foreign currency or traveler's checks, but you will have a few seni deducted for stamp tax. The banks have offices in the baggage claim area at Faleolo Airport, which are open when international flights arrive and depart. You can get cash advances against your MasterCard or Visa cards at the banks' main offices on Beach Road. There were no ATMs in Samoa during my recent visit.

CREDIT CARDS American Express, Visa, MasterCard, and Diners Club credit cards are accepted by the major hotels and car-rental firms. Elsewhere, carry enough cash to cover your anticipated expenses.

7 When to Go

THE CLIMATE

Both Samoas enjoy a humid tropical climate, with lots of very intense sunshine even during the wet season (December to May). Average daily high temperatures range from 83°F (28°C) in the drier and somewhat cooler months of June through September to 86°F (30°C) from December to April, when midday can be hot and sticky. Evenings are usually in the comfortable 70s (21°C to 26°C) all year round.

EVENTS

The **Arts and Crafts Fair** during the third week in March is dedicated to reviving the ancient handcrafts. **Easter Week** sees various religious observances, including hymn singing and dramas. The **Independence Celebrations** in early June are the biggest event here, featuring dances, outrigger-canoe races, marching competitions, and horse racing. Samoans living overseas are invited to come home and perform in the **Musika Extravaganza** on the next to last weekend in July. The **Teuila Tourism Festival** during the first week of September displays a variety of entertainment, including canoe races, dance competitions, and traditional games, and culminating in the Miss Samoa beauty pageant. The **Miss Drag Queen Pageant** in early October sees the fa'afafines dressed in their finest. The second Sunday in October is observed as **White Sunday,** during which children go to church dressed in white, lead the services, and are honored at family feasts. **Christmas week** is celebrated with great gusto.

In addition to the man-made holidays and events, late October or early November will see hundreds if not thousands of Samoans out on the reefs with lanterns and nets to snare the wiggly *palolo,* a coral worm that comes out to mate on the seventh day after the full moon. Palolo are considered by Pacific Islanders to be the caviar of their region.

The visitors bureau can tell you the precise dates and the schedules for these events (see "Visitor Information & Entry Requirements," above).

HOLIDAYS

Offices and schools are closed both January 1 and January 2 for New Year's; Good Friday and Easter Monday; April 25 as ANZAC Day, to remember those who died in the two World Wars; the Monday after the second Sunday in May as Mother's Day of Samoa; June 1 through June 3, for the annual Independence Celebrations; the first Friday in August as Labour Day; the Monday after the second Sunday in October, in honor of the preceding White Sunday; the first Friday in November as Arbor Day, to encourage the planting of trees and appreciation of conservation; Christmas Day; and December 26 as Boxing Day.

8 Getting There & Getting Around

GETTING THERE

Air New Zealand and **Polynesian Airlines** have direct flights between Los Angeles and Apia, with a brief stop in Honolulu. (Polynesian's seats are on Air New Zealand's planes). Those flights go on to Tonga and Auckland. Polynesian flies its own plane between Apia and Sydney, Melbourne, Auckland, Wellington, and Tonga. **Air Pacific** has service between Apia and Fiji. **Royal Tongan Airlines** links Apia to Tonga and New Zealand.

A less desirable way to get to Apia is on **Hawaiian Airlines,** which flies between several West Coast cities and Honolulu, thence to Pago Pago in American Samoa. Connections to Samoa can then be made on **Polynesian Airlines** or **Samoa Air** (☎ 22-321 in Apia or 633-4331 in American Samoa). Samoa Air also flies nonstop between Pago Pago and Maota Airstrip on Savai'i. That fare is US$81 one-way, US$120 round-trip.

For more information, see "Getting There" in Chapter 2.

Flights into and out of the Samoas are often packed with Samoans leaving and returning to the islands, so reserve your seat as soon as possible.

ARRIVING

Unless you're coming from Pago Pago, your flight will arrive at **Faleolo Airport,** on the northwest corner of Upolu about 32km (19 miles) from Apia. **Fagali'i Airport** near Apia is used only for flights between Samoa and Pago Pago.

There are duty-free shops and two currency exchange windows in the baggage claim area at Faleolo Airport, so you can shop and change money while waiting for your luggage. There's a bank and a small duty-free shop at Fagali'i.

Transportation from the Faleolo Airport is by taxi or by a relatively small Polynesian Airlines bus that meets all international flights (you will be astounded by how many passengers and their baggage can be crammed into one of these vehicles). The bus ride costs S$7 ($2.30) each way. The government-regulated taxi fare into town is S$35 ($11.55).

Transportation from Fagali'i Airstrip is by taxi only. The fare into downtown Apia is S$5 ($1.65).

The airline buses also transport passengers from the Apia hotels to Faleolo Airport for departing international flights. They arrive at the hotels 2 hours before departure time. Be sure to tell your hotel what flight you are leaving on; otherwise, the bus could leave you behind.

When leaving the country, get your boarding pass and then pay S$20 ($6.60) **departure tax** at one of the banks in the main concourses at Faleolo and Fagali'i airports.

There is no bank in the departure lounges of either airport, so change your leftover talas before clearing Immigration. Remember, Samoan currency cannot be exchanged outside the country, even in American Samoa.

GETTING AROUND
BY PLANE
Polynesian Airlines (☎ **800/644-7659** in the U.S. and Canada or 22-737 in Apia) flies several times a day between Fagali'i Airstrip near Apia and Maota Airstrip, near Salelologa on the southeast corner of Savai'i, less frequently between Faleolo and Maota. The Fagali'i–Savai'i fares are S$34 ($11.25) one-way, S$60.50 ($20) round-trip.

BY FERRY
The *Lady Samoa,* a passenger and automobile ferry, operates three times daily between Mulifanua Wharf on Upolu and Salelologa on Savai'i. The one-way fare is S$7 ($2.30). Local buses leave regularly from the Apia market and pass Mulifanua Wharf on their way to Pasi O Le Vaa. Bus fare to the wharf is S$1.50 (50¢). For more information, ask at the visitors bureau or contact the **Samoa Shipping Corporation** (☎ **20-935**), on Beach Road opposite the main wharf.

BY RENTAL CAR
The car-rental firms will arrange to pick you up at the airport if you have reservations. Most of them quote their rates in U.S. dollars, and all accept American Express, Diners Club, MasterCard, and Visa credit cards. Insurance policies do not cover damage to the vehicles' undercarriages, which may occur on some rocky, unpaved roads. Don't count on buying gasoline outside of Apia. Depending on your own insurance policies, you may also want to buy optional personal accident coverage, which covers you and your passengers.

The main roads on both islands are paved and in good condition, but none of Apia's car-rental firms will allow you to drive on unpaved roads, or take your rented vehicle on the ferry to Savai'i.

The largest and best rental firm here is ✪ **Funway Rentals,** which has a modern depot on Beach Road opposite the main wharf (☎ **22-045;** fax 25-008; e-mail funwayrentals@samoa.net). It rents Suzuki four-wheel-drive vehicles starting at S$110

The Samoa Islands

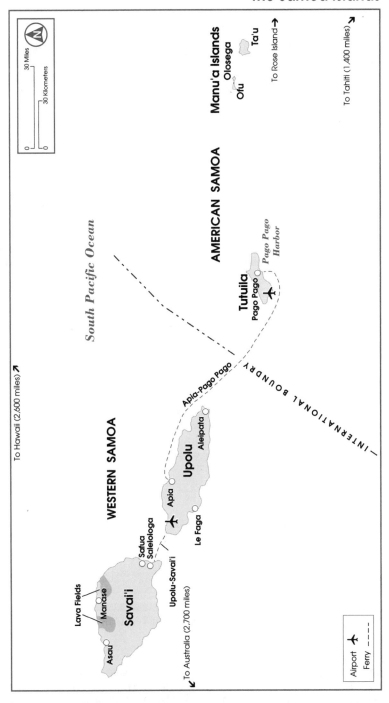

($36.50) a day, plus S$20 ($6.60) a day for insurance. MasterCard and Visa credit cards are accepted.

Budget Rent-A-Car has an office in the National Provident Fund building opposite the Town Clock in Apia (☎ **800/527-0700** or 20-561). Rates range from US$48 to US$57 a day, including unlimited miles. There's a mandatory US$7 per day for insurance on all models.

Avis (☎ **800/831-2847** or 20-486) charges US$55 a day for a Toyota Tercel or US$65 for a Toyota Corolla, plus US$10 per day for insurance. Avis also has an agency in American Samoa and will reserve a car for you in Pago Pago at no extra charge, but give them a day's notice.

Whichever firm you chose, you pay for the gasoline; bring it back full.

DRIVING RULES   You drive on the right-hand side of the road in the American fashion, stopping for pedestrians in crosswalks, and not exceeding the speed limits of 35 m.p.h. on the open road or 25 m.p.h. in Apia and the villages. Samoans and their dogs, chickens, and pigs have a habit of walking in the middle of the roads that pass through their villages, so proceed with care. Even if the way is clear, local courtesy dictates that you slow down when going through the villages so as not to kick up a lot of dust. Special care is required on Sundays, when Samoans usually lounge around the village after going to church.

Visitors technically are required to get a local **driver's license** from the police department traffic office on Ifi'ifi Street. You neglect this cumbersome procedure at your own risk; that having been said, I've never bothered to get one, nor do I know anyone who has. The car-rental firms will ask to see your home driver's license.

By Bus

Samoa has a system of "aiga buses" (similar to those in American Samoa), most of which have wooden passenger compartments built on the back of flatbed trucks. The main **bus station** is behind the Old Apia Market on Beach Road, but the buses stop at the New Market before leaving town. They have the names of their villages written on the front. The first buses leave their villages usually between 5 and 7am, with the last departure between 2 and 2:30pm. They turn around in Apia and go back to the villages. The last departure from town is about 4:30pm. They do not run on Saturday afternoon or Sunday. The buses are always crowded.

The Western Samoa Visitors Bureau has the schedules and fares. Here are the destinations most often visited, followed by the names of the village buses that go there:

To Piula Cave Pool: Falefa or Saoluafata.

To Return to Paradise Beach: Lefaga. They run every 3 hours.

To Papase'a Sliding Rocks: Se'ese'e, Tagaigata or Ale.

To Muliafanua Wharf: Pasi o le Vaa.

The Si'umu bus is the only one which goes all the way to the south coast via the Cross Island Road.

In general, 50 sene (17¢) will take you around Apia and into the hills above the town. The maximum fare is about S$3 ($1) to the most distant villages and to Mulifanua Wharf, where the Savai'i ferries land on Upolu's western end (see "Savai'i" later in this chapter).

By Taxi

Silver Star Taxis (☎ **21-770**), **Marlboro Taxis** (☎ **20-808**), **Vailima Taxis** (☎ **22-380**), **Heini Taxis** (☎ **24-431**), and **Town Taxis** (☎ **21-600**) all provide taxi service in Apia. They have stands at the Town Clock on Beach Road and nearby on Vaea Street. **Town Taxis** also has a stand at the airport.

The cabs do not have meters, but **fares** are set by the government. A pamphlet listing them is available at the visitors bureau or at the Ministry of Transport. In general, S$2 (67¢) will take you around Apia and its hotels. One-way fares are S$5 ($1.65) from Apia to Vailima; S$5 ($1.65) to Fagali'i Airstrip; S$35 ($11.55) to Faleolo Airport; S$35 ($11.55) to Coconuts Beach Club & Resort; S$45 ($15) to Lefaga and Return to Paradise Beach; and S$25 ($8.25) to Piula College and Cave Pool.

Fast Facts: Samoa

American Express   There is no American Express representative in Samoa. See "Money" in chapter 2 for what to do if you lose your American Express credit card or traveler's checks.

Area Code   The international country code for Samoa is **685.**

Baby-Sitters   Your hotel can arrange for qualified baby-sitters.

Bookstores   Aggie's Gift Shop (☎ 22-880), next to Aggie Grey's Hotel on Beach Road, carries books on Samoa and the South Pacific and a few paperback novels. **Le Moana Cafe** (☎ 24-828), in the Lotemau Centre at Vaea and Convent Streets, has the latest editions of *Time* and *Newsweek,* the latter in *The Bulletin.* **Matafele (Wesley) Bookshop,** on Beach Road opposite the visitors bureau (☎ 24-231), carries classic novels and excellent maps.

Business Hours   Most shops and government offices are open Monday through Friday from 8am to noon and 1:30 to 4:30pm, Saturday from 8am to noon. Except for the major hotels, the only businesses open on Sunday are the scores of mom-and-pop grocery shops in Apia and some villages.

Camera/Film   Photomart Camerahouse, in the first block of Vaea Street off Beach Road (☎ 22-868), carries a wide range of color print film and has 1-hour processing.

Clothing   Lightweight, informal summer clothing is best throughout the year, although a light sweater or wrap could come in handy for evening wear from June through September. Men can wear shorts and shirts almost anywhere, but women should stick to dresses away from the hotels and should never wear bathing suits or skimpy clothing away from the beach or swimming pool. Topless or nude bathing is outlawed. Outside Apia most Samoans still wear wraparound lavalavas, which come well below the knees of men and to the ankles on women.

Currency Exchange   See "Money," above.

Doctor   There are doctors with private clinics in Apia; ask your hotel staff to recommend one. Also see "Hospitals," below.

Drugstores   Samoa Pharmacy (☎ 22-595) and **Apia Pharmacy** (☎ 22-703) are both on Beach Road west of the Town Clock. They carry cosmetics, nonprescription remedies, and prescription drugs—most of New Zealand or Australian manufacture.

Electricity   Electricity in Samoa is 240 volts, 50 cycles, and most plugs have angled prongs like those used in New Zealand and Australia. Aggie Grey's Hotel and the Kitano Tusitala Hotel supply 110-volt current for electric shavers only; you will need a converter and adapter plugs for other American appliances.

Embassies/Consulates   The **U.S. Embassy** (☎ **21-631**) is in the John Williams Building on Beach Road at Falealili Street (the Cross Island Road). Hours are Monday through Friday from 9:30am to 12:30pm. New Zealand and Australia both have high commissions on Beach Road.

E-mail   CLS Internet Cafe (☎ **20-926**) and **Cyber Booth** (☎ **21-016**), both in the Lotemanu Centre, corner of Vaea and Convent Streets, have computer terminals for Internet access. Both charge S$5 ($1.65) for 5 minutes and are open Monday through Friday 8am to 4pm, Saturday 8am to noon. Despite its name, the former is a computer shop, not a cafe.

Emergencies   The emergency phone numbers are **995** for police, **994** for fire, and **996** for an ambulance.

Eyeglasses   Try the **National Hospital** (see "Hospitals" below); if they can't be fixed there (replacements must be ordered from New Zealand), try the Lyndon B. Johnson Tropical Medical Center in Pago Pago.

Hairdressers/Barbers   Aggie Grey's Hotel has a beauty parlor (☎ **23-277**).

Hospitals   The best doctors are at the **MedCen Private Hospital,** a modern facility on the Cross Island Road (☎ **26-519**). The government-run **National Hospital,** on Ifi'ifi Street in Apia (☎ **21-212**), has an outpatient clinic open daily from 8am to noon and from 1 to 4:30pm.

Insects   There are no dangerous insects in Samoa, and the plentiful mosquitoes do not carry malaria. Bring a good insect repellent with you, and consider burning mosquito coils at night.

Liquor Laws   The legal drinking age is 18. Except for a prohibition of Sunday sale of alcoholic beverages outside the hotels or licensed restaurants, the laws are fairly liberal. Bars outside the hotels can stay open Monday through Saturday till midnight. Spirits, wine, and beer are sold at private liquor stores.

Maps   The **Samoa Visitors Bureau** distributes a one-sheet collection of maps of Upolu, Savai'i, and Apia town. See "Visitor Information & Entry Requirements," above. **Aggie's Gift Shop** (☎ **22-880**), next to Aggie Grey's Hotel on Beach Road, and **Matafele (Wesley) Bookshop,** on Beach Road opposite the visitors bureau (☎ **24-231**), sell detailed maps.

Newspapers/Magazines   The daily *Samoa Observer* and *Newsline* carry local and world news. **Le Moana Cafe** (☎ **24-828**), in the Lotemau Centre at Vaea and Convent Streets, has the latest editions of *Time* and *Newsweek,* the latter in *The Bulletin.*

Police   The **Police Station** (☎ **22-222**) is on Ifi'ifi Street, inland from the prime minister's office.

Post Office   The **Chief Post Office** is on Beach Road, east of the Town Clock. Airmail letters to North America cost 90 sene (30¢), postcards 80 sene (27¢). Hours are Monday through Friday from 9am to 4:30pm.

Radio/TV   Samoa has two broadcast television stations, one owned by the government and one by a Christian religious organization. The government channel has New Zealand programming daily from 5 to 11pm (earlier or later if there's a rugby game on). Many homes on Upolu's north shore can receive the American Samoan channels, one of which has the NBC "Today" show followed by MSNBC and CNN during the mornings, and two American channels at night, one commercial channel and one with Public Broadcasting System programs. The government also operates two AM radio stations, on which most programming is in

Samoan. The world news is rebroadcast from Radio Australia and Radio New Zealand several times a day. A privately owned FM station broadcasts lots of music on FM 98.8.

Safety   Remember that the communal property system still prevails in the Samoas, and items such as cameras and bags left unattended may disappear. Street crime has not been a serious problem, but be on the alert if you walk down dark streets at night. Women should not wander alone on deserted beaches. Samoans take the Sabbath seriously, and there have been reports of local residents tossing stones at tourists who drive through some villages on Sunday. If you plan to tour by rental car, do it during the week.

Taxes   Samoa imposes a 10% General Services Tax, which is included in restaurant and bar bills and is added to the cost of some other items, including rental cars, but be sure to ask if your hotel has included the tax in its room rates. Also, an airport departure tax of S$20 ($6.60) is levied on all passengers leaving Samoa at both Faleolo and Fagali'i airports. No such tax is imposed on domestic flights or on the ferry to Pago Pago.

Telephone/Telex/Fax   International calls can be directly dialed into Samoa from most parts of the world. The international country code is **685.**

The easiest way to call home is via a phonecard public telephone, which you will find at post offices and elsewhere. Buy the cards at the post office. Domestic long-distance and international calls may be placed at the **International Telephone Bureau** just inside the Chief Post Office on Beach Road. You place your call with the clerk at the central booth and wait to be paged to one of the side booths. The bureau does not accept credit cards, so you must reverse the charges or pay cash in advance of having your call placed. Station-to-station calls to North America cost S$13.50 ($4.46) for the first 3 minutes, then S$4.50 ($1.50) a minute thereafter. Calls to Australia and New Zealand cost about half that amount. The bureau is open daily from 8am to 10pm, but fax services are available daily from 8am to 4pm.

Pay telephones are in post offices in the villages. Phonecard phones are replacing those which accept coins. They are operated by lifting the handset, inserting the phonecard, and dialing the number. Old-fashioned coin phones require a 20-sene coin.

The number for directory assistance is **933;** for the international operator, **900;** for international directory assistance, **910;** and for the domestic long-distance operator, **920.**

Time   Local time in Samoa is 11 hours behind GMT. That means it's 3 hours behind Pacific Standard Time (4 hours behind during daylight saving time). If it's noon standard time in California and 3pm in New York, it's 9am in Apia. During daylight saving time, it's 8am in Samoa.

The islands are east of the international date line; therefore, they share the same date with North America and are 1 day behind Tonga, Fiji, Australia, and New Zealand. That's worth remembering if you are going on to those countries or will be arriving in Samoa from one of them.

Tipping   There is no tipping in Samoa except for extraordinary service, and the practice is discouraged as being contrary to the traditional way of life. One exception is the practice of throwing money on the dance floor to show appreciation of a show well performed.

Water   All tap water should be boiled before drinking. Safe bottled water is produced locally and is available at most grocery stores.

Weights/Measures   Samoa officially is on the metric system, but in their every-day lives, most residents still calculate distances by the British system used in American Samoa and in the U.S. Speed limits are posted in miles per hour, and the speedometers of many local vehicles (all of which have the steering wheels on the left side in the American and European fashion) are calculated in miles.

9 Exploring Apia & Upolu

The town of Apia sits midway along the north coast of Upolu, which makes it a centrally located base from which to explore the main island. The Cross Island Road runs 14 miles from town across the range of extinct volcanoes that form Upolu, thereby bringing the south coast within easy reach of town.

THE TOP ATTRACTION

○ Robert Louis Stevenson Museum & Grave. Vailima, on the Cross Island Road, 3 miles south of Apia. ☎ **20-798.** Admission S$15 ($5) adults, S$5 ($1.65) children under 11. Mon–Fri 9am–4pm, Sat 8am–noon. Guided Mon–Fri 1pm.

When Robert Louis Stevenson and his wife, Fanny, decided to stay in Samoa in 1889, they bought 314 acres of virgin land on the slopes of Mount Vaea above Apia and named the estate **Vailima**—or "Five Waters"—because five streams crossed the property. They cleared about 8 acres and lived there in a small shack for nearly a year. The American historian Henry Adams dropped in unannounced one day and found the Stevensons dressed in lavalavas, doing dirty work about their hovel. To Adams, the couple's living conditions were repugnant. Their Rousseauian existence didn't last long, however, for in 1891 they built the first part of a mansion that was to become famous throughout the South Pacific.

When completed 2 years later, the big house had five bedrooms, a library, a ballroom large enough to accommodate 100 dancers, and the only fireplace in Samoa. The Stevensons shipped 72 tons of furniture out from England, all of which was hauled the 3 miles from Apia on sleds pulled by bullocks. A piano sat in one corner of the great hall in a glass case to protect it from Samoa's humidity. There were leather-buttoned chairs, mahogany tables, a Chippendale sideboard, Arabian curtains of silver and gold, paintings by the masters, a Rodin nude given them by the sculptor, a damask tablecloth that was a gift from Queen Victoria, and a sugar bowl that had been used by both Robert Burns and Sir Walter Scott.

The Stevensons' lifestyle matched their surroundings. Oysters were shipped on ice from New Zealand, Bordeaux wine was brought by the cask from France and bottled at Vailima, and 1840 vintage Madeira was poured on special occasions. They dressed formally for dinner every evening—except for their bare feet—and were served by Samoans dressed in tartan lavalavas, in honor of the great author's Scottish origins.

Vailima and this lavish lifestyle baffled the Samoans. As far as they could tell, writing was not labor; therefore, Stevenson had no visible way of earning a living. Yet all this money rolled in, which meant to them that Stevenson must be a man of much mana. He was also a master at one of their favorite pastimes—storytelling—and he took much interest in their own stories, as well as their customs, language, and politics. When the followers of the defeated Mataafa were released from prison, they built a road from Apia to Vailima in appreciation for Stevenson's support of their unsuccessful struggle against the Germans. And when he died in 1894, they cut the "Road of the Loving Hearts" to his grave on Mount Vaea overlooking Vailima.

Stevenson's wife, Fanny, died in California in 1914, and her ashes were brought back to Vailima and buried at the foot of his grave. Her Samoan name, Aolele, is engraved on a bronze plaque.

Apia

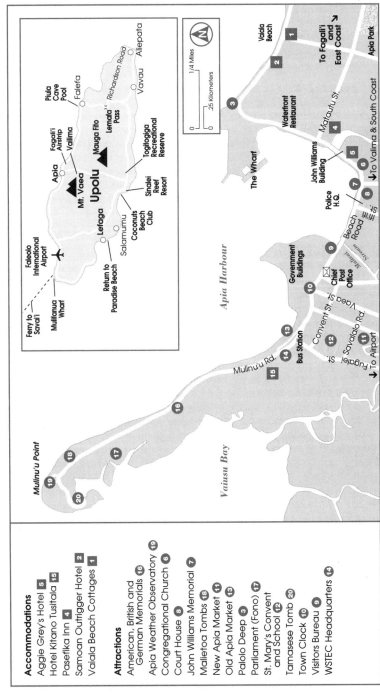

Accommodations
Aggie Grey's Hotel **5**
Hotel Kitano Tusitala **15**
Pasefika Inn **4**
Samoan Outrigger Hotel **2**
Vaiala Beach Cottages **1**

Attractions
American, British and
  German Memorials **16**
Apia Weather Observatory **19**
Congregational Church **6**
Court House **8**
John Williams Memorial **7**
Malietoa Tombs **18**
New Apia Market **11**
Old Apia Market **13**
Palolo Deep **3**
Parliament (Fono) **17**
St. Mary's Convent
  and School **12**
Tamasese Tomb **20**
Town Clock **10**
Visitors Bureau **9**
WSTEC Headquarters **14**

Our place is in a deep cleft of Vaea Mountain, some six hundred feet above the sea, embowered in a forest, which is our strangling enemy, and which we combat with axes and dollars.

—Robert Louis Stevenson, 1890

Samoa's head of state lived in Vailima until hurricanes severely damaged the mansion in 1990 and 1991. Since then, an extraordinary renovation has turned it into the **Robert Louis Stevenson Museum.** It now appears as it did when Stevenson lived here. A sitting room matches exactly that seen in a photo made of Fanny on a chair. Another photo of Stevenson dictating is hung in his library where he stood at the time.

The "Road of the Loving Hearts" leading to **Stevenson's Grave** passes a lovely cascade, which Stevenson turned into a swimming pool. A short, rather steep walking track to the grave takes about 30 strenuous minutes; a longer but easier path takes about 1 hour. Mount Vaea is best climbed in the cool of early morning.

A STROLL THROUGH APIA

Like most South Pacific towns, Samoa's capital and only town has expanded from one small Samoan village to include adjacent settlements and an area of several square miles, all of which is now known collectively as Apia (the name of the village where Europeans first settled). The town now has a population approaching 40,000. Most points of interest lie along **Beach Road,** the broad avenue that curves along the harbor, a waterfront promenade on one side and churches, government buildings, and businesses on the other.

Apia can be brutally hot at midday, so the best time to make this walk is right after the **Samoa Police Brass Band** marches along Beach Road to Government House, where they raise the national flag daily at 8am. It's worth watching the cops in their white helmets, light blue uniforms, and lavalavas even if you don't make the walking tour. If you take photos, don't get between the band and the flag pole.

We start our walking tour of downtown at **Aggie Grey's Hotel,** on the banks of the Vaisigano River. This famous hotel and its founder are stories unto themselves, which I have recounted in "Accommodations," below. From Aggie's, head west, or to the left as you face the harbor.

The two large churches on the left are both Protestant, legacies of the Rev. John Williams, for whom the modern high-rise office building at the corner of Falealili Road is named. On the waterfront across Beach Road is a memorial to this missionary who brought Christianity to Samoa and many more South Pacific islands. Williams's bones are reputedly buried beneath the clapboard **Congregational Christian Church,** directly across Beach Road from the memorial. The missionary was eaten after the natives did him in on Erromango in what now is Vanuatu; the story has it that his bones were recovered and brought to Apia.

During business hours there's usually a line outside the **New Zealand High Commission** office, just beyond the church, as Samoans wait to apply for visas. Like their American Samoan cousins who flock to the U.S., they migrate to Auckland for better jobs and higher pay. Unlike them, however, Samoans do not have unrestricted access to the larger country and must apply for visas to enter New Zealand, their former "Mother Country."

The clapboard, colonial-style **Courthouse** on the next corner formerly housed the Supreme Court and prime minister's office before they moved into the big high-rise buildings across the road. In colonial times, it was headquarters of the New Zealand trusteeship administration, and site of the Mau Movement demonstration and shootings in 1929.

The Marist Brothers' Primary School is on the banks of Mulivai Stream. Across the bridge stands **Mulivai Catholic Cathedral,** begun in 1885 and completed some 20 years later. Farther along, the imposing **Matafele Methodist Church** abuts the shops in the **Wesley Arcade.** According to a monument across Beach Road, Chief Saivaaia of Tafua in Tonga brought Methodism to Samoa in 1835. The Methodist Church of Australia had responsibility for the Samoas from 1859 until an independent conference was established in Samoa in 1964.

The remains of the German warship *Adler* are buried under the reclaimed land, now the site of two huge, fale-topped government office buildings. Built in the mid-1990s with foreign aid from China, the huge structures house the prime minister's offices, government departments, and the central bank. On the water side of Beach Road stands a memorial to the Samoans who fought alongside the New Zealanders during World War II.

The center of modern Apia's business district is the **Town Clock,** the World War I memorial at the foot of Vaea Street. Across the street, the **Chan Mow & Co.** building, formerly the home of Burns Philp trading corporation, is a fine example of late colonial architecture; its arches and red tile roof make it look almost Spanish. Between the clock and the water stands a large Samoan fale known as **Pulenu'u House,** where local residents can be seen lounging or eating their lunches. Next to the clock on the water side is **Nelson Memorial Public Library,** which has a collection of South Pacific literature in the Pacific Room, to the right after you enter. The clock and library were gifts from the family of Olaf Nelson, a Swede who arrived in 1868 and built a sizeable trading empire.

Continuing west on Beach Road, you come to the sprawling **Old Apia Market.** Once the vegetable market, this large covered space is now home to flea-market stalls selling a wide range of items, from sandals to toothpaste. One area is devoted to handcraft vendors, and you can stop and watch local women weaving pandanus mats, hats, and handbags. This is a good place to shop for wood carvings and tapa cloth (see "Shopping," below). I haven't had the stomach for such local fare since my days as a young backpacker, but the food stalls along the market's water side are the cheapest (and dirtiest) places in town to get a meal.

Fugalei Street, which leaves Beach Road across from the market, goes to the airport and west coast. Walk down it a block, and turn left and go east on Convent Street past picturesque **St. Mary's Convent and School.** At the next corner, turn right on Saleufi Street and walk inland 2 blocks to the **New Market,** a modern, tin-roofed pavilion where Samoan families sell a wide variety of tropical fruits and vegetables, all of which have the prices clearly marked (there is no bargaining). Like everywhere else in the islands, the market is busiest on Saturday morning.

Impressions

Many an English village is bigger by far than Apia. And the whole place had an air of faded obsolescence, as if somebody had decided that it was hardly worth nailing the buildings to the ground or giving them a lick of paint because the inevitable hurricane was bound to blow them away.

—John Dyson, 1982

⭐ **Frommer's Favorite Samoa Experiences**

Visiting Stevenson's Museum & Grave. Anyone who has ever put words on paper or a computer screen will feel a sense of awe when reading Robert Louis Stevenson's requiem carved on his grave up on Mount Vaea overlooking Apia. The climb isn't easy, but it's worth it if you have a single literary bone in your body. The museum is one of the finest literary shrines I've ever seen: you almost expect Stevenson to walk in at any second, so much does Vailima look like it did when he was alive.

Lazing the Day Away on a Beautiful Beach. A Sunday afternoon at one of the South Pacific's most beautiful beaches is on my agenda every time I come here. Return to Paradise Beach, where Gary Cooper filmed *Return to Paradise,* is what all beaches should be like: surf breaking around black rock outcrops, palm trees draped over white sand. But I'm also enamoured of Aliepata Beach, where a clif-flike mountain provides a backdrop, and offshore islands enhance the sea view.

Enjoying Fiafia Night at Aggie Grey's. The dancing is more suggestive in French Polynesia and the Cook Islands, but there is a warmth and charm to Aggie's fiafia nights that no other establishment comes close to matching. The concluding fire dance around the pool is nothing short of spectacular.

Walking in Apia. A Hollywood set designer would be hard pressed to top Apia as an old South Seas town. I love to stroll along the perfect half-moon curve of Beach Road and let the old churches and clapboard government buildings tell me how things used to be. Locals fishing or idling the time away along the seawall tell me what's going on today.

Touring Savai'i. The best way to see the desolate lava fields of Savai'i is with retired Australian geologist Warren Jopling. Having lived on Savai'i for many years, he is also an expert on Samoan customs and lifestyles (everyone on the island knows him). Touring with Warren is like having your own personal guide through a living geological and cultural museum.

THE MULINU'U PENINSULA

Beyond the market, Beach Road becomes Mulinu'u Road, which runs about a mile to the end of **Mulinu'u Peninsula,** a low arm separating Apia Harbor to the east and shallow Vaiusu Bay on the west.

Just beyond the market on the left is the **Samoan Trust Estates Corporation,** which took over ownership of the copra plantations when the Germans were kicked out of the islands at the beginning of World War I. The WSTEC building was originally headquarters of the German firms that owned and managed the plantations. The Kitano Tusitala Hotel just up the way was built where once stood a boarding house for the German employees of the original company.

About halfway out on the peninsula are the **German, British, and American Memorials,** one dedicated to the German sailors who died in the 1889 hurricane, one to the British and American sailors who were drowned during that fiasco, and one to commemorate the raising of the German flag in 1900.

The Mulinu'u Peninsula is home of the **Fono,** Samoa's parliament. The new Fono building sits opposite a memorial to Samoa's independence, the two separated by a wide lawn. The Fono's old home is next to the road in the same park. A tomb on the lawn holds the remains of Iosefa Mataafa, one of the paramount chiefs.

Beyond the Apia Yacht Club stand the tombs of the Malietoa family of paramount chiefs, which makes this the **burial grounds** of Samoa's incumbent "royalty." At the end of the paved road, a dirt path goes left past a gravel quarry to the tombs of Tuimalaeali'ifano and Tupua Tamasese, two other paramount chiefs.

At the end of the peninsula you'll find the **Apia Weather Observatory,** originally built by the Germans in 1902 (they apparently learned a costly lesson from the unpredicted, disastrous hurricane of March 1889).

EXPLORING UPOLU

To travel along the roads of Upolu away from Apia is to see Polynesia relatively unchanged from the days before the Europeans arrived in the islands. Bring your swimming gear, for you'll also visit some of the South Pacific's most stunningly beautiful beaches.

If you're driving, be sure to buy a map from the visitors bureau (see "Visitor Information & Entry Requirements" above).

✪ **ALEIPATA**   One of the most popular sightseeing tours makes a loop from Apia to the long white beaches of Aleipata District on Upolu's eastern end. Most of Upolu is a volcanic shield that slopes gently to the sea, but since the east is older—and therefore more eroded and rugged than the central and western portions—this area has the island's most dramatic scenery. Serrated ridges come down to the sea, giving the eastern third of the island a tropical beauty reminiscent of Moorea in French Polynesia.

The East Coast Road follows the shore for 16 miles to the village of Falefa, skirting the lagoon and black-sand surf beaches at Lauli'i and Solosolo. Look for **Piula College,** a Methodist school on a promontory overlooking the sea about 2 miles before Falefa, turn in at the playing field, and drive around to the school on the right. Park there and follow the steps down to the freshwater ✪ **Piula Cave Pool,** cut into the cliff below the church. Bring snorkeling gear to swim through an underwater opening at the back of the pool into a second chamber. The cave pool is open from 8am to 4:30pm Monday through Saturday; admission is S$1 (33¢), and there is a rudimentary changing room for visitors. No alcoholic beverages are allowed on the grounds.

To the left of the bridge beyond Falefa village lie **Falefa Falls,** impressive during the rainy season. The road then slowly climbs toward 950-foot-high **Le Mafa Pass** in the center of the island, with some great views back toward the sea. Another rugged, winding road to the left just before the pass dead-ends at picturesque **Fagaloa Bay,** once a volcanic crater that exploded seaward, leaving a mountain-clad bay cutting deep into the island. The Fagaloa road should be traveled only in a four-wheel-drive vehicle—and even then with the utmost caution.

Once over the pass, the main paved road crosses a bridge. Just beyond, an unpaved and unmarked road goes to the right and cuts through the forests down to the south coast. We will come back this way, road conditions permitting, but for now go straight ahead on the **Richardson Road.** Once a bush path, this paved road crosses a refreshingly cool high plateau and skirts **Afulilo Lake,** formed by the country's hydroelectric dam. From there it gently descends to ✪ **Aleipata,** a picturesque district whose villages sit beside one of the most gorgeous white-sand beaches in the South Pacific. Four small islands offshore enliven the view, and on a clear day you can see the jagged blue outline of American Samoa on the horizon.

As you turn the corner to the south coast, stop at the overlook. The villagers may ask for S$2 (67¢) for the privilege, but your photos from here should be among the best you'll take in Samoa, for the view includes the clifflike escarpment which leaves a narrow shelf of land bordered by a long, white sand beach. There's not enough space

Samoa is different. Of all the Polynesian nations, it is the one with the most peculiar life-style, the strangest customs, the greatest resistance to foreign encroachment; and yet, paradoxically, it is the nation that offers itself most proudly for public inspection.

—Ron Hall, 1991

here for villages, but on these sands stands a collection of rustic **beach fales** available for camping (see "Accommodations," below). You can refuel your body at **Boomerang Creek** (☎ 40-3580), where the Kangarumu Restaurant and Harro's Bar offer inexpensive meals and libation.

Keep going along the southeast shore to Vavau village, where the paved Le Mafa Pass Road begins (don't take the unpaved road to the left; it dead-ends at a river). Le Mafa Pass Road climbs steadily uphill to a viewpoint overlooking 175-foot-high ✪ **Sopo'aga Falls.** The villagers have built a small park on a cliff overlooking the deep and narrow gorge, complete with picnic tables and toilets. They charge S$3 ($1) per vehicle, but that's a small price to pay for this view.

THE CROSS ISLAND ROAD The Cross Island road runs for 14 miles from the John Williams Building on Beach Road in Apia to the village of Si'umu on the south coast. Along the way it passes first the Robert Louis Stevenson Museum at Vailima and then the **Malololeilei Scenic View,** a park on the east side of the road. Pull off here and take the short walks to views over Apia, the sea, and a waterfall. Back on the road, you'll later pass the modern, nine-sided **House of Worship,** one of six Baha'i Faith temples in the world. Open for meditation and worship, the temple was dedicated in 1984. An information center outside the temple makes available materials about the Baha'i Faith.

After passing the temple, the road winds its way through cool, rolling pastures and then starts its descent to the east coast. Watch on the right for a parking area overlooking **Papapai-tai Waterfalls,** which plunge 300 feet into one of the gorges that streams have cut into central Upolu's volcanic shield. Of the many waterfalls on Upolu, Papapai-tai is the most easily seen.

THE SOUTHWEST COAST A left turn at the end of the Cross Island Road in Si'umu village on the south coast leads to **O Le Pupu-Pue National Park** and the **Togitogiga National Forest.** The park contains the best remaining tropical rain forest on Upolu, but you'll have to hike into the valley to reach it. Some 51 species of wildlife live in the park: 42 species of birds, five of mammals, and four of lizards. Lovely ✪ **Togitogiga Falls** are a short walk from the entrance, from where a trail to **Peapea Cave** also begins. It's a 2-hour round-trip hike to the cave. Another walking trail leads seaward to arches cut by the surf into the south coast. **Mount Le Pu'e,** in the northwest corner of the park, is a well-preserved volcanic cinder cone. The park and reserve are open during the daylight hours 7 days a week, and there's no admission fee.

Heading west from Si'umu, the road soon passes the Coconuts Beach Club & Resort and then the nearby **Togo Mangrove Estuary,** a tidal waterway alive with birds, flowers, bees, and other wildlife. Coconut Watersports, based at Coconuts Beach Club & Resort, rents kayaks for exploring the waterways through this enchanting, swamp-like preserve (see "Water Sports, Golf & Other Outdoor Pursuits," below).

Some of Upolu's most beautiful beaches are on the southwest coast, particularly in the Lefaga district. One of these is at the village of **Salamumu.** Farther on the south coast road, Matautu village boasts ✪ **Return to Paradise Beach,** one of the most gorgeous coves in the South Pacific. Palms hang over a sandy beach punctuated by large boulders that confront the breaking surf. It gets its name from the movie starring Gary Cooper, which was filmed here in 1951. The S$5 ($2) per-person custom fee charged by Matautu village is well worth it.

From Matautu the main road winds across the center of the island to the north coast.

ORGANIZED TOURS   Based at Aggie Grey's Hotel, **Samoa Scenic Tours** (☎ 22-880) offers a variety of tours which stop for photographs and a swim at beautiful beaches and waterfalls. The Apia and surroundings tour includes a stop at the Robert Louis Stevenson Museum. A morning excursion goes to Piula Cave Pool and Falefa Falls. They both run Monday through Saturday and cost S$38 ($12.50) per person. One full-day trip goes to Lefaga and Matareva village, with a swim at Return to Paradise Beach when you get there. Another takes in Aleipata and the northeast coast, including Togitogiga waterfalls. These cost S$70 ($23) per person. A third full-day excursion goes out to Manono Island, for about S$83 ($27.50). The full-day trips usually go twice a week. Full-day tours include a beachside barbecue lunch (beers and soft drinks, too). On Sunday there's a beach outing to the southwest coast, with juice and towels included for S$55 ($18) per person. Each day's offerings are written on a notice board in the lobby at Aggie's.

Outrigger Adventure Tours, based at The Samoan Outrigger Hotel (☎ 20-042), has excursions to Aleipata on Sunday, and to Paradise and Matareva beaches and Togitogiga Waterfall on Wednesday. Both cost S$50 ($16.50) per person, including lunch. Bring your bathing suit, towel, and snorkeling gear.

ENVIRONMENTAL TOURS   The sightseeing tours don't go to the remote areas visited by Dr. Steve Brown and his Samoan wife Lumaava Sooaemalelagi of **Eco-Tour Samoa,** P.O. Box 4609, Matautu-uta (☎ 22-144 or 25-993, or 800/255-8732 in the U.S.; e-mail ecotour@samoa.net). Leading proponents of nature-sensitive "sustainable tourism," the Browns have a number of 2- to 6-day tours that explore the wildlife and fauna of such places as the Mount Vaea rain forest, remote Fagaloa Bay, the south coast estuaries and wetlands, Monono Island, and Lake Lanotoo, a crater lake in the center of Upolu that should be seen only with a guide. They also have expeditions to Savai'i. See "Accommodations," below, for information about their Rainforest Ecolodge.

10 Water Sports, Golf & Other Outdoor Pursuits

You'll soon get to know Americans Roger and Gayle Christman of **Pacific Quest Divers** (☎ and fax 24-728; e-mail pqdivers@samoa.net), who offer not just scuba diving but a host of activities, including fishing charters, snorkeling trips, kayak rentals and guided tours, and sunset cruises. They have an office at Samoa Marine, opposite the main wharf on Beach Road, and at Coconuts Beach Club (see "Accommodations," below).

FISHING   **Pacific Quest Divers** (☎ 24-728) has sport fishing charters, while **Samoa Marine** (☎ 22-271) does the deep-sea fishing here. Both are near the Main.

GOLF   The **Royal Samoan Golf Club** has a nine-hole course at Fagali'i, on the eastern side of Apia, and visitors are welcome to use the facilities. Call the club's secretary (☎ 20-120) for information and starting times. The Samoa Open Golf Championship tournament is played each year in August.

KAYAKING   Rentals and self-guided tours are available from **Pacific Quest Divers** (☎ 24-728). One self-guided tour goes through the Togo Mangrove Estuary, whose entrance is a short paddle west of Coconuts Beach Club & Resort. Another goes east to lava walls and arches along the coast near the Togitogiga National Forest. Kayaks cost S$12 ($4) per hour for a single, S$24 ($8) for a double.

As part of his **Eco-Tour Samoa** (☎ **22-144** or 25-993; e-mail ecotour@samoa.net), Dr. Steve Brown will take you sea-kayaking out to Manono Island. These trips usually are part of his environmentally friendly tour packages (see "Environmental Tours," above).

SCUBA DIVING   **Pacific Quest Divers** (☎ and fax **24-728**; e-mail pqdivers@ samoa.net) will pick you up in Apia for dives on the south coast rocks and reefs. Two-tank dives cost US$64 per dive (plus equipment rental if needed). They also do a short resort course and teach PADI certification courses.

Claus Hermansen of **Outrigger Adventure Tours,** at The Samoan Outrigger Hotel (☎ **20-042;** fax 23-880; e-mail outrigger@samoa.net), takes his divers to a turtle nesting area on the southeast coast. He charges S$150 ($50) for a two-tank dive. He also teaches C-MAS certification courses.

SWIMMING & SNORKELING   The best swimming and snorkeling is on the beaches of Aleipata and the southwest coast (see "Exploring Upolu," above). In town, just east of the main wharf, canyons in the reef at ✪ **Palolo Deep Marine Reserve** (no phone) make for good snorkeling without having to leave town. The reserve is open daily during the daylight hours, and has changing rooms; a bar; and snorkeling gear, reef shoes, and bicycles for hire. A contribution of S$2 (67¢) to the preservation fund is required.

Some people think a trip to **Papase'a Sliding Rocks** is a highlight of a trip to Apia. You of strong bottom can slide down this waterfall into a dark pool. Take a taxi or the Se'ese'e village bus. The rocks are about 2 kilometers (1.2 miles) from the paved road; the bus driver may go out of his way to take you there, but you will have to walk back to the bus route. The villagers extract S$5 ($1.65) custom fee per person.

Another popular outing away from Apia is to **Piula Cave Pool** and the outlying beaches. See "Exploring Upolu," above, for details.

On the south coast, **Pacific Quest Divers** (☎ **24-728**) has guided snorkeling expeditions for US$25, including gear.

11 Shopping

Economic hard times and encouragement by local dealers has led to an increase in quantity and quality of Samoan handcrafts in recent years, so your best buys here will be handmade baskets, sewing trays, purses, floor mats, napkin rings, place mats, and fans woven from pandanus and other local materials, plus some wood carvings.

Except for the Old Apia Market, which is open all day, the stores below observe regular business hours (see "Fast Facts: Samoa," above).

✪ **Aggie's Store.** Beach Rd., next to Aggie Grey's Hotel. ☎ **22-880.**

The hotel's gift shop has Apia's best selection of handcrafts and Samoan products such as sandalwood soap, small bags of kava, and watercolors by local artists. The handcrafts include shell and black coral jewelry and tapa cloth *(siapo* in Samoan), carved wooden war clubs, ceremonial kava bowls, and high talking chiefs' staffs (known as *tootoo).* Among clothing items are hand-screened lavalavas, T-shirts, shorts, and dresses. The shop also carries books about the Samoas and has a snack bar just inside the front door.

✪ **Kava Kavings Handicraft.** Beach Rd., west of John Williams Building. ☎ **24-145.**

Harry Paul has been encouraging Samoans to resume making handcrafts, and he carries some of the resulting works: bone fishhooks, carved war clubs, spears, and orator's staffs and "horses tails" of the type carried by high talking chiefs, hair clasps and ukuleles made from coconut shells, and many other items. He also has imported hand-crafts from Tonga, Fiji, and other South Pacific islands. Kava Kavings will pack and ship your purchases home. Along with Aggie's Gift Shop, this is the best place in town to shop for handcrafts.

Old Apia Market. Beach Rd., west of Town Clock. No phone.

Once the town's vegetable market, this giant shed is now a crowded and very active flea market, with vendors selling everything from cosmetics to shoes (local wags say it's better stocked than Apia's regular stores, since some goods may have been slipped past Customs on their way from American Samoa). Your best buys here are fine mats and other Samoan handcrafts; in fact, you can even watch local women at work in their stalls. The other handcraft shops usually have better quality pieces, but you may find an exceptional one here. Especially look for the merchant who sells intricately carved tanoa (kava) bowls.

12 Accommodations

A bed-and-breakfast option here is **The Rainforest Ecolodge,** which in reality is the home of Steve and Lumaava of Eco-Tour Samoa, P.O. Box 4609, Matautu-uta (☎ **22-144** or 25-993; e-mail ecotour@samoa.net). Their German colonial homestead is up in the hills 6 miles from Apia and is surrounded by 150 acres of a working plantation, complete with a botanical garden. They rent three rooms (none with bathroom) for US$40 double a night. Breakfast costs extra. See "Exploring Apia & Upolu," above, for information about their environmental tours.

HOTELS IN APIA
✪ **Aggie Grey's Hotel.** P.O. Box 67, Apia (Beach Rd., on the waterfront). ☎ **800/448-8355** or 22-880. Fax 23-626. E-mail: aggiegreys@samoa.net. 144 units, 25 bungalows. A/C TV TEL. US$100–US$145 double. AE, DC, MC, V.

The late Aggie Grey's son Alan Grey, his wife Marina, and their son and daughter, Fred and Tonya, are making sure that the hotel has the same warm, family feeling instilled by Aggie when she opened it in 1943 (see the "Hot Dogs and Hamburgers" box, below). The fire marshal made Alan tear down the charming old clapboard hotel a few years ago—Aggie's Store next door will show you what this venerable establishment once looked like. Alan has replaced it with a beautiful building housing the reception area, the air-conditioned Le Tamarina restaurant, an open-air bar facing the harbor, and two floors of modern rooms and suites with private verandas overlooking the water, the curve of Beach Road, and the town of Apia. Most impressively, the Victorian-style building looks like it belongs on Apia's historic waterfront, with siding that looks like clapboard, a roof of corrugated tin, and verandas trimmed in gingerbread fretwork.

The new facility hasn't changed the relaxed atmosphere back in the large, exquisite fale beside the swimming pool with a palm tree growing in the middle. Guests can still take their meals under the great turtle-shaped roof or wander over to the bar for a cold Vailima beer and a chat with friendly strangers. The efficient staff prepares feasts and barbecues in which the quantity of food dished out is, as always, astounding. And the Greys maintain Aggie's tradition of circulating among their guests. Marina Grey now dances the siva during the weekly fiafias (see "Island Nights," below).

Most rooms here are in modern, stone-accented, two-story buildings rambling through a garden so thick with tropical vegetation that it's easy to get lost trying to find your way from one room to another. Recently renovated, they are all comfortable,

Hot Dogs & Hamburgers

Back in 1919, a young woman of British and Samoan descent named Agnes Genevieve Grey started the Cosmopolitan Club on a point of land where the Vaisigano River flows into Apia Harbor. It was just a small pub catering to local businessmen and the occasional tourists who climbed off the transpacific steamers stopping in Apia.

And then the U.S. Marines landed.

That was in 1942, when thousands of American servicemen arrived in Samoa to train for the South Pacific campaigns against the Japanese. Aggie Grey started selling them much-appreciated hot dogs and hamburgers. Quickly her little enterprise expanded into a three-story clapboard hotel, with a bar at ground level, a dining room on the next, and rooms to rent on the third. Many of those young Marines, including future U.S. Secretary of State George Shultz, left Samoa with fond memories of Aggie Grey and her hotel.

Another serviceman who came to Aggie's was a U.S. naval historian named James A. Michener. Everyone in Samoa believes Michener used Aggie as the role model for Bloody Mary, the Tonkinese woman who provided U.S. servicemen with wine, song, and other diversions in his *Tales of the South Pacific.*

Although her hotel grew after the war to include more than 150 rooms, Aggie always circulated among her guests, making them feel at home. Everyone sat down family-style when taking a meal in the old clapboard building on Beach Road, and afterward moseyed over for coffee in the lounge. Afternoon tea was a time for socializing and swapping gossip from places far away. And on *fiafia* nights, when the feasts were laid out, Aggie herself would dance the graceful Samoan *siva.*

Like Robert Louis Stevenson before her, Aggie Grey was revered by the locals. They made her the only commoner ever to appear on a Samoan postage stamp. And when she died in 1988 at the age of 90, Head of State Malietoa Tanufafili II and hundreds of other mourners escorted her to her final resting place in the hills above Apia.

and although air conditioned, have good natural ventilation (fans swing from the ceiling or oscillate from a wall to help out the usual breeze). Each has a veranda or balcony where guests can sip their morning tea or coffee made right in the rooms.

Individual "VIP fale suites" are scattered around the other buildings, each of enormous size and bearing the name of one of Aggie's famous past guests, such as actors Gary Cooper, William Holden, and Marlon Brando. They have old-fashioned touches like fold-down ironing boards, irons mounted in their own wooden holders, and comfy, wicker furniture.

Dining/Diversions: No one goes hungry at Aggie's. Hearty breakfasts—either continental or a 1943 version of bacon and scrambled eggs—are served in the big fale. Sandwiches, hamburgers, and other light items are available in the Marlon Brando coffee shop off the lobby. And for fine dining, Le Tamarina Restaurant faces the harbor (see "Dining," below).

Traditionally on Wednesday, fiafia nights feature an enormous buffet of European, Chinese, and Samoan selections (look the table over before going through the line, and watch for the Samoan dishes along the front). A similar spread, plus charbroiled steaks, chicken, and sausages is laid out on Sunday barbecue night, when many restaurants in

Apia are closed. The all-you-can-eat fiafias cost about S$44 ($14.50), while the barbecues are S$35 ($11.50).

Nonguests are welcomed at all meals.

Hotel Insel Fehmarn. P.O. Box 3272, Apia (on Cross Island Rd., 1¼ miles uphill from Beach Rd.). ☎ **23-301.** Fax 22-204. E-mail: insel@samoa.net. 54 units. A/C TV TEL. US$85 double. AE, DC, MC, V.

This modern, well-kept establishment sits on the side of the hill above Apia, affording some of its motel-style rooms with views of town and the offshore reef from their balconies, especially those on the third (top) floor. Each identical room in this beige structure has two double beds, chairs, table, tiled shower-only bathroom, and kitchenette. There are a dining room and bar on the premises, as well as a convenience store, two tennis courts, and a pool. It's popular with business travelers looking for kitchen-equipped accommodations. Giordano's Cafe & Pizzeria is across the road (see "Dining," below).

Hotel Kitano Tusitala. P.O. Box 101, Apia (Beach Rd., Mulinu'u Peninsula). ☎ **800/ 448-8355** or 21-122. Fax 23-652. E-mail: kitano@samoa.net. 94 units. A/C MINIBAR TV TEL. US$60–US$140. AE, DC, MC, V.

Built in 1974 by the government and named the Tusitala in honor of Robert Louis Stevenson, this hotel is now owned by Kitano, a Japanese construction company. The modern structure is similar in appearance to the Rainmaker Hotel in Pago Pago in that its three main buildings are under huge turtle-shaped thatch roofs. They ring a tropical garden featuring a children's wading pool, from which water falls two levels into a larger adult swimming pool. Nearby are two hard-surface tennis courts. The hotel also has a tour desk, hair salon, and gift shop.

The rooms are all in five 2-story motel-style buildings grouped beyond the swimming pools. Those facing the pool have been refurbished and are in much better condition than the others, which have been repainted but still show their age. All have typical Australian and New Zealand features: a double bed with a single bed serving as a settee, tropical-style lounge chairs, bathroom with shower, refrigerator, tea/ coffee-making facilities, and sliding glass door opening onto either a private patio or balcony. They are air conditioned, but you won't feel any cross-ventilation unless you leave the back door open.

A bar and lounge in an open-air Samoan fale stands next to the pool, as does the Apaula Snackbar, open throughout the day. One of the three big common buildings houses Stevenson's Restaurant (with portraits of R.L.S. himself). The Tusitala usually has its fiafia night on Thursday. A band plays for dancing on Saturday evening.

Pasefika Inn. P.O. Box 4213, Apia (Matautu St., 100 yards from Beach Rd.). ☎ **20-971.** Fax 23-303. E-mail: pinn@samoa.net. 30 units (all with private bathroom), 18 dorm beds. A/C TEL. US$45–US$65 double, US$10 dorm bed. Rates include continental breakfast. MC, V.

This 3-story, walk-up establishment around the corner from Aggie Grey's Hotel has simple but bright rooms occupying its upper two floors (downstairs is commercial office space). Central hallways run through the building, separating the rooms into two categories. Those on one side are larger and have balconies, desks, dressers, and spa tubs. Those without balconies (including all on the third floor) are smaller and have shower-only bathrooms. All rooms are air conditioned and have tapa drapes and spreads, phones, and refrigerators. The dormitory units open to a communal kitchen, and there's a restaurant and bar available to guests only except on Friday nights, when it has live music for dancing, and for Samoan-style feasts on Sunday afternoon (see "Dining," below).

Vaiala Beach Cottages. P.O. Box 2025, Apia (Vaiala Beach, 1 mile east of Main Wharf). ☎ **22-202.** Fax 22-008. 7 bungalows. US$75 double. MC, V.

These comfortable, modern, and airy bungalows share a yard with frangipani, crotons, and other tropical plants across the street from Vaiala Beach. Except for the tropical furnishings and decor, such as cane furniture and woven floor mats, the bungalows are all identical: a full kitchen with stainless-steel sink, a bedroom with either one double or two twin beds, a spacious bathroom with a shower dispensing hot water, and a narrow balcony off a bright living room. They were built in 1984 of New Zealand–treated pine, including the varnished interior walls. The living rooms have ceiling fans hanging over the sitting area, but the large, screened, louvered windows and sliding doors leading to the balconies usually allow the trade winds to cool the house without such assistance. Reservations are advised.

RESORTS ON THE SOUTH COAST

Coconuts Beach Club & Resort. P.O. Box 3684, Apia (in Si'umu, 30 min. south of Apia). ☎ **24-849** or 800/227-5317. Fax 20-071. www.coconutsbeachclubsamoa.com. E-mail: cbc@samoa.net or cbcsamoa@aol.com. 15 units, 5 bungalows. A/C MINIBAR. US$89–US$139 double; US$239–US$289 bungalows. Rates for bungalows include rental car. AE, DC, MC, V. Turn right at end of cross-island road.

Former Hollywood show-biz lawyers Barry and Jennifer Rose developed this eclectic resort on a piece of land abutting the Togo Mangrove Estuary (mosquitoes can be plentiful at times here). They chopped down enough of this dense growth for three bungalows, each facing the lagoon, and a 2-story, motel-style block of eight rooms reached by tree-house-like stairs. They have added over-water bungalows—two luxuriously appointed hexagonal cottages with floor-to-ceiling glass walls and coffee tables with see-through tops for looking into the lagoon (use of a four-wheel-drive vehicle is included in their rates). Ashore, the spacious thatch-roofed, clapboard-sided bungalows (one has two bedrooms) have a rustic look without giving up luxuries. They have outdoorsy screened bathrooms with showers pouring down rock walls into sunken tubs. In the rooms, you can step from oval bathtubs directly onto 24-foot-long covered patios or balconies. Lots of natural wood creates unusual accents, such as tree limbs used as posts for the king-size beds, towel racks in the bathrooms, and legs for coffee tables. Another European-style building holds seven standard units with mat-lined walls and separate air-conditioned bedrooms. Another four bungalows were being built during my last visit.

A bearded, former Hawaii restaurateur named Mika holds forth under an open-sided thatch pavilion with a friendly beachfront bar. He specializes in fresh seafood, especially local lobster and mud crabs from the nearby mangrove estuary. A string band plays evenings, and Wednesday is usually fiafia night.

Erosion has wiped away the beach here, now replaced by a rock breakwater across most of the property. You can walk around the breakwater, however, and swim out to a lava wall which creates a good snorkeling area. A gecko-shaped swimming pool (it also has a gecko tile mosaic in the bottom) with swim-up bar sits just behind the breakwater but away from the main building. Roger and Gayle Christman's Pacific Quest Divers provides a host of activities, most of which cost extra (see "Water Sports, Golf & Other Outdoor Pursuits," above).

Sinelei Reef Resort. P.O. Box 1510, Apia (in Si'umu, 30 min. south of Apia). ☎ **25-191** or 25-794. Fax 20-285 or 25-490. E-mail: sinelei@samoa.net. 20 bungalows. A/C TEL. US$180–US$190 double. Rates include tropical breakfast, afternoon tea, town shuttle daily. AE, DC, MC, V.

More formal and reserved than Coconuts Beach Club, this fine resort sits on a rise over-looking the lagoon, but it has a path down to its end at a magnificent crescent-shaped beach—backed by the proverbial palm grove—which separates it from Coconuts. There's also a second, more private beach area here with "beach fales" for lounging or escaping the sun. A group of three open, Samoan-style thatch-roof buildings comprise the central complex, one each covering reception and gift shop, dining room, and bar.

The square bungalows sit to either side of the central buildings, with the choice units having sea views. They are of European construction, with peaked shingle roofs and glass walls across the front. Ventilation is at a premium, but they are all air conditioned. They have red terra-cotta floors, tropical furniture including wicker chairs and glass-top tables, refrigerators, tea/coffee-making facilities, and outdoor showers with sea-life designs in their rock floors. Some also have ceiling fans and separate bedrooms (these latter are considered to be suites and have minibars).

Dining/Diversions: With a view down over the sea, the dining room provides European and Polynesian fare, and Samoans strum guitars for evening entertainment (there's usually a fiafia night on Sunday). Down at the beach, another restaurant provides grilled steaks and fish from a perch overlooking freshwater welling up from a spring beneath the lagoon.

Amenities: Guests can use nonmotorized water sports equipment for free, and pay extra for village visits and excursions to the mangrove swamp and freshwater springs. Scuba diving and sport fishing cost extra. The bar opens to an unusual hilltop pool with a waterfall and huge lava rocks at its edge.

HOSTELS

✪ **The Samoan Outrigger Hotel.** P.O. Box 4074, Apia (Vaiala Beach, 0.5 mile east of Main Wharf). ☎ **20-042.** Fax 23-880. E-mail: outrigger@samoa.net. 7 units (2 with private bathroom), 24 dorm beds. S$55–S$88 ($22–$35) rooms, S$22 ($9) dorm bed (including tropical breakfast). MC, V.

Claus Hermansen liked what he saw so much during a visit to Samoa that he gave up a banking career in Denmark to give one of the 1894-vintage colonial homes lining Vaiala Beach a thorough painting and turned it into one of the best backpackers' hostels in the South Pacific. Once the American consulate's home, this tin-roofed house has a large central room with sea view. Claus installed a bar there so that his guests could sip a cold Vailima beer and enjoy the sunsets from the front stoop. Another room to the side serves as reading area and TV lounge with billiards table, and to the rear is a pleasant communal kitchen and dining area. The choice guest room here is in the front, where it catches the breezes off the lagoon. It and another room have their own toilets and showers. Other guests share five showers, four toilets, and laundry facilities. All rooms have fans, however, as well as mosquito nets over their beds. This establishment has been spotlessly clean throughout during my recent visits. Guests get free use of 5-speed bikes. Outrigger Adventure Tours is based here (see "Exploring Upolu," above), and Claus will take you diving or teach you to scuba (see "Water Sports, Golf & Other Outdoor Pursuits," above).

BEACH FALES AT ALEIPATA

Samoa has seen an explosion of **beach fales** in recent years. Although included in many accommodation listings, these rustic little structures belong in the camping category. They are miniature Samoan fales, with oval thatch roofs covering open-air platforms, and most provide mosquito nets, foam mattresses, and pull-down canvas or colorful plastic sides to afford some privacy and protection against the elements. Guests share communal toilets and showers in separate buildings.

The very best of these is **Tanu Beach Fales** on Savai'i (see "Savai'i," below). The best of Upolu's lot are in Aleipata, 1 hour by car from Apia on Upolu's southeastern corner. I say "best" not because of the quality of the accommodation, but because they sit right on one of Samoa's best beaches.

Directly on the beach, **Tafua Beach Fales** (☎ **20-180**) has a restaurant and bar across the road. **Litia Sini's Beach Fales** (☎ **24-327**) actually has wood sides on four of its fales. Others within an easy walk are **Sieni's & Ropert's Beach Fales** and **Romeo's Beach Fales** (both ☎ **20-878**). Rates at all are about S$40 ($13.20) per person, including meals, cash only.

Boomerang Creek (☎ **40-358**) is on the mountain side of the road, thus defeating the "beach" in beach fale, but it has the most "luxurious" fales here—well, they have lattice around them, which the others don't, thus providing at least some privacy. It also has the Kangarumu Restaurant, where you can order sandwiches, steaks, local lobster, and other simply prepared fare from a blackboard menu, and Harro's Bar dispensing libation. Fales cost S$50 ($16.50) double with breakfast, S$85 ($28) double with all meals. No credit cards.

Namu'a Beach Fales (☎ **20-566** or 41-079), actually are on Namu'a, one of the rocky islets off Aleipata Beach. A boat ferries guests from Mutiatele village to a deep-sand beach on the island. From there you have a splendid view back to Upolu. Rates are S$50 ($16.50) per person, including all meals. It's all very rustic, with no electricity or even running water on the island (water for showers is hauled in), but owner Tuisala (he's the high chief of this district) and his family will make you feel at home despite the inconveniences.

13 Dining

Think seafood. A small but thriving local fishing industry means Apia is one of the best places in the South Pacific to dine on fresh yellowfin tuna (great for sashimi) and light, flaky mahimahi (known here as *masi masi*). Tropical lobsters are available here, too, although not in the numbers harvested in Tonga.

The local **McDonald's** is on Vaea Street, a block inland from the Town Clock. A Big Mac combo will set you back about S$11 ($3.65).

SAMOAN FIAFIAS   Like other islanders, the Samoans gave up the use of pottery at least a thousand years before the Europeans arrived in the South Pacific. As did their fellow Polynesians, they cooked their foods in a pit of hot stones, which the Samoans call an *umu*. When it had all steamed for several hours, they threw back the dirt, unwrapped the delicacies, and sat down to a ✪ **fiafia.** Favorite side dishes were fresh fruit and *ota* (fish marinated with lime juice and served with vegetables in coconut milk, in a fashion similar to poisson cru in Tahiti). If you happen to be in Samoa on the seventh day after the full moon in late October or early November, the meal may include the coral worm known as *palolo.*

Aggie Grey's Hotel (☎ **22-880**), the **Hotel Kitano Tusitala** (☎ **21-122**), **Coconuts Beach Club** (☎ **24-849**), and **Sinalei Reef Reef Resort** (☎ **25-191**) each have at least one fiafia a week for about S$45 ($15) per person. Guests pass a long buffet table loaded with European, Chinese, and Samoan dishes. After stuffing down the food, they watch a show of traditional Samoan dancing. Check with the hotels to find out when they have their fiafia nights.

You can also sample genuine Samoan foods at noon on Sunday at the **Pasifika Inn,** on Matautu Street (☎ **20-972**), whose feast includes many items fresh from an umu. It costs S$35 ($11.50). Except for the hotel dining rooms, restaurants in town are closed for lunch on Sunday, so this is an attractive way to fill up if you aren't headed to the beach.

MODERATE

Le Tamarina Restaurant. Beach Rd., in Aggie Grey's Hotel. ☎ **23-626.** Reservations recommended. Main courses S$30–S$40 ($10–$13.50). AE, DC, MC, V. Mon–Sat noon–2pm and 7–10pm. INTERNATIONAL.

Tropical plants and furnishings lend appropriate atmosphere to this elegant, air-conditioned dining room with a view of Apia from the ground floor of Aggie's. Guests can wear shorts for buffet lunches, but slacks and dresses are required for evening meals, which feature local and New Zealand produce in a variety of preparations. Fresh lobster came with a tasty orange, pine nut, and butter sauce, while prime New Zealand steak with pepper and garlic sauce also appeared. Saturday evenings usually see an extensive seafood buffet laid out.

✪ **Sails Restaurant and Bar.** Beach Rd., between Ifiifi St. and Mulivai Stream. ☎ **20-628.** Reservations recommended for dinner. Lunch S$12.50–S$25 ($4.25–$8.25); main courses S$24.50–S$40 ($8–$13.50). AE, DC, MC, V. Mon–Sat 11am–11pm, Sun 6–11pm. SEAFOOD/STEAKS.

I first met Ian and Lyvia Black, a charming Australian-Samoan couple, when they were expertly managing hotels in Fiji. Now they've turned the second floor of this historic clapboard store—the first place Robert Louis Stevenson lived when he arrived here in 1889—into one of the South Pacific's best and most charming restaurants. Be sure to reserve a table out on the front porch above Beach Road, where you'll get a view over the white-and-blue railing of Apia Harbour. And by all means start with Sail's signature dish, Commodore Sashimi. Ian makes this mouthwatering concoction by rolling a tenderloin-size cut of fresh yellowfin tuna in Jamaican jerk and other spices, and then slightly searing it on the outside. You won't find anything quite like it in these islands. The creamy lobster bisque loaded with chunks of lobster is out of this world, too. Also superb is smoked marlin with fresh tropical fruits, from a recipe Ian stole from Roy's Restaurants in Hawaii. For a main course, move on to a daily special, such as mahimahi in a luscious cream, lemon, and fruit juice sauce. If you're a meat eater, opt for the tender New Zealand filet in chili and ginger sauce (it starts out gingery but leaves a spicy bite to the tongue). The lunch menu features salads, sandwiches, and burgers, and Ian and Lyvia keep the bar open all day for drinks, the best cappuccino in town, and snacks (including Commodore Sashimi). Nautical decor and jazz on the speakers add to a relaxed, friendly atmosphere.

INEXPENSIVE

✪ **Giodano's Cafe & Pizzeria.** Cross Island Rd., opposite Hotel Insel Fehmarn. ☎ **25-985.** Reservations not accepted. Pizzas S$10–S$33 ($3.50–$10); pasta S$18 ($6). MC, V. Tues–Sat 3–10pm, Sun 5–9pm. PIZZA/PASTA.

Follow your nose around the take-away counter to Alex Stanley's romantic courtyard where patio tables with candles sit under a breadfruit and other tropical trees. Small- or large-size pizzas come with a choice of several toppings. Pasta dishes, which all cost the same, consist of lasagna with beef sauce or spaghetti under bolognaise, marinara, carbonara, or a spicy vegetarian sauce. With jazz on the speaker system, this is a very popular establishment with local expatriate residents.

✪ **Gourmet Seafood & Grille.** Convent St., 1 block behind Central Post Office. ☎ **24-625.** Sandwiches and burgers S$2–S$10 (67¢–$3.30); main courses S$8–S$22 ($2.50–$7.25). No credit cards. Mon–Sat 7am–10pm. SEAFOOD/STEAKS.

You can start your day with fresh fruit pies and muffins at this popular local establishment, which would win all awards for charm in the inexpensive-restaurant category anywhere. Large tree trunks hold up the roof, under which fishnets form a ceiling. Buoys and other nautical items add to the atmosphere. There's nothing gourmet here, but the hallmark is fresh fish. I had a monstrous slab of grilled mahimahi that obviously had been caught that day; served with French fries and a salad, it also was an unbelievable value at just S$12 ($4). You can also get fish and chips, New Zealand steaks, and Apia's best *oka* (marinated raw fish with coconut cream and vegetables). Order at the counter; they will call your number.

Le Moana Cafe & Steakhouse. Vaea St. at Convent St., in Lotemau Centre. ☎ **24-828.** Breakfast S$5–S$12 ($1.65–$3); sandwiches, burgers, and snacks S$4–S$8 ($1.25–$2.50); meals S$12 ($4). MC, V. Mon–Fri 7:30am–3pm and 6:30–9:30pm, Sat 7am–1pm and 6:30–9:30pm, Sun 9am–1pm and 5:30–9:30pm. SNACK BAR.

You can cool off in this spotlessly clean, air-conditioned cafeteria-cafe in the modern Lotemau Centre mall, perhaps with a cold coconut, fresh fruit, sandwiches, meat pies, or two daily specials such as beef curry or roast chicken. No smoking is allowed inside, but you can puff or not on an outside terrace. Evening meals are à la carte grilled steaks and fish, except barbecue buffets on Wednesday and Friday for S$25 ($8.25) per person.

14 Island Nights

SAMOAN DANCE SHOWS Samoa is no different from the other Polynesian countries in that watching a traditional dance show as part of a fiafia night is a high-light of any visit. Samoan dance movements are graceful and emphasize the hands more than the hips; the costumes feature more tapa cloth and fine mats than flowers. While the dances are not as lively nor the costumes as colorful as those in Tahiti and the Cook Islands, they are definitely worth seeing.

✪ **Aggie Grey's Hotel** (☎ **22-880**) consistently has the best fiafia night in town, usually on Wednesday, and the show just keeps getting better. This isn't a Las Vegas floor show, but the fire dance around the swimming pool is nothing short of spectac-ular for these parts. Aggie's fiafia night traditionally is on Wednesday at 6:45pm. But don't be late, for the show starts promptly at 6:45pm, with dinner served afterward.

Hotel Kitano Tusitala (☎ **21-122**) usually has its show in one of its huge fales on Thursday at 7pm.

On the south coast, **Sinalei Reef Reef Resort** (☎ **25-191**) puts on its fiafia on Friday nights, and **Coconuts Beach Club** (☎ **24-849**) does its on Saturday.

The dinners and shows cost about S$45 ($15) at all the hotels. Compared to what you'll pay elsewhere in the South Pacific, that's a steal.

CABARET SHOWS Set aside Thursday night to join the crowd at ✪ **Cindy's Cabaret Show,** starting at 9pm in Margrey-Ta's Lagoon Beer Garden on Beach Road near the Main Wharf (☎ **25-395**). Cindy's drag show is so entertaining that he (or is it she?) has taken it to Auckland (and San Francisco could be next). The troupe lip-syncs to recorded popular tunes, but there's definitely a Samoan influence in their col-orful costumes, elegant dance steps, and satirical humor. There's a S$10 ($3.30) cover charge.

PUB CRAWLING Nights are quiet in Apia from Sunday to Thursday. Then everyone heads down Beach Road, hitting one pub after another. Most of these have live bands on Friday (the biggest night) and Saturday. Thanks largely to citizens out-raged by bars opening in residential neighborhoods, pubs legally must close at mid-night throughout the week (none are open on Sunday). As a practical matter, some of them keep right on going into the wee hours, especially on Friday night.

Note: Don't sit near the door, since this is where fights are most likely to erupt as bouncers evict drunken and unruly customers who don't want to leave.

Margrey-Ta's Lagoon Beer Garden (☎ 25-395) is the beginning of Apia's pub crawl along Beach Road, which goes from there westward around the harbor. Next stop is **Evening Shades,** just across the bridge from Aggie Grey's Hotel (☎ 23-906), a dance club with pulsating music, especially "Jamoa," a variation on rap that is popular among the Samoans living down in Auckland.

Continuing past Aggie Grey's Hotel and Ifiifi Street, you'll come to the slapped-together facade and worse-than-plain furniture at ✪ **Otto's Reef** (☎ 22-691), the most popular bar in town with both locals and expatriate residents. You can look right into this open-air establishment. Two doors down is the air-conditioned **On the Rocks** (☎ 20-093), Apia's only real cocktail bar. The crawl then skips past the Town Clock to the **RSA Club** (☎ 20-171) and the **Hotel Kitano Tusitala** (☎ 21-122), which turns one of its big fales into a dance floor on Saturdays.

The young set end their night at the **Mount Vaea Club** (☎ 21-627) on Vaitele Street near Tofafuafua Road. Don't expect much charm here, just loud music, much talk, a packed house of young Samoans, and an occasional fight around midnight on Friday and Saturday. Women should exercise caution if visiting this old-time South Seas joint alone.

15 Savai'i

You may wish you had stayed longer on Savai'i, whose green mountains rise out of the sea and into the clouds across the 13-mile-wide Apolima Strait. Savai'i is half again as large as Upolu, yet it has only a third as many people as its smaller and more prosperous sister, and they live in villages mainly along the east and south coasts. Elsewhere, Savai'i is made up of practically deserted lava fields and forests. Its 470 volcanic craters are considered to be dormant (the last major eruption occurred in 1911).

On Savai'i, rural Samoan life has changed less than on any other island, and travelers can visit picturesque villages sitting on the edge of the lagoon.

On the trip over, you will see the picturesque islands of **Manono** and **Apolima** sitting in the Apolima Strait between Upolu and Savai'i. Apolima is a small volcanic crater. The beachside village of Apolima-tui sits on the shore where the crater collapsed on one side. Small boats shuttle between Apolima Island and the village of Apolima-uta on Upolu's western end. Boats to Manono leave from Mulifanua Wharf. **Samoa Scenic Tours** (☎ 22-880) at Aggie Grey's Hotel operates popular day trips to Manono and its beautiful surrounding reef, and Dr. Steve Brown of **Eco-Tour Samoa** (☎ 22-144 or 25-993) has sea kayaking expeditions to Manono (see "Exploring Apia & Upolu," above).

GETTING THERE & GETTING AROUND

See "Getting There & Getting Around" earlier in this chapter for air services to Savai'i provided by **Polynesian Airlines** and **Samoa Air,** and the *Lady Samoa* ferry service between Upolu and Savai'i.

You can organize a trip to Savai'i yourself, but the easiest way is to contact one of the tour operators in Apia (see "Organized Tours," earlier in this chapter).

For example, **Oceania Tours** (☎ 24-443) has a 2-day, 1-night package for about US$160, including round-trip transportation, transfers, and a half-day tour of Savai'i. Oceania's day trips to Savai'i cost about US$110 per person.

Eco-Tour Samoa (☎ 25-144 or 25-993 in Apia) has 2- and 3-day expeditions around Savai'i, with an emphasis on exploring the volcanic craters, lava fields, wetlands, and rain forests. See "Exploring Upolu," above, for more information about this company.

Taxis meet the planes and ferry. One-way fare from Maota Airstrip to Safua on the east coast is S$15 ($5). From the ferry wharf to the east coast hotels costs S$10 ($3.30) one-way. The fare is S$100 ($33) one-way to Asau village, 55 miles away on the opposite side of Savai'i.

Local **buses** operate frequently along the east coast. Those headed to Puapua and Tuasivi pass the hotels. The fare is WS60¢ (20¢). Long-distance buses leave Salelologa shortly after each ferry arrival. It's possible to take a bus as far as Asau and back.

Savai'i Car Rentals (☎ **51-206;** fax 51-291; e-mail cars@samoa.net), rents Jeeps for S$110 to S$135 ($36.50 to $44.50) a day. A deposit of S$250 ($82.50) is required, or you can pay by MasterCard and Visa credit cards. It is part of **Savai'i Travel & Tours,** at the intersection of the wharf and main roads in Salelologa. They can assist with reconfirming your return flight on Polynesian Airlines or Samoa Air. If you rent a vehicle in Apia, be sure to ask if you can bring it to Savai'i on the ferry.

The round-island road is completely paved.

EXPLORING SAVAI'I

Unless you have a week or more and plenty of energy, take a tour of this large and sparsely populated island with so little public transport and few road signs. Even then, you'll need 3 days to see all of the readily accessible sights, with no time for the beach.

✪ **Safua Tours,** based at the Safua Hotel (☎ **51-271;** fax 51-272), offers excursions, usually guided by Warren Jopling, a retired Australian geologist who has lived on the island many years. I have toured the island with Warren and have found him to be a font of information, especially about the desertlike lava fields. He will tailor any tour to suit your interests. It will take a full day to see most of the sights, with half the day spent going along the east and north coasts, the other half along the south shore. Half-day tours cost US$27, while full-day excursions costs US$45 per person. Reservations are required.

THE EAST & NORTH COASTS

Leaving the Safua Hotel, the east coast road soon passes a memorial to the Rev. John Williams, then goes up a rise to **Tuasivi,** the administrative center of the island and site of the hospital and police station. From there it drops down to **Faga** and **Siufaga,** two long, gorgeous beaches. Many villages along this stretch have bathing pools fed by fresh water running underground down from the mountains. Only the south side of Savai'i has rivers and streams. Rainwater seeps into the porous volcanic rock elsewhere and reappears as springs along the shoreline.

Mount Matavanu last erupted between 1905 and 1911, when it sent a long lava flow down to the northeast coast, burying villages and gardens before backing up behind the reef. Today the desertlike **Matavanu lava field** is populated primarily by primitive ferns. The flow very nearly inundated the village of **Mauga,** which sits along the rim of an extinct volcano's cone. The villagers play cricket on the crater floor. Past Mauga is the **Virgin's Grave,** a hole left around a grave when the lava almost covered a nearby church. The steeple still sticks out of the twisted black mass. The villagers charge S$2 (66¢) to visit the grave.

The north-coast road past the lava fields is picturesque but holds little of interest other than gorgeous tropical scenery. A drink at **Le Lagoto Bar,** between Fagamalo and Lelepa, or lunch at **Stevenson's at Manase,** just west of Manase village, makes a nice refueling stop if you get that far (see "Accommodations & Dining," below).

THE SOUTH COAST

On the south coast near Vailoa, on the Letolo Plantation, stands the ancient **Pulemelei Mound,** a collection of rocks similar to the ceremonial temples, or maraes, in French Polynesia and the Cook Islands. It's the largest archaeological ruin in Polynesia: A 2-tiered pyramid 240 feet long, 193 feet wide, and 48 feet high. This one is so old, however, that the Samoans no longer have legends explaining their original function. A New Zealand-funded project is underway to clear the ruins and improve access. The side road, which passes Afu'a'au Waterfall, ends some 1½ miles from the mound. A steep and often muddy track leads down to the waterfall.

From the mounds, the south-coast road continues to Gautavai Waterfall, a lovely black-sand beach at Nu'u, and geyserlike blowholes at Taga on the island's southernmost point.

ACCOMMODATIONS & DINING

Like Upolu, Savai'i has seen an explosion of beach fales during the past few years. The pick here is ✪ **Tanu Beach Fales,** Post Office, Fagamalo (☎ and fax **54-050**), which shares a north shore beach with the much more expensive Stevenson's at Manase (see below). Six of its 20 fales sit right by the lagoon, while the others are in a grove of tropical trees. Guests share cold-water showers. A central, European-style building provides a lounge and dining area, and guests can also wander into the owner's traditional Samoan fale. There's a communal kitchen and grocery shop, and you can walk along the beach to Stevenson's for lunch. Rates are S$40 ($13) per person, including breakfast and dinner, mosquito net, linen, mattress, and pillow. No credit cards are accepted, so bring cash or traveler's checks.

Le Lagoto Beach Resort. P.O. Box 34, Fagamalo, Manase (between Fagamalo and Lelepa villages, 28 miles north of ferry wharf). ☎ **58-189.** Fax 58-249. 8 units (all with private bathroom). TV TEL. US$99 double. MC, V.

Kuki and Sara Retzlaff have four cottage-like fales and three rooms in a 2-story, European-style house at the end of their property, which has a beautiful sunset view from its lovely beachside perch (*lagoto* means sunset in Samoan). The fales are equipped with double beds, mosquito nets, toaster ovens, refrigerators, fans, TVs, phones, and shower-only bathrooms. The Retzlaffs also serve breakfast, lunch, and dinner in a screened Samoan-style fale, or you can do your own cooking in the 2-story house. They provide snorkeling gear and canoes for guests to explore a marine reserve offshore.

Safua Hotel. Private Bag, Salelologa, Savai'i (in Safua village, 4 miles north of wharf). ☎ **51-271.** Fax 51-272. E-mail: tuisafua@samoa.net. 10 fales (all with private bathroom). US$98 double. Rates include meals. AE, MC, V.

This rustic hotel is known not so much for the quality of its accommodations as for its owner, Moelagi Jackson, who holds two chiefly titles in her own right. Her main fale holds a bar and dining room, where family-style meals feature Samoan favorites such as chicken curry and whole fish in ginger. The fales scattered about her lawn are of clapboard construction, with front porches, screened windows, basic electric lights, and bathrooms with cold-water showers. Don't be surprised to hear a cat fight or the grunts of pigs running loose at night. The Safua will arrange village accommodation for US$25 per person, including meals.

The Savaiian Hotel. P.O. Box 5082, Salelologa, Savai'i (in Lalomalava village, 4 miles north of ferry wharf). ☎ **51-206.** Fax 51-291. E-mail: savaiian@samoa.net. 6 units, 4 bungalows (all with private bathroom). A/C MINIBAR. S$135 ($44.50) double room, S$66 ($22) double bungalow. MC, V.

Built and opened in 1992, this lagoonside establishment is the most modern and up-to-date accommodation on Savai'i. There's no beach here, only a breakwater, but there is a restaurant serving breakfast, lunch, and dinner. It's in large main building which often hosts official functions on weekend evenings. The six identical rooms are in three duplex, concrete block structures with peaked roofs. They all have sliding doors opening to porches with views of the lagoon. They come with double and single beds, kitchenettes, and adequate shower-only bathrooms with hot water. The four Samoan-style bungalows sit away from the beach. They are much more basic, with real thatch roofs, screened windows, ceiling fans (but not air conditioners), and cold-water showers.

Siufaga Beach Resort. P.O. Box 8002, Tuasive, Savai'i (in Faga village, 8 miles north of ferry wharf). ☎ **53-518.** Fax 53-535. 8 units (all with private bathroom). US$45–US$55 double. MC, V.

Dr. Peter Cafarelli, an Italian who has lived on Savai'i since the late 1960s, actually owns the 7 acres of lawn under his six Samoan-style fales facing Faga Beach and an emerald lagoon speckled with coral heads. Two new fales are equipped with front porches, full kitchens, and hot water showers. They are much larger than the other six somewhat basic, tin-roofed guest fales, which have small refrigerators, hot plate, and cold-water showers. All units are cooled by the trade winds but have electric fans just in case. Also on the premises, the upstairs **Parenzo's Bar/Restaurant** (same phone number) offers inexpensive Italian fare. You can dine at tables inside or outside on a porch with lagoon views.

Stevenson's at Manase. P.O. Box 210, Apia (at Manase village, 30 miles north of ferry wharf). ☎ **58-219.** Fax 58-219. 10 units (all with private bathrooms), 10 beach fales (none with private bathroom). A/C TV. US$66 double room, US$125 bungalow, US$10 per person in beach fale. MC, V.

The best features of this establishment, on a lovely beach just west of Manase village, are two stunning thatch-roofed, sawdust-floored buildings holding Fanny's Restaurant and the Admiral Benbow Bar. Across the road on the beach, 10 bungalows have leaf exteriors to make them look rustic, but inside they are relatively modern, with air conditioners and televisions plus woven mat walls, tapa-lined ceilings, and outdoor hot-water showers enclosed by rock walls. Backpackers can share beach fales. Stevenson's is a popular local beach on weekends, when a bar opens in a beachside pavilion. Guests can use paddleboats, canoes, and snorkeling gear.

American Samoa 13

The main reason to visit American Samoa is to see its incredible beauty, and you'll get an eyeful of that on the 7-mile ride from the airport at Tafuna into the legendary port of Pago Pago. Instead of following a gentle shoreline like the west coast road does over in independent Samoa, here it twists and turns along the gorgeous rocky coastline of Tutuila, one of the South Pacific's most dramatically beautiful islands. At places it rounds the cliffs of headlands that drop down to the sea; at others it curves along beaches in small bays backed by narrow valleys. All the way, the surf pounds on the reef. When you make the last turn at Blount's Point, there before you are the green walls dropping precipitously into Pago Pago Harbor. The physical beauty of this little island competes with the splendor of Moorea and Bora Bora in French Polynesia.

But you'll also pass through Nu'uli, once a sleepy Samoan village but now a bustling suburb with a small shopping mall and a modern multi-screen cinema. You'll notice right away that the roads here are crowded with automobiles and buses and are patrolled by policemen bedecked with revolvers in big American-style cruisers. And when you reach Pago Pago, you'll find the view across the fabled harbor—if it isn't obscured by a veritable mountain of rusting shipping containers—reveals two smelly tuna canneries. It's little wonder, therefore, that many visitors see American Samoa as ruined by modern commercialism, as crowded, littered, seedy, and run-down.

Yet despite the inroads of Western ways and American money, the local residents still cling to *fa'a Samoa,* the ancient Samoan way of life (see "The Samoan People" in chapter 12). While many young American Samoans wear Western clothes and speak only English—with a pronounced Hawaiian or Californian accent—out in the villages the older folk still converse in Samoan and abide by the old ways.

Nevertheless, the Samoan culture is best experienced in independent Samoa. I usually stay in Apia and make a day trip from there to Pago Pago.

1 American Samoa Today

The seven islands of American Samoa are on the eastern end of the 300-mile-long Samoa Archipelago. Together they comprise a land area of 77 square miles, 53 of which are on **Tutuila,** the slender remains of an ancient volcano. One side of Tutuila's crater apparently blew away,

The melancholy irony of this smug little island is that American Samoa epitomizes the state of comfortable dependence on cash and Western goods to which so many aspire.
—John Dyson, 1982

almost cutting the island in two. Thus was created the long, bent arm of **Pago Pago Harbor,** one of the South Pacific's most dramatically scenic spots.

American Samoa is the only United States territory south of the equator. American Samoans are nationals, not citizens, of the United States. They often refer to the islands—not to the United States—as their "country." Although they carry American passports, have unrestricted entry into the U.S., and can serve in the U.S. armed forces, they cannot vote in American presidential elections.

Only half as many American Samoans live in their home islands as reside in the U.S., where a number of them have made names for themselves as college and professional football players. They have been replaced at home by Western Samoans and some Tongans, who have swelled the population to some 55,000, up from 30,000 in the early 1990s.

GOVERNMENT   The United States Department of the Interior in Washington has jurisdiction over American Samoa, but the territory has considerable say over its local affairs. The territorial government is patterned after that of the United States, with some important local wrinkles. American Samoans elect their own governor, who's head of the executive branch. But they elect only members of their House of Representatives, the lower house of the bicameral legislature known as the Fono, while senators are chosen by the chiefs in accordance with Samoan custom. The Fono has authority over the budget and local affairs, although both the Interior Department and the governor can veto the laws it passes. Local government is organized by counties and villages under a secretary of Samoan affairs, a position traditionally held by a ranking chief. A third branch of government, the High Court of American Samoa, has a special department that deals exclusively with land ownership and matai titles.

American Samoans also elect a nonvoting delegate to the U.S. House of Representatives in Washington.

The American Samoan government's annual budget is considerably larger than that of independent Samoa, which has a population some four times larger. Washington provides about half the American Samoan government's revenue. Some 80% of the taxes raised locally go to pay more than 40% of the local work force.

THE ECONOMY   The American Samoa islands are small, rugged, and relatively unproductive. Money from Washington and the tuna canneries are the major sources of income. The canneries employ some 4,000 workers, most of them Western Samoans. They have faced increased competition from Asian canneries in recent years, however, and lower protective tariffs have reduced their advantage in selling to the U.S. mainland.

Most other workers are employed by retail establishments, a few small manufacturers, and service businesses, especially shipping companies, which have made Pago Pago a major transshipment point (the Budweiser beer sold in Western Samoa and Tonga is shipped through Pago Pago).

2 History 101

As friendly as American Samoans are today, their ancestors did anything but warmly welcome a French expedition under Jean La Pérouse, which came ashore in 1787 on

---

Unfriendly Fire

Except during World War II, the United States Navy did very little during its half century in control of American Samoa. When the war with Japan broke out, Tutuila became a major forward training base for the U.S. Marine Corps. The Marines installed shore batteries in the hills above the entrance to Pago Pago Harbor and built concrete pillboxes along Tutuila's shoreline. Many of them are still standing.

Thousands of American Samoans joined the Marines during the war, and thousands of others formed a home guard militia. Enlisting in the United States armed services—especially the Marines—is to this day considered an honorable undertaking for American Samoans.

The home guard militia had only one chance to see action during World War II. That occurred when a Japanese submarine surfaced offshore and lobbed a few shells toward Tutuila. Ironically, their target was a store owned by Frank Shimasaki, the island's only resident of Japanese descent.

---

the north coast of Tutuila. Samoan warriors promptly attacked, killing some 12 members of the landing party, which in turn killed 39 Samoans. The site of the battle is known as **Massacre Bay.** La Pérouse survived that incident, but he and his entire expedition later disappeared in what is now Solomon Islands.

American businessmen cast an eye on Pago Pago in the mid-1800s, and in 1872, the U.S. Navy negotiated a treaty with the chiefs of Tutuila to permit it to use Pago Pago as a coaling station. The U.S. Congress never ratified this document, but it helped keep the Germans out of Eastern Samoa, as present-day American Samoa was then known.

In 1900, the chiefs on Tutuila ceded control of their island to the United States, and the paramount chief of the Manu'a Group of islands east of Tutuila did likewise in 1905. Finally ratified by the U.S. Senate in 1929, those treaties are the legal foundation for the U.S. presence in American Samoa. "Presence" is the accurate term, for under those treaties the U.S. does not "possess" American Samoa; instead, it is here subject to the conditions of the treaties, one of the most important of which is a U.S. obligation to preserve the system of chiefs and to retain the traditional ways of fa'a Samoa, including the communal ownership of Samoan land.

ON THE DOLE   From 1900 until 1951, American authority in Samoa rested with the U.S. Navy, which maintained the refueling station at Pago Pago and for the most part left the local chiefs alone to conduct their own affairs. Tutuila became a training base for U.S. servicemen during World War II, but things quickly returned to normal after 1945. Since it had little military value, control of the territory was shifted from the Navy to the U.S. Department of the Interior in 1951.

The Interior Department did little in the islands until 1961, when *Reader's Digest* magazine ran a well-publicized article about "America's Shame in the South Seas." The story took great offense at the lack of roads and adequate schools, medical care, water and sewer service, and housing. The U.S. federal government reacted by building sealed roads, an international airport, water and electrical systems, the then-modern Rainmaker Hotel, and a convention center. A mile-long cable was strung across Pago Pago Harbor to build a television transmitter atop 1,610-foot Mount Alava, from which education programming was beamed into the schools. The territory's duty-free status and relatively low wages enticed American firms to build the two tuna canneries.

For fear of losing all that federal money, American Samoans were reluctant to tinker with their political relationship with Washington during the 1960s and 1970s, when other South Pacific colonies were becoming independent. The United States offered to let them have local autonomy, but they refused. That attitude finally changed in the mid-1970s, when an appointed governor turned out to be very unpopular. After twice turning down the proposal, American Samoans voted in 1976 to elect their own governor, and did so for the first time in 1977.

3 Visitor Information & Entry Requirements

VISITOR INFORMATION

The **American Samoan Office of Tourism,** P.O. Box 1147, Pago Pago, AS 96799 (☎ 633-1091; fax 633-1094; www.samoanet.com/americansamoa; e-mail samoa@ samoatelco.com), has offices in Utulei, next to the yacht club. It also acts as a booking agent for the *Fale, Fala Ma Ti,* or homestay program (see "Accommodations," below). The office is open Monday through Friday 7:30am to 4pm.

The delegate from American Samoa to the U.S. Congress also dispenses some tourist information. The address is U.S. House of Representatives, Washington, D.C. 20515 (☎ **202/225-8577**).

You can also get advance information from the **Tourism Council of the South Pacific** (see "Visitor Information & Entry Requirements" in chapter 2).

ENTRY REQUIREMENTS

Visas are not required for stays of up to 30 days. Technically, U.S. citizens need only proof of citizenship (such as a birth certificate) to enter American Samoa. They will need valid passports to enter independent Samoa, however, and having one speeds entry here and back into the United States. Citizens of other nations must have passports to enter American Samoa. Everyone must possess a ticket for onward passage.

Immunizations are required only if a person has been in an infected yellow fever or cholera area within 14 days of arrival at Pago Pago.

Customs allowances (you pay no duty) are 1 liter of liquor or wine and 1 carton of cigarettes. Illegal drugs and firearms are prohibited, and pets will be quarantined. Returning American citizens get larger Customs allowances for purchases made in American Samoa, provided they have been in the territory for at least 48 hours.

4 Money

U.S. bank notes and coins are used in American Samoa. Western Samoan currency is not accepted, nor can it be exchanged in American Samoa. There is no bargaining over prices.

HOW TO GET LOCAL CURRENCY The **Bank of Hawaii** and the **Amerika Samoa Bank,** both in Fagatogo, are open Monday through Friday from 9am to 3pm. Transacting business with them is virtually the same as doing business with a bank in the United States. You can get cash advances using your MasterCard or Visa cards at the banks. Both have ATMs.

CREDIT CARDS American Express, Visa, MasterCard, and Diners Club credit cards are accepted by the hotels, car-rental firms, and airlines. Otherwise, it's best to carry enough cash to cover your anticipated expenses.

5 When to Go

"It did not pour, it flowed," wrote W. Somerset Maugham in his 1921 short story "Rain," the famous tale of prostitute Sadie Thompson, who seduces a puritanical missionary while stranded in American Samoa. This description, however, applies mainly to Pago Pago, which, because of its location behind appropriately named Rainmaker Mountain, gets an average of over 200 inches (500cm) of rain per year. For the most part, American Samoa enjoys a typically tropical climate, with lots of very intense sunshine even during the wet season from December to April. Average daily high temperatures range from 83°F (28°C) in the drier and somewhat cooler months of June through September to 86°F (30°C) from December to April, when midday can be hot and sticky. Evenings are usually in the comfortable 70s (21°C to 26°C) all year round.

EVENTS & HOLIDAYS

The biggest celebration is on April 17, when **Flag Day** commemorates the raising of the Stars and Stripes over Tutuila in 1900. The second Sunday in October is observed as **White Sunday,** when children attend church dressed in white and later are honored at family feasts.

American Samoa observes New Year's Day, President's Day (the third Monday in February), Good Friday, Flag Day (April 17), Memorial Day (the last Monday in May), the Fourth of July, Labor Day (the first Monday in September), Columbus Day (the second Monday in October), Veteran's Day (November 11), Thanksgiving (the fourth Thursday in November), and Christmas Day.

6 Getting There & Getting Around

GETTING THERE

FROM WESTERN SAMOA   Some travel agents in Apia offer packages for day trips to Pago Pago. For example, **Oceania Travel & Tours** (☎ **24-443** in Apia; fax 22-255) offers 1-day tours for about $150 per person, including round-trip airfare, a guided tour of Pago Pago, and lunch. Oceania Tours has a desk in the Kitano Tusitala Hotel in Apia.

Polynesian Airlines (☎ **800/644-7659,** 22-737 in Apia, or 633-4331 in Pago Pago) and **Samoa Air** (☎ **22-321** in Apia or 699-9126 in Pago Pago) both shuttle back and forth between Fagali'i Airstrip near Apia and Pago Pago several times a day. Round-trip fares on both airlines are $191 ($63) if purchased in Apia, $89 if bought in American Samoa. That saving is one more reason to make your Samoan base in Apia.

For the adventurous, a relatively modern ferry, the *Lady Naomi,* makes the 8-hour voyage between Pago Pago and Apia once a week, usually leaving the main wharf in Apia at 11pm on Wednesday and departing Pago Pago's marine terminal at 4pm Thursday for the return voyage. Tickets should be bought at least a day ahead of time. One-way tickets purchased in Apia cost S$40 ($13) for a seat, S$50 ($16.50) for a bunk. Round-trip fares purchased in Apia are S$60 and S$80 ($20 and $26.50), respectively. The *Lady Naomi* is operated by the **Western Samoa Shipping Corporation,** whose ticket office is on Beach Road opposite the main wharf in Apia (☎ **20-935**). The American Samoa agent is **Polynesia Shipping Services** (☎ **633-1211**), whose office is opposite Sadie's Restaurant in Pago Pago. Since the trade winds prevail from the southeast, the trip going west with the wind toward Apia is usually somewhat smoother.

FROM OTHER COUNTRIES   The only international carrier serving American Samoa is **Hawaiian Airlines,** which flies from several West Coast cities to Pago Pago, with a change of planes at its base at Honolulu. Otherwise, you can fly to Faleolo Airport in Western Samoa on **Air New Zealand, Air Pacific,** or **Polynesian**

Airlines, then connect on to Pago Pago. For more information, see "Getting There" in chapter 2.

ARRIVING & DEPARTING The runways at **Pago Pago** International Airport extend for half their length on landfills over the reef near the village of Tafuna, about 7 miles (11km) west of The Rainmaker Hotel. Taxi fare is $10 from the airport to Pago Pago. Local buses shuttle along the Tafuna road. The bus fare to town is 50¢. There is no departure tax on passengers leaving Pago Pago.

GETTING AROUND
BY RENTAL CAR The only international car-rental firm in American Samoa is **Avis** (☎ 800/331-1212 or 699-4408), which rents non-air-conditioned cars for $45, air-conditioned models for $55 to $65 a day including unlimited mileage, plus $10 for insurance. The Avis office in Apia (☎ 20-486) will reserve a car in Pago Pago for you. Local firms include **Royal Samoan Car Rental** (☎ 633-2017 or 633-4545) and **Pavitt's U-Drive** (☎ 633-1456).

Your valid home driver's license will be honored in American Samoa. Driving is on the right-hand side of the road, and traffic signs are the same as those used in the U.S. Speed limits are 15 m.p.h. in the built-up areas and 25 m.p.h. on the open road.

BY BUS It sometimes seems that every extended family on Tutuila owns an "aiga bus," since so many of these gaily painted vehicles prowl the roads from early in the morning until sunset every day except Sunday, when they are put to use to haul the family to church. Basically they run from the villages to the market in Pago Pago and back, picking up anyone who waves along the way. To get off, push the button for the bell as you approach your destination. Some buses leave the market and run to Fagasa on the north coast or to the east end of the island; others go from the market to the west. None goes from one end of the island to the other, so you'll have to change at the market in order to do a stem-to-stern tour of Tutuila. The drivers are friendly and helpful, so just ask how far they go in each direction. Fares are between 25¢ and $1 a ride.

BY TAXI There are **taxi stands** at the airport (☎ 699-1179) and at the Pago Pago market (no phone). The taxi companies are **Aeto Cab** (☎ 633-2366), **Black Ace** (☎ 633-5445), **Island Taxi** (☎ 633-5645), and **Samoa Cab Service** (☎ 633-5870 or 633-5871). None of the taxis has a meter, so be sure to negotiate the fare before driving off. As a starting point for your discussions, the fares should be about $1 a mile.

Fast Facts: American Samoa

American Express There is no American Express representative in American Samoa.

Area Code The international country code is **684.**

Bookstores Transpac, under Sadie's Restaurant in Pago Pago and in Nu'uli Shopping Center on the main road west of the airport, and **Polynesian Picks,** the gift shop in the Rainmaker Hotel, both carry some paperback books, and Polynesian Picks has some current U.S. magazines.

Business Hours Normal shopping hours are Monday through Friday from 9am to 6pm and Saturday from 9am to 2. Government offices are open Monday through Friday from 7:30am to 4pm.

Camera/Film A wide variety of film is available at reasonable prices. **Samoa Photo Express,** opposite the Fono building in Fagatogo (☎ 633-2374), has 1-hour developing of color print film.

Clothing   Lightweight, informal summer clothing is appropriate all year, with perhaps a light sweater or wrap for evenings from June through September. I always carry a folding umbrella or plastic raincoat, since it can rain any time of the day or night in Pago Pago. Young American Samoans have adopted Western-style dress, including blue jeans and shorts of respectable length, although the traditional wraparound lavalava still is worn by many older men and women. In keeping with Samoan custom regarding modesty, visitors should not wear bathing suits or other skimpy clothing away from the hotels. This is not a French territory, so women must wear their bikini tops.

Drugstores   See "Hospital," below.

Electricity   American Samoa uses 110-volt electric current and plugs identical to those in the U.S.

Embassies/Consulates   The governor of American Samoa is a consular official of the U.S. federal government and can issue temporary passports to U.S. citizens and nationals who lose theirs, provided they have some other proof of citizenship. Applications should be made to the **Immigration Office** (☎ **633-4203**), in the Department of Legal Affairs. The Republic of Korea has a consulate, and the Republic of China (Taiwan) maintains a liaison office in Pago Pago, primarily to assist the Korean and Taiwanese crews of the tuna boats unloading their catches at the tuna canneries.

Emergencies   The emergency telephone number for the police, fire department, and ambulance is **911.** The emergency room at the **Lyndon B. Johnson Tropical Medical Center** (☎ **633-5555**) in Faga'alu is open 24 hours a day.

Firearms   They are tightly controlled, and permits will be required.

Gambling   There are no casinos or other organized forms of gambling in American Samoa except for slot machines in some stores and private clubs. Money is also wagered at very popular bingo games.

Hospital   The **Lyndon B. Johnson Tropical Medical Center** in Faga'alu west of Pago Pago (turn off the main road at Tom Ho Chung's store) may be a classic example of socialized medicine, but it's one of the better hospitals in the South Pacific. The outpatient clinic is open 24 hours a day. The medical center's main phone number is ☎ **633-1222.** The emergency line is ☎ **633-5555.**

Insects   There are no dangerous insects in American Samoa, and the plentiful mosquitoes do not carry malaria.

Libraries   **Feleti Pacific Library,** north of The Rainmaker Hotel, has a good collection of books about the South Pacific.

Liquor Laws   There are no unusual laws to worry about. Most of the beer consumed is imported from the U.S.

Maps   The American Samoa Office of Tourism distributes a one-sheet set of maps of the islands (see "Visitor Information & Entry Requirements," above).

Newspapers/Magazines   American Samoa has two tabloid newspapers that carry local news: the weekly *Samoa Journal* and the daily *Samoa News.* Both papers' coverage of local events can be quite colorful.

Post Office   The United States Postal Service's main post office is in Fagatogo. U.S. postage rates apply, and first-class and priority letters and packages go by air between American Samoa and the United States—33¢ for a letter at press time. Unless you pay the first-class or priority mail rate, however, parcel post is sent by ship and will take several weeks to reach the U.S. The main post office is open

Monday through Friday from 8am to 4pm and Saturday from 8am to noon. The ZIP Code for all of American Samoa is 96799.

Radio/TV   Those transmitters atop Mount Alava are used during the day to send educational TV programs to the territory's public schools and to transmit CNN and live sporting events. At night they broadcast two channels of U.S. network entertainment programs. The broadcasts can be seen 80 miles away in Samoa. Many homes in American Samoa also have cable television.

The territory has one FM radio station, which transmits American network news broadcasts on the hour.

Safety   Street crime is not a serious problem in American Samoa except late at night around Pago Pago Harbor. Fa'a Samoa and its rules of communal ownership are still in effect, however, so it's wise not to leave cameras, watches, or other valuables lying around unattended.

Taxes   The government of American Samoa charges no sales tax; however, an import tax of 5% is imposed on most merchandise (it's much stiffer on tobacco and alcoholic beverages). There is no airport departure tax.

Telephone/Fax   Telephone calls can be dialed directly into American Samoa from most parts of the world. The international country code is **684.**

The local telephone system is identical to that in the U.S. The pay telephones are the same type used in phone booths throughout the U.S. The number for directory assistance is **411.** For emergencies, dial **911.**

Visitors can place overseas calls from the **Office of Communications,** diagonally across the Fagatogo *malae* (village green) from the Fono building. Station-to-station calls to the U.S. mainland cost about $7 for the first 3 minutes and 90¢ for each additional minute. The office accepts AT&T credit cards, or you can pay cash in advance or reverse the charges. The office is open 24 hours every day. You can also use MCI credit and prepaid cards by dialing ☎ **633-2624** from a pay phone.

Time   Local time in American Samoa is the same as in independent Samoa: 11 hours behind Greenwich Mean Time. That's 3 hours behind Pacific Standard Time (4 hours behind during daylight saving time). In other words, if it's noon standard time in California and 3pm in New York, it's 9am in Pago Pago. If daylight saving time is in effect, it's 8am in American Samoa. American Samoa is east of the International Date Line and shares the same date with North America, 1 day behind Tonga, Fiji, Australia, and New Zealand.

Tipping   Although this is an American territory, there is no tipping in American Samoa.

Weights/Measures   American Samoa is the only country or territory in the South Pacific whose official system of weights and measures is the same as that used in the U.S.: pounds and miles, not kilograms and kilometers.

7 Exploring American Samoa

A STROLL THROUGH PAGO PAGO

Although the actual village of Pago Pago sits at the head of the harbor, everyone refers to the built-up area on the south shore of the harbor, including Fagatogo, the government and business center, as Pago Pago. The harbor is also called the Bay Area. Despite development that has come with economic growth of the territory, Pago Pago still has

Pago Pago

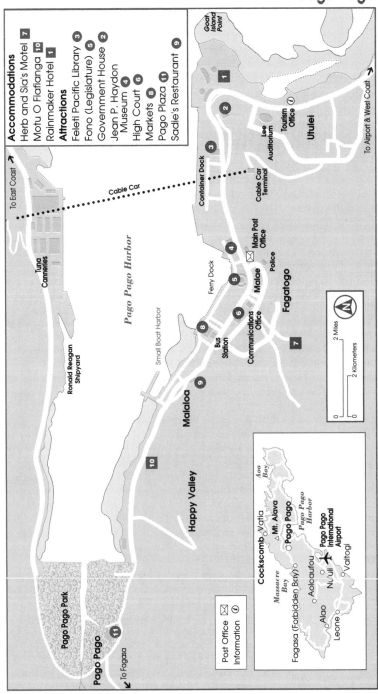

Accommodations
Herb and Sia's Motel `7`
Motu O Fiafianga `10`
Rainmaker Hotel `1`

Attractions
Feleti Pacific Library `3`
Fono (Legislature) `5`
Government House `2`
Jean P. Haydon Museum `4`
High Court `6`
Markets `8`
Pago Plaza `11`
Sadie's Restaurant `9`

Cable Car

To East Coast

To Airport & West Coast

Goat Island Point

Tourism Office

Utulei

Lea Auditorium

Container Dock

Cable Car Terminal

Tuna Canneries

Pago Pago Harbor

Main Post Office

Police

Malae

Fagatogo

Ferry Dock

Small Boat Harbor

Ronald Reagan Shipyard

Bus Station

Communications Office

Malaloa

Happy Valley

Pago Pago Park

Pago Pago

To Fagasa

Post Office
Information

N

2 Miles
2 Kilometers
0

Cockscomb
Vatia
Mt. Alava
Pago Pago

Aoa Bay

Massacre Bay

Pago Pago Harbor

Fagasa (Forbidden Bay)

Aoloaufou
Nu'uli

Alao
Leone
Vaitogi

Pago Pago International Airport

Seeing American Samoa as a Day Trip from Apia

In brief, here's how to see American Samoa in 1 day as a side trip from independent Samoa. Fly early in the morning from Fagali'i Airstrip in Apia to Pago Pago, then take a taxi to The Rainmaker Hotel. Take the walking tour of Pago Pago described below, then stop for lunch. If you haven't rented a car, grab an aiga bus at the market for a ride out to the east end, followed by another bus ride to the west end. On the way back, you can get off and call a taxi, catch a Tafuna aiga bus, or walk the 1½ miles from the main road to the airport for a late-afternoon return flight to Apia.

See "Getting There & Getting Around," above, for information about Apia travel agents' day trips.

---

much of the old South Seas atmosphere that captivated W. Somerset Maugham when he visited and wrote "Rain" in the 1920s.

We'll begin our tour at **The Rainmaker Hotel** on the east end of the inner harbor, actually in the village of Utulei. Just across the main road from the hotel, a set of concrete steps climbs to **Government House,** the clapboard mansion built in 1903 to house the governor of American Samoa. Unless you have business with the governor, the mansion is not open to the public. There is a nice view, however, from the top of the steps looking back over the hotel and across the harbor to flat-top Rainmaker Mountain.

Back on the main road heading north toward town, we pass a mountain of shipping containers standing idle on the main wharf before we reach **Feleti Pacific Library,** which has a good collection of books on the South Pacific. Beyond the busy port terminal is the **Jean P. Haydon Museum** (☎ 633-4347), featuring exhibits on Samoan history, sea life, canoes, kava making, and traditional tools and handcrafts, including the finely woven mats that have such great value in Samoa and Tonga. The old iron-roofed building housing the museum was once the U.S. Navy's commissary. The museum is open Monday through Friday from 9am to 3pm, except on holidays. Admission is free but donations are accepted.

Every Samoan village has a **malae,** or open field, and the area across from the museum is Fagatogo's. The chiefs of Tutuila met on this malae in 1900 to sign the treaty that officially established the U.S. in Samoa. The round modern building across the road beside the harbor is the **Fono,** American Samoa's legislature; the visitors' galleries are open to the public. The ramshackle stores along the narrow streets on the other side of the malae were for half a century Pago Pago's "downtown," although like any other place under the Stars and Stripes, much business now is conducted in suburban shopping centers. On the malae, the **American Samoa Archives Office** occupies the old stone jail built in 1911.

Just beyond the malae on the main road, the big white clapboard building with columns, which from its colonial style looks as if it should be in South Carolina rather than the South Pacific, is the **Judicial Building,** home of the High Court of American Samoa (everyone calls it the Court House). Across the road on the waterfront stands **Fagatogo Plaza,** a modern shopping center. You can take a refreshment break here at **Billy's,** on the water side of the center (see "Dining," below).

In marked contrast are the **produce and fish markets** a few yards farther on. They usually are poorly stocked, and when they do have produce, it most likely comes by ferry from Western Samoa. The markets also serve as the bus terminal.

Continuing north along the harbor, we soon come to the **Sadie Thompson Building,** a large wooden structure now housing Sadie's Restaurant and the Transpac store. This was the rooming house where W. Somerset Maugham was marooned during a measles epidemic early in this century. It provided the grist for his famous short story "Rain."

The Asian-style building across the playing fields at the head of the harbor may look like a Chinese restaurant, but in reality it is **Korea House,** a hospitality center for the Korean sailors who man many of the boats that bring tuna to the canneries. The canneries are in the large, industrial buildings on the north side of the harbor at the base of Mount Alava. No need to go around there; turn around and repeat your steps.

A TOUR OF TUTUILA

THE NORTH COAST   A paved road turns off the main highway at Spenser's Store in Pago Pago village and leads up **Vaipito Valley,** across a ridge, and down to Fagasa, a village huddled beside picturesque Fagasa, or **Forbidden Bay,** on Tutuila's north shore. The road is steep but paved all the way, and the view from atop the ridge is excellent. The track up Mount Alava begins on the saddle (see "The National Park of American Samoa," below). Legend says that porpoises long ago led a group of three men and three women to safety in Fagasa Bay, which has long been a porpoise sanctuary.

THE EAST SIDE   The 18-mile drive from Pago Pago to the east end of Tutuila skirts the harbor, passes the canneries and their fishy odor, and then winds around one headland after another into small bays, many of them with sandy beaches and good swimming holes over the reef. Watch particularly for **Pyramid Rock** and the **Lion's Head,** where you can wade out to a small beach.

From Aua, at the foot of Rainmaker Mountain, a switch-backing road runs across Rainmaker Pass (great views from up there) to the lovely north shore village of **Vatia,** on a bay of the same name. World War II pillboxes still dot the beach here. At the north end of Vatia Bay sits the skinny, offshore rock formation known as **The Cockscomb,** one of Tutuila's trademarks.

Another paved road leaves Faga'itua village and climbs to a saddle in the ridge, where it divides. The left fork goes down to Masefau Bay; the right goes to Masausi and Sa'ilele villages. Near the east end, a road from Amouli village cuts across Lemafa Saddle to **Aoa Bay** on the north coast.

Aunu'u Island will be visible from the main road as you near the east end of Tutuila. Aunu'u is the top of a small volcanic crater and has a village near a famous quicksand pit. Motorboats leave for it from the small-boat harbor at Au'asi on the southeast coast.

Alao and **Tula** villages on the east end of Tutuila are the oldest settlements in American Samoa. They have long, gorgeous surf beaches, but be careful of the undertow from waves driven by the prevailing southeast trade winds.

THE WEST SIDE   You saw some of Tutuila's rugged coast on the drive in from the airport west of Pago Pago, including the **Flower Pot,** a tall rock with coconut palms growing on its top sitting in the lagoon. About halfway from the airport to the Rainmaker Hotel is a road inland (at Tom Ho Chung's store) leading to the **Lyndon B. Johnson Tropical Medical Center** in the Faga'alu Valley. If you feel like a hike, take the left fork in the road past the medical center, and when the pavement ends, follow the track to **Virgin Falls.** It's not the easiest walk, but the falls have a nice pool beneath them. Give yourself several hours for this sweaty outing.

The **airport** sits on the island's only sizable parcel of relatively flat land, and the main road from there west cuts through rolling hills and shopping centers until emerging on the rugged west end.

At Pava'ia'i village a road goes inland and climbs to the village of A'oloaufou, high on a central plateau. A hiking trail leads from the village down the ridges to the north coast; from here it drops to A'asutuai on **Massacre Bay,** where Samoans attacked the La Pérouse expedition in 1787. The French have put a monument there to the members of the expedition slain by Samoan warriors.

Back on the main road, head west and watch for a sign on the left marking the turn to the villages of Illi'ili and Vaitogi. Follow the signs to **Vaitogi,** and once in the village, bear right at the fork to the beach. Take the one-lane track to the right along the beach, past some graves and the stone remains of an old church, and up a rocky headland through pandanus groves. When you reach the first clearing on the left, stop the car and walk over to the cliff. According to legend, Vaitogi once experienced such a severe famine that a blind old woman and her granddaughter jumped off this cliff and were turned into a shark and a turtle. Today the villagers reputedly can chant their names and the turtle and the shark will appear. You may not be lucky enough to see them, but the view of the south coast from **Turtle and Shark Point,** with the surf pounding the rocks below you, is superb.

The picturesque village of **Leone,** which sits on a white sand beach in a small bay, was chosen by the Rev. John Williams as his landing place on Tutuila in 1830, and it became the cradle of Christianity in what was to become American Samoa. There is a monument to Williams in the village. The road beside the Catholic church leads about a mile and a half to **Leone Falls,** which has a freshwater pool for swimming (but never on Sunday).

The road from Leone to the western end of the island is quite scenic, as it winds in and out of small bays with sandy beaches and then climbs spectacularly across a ridge to Poloa village on the northwest coast.

8 The National Park of American Samoa

The **National Park of American Samoa** was authorized by the U.S. Congress in 1988, and although its facilities have been slow in coming, the park has amassed some 10,000 pristine acres—3,000 of them on Tutuila and another 6,000 in the Manu'a Islands (5,000 acres on T'au and 1,000 on Ofu). In all, they protect some extraordinarily beautiful shoreline, magnificent beaches, cliffs dropping into the sea, colorful reefs, and rain forest reaching up to serrated, mist-shrouded mountain peaks.

Since development is ongoing, stop by the **Park Visitors Center,** in the Pago Plaza shopping center at the head of the bay, or contact them at NPAS, Pago Pago, AS 96799 (☎ **633-7082;** fax 633-7085; www.nps.gov; e-mail charles_cranfield@nps. gov). The center has exhibits explaining Samoa's prehistory.

On Tutuila, the park essentially starts along the ridge atop Mount Alava and drops down sharp ridges and steep valleys to the north coast. It includes The Cockscomb off the north coast and the scenic Amalau Valley, near the picturesque north shore village of Vatia, where you can see many of Samoa's native bird species, including flying foxes (fruit bats). See "A Tour of Tutuila," above, for directions to Vatia.

Hikers can scale 1,600-foot Mount Alava via a four-wheel-drive trail, which begins in the Fagasa Pass and ascends steeply through the rain forest. It's a 3-hour walk uphill along a seldom used four-wheel-drive track, and about 2 hours to get back down, but you'll be rewarded with a view straight down over the entirety of Pago Pago Harbor and most of Tutuila Island. It's one of the most spectacular vistas in the South Pacific, if not the world. Be sure to take plenty of water.

Rory West of **North Shore Tours** (☎ **644-1416** or 733-3047) has various expeditions to the north coast, including hiking, camping, and fishing trips. Prices start at $25.

Unlike other U.S. National Parks, in which the federal government buys property outright, here the National Park Service has leased the land from the villages for 50 years, thereby protecting both the natural environment and traditional Samoan ownership customs.

9 Accommodations

The lack of accommodations, and the apparent lack of interest by the government or anyone else to do anything about it, is a major reason you should consider making Pago Pago a day trip from Apia instead of staying here.

Most package tours put visitors up at **The Rainmaker Hotel,** P.O. Box 996, Pago Pago, AS 96799 (☎ **633-4241;** fax 633-5959). This place was built with government backing in the 1960s, and under government management went steadily downhill. A $3 million improvement project had been announced as we went to press, but until it's complete, avoid this hotel. The Rainmaker originally had 184 rooms; no more than 40 were serviceable during my last visit. If you must stay here before the renovations are complete, demand an upstairs room in the Beach Wing. Avoid any attempt to put you in the Harbor Wing or in a downstairs room in the Beach Wing. Even in the Beach Wing, inspect the room thoroughly before moving in. Make sure that the air conditioner works, the night latches engage properly, the plumbing actually does what it's supposed to do, and the sheets and towels are clean. Leave absolutely no valuables in your room, and lock the safety latch when you're inside. A restaurant, snack bar, beauty salon, and tour desks are on the premises. Upstairs rooms in the Beach Wing cost $85 (an exorbitant amount compared to what you get at Aggie Grey's Hotel in Apia for the same price).

Given this situation, the American Samoa Office of Tourism matches visitors seeking inexpensive accommodations with local families willing to take in paying guests. This **homestay program** is known as Fale, Fala Ma Ti. Prices vary from $10 to $45 a night, depending on the homes. Some are Western-style houses; others are Samoan fales. All of them have modern toilets and showers. Some homes also have space for campers who bring their own tents. The Samoan hospitality will more than make up for the simple accommodations. Prior arrangements are required. Contact the Office of Tourism (see "Visitor Information & Entry Requirements," above).

A new property opened shortly before we went to press, which should help the accommodations situation here. Near the airport, **Tessarea Vaitogi Inn,** P.O. Box 2511, Pago Pago, AS 96799 (☎ **699-7793;** fax 699-7790; e-mail tessa@samoatelco. com), has eight hotel rooms and five apartments, all air-conditioned, with phones, televisions, and private bathrooms. There's a swimming pool and guest laundry. Rooms cost $85 double, apartments are $100 to $145. MasterCard and Visa cards accepted.

Motu O Fiafianga. P.O. Box 1554, Pago Pago, AS 96799 (on main road near head of harbor in Pago Pago). ☎ **633-7777.** Fax 633-4767. 12 units (none with private bathroom). A/C TV. $60 single or double, $50 single or double for stays of 2 nights or more. Rates include continental breakfast. AE, MC, V.

Evalani Pearson Viena's little place perched at the foot of a cliff has the best digs in town, provided you don't need a private bathroom and don't mind staying next to Evalani's Cabaret next door. The inside is a bit gaudy, with brass light fixtures and lots of paintings of James Dean and Marilyn Monroe. The 12 rooms, all off a narrow hallway, share four toilets and four showers, two each for men and women. Guests can use a common lounge with a bar, an exercise room, and a sauna. Each room has a queen-size bed, a writing desk, an open closet, and a small table with two chairs. All rooms have TVs with cable.

Pago Airport Inn. P.O. Box 783, Pago Pago, AS 96799 (Tafuna, 3 min. from airport). ☎ **699-6333.** Fax 699-6336. E-mail: pagairin@samoatelco.com. 20 units. A/C TV TEL. $85 double. MC, V.

In a village setting, this 2-story motel was built in 1997 and was the pick of the lot here during my last visit. The motel-style rooms open to veranda-like walkways across the front of the white stucco building. The units are simple but clean and equipped with double and single beds, cable-fed TVs mounted on their walls, desks and chairs, and tiled shower-only bathrooms. Coffee is supplied in the morning, but there's no restaurant here or nearby (consider renting a car).

10 Dining

Billy's. Fagatogo, in Fagatoga Square behind Tedi of Samoa. ☎ **633-1199.** Fried chicken, sandwiches, burgers, and hot dogs $1.50–$6. No credit cards. Mon–Sat 7am–9pm, Sun 9am–4pm. PIZZA/SNACK BAR.

The best place to stop for refreshment during a walking tour of Pago Pago, this waterfront establishment offers pizzas, fried chicken, sandwiches, hamburgers, hot dogs, nachos, fish and chips, and daily specials such as corned beef and cabbage. It's not as fast as it could be, since all items are cooked to order. Even if you don't eat here, stop by for a cold soda and enjoy the magnificent view of the harbor.

✪ **Rubbles Tavern.** Main Road, in Nu'uli Shopping Center (east of airport turnoff). ☎ **633-4403.** Reservations not accepted. Burgers, sandwiches, and salads $5–$8; main courses $7–$22. MC, V. Mon–Sat 11am–11pm. Bar open later. AMERICAN/MEXICAN.

It's a long way from town if you're here on a day tour, but this friendly air-conditioned pub is a great place to cool off while you're waiting for the last plane back to Apia. Except for the bamboo lining the walls of one dining room and the mat panels and huge Samoan war canoe rudder adorning the other, Rubbles could be in any Western city. You can even watch live contests on the two sports TVs behind the long bar. The very decent pub fare includes salads, nachos, stuffed potato skins, burgers, sandwiches, spicy chicken wings, grilled steaks and fish, sashimi, and onion rings and fish-and-chips in a beer batter made with Vailima beer from Apia.

Sadie's Restaurant. Pago Pago, west of market in Malaloa area. ☎ **633-5981.** Reservations recommended. Lunch $7–$16; main courses $17–$23. MC, V. Mon–Sat 11am–2pm and 6–10pm. AMERICAN.

Appropriately located upstairs in the old building where W. Somerset Maugham stayed and set his short story "Rain," Sadie's has in recent years taken on that elegantly deteriorating look that Maugham would have loved. That is, it's seen just enough wear and tear to its cut-glass-and-mauve style to look the South Seas outpost part. Nevertheless, it's the only semi-refined dining spot here. The best seats are on the now-enclosed front porch with a commanding view of the harbor, but reserve early or the local palagis and affluent American Samoans will beat you to those tables. Lunches offer a wide variety of sandwiches, diet plates, and seafood and chicken platters. Dinners include seafood, steaks, and chicken in various styles.

The Kingdom of Tonga

Thanks to a quirk of humankind and not of nature, the International Date Line swings eastward from its north-south path down the middle of the Pacific Ocean just enough to make the last Polynesian monarch the first sovereign to see the light of each new day. When the king greets the dawn and looks out on his realm from the veranda of his whitewashed Victorian palace, he sees a country of low but extremely fertile islands, of gorgeous sandy beaches, and of colorful coral reefs waiting to be explored.

His is a nation protected but never ruled by a Western power. Like Samoa to the north, Tonga has managed to maintain its Polynesian culture in the face of modern change. As the Tonga Visitors Bureau says, the kingdom "still remains far away from it all; still different, still alone, and to the joy of those who find their way to her—essentially unspoiled."

While this description is true of the perfectly flat main island Tongatapu, it is especially applicable to Vava'u, a group of hilly islands whose fjordlike harbor makes it one of the South Pacific's most popular yachting destinations, and to Ha'apai, a group of low islands which seems to have changed little since the crew of H.M.S. *Bounty* staged their mutiny just offshore in 1789. Visiting Vava'u is extremely pleasant to the eyes, and a trip to Ha'apai is like traveling back in time to the old South Seas.

Bring your sense of adventure to Tonga, for this is the poorest county in the South Pacific. The electricity may go off while you're here, and the tap water may be turned off (not that you can drink it when it's running). You'll see multitudes of dogs, chickens, and even pigs almost everywhere, even wandering the streets of Nuku'alofa, the capital. And with a few exceptions, you'll stay in accommodations that make a Motel 6 seem luxurious.

1 Tonga Today

In other Polynesian languages, the word *tonga* means "south." It stands to reason that Tonga would be so named because the kingdom lies south of Samoa, the first islands permanently settled by Polynesians and presumably the launching site for the colonization of Tonga and the rest of Polynesia. But to the Tongans the name means "garden," and when you drive from the airport into **Nuku'alofa,** the nation's capital, you can see why. It seems that every square yard of the main island of **Tongatapu** ("Sacred Garden") not occupied by a building or by the road is either under cultivation or lying fallow but ready for the next planting of bananas, tapioca, taro, yams, watermelons, tomatoes, squash, and a plethora of other fruits and vegetables. Crops grow in small plots under towering coconut palms so numerous that this flat island appears to be one huge copra plantation. The Tongans are generally poor in terms of material wealth, but they own some of the South Pacific's most fertile and productive land.

There just isn't much of it. The kingdom consists of 170 islands, 36 of them inhabited, scattered over an area of about 100,000 square miles, an area about the size of Colorado. The amount of dry land, however, is only 700 square kilometers (269 square miles). That's smaller than New York City.

The largest island in the kingdom, Tongatapu has about a third of the country's land area and about two-thirds of its population. It's a flat, raised atoll about 40 miles across from east to west and 20 miles across from north to south at its longest and widest points. In the center is a sparkling lagoon now unfortunately void of most sea life.

The government and most businesses and tourist activities are in Nuku'alofa (pop. 22,000), but there is much to see outside of town, including some of the South Pacific's most important and impressive archaeological sites.

There are three major island groups in the country. Tongatapu and the smaller **'Eua** comprise the southernmost group. About 155 kilometers (96 miles) north are the islands of the **Ha'apai Group,** and about 108 kilometers (67 miles) beyond them is the beautiful **Vava'u Group.** Even farther north, and definitely off the beaten path, are the **Niuas Islands.** The most frequently visited islands are Tongatapu and the sailor's paradise of Vava'u.

THE NATURAL ENVIRONMENT   Tonga lies roughly north-south along the edge of the Indo-Australian Plate. The Tonga Trench, one of the deepest parts of the Pacific Ocean, parallels the islands to the east where the Pacific Plate dips down and then under the Indo-Australian Plate. The resulting geological activity puts Tonga on the "Ring of Fire" that encircles the Pacific Ocean. One of Tonga's islands, Tofua, is an active volcano, and the entire country experiences frequent earth tremors. Legend says that earthquakes are caused when the Polynesian goddess Havea Hikule'o moves around underground; consequently, Tongans customarily stomp the shaking ground to get her to stop whatever she's doing down there.

Most of the islands are raised coral atolls. The exceptions are the Niuas and, in the Ha'apai Group, the active volcano Tofua and its sister volcanic cone, Kao. Geologists say that the weight of the growing Ha'apai volcanoes has caused the Indo-Australian Plate to sag like a hammock, thereby raising Tongatapu and 'Eua on the south end of the Tongan chain and Vava'u on the north end. As a result, the sides of Tongatapu and Vava'u facing Ha'apai slope gently to the sea, while the sides facing away from Ha'apai end in cliffs that fall into the ocean.

Impressions

Nature, assisted by a little art, no where appears in a more flourishing state than at this Isle.
                                                                                            —Capt. James Cook, 1773

What could the Tongan people do? "Not much," he reflected. "All we can do is resign ourselves to our lot, become very religious, and pray that there will be more land available in Heaven."
                                                                                            —John Dyson, 1982

GOVERNMENT   Although Tonga technically is a constitutional monarchy, the king in reality is head of a system of hereditary Polynesian chiefs who happen to have titles derived from England. The present king, Taufa'ahau Tupou IV, picks his own Privy Council of advisors and appoints seven cabinet members and the governors of Ha'apai and Vava'u. With few exceptions they all are nobles. The cabinet members and the governors serve until they retire or die, and they hold 12 of the 30 seats in Parliament—in effect, for life. Of the 16 other members of the Parliament, the nobles choose nine from among their ranks, leaving nine to be elected by the tax-paying commoners.

It would be an understatement to say that the royal family has a hand in every important decision made in Tonga; in fact, very little gets done without its outright or tacit approval or involvement.

With more and more Tongans living abroad, and those at home being exposed more and more to news of the world, the monarchy has been under increasing pressure to move to a democracy. This is not likely to happen as long as King Taufa'ahau Tupou IV—now in his 80s—is on the throne. What happens after he dies was very much up in the air during my recent visit (see "History 101," below).

THE ECONOMY   Tonga has few natural resources other than its fertile soil and the fish in the sea within its exclusive economic zone. The world markets for its major exports—vanilla, kava, bananas, coconut oil, pineapples, watermelons, tomatoes, squash, and other vegetables—has been unstable and even depressed at times in recent years. The country imports far more than it exports.

In addition, the kingdom has run out of land to apportion under the rule that gives each adult male 8¼ acres for growing crops. Given this lack of land, plus little chance of upward economic or social mobility, many thousands of Tongans have left the country and now live in Australia, New Zealand, and the United States. Money sent home by them is a major source of foreign exchange for the country.

For the commoners who remain behind, labor unions are illegal, and the primary chance for economic advancement is in small businesses. Although some of these are flourishing when compared to those of other South Pacific island countries, the royal family can get involved when leases or permits are required from the government. The royals are partners in many businesses operated here by both Tongans and expatriate residents, and they reportedly own majority interests in the corporations that control Tonga's communications satellite slot above the Pacific and the allocation of Internet address using its extension ".to".

2 History 101

Legend has it that the great Polynesian god Maui threw a fishhook into the sea from Samoa and brought up the islands of Tonga. He then stepped on some of his catch, flattening them for gardens. Tofua and Kao in the Ha'apai Group and some of the Niuas were left standing as volcanic cones.

Polynesian settlers found and settled these gardens sometime around 500 B.C. on their long migration across the South Pacific. Around A.D. 950, according to another myth, the supreme god Tangaloa came down to Tongatapu and fathered a son by a lovely Tongan maiden named Va'epopua. The son, Aho'eitu, thus became the first Tui Tonga—King of Tonga—and

Dateline

- **500 B.C.** Polynesians from Samoa settle in Tonga.
- **950 A.D.** By legend, supreme god Tangaloa comes to earth, fathers a son by beautiful virgin, thus founds Tui Tonga dynasty.
- **1642** Dutchman Abel Tasman is first European to set foot in Tonga.
- **1777** Captain Cook is feted by Finau I in Ha'apai, names

continues

- them "The Friendly Islands," leaves as Finau plans to kill him.
- **1781** Spaniard Francisco Mourelle discovers Vava'u.
- **1789** Mutiny on the *Bounty* takes place off Ha'afeva in Ha'apai Group.
- **1798** First missionaries land in Ha'apai Group during Tongan wars; two are killed, and the rest flee to Australia.
- **1806** Chief Finau II captures the *Port au Prince,* slays all its crew except young Will Mariner, who becomes the chief's favorite, later writes a book about his adventures.
- **1823** Wesleyan missionaries settle on Lifuka in Ha'apai Group; Chief Taufa'ahau begins his rise to power.
- **1831** Taufa'ahau converts to Christianity, names self George, with missionary help launches wars against his rivals.
- **1845** Taufa'ahau conquers all of Tonga, proclaims self King George.
- **1860** Rev. Shirley Baker arrives, exercises influence over Tonga for next 30 years.
- **1862** King George I frees commoners, makes his chiefs "Nobles of the Realm," establishes Privy Council, gives land to every male.
- **1875** King George I adopts Constitution, including "Sabbath-is-sacred" clause, essentially shutting Tonga down on Sunday.
- **1890** Under Treaty of Berlin, Great Britain establishes protectorate over Tonga, kicks out Rev. Baker, straightens out kingdom's finances.
- **1893** King George I dies, ending reign of 48 years. King George II assumes throne.
- **1900** King George II turns Tonga's foreign affairs over to

continues

launched one of the world's longest-running dynasties. Under subsequent Tuis, Tonga became a power in Polynesia; its large war canoes loaded with fierce warriors conquered and dominated the Samoas and the eastern islands of present-day Fiji.

The first Tuis Tonga ruled from the village Niutoua on the northwest corner of Tongatapu. They moved to Lapaha on the shore of the island's interior lagoon about 800 years ago, apparently to take advantage of a safer anchorage for the large, double-hulled war canoes they used to extend their empire as far as Fiji and Samoa. At that time, a deep passage linked the lagoon to the sea; it has been slowly closing as geological forces raise the island and reduce the entrance to the present shallow bank.

Over time, the Tui became more of a figurehead, and his power was dispersed among several chiefs, all of them descendants of the original Tui. For centuries the rival chiefs seemed to stop warring among themselves only long enough to make war on Fiji and Samoa. One of the domestic wars was in full swing when missionaries from the London Missionary Society arrived in 1798 and landed on Lifuka in the Ha'apai Group. Two of the missionaries were killed. The rest fled to Sydney, leaving Tonga to the warring heathens.

EUROPEANS ARRIVE   Tongatapu and Ha'apai had been sighted by the Dutch explorers Schouten and Lemaire in 1616, and the Dutchman Abel Tasman had landed on them during his voyage of discovery in 1643. The missionaries knew of the islands, however, from the visits of British Captains Samuel Wallis, James Cook, and William Bligh in the late 1700s. During his third voyage in 1777, Captain Cook was feted lavishly on Lifuka by a powerful chief named Finau I. Cook was so impressed by this show of hospitality that he named the Ha'apai Group "The Friendly Islands." Unbeknownst to Cook, however, Finau I and his associates apparently plotted to murder him and his crew, but they couldn't agree among themselves how to do it before the great explorer sailed away. The name he gave the islands stuck, and today Tonga uses "The Friendly Islands" as its motto.

Captain Bligh and H.M.S. *Bounty* visited Lifuka in 1789 after gathering breadfruit in Tahiti. Before he could leave Tongan waters, however, the famous mutiny took place near the island of Ha'afeva in the Ha'apai Group.

Some 20 years later Chief Finau II of Lifuka captured a British ship named the *Port au Prince,* brutally slaughtering all but one member of its crew, stealing all of its muskets and ammunition, and setting it on fire. The survivor was a 15-year-old Londoner named Will Mariner. He became a favorite of the chief, spent several years living among the Tongans, and was made a chief. Mariner later wrote an extensive account of his experiences, telling in one of the four volumes how the Tongans mistook 12,000 silver coins on the *Port au Prince* for gaming pieces they called *pa'angas*. The national currency today is known as the pa'anga.

The arrival of the Wesleyan missionaries on Lifuka in the 1820s coincided with the rise of Taufa'ahau, a powerful chief they converted to Christianity in 1831. With their help, he won a series of domestic wars and by 1845 had conquered all of Tonga. He made peace with Fiji, took a wife of the incumbent Tui Tonga as his own, and declared himself to be the new Tui Tonga. The deposed Tui, last of the direct descendants of the original Tui Tonga, lived on until 1865.

ROYALTY ARRIVES   Meanwhile, Taufa'ahau took a Christian name and became King George I of Tonga. In 1862 he made his subordinate chiefs "nobles," but he also freed the commoners from forced labor on their estates and instituted the policy of granting each adult male a garden plot and house lot. He created a Privy Council of his own choosing and established a legislative assembly made up of representatives of both the nobles and commoners. This system was committed to writing in the Constitution of 1875, which still is in effect today, including its "Sabbath-is-sacred" clause. The legislative assembly is known now as Parliament.

- **1918** King George II dies, Queen Salote begins 47-year reign during which Tonga remains a backwater.
- **1953** Queen Salote comes to world attention by going bareheaded during rainstorm at coronation of Queen Elizabeth II in London.
- **1965** Queen Salote dies; new King Taufa'ahau Tupou IV begins opening Tonga to tourists.
- **1967** King Taufa'ahau Tupou IV crowned among pomp and circumstance; International Dateline Hotel opens.
- **1970** King ends treaty with Great Britain; Tonga resumes own foreign affairs.
- **1989** Commoner members of Parliament begin push for more accountability from king's government.
- **1990** Passport scandal rocks the government.
- **1992** Pro-democracy conference calls for new elections.
- **1993** New elections bring same old results.

King George I was dominated during his later years by the Rev. Shirley W. Baker, a missionary who came to Tonga from Sydney in 1860 under the auspices of the Wesleyan Church. Over the next 30 years he held almost every important post in the king's government. When the British established their protectorate over Tonga according to the terms of the 1889 Berlin treaty, which also divided the Samoas between Germany and the U.S., they found the kingdom's finances to be in a shambles. In cleaning up the mess, they arranged to have Baker deported to New Zealand, where he stayed for 10 years. Baker returned to Tonga in 1900 as a lay reader licensed by the Anglican church and died there in 1903. His children erected a large statue of his likeness at his grave on Lifuka, in the Ha'apai Group.

King George I died in 1893 at the age of 97, thus ending a reign of 48 years. His great-grandson, King George II, ruled for the next 25 years and is best remembered for signing a treaty with Great Britain in 1900. The agreement turned Tonga's foreign

[Great Britain, preventing further colonial encroachments.]

Impressions

The good natured old Chief interduced me to a woman and gave me to understand that I might retire with her, she was next offered to Captain Furneaux but met with a refusal from both, tho she was neither old nor ugly, our stay here was but short.
—Capt. James Cook, 1773

The people were hospitable and, as you sailed in, local boats really did come alongside as they did in voyagers' tales, to invite you to their villages for a feast. Only when arrangements were finalized does the awful truth dawn: it is not natural hospitality being pressed so warmly upon you, but salesmanship.

—John Dyson, 1982

affairs over to the British and prevented any further encroachments on Tonga by the Western colonial powers. As a result, the Kingdom of Tonga is one of the few Third World countries never to have been colonized.

King George II died in 1918 and was succeeded by his daughter, the 6-foot 2-inch Queen Salote (her name is the Tongan transliteration of "Charlotte"). For the next 47 years Queen Salote carefully protected her people from Western influence, even to the extent of not allowing a modern hotel to be built in the kingdom. She did, however, come to the world's attention in 1953, when she rode bareheaded in the cold, torrential rain that drenched the coronation parade of Queen Elizabeth II in London (she was merely following Tongan custom of showing respect to royalty by appearing uncovered in their presence).

KING TAUFA'AHAU TUPOU IV   Queen Salote died in 1965 and was succeeded by her son, the present King Taufa'ahau Tupou IV. Trained in law at Sydney University in Australia, the new king—then 49 years old—set about bringing Tonga into the modern world. On the pretext of accommodating the important guests invited to his elaborate coronation scheduled for July 4, 1967, the then-modern International Dateline Hotel was built on Nuku'alofa's waterfront, and Fua'amotu Airport on Tongatapu was upgraded to handle jet aircraft. Tourism, albeit on a modest scale, had finally arrived in Tonga.

The king ended the treaty of protection with Great Britain, and in 1970 Tonga reassumed her small role on the world's stage. This enabled her to acquire aid from other countries with which to make further improvements.

Although not as tall as his mother, the king stands above 6 feet and once weighed on the order of 460 pounds (the large statue of him beside the old terminal at Fua'amotu Airport is only a slight exaggeration of his former size). He has slimmed down in recent years to just over 300 pounds, thanks in part to an exercise program including bicycling and rowing, his bodyguards puffing along behind. He has been seen wearing ski goggles and a motorbike helmet when flying from island to island. Watching him arrive at an airport should not be missed.

DEMOCRACY DOESN'T ARRIVE   The king and his government have had their problems, thanks to more and more of his commoner subjects going overseas to work in the Western democracies, and to those at home becoming better educated and more aware of what's going on both in Tonga and in the world. In the late 1980s a group of commoners founded *Kele'a*, a newspaper published without the king's input. The paper created a ruckus almost from its first issue by revealing that some government ministers had rung up excessive travel expenses on trips abroad.

Then came news that the government had stashed millions of dollars in U.S. banks, money earned from selling Tongan passports to overseas nationals (most of them Hong Kong Chinese but including Imelda Marcos, wife of the deposed Philippine dictator). For $20,000 the buyers received a passport declaring them to be "Tongan protected persons." The documents didn't allow the person to live in Tonga, however, so other nations refused to recognize them. To compound the problem, the Tongan High

Court ruled the sales to be unconstitutional. Rather than refund the money, Parliament held a special session in 1991 and amended the constitution—a document that had not been significantly changed since 1875. It also raised the price to $50,000. The new passports also allow the holders to live in Tonga.

Incensed, several hundred Tongans marched down Nuku'alofa's main street in a peaceful protest. Nothing like that had ever happened in Tonga before, but it was just the beginning. When the king kept on selling passports, the leaders held a pro-democracy conference in late 1992. That led to fresh elections in 1993—with the same old results. It was difficult at press time to predict what future course Tongan politics would take. Many observers believe the monarchial system will stay intact as long as King Taufa'ahau Tupou, now about 80 years old, is in power. The crown prince has indicated that some changes eventually will occur, but those aren't likely to be known until Tonga gets a new king.

3 The Tongans

The population of Tonga is estimated at somewhere around 100,000 (no one knows for sure). Approximately 98% of the inhabitants are pure Polynesians, closely akin to the Samoans in physical appearance, language, and culture.

As in Samoa, the bedrock of the Tongan social structure is the traditional way of life—*faka Tonga*—and the extended family. Parents, grandparents, children, aunts, uncles, cousins, nieces, and nephews all have the same sense of obligation to each other as is felt in Western nuclear families. Although Tongans are poor by Western standards, the extended-family system makes sure that no one ever goes hungry or without a place to live.

THE TONGAN SYSTEM The extended family aside, some striking differences exist between Tonga, Samoa, and the other Polynesian islands. Unlike the others, in which there is a certain degree of upward mobility, Tonga has a rigid two-tier caste system. The king and 33 "Nobles of the Realm"—plus their families—make up a privileged class at the top of society. Everyone else is a commoner, and although commoners can hold positions in the government, it's impossible for them to move up into the nobility even by marriage. Titles of the nobility are inherited, but the king can strip members of the nobility of their positions if they fail to live up to their obligations (presumably including loyalty to the royal family).

The king owns all the land in Tonga, which technically makes the country his feudal estate. Tonga isn't exactly like the old European feudal system, however, for although the nobles each rule over a section of the kingdom, they have an obligation to provide for the welfare of the "serfs" rather than the other way around. The nobles administer the villages, look after the people's welfare, and apportion the land among the commoners.

Under Tonga's constitution, each adult male is entitled to a garden plot of 8¼ acres and a site for a house in the village. Unfortunately, the population has outstripped the amount of available land, but this system is primarily responsible for the intensely cultivated condition of Tongatapu and the other islands and for the abundance of food in the country.

Foreigners are absolutely forbidden to own land in Tonga, and leases require approval of the Cabinet, which for all practical purposes means the king.

TONGAN DRESS Even traditional Tongan dress reflects this social structure. Western-style clothes have made deep inroads in recent years, especially among young persons, but many Tongans still wear wraparound skirts known as *valas*. These come to well below the knee on men and to the ankles on women. To show their respect for

What Day Is It?

Tonga was the first nation to welcome the new millennium because of a capricious quirk in the International Date Line. Established in 1884, this imaginary line marks the start of each calendar day. Theoretically, it should run for its *entire length* along the 180th Meridian, halfway around the world from the Zero Meridian, the starting point for measuring international time.

If it followed the 180th Meridian precisely, however, most of the Aleutian Islands would be a day ahead of the rest of Alaska, and Fiji would be split into 2 days. To solve these problems, the date line swings west around the Aleutians, leaving them in the same day as Alaska. In the South Pacific, it swerves east between Fiji and Samoa, leaving all of Fiji a day ahead of the Samoas.

Since Tonga and Samoa lie east of the 180th Meridian, both countries logically should be in the same day. But Tonga wanted to have the same date as Australia and New Zealand, so the line was drawn arbitrarily east of Tonga, putting it 1 day ahead of Samoa.

To travelers, it's even more confusing, since Tonga and Samoa are in the same time zone. When traveling from one to the other, therefore, only the date changes, not the time of day. For example, if everyone is going to church at 10am on Sunday in Tonga, everyone's at work on Saturday in Samoa.

Tonga's Seventh-Day Adventists, who celebrate the Sabbath on Saturday but work on Sunday, have taken advantage of this abnormality to avoid running afoul of Tonga's tough Sunday blue laws. In God's eyes, they say, Sunday in Tonga really is Saturday. Accordingly, Tonga is the only place in the world where Seventh-Day Adventists observe their Sabbath on Sunday.

the royal family and to each other, traditional men and women wear finely woven mats known as *ta'ovalas* over their valas. Men hold these up with waistbands of coconut fiber; women wear decorative waistbands known as *kiekies*. Tongans have ta'ovalas for everyday wear, but on special occasions they will break out mats that are family heirlooms, some of them tattered and worn. The king owns ta'ovalas that have been in his family for more than 500 years.

Tongan custom is to wear black for months to mourn the death of a relative or close friend. Since Tongan extended families are large and friends numerous, the black of mourning is seen frequently in the kingdom.

In keeping with Tonga's conservatism, it's against the law for men as well as women to appear shirtless in public. While Western men can swim and sunbathe shirtless at the hotel swimming pools and beaches frequented by visitors, you will see most Tongans swimming in a full set of clothes.

RELIGION Wesleyan missionaries gained a foothold in Tonga during the early 1820s and by 1831 had converted Taufa'ahau, the high chief of the Ha'apai Islands. As happened with the converted chief named Pomare in Tahiti, Taufa'ahau then used missionary support—and guns from other sources—to win a series of wars and become king of Tonga. Tonga quickly became a predominantly Christian nation—apparently an easy transition, as Tongan legend holds that their own king is a descendant of a supreme Polynesian god and a beautiful earthly virgin.

When Taufa'ahau instituted a constitution in 1862, a clause in that document declared, "The Sabbath Day shall be sacred in Tonga forever and it shall not be lawful to work, artifice, or play games, or trade on the Sabbath." The penalty for breaking

Impressions

The people stay home on Sundays and entertain each other with good food, even if they have to semi-starve all week.

—John Dyson, 1982

this stricture is a T$10 ($8) fine or 3 months in the slammer at hard labor. Although there now is some flexibility that allows hotels to cater to their guests on Sunday, almost everything else comes to a screeching halt on the Sabbath. Taxis don't run, airplanes don't fly, most restaurants other than those in the hotels don't open. Tongans by the thousands go to church, then enjoy family feasts and a day of lounging around in true Polynesian style.

About half of all Tongans belong to the Free Wesleyan Church of Tonga, founded by the early Methodist missionaries and headed by the king. The Free Church of Tonga is an offshoot that is still allied with the Methodist synods in Australia and New Zealand. There are also considerable numbers of Roman Catholics, Anglicans, Seventh-Day Adventists, and Mormons. Church services are usually held at 10am on Sunday, but very few of them are conducted in English. St. Paul's Anglican Church, on the corner of Fafatehi and Wellington Roads, usually has communion in English on Sunday at 8am. The royal family worships at 10am in the Free Wesleyan Church on Wellington Road, a block behind the Royal Palace.

The red national flag has a cross on a white field in its upper corner to signify the country's strong Christian foundation.

The Mormon church has made inroads in Tonga. Gleaming white Mormon temples have popped up in many Tongan villages, along with modern schools that offer quality education and the chance for students to go on to Mormon colleges in Hawaii and Utah. Many Tongans have joined the church, reportedly for this very reason, and there are now sizable Tongan communities in Honolulu and around Salt Lake City, headquarters of the Mormon church. Unlike the Samoans and Cook Islanders, Tongans do not have unlimited access to a larger Western country such as the U.S. or New Zealand, and the promise of Mormon help in settling in America is an appealing prospect in light of the population pressures at home.

Tongans of all religions bury their dead in unique cemeteries set in groves of frangipani trees. The graves are sandy mounds decorated with flags, banners, artificial flowers, stones, and seashells. Many of them are bordered by brown beer bottles turned upside down.

As was the case throughout Polynesia, the Tongans accepted most of the puritanical beliefs taught by the early missionaries but stopped short of adopting their strict sexual mores. Today Tongan society is very conservative in outlook and practice in almost every aspect of life except the sexual activities of unmarried young men and women.

In keeping with Polynesian custom described earlier in this book, Tongan families without enough female offspring will raise boys as they would girls. They are known in Tongan as *fakaleitis* ("like a woman") and live lives similar to those of the mahus in Tahiti and the fa'afafines in the Samoas. In Tonga they have a reputation for sexual promiscuousness and for persistently approaching Western male visitors in search of sexual liaisons.

4 The Tongan Language

The official language is Tongan, but English is taught in the schools and is widely spoken in the main towns.

Tongan is a Polynesian language similar to Samoan. One major difference between them is the enormous number of glottal stops (represented by an apostrophe in writing) in the Tongan tongue. These are short stops similar to the break between "Oh-oh" in English.

Every vowel is pronounced in the Latin fashion: *ah, ay, ee, oh,* and *oo* (as in kan-ga*roo)* instead of *ay, ee, eye, oh,* and *you* as in English. The consonants are sounded as they are in English.

An extensive knowledge of Tongan will not be necessary for English-speakers to get around and enjoy the kingdom, but here are a few words you can use to elicit smiles from your hosts and to avoid the embarrassment of entering the wrong restroom.

English	Tongan	Pronunciation
hello	malo e lelei	mah-low ay lay-lay
welcome	talitali fiefia	tah-lay-tah-lay fee-ay-fee-ah
how do you do?	fefe hake?	fay-fay hah-kay?
fine, thank you	sai pe, malo	sah-ee pay, mah-low
good-bye	'alu a	ah-loo ah
thank you	malo	mah-low
how much?	'oku fiha?	oh-koo fee-hah?
good	lelei	lay-lay-ee
bad	kovi	koh-vee
woman	fefine	fay-feen-ay
man	tangata	tahn-got-ah
house	fale	fah-lay
transvestite	fakaleiti	fah-ka-lay-tee

For more information, the Friendly Islands Bookshop on Taufa'ahau Road carries language books, and the Tonga Visitors Bureau on Vuna Road distributes a brochure of Tongan phrases.

5 Visitor Information & Entry Requirements

VISITOR INFORMATION

The friendly staff have many brochures, maps, and other materials available at the **Tonga Visitors Bureau,** P.O. Box 37, Nuku'alofa, Kingdom of Tonga (☎ **21-733;** fax 23-507; www.vacations.tvb.gov.to; e-mail tvb@kalianet.to). The office is on Vuna Road near the International Dateline Hotel. Especially good are the bureau's brochures on Tongan dancing, handcrafts, archaeology, construction skills, and a walking tour of central Nuku'alofa. A stop by the "TVB" is a must before setting out to see the country. Hours are Monday through Friday from 8:30am to 4:30pm and Saturday from 9am to 1pm.

Other sources of information are:

North America: Tonga Consulate, 360 Post St., Suite 604, San Francisco, CA 94108 (☎ **415/781-0365;** fax 415/781-3964).

Australia: Tonga Visitors Bureau, 642 King St., Newton, NSW 2042 (☎ **02/9519-97009;** fax 02/9519-9419).

New Zealand: Tonga Visitors Bureau, P.O. Box 24–054, Royal Oak, Auckland (☎ **09/634-1519;** fax 09/636-8973).

United Kingdom: Tonga High Commission, 36 Molyneux St., London W1H 6AB (☎ **724-5828;** fax 723-9074).

You can also get advance information from the **Tourism Council of the South Pacific** (see "Visitor Information & Entry Requirements" in chapter 2).

Once you're in Tonga, be on the lookout for *'Eva: Your Holiday Guide to Tonga,* a slick bimonthly tabloid full of news about Tongan tourism and advertisements for the hotels, restaurants, and nightclubs. It's carried as a supplement in *Matagi Tonga,* an excellent local magazine.

ENTRY REQUIREMENTS

Visas are not required for bona fide visitors to enter Tonga, who are permitted to stay for up to 30 days provided they have a valid passport, an onward air or sea ticket, proof of adequate funds, and relevant health certificates. As a practical matter, your initial permit will likely be limited to the number of days you request on your entry form or the date of your return or onward ticket, whichever is earlier. Expect to have your tickets examined.

Applications for stays of longer than 30 days must be made to the principal immigration officer in Nuku'alofa.

Vaccinations are required only if a traveler has been in a yellow fever or cholera area within 2 weeks prior to arrival in Tonga.

CUSTOMS   Visitors are allowed to bring in 500 cigarettes and 2 liters of alcoholic beverage, as well as personal belongings in use at the time of arrival. Pets, dangerous drugs, firearms, and ammunition are prohibited, and foodstuffs must be declared and inspected. Arriving visitors can buy duty-free merchandise at Fua'amotu Airport after clearing Immigration but before going through Customs.

6 Money

The Tongan unit of currency is the **pa'anga,** which is divided into 100 **seniti.** The pa'anga is abbreviated in this book as **"T$."** Most Tongans will refer to "dollars" and "cents" when doing business with visitors, meaning pa'angas and senitis.

The value of the pa'anga is determined by a basket of currencies. At the time of writing, T$1 was worth about U.S. 60¢. The equivalent U.S. dollar prices given in parentheses are based on this rate of exchange. The rate is not quoted in overseas newspapers, but you can find it on the *Washington Post* newspaper's Worldwide Web site (www.washingtonpost.com).

Tongan coins bear the likeness of the king on one side and such items as bananas, chickens, and pigs on the other.

HOW TO GET LOCAL CURRENCY   The **Bank of Tonga** has an office at the waterfront end of Taufa'ahau Road, Nuku'alofa's main street. It is open Monday through Friday from 9am to 3:30pm and Saturday from 8:30 to 11:30am. **ANZ Bank** has its office at the corner of Railway and Salote Roads, near the market. It is open Monday through Friday from 9am to 4pm and Saturday from 8:30 to 11:30am. **MBf Bank** is on Taufa'ahau Road; it's open Monday through Friday from 9am to 3:30pm, Saturday from 9 to 11:30am. You will need your passport in order to exchange currency or traveler's checks. The International Dateline Hotel will change money at a rate lower than you will get at the banks.

You can get cash advances using your MasterCard and Visa at the Bank of Tonga or ANZ Bank. There were no ATMs in Tonga during my last visit.

CREDIT CARDS   The major hotels, car-rental firms, travel agencies, and Friendly Island Airways accept American Express, Diners Club, MasterCard, and Visa credit cards. Some restaurants and other businesses accept MasterCard or Visa; those who do

The Pa'anga & The U.S. Dollar

At this writing, T$1 = approximately $.60, the rate of exchange used to calculate the U.S. dollar prices given in this chapter. This rate may change by the time you visit, so use the following table only as a guide.

T$	US$	T$	US$
.25	.15	15.00	9.00
.50	.30	20.00	12.00
.75	.45	25.00	15.00
1.00	.60	30.00	18.00
2.00	1.20	35.00	21.00
3.00	1.80	40.00	24.00
4.00	2.40	45.00	27.00
5.00	3.00	50.00	30.00
6.00	3.60	75.00	45.00
7.00	4.20	100.0	60.00
8.00	4.80	125.00	75.00
9.00	5.40	150.00	90.00
10.00	6.00	200.00	120.00

may add 4% or 5% to your bill for doing so. It's a good idea to ask first if you want to put your purchases on plastic.

7 When to Go

THE CLIMATE

Like Rarotonga in the Cook Islands to the east, Tongatapu is far enough south of the equator to have cool, dry, and quite pleasant weather during the austral winter months (July to September), when temperatures range between 60°F (15.5°C) and 70°F (21°C). However, the ends of occasional cold fronts from the Antarctic and periods of stiff southeast trade winds can make it seem even cooler during this period. During the summer (December to March), the high temperatures can reach above 90°F (32°C), with evenings in the comfortable 70s (21°C to 26°C). A sweater, jacket, or wrap will come in handy for evening wear at any time of the year. The islands get about 180cm (70 inches) of rainfall a year (compared to 500cm [200 inches] in Pago Pago, American Samoa), the majority of it falling during the summer months. Vava'u to the north tends to be somewhat warmer and slightly wetter than Tongatapu.

Tonga is in the southwestern Pacific cyclone belt, and hurricanes are possible from November to April. Rest assured, however, that there will be ample warning if one bears down on the islands while you're there. The Tongans have seen enough hurricanes to ensure their guests' safety.

FESTIVALS & EVENTS

The largest annual festival is ✪ **Heilala,** which coincides with the King's Birthday on July 4. Nuku'alofa goes all out for a week of dance and beauty competitions, parades, sporting matches, band concerts, marching contests, yacht regattas, parties, and the lovely Night of Torches on the waterfront. Tongans living overseas like to come home for Heilala, so hotel reservations should be made well in advance. Vava'u stages its own version of Heilala early in May.

The Tongan version of a state fair is the **Royal Agricultural Show.** One show is held in each of the island groups during late August or early September. His Majesty visits them all and examines the best of the crops and handcrafts.

Other festivals are **Red Cross Week** in May, the **opening of Parliament** early in June, and the **Music Festival,** which coincides with the Heilala festival on July 4.

The annual **Vava'u Festival** the first week in May and the **Ha'apai Festival** the first week in June will enliven visits to Tonga's other islands.

The Tonga Visitors Bureau keeps track of when the festivals will occur each year.

Note: You do not want to be here if a key member of the royal family dies, for the country virtually shuts down for a lengthy period of mourning.

HOLIDAYS

Public holidays in Tonga are New Year's Day, Good Friday and Easter Monday, ANZAC (Memorial) Day (April 25), Crown Prince Tupouto'a's birthday (May 4), Emancipation Day (in honor of King George I, June 4), the King's Birthday (July 4), Constitution Day (November 4), King Tupou I Day (December 4), Christmas Day, and Boxing Day (December 26).

8 Getting There & Getting Around

GETTING THERE

Air New Zealand flies between Los Angeles and Tonga at least once a week, with brief stops in Honolulu and Samoa. Those flights go on to Auckland and return over the same route. **Air Pacific** connects Tonga to its flights to Fiji from Los Angeles, Australia, and New Zealand. **Polynesian Airlines** also flies to Tonga from Auckland, Sydney, and Samoa. **Royal Tongan Airlines** flies between Tongatapu and Auckland, Wellington, Sydney, and Apia, and it also has weekly flights between Nadi and Vava'u. **Samoa Air,** based in American Samoa, flies its small planes between Pago Pago and Vava'u.

There are no flights into, out of, or in Tonga on Sunday, when the local airports are closed.

For more information, see "Getting There" in chapter 2.

ARRIVING AND DEPARTING   Except for the few international flights destined for Vava'u, most land at **Fua'amotu Airport** on Tongatapu, 24km (14 miles) from Nuku'alofa. The terminal has currency exchange counters, a duty-free shop, a snack bar, and a small handcraft outlet. International passengers can purchase duty-free liquor and cigarettes after clearing Immigration but before going through Customs.

Transportation from the airport into Nuku'alofa is by hotel minibuses or taxi. The bus ride to town costs T$6 ($3.60). The one-way taxi fare into Nuku'alofa is about T$12 ($7.20); the drivers will be happy to take U.S., New Zealand, or Australian currency.

A **departure tax** of T$20 ($12) is charged of all passengers leaving on international flights. You pay it in Tongan currency at Fua'amotu Airport, at a separate booth outside Immigration. There is no departure tax for domestic flights.

There is no currency exchange facility in the departure lounge, so swap your money before clearing Immigration.

GETTING AROUND

BY PLANE   **Royal Tongan Airlines** (☎ **800/486-6426** or 23-414) has a monopoly on air travel within the country, providing at least three round-trip flights a day between Tongatapu and Vava'u. Daily service is also provided between Tongatapu,

'Eua, and Ha'apai. The round-trip fare from Tongatapu to Vava'u is about T$248 ($149); to 'Eua, T$36 ($21.50); and to Ha'apai, T$124 ($74.50).

It's always a good idea to book your flights as far in advance as you can. Always reconfirm your return flight as soon as possible after arriving on an outer island.

The airlines' offices are in the Royco Building on Fatafehi Road at Wellington Road.

Pacific Island Seaplanes (☎ 25-177; fax 25-165) provides charter service throughout the islands in its eight-seat floatplane. Transfers to the resorts off Nuku'alofa cost T$85 ($51) per person, with a minimum of four persons, or F$585 ($351) per hour of flying time.

BY FERRY   It's not for everyone, but the **Shipping Corporation of Polynesia** (☎ 21-699) operates weekly ferry service from Nuku'alofa to Ha'apai and Vava'u, using the M.V. *Olovaha,* a car-ferry with a few passenger cabins. It usually leaves Nuku'alofa 1 day a week at 5:30pm and takes about 16 hours to make the 163-mile trip to Vava'u, stopping at Lifuka in the Ha'apai Group on the way. The ship then turns around and arrives back in Nuku'alofa late the next afternoon. One-way fares between Nuku'alofa and Vava'u are T$42 ($25) for deck passage. **Walter Shipping Corporation** (☎ 23-855) operates the *Taufahi* over the same route. Its fares are slightly less than on the *Olovaha.*

The Shipping Corporation of Polynesia also runs a boat between Nuku'alofa and nearby 'Eua Island, and the roll-on, roll-off ferry *Alai Moana* (☎ 21-326) covers this same route. One-way fare on both is T$6 ($3.60). Call for schedules. Small, privately owned boats leave Faua jetty for 'Eua around midday, except on Sunday.

BY RENTAL CAR   **E. M. Jones Ltd.** (☎ 23-422 or 29-858) and **Makalita Rental Cars** (☎ 24-823) both rent cars, with rates starting at T$50 ($30) a day, including unlimited mileage and insurance.

Gasoline (petrol) is readily available only at stations in Nuku'alofa, so fill up before leaving town. It cost about T$62¢ (37¢) a liter during my recent visit, or about $1.40 for a U.S. gallon.

Before you can officially drive in Tonga, you must obtain a **local driver's license** from the Registration and Licensing Department at the Central Police Station in Nuku'alofa. You will need your home driver's license and T$10 ($6) for rental cars, T$4 ($2.40) for scooters.

Driving in Tonga is on the left-hand side of the road. Speed limits are 65kmph (39 m.p.h.) on the open road and 40kmph (24 m.p.h.) in the towns and villages. Be alert for pigs, dogs, horses, and chickens, and pull over for policemen on motorcycles escorting the king in his long black limousine bearing license plates with no numbers, only a crown.

BY TAXI   Taxis usually gather near Maketi Talamahu at the corner of Salote and Railway Roads in Nuku'alofa. The largest firm is **Five Star Taxis** (☎ 21-595 or 21-429). **Nuku'alofa Taxis** (☎ 22-624) are radio dispatched. Others are **Holiday Taxis** (☎ 21-858), **One-Way Taxis** (☎ 21-741), **Friendly Island Taxis** (☎ 21-023), **Malolala Taxis** (☎ 22-500), and **City Taxis** (☎ 24-666).

Fares are T$1 (60¢) in town. Longer distances cost T$1.50 (90¢) for the first kilometer plus T30¢ (18¢) for each additional kilometer, but since the taxis have no meters, make sure you and the driver agree on just how much the fare will be. The fares are doubled on Sundays, when taxis officially are permitted only to take passengers to church and back (some of them will carry tourists from their hotels or guesthouses to the wharf in order for them to get to the offshore islands).

BY BUS   Buses use the **Vuna Road waterfront** as their terminal. Town buses stop in front of the Tonga Visitors Bureau; long-distance ones stop in front of the government buildings. They fan out from there to all parts of Tongatapu, but there are no reliable schedules. Simply ask the bus drivers at the market where they are going. If you take one into the countryside, remember that they make their last runs back to Nuku'alofa at about 3pm daily, in time to pick up passengers who are just getting off work. Once they make their last runs to the villages, they don't come back to town until the next morning. About T$1 (60¢) will take you to the end of the island in either direction.

BY BICYCLE   Tongatapu is virtually flat, making it an ideal island on which to ride a bicycle. "Pushbikes" can be rented from **Niko's Bike Rental** (no phone) on the Vuna waterfront near the International Dateline Hotel. One-speed models cost T$2 ($1.20) per hour, T$8 ($4.80) for a full day, or T$18 ($10.80) for 3 days.

Fast Fasts: Tonga

American Express   American Express has no representative in Tonga. See "Money" in chapter 2 for what to do if your lose your American Express card or traveler's checks.

Area Code   The international country code is **676.**

Bookstores   **Friendly Islands Bookshop,** on Taufa'ahau Road near the Pacific Royale Hotel (☎ **23-787**), carries greeting cards made from tapa cloth, paperback books, postcards, international news magazines, week-old Australian newspapers, books about Tonga and the South Pacific, and a sheet of maps of Tonga.

Business Hours   In general, Tonga's shops are open Monday through Friday from 8am to 1pm and 2 to 5pm, Saturday from 8am to noon. Government offices are open Monday through Friday from 8:30am to 12:30pm and 1:30 to 4:30pm.

Camera/Film   **Foto Fix,** on Taufa'ahau Road south of Wellington Road (☎ **23-466**) sells Kodak and Fuji film and provides 1-hour color film processing.

Clothing   Summer clothing is in order during most of the year, but a sweater, jacket, or wrap should be taken for evening wear throughout the year. Tongans are very conservative, and visitors should not wear bathing suits or skimpy attire away from the hotel pools or beaches frequented by foreigners. In fact, appearing in public without a shirt is a punishable offense for both men and women, as is nudity of any degree.

Currency Exchange   See "Money," above.

Dentist   **Vaiola Hospital** (☎ **21-200**) provides dental service in Nuku'alofa; the outpatient clinics are open from 8:30am to 4:30pm daily.

Doctor   German-trained Dr. Heinz Betz (☎ **22-736**) practices on Wellington Road at Fatafehi Road.

Drug Laws   A drug-sniffing dog roams the baggage claim area, so don't even think about bringing illegal narcotics or dangerous drugs into Tonga.

Drugstores   The **Nuku'alofa Pharmacy Clinic** (☎ **21-007**) is on Salote Road in the block west of Taufa'ahau Road. Hours are Monday through Friday from 9:30am to 5pm and Saturday 9am to noon. For toiletries, go to the big Morris Hedstrom department store on Salote Road near the market.

Electricity   Electricity in Tonga is 240 volts, 50 cycles, and the plugs are the heavy, angled type used in Australia and New Zealand. You will need a converter and adapter plug to operate American appliances.

E-mail   The **Royal School of Science,** on the fifth level of the National Reserve Bank building on Salote Road at Tupoulahi Road (☎ **23-373**), lets visitors use its computers to access the Internet. Rates start at T$2 ($1.20) for 1 hour.

Embassies/Consulates   The nearest U.S. embassy is in Suva, Fiji. There is an office of the United States Peace Corps in Nuku'alofa (☎ **21-467**). Consular offices in Tonga are the Australian High Commission (☎ **21-244**), the British High Commission (☎ **21-021**), the New Zealand High Commission (☎ **21-122**), the Honorary Consulate of France (☎ **21-830**), the Honorary Consulate of West Germany (☎ **21-477**), and the Honorary Consulate of Nauru (☎ **22-109**).

Emergencies   The emergency telephone number for the police, fire department, and hospital is **911.**

Eyeglasses   **Vaiola Hospital** is the only place to get glasses fixed or replaced. See "Hospital," below.

Firearms   They are illegal in Tonga.

Gambling   There is no casino or other form of organized gambling in Tonga.

Hitchhiking   It's not against the law, but Tongans are not particularly accustomed to picking up strangers.

Hospital   **Vaiola Hospital** (☎ **21-200**) provides medical, dental, and optical service, but it's considerably below Western standards. The outpatient clinics are open from 8:30am to 4:30pm daily.

Insects   There are no dangerous insects in Tonga, and the mosquitoes do not carry malaria. Vava'u, warmer and more humid than Tongatapu, tends to have more mosquitoes and has tropical centipedes that can inflict painful stings if touched; watch your step if walking around with bare feet.

Library   **'Utue'a Public Library,** on the ground floor of Basilica of St. Anthony of Padua on Taufa'ahau Road, usually is open Monday through Friday from 3 to 9pm and Saturday from 10am to 3pm.

Laundry/Dry Cleaning   **Savoy Dry Cleaners,** on Fatefehi Road (☎ **23-314**), has 1-day laundry and dry cleaning service. Open Monday through Friday 7:30am to 6pm, Saturday 7:30am to 3pm.

Liquor Laws   The legal drinking age is 18. Licensed hotels can sell alcoholic beverages to their guests 7 days a week; otherwise, sale is prohibited from midnight Saturday through midnight Sunday. Royal beer is brewed here (Ikale is the higher quality export brand).

Maps   Free maps of Nuku'alofa, Tongatapu, and Vava'u are available at the Tonga Visitors Bureau.

Newspapers/Magazines   The *Tonga Chronicle* is a government-owned weekly newspaper appearing on Friday. It carries local news in both Tongan and English, but there are so many stories about the king and his family that many locals facetiously call it the "Royal Diary." For a different view, look for *Matangi Tonga,* a fine monthly magazine edited by the noted Tongan writer and publisher Pesi Fonua. It carries features about the kingdom and its people.

Police   The main station is on Salote Road at Railway Road. The emergency phone number is **911.**

Post Office   The Nuku'alofa Post Office is at the corner of Taufa'ahau and Salote Roads. It's open Monday through Friday from 8:30am to 4pm. Airmail

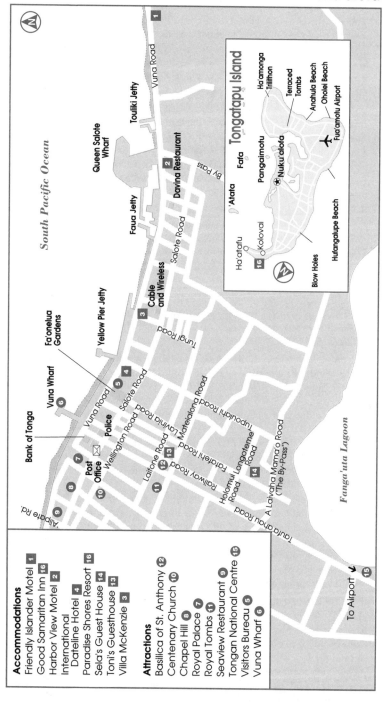

Accommodations

Friendly Islander Motel **1**
Good Samaritan Inn **16**
Harbor View Motel **2**
International
 Dateline Hotel **4**
Paradise Shores Resort **16**
Sela's Guest House **14**
Toni's Guesthouse **13**
Villa McKenzie **3**

Attractions

Basilica of St. Anthony **12**
Centenary Church **10**
Chapel Hill **8**
Royal Palace **7**
Royal Tombs **11**
Seaview Restaurant **9**
Tongan National Centre **15**
Visitors Bureau **5**
Vuna Wharf **6**

letters to the U.S. cost T80¢ (48¢); postcards are T45¢ (27¢). Tongan stamps, some of which are in the shape of bananas and pineapples, are collectors' items. They are available from the post office clerks or at the Philatelic Bureau, to the left of the counters.

Radio/TV   The government-owned radio station, A3Z or "Radio Tonga," broadcasts in both the AM and FM bands. Most programming on the AM station is in Tongan, although the music played is mostly American, Australian, or British popular tunes. The news in English is relayed from the BBC or Radio Australia several times a day. Some programming is provided by the Voice of America. Four privately owned FM stations in Nuku'alofa play popular music.

Tonga has one television channel, which carries predominantly Christian programming with CNN International off and on during the day. It can be received only on Tongatapu and 'Eua.

Safety   Although crimes against tourists have been rare in Tonga, remember that the communal property system still prevails in the kingdom. Items such as cameras and bags left unattended may disappear, so take the proper precautions. Street crime is not a problem, but it's a good idea to be on the alert if you walk down dark streets at night. Women should not wander alone on deserted beaches.

Taxes   The government imposes a 5% sales tax on all items purchased in Tonga, 7½% on hotel rooms. The tax is added to some bills in the American fashion and included in others. All passengers on international flights pay a departure tax of T$20 ($16).

Telephone/Telex/Fax   Calls can be dialed directly into Tonga from most areas of the world. The international country code is **676.**

International calls, telegrams, and telex messages can be placed from your hotel or at the office of Cable and Wireless Ltd., on Salote Road at the corner of Takaunove Road. The office is open 24 hours a day, 7 days a week for collect calls. Otherwise, you can pay cash or use your MasterCard, Visa, or AT&T credit cards Monday through Saturday 7am to midnight, Sunday 4pm to midnight. Station-to-station phone calls to the U.S. cost T$9.50 ($5.70) for the first 3 minutes, T$12 ($7.20) for person-to-person. The rates to Australia and New Zealand are about half those amounts.

It's less expensive to call from Cardphone public telephones at Cable and Wireless, at the post offices, and at the airport. These use plastic credit cards, which you can buy at the post offices or at Cable and Wireless. Lift the receiver, insert the card in the slot, and dial your number. A digital read-out tells you how much money you have left. Direct-dial calls to North America using Cardphones cost about T$3 ($1.80) a minute.

The number for directory assistance is **910** or **919;** for emergencies, **911;** and for the international operator, **913.**

Time   Local time in Tonga is 13 hours ahead of Greenwich Mean Time. It's in the same day as Australia, New Zealand, and Fiji, and a day behind the U.S., the Samoas, the Cook Islands, and French Polynesia. Translated, Tonga is 3 hours behind the U.S. West Coast during standard time (4 hours behind during daylight saving time)—and 1 day ahead. If it's noon on Tuesday in Tonga, it's 3pm Pacific Standard Time on Monday in Los Angeles and 6pm Eastern Standard Time on Monday in New York.

Tipping   Although it has gained a foothold, tipping is officially discouraged in Tonga because it's considered contrary to the Polynesian tradition of hospitality to guests. One time it is encouraged is during Tongan dance shows, when members of the audience rush up to the female dancers and stick notes to their well-oiled bodies.

Water   Don't drink the tap water. Bottled water is available at most groceries in Nuku'alofa. Since tap water here comes from wells in the limestone bedrock, it's very hard and doesn't easily rinse off soap and shampoo.

Weights/Measures   Tonga uses the metric system of weights and measures.

9 Exploring Tongatapu

This quaint little kingdom has a lot for visitors to see and do 6 days a week. **Sunday in Tonga** is more of a challenge, since nearly everyone goes to church, followed by a family feast and an afternoon of lounging around. You can worship with the royal family at 10am in the Centenary Church on Wellington Road. Tongan men wear neckties, but tourists get by without if they're neatly dressed. Women should wear dresses that cover the shoulders and knees. **Paea Tours** (☎ 21-103) usually offers a special Sunday outing that begins with church, then a tour of eastern Tongatapu, a stop for a traditional lunch with a Tongan family, and a tour of the island's western side. It is a good value at T$35 ($21) per person. Many of us visitors—and a good many Westernized Tongans, too— head for one of the offshore resorts (see "Island Excursions, Water Sports & Other Outdoor Pursuits," below), where we can get a meal, some libation, and a legal swim.

If you're interested in native cultures, make a point to visit the ✪ **Tongan National Center** (☎ 23-022), one of the South Pacific's best facilities. Located on the lagoon shores across from Vaiola Hospital, about 1.5 kilometer (1 mile) south of Nuku'alofa on Taufa'ahau Road, the center's fale-style buildings house displays of Tongan history, geology, and handcrafts. In fact, artisans work daily on their crafts and sell their wares to visitors. In other words, you can see how Tonga's remarkable handcrafts are made, which should help as you later scour the local shops for good buys. The center is open from Monday through Friday from 8:30am to 4:30pm. The exhibitions and handcraft shop are also open Saturday from 8:30am to noon. Regular admission is T$2 ($1.20). A lunch of Tongan food is followed by special displays from 2 to 4pm featuring demonstrations of carving, weaving, tapa making, food preparation, kava ceremony, and dance. The price is T$12 ($7.20) for lunch and tour, T$8 ($4.80) for tour only. A travel agent or hotel tour desk will make reservations, which are essential.

A highlight in the history section is the long robe Queen Salote wore at the coronation of Queen Elizabeth II in 1953, and the carcass of Tui Malila, the Galapagos tortoise Capt. James Cook reputedly gave the Tui Tonga in 1777. The beast lived until 1968.

A STROLL THROUGH NUKU'ALOFA

Before you start out to see Nuku'alofa, drop by the Tonga Visitors Bureau office on Vuna Road near the International Dateline Hotel and pick up a copy of the excellent brochure, "Walking Tour of Central Nuku'alofa." A morning's stroll around this interesting town will be time well spent, for in many respects it's a throwback to times gone by in the South Pacific. Although there are no street-name posts, the visitors bureau has put up signs giving general directions to the main sights. In addition, Nuku'alofa more or less is laid out on a grid, so you shouldn't have trouble finding your way around. It's also flat, with no hills to climb.

Start at the **Tonga Visitors Bureau** and walk west along Vuna Road toward the heart of town. The park on the left as you leave the visitors bureau is known as

⚫ Frommer's Favorite Tonga Experiences

Seeing the King. Being an American and therefore not particularly enamored of royalty, I nevertheless enjoy watching King Taufa'ahau Tupou IV being chauffeured around his kingdom—sometimes in the back seat of a stretched pickup truck—and being given the royal treatment whenever he arrives somewhere.

Spending Sunday on an Islet. I usually stay very busy revising this guide, but I am forced by law to put it aside and relax on Sunday in Tonga. I like to spend my day doing nothing at one of the little resorts off Nuku'alofa.

Watching the Blow Holes. Having crossed the Pacific several times in U.S. Navy ships and sailed across it once in a small boat, I am acutely aware of the power of the sea. It's strangely comforting to watch it explode through the Blow Holes on Tongatapu's south coast. Maybe it's because I know those waves can't get me up there on dry land.

Exploring Vava'u. There are a lot of South Pacific places where I would like to stay just a little longer, and beautiful Vava'u is at the top of the list. Visiting this boating paradise is a very different experience from visiting Tongatapu. The main village of Neiafu is a trip even farther back in time than Nuku'alofa.

Fa'onelua Gardens. The modern 3-story building before Railway Road houses the government ministries of works, agriculture, health, education, lands and survey, and civil aviation. As a resident of the Washington, D.C. area, every time I see this building I think of my own nation's capital, where it takes several huge buildings and hundreds of acres of land to house that many departments of the U.S. government.

Turn left on Railway Road. The small colonial-era wooden structure on the left in the first block serves as both the **Court House** and **parliament** when it meets from June to September. Both court and parliament sessions are open to the public. Now return to Vuna Road and turn left.

Vuna Wharf, at the foot of Taufa'ahau Road, Nuku'alofa's main street, was built in 1906, and for some 60 years most visitors to Tonga debarked from ships that tied up here. It became less trafficked when Queen Salote Wharf was erected east of town in 1966 to handle large ships, and a major earthquake in 1977 damaged Vuna Wharf so extensively that it has been used since only in emergencies. A railroad once ran through town along Railway Road to transport copra and other crops to Vuna Wharf.

Directly across Vuna Road from the wharf is the low **Treasury Building.** Constructed in 1928, it's a fine example of South Pacific colonial architecture. Early in its life it housed the Tongan Customs service and the post office as well as the Treasury Department.

The field to the west of the wharf is the **Pangai,** where royal feasts, kava ceremonies, and parades are held. Overlooking the Pangai and surrounded by towering Norfolk pines is the ⚫ **Royal Palace,** a white Victorian building with gingerbread fretwork and gables under a red roof. The palace was prefabricated in New Zealand, shipped to Tonga, and erected in 1867. The second-story veranda was added in 1882. You can get a good view over the low white fence built of coral blocks (the best spot for photographs is on the east side, so save some film until we get around there). The king and queen usually live on a large spread west of town.

Now walk up Taufa'ahau Road past the huge rain tree in front of the modern Bank of Tonga (a local gathering place). Across the street stands the colonial-style **prime minister's office** with its quaint tower.

Turn right at the post office on Salote Road. The **Nuku'alofa Club** on the left, about halfway down the block, is another holdover from the old South Pacific: It's a private club where Tonga's elite males gather to relax over a game of snooker and a few Australian beers. The next block of Salote Road runs behind the Royal Palace. You can look over the backyard fence and observe the royal geese. Turn right on Vaha'akolo Road and walk along the west side of the palace toward the sea. The highest point on Tongatapu, **Chapel Hill** (or Zion Hill) to the left, part of the Royal Estate, was a Tongan fort during the 18th century and the site of a missionary school opened in 1830 and a large Wesleyan church built in 1865. The school is now located 4 miles west of Nuku'alofa and is known as **Sia'atoutai Theological College.** The church has long since been torn down.

When you get to the water, look back and take your photos of the palace framed by the Norfolk pines.

Picturesque **Vuna Road** runs west from the palace, with the sea and reef on one side and stately old colonial homes on the other. The house at the end of the first block was the home of a Tongan noble who on several occasions in the 1800s went to England, where he stayed with friends in Newcastle; accordingly, he named the house **Niukasa.** The British High Commissioner's residence, in the second block, sports a flagpole surrounded by four cannons from the *Port au Prince,* the ship captured and burned by the Tongans at Ha'apai in 1806 after they had clubbed to death all its crew except young Will Mariner. King George I had two wives—not concurrently—and both of them are buried in casuarina-ringed Mala'e'aloa Cemetery, whose name means "tragic field." The clapboard house in the next block is known as **Ovalau** because it was built in the 1800s at Levuka, the old capital of Fiji on the island of Ovalau, and was shipped to Tonga in the 1950s.

Turn inland at the corner, walk 2 blocks on 'Alipate Road, take a left on Wellington Road, and walk 2 blocks west to **Centenary Church.** The mansion just before the church was reputed to have been built about 1871 by the Rev. Shirley W. Baker, the missionary who had so much influence over King George I. Now it's the home of the president of the Free Wesleyan Church of Tonga. Centenary Church was built by the Free Wesleyan Church of Tonga between 1949 and 1952. Most of the construction materials and labor were donated by members of the church. While construction was going on, the town was divided into sections that fed the workers three meals a day on a rotating basis. The amount of money spent on the building was about T$80,000 ($72,000); the actual value of the materials and labor was many times that amount. The church seats about 2,000 persons, including the king and queen, who worship there on Sunday mornings.

Turn right past the church and proceed inland on Vaha'akolo Road. On the right behind the Centenary Church is the old **Free Wesleyan Church of Tonga,** built in 1888 and an example of early Tongan church architecture. Past the old church is **Queen Salote College,** a girls' school named for a wife of King George I and not for his great-great-granddaughter, the famous Queen Salote.

Turn left at the first street, known as Laifone Road, and walk along a large open space to your right. Since 1893 this area has been known as the ♻ **Royal Tombs,** and King George I, King George II, Queen Salote, and most of their various wives and husbands are buried at the center of the field. For many years the rest of the area was used as a golf course; today, however, the king's cattle keep the grass mowed. On Taufa'ahau Road, behind this open expanse, stands the modern **Queen Salote Memorial Hall,** the country's national auditorium, which opened in 1994.

On the other side of Taufa'ahau Road, opposite the Royal Tombs, rises the tent-shaped **Basilica of St. Anthony of Padua,** the first basilica built in the South Pacific

We had come to see the island and the islanders had come to see us and both sides were having a fine time.
—John Dyson, 1982

islands. On the ground level are the Loki Kai Cafeteria (more commonly known as Akiko's Restaurant) and the 'Utue'a Public Library.

Now follow **Taufa'ahau Road** toward the waterfront. This is Nuku'alofa's "main street," and you'll pass shop after shop, some of them carrying handcrafts and clothing. Between Wellington Road and Salote Road is an old house that now is the home of the **Langafonua Women's Association Handicraft Center** (see "Shopping," below). The clapboard house was built by William Cocker, a local merchant, for his five daughters, who lived in New Zealand but spent each winter in Nuku'alofa.

Turn right on the next street—Salote Road—and walk past the police station on the left to **Maketi Talamahu** in the second block, the lively produce market where vendors sell a great variety of fresh produce ranging from huge taro roots and watermelons to string beans and bananas. Tongatapu's climate is just cool enough during the winter months that both European and tropical fruits and vegetables grow in great bounty. Upstairs, several stalls carry handcraft items, such as tapa cloth and straw baskets and mats.

After looking around the market and perhaps munching on a banana or sipping a fresh young coconut, continue walking east. In the next block is the park known as Fa'onelua Gardens; walk through it to the Tonga Visitors Bureau, where we began our tour and where we end it.

TOURING TONGATAPU

Most visitors see Tonga's main island in two parts: first the eastern side and its ancient archaeological sites, then the western side for its natural spectacles. You can do these on your own via rental car or go with one of the local tour operators (see "Organized Tours," below). Either way, pick up a copy of the visitor bureau's "The Capital Places Tour," which covers the entire island.

THE EASTERN TOUR Take Taufa'ahau Road out of Nuku'alofa, making sure to bear left on the paved road. If you want to see tropical birds in captivity, watch for the signs on the right-hand side of the road directing you to the ✪ **Bird Park** and follow the dirt track about 3 kilometers (1.8 miles). There you will find the Tongan Wildlife Centre with a collection of birds from Tonga and other South Pacific islands kept in cages carefully planted with native vegetation. A star is the Tongan megapode, a native only of Niuafo'ou in the Niuas islands; it buries its eggs in volcanic vents where the temperature is a constant 35°C (95°F), and then flies away, never to see its offspring. Admission is F$3 ($1.80). The exhibit is open Monday through Friday 9am to 5pm, Saturday and Sunday 9am to 6pm.

Now backtrack to the main road and turn right toward the airport. Keep left, especially at Malapo (where the road to the airport goes to the right), and follow the Tonga Visitors Bureau's excellent signs, which will show you the way to **Mu'a.** When the road skirts the lagoon just before the village, watch for ✪ **Captain Cook's Landing Place,** a grassy area beside the water where Capt. James Cook landed and rested under a large banyan tree in 1777. Cook came ashore to meet with Pau, the reigning Tui Tonga, and attended the traditional presentation of first fruits marking the beginning of the harvest season. The banyan tree is long gone; in its place is a stone-and-brass monument.

The next village is ✪ **Lapaha,** seat of the Tui Tonga for 6 centuries beginning about A.D. 1200. All that remains of the royal compound is a series of *langa,* or ancient terraced tombs, some of which are visible from the road. A large sign explains how the supreme Polynesian god, Tangaloa, came down from the sky about A.D. 950 and sired the first Tui Tonga. The last Tui Tonga, who died in 1865 after being deposed by King George I in 1862, is buried in one of the tombs. The 28 tombs around Lapaha and Mu'a are among the most important archaeological sites in Polynesia, but none of them has been excavated. Walk down the dirt road near the sign to see more of the tombs.

From Lapaha, follow the scenic paved road along the coast until reaching the ✪ **Ha'amonga Trilithon,** near the village of Niutoua on the island's northeast point, 32 kilometers (19 miles) from Nuku'alofa. This huge archway, whose lintel stone is estimated to weigh 35 tons, is 16 feet high and 19 feet wide. Tradition says it was built by the 11th Tui Tonga about A.D. 1200, long before the wheel was introduced to Tonga, as the gateway to the royal compound. The present King Taufa'ahau Tupou IV advanced a theory that it was used not only as a gateway but also for measuring the seasons. He found a secret mark on top of the lintel stone and at dawn on June 21, 1967, proved his point. The mark pointed to the exact spot on the horizon from which the sun rose on the shortest day of the year. You can stand under this imposing archway and ponder just how the ancient Tongans got the lintel stone on top of its two supports; it's the same sense of mysterious wonderment you feel while looking at Stonehenge in England or contemplating the great long-nosed heads that were carved and somehow erected by those other Polynesians far to the east of Tonga, on Easter Island.

The paved road ends at **Niutoua,** but a narrow dirt track proceeds down the east coast. **Anahulu Beach** has a cave with limestone stalactites near the village of Haveluliku. A gorgeous sand beach begins here and runs to **Oholei Beach.** 'Eua Island is visible on the horizon.

On the way back to Nuku'alofa you can take a detour to **Hufangalupe Beach** on the south coast for a look at a large natural bridge carved out of coral and limestone by the sea.

THE WESTERN TOUR   Proceed out of Nuku'alofa on Mateialona Road and follow the Visitors Bureau signs to the ✪ **blowholes** near the village of Houma on the southwest coast. At high tide the surf pounds under shelves, sending geysers of seawater through holes in the coral. These are the most impressive blowholes in the South Pacific, and on a windy day the coast for miles is shrouded in mist thrown into the air by hundreds of them working at once. They perform best on a day when the surf is medium—that is, just high enough to pound under the shelves and send water exploding up through holes in them. Lime sediments have built up terraces of circles, like rice paddies, around each hole, and the local women come just before dusk to gather clams in the shallow pools formed by the rings. There is a park with benches and a parking area at the end of the road near the blowholes, but you'll need shoes with good soles to walk across the sharp edges of the top shelf to get the best views. This area once was an underwater reef, and corals are still very much visible, all of them now more than 50 feet above sea level. (Look for what appear to be fossilized brains; they are appropriately named brain corals.) The blowholes are known in Tongan as *Mapu'a a Vaea,* "the chief's whistle."

From Houma, proceed west to the village of Kolovai and watch for the trees with strange-looking fruit. The sounds you hear and the odors in the air are coming from what appear to be black fruit hanging on the trees. In reality, these are the **Flying Foxes of Kolovai,** a type of bat with a foxlike head found on many islands in the

Pacific. They are nocturnal creatures who spend their days hanging upside down from the branches of trees like a thousand little Draculas awaiting the dark, their wings like black capes pulled tightly around their bodies. They don't feed on blood but on fruit; hence they are known as fruit bats. On some islands they are considered a delicacy. In Tonga, however, where they live in trees throughout the villages of Kolovai and Ha'avakatolo, they are thought to be sacred, and only members of the royal family can shoot them. Legend says that the first bats were given to a Tongan navigator by a Samoan princess.

A road from Kolovai goes about a mile west of **Kolovai Beach** and the Good Samaritan Inn, a good place to sip a drink while watching the sun set or to enjoy a Tongan feast on Sunday afternoons. Near the end of the island is **Ha'atafu Beach,** site of an offshore reef preserve.

The first missionaries to land in Tonga came ashore at the end of the peninsula on the northwest coast, and a sign now marks the spot at the end of the road. They obviously got their feet wet—if they were not inadvertently "baptized"—wading across the shallow bank just offshore.

You've now toured Tongatapu from one end to the other. Turn around and head back to town.

ORGANIZED TOURS

Kingdom Tours, in the Air New Zealand office on Taufa'ahau Road (☎ **25-200**), has a selection of tours of Nuku'alofa and the island. Its full-day town tour is divided into two parts: sightseeing in the morning for T$25 ($15) per person, and a cultural tour of the Royal Palace and Tongan National Center in the afternoon for T$17 ($10). Its history tour to the east end takes 2 to 3 hours and costs T$25 ($15). Its west end tour takes 4 hours and costs T$53 ($32), including lunch at the Good Samaritan Inn (see "Accommodations," below).

You also can see the island with **Paea Tours** (☎ **21-103**), **Teta Tours** (☎ **21-688**), **Quick Tours** (☎ **29-910**), and **Toni's Tours** (☎ **21-049**). The latter is run by Englishman Toni Matthias of Toni's Guesthouse (see "Accommodations," below). He stops at Anahulu Beach, where you can swim inside the cave.

FLIGHTSEEING

Larry Simon of **Pacific Island Seaplanes** (☎ **25-177** or 25-165) has a variety of tours in his 1951 refurbished DH-2 floatplane, a veteran of flying in Canada's north (from whence Larry hails, too). A 30-minute sightseeing flight over Tongatapu and the nearby islands costs T$85 ($51) per person. He'll fly you to up to the Ha'apai Group and actually land in the crater lake of Tofua Island. You can even scuba dive in the crater lake and later on a reef. These all-day excursions cost T$250 ($150) per person. And he'll fly you to a deserted island, where you can camp for a week before he picks you up. These cost T$450 ($270), including the flights, food, tent, and supplies. A minimum of four passengers is required for all his excursions, or you'll have to pay the T$580 ($348) per hour flying time.

10 Island Excursions, Water Sports & Other Outdoor Pursuits

✪ **ISLAND EXCURSIONS**   Water sports activities are concentrated in the huge lagoon on Tongatapu's north shore, especially at resorts on the small islets off Nuku'alofa. In fact, the most popular way to spend a day—particularly a very slow Sunday in Tonga—is swimming, snorkeling, sunbathing, dining, or just hanging out at the flat, small islands of Pangaimotu, Fafa, or 'Atata, each of which has a resort just a few miles off Nuku'alofa. These little beachside establishments have restaurants and bars, too.

Tongan Beachcomber Island Village (☎ 23-759) on Pangaimotu is the oldest and closest of the offshore resorts, and it's also the most popular. Virtually hanging over a lovely beach, its main building oozes slapped-together, old South Seas charm. Its boat usually leaves Faua Jetty on Vuna Road at 10 and 11am Monday through Saturday, and at 10am, 11am, noon, and 1pm on Sunday. They return at 5pm Monday through Saturday, and at 4, 5, and 6pm on Sunday. Round-trip fare is T$10 ($6). Once there, a chalkboard menu offers burgers and sandwiches, and owner Earl Emberson serves icy cold brews from a giant ice box behind the bar. There's a children's playground.

Fafa Island Resort (☎ 22-800), a German-owned Robinson Crusoe–like establishment, operates its own sailboat from Faua Jetty daily at 11am. Round-trip transfers and lunch cost T$31.50 ($19).

Royal Sunset Island Resort (☎ 21-155) on 'Atata, the most modern and comfortable of the resorts, welcomes day-trippers only on Sunday. Cost there is T$31.50 ($19), including transfers and lunch.

See "Accommodations," below, for more information about these offshore resorts.

FISHING You won't be able to rely on going when you want to, but the **Tonga International Gamefishing Association (TIGFA)** pairs its members with visitors who like to fish, especially on weekends. Ask the Tonga Visitors Bureau for TIGFA's contact numbers. You'll have to share the cost of fuel, usually about T$40 ($24) per person for a day's fishing.

GOLF You won't be playing any golf on Sunday, but you can every other day at the flat, nine-hole **Manamo'ui Golf Course,** home of the Tonga Golf Club. The tour desk at the International Dateline Hotel (☎ 21-411) can arrange equipment rentals and tee-off times on this somewhat-less-than-challenging course, which is on the main road between the airport and town.

SAILING In addition to the charter yachts based in Vava'u (see "Vava'u," below), **Royal Sunset Cruising,** based at Royal Sunset Island Resort on 'Atata Island (☎ 21-254), has the 51-foot yacht *Impetuous* available for charter anywhere in Tonga (it's one of the best ways to explore the more remote islands in the Ha'apai Group). This crewed craft has three cabins, each with own head (restroom) with shower. Cost is T$750 ($450) a day, including skipper, cook, and provisions.

SCUBA DIVING & SNORKELING Although diving off Tongatapu must play second fiddle to Vava'u, the reefs offshore have some colorful coral and a great variety of sea life. **Deep Blue Diving Centre** (☎ and fax 25-392), on Vuna Road at Faua Jetty, has dives to Hakaumana'o and Malinoa Reef Reserves, two protected underwater parks. Two-tank dives cost T$120 ($72) including all equipment. The company also teaches PADI advanced and open water. Nondivers can go for T$35 ($21), including equipment.

11 Shopping

Tonga is the best place to shop for extraordinary Polynesian handcrafts, such as tapa cloth, mats, carvings, shell jewelry, and other exquisite items. Your large laundry basket will take at least 3 months to get home via ship if you don't send it by air freight or check it as baggage on your return flight, but the quality of its craftsmanship will be worth the wait.

Tapa cloth and finely woven pandanus mats are traditional items of clothing and gifts in Tonga, and the women of the kingdom have carried on the ancient skills, not only out of economic necessity but also out of pride in their craft. Collectively they produce thousands of items a day, every one made by hand and no two exactly alike. The sounds of hammers beating tapa cloth from the bark of the paper mulberry tree is a familiar sound in many Tongan villages.

For an excellent description of how tapa cloth is made and the process by which the women weave baskets, mats, and other items from natural materials, pick up a copy of the Tonga Visitors Bureau's brochure "Tongan Handicrafts."

A few artisans have shops on Vuna Road next to the Tonga Visitors Bureau, where they sell jewelry made from shells and black coral. The quality of some items is quite good, especially at Miki's Curio Shop, reviewed below.

There are handcraft stalls on the second level of **Maketi Talamahu** on Salote Road, where occasionally you can find an excellent basket or other item.

Important advice: I recommend you purchase items already made and on display rather than ordering for future production and delivery after you have left Tonga.

Except for tobacco products and liquor, Tonga has little to offer in the way of duty-free shopping. Get your booze and smokes at the airport, or order them at least 1 day prior to departure at Leiola Duty Free Shop in the International Dateline Hotel.

Kalia Handicrafts (FIMCO). Taufa'ahau Rd., opposite Air New Zealand. ☎ **23-155.**

The retail outlet of the Friendly Islands Marketing Cooperative (FIMCO) offers a large variety of baskets, mats, tapa, shell jewelry, and other handcrafts. You can pay with American Express, MasterCard, and Visa credit cards, and the staff will pack and ship your purchases home. The shop is open Monday through Friday from 8am to 8pm and Saturday from 8am to noon.

✪ **Langafonua Women's Association.** Taufa'ahau Rd., second block inland. ☎ **21-014.**

This shop in the colonial house on Taufa'ahau Road was founded by Queen Salote in 1953 in order to preserve the old crafts and provide a market. It has an excellent collection, and some items may be priced somewhat lower than elsewhere. It does not accept credit cards, nor will it pack and ship your purchases. Open Monday through Friday from 8:30am to 4:30pm, Saturday from 8:30am to noon.

Miki's Curio Shop. Vuna Rd., next to the International Dateline Hotel. ☎ **32-083.**

This small emporium is run by veteran carver Mickey Guttenbeil and his family, who export their black coral, mother-of-pearl, wood, bone carvings, and scrimshaw to other South Pacific and Hawaiian shops. Open Monday through Friday from 9:30am to 4:30pm, Saturday from 9am to noon.

Tongan National Centre. Taufa'ahau Rd., 1 mile south of Nuku'alofa. ☎ **23-022.**

Artisans at this fine cultural center reviewed in "Exploring Tongatapu," above, actually make traditional handcrafts before your eyes, then put them up for sale at the centre's gift shop. They'll pack and ship your choices. Open Monday through Friday 9am to 4:30pm, Saturday 9am to noon.

12 Accommodations

Let's put it this way: If an expensive, super-luxurious vacation or honeymoon is your primary reason for coming to the South Pacific, go to Fiji or French Polynesia, not to Tonga. There are no large luxury resorts at all in Tonga, although there are comfortable—though far from deluxe—hotels and island hideaways to choose from.

That's not to say some establishments here don't have considerable charm, especially Tonga's **offshore resorts,** those little hideaways sitting all by themselves on small islands off Tongatapu's north shore. Go there to rest, relax, sunbathe, swim, snorkel, dive, dine, get drunk, or do whatever comes naturally in a romantic South Seas bungalow. On the other hand, don't spend your entire holiday at an offshore resort if you want to see much of the country or to sample exciting nightlife, since to get anywhere else requires a rather lengthy boat ride. Consider spending a weekend out in the islands, since everyone else will be there on Sunday anyway.

HOTELS

Friendly Islander Hotel. P.O. Box 142, Nuku'alofa (Vuna Rd., on the waterfront 3km [2 miles] east of downtown Nuku'alofa). ☎ **23-810.** Fax 24-199. E-mail: papiloa@kalianet.to. 26 units. A/C TEL. T$60–T$95 ($36–$57). MC, V.

Papiloa Foliaki, once Tonga's only female member of Parliament, started this motel in 1980 with 12 self-contained units. She added a swimming pool, restaurant, and 14 bungalows. The older rooms are in a two-story building facing the sea on one side and a courtyard full of tropical plants on the other. Those on the ocean side are small suites with separate bedrooms and sitting areas. The rooms aren't air conditioned, but they do have basically equipped kitchenettes, tile bathrooms, wall-mounted fans, radios, and sliding glass doors leading either to a patio on ground level or to a balcony on the second story. Built of modern materials, the bungalows are across a side street or behind the main complex. Eight of them have one room; the others have a separate bedroom and are called "Family Fales." All bungalows have shower-only bathrooms and both air conditioners and ceiling fans. A dining room here specializes in dishes featuring fresh local produce.

Harbor View Motel. P.O. Box 83, Nuku'alofa (Vuna Rd., opposite Queen Salote Wharf). ☎ **25-488.** Fax 25-490. 12 units (5 with private bathroom). A/C TV. T$60–T$170 ($36–$102) double. Rates include continental breakfast. MC, V.

Built in 1997, this 3-story concrete building offers a variety of simple but clean rooms. The location on the waterfront is convenient if not particularly quiet, since the town's commercial wharf is across the road in front and the Billfish Bar and Restaurant is one door removed. Nevertheless, the New Zealand High Commission and other organizations put people here as an alternative to the International Dateline Hotel (it's very popular, so book early). Choice quarters are the huge executive suite on the third floor; it has windows on three sides, a TV, a kitchen, both queen and double beds, and a huge bathroom with whirlpool tub. On the second floor, spacious deluxe rooms come equipped with TVs, refrigerators, sofas, and combination tub-shower bathrooms. Seven budget rooms share five bathrooms; four of these have double beds, but one has only a single (it's the least expensive room here). The first floor also has a breakfast room, a lounge with television, and a small bar. This is a walk-up establishment with external stairways leading to verandas on each floor.

International Dateline Hotel. P.O. Box 39, Nuku'alofa (Vuna Rd. at Tupoulahi Rd., on the waterfront). ☎ **23-411.** Fax 23-410. E-mail: idh@kalianet.to. 76 units. A/C MINIBAR TEL. T$94–T$132 ($56.50–$79) double. AE, DC, MC, V.

Built prior to the king's coronation in 1967, this is Tonga's most widely known place to stay, and most tour packages will put you here. The property enjoys a choice location facing the harbor across Vuna Road on Nuku'alofa's waterfront, a few blocks from downtown, and it's the only hotel on Tongatapu with spacious grounds featuring a swimming pool.

Although the hotel received a face-lift prior to the millennium celebrations at the end of 1999, it's still not up to international standards. Only six rooms are completely up to snuff. They're in a newer wing, built along a side street, whose other rooms show wear but are in better shape than those in the original wing across the front of the building. You won't get a direct view of the lagoon, but the additional comforts—and showers with reasonably reliable hot water—will be worth the extra money. The smaller old wing rooms received new furniture in 1999, including sofas and dinette tables with chairs, but they kept their same double-bed mattresses, and little was done to the bathrooms, whose stall showers are notorious for running out of hot water. These old rooms also have air-conditioning units mounted near the bottom of floor-to-ceiling front windows, which means you have to prop the full-length drapes over a chair to get any cold air.

In good weather, the Tu'imalila Dining Room has tables and plastic chairs outside and some form of entertainment after dinner each evening, including traditional Tongan dance shows. The food is plain but adequate. The activities desk will tell you what's on during your stay.

✪ **Villa McKenzie.** P.O. Box 1892, Nuku'alofa (Vuna Rd., at Tungi Rd.). ☎ **24-998.** Fax same as phone. 4 units (all with private bathroom). A/C. T$95–T$120 ($57–$72) double. Rates include full breakfast and taxes. MC, V.

New Zealanders Anne and Milton McKenzie, who have lived in Tonga for many years, have turned their old colonial clapboard home on the waterfront into one of the few real bed-and-breakfasts in the islands. A central hallway is flanked on one side by a large lounge room (equipped with television and VCR), an old-fashioned dining room with chintz curtains, and a huge country kitchen. To the other side, the four rooms all have tongue-in-groove walls, mosquito nets over their beds (doubles in three rooms, twins in one), and tiny, closetlike bathrooms with shower stalls, pullman sinks, and toilets. The McKenzies also built in small closets and vanities, and they move a desk from room to room at their guests' request. They also have a rental-car available, and they serve snacks in the rear garden Wednesday through Friday evenings. This is a clean and comfortable choice, and it's the only one in town with old South Seas charm—so book several months in advance.

HOSTELS

Good Samaritan Inn. P.O. Box 306, Nuku'alofa (Kolovai Beach, 11 miles west of Nuku'alofa). ☎ **41-022.** Fax 24-102. 12 units (4 with private bathroom). T$40 ($24) double without private bathroom; T$60 ($36) double with private bathroom; camping T$10 ($6) per person. Rates include breakfast and airport transfers. MC, V.

Run by Irene Mo'ungaloa, this basic, low-budget resort has a popular Friday night Tongan feast and dance show (see "Dining," below) and is a favorite Sunday retreat because of its pleasant dining room, bar, and concrete terrace perched right on Kolovai Beach. Accommodation is in very basic bungalows suitable for backpackers and others who seek no frills whatsoever. All units have electric lights, and all private and communal showers have hot water. A comfy beachside lounge is available for guest use only. A cyclone damaged the beach here in 1993, so you will have to walk a short distance for swimming and snorkeling. Campers can pitch their tents near the beach. Cars, bicycles, and snorkeling gear can be rented on the premises.

Heilala Holiday Lodge. P.O. Box 1698, Nuku'alofa (3km [2 miles] south of town). ☎ **29-910.** Fax 29-410. www.kalianet.to/quick. E-mail: quick@kalianet.to. 12 units (7 with bathroom). T$40 ($24) double; T$45 ($27) double bungalow; T$10 ($6) per person camping. MC, V.

When I visited, Waltrand Quick and her son Sven Quick, both natives of Germany, were in the process of enlarging this hostel set among gardens plots, coconut palms, and fruit trees (you'll hear the neighborhood roosters before dawn).

By the time you arrive, they will have four new deluxe bungalows with private bathrooms, ceiling fans, and big verandas with hammocks. They'll be next to a thatch-roof restaurant and bar. In their original house, five upstairs rooms share two bathrooms (one upstairs, one down), a communal kitchen, and a second-story porch (where smokers can light up). The simple rooms have table fans, platform beds that can be pushed together, and screened windows with Venetian blinds. In the backyard stand three Tongan-style fales made completely of thatch and other natural materials: a poor person's version of the more deluxe models at Fafa Island Resort (see "Offshore Resorts," below), they have fans, lofts with beds, round porches with hammocks, and bathrooms. A camping area across the lane has its own kitchen and toilet block. The Quicks provide free bikes (except to campers) to go to town, a shuttle to the beach, and a free introductory tour of Nuku'alofa. They also operate **Quick Tours,** which provides low-budget island tours in both German and English.

Paradise Shores Resort. P.O. Box 976, Nuku'alofa (Ha'atafu Beach, 48km [30 miles] west of town). ☎ **41-158.** Fax 41-158 or 24-868. www.kalianet.candw.to/parashor/resort. E-mail: paradise-shores@kalianet.to. 12 units (none with private bathroom). T$35 ($21) double, T$10 ($6) dorm bed. MC, V.

Operated by American Dave Bergeron and Australian Alan Karst, this friendly backpackers resort sits on Ha'atafu Beach, one of the island's best, with much better sands than in front of the Good Samaritan Inn (see above). They plan to build a big Tongan fale by the beach; until then, a Western-style house with big veranda holds a restaurant and bar with jazz coming from speakers. It looks across a lawn, upon which stands an outdoor whirlpool tub under the palm trees. Their basic but charming guest fales are made of natural materials and have a double or two single beds with mosquito nets, ceiling fans, tables, chairs, and dressers. Guests share toilets and showers in a rustic communal building. Guests can ride to town for free once a day. Tongans and local expatriate residents like to spend Sunday afternoons here, having lunch, drinking at the bar, and going for a swim.

Toni's Guesthouse. P.O. Box 3084, Nuku'alofa (corner of Railway and Mateialona Rds.). ☎ **21-049.** Fax 22-970. 8 units (none with private bathroom). T$10.75 ($6.45) per person. Rates include tax. No credit cards.

Englishman Toni Matthias manages this basic but clean establishment, the most popular backpacker accommodation here. The rooms are in a long, Day-Glo green building fronted by a communal kitchen and covered gathering area on the carport. Toni does a kava ceremony some evenings and runs all-day island tours in his own truck for T$20 ($12) per person, with a T$60 ($36) minimum.

OFFSHORE RESORTS

Fafa Island Resort. P.O. Box 1444, Nuku'alofa (Fafa Island, 10km [6 miles] off Nuku'alofa). ☎ **22-800.** Fax 23-592. E-mail: fafa@kalianet.to. 16 units. T$99–T$172 ($59.50–$103) double. Meal plans T$70 ($42) per person per day. Round-trip transfers T$21 ($12.50) per person. AE, DC, MC, V.

German Rainer Urtel has stocked his little resort with bungalows made entirely of local materials: coconut timbers and shingles and lots of thatch. Although rustic and definitely not for anyone looking for all the comforts of home, they have Robinson Crusoe charm that has attracted a largely European clientele.

He started out with eight very basic fales circling a central building, all set in the center of this 17-acre, atoll-like island studded with coconut palms. He has replaced his original central fale with a much-improved version right on the beach and added eight much larger guest bungalows, also on the beach. These newer models have shingle roofs and front porches; over two of the porches are romantic "honeymoon" sleeping lofts with a lagoon view. An unusual feature has the toilets and lavatories on rear porches and showers actually sitting in the middle of fenced courtyards. The push-out windows aren't screened, so each of the platform beds has its own mosquito net. Early morning coffee and tea are delivered to the deluxe units.

The beachside central building houses a bar and a restaurant that features excellent German and Tongan seafood specialties. Guests can use Windsurfers, snorkeling gear, and surf skis for free; they pay extra for Hobie Cats and trips to an uninhabited island for snorkeling.

✪ **Royal Sunset Island Resort.** P.O. Box 960, Nuku'alofa ('Atata Island, 10km [6 miles] off Nuku'alofa). ☎ **800/227-5317** or 24-923. Fax 21-254. E-mail: royalsun@kalianet.to. 26 units. T$120–T$170 ($72–$102) double. Meals T$45 ($27) per person per day. Round-trip transfers T$40 ($24) per person. AE, DC, MC, V.

New Zealanders David and Terry Hunt's resort shares small, tadpole-shaped 'Atata Island with a native Tongan village. One of the South Pacific's finest beaches swings around their end, the "tail" of the tadpole, and the surrounding lagoon attracts swimmers, snorkelers, scuba divers, and anyone who loves to fish. Two large shingle-roofed fales house a dining room and a triangular sunken bar, which opens to a swimming pool surrounded by a deck dotted with lawn tables and umbrellas.

Each of the guest bungalows sits behind privacy-providing foliage just off the shore-line. About half face the prevailing southeast trade winds; these can be chilly from June to August but provide nature's air-conditioning during the warmer months of December to March. You pay more for the other units facing the lagoon, but they have a much better beach, plus views of the royal sunsets. Of modern construction, they have their own spacious shower-only bathrooms with hot and cold water, kitchenettes, ceiling fans in both rooms, and large, fully screened windows. A few bungalows are "mini-suites"—one room with sitting areas and tea/coffee-making facilities but no kitchens.

The dining room serves fine meals, always featuring a choice of at least one meat and one fish main course. Tongans strum guitars and sing during the evenings, and there's at least one Tongan dance show every week. Guests can use snorkeling gear, sailboats, and Windsurfers for free, and pay to sport fish and dive (you must be certified in advance to go diving).

Tongan Beachcomber Island Village. Private Bag 49, Nuku'alofa (Pangaimotu Island, 3km [2 miles] off Nuku'alofa). ☎ **11-236.** Fax 23-759. 4 units (all with private bathroom). T$55 ($33) bungalow; T$20 ($12) dorm bed; camping T$10 ($6) per person. Round-trip transfers T$10 ($6). MC, V.

Usually referred to as "Pangaimotu Island Resort," Earle Emberson's lively little retreat is usually packed on Sunday afternoons when it becomes the playground of tourists, local expatriate residents, and Westernized Tongans. The key here is one of the South Pacific's more charming pubs: a rickety lagoonside building where Earle plays jazz compact discs at the bar while the staff whips up meals or burgers and sandwiches served on an adjacent sundeck hanging over a lovely beach. All meals feature fresh local seafood. Guests can swim in one of the safest lagoons in Tonga. The four basic but comfortable guest fales are built of natural materials. They have separate sitting and sleeping areas, platform double beds with mosquito nets, and their own simple bathrooms with hot-water showers. All face the beach. Dorm beds are in a larger communal fale. Campers can pitch their tents on the lawns. Dorm dwellers and campers share communal showers, toilets, and kitchen facilities, and there's a small store dispensing groceries.

13 Dining

Nuku'alofa is blessed with a few restaurants that serve continental cuisine of remarkably high quality for such a small and unsophisticated town. Most are operated by expatriates, especially from Germany and Italy. This also means a high turn-over factor, since not all expatriates stay in the islands forever. I've listed the establishments below that were open when I was here recently. There may be more by the time you arrive—or these may be gone.

There's no McDonald's here yet, but you can get inexpensive burgers, curries, Chinese dishes, and other quick fare at **John's Place Takeaway,** in the business district on Taufa'ahau Road (☎ **21-426**). It's open Monday through Thursday from 8am to midnight, and from 8am Friday straight through until midnight Saturday.

MODERATE

Billfish Bar and Restaurant. Vuna Rd., opposite Queen Salote Wharf. ☎ **24-084.** Reservations recommended for dinner. Lunch T$5–T$10 ($3–$6); main courses T$10–T$23 ($6–$14). MC, V. Mon–Fri 11:30am–10pm, Sat 6–11pm. Bar open later. INTERNATIONAL.

Primarily a socializing and drinking spot (see "Island Nights," below), come to dine at the Billfish after you've exhausted the other options here. It serves meals under its thatch-lined, lean-to roof. A floor of crushed coral and white picnic tables also help create a tropical ambiance. Look for lasagna, spicy Thai-style chicken curry, pepper steaks, and fresh fish steamed with fresh herbs and coconut milk. I opted for king prawns in a garlic cream sauce; it wasn't gourmet quality, but the sauce had a spicy bite. For lunch you can opt for burgers, sandwiches, fish and chips, grilled chops, and curries.

Davina's Restaurant and Bar. Vuna Rd., at Faua Jetty. ☎ **23-385.** Reservations recommended at dinner. Breakfast T$4.50–T$12.50 ($2.50–$7.50); sandwiches and snacks T$7.50–T$12.50 ($4.50–$7.50); main courses T$12.50–T$26 ($7.50–$15.50). MC, V. Mon–Sat 9am–11pm (breakfast all day, lunch noon–3pm, snacks 3–6pm, dinner 6–11pm). REGIONAL.

Englishman David Foy has operated this pleasant restaurant in a pink stucco-over-cinderblock house since 1989. He keeps it open all day for breakfast, lunch, afternoon snacks, and dinners. You can take your afternoon tea at the bar on the front porch or under a small Tongan fale in the front yard. Other meals are eaten in a dining room attractively furnished with cane. Ceiling fans whirring overhead add to the tropical atmosphere. Main courses feature the best steaks in town, plus fish, chicken, and local lobsters. The long front porch bar is a favorite drinking spot for expatriate residents, and David's satellite TV draws a crowd during rugby games.

✪ Seaview Restaurant. Vuna Rd., 3 blocks west of Royal Palace. ☎ **23-709.** Reservations essential. Main courses T$17–T$25 ($10–$15). AE, DC, MC, V. Mon–Fri 6–10pm. CONTINENTAL.

Offering consistently the best cuisine in town, this extremely pleasant establishment is in an old colonial clapboard house tastefully decorated inside with tapa cloth and mats to give the dining room an appropriately tropical atmosphere. Daily specials depend on the availability of fresh lobster and quality meats imported from New Zealand, which the German owners usually prepare with heavy continental sauces. Some items that might appear are filet mignon wrapped in bacon and grilled, pepper steak, and fresh lobster or fish "Polynesia" (made sweet by papaya and other tropical fruits). Start with a lobster cocktail and finish with homemade German pastries for dessert. Try to get a table on the breezy front porch.

Tongan Feasts

Like most Polynesians, the Tongans in the old days cooked their food over hot rocks in a pit—an *umu*—for several hours. Today they roast whole suckling pigs on a spit over coals for several hours (larger pigs still go into the umu). The dishes that emerge from the umu are similar to those found elsewhere in Polynesia: pig, chicken, lobster, fish, octopus, taro, taro leaves cooked with meat and onions, breadfruit, bananas, and a sweet breadfruit pudding known as *faikakai-lolo,* all of it cooked with ample amounts of coconut cream. Served on the side are fish *(ota ika)* and clams *(vasuva),* both marinated in lime juice.

The best places to sample Tongan food is during evening buffets and dance shows at the **Tonga National Centre** (☎ 23-022), the **Waterfront Cafe** (☎ 24-962), the **International Dateline Hotel** (☎ 23-411), and the **Good Samaritan Inn** (☎ 41-022). See "Island Nights," below, for details.

○ **Waterfront Cafe.** Vuna Rd., opposite Faua Jetty. ☎ **24-962.** Reservations recommended Thurs and Fri. Main courses T$12–T$25 ($7–$15). MC, V. Mon–Sat 10:30am–10:30pm, Sun 6–9pm. INTERNATIONAL.

Under a big tin roof, this open-air creation of Italians Daniella Orbessano and Grace Ansaldi, who once worked on Princess Cruise Line's ships, is another popular watering hole, but unlike the Billfish (see above), the products of Daniella's kitchen are reason enough to come here. Her menu changes every month, but you can always choose from homemade pastas, freshly caught red snapper, and tender steaks. I started with New Zealand mussels steamed with coconut cream and onions and laced with red chilies, which rendered a pleasant bite to my taste buds. Of several treatments of snapper, I picked an islandy version steamed in parchment paper with coconut cream and taro leaves. A lovely rendition of tiramisu made a fine exclamation point to my meal. Most of a good selection of Australian, New Zealand, and Italian wines are available by the glass. Forget dining à la carte on Thursday nights, when Daniella and Grace put out a buffet of Tongan foods, followed by a traditional dance show (see "Tongan Feasts," above).

INEXPENSIVE

Akiko's Restaurant (Loki Kai). Taufa'ahau Rd., in Basilica of St. Anthony of Padua. No phone. Reservations not accepted. Lunch specials T$2–T$4 ($1.25–$2.50); main courses T$3.50–T$8.50 ($2–$5). No credit cards. Mon–Fri 11:30am–2pm and 6:30–8pm. EUROPEAN/ JAPANESE/CHINESE.

Known as Akiko's in honor of its former Japanese owner, this plain but spotlessly clean establishment provides a selection of European, Chinese, and—yes—Japanese selections that are marvelous bargains. Local expatriates bring the kids here for dinner when they don't want to dress up. No alcoholic beverages are served.

○ **Friends Cafe.** Taufa'ahau Road, between Salote and Wellington Rds. ☎ **21-284.** Reservations not accepted. Breakfast T$2.50–T$6 ($1.50–$3.50); lunch T$3–T$6.50 ($2–$4). Mon–Fri 8:30am–5:30pm, Sat 8:30am–2pm. Ask about evening hours. INTERNATIONAL.

This sophisticated coffee shop and cafe provides a delightful oasis in Taufa'ahau Road's dusty business scene. Order cappuccino, espresso, the town's best cakes and pastries, luscious fruit plates, and made-to-order sandwiches at the counter, then sip or dine at the round wooden tables while listening to jazz or classical music on the sound system. A blackboard menu offers specials such as quiche and salad, braised lamb shanks in tomato sauce, or a sweet, New Orleans-style gumbo over rice. The "friends" here are

Tonga-born Paul Johansson and his Australian partner, Geoff Smith, who once lived in Dallas, Texas.

✪ **Pizzeria Little Italy.** Vuna Rd., 5 blocks west of Royal Palace. ☎ **21-053.** Reservations recommended. Pizzas T$7–T$12.50 ($4.25–$7.50); pastas T$9.50–T$16.50 ($5.50–$10). MC, V. Mon–Sat noon–2pm and 6:30–11pm, Sat 6:30–10:30pm. PIZZA/PASTA.

Angelo Crapanzano, who learned his trade as a pizza chef in Milan, Italy, now scurries around the open kitchen in this unusual restaurant: it's a genuine, thatch-roofed Tongan fale, but empty Ruffino wine bottles dangle from the support posts, and hats of every imaginable description adorn the walls. Don't be in a hurry, for Angelo makes everything from scratch, including the pizza dough and pasta. I started with a focaccia of thin, crispy pizza crust, and went on to an Italian-style side salad with virgin olive oil, oregano, and salt. My main course was a delicious helping of penne pasta in a medium-thick cream sauce accented with smoked salmon. And I finished with a cup of real cappuccino. You can also pick from a limited list of Italian wines.

14 Island Nights

TONGAN DANCE SHOWS   As in Samoa, traditional **Tongan dancing** emphasizes fluid movements of the hands and feet instead of gyrating hips, as is the case in French Polynesia and the Cook Islands. There also is less emphasis on drums and more on the stamping, clapping, and singing of the participants. The dances most often performed for tourists are the *tau'olunga,* in which one young woman dances solo, her body glistening with coconut oil; the *ma'ulu'ulu,* performed sitting down by groups ranging from 20 members to as many as 900 for very important occasions; the *laklaka,* in which rows of dancers sing and dance in unison; and the *kailao,* or war dance, in which men stamp the ground and wave war clubs at each other in mock battle.

The **Tonga National Centre** (☎ 23-022) stages a full Tongan-style feast complete with traditional kava welcoming ceremony and dance show Tuesday and Thursday evenings. What makes the evening special is an explanation, in English, of what each dance represents. Cost is T$21 ($12.50). Book by 4:30pm.

Also in town, the **Waterfront Cafe,** on Vuna Road opposite Faua Jetty (☎ 24-962), has a buffet of Tongan foods followed by a dance show on Thursday evenings. It costs T$18 ($11).

Another good choice is the Friday night feasts at the **Good Samaritan Inn** (☎ 41-022), on the beach 11 miles west of Nuku'alofa (see "Accommodations," above). There's an extensive buffet of Tongan and Western foods, followed by a dance show beside the lagoon. The meal and show cost T$18 ($11), plus T$5 ($3) for round-trip transportation from town if you need it. Reservations are advised.

You'll also have a chance to see Tongan dancing in Nuku'alofa at the **International Dateline Hotel** (☎ 23-411), where floor shows start about 9pm after buffet-style dinners (the nights and prices change, so check with the hotel).

PUB CRAWLING   Since all pubs and nightclubs must close at the stroke of midnight Saturday, Friday is the busiest and longest night of the week in Tonga. That's when some establishments stay open until 2am or even 5am. Many Tongans start their weekends at one of the local bars, then adjourn to a nightclub for heavy-duty revelry.

Clubs change in popularity quickly here, so it's best to ask around to find out which ones are drawing the crowds. During my recent visit, everyone started the Friday revelry with drinks at either **Davina's Restaurant** or the **Billfish Bar & Restaurant,** both on Vuna Road opposite Queen Salote Wharf (see "Dining," above). They then adjourned for late-night dancing at the **Blue Pacific Club,** on the Fang'uta Lagoon east of town (access is by dirt road, so take a taxi).

15 Vava'u

Approximately 260 kilometers (163 miles) north of Tongatapu lies enchanting Vava'u, the second-most-visited group of islands in the kingdom and one of the South Pacific's most unusual destinations.

Often mispronounced "Va-vow," the group consists of one large, hilly island shaped like a jellyfish, its tentacles trailing off in a myriad of waterways and small, sand-ringed islets. In the middle is the magnificent fjord-like harbor known as **Port of Refuge,** one of the finest anchorages and most popular yachting destinations in the South Pacific. From its picturesque perch above the harbor, the main village of **Neiafu** (pop. 5,000) evokes scenes from the South Pacific of yesteryear.

Vava'u has its own unique history. The first European visitor was Spanish explorer Francisco Antonio Mourelle, who happened upon the islands in 1781 on his way to the Philippines from Mexico. He gave Port of Refuge its name. At the time, Vava'u was the seat of one of three chiefdoms fighting for control of Tonga. Finau II, who captured the *Port au Prince* in 1806, built a fortress at Neiafu and kept Will Mariner captive there until the young Englishman became one of his favorites. Two years later the brutal Finau won a major victory by faking a peace agreement with rival chiefs. He then tied them up and let them slowly sink to their deaths in a leaky canoe.

Finau II's successor, Finau 'Ulukalala III, converted to Christianity but died before his successor was old enough to rule. Before dying he asked George Taufa'ahau, who was then chief of Ha'apai, to look after the throne until the young boy was old enough. George did more than that; he took over Vava'u in 1833. Twelve years later he conquered Tongatapu and became King George I, ruler of Tonga.

To the south of Neiafu, the reef is speckled with 33 small islands, 21 of them inhabited. The others are spectacularly beautiful little dots of land that fall into the Robinson Crusoe category of places to escape from it all for a day. The white beaches and emerald surrounding lagoon are unsurpassed in their beauty.

Vava'u is heaven for water-sports enthusiasts and sailors. Getting out on the water for a day is easy. When you see these protected waterways, you'll know why cruising sailors love Vava'u. If you like walking on unspoiled white sandy beaches on uninhabited islands, swimming in crystal-clear water, and taking boat rides into mysterious caves cut into cliffs, you'll like Vava'u, too.

Vava'u is the most seasonal destination in the South Pacific. Sleeping for 6 months of the year, it virtually comes alive during the yachting season from May to October, when more than 100 boats can be in port at any one time. This is also the time of year when humpback whales migrate from the Antarctic to frolic in Tongan waters. You can often see them close inshore at Vava'u.

I recommend that side trips to Vava'u be made early in a visit to Tonga in order to allow a day or two leeway in case you can't get back to Nuku'alofa on the day your international flight leaves.

As with Savai'i in Samoa, you will wish you had stayed longer in this most beautiful and enchanting part of Tonga.

GETTING THERE

Royal Tongan Airlines (☎ 800/486-6426 or 23-414 in Nuku'alofa) has several flights a day from Tongatapu to Vava'u, and once a week to and from Nadi in Fiji. **Samoa Air** flies very small planes between Pago Pago and Vava'u twice a week. See section 8, "Getting There & Getting Around," in this chapter for details.

Lupepa'u International Airport is on the north side of Vava'u, about 7 kilometers (4 miles) from Neiafu. The Paradise Hotel's bus provides airport transfers for its guests

---

Impressions

Despite the lack of green fields and church spires, in the pearly dawn from the ship's bridge the Vava'u Group had the appearance of a lump of Cornwall or Brittany that had been dropped on a hard surface from a height just sufficient to scatter the thirty-four fragments and create deep channels, scarcely wider than rivers, between them. As the ship wandered among the scrub-covered limestone tableaux I thought it was the nearest thing in cruise-liner terms to cross-country driving.

—John Dyson, 1982

---

for free and for anyone else for T$4 ($2.50), or you can take one of the island's few taxis to Neiafu for about T$7 ($4.25).

Don't forget that it's imperative to reconfirm your return flight to Tongatapu as soon as possible after arriving on Vava'u. The staff at your hotel can take care of this for you, or you can visit the office of Royal Tongan Airlines, on the main street in Neiafu.

The ferries from Nuku'alofa land at Uafu Lahi, the Big Wharf, in Neiafu. From there you can walk or take a taxi ride to your hotel or guesthouse. If on foot, turn right on the main street to reach the center of town and the accommodations.

The road from the airport dead-ends at a T-intersection atop the hill above the wharf. The main street runs from there in both directions along the water, with most of the town's stores and government offices flanking it. The government used convicted adulteresses to help build this road; hence, its Tongan name is Hale Lupe (Road of the Doves). There are no street signs, but the Tonga Visitors Bureau's helpful signs point the way to most establishments and points of interest.

GETTING AROUND

Public transportation on Vava'u is limited. If you book an excursion, ask about the availability of transportation to and from the event. **Taxis** are not metered, so be sure you determine the fare before getting in. **Falepiu Taxi** (☎ **70-671**) has a stand opposite the Bank of Tonga; **Liviela Taxi** (☎ **70-240**) is opposite the big Frisco store; **Hamana Taxi** (☎ **70-257** or 70-157) is near the market; and **Lopaukamea Taxi** (☎ **70-153**) is opposite the market. Fares are T$1.50 (90¢) in town, or you can hire one for about T$10 ($6) per hour or T$25 ($15) a day, but be sure to negotiate a fare in advance. **Buses** and pickup trucks fan out from the market in Neiafu to various villages, but they have no fixed schedule. If you take one, make sure you know when and whether it's coming back to town.

FAST FACTS: VAVA'U

If you don't see an item here, check the "Fast Facts: Tonga" earlier in this chapter, or just ask around. Vava'u is a very small place where nearly everyone knows everything.

Bookstores   Friendly Islands Bookshop has a branch on the main street.

Currency Exchange   The **Bank of Tonga** office, on the main street in Neiafu, is open Monday through Friday from 9:30am to 3:30pm; and **ANZ Bank** nearby is open Monday through Friday from 9am to 3:30pm. When they are closed, traveler's checks can be exchanged at the Paradise Hotel.

Doctor & Dentist   **Dr. Alfredo Carafa** (☎ **70-607**), an engaging Italian, has a private clinic with two doctors and a dentist next to the Bank of Tonga. Open Monday through Friday 9am to 2pm.

Hospital   The government has a 40-bed hospital with dental service in Neiafu. Take my advice and call "Dr. Alfredo" at his clinic.

Information   The **Tonga Visitors Bureau** (☎ **70-115;** fax 70-666; e-mail tvbvv@kalianet.to) has an office on the main road in Neiafu. Check there for lists of local activities while you're in town. The staff can also help arrange road tours of the island and boat tours of the lagoon. The office is open Monday through Friday from 8:30am to 4:30pm, Saturday from 8:30am to noon. The address is P.O. Box 18, Neiafu, Vava'u.

Police   The telephone number for the police is **70-234.**

Post Office/Telephone/Fax   The post office opposite the wharf is open Monday through Friday from 8:30am to 12:30pm and 1:30 to 3:30pm. Local calls can be made at the post office, which has the island's only public telephone.

Telephone   Tonga Telecom next to the post office is open 24 hours a day, 7 days a week for domestic and long-distance calls.

Water   Don't drink the tap water.

EXPLORING VAVA'U

You can take a walking tour of Neiafu, the picturesque little town curving along the banks of Port of Refuge. The Tonga Visitors Bureau (☎ **70-115**) might also be able to organize a walking tour for a small group.

For sure, make the walk along Port of Refuge from the Paradise Hotel into town, a stroll of about 15 minutes.

The flat-topped mountain across the harbor is **Mo'unga Talau,** at 204 meters (675 feet) the tallest point on Vava'u. A hike to the top takes about 2 hours round-trip. To get there, turn inland a block past the Bank of Tonga on the airport road, then left at Sailoame Market. This street continues through the residential area and then becomes a track. The turnoff to the summit starts as the track begins to head downhill. It's a steep climb and can be slippery in wet weather.

Both the **Paradise Hotel** (☎ **70-211**) and the **Tonga Visitors Bureau** (☎ **70-115**) will arrange **sightseeing tours** of the island. Cost is about T$25 ($15) per person, with a minimum of three persons required. You will see lovely scenery of the fingerlike bays cutting into the island, visit some beautiful beaches, and take in the sweet smell of vanilla—the principal cash crop on Vava'u—drying in sheds or in the sun.

ISLAND TOURS, WATER SPORTS & OUTDOOR PURSUITS

As noted above, Vava'u has a very busy yachting and whale-watching season from May to October. Some of the activities mentioned below, especially sailing and fishing boats, operate only during this period, then clear out of Tonga entirely during the hurricane season from November to April. It's best to inquire in advance whether any particular activity is available when you will be here.

✪ **BOAT TOURS**   The thing to do in Vava'u is to get out on the fabulous fjords for some swimming, snorkeling, and exploring of the caves and uninhabited islands.

The typical boat tour follows Port of Refuge to **Swallows Cave** on Kapa Island and then to **Mariner's Cave** (named for Will Mariner, the young Englishman captured with the *Port au Prince* in 1806) on Nuapapu Island. Both of these have been carved out of cliffs by erosion. Boats can go right into Swallows Cave for a look at the swallows flying in and out of a hole in its top. Swimmers with snorkeling gear and a guide can dive into Mariner's Cave. Both caves face west and are best visited in the afternoon, when the maximum amount of natural light gets into them. Most trips also include a stop at one of the small islands for some time at a sparkling beach and a swim over the reefs in crystal-clear water.

Every hotel and guest house here can arrange boat tours, or contact **Natural Mystic Adventures,** in the Puataukanave Centre on the main street in Neiafu (☎ **70-458;** fax

Impressions

If I could repeat just one of my excursions in Polynesia, it would be that spent in a fast little jet-boat, exploring this maze of beaches, cliffs, caves, reefs, and lagoons—or at least, what small proportion of it could be fitted into a single day.

—Ron Hall, 1991

70-080; e-mail nmystic@kalianet.to). Half-day tours cost T$25 ($15) per person, with a minimum charge of T$50 ($30), while full-day trips go for T$40 ($24) per person. Natural Mystic Adventures also has sunset and full-moon cruises for T$15 ($9) per person, and it rents motorboats for T$60 ($36) half day, T$95 ($57) full day. Camping, spear-fishing, and personalized tours can be arranged.

Sailing Safaris (☎ and fax **70-650**) uses sailboats for its island tours, which include snorkeling in the caves, tea and coffee, and lunch for T$55 ($33) per person. See "Sailing," below, for more information.

Beluga Diving (☎ and fax **70-087**) and **Dolphin Pacific Diving** (☎ and fax **70-292**) have snorkeling trips for T$30 ($18) and T$25 ($15) per person, respectively (see "Scuba Diving," below).

FISHING   The waters off Vava'u hold a large number of sizeable blue marlin, sailfish, yellowfin and dogtooth tuna, mahimahi, and other species, and you can charter one of several boats here to go get 'em.

New Zealanders Keith and Pat McKee of *Kiwi Magic* (☎ and fax **70-441;** www.invited.to/kiwi.magic.to; e-mail kiwifish@kalianet.to) take visitors offshore for a full day of sports fishing, and snorkelers can go along by arrangement. Based at the Vava'u Guesthouse, the McKees operate year-round, as do their fellow Kiwis, Henk and Sandra Gross of **Target One** (☎ and fax **70-647;** www.kalianet.to/target1; e-mail fishtarget@kalianet.to). Both the McKees and Grosses charge T$150 ($90) per person per day, including bait, tackle, and lunch. There's a minimum of two persons and maximum of four persons on board.

KAYAKING   Not only yachties can enjoy the multitude of protected waterways here. So can kayakers. **Friendly Islands Kayak Company** (☎ **70-173;** fax 70-173 or 22-970; e-mail fikco@kalianet.to), a New Zealand firm which is based at the Tongan Beach Resort from May to January, rents sea kayaks and conducts guided tours. It has scheduled 6-, 8-, and 10-day trips through the islands, using double- and single-seat kayaks. Or you can call when you get here for a guided day trip—for T$50 ($30), including kayak, snorkeling gear, and lunch—or multi-day trips for T$100 ($60) per day, including boat, snorkeling gear, meals, and tents for camping overnight. You can contact the company during the off-season at P.O. Box 142, Waitati, Otago, New Zealand (☎ and fax **3/482-1202**).

Do-it-yourselfers can rent kayaks from the **Paradise Hotel** (☎ **70-211**).

SCUBA DIVING   There's good diving in these clear waters, especially since you don't have to ride on a boat for several hours just to get to a spot with colorful coral and bountiful sea life. In Port of Refuge, divers can explore the wreck of the copra schooner *Clan McWilliam,* sunk in 1906.

The Dutch-New Zealander couple of Huib and Sybil Kuilboer of **Beluga Diving,** P.O. Box 11, Neiafu (☎ and fax **70-087;** www.kalianet.to/beluga; e-mail beluga@kalianet.to), offer a variety of diving excursions as well as parasailing and Windsurfer rentals. Two-tank dives cost T$75 ($45) without equipment (rentals are available) and teach PADI open-water courses for T$350 ($210). They also organize

2-night diving and camping trips to the outer islets. These cost T$330 to T$395 ($198 to $237) per person, depending on how many people go, including six dives, food, drinks, and camping gear. The Kuiboers also offer parasailing for T$40 ($24) for a 20-minute ride, and they rent Windsurfers for T$30 ($18) for half a day.

Dolphin Pacific Diving, P.O. Box 131, Neiafu (☎ and fax **70-292;** e-mail dive-adi@wave.co.nz), offers two-tank dives for T$90 ($54), including tanks and weight belts, and a short introductory course for T$120 ($72). They teach PADI courses from open-water to dive master.

SAILING   The Florida-based company **The Moorings** (☎ **800/534-7289** or 70-016; e-mail moorings.tonga@kalianet.to), which pioneered charter sailboats in the Caribbean, has one of its South Pacific operations on the main street in Neiafu. Boats range in length from 36 feet to 51 feet and in price from US$1,940 to US$4,760 a week per boat for bareboat charters (that is, you hire the "bare" boat and provide your own skipper and crew). If a boat is available, day rates start at US$200. The Moorings requires that its clients be qualified to handle sailboats of the size it charters, and the staff will check out your skills before turning you loose. A skipper or guide is available at extra cost. The Moorings will do your shopping and have the boat provisioned with food and drink when you arrive. For more information and reservations, contact **The Moorings,** 19345 US19 North, Suite 402, Clearwater, FL 34624 (☎ **800/535-7289** or 727/535-1446; www.moorings.com; e-mail yacht@moorings.com).

Also here is the New Zealand-based **Sunsail Yacht Charters,** Private Bag, Neiafu (☎ **800/227-5317** or phone and fax 70-646 in Vava'u; www.sunsail.co.nz; e-mail res.v@sunsail.co.nz). Its boats range from 38 feet to 46 feet in length and cost from US$300 to US$700, depending on size and season.

American Vern Kirk provides cruises on his trimaran sailboat *Orion.* He charges T$45 ($27) per person for a full day's cruise around the lagoon, with a three-person minimum. Bring your own lunch. Find him or book the *Orion* at the Paradise Hotel (☎ **70-211**).

Sailing Safaris, P.O. Box 153, Neiafu (☎ and fax **70-650;** e-mail sailingsafari@kalianet.to), whose office is in the "Whale Excursions Centre" near the Paradise Hotel, has 26-foot to 51-foot yachts available from T$180 to T$900 ($108 to $540) a day. This company also has "Day Safaris" to the outer islands for T$55 ($33) per person, including gear, snorkeling in the caves, tea and coffee, and lunch. See "Whale Watching," below.

WHALE WATCHING   Humpback whales regularly breed in the waters off Vava'u from June to October, and going out to see them—and even swim with them—is a highlight of a visit here during the season. Both **Whale Watch Vava'u** (☎ 70-576) and **Sailing Safaris** (☎ and fax **70-650**) take guests out to snorkel among these huge animals for T$65 ($39) per person. Book Whale Watch Vava'u at the Bounty Bar & Cafe in Neiafu (see "Dining," below). Sailing Safaris has its office in the "Whale Excursion Centre," on the main road near the Paradise Hotel.

SHOPPING

If you depart Vava'u directly for Pago Pago or Nadi, you can buy some duty-free merchandise at **Leiola Duty Free Shop,** which has shops in the Paradise Hotel and next door to the Tonga Visitors Bureau on the main street.

As noted earlier in this chapter, Vava'u produces some of the finest handcrafts in Tonga. The establishments listed below will pack and ship your purchases home. Also look in the small jewelry shops along the main street for items of black coral and shell.

FaSea Souvenir. Main St., in Whale Excursion Centre. ☎ **70-853.**

Best offerings at this little shop are wood and whale bone carvings produced on the premises (though remember, you can't legally bring whale bones home). You'll also find a small selection of black coral and other jewelry and a few aloha shirts. Open Monday through Saturday 7:30am to 10pm.

Friendly Islands Marketing Cooperative (FIMCO). Main St., next to Royal Tongan Airlines. ☎ **70-242.**

The Vava'u branch of FIMCO has some good items, but most of the best is shipped to the main store in Nuku'alofa for sale. Open Monday through Friday from 8:30am to 4:30pm (to 5pm June through November) and Saturday 8:30am to noon.

Langafonua Handicrafts. Main St., in Tonga Visitors Bureau. ☎ **70-356.**

The Vava'u branch of Langafonua, the women's handcraft organization founded by Queen Salote, has a shop in a Tongan fale adjacent to the Tonga Visitors Bureau. It has a good variety of baskets, mats, wood carvings, and other items at reasonable prices. Open Monday through Friday 8:30am to 4pm, Saturday 8:30am to noon.

ACCOMMODATIONS
HOTELS & RESORTS
Mounu Island Resort. Private Box 7, Neiafu (Mounu Island, 25 min. by speedboat from Neiafu). ☎ **70-747.** Fax 70-493. www.kalianet.to/mounu. E-mail: mounu@kalianet.to. 4 units. T$125 ($75) double. Meals T$45 ($27) per person per day. Transfers T$45 ($27) per person. MC, V.

The long-time dream of New Zealanders Allan and Lyn Bowe, this little resort sits beside a wraparound beach of deep white sand on Mounu ("Bait Fish" in Tongan), an atoll-like, 6-acre islet near the southern end of Vava'u's outer islands. Cruising yachties moor their boats over the colorful corals and row their dinghies ashore to imbibe and dine on freshly caught seafood in the Bowe's main building, a lovely mat-lined Tongan fale right on the beach.

Their four widely spaced guest fales are rustic but charming, with futon beds covered with mosquito nets (necessary since the windows aren't screened), rattan easy chairs and glass-topped coffee tables, bathrooms with hot-water showers, and front porches facing the lagoon. Solar power generates the electricity, and rain provides all the fresh water here.

You can swim, snorkel, kayak, fish, go on village visits, and observe seabirds at a nearby breeding colony. This is a very popular retreat during the June to October whale-watching season, when Alan operates Whale Watch Vava'u (see "Island Tours, Water Sports & Outdoor Pursuits," above).

✪ **Paradise Hotel.** P.O. Box 11, Neiafu, Vava'u, Tonga (east end of Neiafu). ☎ **70-211.** Fax 70-184. www.kalianet.to/paradise. E-mail: paradise@kalianet.to. 48 units. A/C TEL. T$52–T$110 ($31–$66) double. AE, DC, MC, V.

Perched on a grassy ridge overlooking Port of Refuge and a short walk from Neiafu, this is the most comfortable hotel in Tonga. Kentuckian Carter Johnson, who made his fortune building pipelines in the U.S. and Australia, bought the Paradise at auction in 1981 as "something to do" during an early retirement. What he has done is create an unusual property whose blocks of humongous rooms are joined by covered walkways sided with white pipe railings (a testament to his abilities with a welding torch). A large central building houses the reception area, a gift shop, bar, restaurant, and dance area. Next to it on a grassy lawn is a swimming pool with a panoramic view of the harbor below. A path leads down to the water's edge, where the hotel has its own pier, a popular spot for "yachties" from May to October, who congregate in the bar and contribute to a very friendly, informal atmosphere. Incidentally, the airplane engine hanging near the bar once was part of the hotel's aircraft that Carter crash-landed in 1985. Fortunately, no one was seriously injured.

The American-size rooms, in 1- and 2-story buildings, are devoid of any tropical charms except the views from their balconies (the most expensive have unimpeded views of Port of Refuge). They have various bed combinations, recliner chairs, coffee tables, coffeemakers, refrigerators, and ample bathrooms with combo tub-showers. A few older "economy" rooms have ceiling fans but no air conditioners, tea/coffee-making facilities, hot water, or harbor views.

The dining room opens to the hilltop pool. The hotel has a game room in which video movies are shown in the evenings, and a local musical group plays in the dance area off the bar beginning at 8pm Monday through Saturday during the sailing season. The reception staff can tell you what's happening while you're there and can also arrange tours and boat trips.

Tongan Beach Resort. P.O. Box 104, Neiafu, Vava'u (on 'Utungake Island, 8.8km [5.5 miles] from Neiafu, 14.5km [9.5 miles] from airport via dirt road and causeway). ☎ and fax **70-380.** www.thetongan.com. 12 units. T$108–T$220 ($65–$132). Meals T$50 ($30) per person per day. Round-trip airport transfers T$20 ($12). MC, V.

This isolated resort sits beside a lovely narrow channel south of Port of Refuge, giving guests their own swimming beach and jumping-off point for scuba diving, kayaking, and other water sports. The main building here is an open Tongan fale housing a restaurant, whose menu varies each day depending on the catch, the emphasis being on fresh seafood. A sand-floored bar has its own fale next door. The star accommodations here are two partially over-water bungalows with thatch-covered tin roofs and steps down into the lagoon. Ashore, comfortable, motel-like guest rooms flank the main complex. They are of New Zealand–style construction and furnishings. All have tile floors, ceiling fans, refrigerators, dressing areas, one queen and one single bed, and shower-only bathrooms.

HOSTELS

Hilltop Guest House. Private Bag, Neiafu, Vava'u (off the airport road; follow TVB signs). ☎ and fax **70-209.** 12 units (2 with private bathroom). T$18–T$25 ($11–$15) double. MC, V.

Low-budget travelers can get a bit of everything at this guesthouse overlooking Port of Refuge. The two rooms with their own bathrooms here provide a gorgeous vista, as do the communal lounge and kitchen. Otherwise, you get small, very basic but clean rooms. There's a swimming pool behind the house (it has a view of both harbors), and an adjoining lean-to roof covers a barbecue venue.

Vava'u Guest House. P.O. Box 148, Neiafu, Vava'u (east end of Neiafu, opposite Paradise Hotel). ☎ **70-300.** E-mail: kiwifish@kalianet.to. 9 units (4 with bathroom). T$25 double ($15) double. No credit cards.

You can get a room or stay in your own very basic bungalow at this convenient establishment across the road from the Paradise Hotel. The four Tongan-fale bungalows are comfortable (albeit with cold-water showers). A European-style house on the property contains 10 rooms sharing two bathrooms. There are no guest cooking facilities here, but a restaurant offers a mix of Chinese and Tongan dishes. Full dinners cost about T$9 ($7); guests should book by 3pm.

DINING IN VAVA'U

If you missed a Tongan feast in Nuku'alofa, or just liked it so much you want to try again, **Hinakauea Beach Feast** takes place Thursday on lovely Lisa Beach. It costs T$20 ($12) per person. Inquire at the Paradise Hotel or the Tonga Visitors Bureau.

'Ana's Waterfront Cafe. Neiafu, main street next to The Moorings. ☎ **70-664.** Reservations not accepted. Breakfast T$3.50–T$6 ($2–$3.50); lunch T$3.50–T$13 ($2–$8); main courses T$9.50–T$13 ($5.50–$8). MC, V. Mon–Fri 8am–10pm, Sat 8am–3pm. REGIONAL.

Go down the steep steps next to The Moorings to reach this friendly cafe on a covered dock by the bay. Actually, you can sit on the dock, or in a lighted cave in the cliff that drops from the main road to the harbor ('Ana is not a woman's name; it means "cave" in Tongan). The Moorings actually owns this restaurant, which explains the "Eggs McMoorings" on the breakfast menu—along with fruit plates, omelets, sandwiches, and pancakes. Lunchtime sees big burgers, fish and chips, and the like. For dinner, the menu shifts to grilled fish, steaks, and local lobster. You'll find all the town's expatriate residents and most of the yachties here.

Bounty Bar & Cafe. Neiafu, main street in heart of town. ☎ **70-576.** Reservations required for dinner. Breakfast T$2–T$4 ($1.20–$2.50); snacks and meals T$4–T$15 ($2.50–$9). No credit cards. Sept–May, Mon–Fri 8:30am–7pm; June–Aug, Mon–Fri 8:30am–10pm. SNACKS/REGIONAL.

With its great view overlooking Port of Refuge, the Bounty Bar is a popular establishment for morning tea. You also can order cooked breakfasts, burgers and sandwiches, and meals of sashimi, fried rice, and fresh local fish. Full dinners and live entertainment are offered on Friday during the yachting season from June to August, but you must reserve in advance for the 7pm seating.

Mermaid Restaurant. Neiafu, main street on the water next to The Moorings. ☎ **70-730.** Reservations required. Main courses T$8–T$20 ($5–12). No credit cards. May–Dec, Mon–Sat 5–10pm. Closed Jan–Apr. SEAFOOD.

Canadian chef Ron Cherry presides in this thatch building beside Port of Refuge (it's on the property of Coleman Marine, next to The Moorings). Seafood is his specialty, particularly local lobster in a variety of sauces. There's music and a Tongan floor show Monday, Wednesday, and Friday.

✪ **Ocean Breeze Restaurant.** Neiafu, on the Old Harbor. ☎ **70-582.** Reservations required. Main courses T$11.50–T$26.50 ($7–$16). MC, V. Mon–Sat noon–2pm and 6–10pm, Sun by prior arrangement only. REGIONAL.

Born in Tonga, Amelia Dale lived for 15 years in England, where she met and married husband John. She and John have converted their living room and veranda overlooking the Old Harbour into a restaurant where you will find the best curries in Tonga. I love her lobster with banana, pineapple, and Bombay potatoes, which is right up there with any curry I've had anywhere, and that includes India and Pakistan. Ask her to turn down the chilies if you have a tender tongue! You can have a drink out in the Bistro Bar on the lawn. The trail across the peninsula from Port of Refuge and the Paradise Hotel is narrow and can be muddy. Take a cab for T$2 ($1.20) each way.

ISLAND NIGHTS

A dance band usually plays from 8pm nightly in the **Paradise Hotel** bar (☎ 70-211) during the busy yachting season from May to October, on Fridays and Saturdays during the rest of the year. Also in season, the **Mermaid Restaurant** on the waterfront (☎ 70-730) has a Tongan floor show on Monday, Wednesday, and Friday. Otherwise, there's not much to do except hang out with all the expatriates playing billiards and darts, drinking, and gossiping at the **Neiafu Club** (☎ 70-566) overlooking the harbor on the main road just east of the Paradise Hotel. Members welcome overseas visitors to use their rustic lounge with shelf of books and bar. The club is open daily from 3 to 11pm, including all holidays, with happy hour daily from 6 to 7pm. The club will stay open after 11pm if those still present ante up to pay the bartender.

16 Ha'apai

Off the beaten path but easily accessible, the Ha'apai group of islands are central both to Tonga's geography and to its history. In the middle of the kingdom, 155 kilometers (96 miles) north of Nuku'alofa and 108 kilometers (67 miles) south of Vava'u, Ha'apai consists of numerous small, atoll-like islands scattered across the sea. The largest and most often visited, **Lifuka** and **Foa,** are linked by a causeway. On the horizon to their west sit the active volcano **Tofua,** where puffs of steam spew from the rim of its crater lake, and the perfectly shaped cone of its inactive neighbor, **Kao.**

The Dutchman Abel Tasman landed on one of the islands in 1643. Captain James Cook was so impressed with the Tongans' hospitality when he visited Lifuka in 1773 and 1777 that he named the group the "Friendly Islands" (he sailed away unaware that the local chief had plotted to do him in). Fletcher Christian and the *Bounty* mutineers cast Capt. William Bligh adrift in a longboat off Tofua in 1789. In 1806 the locals ransacked the British privateer *Port-au-Prince,* killing all of its crew except the young Will Mariner, who lived to write about his adventure. Tonga's first Wesleyan missionaries arrived here in the 1820s. With their help, the converted local chief Taufa'ahau captured the rest of Tonga, changed his name to King George I, and in 1845 created the realm we visit today. The Rev. Shirley Baker, who dominated King George during his later years, is buried on Lifuka in **Pangai,** Ha'apai's only town.

Today Lifuka and the other islands seem much as they must have been when King George moved his capital to Tongatapu. You'll find some great beaches and fine scuba diving here, but there's not much else to do except relax and explore Pangai's historical sights. In other words, it's a fine place to get away from it all.

GETTING THERE & GETTING AROUND

Royal Tongan Airlines (☎ 800/486-6426 or 23-414) flies from Tongatapu and Vava'u to **Salote Pilolevu Airport,** on Lifuka's northern end, at least once every day except Sunday. The airline's bus will take you from the airport 5 kilometers (3 miles) south to Pangai. You can charter **Pacific Island Seaplanes** (☎ 25-177 in Nuku'alofa) to bring you here or even to land in Tofua's volcanic crater. The **Shipping Corporation of Polynesia** (☎ 21-699 in Nuku'alofa) operates weekly M.V. *Olovaha* ferry service from Nuku'alofa to Ha'apai. For details see section 8, "Getting There & Getting Around," earlier in this chapter.

EXPLORING LIFUKA

Begin your visit at the local **Tonga Visitors Bureau** branch, in the government compound on Palace Road (☎ 60-733), which distributes free maps of the island and a very helpful "Strolling Through Lifuka" brochure (you can pick these up at the TVB in Nuku'alofa, too). The post office, infirmary, Tonga Telekom, and other offices are in the compound.

Australian Trevor Gregory, owner of Mariner's Bar & Cafe (☎ 60-374), guides **walking tours** of town for T$4 ($2.50) per person. See "Dining," below.

Easily explored on foot, the town of Pangai spreads out from **Taufa'ahau Wharf,** on the western, lagoon side of Lifuka. Europeans settled north of the wharf and built colonial-style houses, a clapboard hotel, and a cemetery where the **Rev. Shirley Baker Monument** is a major site today. In those days, the king resided in an impressive palace which stood at the inland end of Palace Road. The incumbent king stays at a much more modest **Royal Palace** on the lagoon south of the wharf.

Billed as "The Smallest Museum in the World," the **Afa Eli Historical Museum & Research Library,** inland near the old palace site (no phone), is the creation of Virginia Watkins, a Vermont native who has lived in Tonga since 1981. The museum actually resides in a window, in which Mrs. Watkins displays small exhibits of Tongan culture and lore. She lives across the road and is always happy to show off the 3,000-year-old pottery shards and other items she has collected. Admission is free but donations are appreciated.

South of town, the tiered **Olovehi Tomb** was constructed of limestone in the late 1700s for the eldest sister of the high chief. The chiefly **Bathing Well at 'Ahau** nearby was dug as an inverted cone to stabilize the porous bedrock. Trees in the bottom provided privacy.

Captain Cook sailed past the **Huluipaongo Tomb,** built on the southern end of Lifuka by harsh chiefs who were notorious for making their subjects work on this and other mounds. Stones for those projects were taken from the **Holopeka Beach Quarry,** northeast of town on Lifuka's ocean side.

SCUBA DIVING & OTHER WATER SPORTS

The largest underwater caves and canyons in the South Pacific beckon divers to the fish-filled seas surrounding these islands. German native Roland Schwara of **Watersports Ha'apai** (☎ and fax **60-097**), who's based at the Niu'akalo Beach Motel, will take you out there on a two-tank dive for T$95 ($57), including all equipment. Roland goes on half-day deep-sea fishing expeditions for T$160 ($96) per person. He rents kayaks and will organize whale-watching voyages and diving-camping trips to Tofua and Kao islands.

Another German, Monika Rahimi of **Happy Ha'apai Divers** (☎ and fax **60-600;** e-mail sandybch@kalianet.to), at Sandy Beach Resort (see "Accommodations," below), charges between T$85 and T$95 ($51 to $57) for two-tank dives, including tanks and weights.

ACCOMMODATIONS

The pick of the basic, low-budget accommodations here is **Fifita Guesthouse** (☎ **60-213;** fax 60-374; e-mail mariners@kalianet.to), over Mariner's Bar & Cafe in the middle of Pangai (see "Dining," below). A simple, share-bath double room costs T$20 ($12). No credit cards.

You'll see gorgeous sunsets from the rocky beach at **Niu'akalo Beach Motel** (☎ **60-023;** fax 60-500), beside the lagoon 1.5 kilometer (1 mile) north of Pangai. Four of the 12 basic units here have private bathrooms. Doubles cost from T$27.50 to T$32 ($16.50 to $19). No credit cards.

Resort at Billy's Place. P.O. Box 66, Pangai, Ha'apai (1.1km [0.7 mile] northeast of Pangai). ☎ **60-336.** Fax 60-200. 4 units (none with bathroom). T$45–T$55 ($27–$33) double. No credit cards.

Tongan Billy Hu'akau and his American wife Sandy operate this basic but friendly and clean little resort on a nearly deserted beach on Lifuka's ocean side. You won't be able to swim here, however, for the waves crash on a shallow coral shelf. Wooden walkways run through a thick tropical forest to their bungalows, which are made of timber over concrete floors. Each has two single beds which can be pushed together. Guests share communal toilets and showers. Inexpensive meals are served under a tent next to a central building, and there's a bar.

✪ **Sandy Beach Resort.** P.O. Box 61, Pangai, Ha'apai (north end of Foa island). ☎ and fax **60-600.** E-mail: sandybch@kalianet.to. 12 units. T$140 ($84) double. Rates include airport transfers. Lunch and dinner T$45 ($27) per person per day. AE, MC, V.

Sigrid ("Siggy") and Juergen Stavenow's resort is aptly named, for it sits beside one of the South Pacific's best beaches, a glorious curving stretch of white sand facing west toward Tofua and Kao on the horizon. You can have a meal or a cold drink while taking in this view from the central building's big concrete veranda. Of modern construction but with Tongan style, the light, airy bungalows all have porches facing the beach and come equipped with cool tile floors, either a double or two single beds, chairs and tables, ceiling fans, refrigerators, coffeemakers, and ample bathrooms with tiled showers. Each also has its own hammock and a thatch cabana out by the beach. To provide privacy, they are staggered and have a solid wall on the side facing their nearest neighbor. Guests get free snorkeling gear, canoes, kayaks, bicycles, nature walks (Juergen's specialty), culture show, and daily shuttle to Pangai. You'll pay extra for diving, horseback riding, boat trips, and tennis at the local Mormon church (bring your own racquet and balls).

DINING

Mariner's Bar & Cafe. Fau Rd., Pangai. ☎ **60-374.** Reservations not accepted. Lunch T$2–T$5 ($1.20–$3), dinners T$5–T$10 ($3–$6). MC, V. Mon–Sat 8am–8pm. REGIONAL.

Australian Trevor Gregory sailed to Ha'apai on a yacht and liked it so much he returned to open the town's only restaurant. A tin roof covers his wooden tables and white plastic chairs. There's nothing fancy here: burgers, curries, steaks, chops, stir-fries, and fish and chips, but the company's friendly and informative.

Appendix:
The South Pacific in Depth

The South Pacific islands have romantically impacted the Western imagination since Tahitians gave a roaring, bare-breasted welcome to an English sea captain and his crew in 1767. To European minds back then, the Pacific Islanders seemed to be Rousseau's "noble savages," living guilt-free lives beside crystal-clear lagoons. Fletcher Christian committed the world's most famous mutiny, in part because of his obsession with a Tahitian *vahine*. Missionaries soon arrived to save these heathen souls, and traders came to sell them whiskey and guns in exchange for sea cucumbers, coconuts, and land. Literary giants such as Herman Melville, Robert Louis Stevenson, W. Somerset Maugham, and James A. Michener spun great yarns about the islands, and actors like Clark Gable and Mel Gibson (both portraying Christian) brought colorful island characters to life on the silver screen.

Despite the inroads of modern materialism and the moral fervor of Christian fundamentalism instilled by the missionaries, today's travel posters don't lie about these languid islands. Palm-draped beaches beckon us to get away from it all. Blue lagoons and colorful reefs offer some of the world's best diving and snorkeling. Steep mountain valleys await hikers to visit islanders who live much as their ancestors did centuries ago. And uninhabited islets beg to be explored under sail.

Best of all, the proud and friendly Pacific Islanders stand ready to welcome you to their shores and to explain their ancient customs and traditions. If the enormous beauty of their islands doesn't charm you, then their highly infectious smiles surely will.

1 History 101

The islanders had been living on their tiny outposts for thousands of years before Europeans had the foggiest notion that the Pacific Ocean existed. Even after Vasco Nuñez de Balboa crossed the Isthmus of Panama and discovered this largest of oceans in 1513, and Ferdinand Magellan sailed across it in 1521, more than 250 years went by before Europeans paid much attention to the islands that lay upon it.

For most of that time, the Pacific was the domain of Spanish sea captains, whose job was not discovery but bringing loot from the rich Spice Islands (now Indonesia and the Philippines) to Peru. Magellan stumbled upon few Pacific islands, and none below the equator. Alvaro de Medaña discovered some of the Solomon, Cook, and Marquesas islands in 1568 and 1595, respectively, and in 1606 Pedro Fernández de Quirós happened upon some of the Tuamotu, Cook, and New

Dateline

- **30,000 B.C.** Australoid peoples settle in Southwest Pacific.
- **7,000–3,500 B.C.** Papuans arrive from Southeast Asia.
- **3,000–1,000 B.C.** Austronesians arrive from Asia, push eastward.
- **1,000 B.C.** Polynesians migrate eastward to Samoa and Tonga.
- **1513** Balboa discovers the Pacific Ocean.
- **1521** Magellan crosses the Pacific.
- **1568** Medaña discovers the Marquesas and some of Cook and Solomon Islands.
- **1606** De Quirós discovers islands in the Tuamotus, Cooks, and New Hebrides (Vanuatu).
- **1642** Abel Tasman explores western Pacific, finds Tonga and Fiji.
- **1722** Roggeveen happens upon Easter Island and Samoa.
- **1764** Byron fails to find Terra Australis Incognita.
- **1767** Wallis discovers Tahiti.
- **1768** Bougainville also discovers Tahiti.
- **1769–71** Captain Cook observes transit of Venus from Tahiti, explores South Pacific.
- **1772–74** On second voyage, Cook finds New Caledonia, Norfolk Island, more of the Cook Islands, and Fiji.
- **1778–79** Cook explores northwest America, dies in Hawaii.
- **1789** Fletcher Christian leads mutiny on the *Bounty*.
- **1797** First missionaries arrive in Tahiti.
- **1800–1810** Whalers, merchants, and sandalwood traders flock to islands, bring guns and whiskey.
- **1808** Last *Bounty* mutineer discovered on Pitcairn.
- **1820–50** *Bêche-de-mer* trade flourishes; Western-style

continues

Hebrides (now Vanuatu) islands. Otherwise, the Spanish missed the South Pacific islands. Dutchman Abel Tasman discovered and explored much of Australia, New Zealand, Tonga, and Fiji in 1642, but the Dutch did nothing to exploit his discoveries, nor did they follow up on those of Jacob Roggeveen, who found Easter Island and Samoa in 1722.

VENUS IN A GRASS SKIRT The South Pacific came to Europe's attention during the latter half of the 18th century when a theory came into vogue that an unknown southern land—a *terra australis incognita*—lay somewhere in the southern hemisphere. It had to exist, the theory went, for otherwise the unbalanced earth would wobble off into space. King George III of Great Britain took great interest in the idea and in 1764 sent Capt. John Byron (the poet's grandfather) to the Pacific in H.M.S. *Dolphin*. Although Byron came home empty handed, King George immediately dispatched Capt. Samuel Wallis in the *Dolphin*. Wallis had no better luck finding the unknown continent, but in 1767 he stumbled upon a high, lush island known as Tahiti. Canoeloads of Tahitians, including multitudes of young women clad only in grass skirts, paddled out to give him a rousing welcome.

Less than a year later, the Tahitians similarly welcomed French explorer Louis Antoine de Bougainville. So enchanted was Bougainville by the Venus-like quality of Tahiti's women that he named their island New Cythère—after the Greek island of Cythera, associated with the goddess Aphrodite (Venus).

Bougainville continued west, discovering several islands in Samoa and exploring the Solomon Islands, of which the island of Bougainville—now part of Papua New Guinea—still bears his name. So does the bright tropical shrub known as bougainvillea. He was the first Frenchman to circumnavigate the globe and was treated to a rousing reception when he returned home in 1769. He brought with him a young Tahitian, whom the Parisians saw as living proof of Rousseau's theory that man at his best lived an uninhibited life as a noble savage.

CAPT. COOK'S TOURS After Wallis arrived back in England, the Lords of the Admiralty put a young lieutenant named

James Cook in command of a converted collier and sent him to Tahiti. A product of the Age of Enlightenment, Cook was a master navigator, a mathematician, an astronomer, and a practical physician who became the first captain of any ship to prevent scurvy among his crewmen by feeding them fresh fruits and vegetables. His ostensible mission was to observe the transit of Venus—the planet, that is—across the sun, an astronomical event that would not occur again until 1874, but which, if measured from widely separated points on the globe, would enable scientists for the first time to determine longitude on the earth's surface. Cook's second, highly secret mission was to find the elusive southern continent.

Cook's measurements of Venus were somewhat less than useful, but his observations of Tahiti, made during a stay of 6 months, were of immense importance in understanding the "noble savages" who lived there.

Cook then sailed southeast to carry out the secret part of his mission. He discovered the Society Islands northwest of Tahiti and the Australs to the south, and then fully explored the coasts of New Zealand and eastern Australia, neither of which had been visited by Europeans since Tasman's voyage in 1642. After nearly sinking his ship on the Great Barrier Reef, he left the South Pacific through the strait between Australia and Papua New Guinea, which he named for his converted collier, the *Endeavor*. He returned to London in 1771.

During two subsequent voyages, Cook visited Tonga and discovered several other islands, among them what now are Fiji, the Cook Islands, Niue, New Caledonia, and Norfolk Island. His ships were the first to sail below the Antarctic Circle; although he failed to sight Antarctica, he put to rest the theory that a large land mass lay in the tropical South Pacific. On his third voyage in 1778–79, he discovered the Hawaiian Islands and explored the northwest coast of North America until ice in the Bering Strait turned him back. He returned to the Big Island of Hawaii, where, on February 14, 1779, he was killed during a petty skirmish with the islanders.

With the exception of the Hawaiians who smashed his skull, Captain Cook was revered throughout the Pacific. Although he claimed many of the islands for Britain, he hoped they never would be colonized. He treated the islanders fairly and respected their traditions.

- towns founded in Tahiti, Samoa, Tonga, Fiji.
- **1842** France annexes Tahiti; Herman Melville arrives in Papeete the same day.
- **1848** Tonga captures eastern Fiji.
- **1858** Fiji asks to become a British colony.
- **1865** First Chinese brought to Tahiti to harvest cotton.
- **1874** Britain accepts Fiji as a colony.
- **1879** First Indians brought to Fiji.
- **1884** International Dateline established.
- **1888** Britain, foiling France, declares protectorate over the Cook Islands.
- **1889** Unrest in Western Samoa; hurricane destroys U.S., British, and German warships at Apia. Robert Louis Stevenson settles in Apia.
- **1890** Germany takes Western Samoa, U.S. gets Eastern Samoa, Britain claims protectorate over Tonga.
- **1891** Painter Paul Gauguin arrives in Tahiti.
- **1894** Robert Louis Stevenson dies in Samoa.
- **1901** Paul Gauguin dies in the Marquesas Islands of French Polynesia.
- **1915** During World War I, German Admiral von Spee shells Papeete.
- **1917** Count von Luckner captured in Fiji after his German raider runs aground in the Cook Islands.
- **1933** Charles Nordhoff and James Norman Hall publish *Mutiny on the* Bounty, a bestseller.
- **1935** *Mutiny on the* Bounty, starring Clark Gable and Charles Laughton, is a smash box-office hit.
- **1941** Japanese bomb Pearl Harbor in Hawaii, begin advance into the South Pacific.

continues

- **1942–44** Allied forces strike Guadalcanal in Solomon Islands, use other islands as bases for attacks on Japanese.
- **1947** James A. Michener's *Tales of the South Pacific* is published; gives rise to musical and movie *South Pacific.*
- **1959–60** International airports open at Tahiti and Fiji.
- **1960** MGM remakes *Mutiny on the* Bounty, starring Marlon Brando.
- **1962** Western Samoa becomes independent.
- **1965** Cook Islands gain local autonomy in association with New Zealand.
- **1966** France explodes first nuclear bomb in Tuamotus.
- **1970** Fiji gains independence from Britain.
- **1978** Solomon Islands become independent.
- **1980** New Hebrides become independent Vanuatu.
- **1985** Treaty of Rarotonga declares South Pacific to be a nuclear-free zone.
- **1987** Fiji's military overthrows elected government.
- **1990** U.S. President George Bush and island leaders meet at summit conference.
- **1992** France halts nuclear testing in Tuamotus; Fiji elects civilian government.
- **1995** French resume limited nuclear testing, protesters riot in Papeete, Japanese tourists boycott Tahiti.
- **1996** French end nuclear testing program.
- **1997** Western Samoa officially changes name to Samoa; French Polynesia embarks on hotel-building campaign.
- **1998** Fiji adopts multiracial constitution.
- **1999** Fiji elects first Indian prime minister.

The Polynesian chiefs looked upon him as one of their own. Today, you'll find a Cook's Bay, a Cooktown, a Cook Strait, any number of Captain Cook's landing places, and an entire island nation named for this giant of an explorer.

MUTINY ON THE *BOUNTY* Based on reports by Cook and others about the abundance of breadfruit, a head-size, potatolike fruit which grows on trees throughout the islands, a group of West Indian planters asked King George III if he would be so kind as to transport the trees from Tahiti to Jamaica as a cheap source of food for their slaves. The king dispatched Capt. William Bligh, who had been one of Cook's navigators, in command of H.M.S. *Bounty* in 1787. One of Bligh's officers was a former shipmate named Fletcher Christian.

Their story is one of history's great sea yarns. The *Bounty* was late arriving in Tahiti, so Christian and the crew frolicked on Tahiti for 6 months waiting for the next breadfruit season. They obviously enjoyed the affections of young Tahitian women as well as the balmy climate, for on April 28, 1789, on the way home, they overpowered Bligh off Tonga. After setting the captain and his loyalists adrift, Christian and eight other mutineers, along with their Tahitian wives and six Tahitian men, disappeared with the ship. Bligh and his men miraculously rowed the *Bounty's* longboat some 3,000 miles to the Dutch East Indies, where they hitched a ride back to England. The Royal Navy then rounded up the *Bounty* crewmen left on Tahiti, of whom three were later hanged.

Christian's whereabouts remained a mystery until 1808, when an American whaling ship discovered the last surviving mutineer on remote Pitcairn Island. The mutineers, after landing there in 1789, had burned and sunk the *Bounty* (the ship's rudder has been recovered and now is on display at the Fiji Museum in Suva). Their descendants still live on Pitcairn and elsewhere in the South Pacific.

See "History 101" in chapter 3 for more about the mutiny.

GUNS & WHISKEY The American ship that found the mutineers' retreat at Pitcairn was one of many whalers roaming the South Pacific in the early 1800s. Their ruffian crews made dens of iniquity of many ports, such as Lahaina and Honolulu in Hawaii, Papeete and Nuku Hiva in what is now French Polynesia,

It would have been far better for these people never to have known us.
—Captain James Cook, 1769

and Levuka in Fiji. Many crewmen jumped ship and lived on the islands, some of them even casting their lots—and their guns—with rival chiefs during tribal wars. With their assistance, some chiefs were able to extend their domain over entire islands or groups of islands.

One such deserter who jumped ship in the Marquesas Islands and later went to Tahiti, in the early 1820s, was Herman Melville. He returned to New England and wrote two books, *Typee* and *Omoo,* based on his South Pacific exploits. They were the start of his literary career.

Along with the whalers came traders. Some of them sailed from island to island in search of sandalwood, pearls, shells, and the sea slugs known as *bêches-de-mer,* which they traded for beads, cloth, whiskey, and guns and then sold at high prices in China. Others established stores that became the catalysts for Western-style trading towns. The merchants brought more guns and alcohol to people who had never used them before. They also put pressure on local leaders to coin money, which introduced a cash economy where none had existed before. Guns, alcohol, and money had far-reaching effects on the easygoing, communal traditions of the Pacific Islanders.

Diseases brought by the Europeans and Americans were even more devastating. The Polynesians had little, if any, resistance to such ailments as measles, influenza, tuberculosis, pneumonia, typhoid fever, and venereal disease. Epidemics swept the islands and killed the majority of their inhabitants.

While the traders were building towns, other arrivals were turning the bush country into plantations: cotton in Tahiti, sugar in Fiji, coconuts everywhere. With the native islanders either disinclined to work or unable to do so, Chinese indentured laborers were brought to a cotton plantation in Tahiti in the 1860s. After it failed, some of them stayed and became farmers and merchants. Their descendants now form the merchant class of French Polynesia. The same thing happened in Fiji, where East Indians were brought to work the sugar plantations.

BRINGING THE WORD OF GOD   The reports of the islands by Cook and Bougainville may have brought word of noble savages living in paradise to some people in Europe; to others, they heralded heathens to be rescued from hell. So while alcohol and diseases were destroying the islanders' bodies, a stream of missionaries arrived on the scene to save their souls.

The "opening" of the South Pacific coincided with a fundamentalist religious revival in England, and it wasn't long before the London Missionary Society (LMS) was on the scene in Tahiti. Its first missionaries, who arrived in the LMS ship *Duff* in 1797, were the first Protestant missionaries to leave England for a foreign country. They chose Tahiti because there "the difficulties were least."

Polynesians, already believing in a supreme being at the head of a hierarchy of lesser gods, quickly converted to Christianity in large numbers. As an act of faith, the puritanical missionaries demanded the destruction of all *tikis,* which they regarded as idols (as a result, today most Polynesian tikis carved for the tourist souvenir trade resemble those of New Zealand, where the more liberal Anglican missionaries were less demanding). The missionaries in Polynesia also insisted that the heathen temples (known as *maraes*) be torn down. Many now have been restored, however, and can be visited in the islands.

The South Pacific in Depth

> *I would get up in the morning, put on my pareu, brew my coffee and suddenly reflect that by rights I should be in a pair of long trousers, jangling a bunch of keys ready to open the store. I had escaped!*
>
> —Tom Neale, 1966

Roman Catholic missionaries made less puritanical progress in Tahiti after the French took over in the early 1840s, but for the most part the South Pacific was the domain of rock-ribbed Protestants. The LMS extended its influence west through the Cook Islands and the Samoas, and the Wesleyans had luck in Tonga and Fiji. Today, thanks to those early missionaries, Sunday is a very quiet day throughout the islands.

COLONIALS TAKE CHARGE   Although Captain Cook laid claim to many islands, Britain was reluctant to burden itself with such far-flung colonies, beyond those it already had—Australia and New Zealand. Accordingly, colonialism was not a significant factor in the history of the South Pacific islands until the late 19th century. The one exception was France's declaring a protectorate over Tahiti in 1842.

The situation changed half a century later, when imperial Germany colonized the western islands of Samoa in the 1890s (at the same time that novelist Robert Louis Stevenson arrived to live there). Britain took over Fiji and agreed to protect the Kingdom of Tonga from takeover by another foreign power; France moved into New Caledonia; and the United States stepped into the eastern Samoan islands, which became known as American Samoa. Britain also claimed the Cook Islands, but they were later annexed by newly independent New Zealand. Thus, within a period of 30 years, every South Pacific island group except Tonga became a colony.

After World War I, when Germany was stripped of its colonies, New Zealand took over in Western Samoa. Otherwise, the colonial structure in the South Pacific remained the same, politically, until the 1960s.

Economically, the islands came under the sphere of Australia and New Zealand. Large Australian companies, such as Burns Philp and Carpenters, built up trading and shipping empires based on the exchange of retail goods for copra and other local produce, and Australian and New Zealand banks came to dominate finance in most islands outside the French and American territories.

THE COUNT & THE CONSTABLES   Although thousands of Pacific Islanders went off to fight with their colonial rulers during World War I, the islands themselves escaped action, with two exceptions.

First, a small German naval force under Admiral Graf von Spee sped across the Pacific during 1915, sinking Allied merchant ships and shelling the town of Papeete.

Two years later, the colorful Count von Luckner brought his German raider *Seeadler* into the Pacific to hunt for merchant prey. After 3 months' prowling, which netted only three small sailing vessels, the *Seeadler* was swept onto the reef at Mopelia atoll in the remote northern Cook Islands. Von Luckner and five crewmen set out in the ship's launch for Rarotonga to commandeer another ship. He could have captured the town of Avarua but steered away when he saw a "ship" in port—in reality, a wreck sitting upright on the reef. He then headed for Fiji, where, deceived as to the actual British force on the island, he surrendered to one armed policeman and 5 unarmed constables sent to investigate.

Missionaries, traders, and broken white folk living on the bounty of the natives, are to be found in almost every isle and hamlet.

—Robert Louis Stevenson, 1889

BASES, ROADS & AIRSTRIPS The South Pacific leaped onto the front pages in World War II. Within weeks after the bombing of Pearl Harbor, in December 1941, the Japanese drove south to New Guinea and the Solomon Islands, where, in July 1942, they began constructing an airfield on Guadalcanal. The U.S. Marines invaded Guadalcanal and nearby Tulagi on August 8, and during the next 6 months one bloody jungle skirmish and sea battle after another took place. By February 1943, with Guadalcanal entirely in U.S. hands, the Japanese advance in the southwestern Pacific had been stopped. The stage was soon set for the Allied counteroffensive that would island-hop its way toward Japan.

Although the South Pacific fighting took place only in Papua New Guinea and the Solomon Islands, many other islands played significant supporting roles. Airstrips and training bases were built all over the South Pacific (many of the airfields are still in use today). Out-of-the-way islands, such as Bora Bora and Aitutaki, became refueling stops on transpacific flights, and the Samoas and Fiji were invaded by thousands of U.S. Marines and GIs preparing for the fighting farther west and north. Entire communities with modern infrastructures were built in weeks—only to be abandoned almost overnight when the war ended.

The war's effect on the islanders was profound. The profusion of new things that arrived on their islands, and the wages paid them for working on the Allied bases, brought a wave of Western influence. The experience was so overwhelming on some Melanesian islands that local "cargo cults" began worshipping Americans or the airplanes with which they brought "mana from heaven."

The soldiers, sailors, and marines also left behind another legacy: thousands of mixed-race children.

CHIEFS, MINISTERS & NUCLEAR BOMBS Colonialism began to crumble in the South Pacific when New Zealand granted independence to Western Samoa in 1962 and, 3 years later, gave complete local autonomy to the Cook Islands. Fiji became independent of Great Britain in 1970. Elsewhere, Britain left the Solomon Islands in 1978, and in 1980 Britain and France gave up their condominium government in the New Hebrides, which became the independent Republic of Vanuatu.

All these young nations have governments based on the Westminster parliamentary system, with wrinkles tailored to fit their citizens' traditions. Almost everywhere there is a council of chiefs to advise the modern-style ministers on custom and tradition. In a modern vestige of the old chiefly system, the national governments tend to have strong individuals at the helm. Elections in these small countries, where everyone seems to know everyone else, often are hard fought and sometimes bitter. Usually, the victors take office, while the vanquished keep on grouching until the polls open again. Fiji's bloodless military coups of 1987, which overthrew that country's first Indian-dominated government, was a shock to observers, since it was directly opposed to this democratic tradition. Fiji has since adopted a constitution providing for an elected parliament.

Of the old colonial powers, only the United States and France remain.

As American nationals, American Samoans are eligible for most U.S. federal aid programs and U.S. passports (about two-thirds of all American Samoans reside in Hawaii or the U.S. mainland). Moreover, except for Washington's control of their budget, they already have almost complete say over their domestic affairs. They are not clamoring for independence.

The problems facing French Polynesia are a good deal thornier. Many Tahitians would like to see their islands free of France and actively campaign for independence. But Paris considers French Polynesia to be an "integral part" of France—so integral, in fact, that France's joining the European Union may force French Polynesia to allow citizens of EU nations to freely migrate and live there—an upsetting thought to many residents of these land-starved islands.

Between 1966 and 1992, the French exploded 210 nuclear weapons in the Tuamotu Archipelago, about 750 miles southeast of Tahiti, first in the air and then underground. The tests were vociferously opposed, especially by New Zealand, where French secret agents sank the Greenpeace protest ship *Rainbow Warrior* in 1985. That same year, the regional heads of government, including the prime ministers of New Zealand and Australia, adopted the Treaty of Rarotonga, calling for the South Pacific to become a nuclear-free zone. After a lull, French President Jacques Chirac decided in 1995 to resume nuclear testing, a move which set off worldwide protests, a day of rioting in Papeete, and a Japanese tourist boycott of French Polynesia. After six underground explosions, the French halted further tests, announced plans to close the testing facility, and in 1996 signed the Treaty of Rarotonga.

THIS LAND IS OUR LAND   Underlying many political issues in the South Pacific is the fundamental question of land rights. There simply isn't much land in these islands, and the indigenous peoples want to maintain their customary ownership of it. Thus, when Vanuatu became independent in 1980, it abolished freehold property and returned all land to its customary owners. Similarly, when it appeared in Fiji that the Indian-dominated government would rewrite the laws protecting Fijian land rights in 1987, the military staged two coups (Fiji has since returned to civilian control and in 1999 elected an Indian as its prime minister).

Despite an occasional riot in Tahiti, the coups in Fiji, and the usual fisticuffs after too many beers on a Friday night, violence is not the usual way by which islanders solve their problems, whether political or personal. They prefer what they call the "Pacific way": discussion, compromise, and consensus, often achieved during all-night sessions over a bowl of kava, the slightly narcotic drink much favored in the islands for ceremonial as well as pleasurable purposes.

Just as the islanders are protective of their land, so they're concerned about the surrounding ocean. For example, the Pacific island states have opposed drift-net fishing; it not only kills dolphins and other sea life unnecessarily, they argue, but also strips them of a vital natural resource. The islanders also are involved in efforts to reduce pollution of the oceans. Many of them see a looming threat in the greenhouse effect: an increase in world temperatures could raise the world's sea level by melting part of the polar ice caps, thus endangering many of the low-lying islands.

2 The Islanders

The early European explorers were astounded to find the far-flung South Pacific islands inhabited by peoples who shared similar physical characteristics, languages, and cultures. How had these people—who lived a late–Stone Age

> *Sentimentalists who moan against natives improving their diet with refrigerators and can openers—"Why, they live on Chinese bread, Australian beef and American pork and beans"—could complain with equal logic that dear old ladies in Boston no longer dip tallow candles because they prefer electricity.*
>
> —James A. Michener, 1951

existence and had no written languages—crossed the vast Pacific to these remote islands long before Europeans had the courage to sail out of sight of land on the Atlantic? Where had they come from? Those questions baffled the early European explorers, and they continue to intrigue scientists and scholars to this day.

THE FIRST SETTLERS

Thor Heyerdahl drifted in his raft *Kon Tiki* from South America to French Polynesia in 1947 to prove his theory that the Polynesians came from the Americas, but most experts now believe that the Pacific islanders have their roots in Southeast Asia. The generally accepted view is that during the Ice Age a race of early humans known as Australoids migrated from Southeast Asia to Papua New Guinea and Australia, when those two countries were joined as one land mass. Another group, the Papuans, arrived from Southeast Asia between 5,000 and 10,000 years ago. Several thousands of years later, a lighter-skinned race known as Austronesians pushed the Papuans inland and out into the more eastern South Pacific islands.

The most tangible remains of the early Austronesians are remnants of pottery, the first shards of which were found during the 1970s in Lapita, a village in New Caledonia. Probably originating in Papua New Guinea, Lapita pottery spread as far east as Tonga. Throughout the area it was decorated with geometric designs similar to those used today on Tongan tapa cloth.

Lapita was the only type of pottery in the South Pacific for a millennium. Apparently, however, the Lapita culture died out some 2,500 years ago. By the time European explorers arrived in the 1770s, gourds and coconut shells were the only crockery used by the Polynesians, who cooked their meals underground and ate with their fingers off banana leaves. Of the islanders covered in this book, only the Fijians still make pottery using Lapita methods.

MELANESIANS

The islands settled by the Papuans and Austronesians are known collectively as Melanesia, which includes Papua New Guinea, Solomon Islands, Vanuatu, and New Caledonia. Fiji is the melting pot of the Melanesians to the west and the Polynesians to the east.

The name Melanesia is derived from the Greek words *melas,* "black," and *nesos,* "island." The Melanesians in general have negroid features—brown-to-black skin, flat or hooked noses, full lips, and wiry hair—but the interbreeding among the successive waves of migrants resulted in many subgroups with varying racial characteristics. That's why the Fijians look more African-American than Polynesian. Their culture, on the other hand, has many Polynesian elements, brought by interbreeding and conquest.

POLYNESIANS

The Polynesians' ancestors stopped in Fiji on their migration from Southeast Asia but later pushed on into the eastern South Pacific. Archaeologists now

Now the cunning lay in this, that the Polynesians have rules of hospitality that have all the force of laws; an etiquette of absolute rigidity made it necessary for the people of the village not only to give lodging to the strangers, but to provide them with food and drink for as long as they wished to stay.

—W. Somerset Maugham, 1921

believe that they settled in Tonga and Samoa more than 3,000 years ago and then slowly fanned out to colonize the vast Polynesian triangle.

These extraordinary mariners crossed thousands of miles of ocean in large, double-hulled canoes capable of carrying hundreds of people, animals, and plants. They navigated by the stars, the wind, the clouds, the shape of the waves, and the flight pattern of birds—a remarkable achievement for a people who on land used no metal tools and gave up the use of pottery of any kind thousands of years before.

Most Polynesians have copper skin and black hair that is straight or wavy rather than fuzzy. A well-built, athletic people, many have become professional football and rugby players in the United States, Australia, and New Zealand. Their ancestors fought each other with war clubs for thousands of years, and it stands to reason that the biggest, strongest, and quickest survived. The notion that all Polynesians are fat is incorrect. In the old days, body size did indeed denote wealth and status, but obesity today is more likely attributable to poor diet. On the other hand, village chiefs still are expected to partake of food and drink with anyone who visits to discuss a problem; hence, great weight remains an unofficial marker of social status.

POLYNESIAN SOCIETY Although Polynesians frequently experienced wars among their various tribes, generally their conflicts were not as bloody as those in Fiji. Nor were they followed as often by a cannibalistic orgy at the expense of the losers.

Polynesians developed highly structured societies, and to this day they place great emphasis on hereditary bloodline when choosing leaders. Strong and sometimes despotic chiefdoms developed on many islands. The present king of Tonga carries on a line of central leaders who were so powerful in the 1700s that they conquered much of Fiji, where they installed many Polynesian customs, including their hereditary chiefly system. Just to make sure, the victorious Tongans forced the conquered Fijian chiefs to take Tongan wives. As a result, today Tongan blood flows in the veins of many Fijian chiefs, some of whom have the Polynesian title *tui*.

In some places, such as Tahiti, the Polynesians developed a rigid class system of chiefs, priests, nobility, commoners, and slaves. Their societies emphasized elaborate formalities, and even today ceremonies featuring kava—a slightly narcotic drink—play important roles in Samoa, Tonga, and Fiji. Everyday life was governed by a system based on *tabu*, a rigid list of things a person could or could not do, depending on his or her status in life. *Tabu* and its variants (*tapu, tambu*) are used throughout the South Pacific to mean "do not enter"; from them derives the English word *taboo*.

Western principles of ownership have made their inroads, but by and large everything in both Polynesia and Fiji—especially land—is owned communally by the family. In effect, the system is pure communism at the family level. If your brother has a crop of taro and you're hungry, then some of that taro belongs to you. The same principle applies to a can of corned beef sitting on

Sex and the Single Polynesian

The puritanical Christian missionaries who arrived in the early 19th century convinced the islanders that they should clothe their nearly naked bodies. They had less luck, however, when it came to sex.

To the islanders, sex was as much a part of life as any other daily activity, and they uninhibitedly engaged in it with a variety of partners from adolescence until marriage.

Even today, they have a somewhat laissez-faire attitude about premarital sex. Every child, whether born in or out of wedlock, is accepted into one of the extended families that are the bedrock of Polynesian society. Mothers, fathers, grandparents, aunts, uncles, and cousins of every degree are all part of the close-knit Polynesian family. Relationships sometimes are so blurred that every adult woman within a mile is known as a child's "auntie"—even the child's mother.

Male transvestism, homosexuality, and bisexuality are facts of life in Polynesia, where young boys are often reared as girls by families with a shortage of female offspring. Some of these youths grow up to be heterosexual; others become homosexual or bisexual and, often appearing publicly in women's attire, actively seek out the company of tourists. In Tahitian, these males are known as *mahus;* in Samoan, *magus;* and in Tongan, *fakaleitis.*

a shelf in a store, which helps explain why islander-owned grocery shops often teeter on the edge of bankruptcy.

While many islanders would be considered poor by Western standards, no one in the villages goes hungry or sleeps without a roof over his or her head. Most of the thatch roofs in Polynesia today are actually bungalows at the resort hotels; nearly everyone else sleeps under tin.

It's little wonder, therefore, that visitors are greeted throughout the islands by friendly, peaceable, and extraordinarily courteous people.

THE OLD GODS Before the coming of Christian missionaries in the 1800s, the Fijians believed in many spirits in the animist traditions of Melanesia. The Polynesians, however, subscribed to a supreme spirit, who ruled over a plethora of lesser deities who, in turn, governed the sun, fire, volcanoes, the sea, war, and fertility. *Tikis* were carved of stone or wood to give each god a home (but not a permanent residence) during religious ceremonies, and great stone *maraes* were built as temples and meeting places for the chiefs. Sacrifices—sometimes human—would be offered to the gods, and cannibalism was not unknown in Polynesia, although it was not as widely practiced there as it was in Fiji and Melanesia.

LANGUAGES

Traced by linguists to present-day Taiwan, the Austronesian family of languages are spoken across a wide area, extending from Madagascar, off the coast of Africa, through Indonesia, Malaysia, the Philippines, and parts of Vietnam, to the South Pacific as far as Easter Island, off the coast of South America. No other group of ancient languages spread to so much of the earth's surface.

Today, the Polynesian islanders still speak similar languages from one major island group to another. For example, the word for "house" is *fale* in Tongan and Samoan, *fare* in Tahitian, *'are* in Cook Islands Maori, *hale* in Hawaiian, and *vale* in Fijian. Without ever having heard the other's language, Cook

Islanders say they can understand about 60% of Tahitian, and Tongans and Samoans can get the gist of each others' conversations.

Thanks to the American, British, New Zealand, and Australian colonial regimes, English is an official language in the Cook Islands, both Samoas, and Fiji. It is spoken widely in Tonga. French is spoken alongside Tahitian in French Polynesia, although English is understood among most hotel and many restaurant staffs.

FEASTS FROM UNDERGROUND OVENS

Before the Europeans arrived, the typical South Pacific diet consisted of bananas, coconuts, and other fruits. Staples were starchy breadfruit and root crops, such as taro, arrowroot, yams, and sweet potatoes. The reefs and lagoons provided abundant fish, lobsters, and clams to augment the meats provided by domesticated pigs, dogs, and chickens. Taro leaves and coconut cream served as complements. Corned beef has replaced dog on today's menu; otherwise, these same ingredients still make up what is commonly called an "island feast."

Like their ancestors, today's islanders still prepare their major meals in an earth oven, known as *himaa* in Tahiti, *lovo* in Fiji, and *imu* or *umu* elsewhere. Individual food items are wrapped in leaves, placed in the pit on a bed of heated stones, covered with more leaves and earth, and left to steam for several hours. The results are quite tasty, with the steam spreading the aroma of one ingredient to the others.

When the meal has finished cooking, the islanders uncover the oven, unwrap the food, and, using their fingers, set about eating their feast of *umukai* (island food) in a leisurely and convivial manner. Then they dance the night away.

The underground oven still is widely used on special occasions and for big family meals after church on Sunday. If you're lucky enough to be invited, don't miss a family feast. Otherwise, many restaurants, especially those at the resort hotels, prepare traditional "island night" feasts for their guests. Don't worry: You can use knives and forks instead of your fingers.

3 The Islands & the Sea

A somewhat less than pious wag once remarked that God made the South Pacific islands on the sixth day of creation so He would have an extraordinarily beautiful place to relax on the seventh day. Modern geologists have a different view, but the fact remains that the islands and the surrounding sea are possessed of heavenly beauty and a plethora of life forms.

HIGH, LOW & IN BETWEEN

The Polynesian islands were formed by molten lava escaping upward through cracks in the earth's crust as it has crept slowly northwestward over the eons, thus building great seamounts. Many of these—called "high islands"—have mountains soaring into the clouds. In contrast, pancake-flat atolls were formed when the islands sank back into the sea, leaving only a thin necklace of coral islets to circumscribe their lagoons and mark their original boundaries. In some cases, geologic forces have once again lifted the atolls, forming "raised" islands whose sides drop precipitously into the sea. Still other, partially sunken islands are left with the remnants of mountains sticking up in their lagoons.

The islands of Tonga and Fiji, on the other hand, were created by volcanic eruptions along the collision of the Indo-Australian and Pacific tectonic plates. Although the main islands are quiet today, they are part of the volcanically active and earthquake-prone "Ring of Fire" around the Pacific Ocean.

A low ribbon of reef and sand encircling a lagoon, an atoll is the very soul of Pacific romance.

—John Dyson, 1982

FLORA & FAUNA

Most species of plants and animals native to the South Pacific originated in Southeast Asia and worked their way eastward across the Pacific, by natural distribution or in the company of humans. The number of native species diminishes the farther east one goes. Very few local plants or animals came from the Americas, the one notable exception being the sweet potato, which may have been brought back from South America by voyaging Polynesians.

PLANTS In addition to the west-to-east difference, flora changes according to each island's topography. The mountainous islands make rain from the moist trade winds and thus possess a greater variety of plants. Their interior highlands are covered with ferns, native bush, or grass. The low atolls, on the other hand, get sparse rainfall and support little other than scrub bush and coconut palms.

Ancient settlers brought coconut palms, breadfruit, taro, paper mulberry, pepper (kava), and bananas to the isolated mid-ocean islands because of their usefulness as food or fiber. Accordingly, they are generally found in the inhabited areas of the islands and not so often in the interior bush.

With a few indigenous exceptions, such as the *tiare Tahiti* gardenia and Fiji's *tagimaucia,* tropical flowers also worked their way east in the company of humans. Bougainvillea, hibiscus, allamanda, poinsettia, poinciana (the flame tree), croton, frangipani (plumeria), ixora, canna, and water lilies all give colorful testament to the islanders' love for flowers of every hue in the rainbow. The aroma of the white, yellow, or pink frangipani is so sweet it's used as perfume on many islands.

ANIMALS & BIRDS The fruit bat, or "flying fox," and some species of insect-eating bats are the only mammals native to South Pacific islands. Dogs, chickens, pigs, rats, and mice were introduced by early settlers. There are few land snakes or other reptiles in the islands. The notable exceptions are geckos and skinks, those little lizards that seem to be everywhere. Don't go berserk when a gecko walks upside-down across the ceiling of your bungalow. They are harmless and actually perform a valuable service by eating mosquitoes and other insects.

The number and variety of species of birdlife also diminishes as you go eastward. Most land birds live in the bush away from settlements and the accompanying cats, dogs, and rats. For this reason the birds most likely to be seen are terns, boobies, herons, petrels, noddies, and others that earn their livelihoods from the sea. Of the introduced birds, the Indian myna is the most numerous. Brought to the South Pacific early in this century to control insects, the myna quickly became a noisy nuisance in its own right.

THE SEA

The tropical South Pacific Ocean virtually teems with sea life, from colorful reef fish to the horrific Great White sharks featured in *Jaws,* from the paua clams that make tasty chowders in the Cook Islands to the deep-sea tuna that keep the canneries going at Pago Pago.

More than 600 species of coral created the great reefs that make the South Pacific a divers' mecca, 10 times the number found in the Caribbean. Billions

The South Pacific in Depth

The South Pacific is memorable because when you are in the islands you simply cannot ignore nature. You cannot avoid looking up at the stars, large as apples on a new tree. You cannot deafen your ear to the thunder of the surf. The bright sands, the screaming birds, and the wild winds are always with you.
　　　　　　　　　　　　　　　　　　　—James A. Michener, 1951

of tiny coral polyps build their own skeletons on top of those left by their ancestors, until they reach the level of low tide. Then they grow outward, extending the edge of the reef. The old skeletons are white, while the living polyps present a rainbow of colors; they grow best and are most colorful in the clear, salty water on the outer edge or in channels, where the tides and waves wash fresh seawater along and across the reef. A reef can grow as much as 2 inches a year in ideal conditions. Although pollution, rising seawater temperature, and a proliferation of crown-of-thorns starfish have greatly hampered reef growth—and beauty—in parts of the South Pacific, there are still many areas where the color and variety of corals are unmatched.

Most island countries have tough laws protecting their environment, so *don't deface the reef.* You could land in the slammer for breaking off a gorgeous chunk of coral to take home as a souvenir.

The lagoons formed by the reefs are like gigantic aquariums filled with a plethora of tropical fish and other marine life, including whales, which migrate to Tonga and Fiji from June to October, and sea turtles, which lay their eggs on some beaches from November through February. Nearly every main town has a bookstore with pamphlets containing photographs and descriptions of the creatures that will peer into your face mask.

Most South Pacific countries restrict the use of spear guns, so ask before you go in search of the catch of your life. Sea turtles and whales are on the list of endangered species, and the importation of their shells, bones, and teeth is prohibited by many countries, including the United States.

SOME WARNINGS　　By and large, the South Pacific's marine creatures are harmless to humans, but there are some to avoid. Always **seek local advice** before snorkeling or swimming in a lagoon away from the hotel beaches. Many diving operators conduct snorkeling tours. If you don't know what you're doing, go with them.

Wash and apply a good antiseptic or antibacterial ointment to all **coral cuts and scrapes** as soon as possible.

Since coral cannot grow in fresh water, the flow of rivers and streams into the lagoon creates narrow channels known as **passes** through the reef. Currents can be very strong in the passes, so stay in the protected, shallow water of the inner lagoons.

Sharks are curious beasts attracted by bright objects such as watches and knives, so be careful what you wear in the water. Don't swim in areas where sewage or edible wastes are dumped, and never swim alone if you have any suspicion that sharks might be present. If you do see a shark, don't splash in the water or urinate. Calmly retreat and get out of the water as quickly as you can without creating a disturbance.

Those round things on the rocks and reefs that look like pin cushions are **sea urchins,** whose calcium spikes can be more painful than needles. If you get stuck with one, soak the injury in hot water, vinegar, or urine for about 15 minutes. That will stop the pain. If you can't get it out, the spike will dissolve and disappear on its own in about 2 weeks.

Jellyfish stings can hurt like the devil but seldom are life-threatening. Adolph's Meat Tenderizer is a great antidote; otherwise, use rubbing alcohol to swab the affected areas, not water or any petroleum-based compound.

The **stone fish** is so named because it looks like a piece of stone or coral as it lies buried in the sand on the lagoon bottom with only its back and 13 venomous spikes sticking out. Its venom can cause paralysis and even death. You'll know by the intense pain if you're stuck. Serum is available, so get to a hospital at once. Sea snakes, cone shells, crown-of-thorns starfish, moray eels, lionfish, and demon stingers also can be painful if not deadly. The last thing any of these creatures wants is to tangle with a human, so keep your hands to yourself.

Rather than list the hundreds of books about the South Pacific, I have picked some of the best that are likely to be available in the United States and Canada, either in bookstores or at your local library. Many other tomes, especially scholarly works, have been published in Australia, New Zealand, and the islands themselves (notably by the University of the South Pacific in Suva, Fiji, and by Vava'u Press in Tonga). Libraries in those countries may have much wider South Pacific selections than do their counterparts in North America.

A number of out-of-print island classics have been reissued in paperback by **Mutual Publishing Company,** Mezzanine B, 1127 11th Ave., Honolulu, HI 96816 (☎ **808/732-1709,** fax 808/734-4094). In some cases, I give a book's original publisher and date of publication, followed by the recent Mutual edition and its date.

4 Recommended Books

GENERAL   If you have time for only one South Pacific book, read *The Lure of Tahiti* (Mutual, 1986). Editor A. Grove Day, himself an islands expert, includes 18 short stories, excerpts of other books, and essays. There is a little here from many of the writers mentioned below, plus selections from Captains Cook, Bougainville, and Bligh.

The National Geographic Society's book *The Isles of the South Pacific* (1971), by Maurice Shadbolt and Olaf Ruhen, and Ian Todd's *Island Realm* (Angus & Robertson, 1974), are somewhat out-of-date coffee-table books but have lovely color photographs. *Living Corals* (Clarkson N. Potter, 1979), by Douglas Faulkner and Richard Chesher, shows what you will see under water.

For reference purposes, *The South Pacific: An Introduction* (Univ. of the South Pacific, 1989), by Ron Crocombe, provides a wealth of political and economic data, as does *Pacific Islands Yearbook* (Fiji Times, 1995), eds. Norman and Ngaire Douglas; both are published in Suva, Fiji.

HISTORY & POLITICS   Several of the early English and French explorers published accounts of their exploits, but *The Journals of Captain James Cook* stand out as the most exhaustive and even-handed. Edited by J.C. Beaglehole, they were published in three volumes (one for each voyage) by Cambridge University in 1955, 1961, and 1967. A. Grenfell Price edited many of Cook's key passages and provides short transitional explanations in *The Explorations of Captain James Cook in the Pacific* (Dover, 1971). Modern prose accounts are given by Lynne Withey in *Voyages of Discovery: Captain Cook and the Exploration of the Pacific* (Morrow, 1987) and by Richard Hough in *Captain James Cook: A Biography* (Norton, 1995).

The explorers' visits and their consequences in Tahiti, Australia, and Antarctica are the subject of Alan Moorehead's excellent study *The Fatal Impact: The Invasion of the South Pacific, 1767–1840* (Harper & Row, 1966), a colorful tome loaded with sketches and paintings of the time.

Mutiny on the Bounty

The most famous movies about the South Pacific are two *Mutiny on the Bounty* films based on the novel by Charles Nordhoff and James Norman Hall. The 1935 version starred Clark Gable as Fletcher Christian and Charles Laughton as a tyrannical Captain Bligh. (It actually was the second film to be based on the *Bounty* story; the first was an Australian production, starring Errol Flynn in his first movie role.) Although the 1935 version contained background shots of 40 Tahitian villages, most of the movie was filmed on Santa Catalina, off the California coast; neither Gable nor Laughton visited Tahiti. The 1962 remake with Marlon Brando and Trevor Howard in the Gable-Laughton roles, however, was actually filmed on Tahiti. It was the beginning of Brando's tragic real-life relationship with Tahiti. A 1984 version, *The Bounty,* not based on Nordhoff and Hall, was filmed in Opunohu Bay on Moorea and featured Mel Gibson as Christian and Anthony Hopkins as a more sympathetic (and historically accurate) Bligh.

Three other very readable books trace Tahiti's post-discovery history. *Tahiti: Island of Love* (Pacific Publications, 1979), by Robert Langdon, takes the island's story up to 1977. *Tahiti: A Paradise Lost* (Penguin, 1985), by David Howarth, covers more thoroughly the same early ground covered by Langdon but stops with France's taking possession in 1842. *The Rape of Tahiti* (Dodd, Mead, 1983), by Edward Dodd, covers the island from prehistory to 1900.

Mad about Islands (Mutual, 1987), by A. Grove Day, follows the island exploits of literary figures Herman Melville, Robert Louis Stevenson, Jack London, and W. Somerset Maugham. Also included are Charles Nordhoff and James Norman Hall, co-authors of the so-called "Bounty Trilogy" and other works about the islands (see "Fiction," below). *In Search of Paradise* (Mutual, 1987), by Paul L. Briand, recounts the Nordhoff and Hall story in detail. *A Dream of Islands* (Norton, 1980), by Gavan Dawes, tells of the missionary John Williams as well as of Melville, Stevenson, and the painter Paul Gauguin, who spent the final years of his life in French Polynesia.

For descriptions of the islands during the 1950s, see Eugene Burdick's *The Blue of Capricorn* (Houghton Mifflin, 1961; Mutual, 1986). In *Tales from Paradise* (BBC Publications, 1986), June Knox-Mawer tells charming yarns of the final years of British rule in Fiji and the Solomons, as seen by a colonial official's wife.

Former *New York Times* reporter Robert Turnbull traveled the islands in the 1970s and reported his findings in *Tin Roofs and Palm Trees* (Univ. of Washington Press, 1977). Scott L. Malcolmson did the same in the late 1980s; his somewhat opinionated views of the political situations in Fiji and French Polynesia are in *Tuturani: A Political Journey in the Pacific Islands* (Poseidon, 1990).

For a political document, order a copy of *Problems in Paradise: United States Interests in the South Pacific* (U.S. House of Representatives, 1990) from the U.S. Government Printing Office in Washington, D.C. It's an excellent report by a 1989 congressional delegation that toured the islands.

PEOPLES & CULTURES Peter Bellwood's *The Polynesians: Prehistory of an Island People* (Thames & Hudson, 1987) examines the Polynesians' history before the coming of Europeans and explains the various island cultures existing at the time. The book contains sketches of island life by the early explorers and photographs of ancient handcrafts that have been unearthed or preserved.

In *We, the Navigators* (Univ. of Hawaii, 1972), Professor David Lewis tells how the islanders managed to sail great distances over open ocean without modern navigation tools.

Some of the most interesting accounts of island life were written by persons who lived among the islanders. Perhaps the most famous is *Coming of Age in Samoa* (1928), in which Margaret Mead tells of her year studying promiscuous adolescent girls in the Manu'a islands of American Samoa. The book created quite a stir when it was published in a more modest time than the present. Her interpretation of Samoan sex customs was taken to task by New Zealander Derek Freeman in *Margaret Mead and Samoa: The Making and Unmaking of an Anthropological Myth* (1983).

Bengt Danielsson, a Swedish anthropologist who has lived in Tahiti since arriving there on Thor Heyerdahl's *Kon Tiki* raft in 1947, paints a much broader picture of Polynesian sexuality in *Love in the South Seas* (Mutual, 1986). He finds that some of the old ways have gone, while others are still hanging on.

Heyerdahl tells his tale and explains his theory of Polynesian migration (since debunked) in *Kon Tiki* (Rand McNally, 1950; translated by F. K. Lyon). In 1936, Heyerdahl and his wife lived for a year in the Marquesas. The resulting book, *Fatu-Hiva: Back to Nature* (Doubleday, 1975), provides an in-depth look at Marquesan life at the time.

Two Americans give unscholarly but entertaining accounts of Polynesian island life during the 1920s. Robert Dean Frisbie spent several years as a trader in the Cook Islands and tells about it charmingly in *The Book of Puka-Puka* (1928; Mutual, 1986). Robert Lee Eskridge spent a year on Mangareva in French Polynesia; his equally charming book is titled, appropriately, *Manga Reva* (Bobbs-Merrill, 1931; Mutual, 1986).

In recent times, noted conservationist Joana McIntyre Varawa married Fijian Male Varawa, half her age, and moved from Hawaii to his home village. In *Changes in Latitude* (Atlantic Monthly Press, 1989), she writes of her experiences, providing many insights into modern Fijian culture.

TRAVELOGUES Although the great novelist Robert Louis Stevenson composed very little fiction about the South Pacific during his years in Western Samoa (see chapter 13), he wrote articles and letters about his travels and about events leading up to Germany's acquisition of the islands in 1890. Many of them are available in two collections: *In the South Seas* (1901) and *Island Landfalls* (Cannongate, 1987). The latter also includes three Stevenson short stories with South Seas settings: "The Bottle Imp," "The Isle of Voices," and "The Beach at Falesá."

Sir David Attenborough, the British documentary film producer, traveled to Papua New Guinea, Vanuatu, Fiji, and Tonga in the late 1950s to film, among other things, Tongan Queen Salote's royal kava ceremony. Sir David entertainingly tells of his trips in *Journeys to the Past* (Penguin, 1983).

John Dyson rode inter-island trading boats throughout the South Pacific and wrote about his experiences in *The South Seas Dream* (Little, Brown, 1982). It's an entertaining account of the islands and their more colorful inhabitants. Julian Evans tells of a more recent trading-boat trip to Fiji, the Samoas, and Tonga in *Transit of Venus* (Pantheon, 1992).

The noted travel writer and novelist Paul Theroux took his kayak along for a tour of the South Pacific and reported on what he found in *The Happy Isles of Oceania: Paddling the Pacific* (Putnam's, 1992). The book is a fascinatingly frank yarn, full of island characters and out-of-the-way places. The King of

I have often been mildly amused when I think that the great American novel was not written about New England or Chicago. It was written about a white whale in the South Pacific.

—James A. Michener, 1951

Tonga reportedly was so upset with what Theroux had to say that he has banned him from returning to the Kingdom.

Few travelogues dedicated to particular island countries are readily available outside of the South Pacific. One of the best is Ronald Wright's enjoyable book *On Fiji Islands* (Penguin, 1986). It's packed with insights about the Fijians and Indians.

FICTION Starting with Herman Melville's *Typee* (1846) and *Omoo* (1847)—semifictional accounts of his adventures in the Marquesas and Tahiti, respectively—the South Pacific has spawned a wealth of fiction. (Though set in the South Pacific Ocean, Melville's 1851 classic, *Moby-Dick,* does not tell of the islands.)

After Melville came Julian Viaud, a French naval officer who fell in love with a Tahitian woman during a short sojourn in Tahiti. Under the pen name Pierre Loti, he wrote *The Marriage of Loti* (1880; KPI, 1986), a classic tale of lost love.

W. Somerset Maugham's *The Moon and Sixpence* (1919) is a fictional account of the life of Paul Gauguin. Maugham changed the name to Charles Strickland and made the painter English instead of French. (Gauguin's own novel, *Noa Noa,* was published in English in 1928, long after his death.) Maugham also produced a volume of South Pacific short stories, *The Trembling of a Leaf* (1921; Mutual, 1985). The most famous is "Rain," the tragic story of prostitute Sadie Thompson and the fundamentalist missionary she led astray in American Samoa. My personal favorite is "The Fall of Edward Bernard," about a Chicagoan who forsakes love and fortune back home for "beauty, truth, and goodness" in Tahiti.

Next on the scene were the aforementioned Charles Nordhoff and James Norman Hall (more about them in chapters 4 and 5). Together they wrote the most famous of all South Pacific novels, *Mutiny on the Bounty* (1932). They immediately followed that enormous success with two other novels: *Men Against the Sea* (1934), based on Bligh's epic longboat voyage after the mutiny; and *Pitcairn's Island* (1935), about the mutineers' sorry demise on their remote hideaway.

Nordhoff and Hall later wrote *The Hurricane* (1936), a novel that has been made into two movies (see "Films," below). Hall also wrote short stories and essays, collected in *The Forgotten One* (Mutual, 1986).

The second most famous South Pacific novel appeared just after World War II—*Tales of the South Pacific* (Macmillan, 1947), by James A. Michener. A U.S. Navy historian, Michener spent much of the war on Espiritu Santo, in the New Hebrides (now Vanuatu), which is the setting for most of the book. Richard Rodgers and Oscar Hammerstein turned the novel into the musical *South Pacific,* one of the most successful Broadway productions ever; it was later made into a popular movie (see "Films," below).

Michener toured the islands a few years later and wrote *Return to Paradise* (Random House, 1951), a collection of essays and short stories. The essays are particularly valuable, since they describe the islands as they were after World War II but before tourists began to arrive via jet aircraft—in other words, near the end of the region's backwater, beachcomber days. His piece on Fiji predicts that country's Fijian-Indian problems.

Index

See also Accommodations index, below.

General Index

General Index

ACCOMMODATIONS

Accommodations Index

FROMMER'S® COMPLETE TRAVEL GUIDES

FROMMER'S® DOLLAR-A-DAY GUIDES

Australia from $50 a Day
California from $60 a Day
Caribbean from $70 a Day
England from $70 a Day
Europe from $60 a Day
Florida from $60 a Day

Hawaii from $70 a Day
Ireland from $50 a Day
Israel from $45 a Day
Italy from $70 a Day
London from $85 a Day
New York from $80 a Day

New Zealand from $50 a Day
Paris from $85 a Day
San Francisco from $60 a Day
Washington, D.C.,
  from $60 a Day

FROMMER'S® PORTABLE GUIDES

Acapulco, Ixtapa & Zihu-
  atanejo
Alaska Cruises & Ports of Call
Bahamas
Baja & Los Cabos
Berlin
California Wine Country
Charleston & Savannah
Chicago

Dublin
Hawaii: The Big Island
Las Vegas
London
Maine Coast
Maui
New Orleans
New York City
Paris

Puerto Vallarta, Manzanillo
  & Guadalajara
San Diego
San Francisco
Sydney
Tampa & St. Petersburg
Venice
Washington, D.C.

FROMMER'S® NATIONAL PARK GUIDES

Family Vacations in the
  National Parks
Grand Canyon

National Parks of the American West
Rocky Mountain

Yellowstone & Grand Teton
Yosemite & Sequoia/
  Kings Canyon
Zion & Bryce Canyon

FROMMER'S® GREAT OUTDOOR GUIDES

New England
Northern California

Southern California & Baja
Washington & Oregon

FROMMER'S® MEMORABLE WALKS

Chicago
London

New York
Paris

San Francisco
Washington D.C.

FROMMER'S® IRREVERENT GUIDES

Amsterdam
Boston
Chicago
Las Vegas

London
Los Angeles
Manhattan

New Orleans
Paris
San Francisco

Seattle & Portland
Vancouver
Walt Disney World
Washington, D.C.

FROMMER'S® BEST-LOVED DRIVING TOURS

America
Britain
California

Florida
France
Germany

Ireland
Italy
New England

Scotland
Spain
Western Europe

THE UNOFFICIAL GUIDES®

Bed & Breakfast in New England	Cruises	London	Skiing in the West
Bed & Breakfast in the Northwest	Disneyland	Miami & the Keys	Walt Disney World
	Florida with Kids	Mini Las Vegas	Walt Disney World for Grown-ups
Beyond Disney	The Great Smoky & Blue Ridge Moun-	Mini-Mickey	
Branson, Missouri	tains	New Orleans	Walt Disney World for Kids
California with Kids	Inside Disney	New York City	
Chicago	Las Vegas	Paris	Washington, D.C.
		San Francisco	

SPECIAL-INTEREST TITLES

Born to Shop: France
Born to Shop: Hong Kong
Born to Shop: Italy
Born to Shop: New York
Born to Shop: Paris
Frommer's Britain's Best Bike Rides
The Civil War Trust's Official Guide to the Civil War Discovery Trail
Frommer's Caribbean Hideaways
Frommer's Europe's Greatest Driving Tours
Frommer's Food Lover's Companion to France
Frommer's Food Lover's Companion to Italy
Frommer's Gay & Lesbian Europe
Israel Past & Present
Monks' Guide to California

Monks' Guide to New York City
The Moon
New York City with Kids
Unforgettable Weekends
Outside Magazine's Guide to Family Vacations
Places Rated Almanac
Retirement Places Rated
Road Atlas Britain
Road Atlas Europe
Washington, D.C., with Kids
Wonderful Weekends from Boston
Wonderful Weekends from New York City
Wonderful Weekends from San Francisco
Wonderful Weekends from Los Angeles